KT-159-751

CHER

ALL HELL'S A-COMING

Karen Berger
VP-Executive Editor

Axel Alonso
Editor-original series

Michael Wright
Editor-collected edition

Nick J. Napolitano
Associate Editor-collected edition

Robbin Brosterman
Senior Art Director

Paul Levitz
President & Publisher

Georg Brewer
VP-Design & Retail Product Development

Richard Brunning
Senior VP-Creative Director

Patrick Caldon
Senior VP-Finance & Operations

Chris Caramalis
VP-Finance

Terri Cunningham
VP-Managing Editor

Dan DiDio
VP-Editorial

Alison Gill
VP-Manufacturing

Lillian Laserson
Senior VP & General Counsel

Jim Lee
Editorial Director-WildStorm

David McKillips
VP-Advertising & Custom Publishing

John Nee
VP-Business Development

Gregory Noveck
Senior VP-Creative Affairs

Cheryl Rubin
VP-Brand Management

Bob Wayne
VP-Sales & Marketing

PREACHER: ALL HELL'S A-COMING
Published by DC Comics.
Cover, introduction and compilation copyright © 2000 DC Comics. All Rights Reserved.
Originally published in single magazine form as PREACHER 51-58, PREACHER: TALL IN THE SADDLE. Copyright © 1999, 2000
Garth Ennis & Steve Dillon. All Rights Reserved. All characters, their distinctive
likenesses and related elements featured in this publication are trademarks of Garth Ennis & Steve Dillon.
The stories, characters and incidents featured in this publication are entirely fictional.
DC Comics does not read or accept unsolicited submissions of ideas, stories or artwork.
DC Comics, 1700 Broadway, New York, NY 10019
A Warner Bros. Entertainment Company
Printed in Canada. Third Printing.
ISBN: 1-56389-617-6
Cover illustration by Glenn Fabry.
Publication design by Louis Prandi.

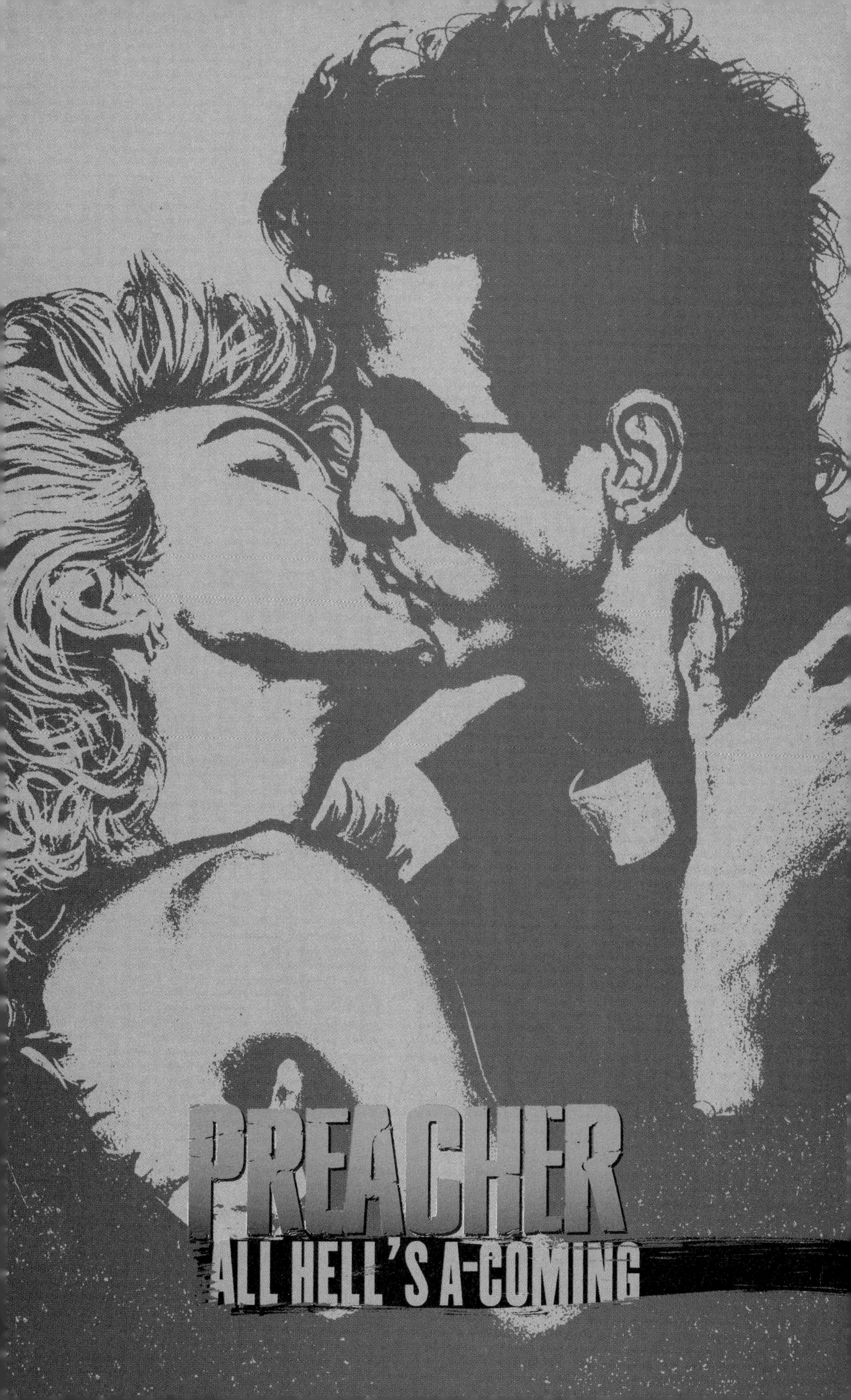
PREACHER
ALL HELL'S A-COMING

GARTH ENNIS
WRITER

STEVE DILLON
PENCILS

STEVE DILLON
JOHN McCREA
INKS

PAMELA RAMBO
PATRICIA MULVIHILL
COLORISTS

CLEM ROBINS
LETTERER

GLENN FABRY
ORIGINAL COVERS

PREACHER created by GARTH ENNIS and STEVE DILLON

PREA

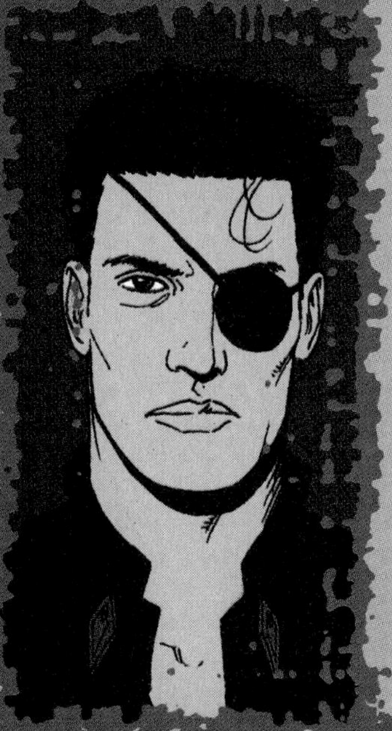

REVEREND JESSE CUSTER

Possessed by the entity Genesis—a child born of a union between Heaven and Hell that should never have existed—Jesse Custer's on a quest to find God and the reason He's abandoned his post. Because of Genesis, Jesse's voice is the literal Word of God, commanding those who hear him to do whatever he says. Jesse drinks too much, smokes too much and has a peculiar habit of taking advice from the spirit of John Wayne.

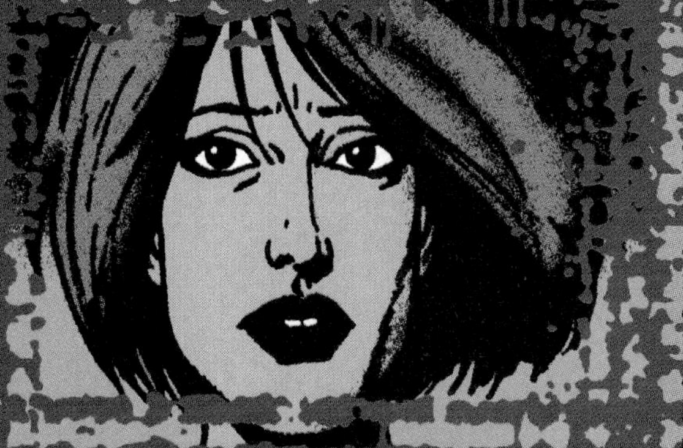

TULIP O'HARE

Five years ago, Tulip and Jesse were pretty much joined at the hip — that is, until Jesse was hauled back to his childhood home of Angelville by good ol' boys Jody and T.C., disappearing on Tulip. Since that time, Tulip made a bungling attempt to be a paid assassin to pay the bills and forget about Jesse Custer. Guns came easy, forgetting Jesse didn't. Now, after bearing witness to the apparent death of her one true love, Tulip again tries to pick up the pieces of her shattered life.

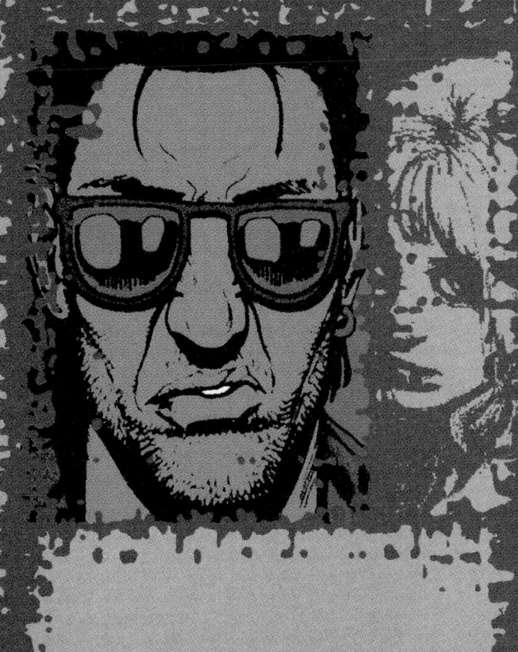

CASSIDY

A hard-drinkin' Irish vampire nearly a hundred years old, Proinsias Cassidy rode with Jesse and Tulip from the time Tulip tried to steal his truck after a botched hit in Texas until Jesse's apparent death in a nuclear firestorm. With Jesse out of the picture, Cassidy now makes his play for his best friend's girl. Call him Cassidy, Cass, or even a total wanker. Just don't ever call him Proinsias.

STARR

Recruited by the centuries-old Grail, Starr rose through the ranks to become the order's most respected agent, answering only to Allfather D'Aronique. Starr killed D'Aronique, realizing that the Grail's efforts were wasted on a tainted messiah. In Jesse Custer, Starr sees the future of the Grail...a future the newly risen Allfather Starr would gladly kill to see a reality.

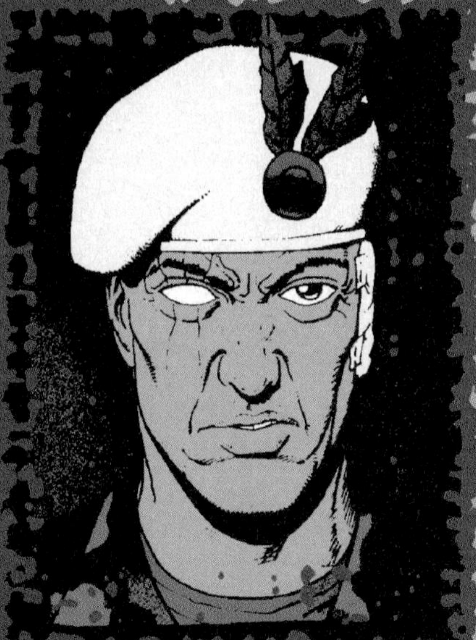

ARSEFACE

Sheriff Hugo Root's only son decided life wasn't worth livin' when Nirvana frontman Kurt Cobain up and killed himself. His father's 12-gauge missed all the vital stuff, and six operations rebuilt the rest. Arseface blamed Jesse Custer for Sheriff Root's suicide, but Jesse and Cass convinced him otherwise. They even got him laid, and helped him land a recording contract. Now he's a pop icon...with a face like an arse. Go figure.

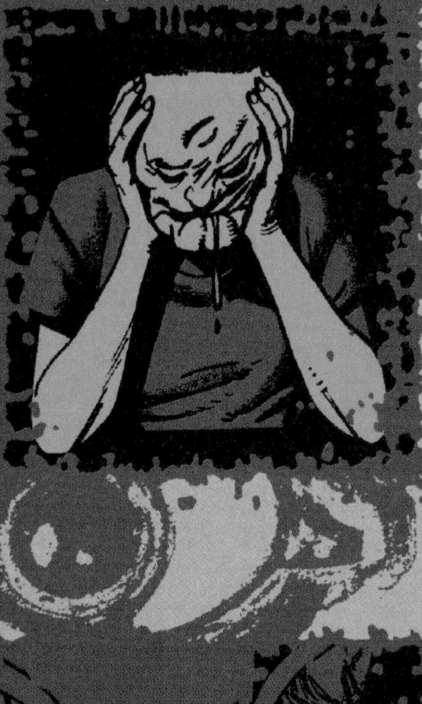

SKEETER

Man's best friend.

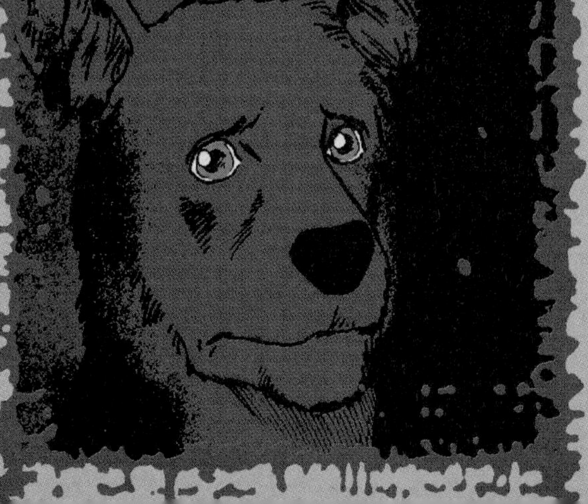

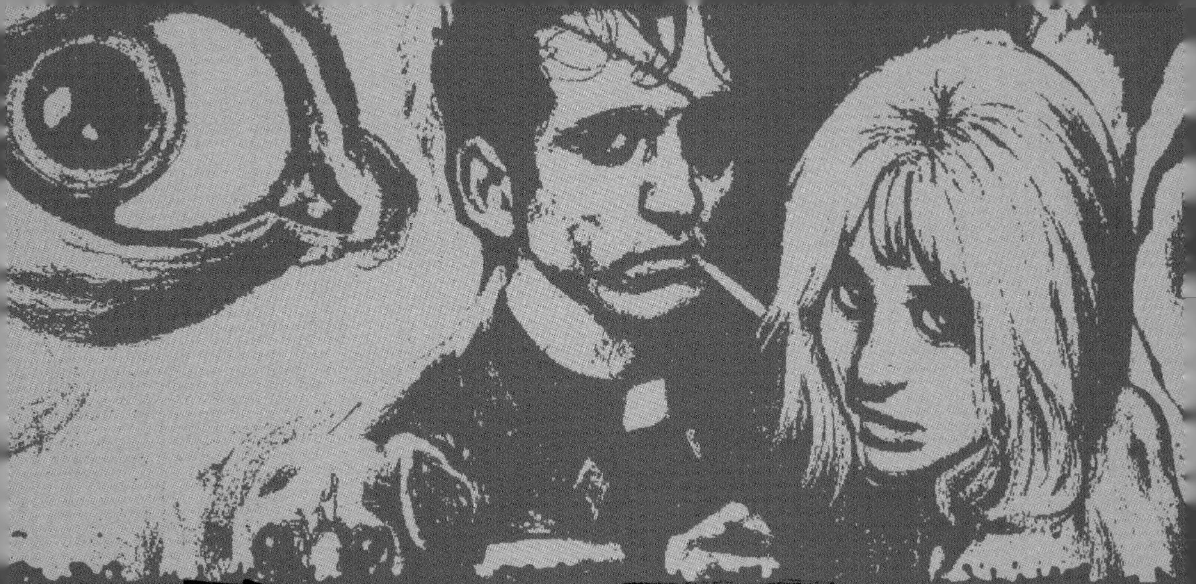

THE STORY SO FAR

The Reverend Jesse Custer may not have been the best minister there ever was, but he was a good man. A drinker with a mouth like a sailor, but a good man all the same.

Then came Genesis.

The spirit conceived from the union of angel and demon, Genesis was a power unlike any other in creation. And when it freed itself from its heavenly fetters, the spirit crash-landed in a small Texas parish, killing everyone except its preacher, Jesse, who somehow bonded with Genesis and assumed its powerful Word of God.

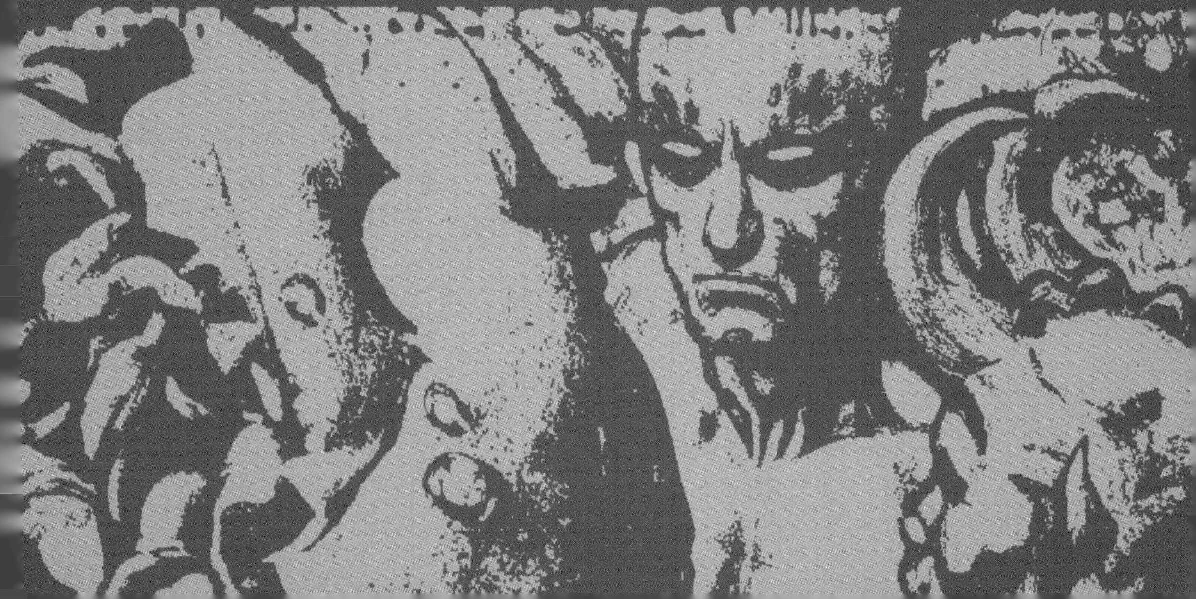

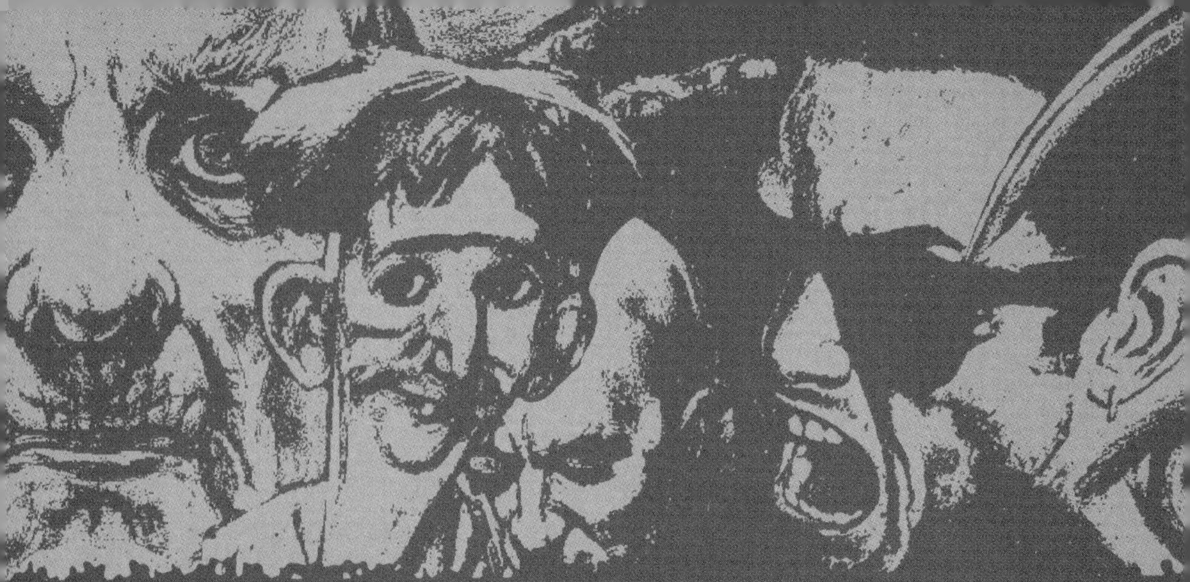

With the help of his long-lost lover, an assassin named Tulip O'Hare, and a hard-drinking Irish vampire named Cassidy, Jesse set out to find God and hold him accountable for his sins. But somewhere along the way, the mission meandered — due in no small part to the machinations of Herr Starr, an agent of a secret society known as the Grail. The Grail sought to manipulate the imminent Armageddon by maintaining control of the new messiah. Starr had his own designs, as he hoped to replace the Grail's messiah with one of his own — Jesse.

But Jesse would not submit to Starr, and their conflict continued to escalate until the day they met in Monument Valley, where Starr attempted to wipe out his foes in a nuclear firestorm. With Jesse presumed dead, Tulip found solace in booze, drugs and the all-too-willing arms of Cassidy. And when Jesse finally found his comrades, he was shocked to discover that they were now lovers, though he had no idea of the many torments this brought for Tulip. And as he left to find himself both as a drifter and a sheriff, Tulip lay wasted in her own personal hell.

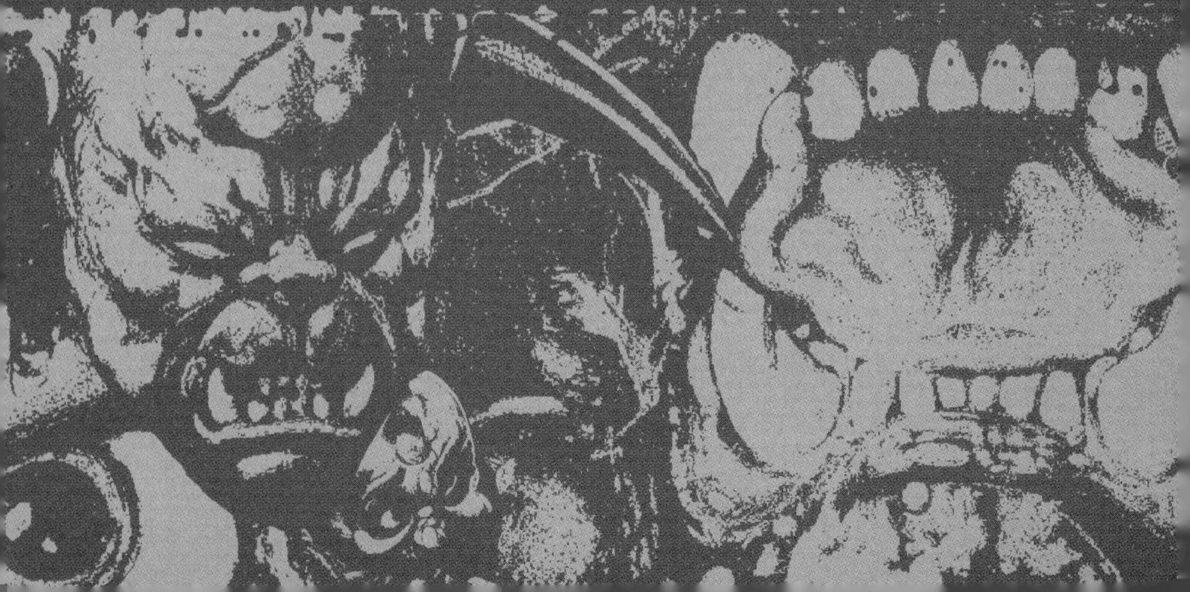

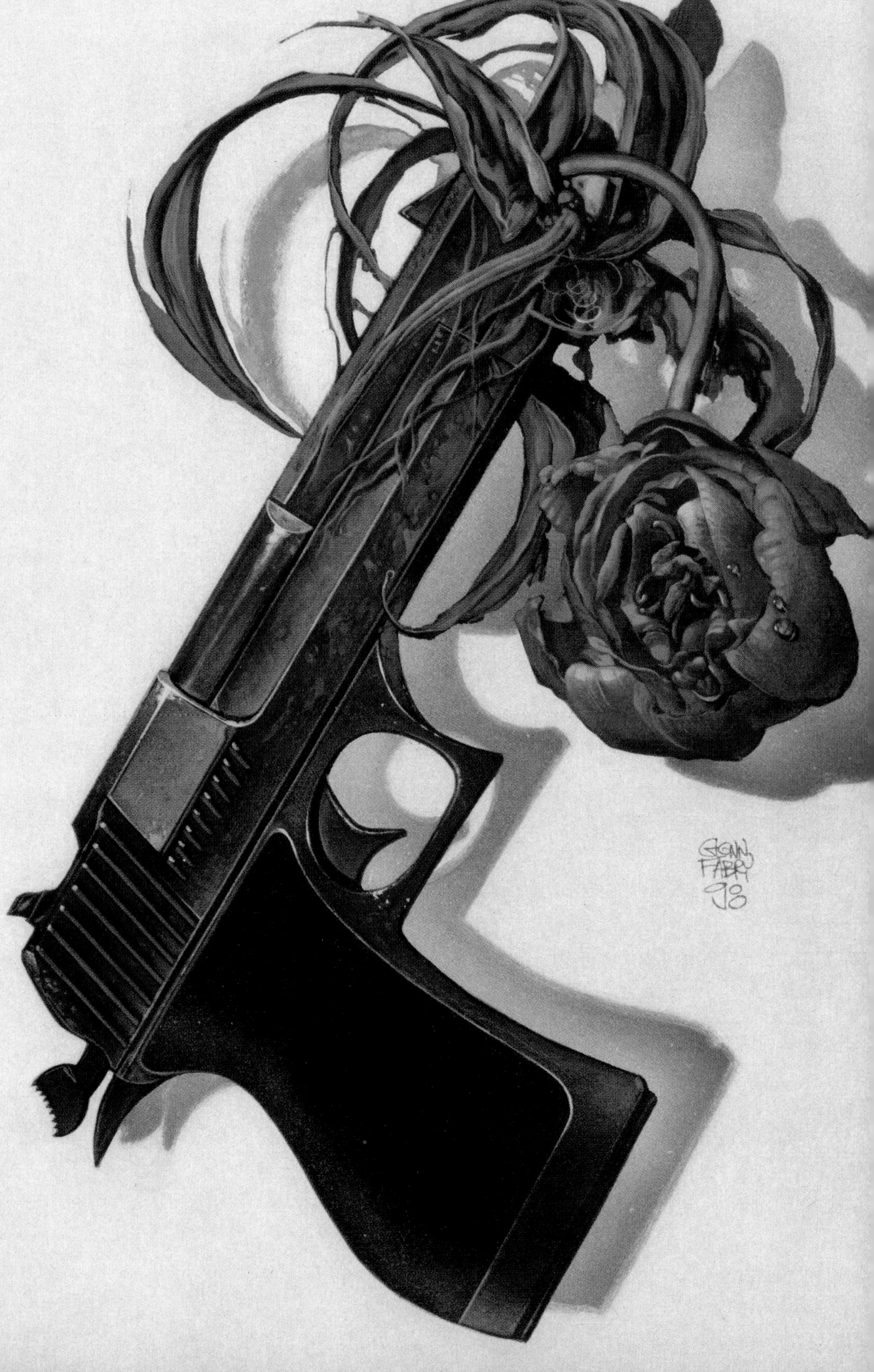
GLENN FABRY 98

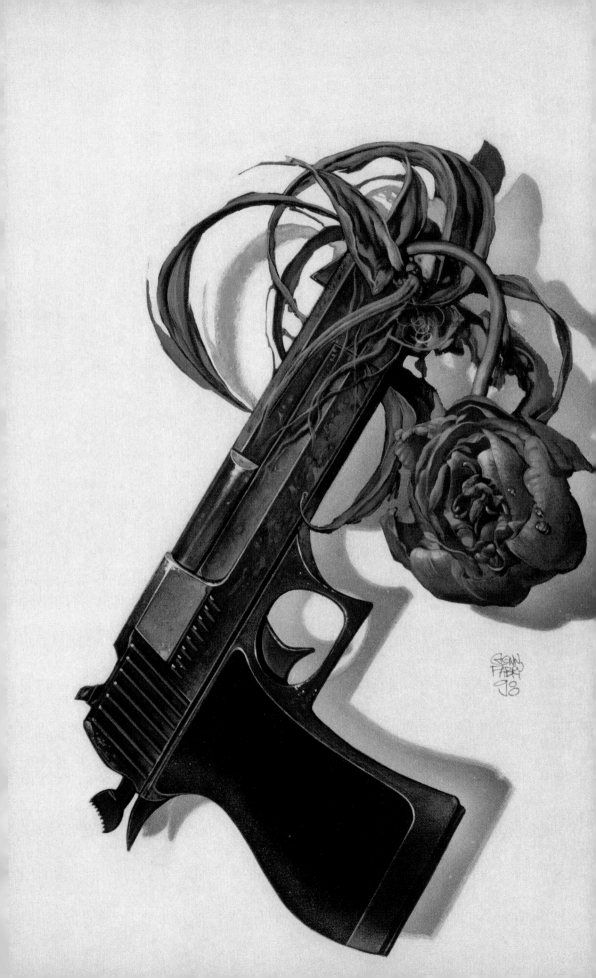

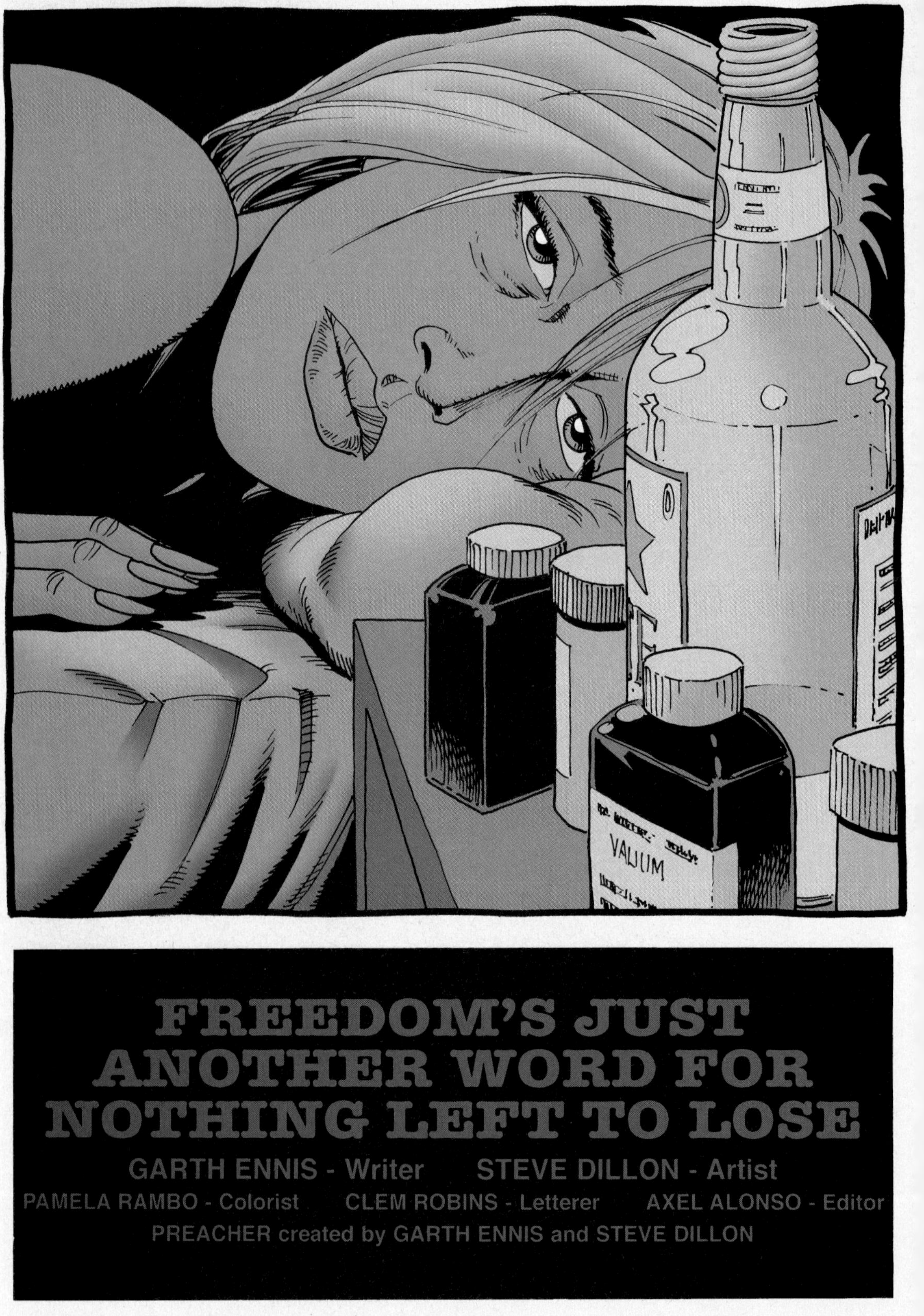
VALIUM

FREEDOM'S JUST ANOTHER WORD FOR NOTHING LEFT TO LOSE

GARTH ENNIS - Writer STEVE DILLON - Artist

PAMELA RAMBO - Colorist CLEM ROBINS - Letterer AXEL ALONSO - Editor

PREACHER created by GARTH ENNIS and STEVE DILLON

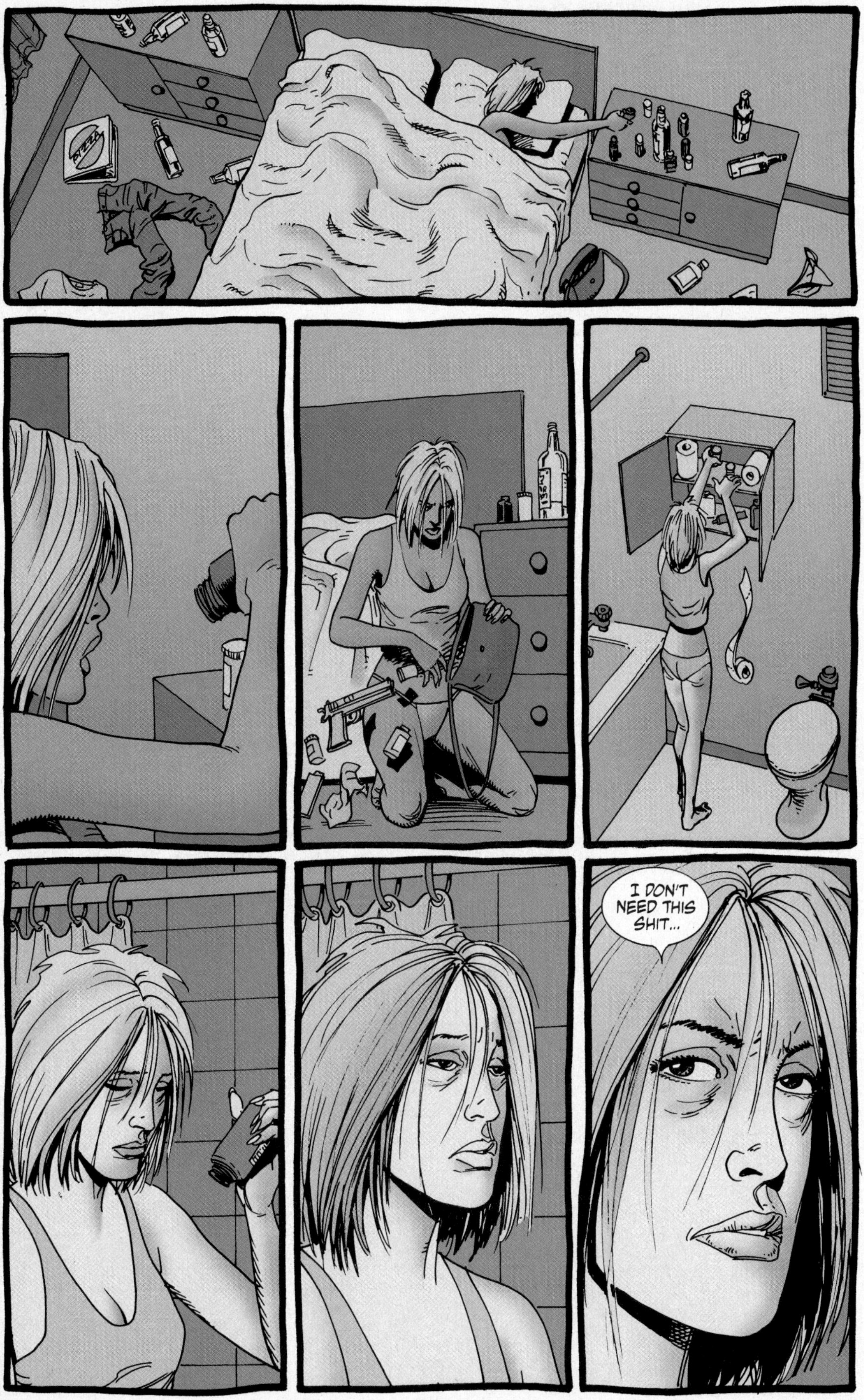
I DON'T NEED THIS SHIT...

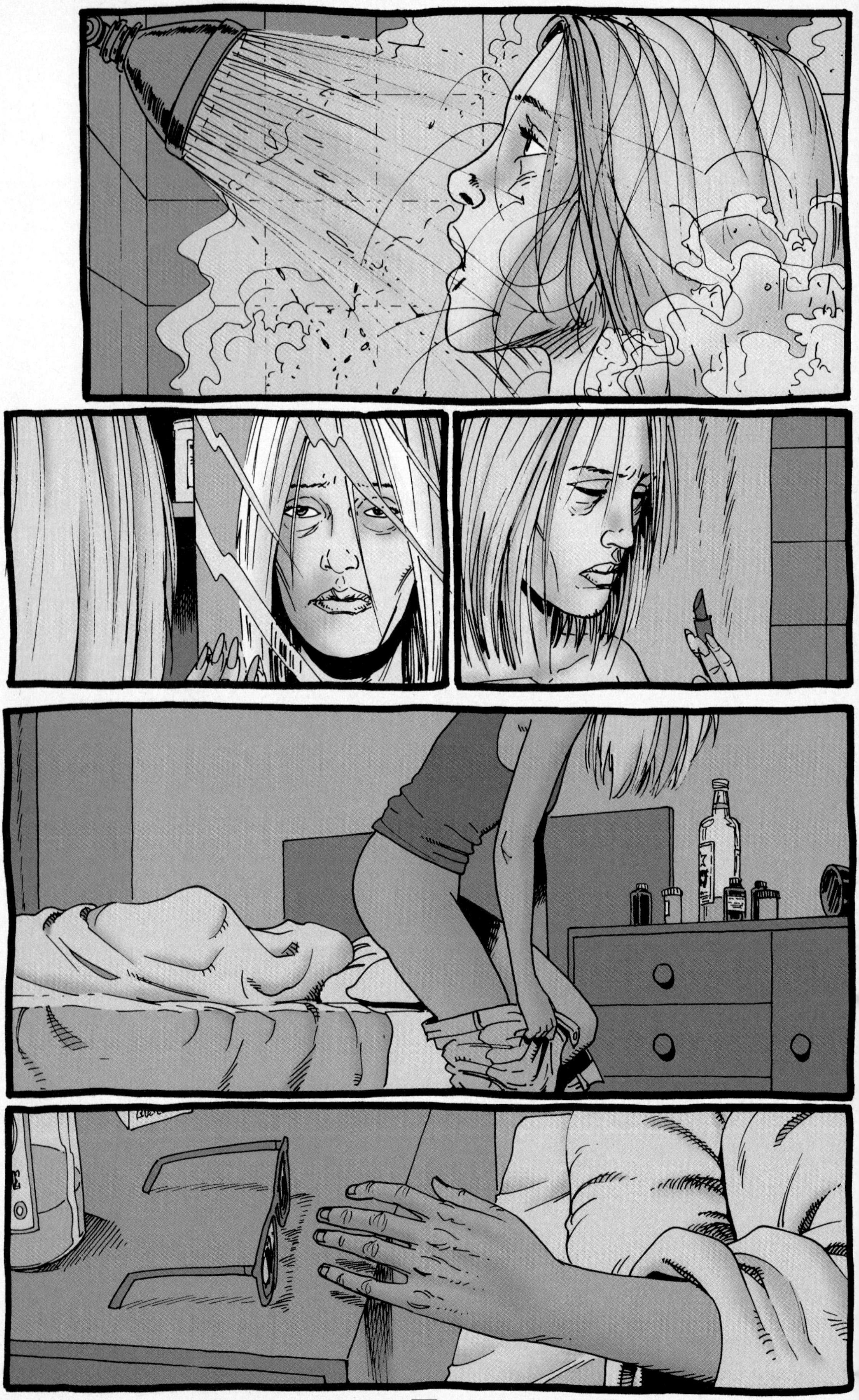

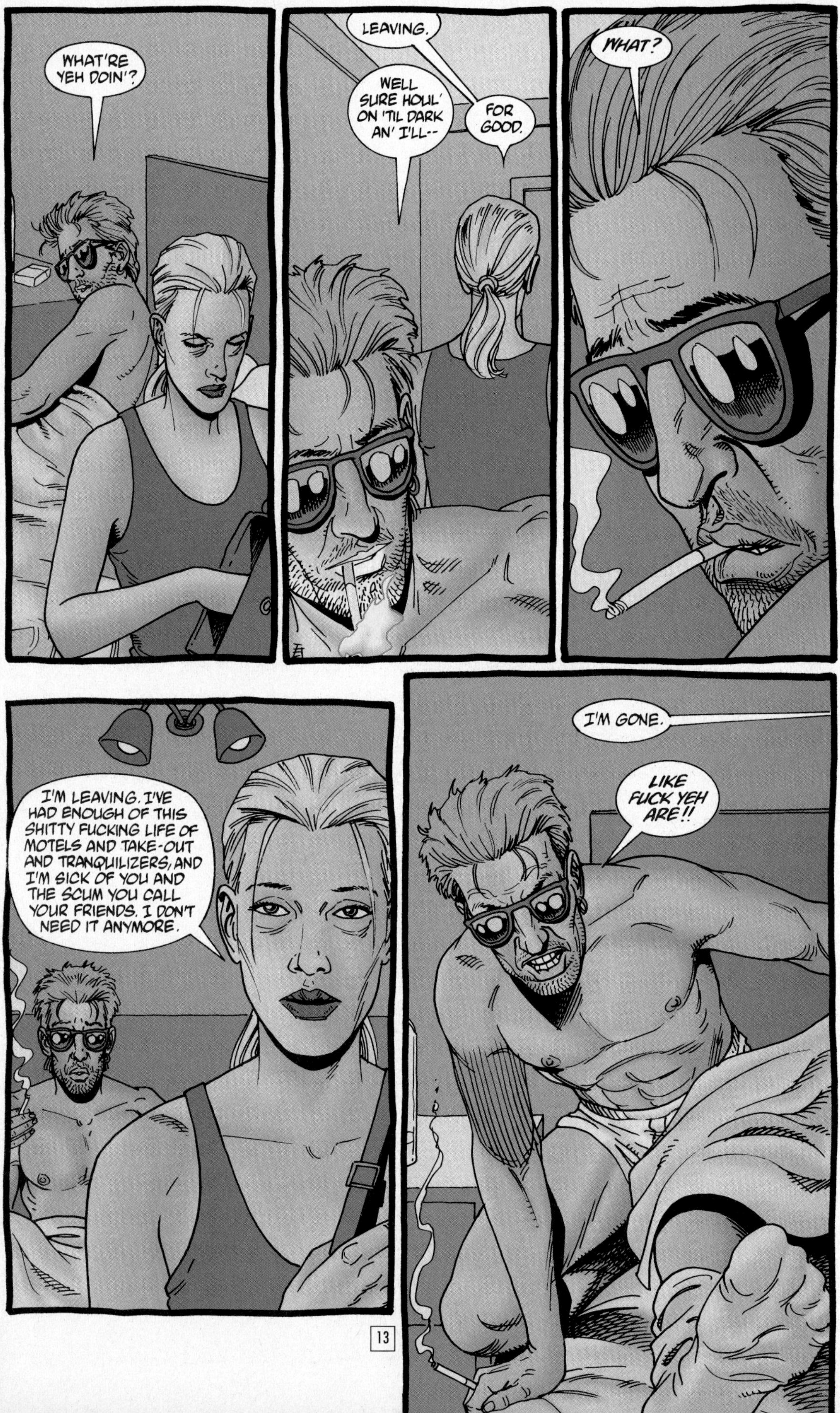
WHAT'RE YEH DOIN'?
LEAVING.
WELL SURE HOUL' ON 'TIL DARK AN' I'LL--
FOR GOOD.
WHAT?
I'M LEAVING. I'VE HAD ENOUGH OF THIS SHITTY FUCKING LIFE OF MOTELS AND TAKE-OUT AND TRANQUILIZERS, AND I'M SICK OF YOU AND THE SCUM YOU CALL YOUR FRIENDS. I DON'T NEED IT ANYMORE.
I'M GONE.
LIKE FUCK YEH ARE!!

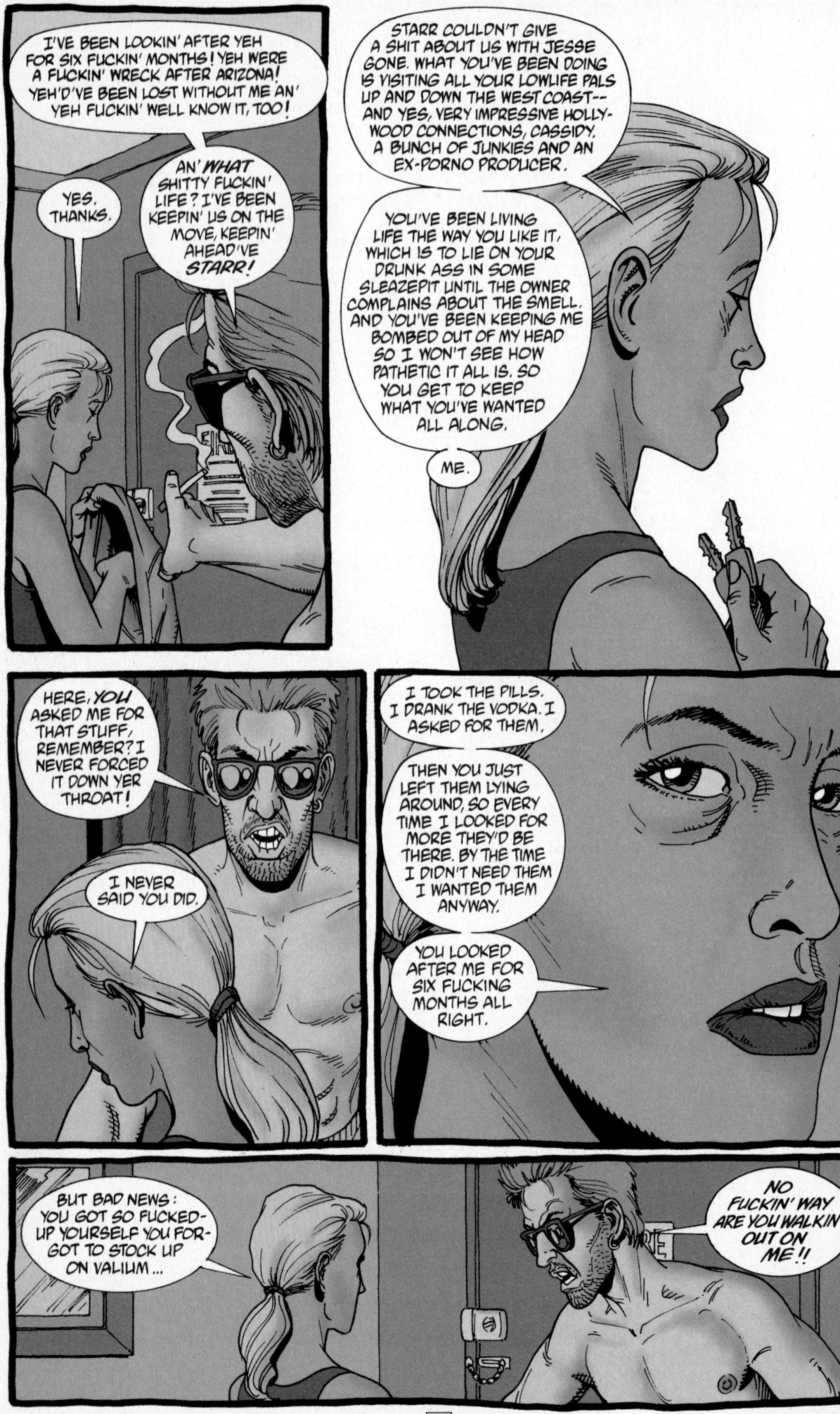
I'VE BEEN LOOKIN' AFTER YEH FOR SIX FUCKIN' MONTHS! YEH WERE A FUCKIN' WRECK AFTER ARIZONA! YEH'D'VE BEEN LOST WITHOUT ME AN' YEH FUCKIN' WELL KNOW IT, TOO!
YES. THANKS.
AN' WHAT SHITTY FUCKIN' LIFE? I'VE BEEN KEEPIN' US ON THE MOVE, KEEPIN' AHEAD'VE STARR!
STARR COULDN'T GIVE A SHIT ABOUT US WITH JESSE GONE. WHAT YOU'VE BEEN DOING IS VISITING ALL YOUR LOWLIFE PALS UP AND DOWN THE WEST COAST-- AND YES, VERY IMPRESSIVE HOLLYWOOD CONNECTIONS, CASSIDY. A BUNCH OF JUNKIES AND AN EX-PORNO PRODUCER.
YOU'VE BEEN LIVING LIFE THE WAY YOU LIKE IT, WHICH IS TO LIE ON YOUR DRUNK ASS IN SOME SLEAZEPIT UNTIL THE OWNER COMPLAINS ABOUT THE SMELL. AND YOU'VE BEEN KEEPING ME BOMBED OUT OF MY HEAD SO I WON'T SEE HOW PATHETIC IT ALL IS. SO YOU GET TO KEEP WHAT YOU'VE WANTED ALL ALONG.
ME.
HERE, YOU ASKED ME FOR THAT STUFF, REMEMBER? I NEVER FORCED IT DOWN YER THROAT!
I NEVER SAID YOU DID.
I TOOK THE PILLS. I DRANK THE VODKA. I ASKED FOR THEM.
THEN YOU JUST LEFT THEM LYING AROUND, SO EVERY TIME I LOOKED FOR MORE THEY'D BE THERE. BY THE TIME I DIDN'T NEED THEM I WANTED THEM ANYWAY.
YOU LOOKED AFTER ME FOR SIX FUCKING MONTHS ALL RIGHT.
BUT BAD NEWS: YOU GOT SO FUCKED-UP YOURSELF YOU FORGOT TO STOCK UP ON VALIUM...
NO FUCKIN' WAY ARE YOU WALKIN' OUT ON ME!!

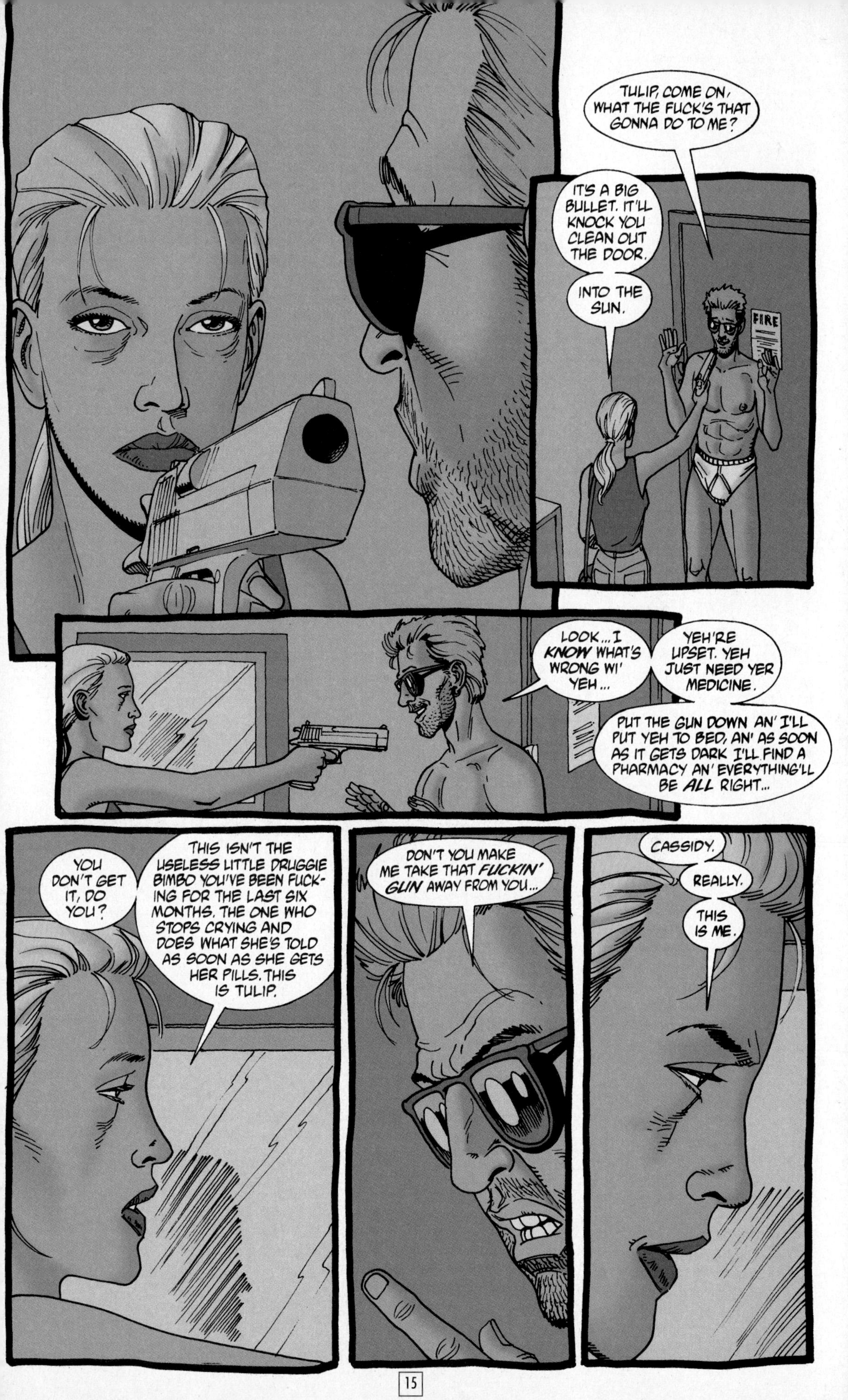

TULIP, COME ON, WHAT THE FUCK'S THAT GONNA DO TO ME?
IT'S A BIG BULLET. IT'LL KNOCK YOU CLEAN OUT THE DOOR.
INTO THE SUN.
FIRE
LOOK... I KNOW WHAT'S WRONG WI' YEH...
YEH'RE UPSET. YEH JUST NEED YER MEDICINE.
PUT THE GUN DOWN AN' I'LL PUT YEH TO BED, AN' AS SOON AS IT GETS DARK I'LL FIND A PHARMACY AN' EVERYTHING'LL BE ALL RIGHT...
YOU DON'T GET IT, DO YOU?
THIS ISN'T THE USELESS LITTLE DRUGGIE BIMBO YOU'VE BEEN FUCKING FOR THE LAST SIX MONTHS. THE ONE WHO STOPS CRYING AND DOES WHAT SHE'S TOLD AS SOON AS SHE GETS HER PILLS. THIS IS TULIP.
DON'T YOU MAKE ME TAKE THAT FUCKIN' GUN AWAY FROM YOU...
CASSIDY.
REALLY.
THIS IS ME.

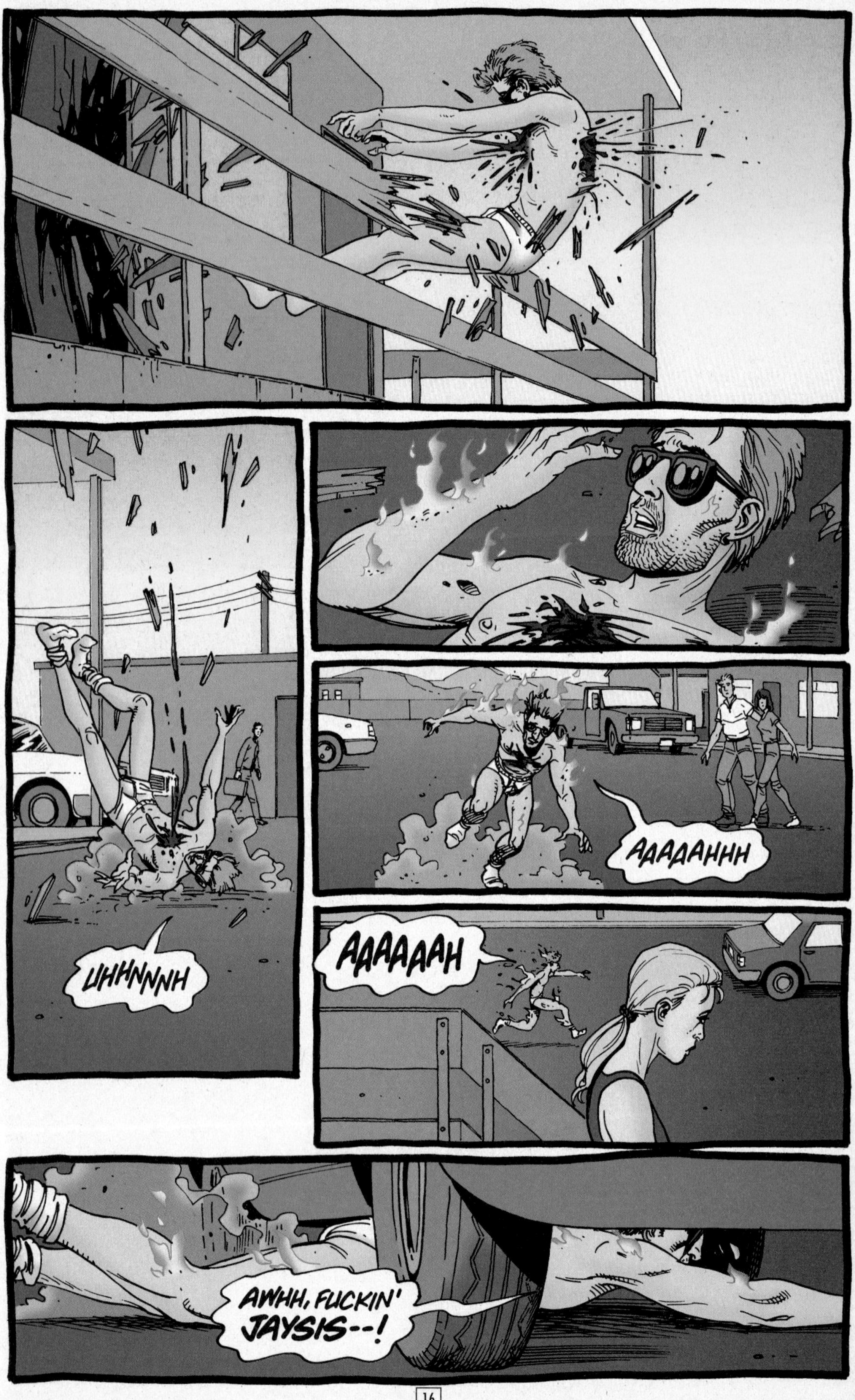
UHHNNNH
AAAAAHHH
AAAAAAH
AWHH, FUCKIN' JAYSIS--!

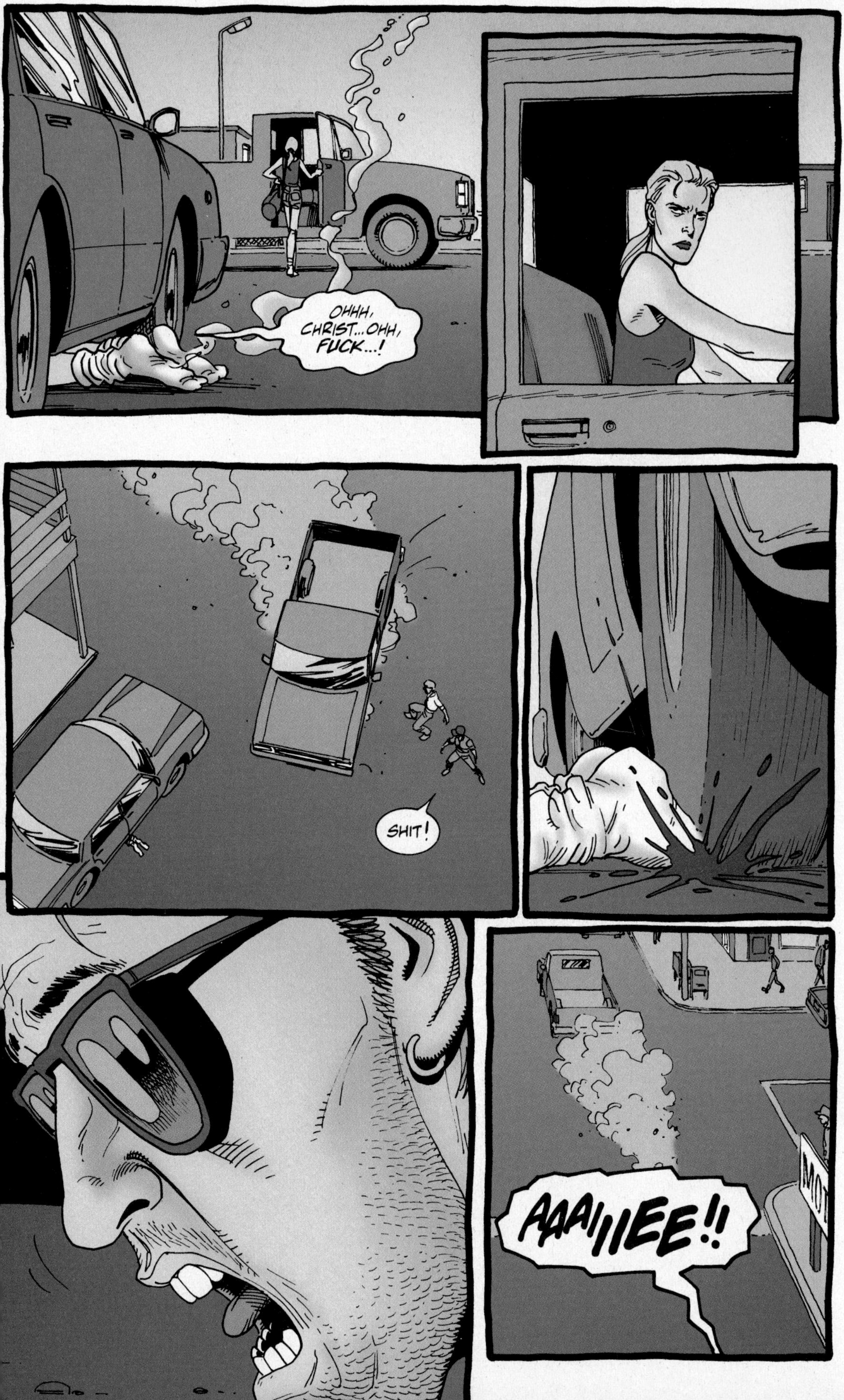
OHHH, CHRIST...OHH, FUCK...!
SHIT!
AAAIIIEE!!

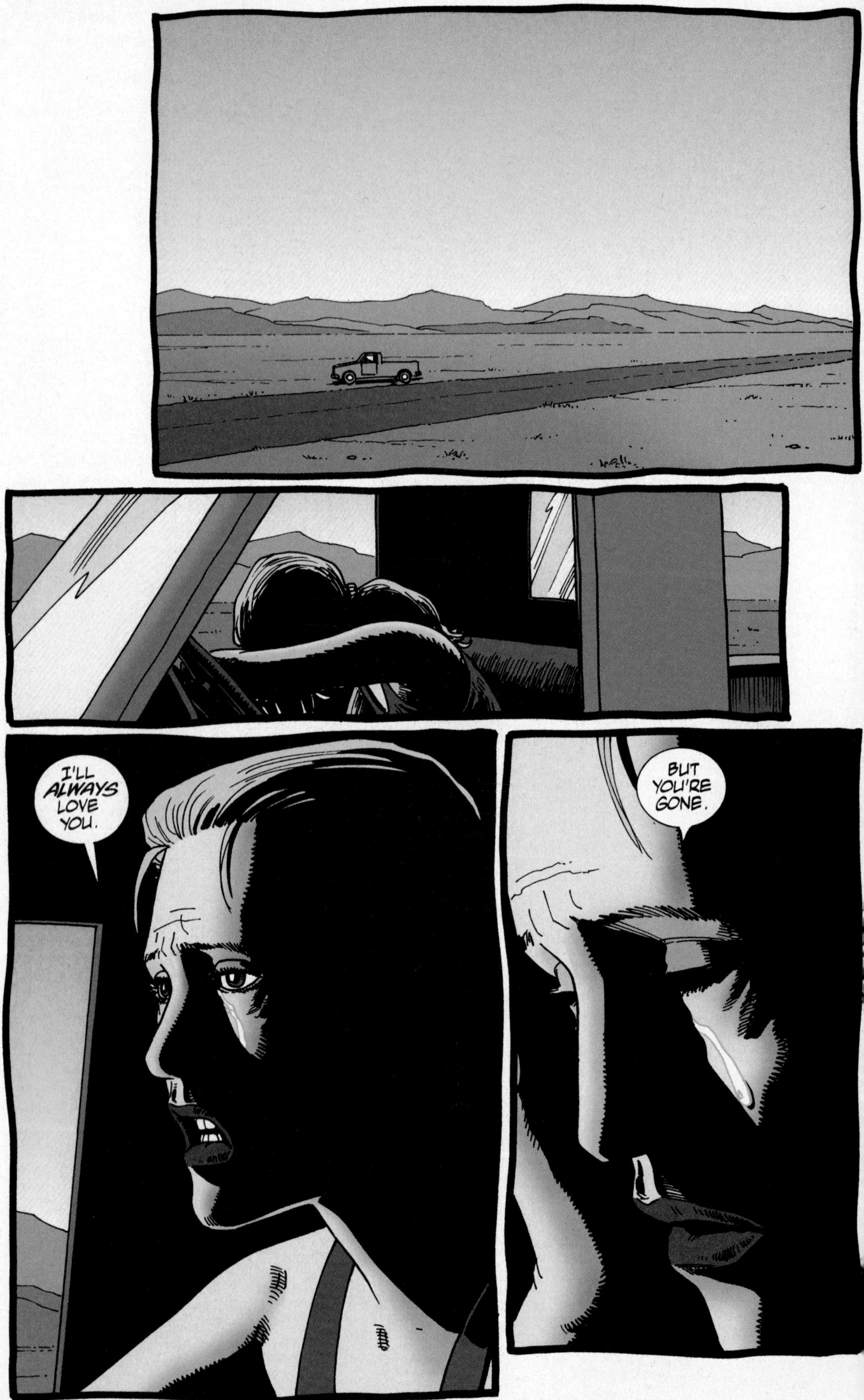
I'LL ALWAYS LOVE YOU.
BUT YOU'RE GONE.

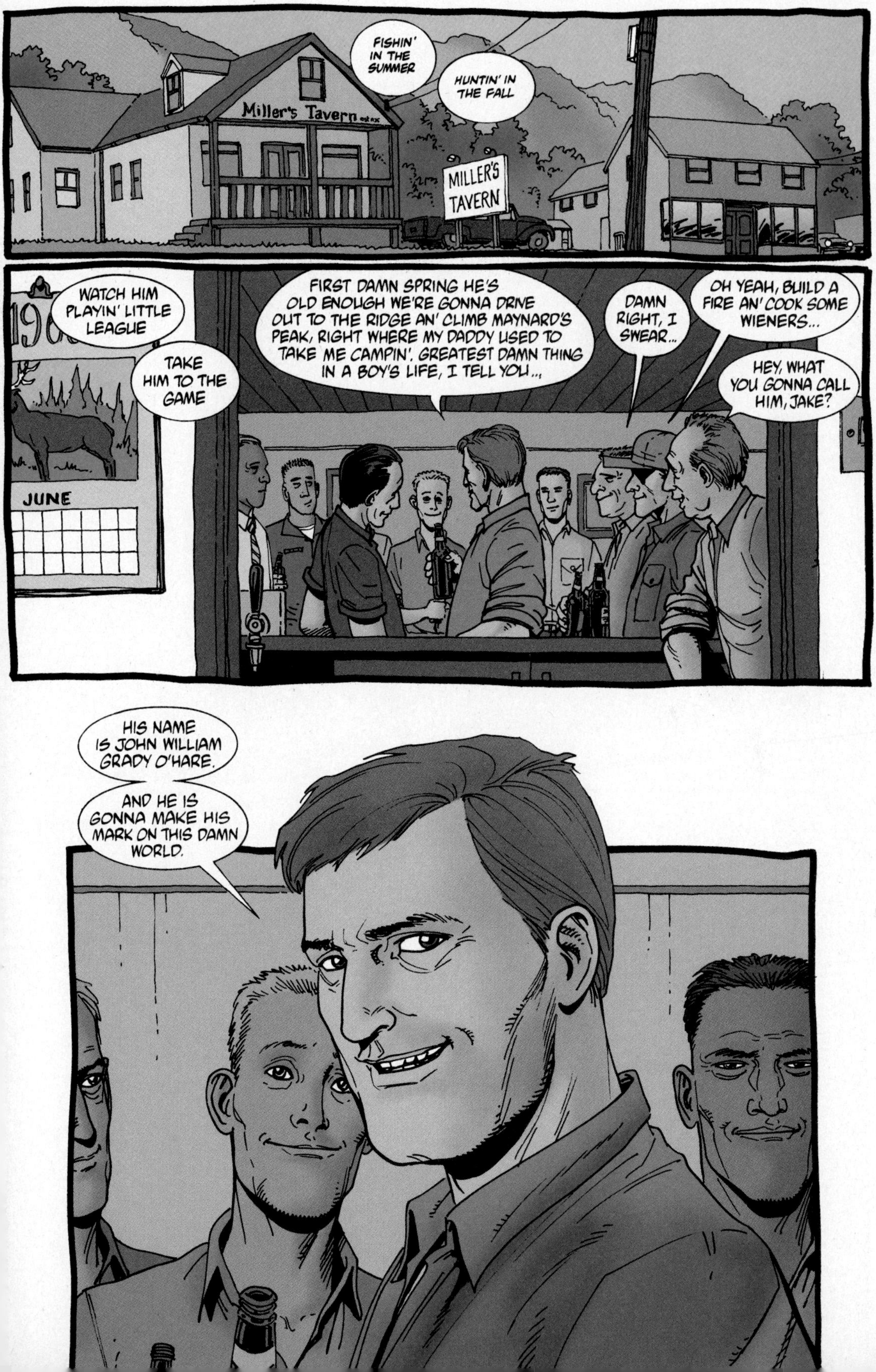
Miller's Tavern
FISHIN' IN THE SUMMER
HUNTIN' IN THE FALL
MILLER'S TAVERN
WATCH HIM PLAYIN' LITTLE LEAGUE
TAKE HIM TO THE GAME
JUNE
FIRST DAMN SPRING HE'S OLD ENOUGH WE'RE GONNA DRIVE OUT TO THE RIDGE AN' CLIMB MAYNARD'S PEAK, RIGHT WHERE MY DADDY USED TO TAKE ME CAMPIN'. GREATEST DAMN THING IN A BOY'S LIFE, I TELL YOU...
DAMN RIGHT, I SWEAR...
OH YEAH, BUILD A FIRE AN' COOK SOME WIENERS...
HEY, WHAT YOU GONNA CALL HIM, JAKE?
HIS NAME IS JOHN WILLIAM GRADY O'HARE.
AND HE IS GONNA MAKE HIS MARK ON THIS DAMN WORLD.

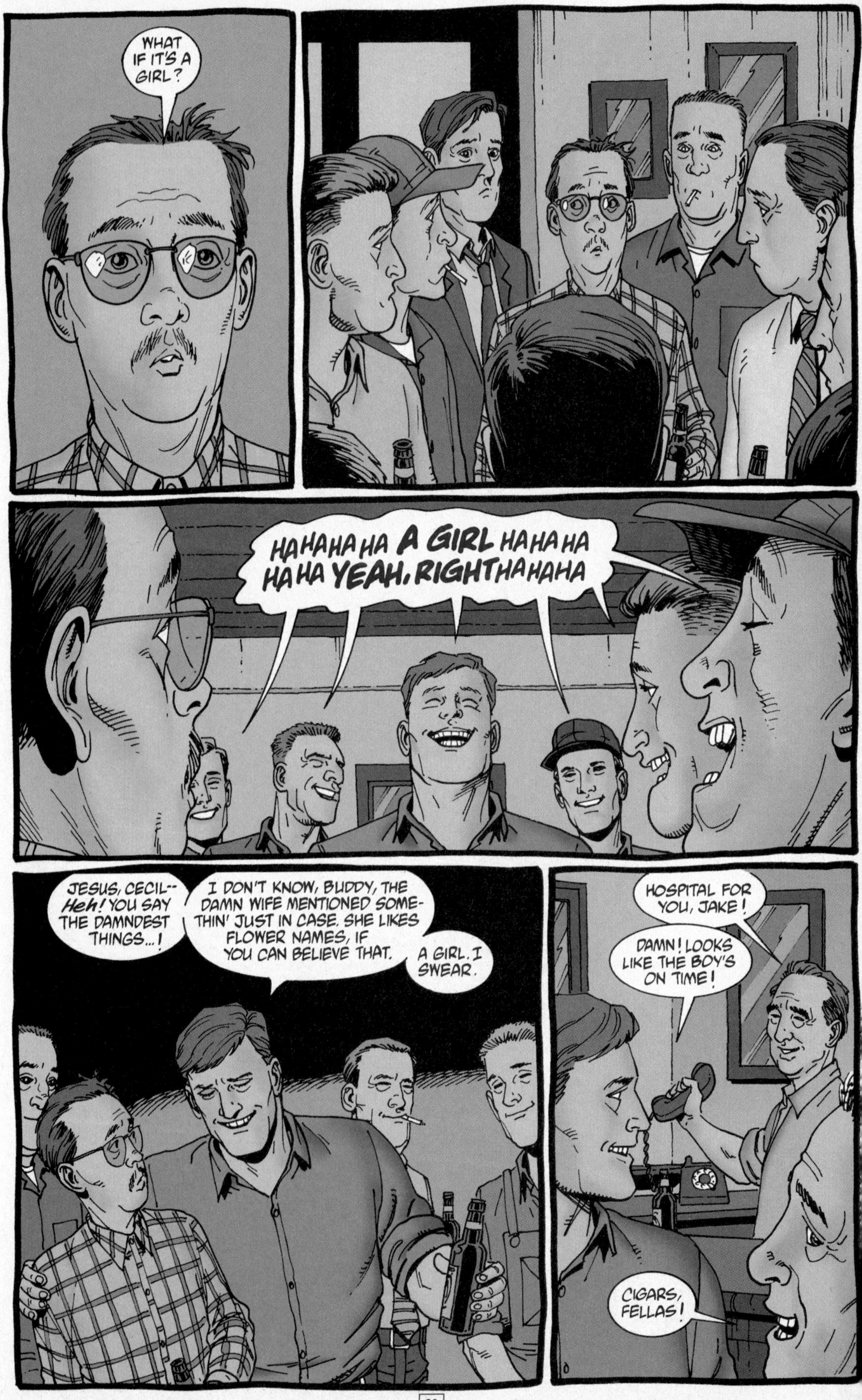
WHAT IF IT'S A GIRL?
HAHAHAHA A GIRL HAHAHA HAHA YEAH, RIGHT HAHAHA
JESUS, CECIL-- Heh! YOU SAY THE DAMNDEST THINGS...!
I DON'T KNOW, BUDDY, THE DAMN WIFE MENTIONED SOME-THIN' JUST IN CASE. SHE LIKES FLOWER NAMES, IF YOU CAN BELIEVE THAT.
A GIRL. I SWEAR.
HOSPITAL FOR YOU, JAKE!
DAMN! LOOKS LIKE THE BOY'S ON TIME!
CIGARS, FELLAS!

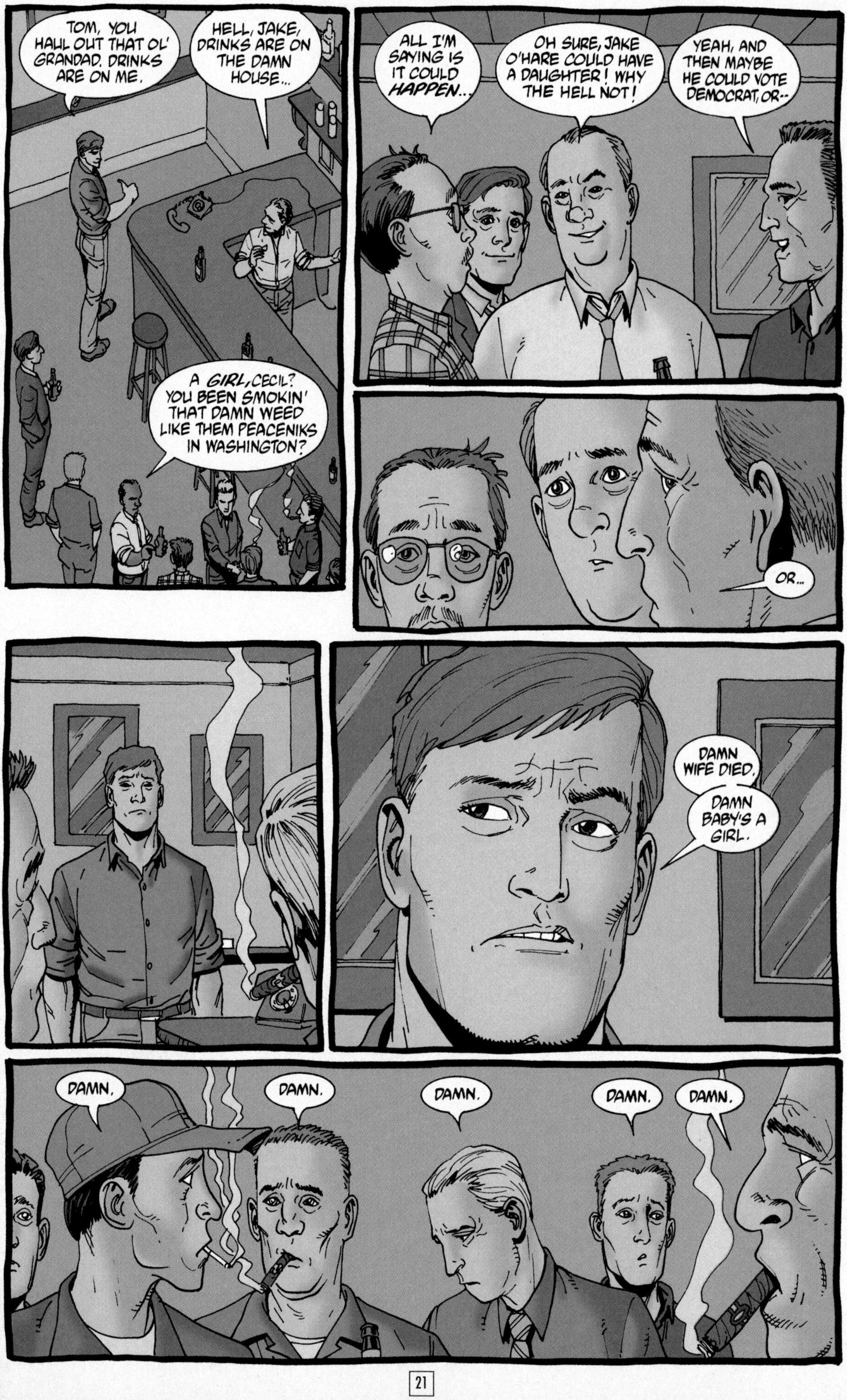
TOM, YOU HAUL OUT THAT OL' GRANDAD. DRINKS ARE ON ME.
HELL, JAKE, DRINKS ARE ON THE DAMN HOUSE...
A GIRL, CECIL? YOU BEEN SMOKIN' THAT DAMN WEED LIKE THEM PEACENIKS IN WASHINGTON?
ALL I'M SAYING IS IT COULD HAPPEN...
OH SURE, JAKE O'HARE COULD HAVE A DAUGHTER! WHY THE HELL NOT!
YEAH, AND THEN MAYBE HE COULD VOTE DEMOCRAT, OR--
OR...
DAMN WIFE DIED.
DAMN BABY'S A GIRL.
DAMN.
DAMN.
DAMN.
DAMN.
DAMN.

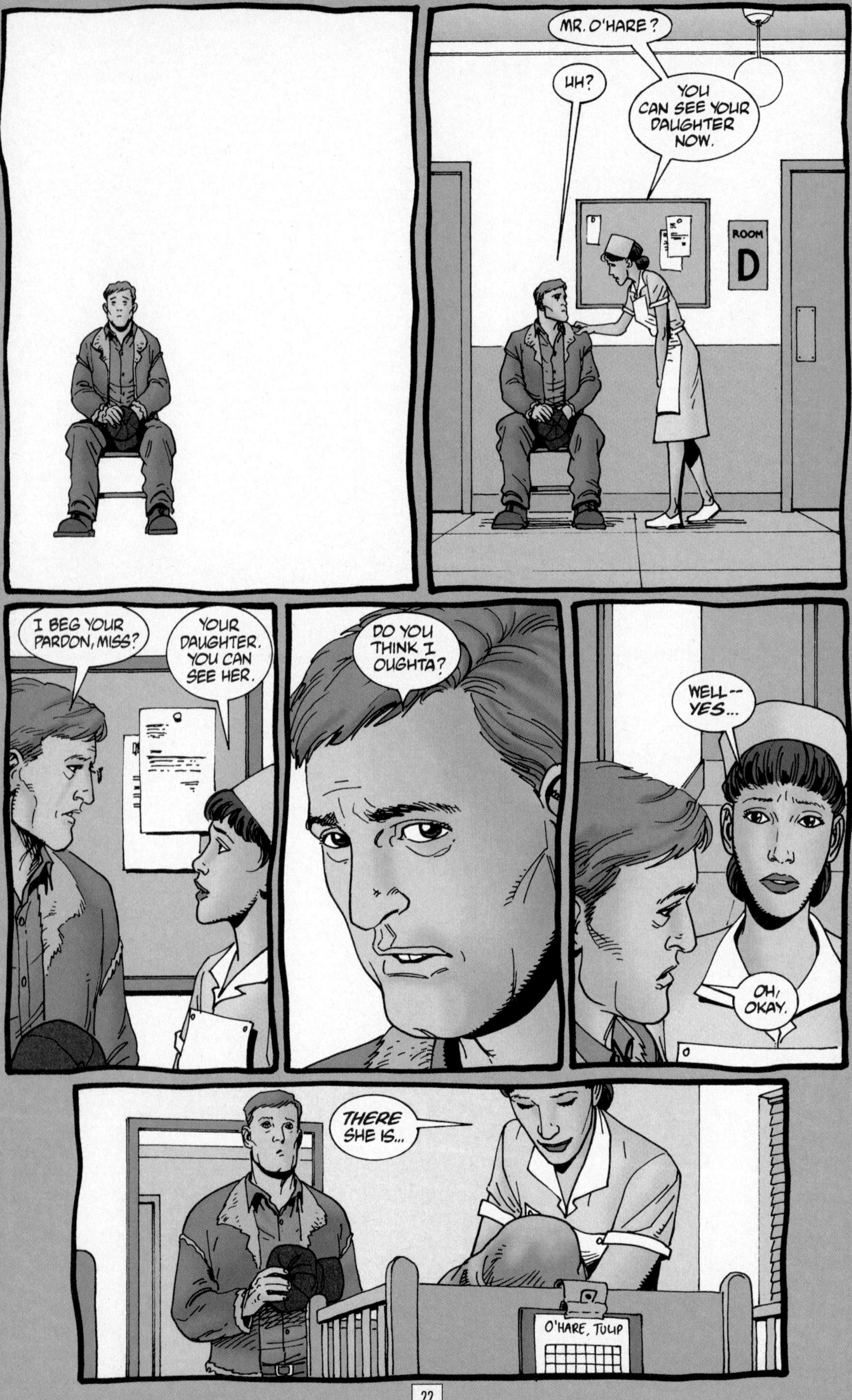
MR. O'HARE?
UH?
YOU CAN SEE YOUR DAUGHTER NOW.
ROOM D
I BEG YOUR PARDON, MISS?
YOUR DAUGHTER. YOU CAN SEE HER.
DO YOU THINK I OUGHTA?
WELL-- YES...
OH, OKAY.
THERE SHE IS...
O'HARE, TULIP

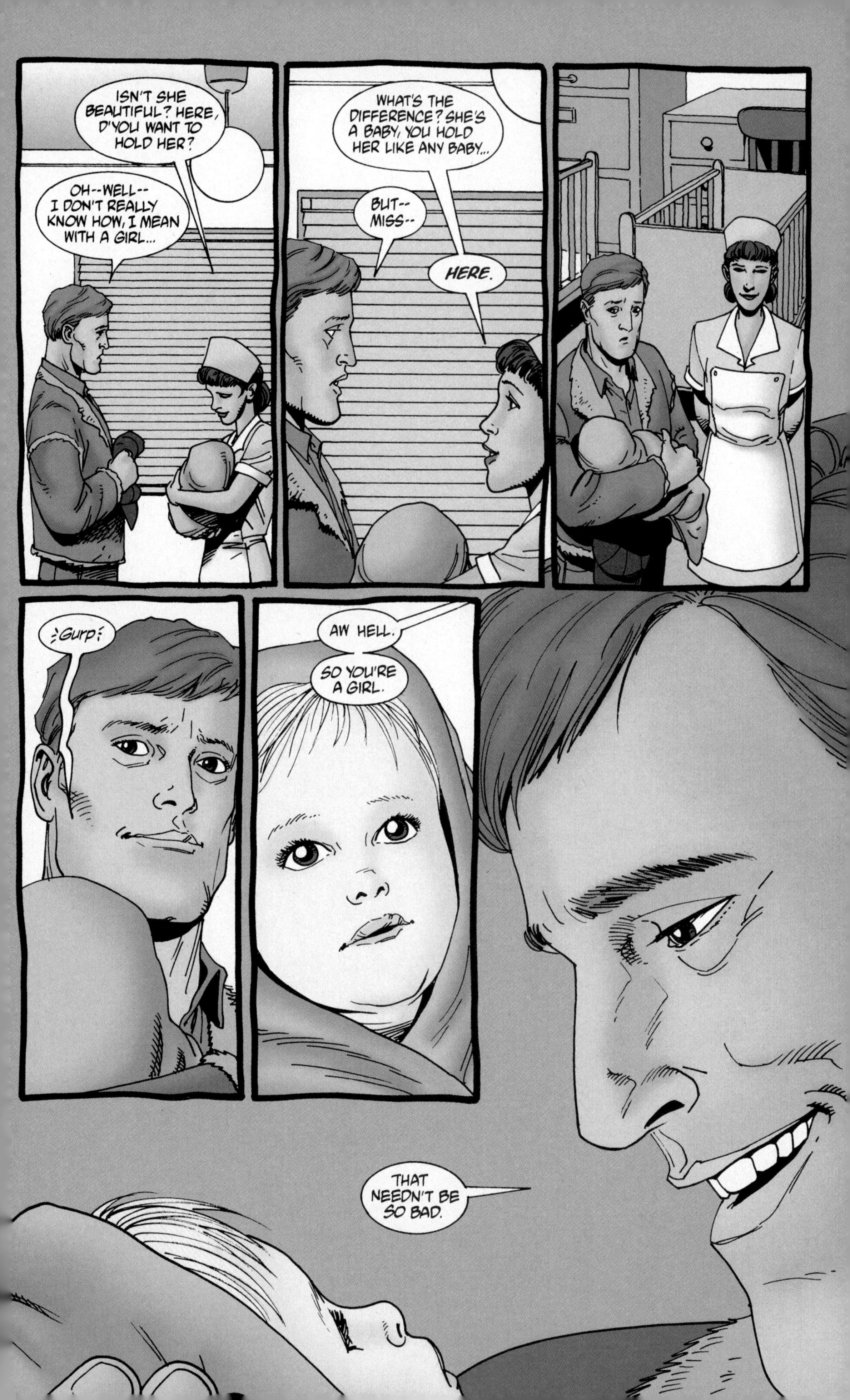
ISN'T SHE BEAUTIFUL? HERE, D'YOU WANT TO HOLD HER?
OH--WELL-- I DON'T REALLY KNOW HOW, I MEAN WITH A GIRL...
WHAT'S THE DIFFERENCE? SHE'S A BABY, YOU HOLD HER LIKE ANY BABY...
BUT-- MISS--
HERE.
Gurp
AW HELL.
SO YOU'RE A GIRL.
THAT NEEDN'T BE SO BAD.

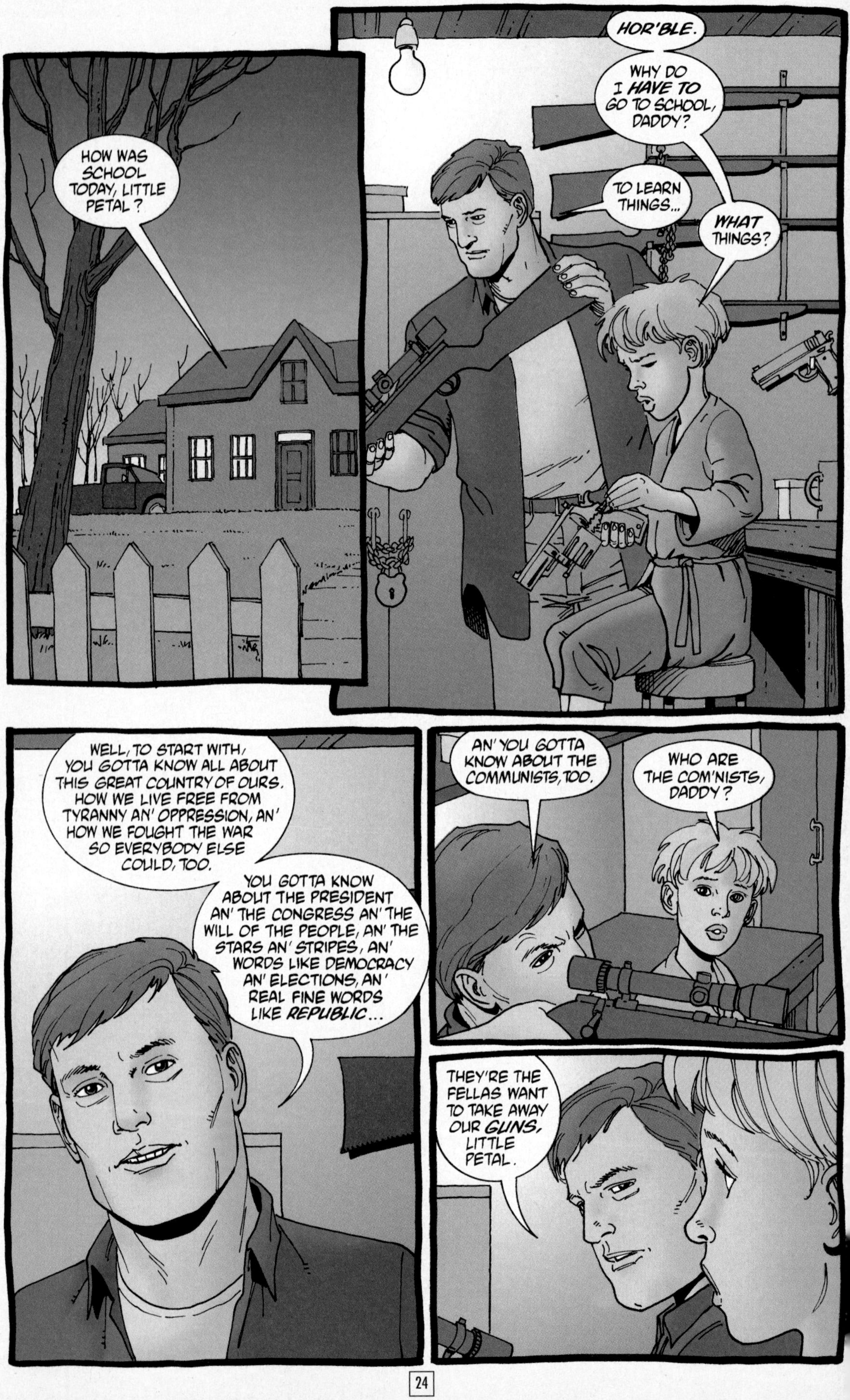

HOW WAS SCHOOL TODAY, LITTLE PETAL ?
HOR'BLE.
WHY DO I HAVE TO GO TO SCHOOL, DADDY?
TO LEARN THINGS...
WHAT THINGS?
WELL, TO START WITH, YOU GOTTA KNOW ALL ABOUT THIS GREAT COUNTRY OF OURS. HOW WE LIVE FREE FROM TYRANNY AN' OPPRESSION, AN' HOW WE FOUGHT THE WAR SO EVERYBODY ELSE COULD, TOO.
YOU GOTTA KNOW ABOUT THE PRESIDENT AN' THE CONGRESS AN' THE WILL OF THE PEOPLE, AN' THE STARS AN' STRIPES, AN' WORDS LIKE DEMOCRACY AN' ELECTIONS, AN' REAL FINE WORDS LIKE REPUBLIC...
AN' YOU GOTTA KNOW ABOUT THE COMMUNISTS, TOO.
WHO ARE THE COM'NISTS, DADDY?
THEY'RE THE FELLAS WANT TO TAKE AWAY OUR GUNS, LITTLE PETAL.

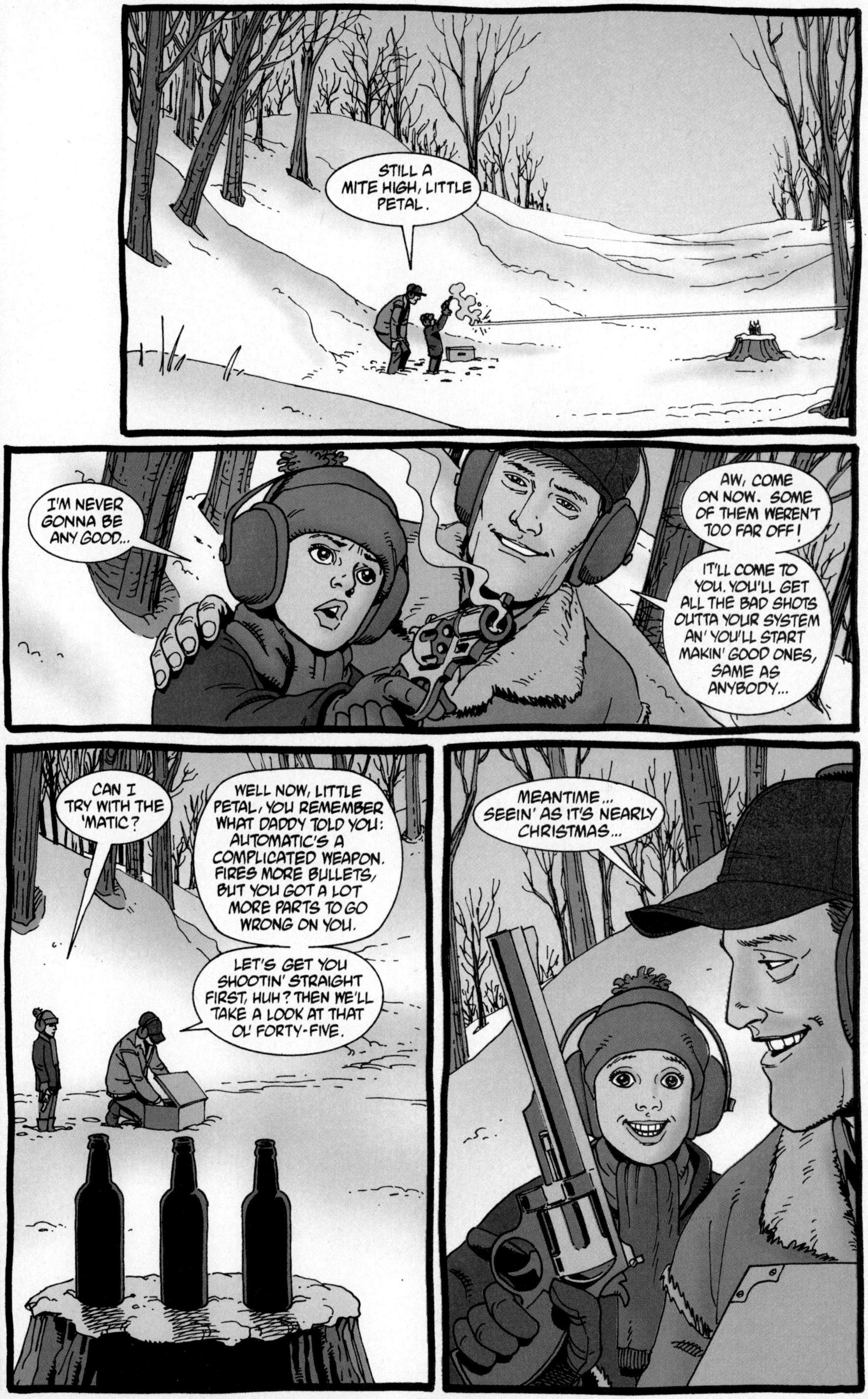
STILL A MITE HIGH, LITTLE PETAL.
I'M NEVER GONNA BE ANY GOOD...
AW, COME ON NOW. SOME OF THEM WEREN'T TOO FAR OFF!
IT'LL COME TO YOU. YOU'LL GET ALL THE BAD SHOTS OUTTA YOUR SYSTEM AN' YOU'LL START MAKIN' GOOD ONES, SAME AS ANYBODY...
CAN I TRY WITH THE 'MATIC?
WELL NOW, LITTLE PETAL, YOU REMEMBER WHAT DADDY TOLD YOU: AUTOMATIC'S A COMPLICATED WEAPON. FIRES MORE BULLETS, BUT YOU GOT A LOT MORE PARTS TO GO WRONG ON YOU.
LET'S GET YOU SHOOTIN' STRAIGHT FIRST, HUH? THEN WE'LL TAKE A LOOK AT THAT OL' FORTY-FIVE.
MEANTIME... SEEIN' AS IT'S NEARLY CHRISTMAS...

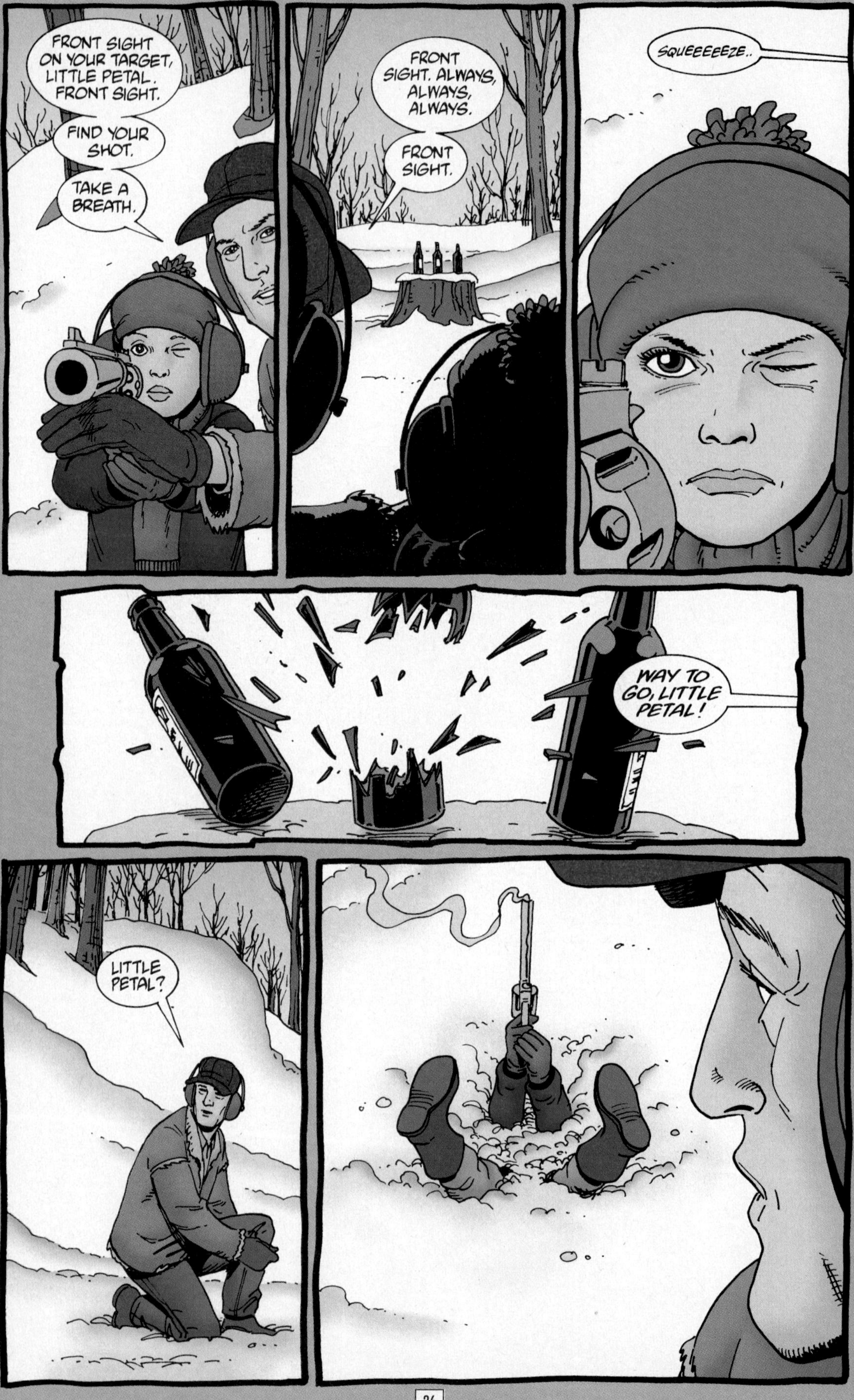
FRONT SIGHT ON YOUR TARGET, LITTLE PETAL. FRONT SIGHT.
FIND YOUR SHOT.
TAKE A BREATH.
FRONT SIGHT. ALWAYS, ALWAYS, ALWAYS.
FRONT SIGHT.
SQUEEEEEEZE..
WAY TO GO, LITTLE PETAL!
LITTLE PETAL?

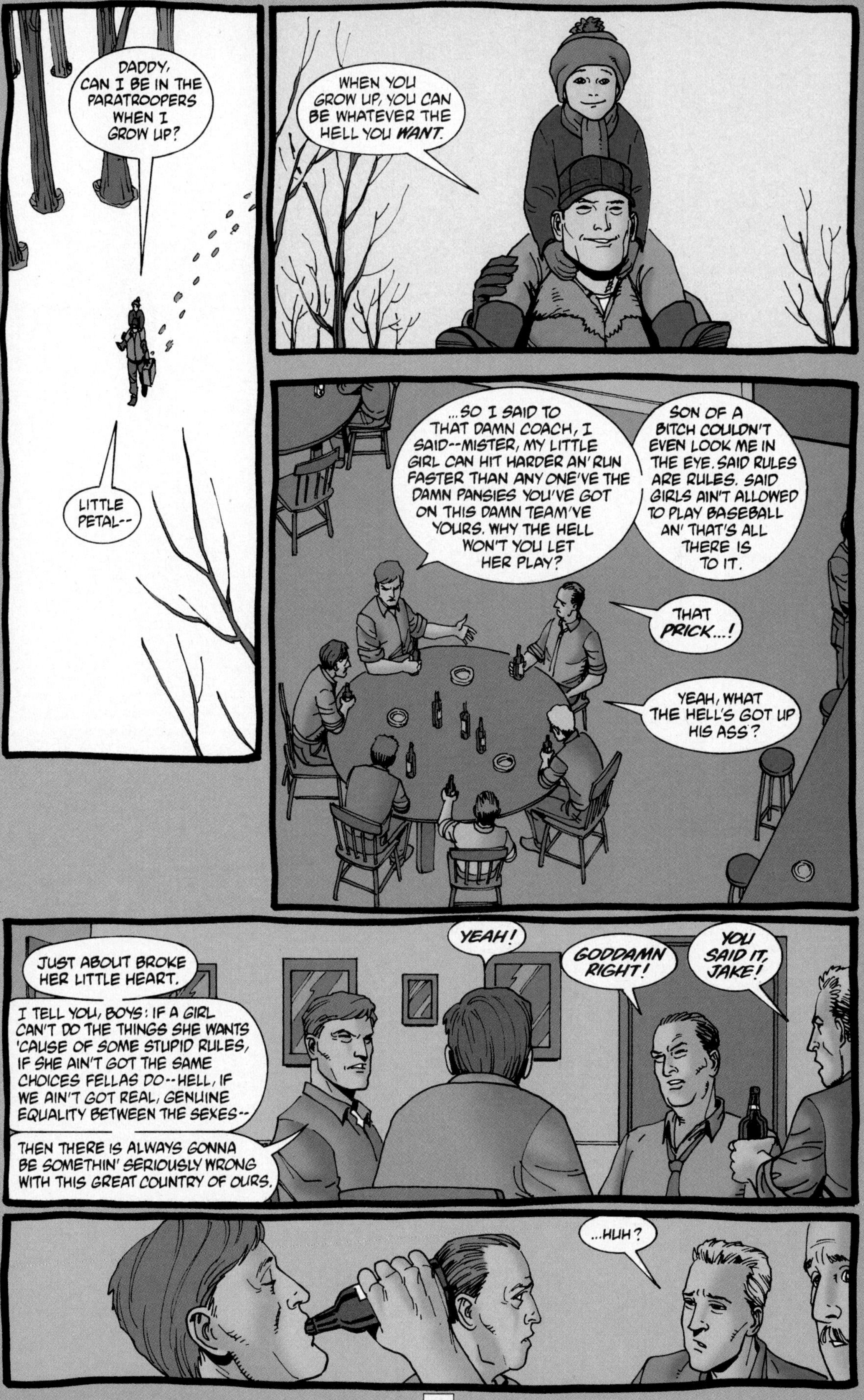
DADDY, CAN I BE IN THE PARATROOPERS WHEN I GROW UP?
LITTLE PETAL--
WHEN YOU GROW UP, YOU CAN BE WHATEVER THE HELL YOU WANT.
...SO I SAID TO THAT DAMN COACH, I SAID--MISTER, MY LITTLE GIRL CAN HIT HARDER AN' RUN FASTER THAN ANY ONE'VE THE DAMN PANSIES YOU'VE GOT ON THIS DAMN TEAM'VE YOURS. WHY THE HELL WON'T YOU LET HER PLAY?
SON OF A BITCH COULDN'T EVEN LOOK ME IN THE EYE. SAID RULES ARE RULES. SAID GIRLS AIN'T ALLOWED TO PLAY BASEBALL AN' THAT'S ALL THERE IS TO IT.
THAT PRICK...!
YEAH, WHAT THE HELL'S GOT UP HIS ASS?
JUST ABOUT BROKE HER LITTLE HEART.
I TELL YOU, BOYS: IF A GIRL CAN'T DO THE THINGS SHE WANTS 'CAUSE OF SOME STUPID RULES, IF SHE AIN'T GOT THE SAME CHOICES FELLAS DO--HELL, IF WE AIN'T GOT REAL, GENUINE EQUALITY BETWEEN THE SEXES--
THEN THERE IS ALWAYS GONNA BE SOMETHIN' SERIOUSLY WRONG WITH THIS GREAT COUNTRY OF OURS.
YEAH!
GODDAMN RIGHT!
YOU SAID IT, JAKE!
...HUH?

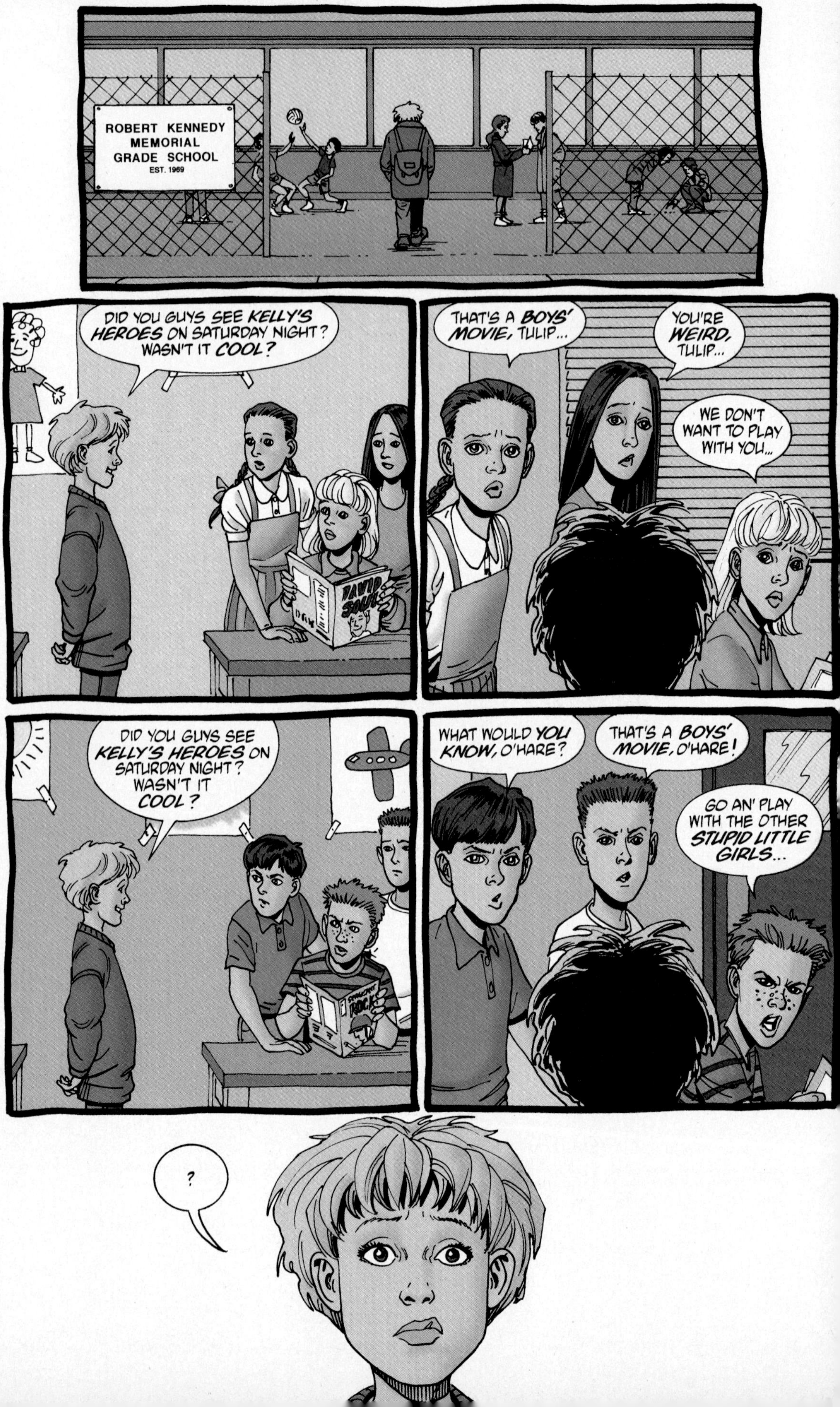
ROBERT KENNEDY MEMORIAL GRADE SCHOOL EST. 1969
DID YOU GUYS SEE KELLY'S HEROES ON SATURDAY NIGHT? WASN'T IT COOL?
THAT'S A BOYS' MOVIE, TULIP...
YOU'RE WEIRD, TULIP...
WE DON'T WANT TO PLAY WITH YOU...
DID YOU GUYS SEE KELLY'S HEROES ON SATURDAY NIGHT? WASN'T IT COOL?
WHAT WOULD YOU KNOW, O'HARE?
THAT'S A BOYS' MOVIE, O'HARE!
GO AN' PLAY WITH THE OTHER STUPID LITTLE GIRLS...
?

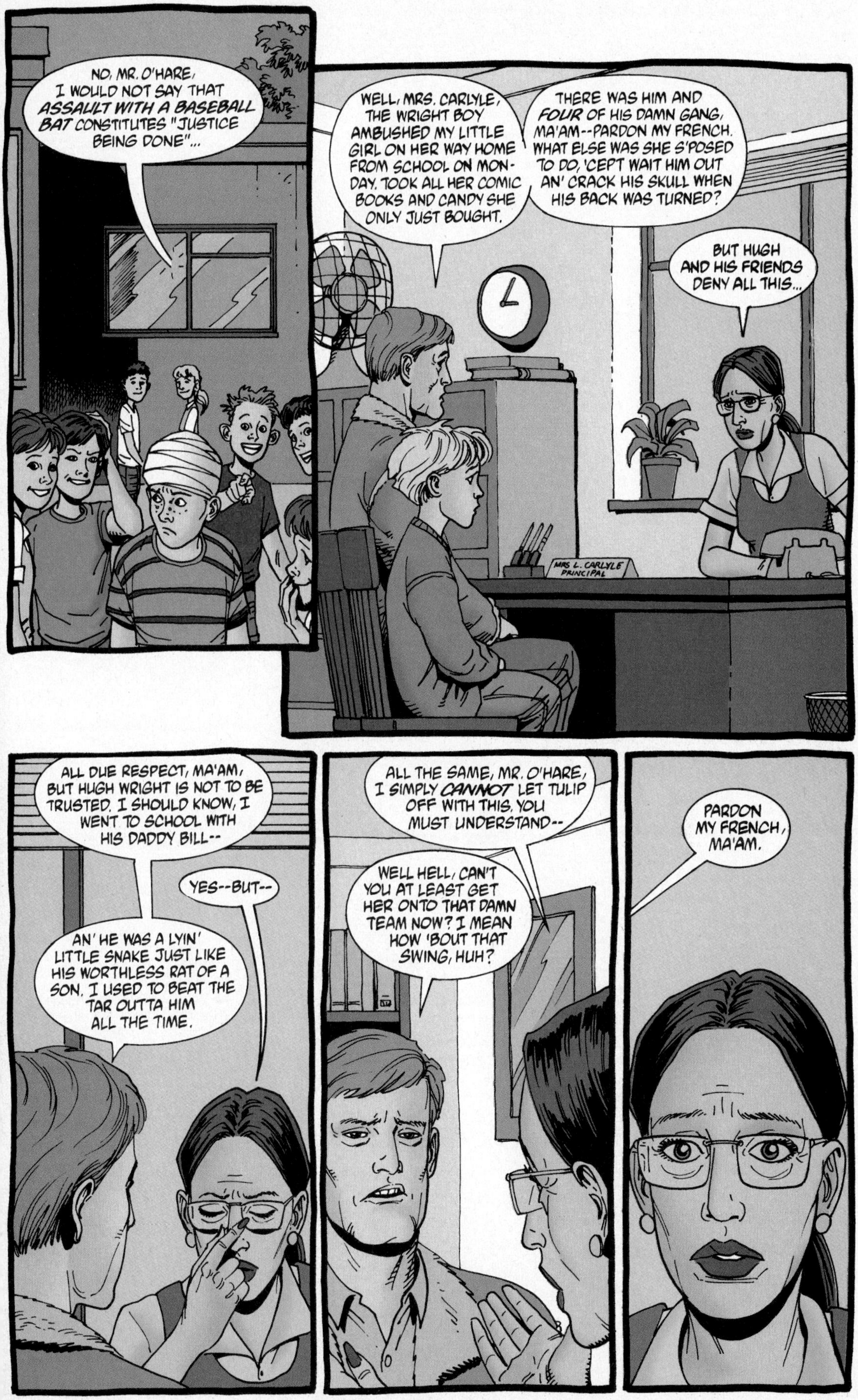
NO, MR. O'HARE, I WOULD NOT SAY THAT ASSAULT WITH A BASEBALL BAT CONSTITUTES "JUSTICE BEING DONE"...
WELL, MRS. CARLYLE, THE WRIGHT BOY AMBUSHED MY LITTLE GIRL ON HER WAY HOME FROM SCHOOL ON MON-DAY. TOOK ALL HER COMIC BOOKS AND CANDY SHE ONLY JUST BOUGHT.
THERE WAS HIM AND FOUR OF HIS DAMN GANG, MA'AM--PARDON MY FRENCH. WHAT ELSE WAS SHE S'POSED TO DO, 'CEPT WAIT HIM OUT AN' CRACK HIS SKULL WHEN HIS BACK WAS TURNED?
BUT HUGH AND HIS FRIENDS DENY ALL THIS...
MRS L. CARLYLE PRINCIPAL
ALL DUE RESPECT, MA'AM, BUT HUGH WRIGHT IS NOT TO BE TRUSTED. I SHOULD KNOW, I WENT TO SCHOOL WITH HIS DADDY BILL--
YES--BUT--
AN' HE WAS A LYIN' LITTLE SNAKE JUST LIKE HIS WORTHLESS RAT OF A SON. I USED TO BEAT THE TAR OUTTA HIM ALL THE TIME.
ALL THE SAME, MR. O'HARE, I SIMPLY CANNOT LET TULIP OFF WITH THIS. YOU MUST UNDERSTAND--
WELL HELL, CAN'T YOU AT LEAST GET HER ONTO THAT DAMN TEAM NOW? I MEAN HOW 'BOUT THAT SWING, HUH?
PARDON MY FRENCH, MA'AM.

...YES, TULIP IS A VERY INTELLIGENT GIRL--HER GRADES ARE EXCELLENT RIGHT ACROSS THE BOARD, IN FACT--

BUT CAN'T YOU *PLEASE* ENCOURAGE HER IN SOME SLIGHTLY MORE--MORE FEMININE PURSUITS? AND ATTITUDES?

WELL, MRS. CARLYLE, NO DISRESPECT INTENDED TO YOUR POINT OF VIEW, MA'AM...

BUT I ALWAYS FIGURED IT WAS BEST TO ENCOURAGE HER IN WHAT SHE *LIKED.*

...
...
...

YOU CAN DISCIPLINE HER, CAN'T YOU? YOU CAN DO THAT, RIGHT?

SURE.

MRS L. CARLYLE PRINCIPAL

WHY WERE YOU BEING SO NICE TO MRS. CARLYLE, DADDY?

US FELLAS HAVE TO BE POLITE TO YOU LADIES, LITTLE PETAL. IT'S HOW WE'RE RAISED.

MENU

HOW COME?

HMMM.

I AIN'T EXACTLY SURE, LITTLE PETAL.

IT MIGHT BE TO MAKE UP FOR LADIES GENERALLY HAVIN' LESS FUN.

30

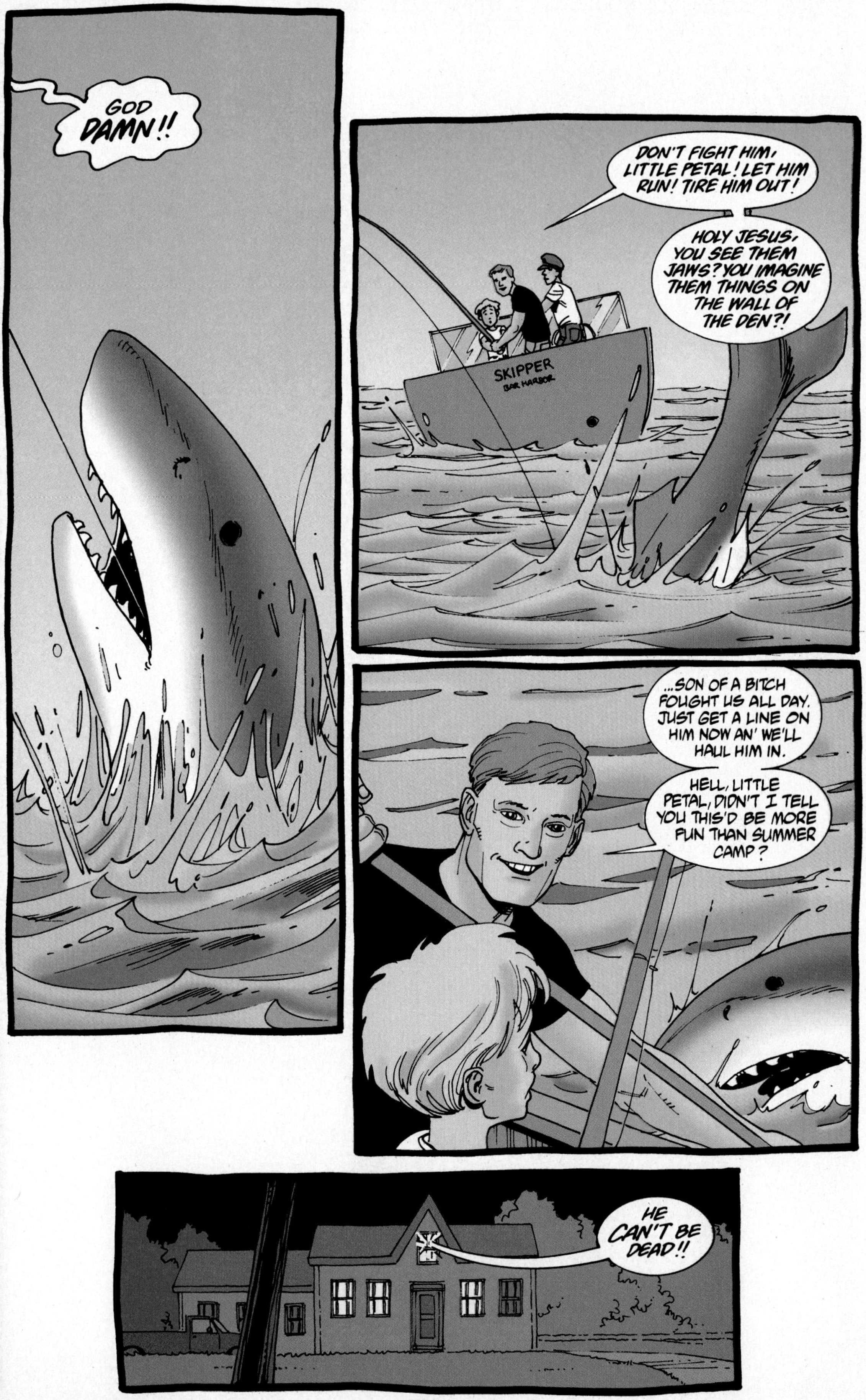
GOD DAMN!!
DON'T FIGHT HIM, LITTLE PETAL! LET HIM RUN! TIRE HIM OUT!
HOLY JESUS, YOU SEE THEM JAWS? YOU IMAGINE THEM THINGS ON THE WALL OF THE DEN?!
SKIPPER
BAR HARBOR
...SON OF A BITCH FOUGHT US ALL DAY. JUST GET A LINE ON HIM NOW AN' WE'LL HAUL HIM IN.
HELL, LITTLE PETAL, DIDN'T I TELL YOU THIS'D BE MORE FUN THAN SUMMER CAMP?
HE CAN'T BE DEAD!!

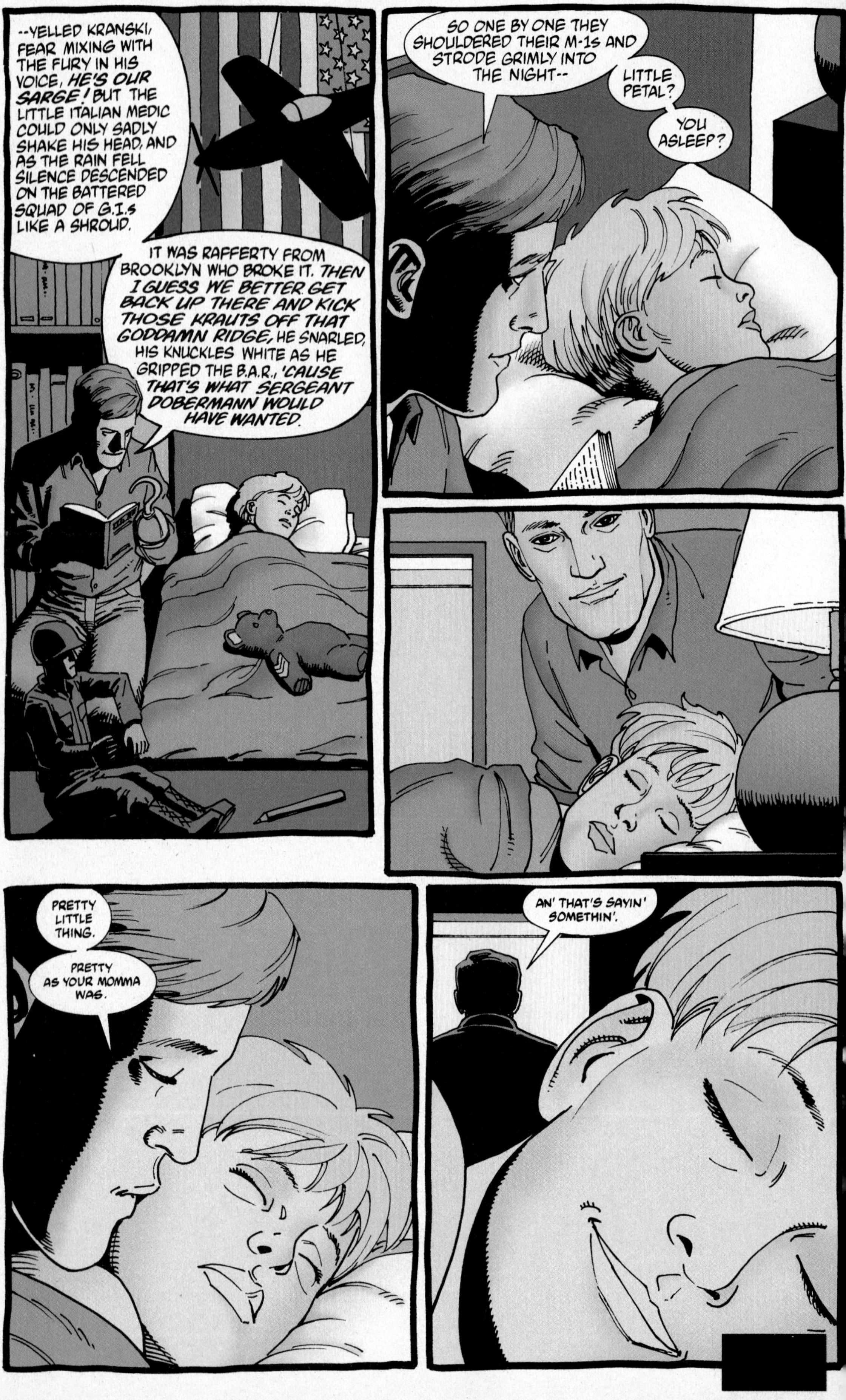
--YELLED KRANSKI, FEAR MIXING WITH THE FURY IN HIS VOICE, HE'S OUR SARGE! BUT THE LITTLE ITALIAN MEDIC COULD ONLY SADLY SHAKE HIS HEAD, AND AS THE RAIN FELL SILENCE DESCENDED ON THE BATTERED SQUAD OF G.I.s LIKE A SHROUD.
IT WAS RAFFERTY FROM BROOKLYN WHO BROKE IT. THEN I GUESS WE BETTER GET BACK UP THERE AND KICK THOSE KRAUTS OFF THAT GODDAMN RIDGE, HE SNARLED, HIS KNUCKLES WHITE AS HE GRIPPED THE B.A.R., 'CAUSE THAT'S WHAT SERGEANT DOBERMANN WOULD HAVE WANTED.
SO ONE BY ONE THEY SHOULDERED THEIR M-1s AND STRODE GRIMLY INTO THE NIGHT--
LITTLE PETAL?
YOU ASLEEP?
PRETTY LITTLE THING.
PRETTY AS YOUR MOMMA WAS.
AN' THAT'S SAYIN' SOMETHIN'.

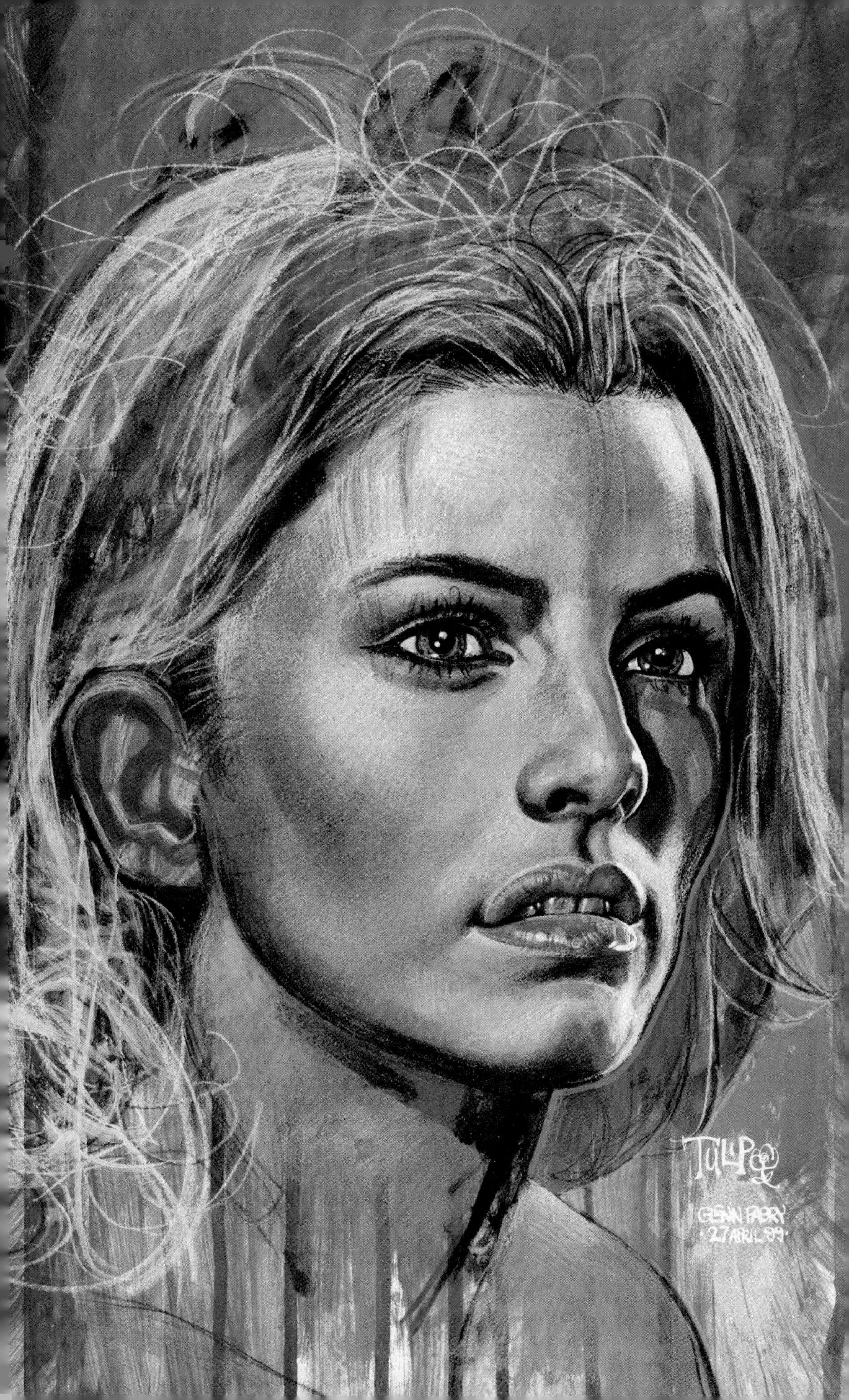
TULIP
GLENN FABRY
27 APRIL '09

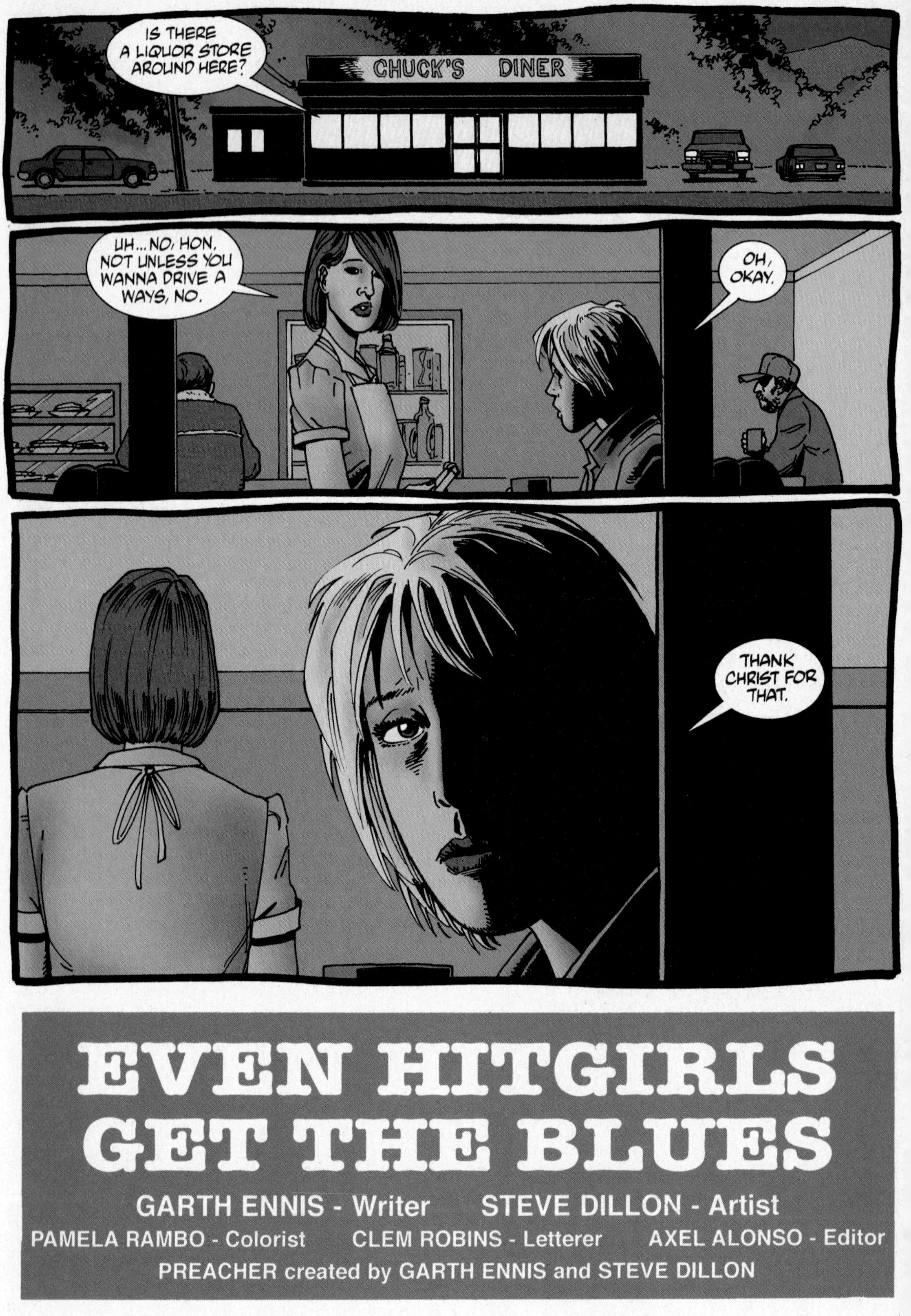
CHUCK'S DINER
IS THERE A LIQUOR STORE AROUND HERE?
UH... NO, HON, NOT UNLESS YOU WANNA DRIVE A WAYS, NO.
OH, OKAY.
THANK CHRIST FOR THAT.

EVEN HITGIRLS GET THE BLUES

GARTH ENNIS - Writer STEVE DILLON - Artist
PAMELA RAMBO - Colorist CLEM ROBINS - Letterer AXEL ALONSO - Editor
PREACHER created by GARTH ENNIS and STEVE DILLON

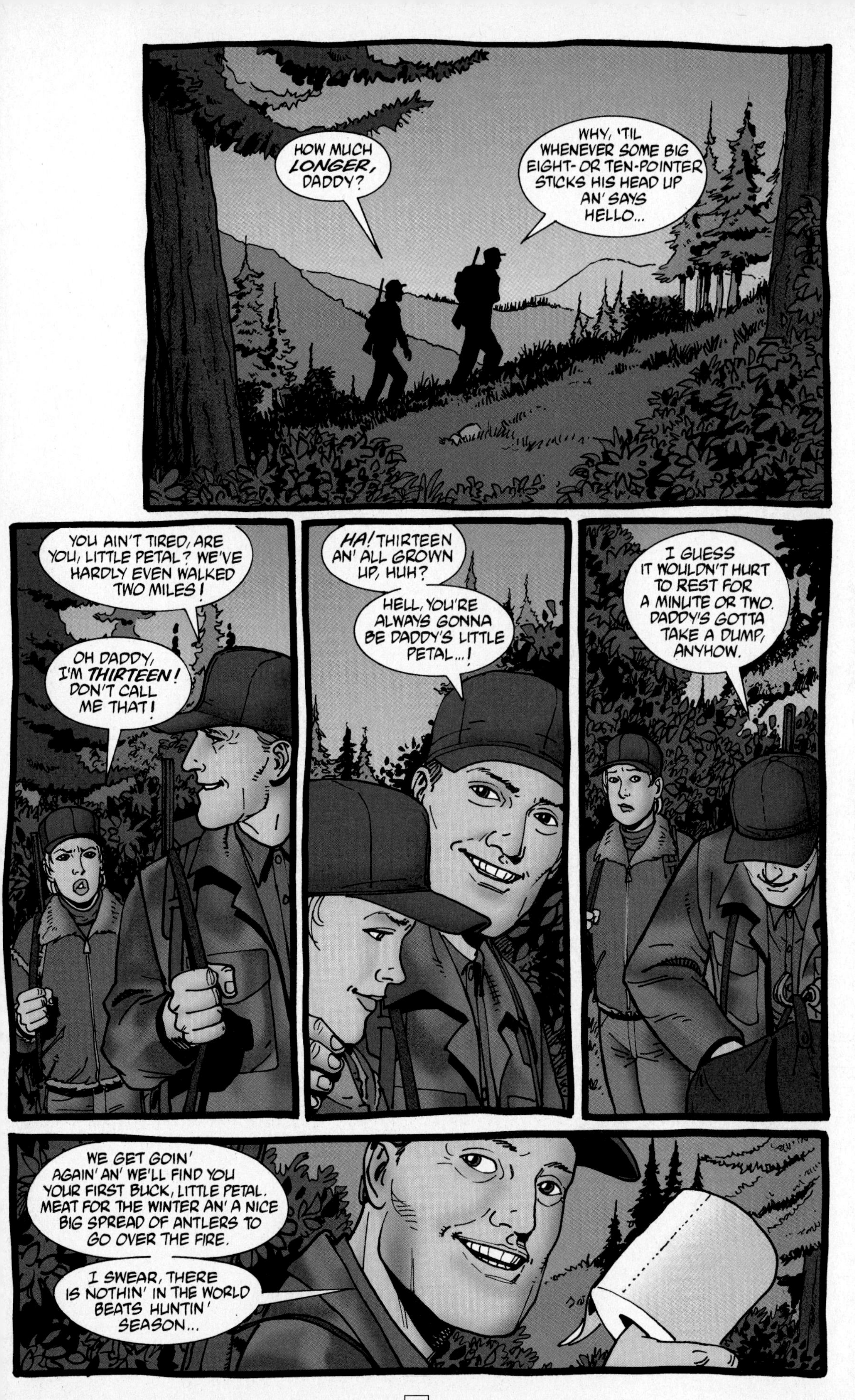
HOW MUCH LONGER, DADDY?
WHY, 'TIL WHENEVER SOME BIG EIGHT- OR TEN-POINTER STICKS HIS HEAD UP AN' SAYS HELLO...
YOU AIN'T TIRED, ARE YOU, LITTLE PETAL? WE'VE HARDLY EVEN WALKED TWO MILES!
OH DADDY, I'M THIRTEEN! DON'T CALL ME THAT!
HA! THIRTEEN AN' ALL GROWN UP, HUH?
HELL, YOU'RE ALWAYS GONNA BE DADDY'S LITTLE PETAL...!
I GUESS IT WOULDN'T HURT TO REST FOR A MINUTE OR TWO. DADDY'S GOTTA TAKE A DUMP, ANYHOW.
WE GET GOIN' AGAIN AN' WE'LL FIND YOU YOUR FIRST BUCK, LITTLE PETAL. MEAT FOR THE WINTER AN' A NICE BIG SPREAD OF ANTLERS TO GO OVER THE FIRE.
I SWEAR, THERE IS NOTHIN' IN THE WORLD BEATS HUNTIN' SEASON...

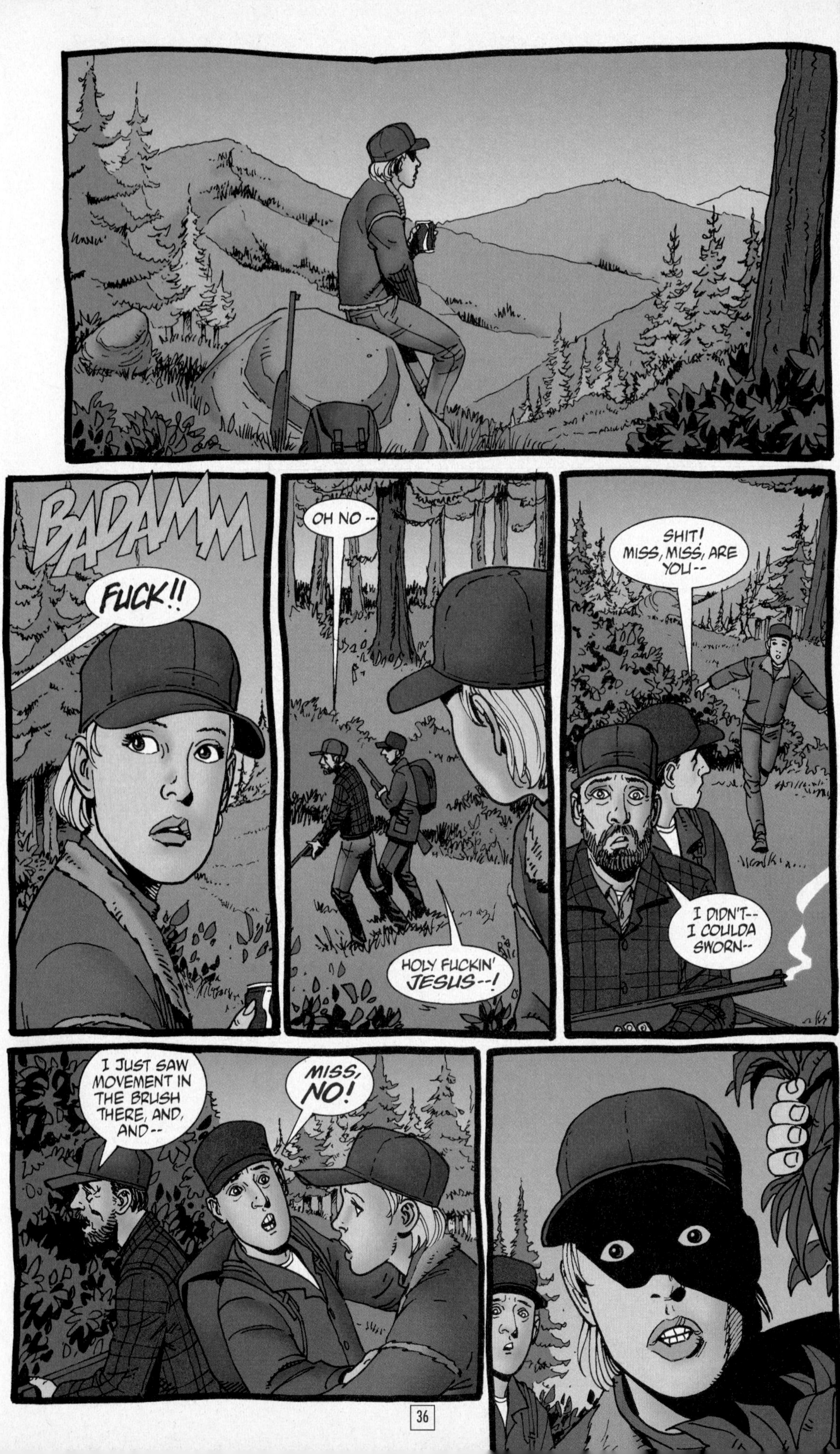
BADAMM
FUCK!!
OH NO --
HOLY FUCKIN' JESUS--!
SHIT! MISS, MISS, ARE YOU--
I DIDN'T-- I COULDA SWORN--
I JUST SAW MOVEMENT IN THE BRUSH THERE, AND, AND--
MISS, NO!

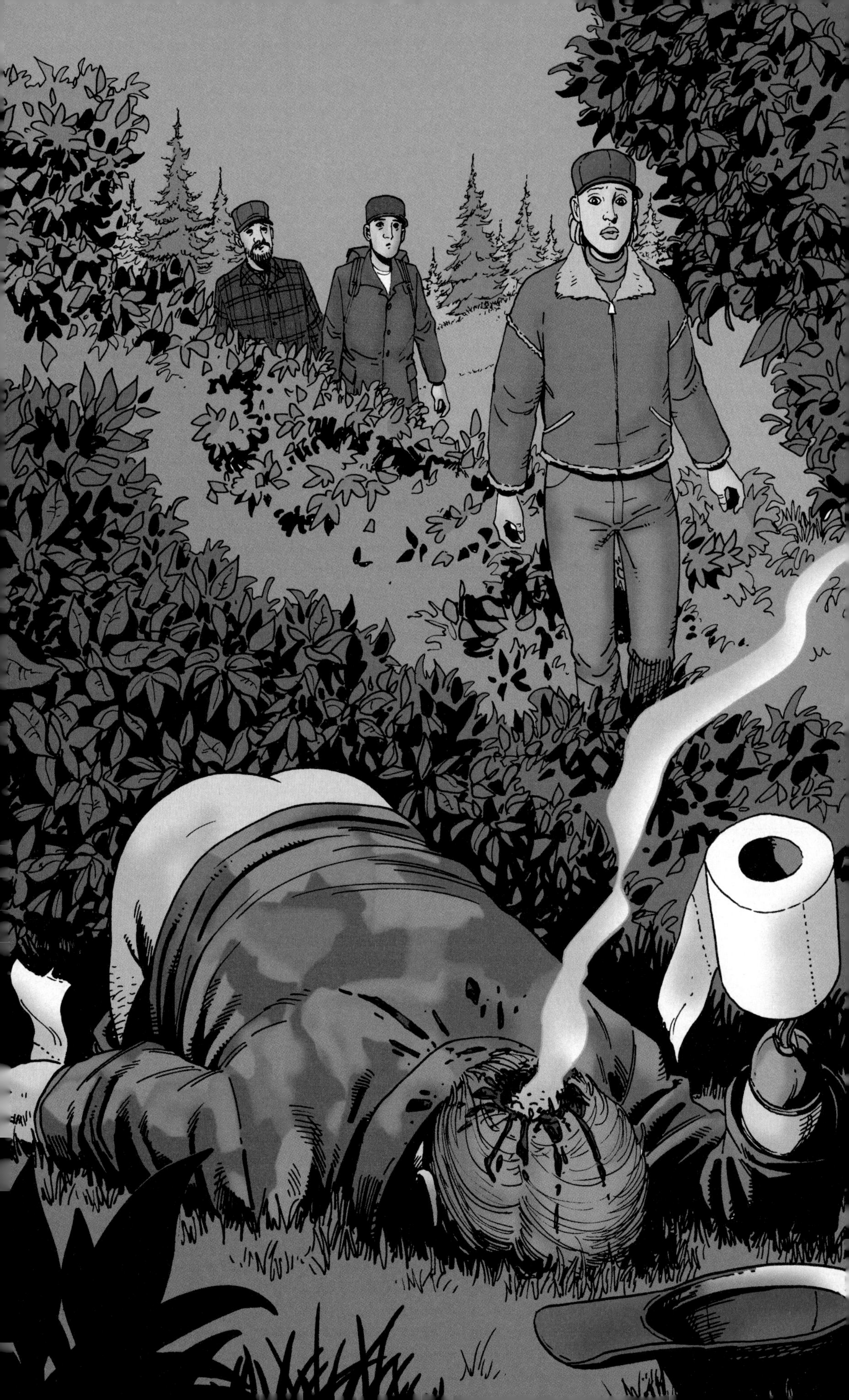

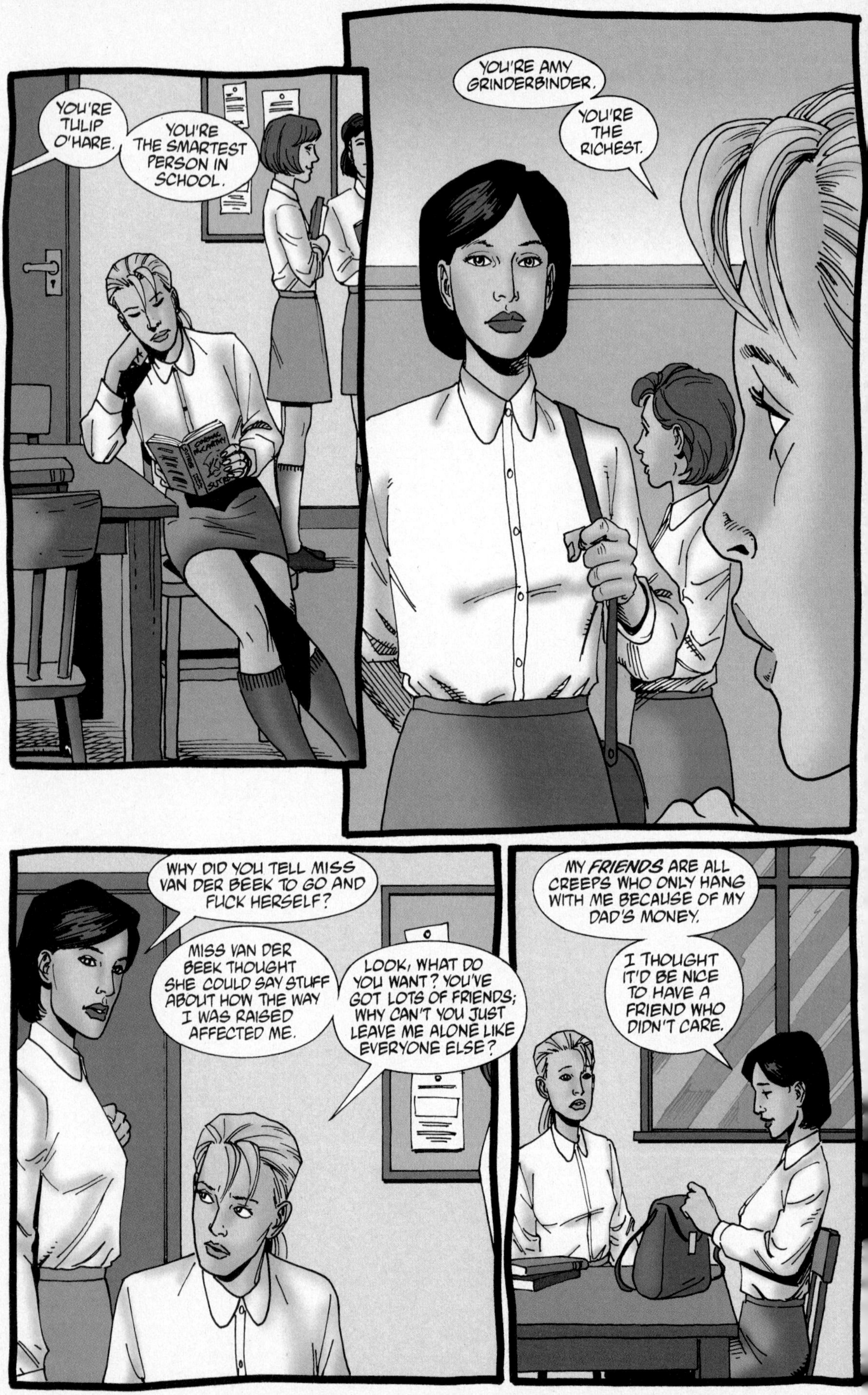

YOU'RE TULIP O'HARE.
YOU'RE THE SMARTEST PERSON IN SCHOOL.
YOU'RE AMY GRINDERBINDER.
YOU'RE THE RICHEST.
WHY DID YOU TELL MISS VAN DER BEEK TO GO AND FUCK HERSELF?
MISS VAN DER BEEK THOUGHT SHE COULD SAY STUFF ABOUT HOW THE WAY I WAS RAISED AFFECTED ME.
LOOK, WHAT DO YOU WANT? YOU'VE GOT LOTS OF FRIENDS; WHY CAN'T YOU JUST LEAVE ME ALONE LIKE EVERYONE ELSE?
MY *FRIENDS* ARE ALL CREEPS WHO ONLY HANG WITH ME BECAUSE OF MY DAD'S MONEY.
I THOUGHT IT'D BE NICE TO HAVE A FRIEND WHO DIDN'T CARE.

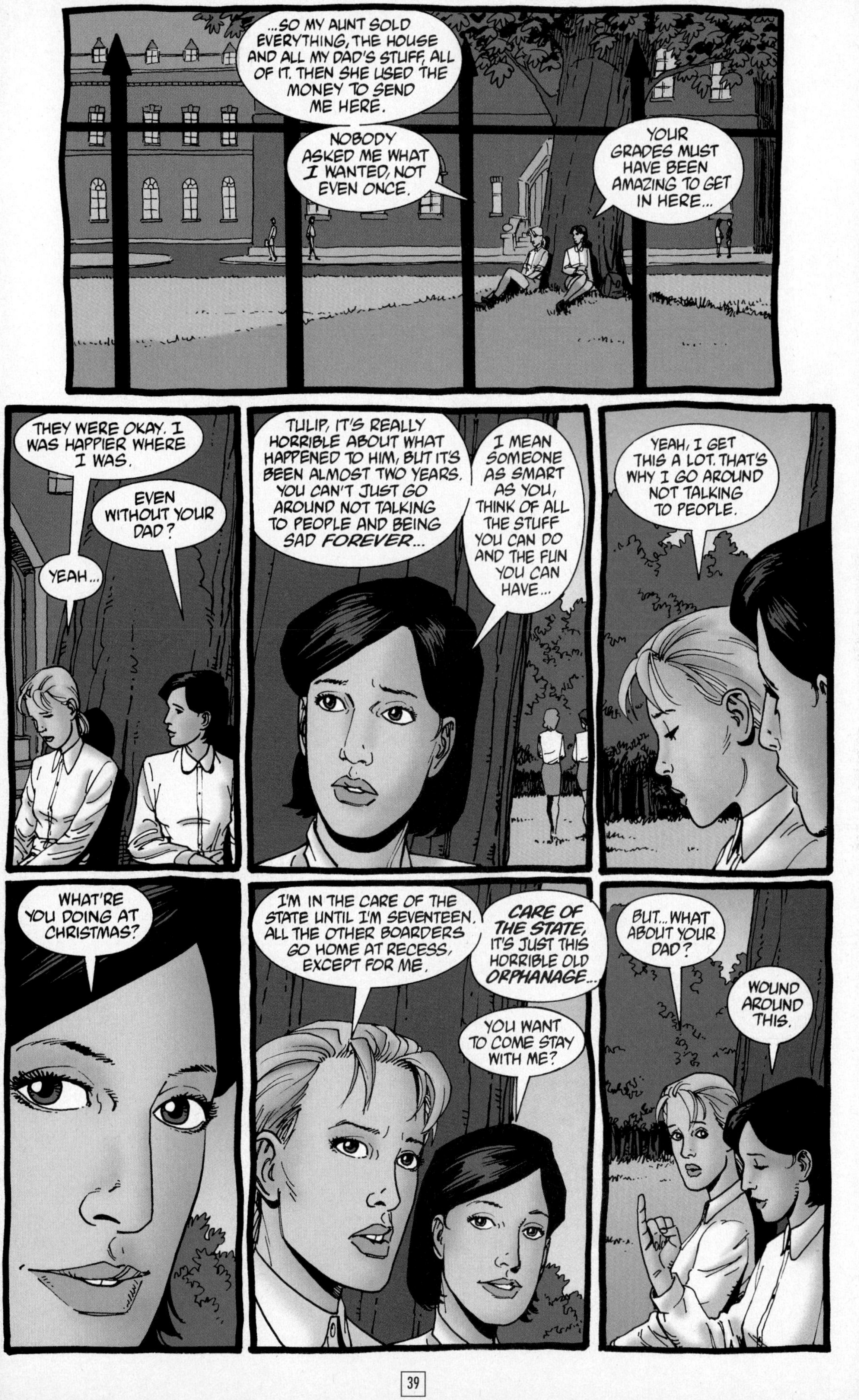
...SO MY AUNT SOLD EVERYTHING, THE HOUSE AND ALL MY DAD'S STUFF, ALL OF IT. THEN SHE USED THE MONEY TO SEND ME HERE.
NOBODY ASKED ME WHAT I WANTED, NOT EVEN ONCE.
YOUR GRADES MUST HAVE BEEN AMAZING TO GET IN HERE...
THEY WERE OKAY. I WAS HAPPIER WHERE I WAS.
EVEN WITHOUT YOUR DAD?
YEAH...
TULIP, IT'S REALLY HORRIBLE ABOUT WHAT HAPPENED TO HIM, BUT IT'S BEEN ALMOST TWO YEARS. YOU CAN'T JUST GO AROUND NOT TALKING TO PEOPLE AND BEING SAD FOREVER...
I MEAN SOMEONE AS SMART AS YOU, THINK OF ALL THE STUFF YOU CAN DO AND THE FUN YOU CAN HAVE...
YEAH, I GET THIS A LOT. THAT'S WHY I GO AROUND NOT TALKING TO PEOPLE.
WHAT'RE YOU DOING AT CHRISTMAS?
I'M IN THE CARE OF THE STATE UNTIL I'M SEVENTEEN. ALL THE OTHER BOARDERS GO HOME AT RECESS, EXCEPT FOR ME.
CARE OF THE STATE, IT'S JUST THIS HORRIBLE OLD ORPHANAGE...
YOU WANT TO COME STAY WITH ME?
BUT...WHAT ABOUT YOUR DAD?
WOUND AROUND THIS.

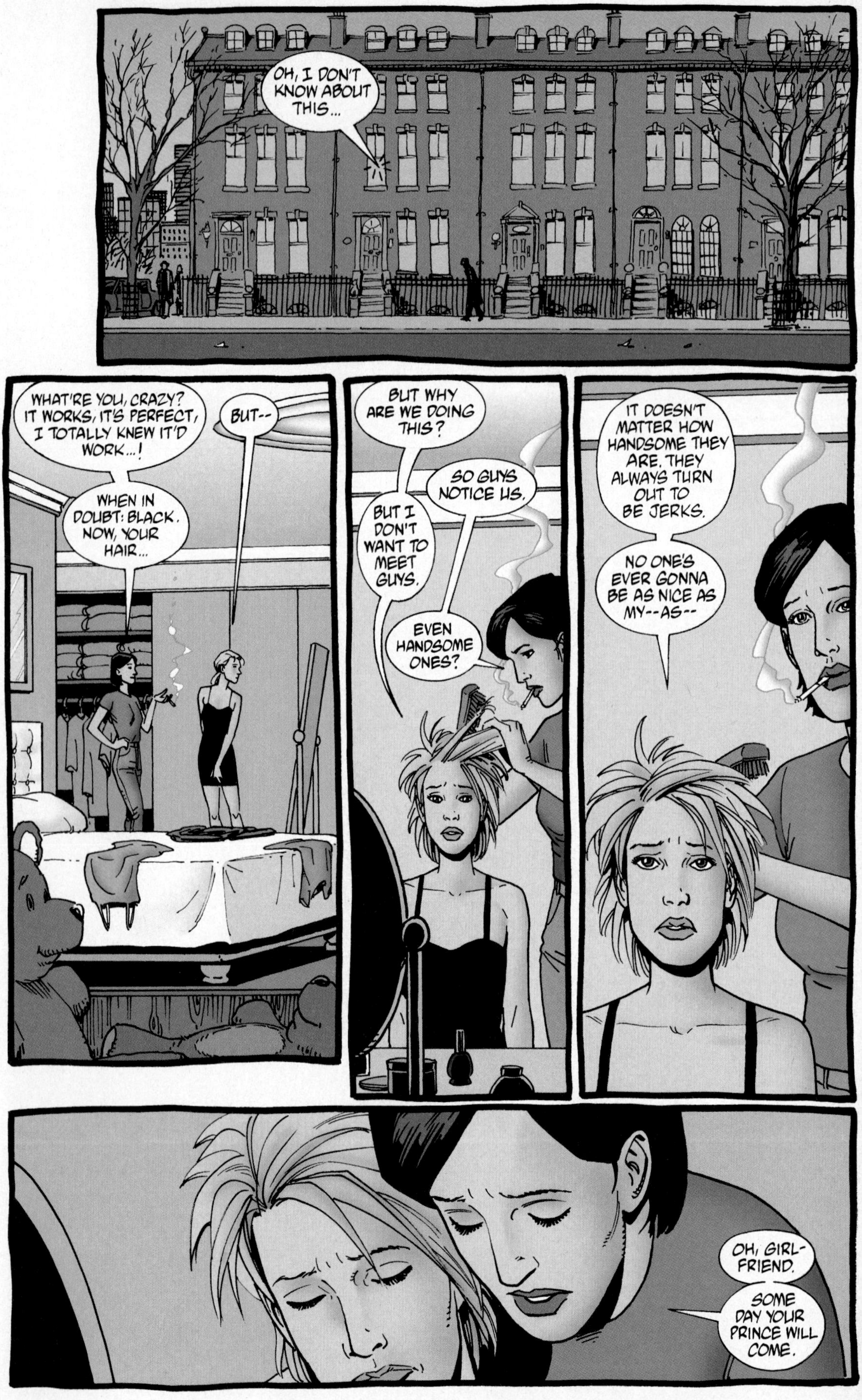
OH, I DON'T KNOW ABOUT THIS...
WHAT'RE YOU, CRAZY? IT WORKS, IT'S PERFECT, I TOTALLY KNEW IT'D WORK...!
WHEN IN DOUBT: BLACK. NOW, YOUR HAIR...
BUT--
BUT WHY ARE WE DOING THIS?
SO GUYS NOTICE US.
BUT I DON'T WANT TO MEET GUYS.
EVEN HANDSOME ONES?
IT DOESN'T MATTER HOW HANDSOME THEY ARE. THEY ALWAYS TURN OUT TO BE JERKS.
NO ONE'S EVER GONNA BE AS NICE AS MY--AS--
OH, GIRL-FRIEND.
SOME DAY YOUR PRINCE WILL COME.

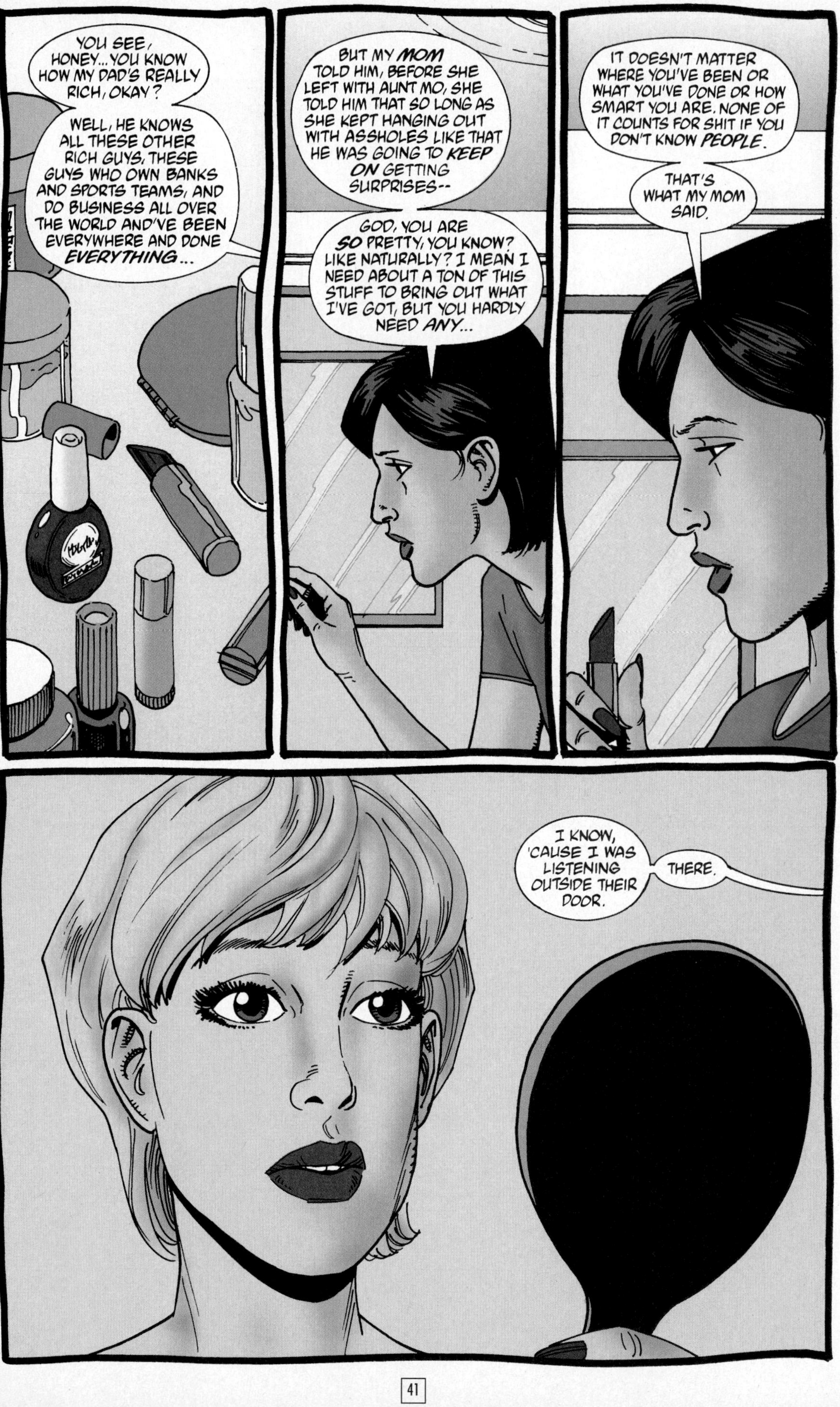
YOU SEE, HONEY... YOU KNOW HOW MY DAD'S REALLY RICH, OKAY?
WELL, HE KNOWS ALL THESE OTHER RICH GUYS, THESE GUYS WHO OWN BANKS AND SPORTS TEAMS, AND DO BUSINESS ALL OVER THE WORLD AND'VE BEEN EVERYWHERE AND DONE EVERYTHING...
BUT MY MOM TOLD HIM, BEFORE SHE LEFT WITH AUNT MO, SHE TOLD HIM THAT SO LONG AS SHE KEPT HANGING OUT WITH ASSHOLES LIKE THAT HE WAS GOING TO KEEP ON GETTING SURPRISES--
GOD, YOU ARE SO PRETTY, YOU KNOW? LIKE NATURALLY? I MEAN I NEED ABOUT A TON OF THIS STUFF TO BRING OUT WHAT I'VE GOT, BUT YOU HARDLY NEED ANY...
IT DOESN'T MATTER WHERE YOU'VE BEEN OR WHAT YOU'VE DONE OR HOW SMART YOU ARE. NONE OF IT COUNTS FOR SHIT IF YOU DON'T KNOW PEOPLE.
THAT'S WHAT MY MOM SAID.
I KNOW, 'CAUSE I WAS LISTENING OUTSIDE THEIR DOOR.
THERE.

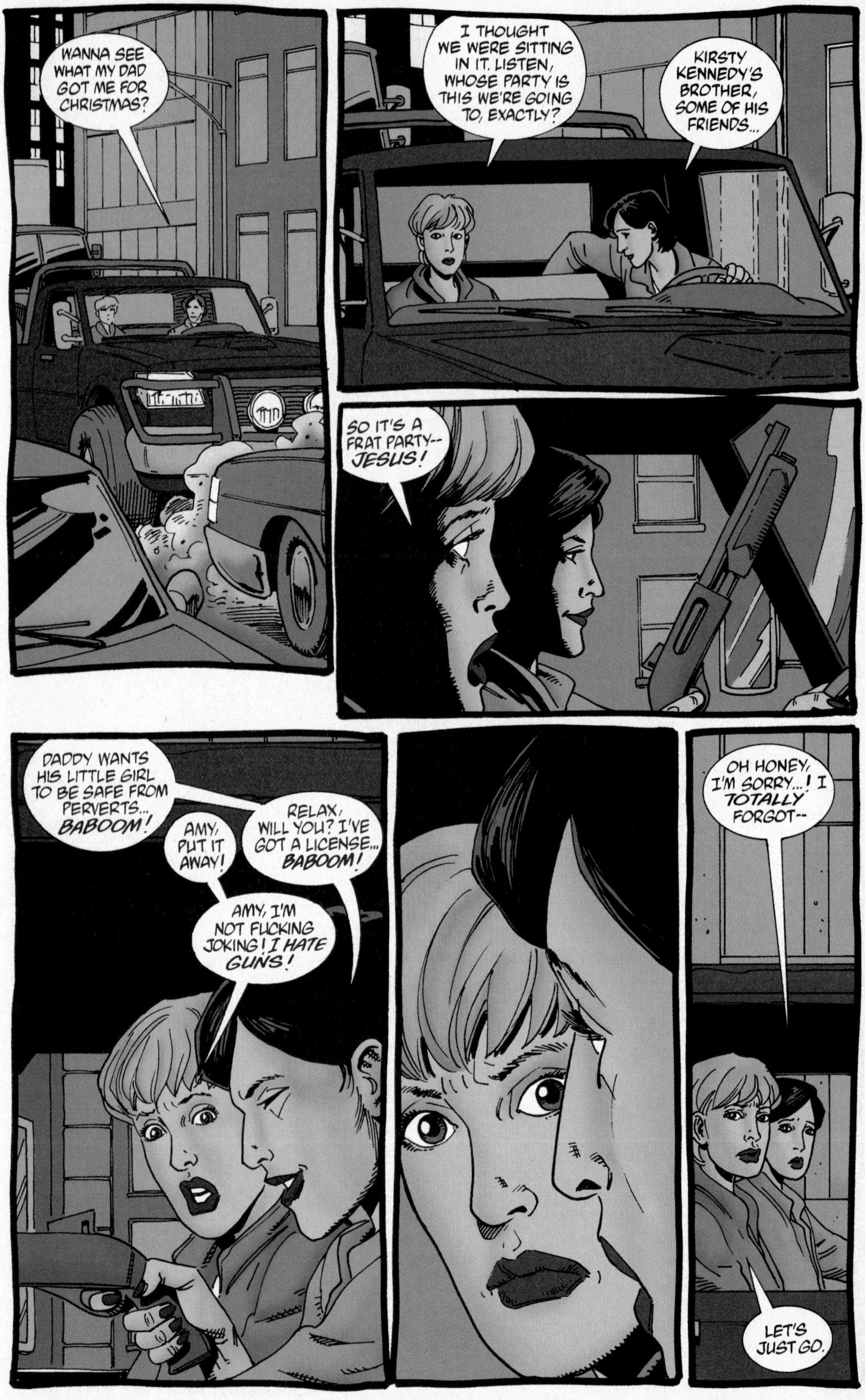
WANNA SEE WHAT MY DAD GOT ME FOR CHRISTMAS?
I THOUGHT WE WERE SITTING IN IT. LISTEN, WHOSE PARTY IS THIS WE'RE GOING TO, EXACTLY?
KIRSTY KENNEDY'S BROTHER, SOME OF HIS FRIENDS...
SO IT'S A FRAT PARTY-- JESUS!
DADDY WANTS HIS LITTLE GIRL TO BE SAFE FROM PERVERTS... BABOOM!
AMY, PUT IT AWAY!
RELAX, WILL YOU? I'VE GOT A LICENSE... BABOOM!
AMY, I'M NOT FUCKING JOKING! I HATE GUNS!
OH HONEY, I'M SORRY...! I TOTALLY FORGOT--
LET'S JUST GO.

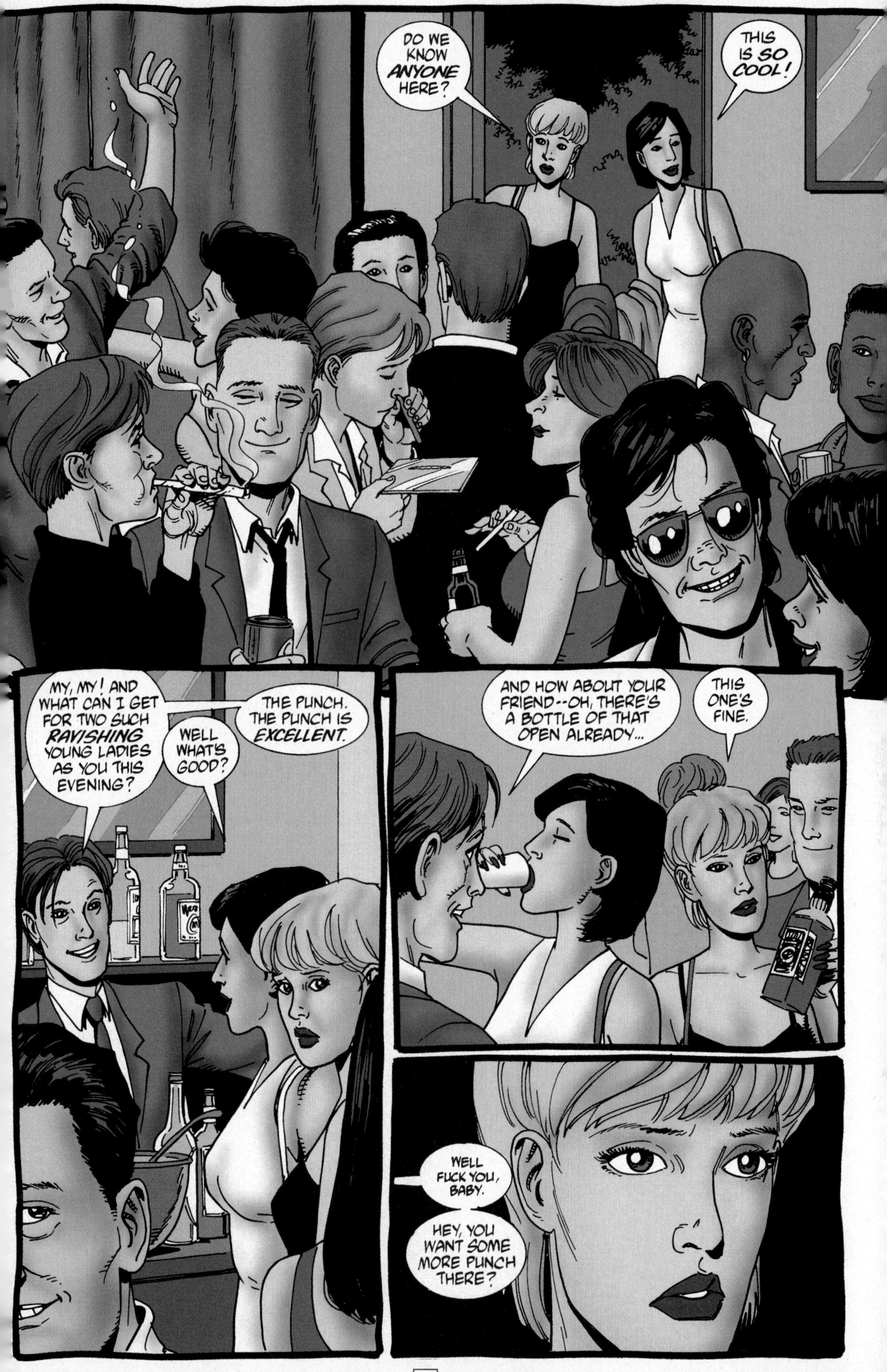
DO WE KNOW ANYONE HERE?
THIS IS SO COOL!
MY, MY! AND WHAT CAN I GET FOR TWO SUCH RAVISHING YOUNG LADIES AS YOU THIS EVENING?
WELL WHAT'S GOOD?
THE PUNCH. THE PUNCH IS EXCELLENT.
AND HOW ABOUT YOUR FRIEND--OH, THERE'S A BOTTLE OF THAT OPEN ALREADY...
THIS ONE'S FINE.
WELL FUCK YOU, BABY.
HEY, YOU WANT SOME MORE PUNCH THERE?

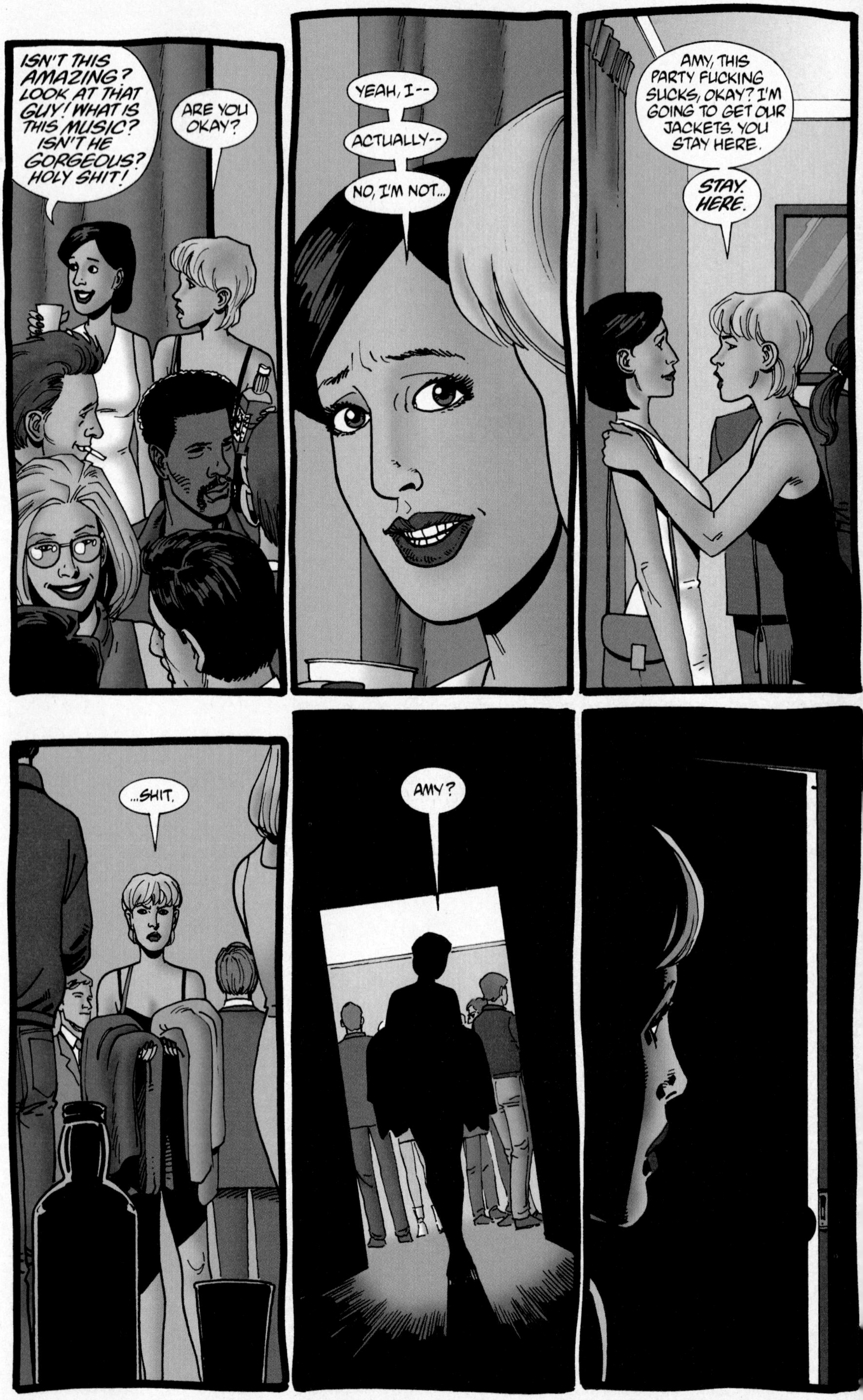
ISN'T THIS AMAZING? LOOK AT THAT GUY! WHAT IS THIS MUSIC? ISN'T HE GORGEOUS? HOLY SHIT!
ARE YOU OKAY?
YEAH, I--
ACTUALLY--
NO, I'M NOT...
AMY, THIS PARTY FUCKING SUCKS, OKAY? I'M GOING TO GET OUR JACKETS. YOU STAY HERE.
STAY. HERE.
...SHIT.
AMY?

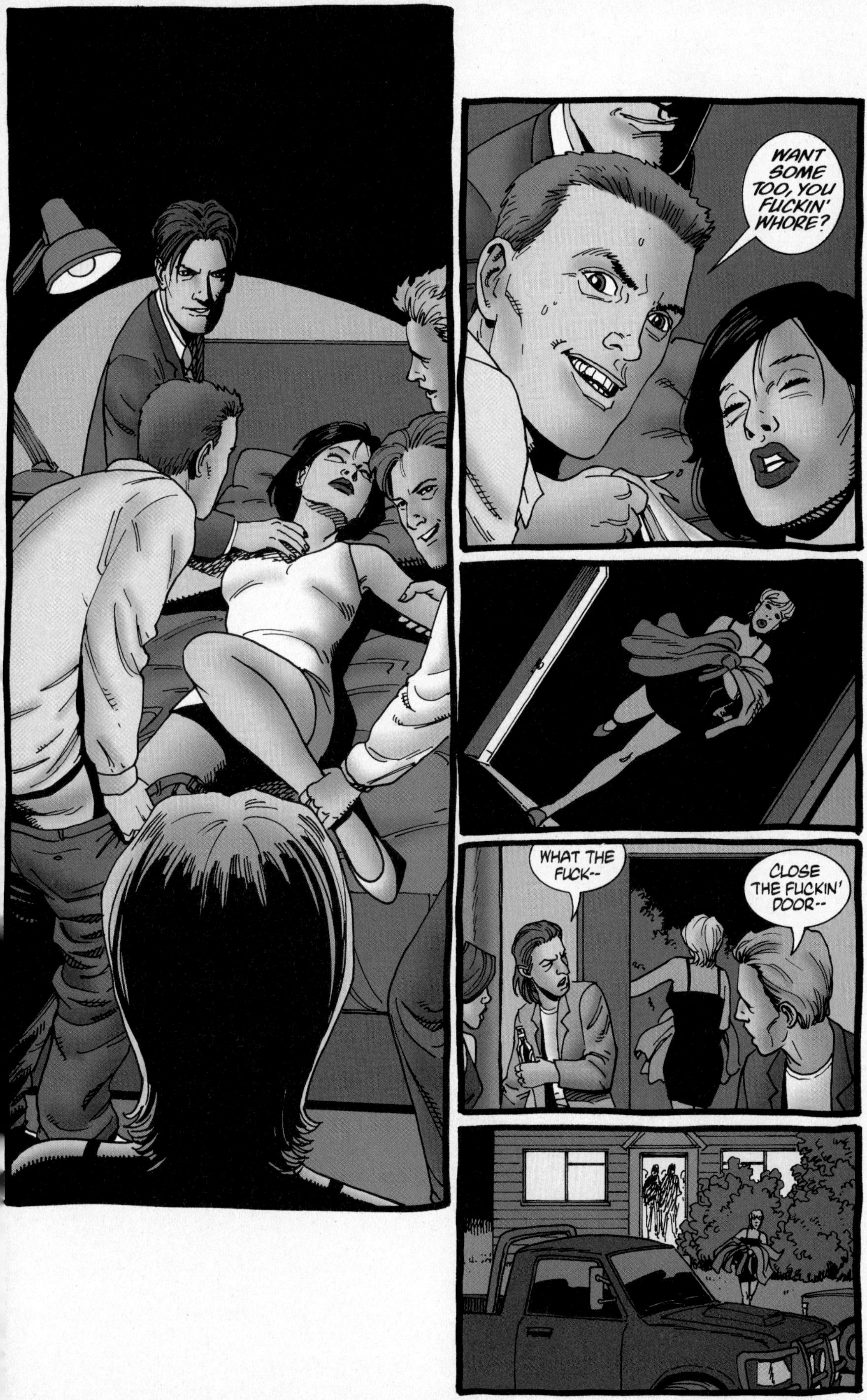
WANT SOME TOO, YOU FUCKIN' WHORE?
WHAT THE FUCK--
CLOSE THE FUCKIN' DOOR--

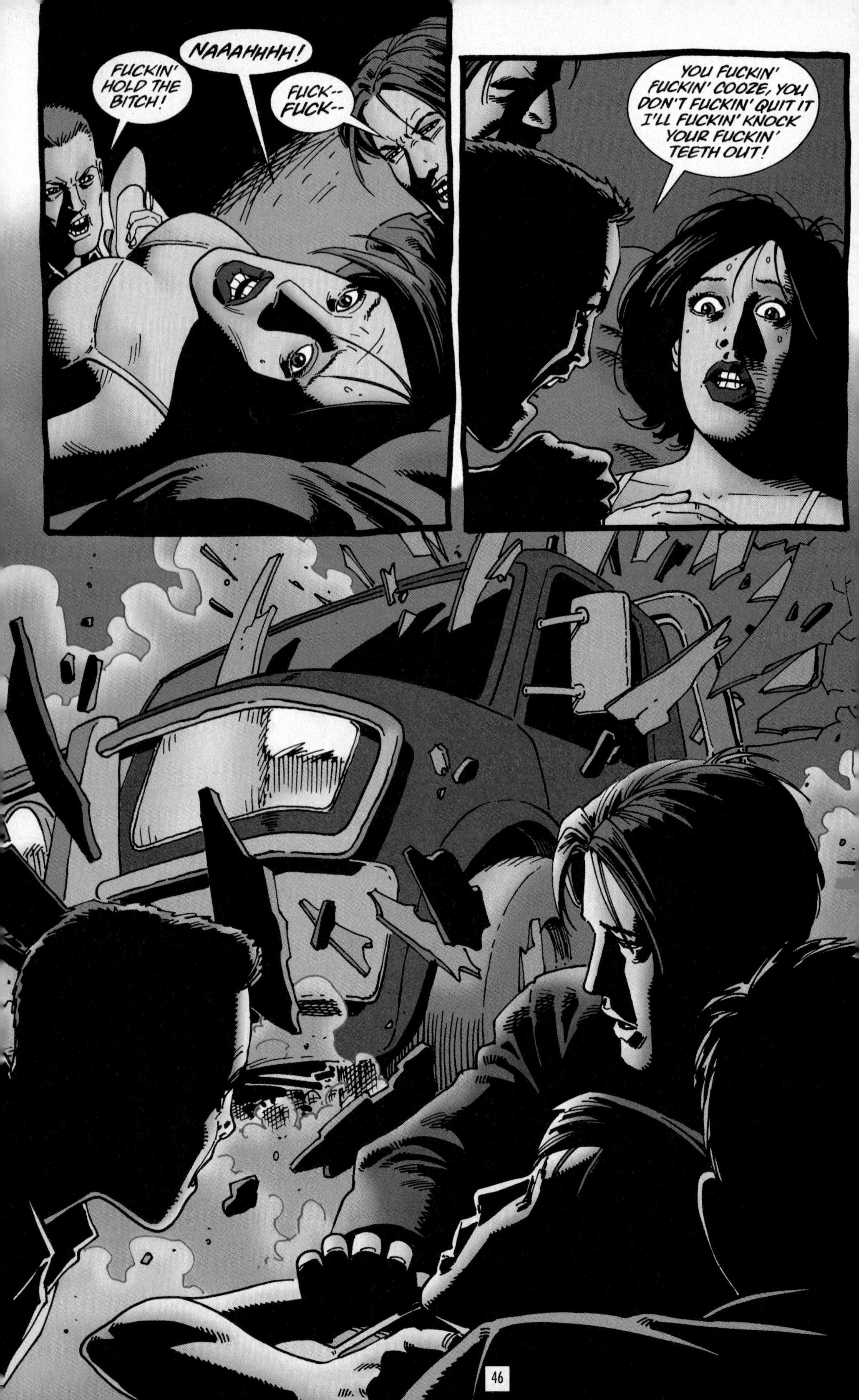
FUCKIN' HOLD THE BITCH!
NAAAHHHH!
FUCK-- FUCK--
YOU FUCKIN' FUCKIN' COOZE, YOU DON'T FUCKIN' QUIT IT I'LL FUCKIN' KNOCK YOUR FUCKIN' TEETH OUT!

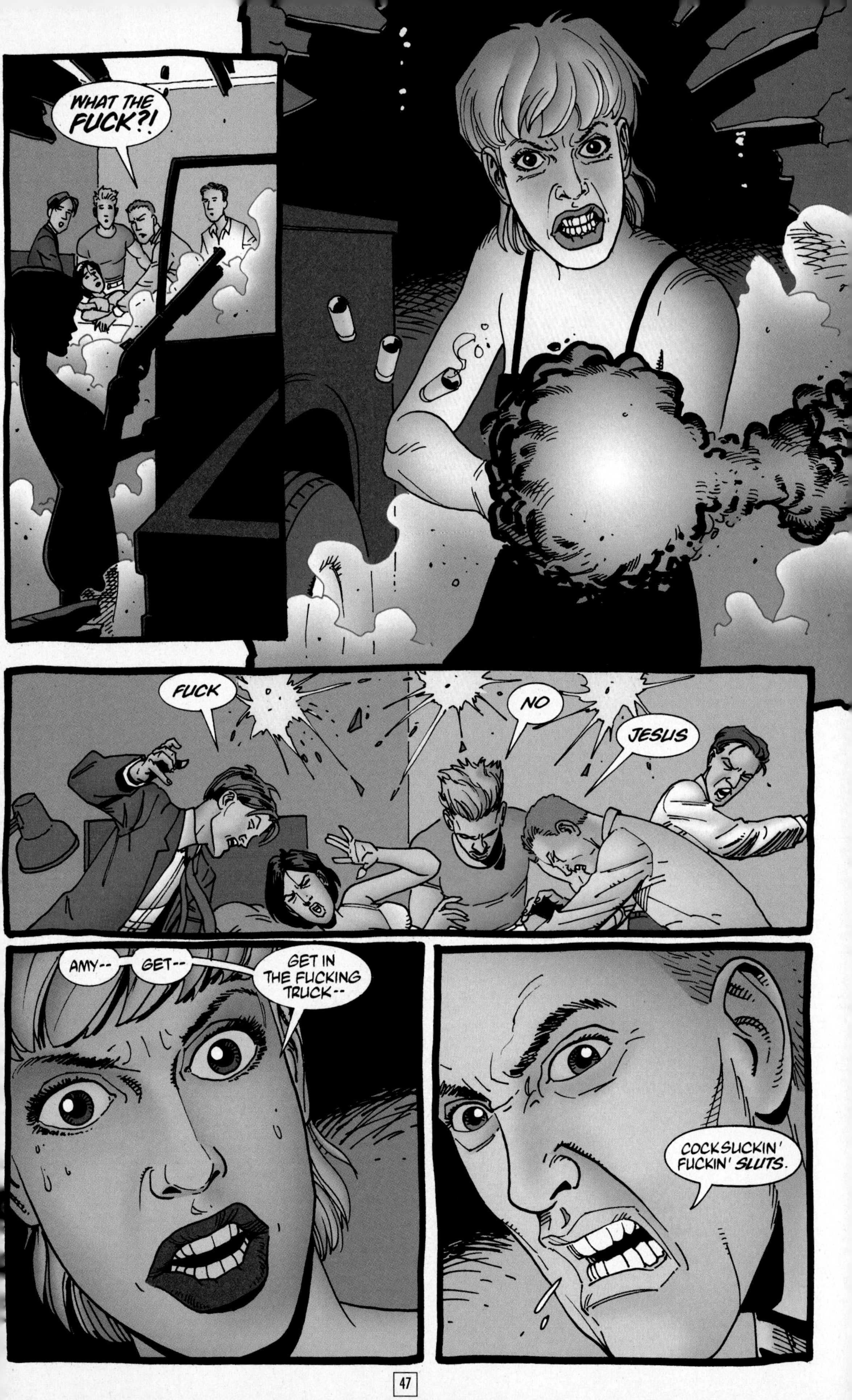
WHAT THE FUCK?!
FUCK
NO
JESUS
AMY--
GET--
GET IN THE FUCKING TRUCK--
COCKSUCKIN' FUCKIN' *SLUTS*.

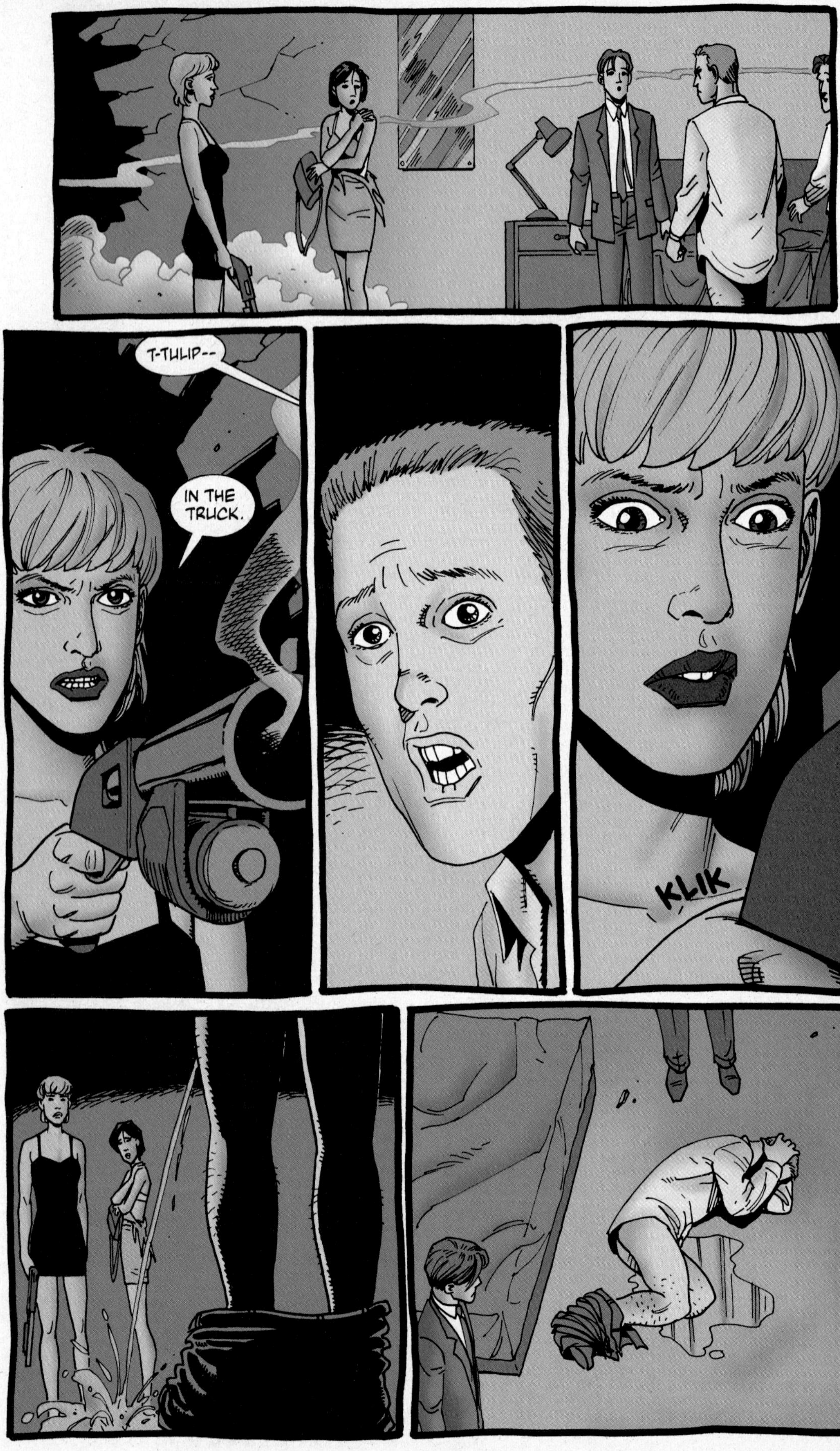
T-TULIP--
IN THE TRUCK.
KLIK

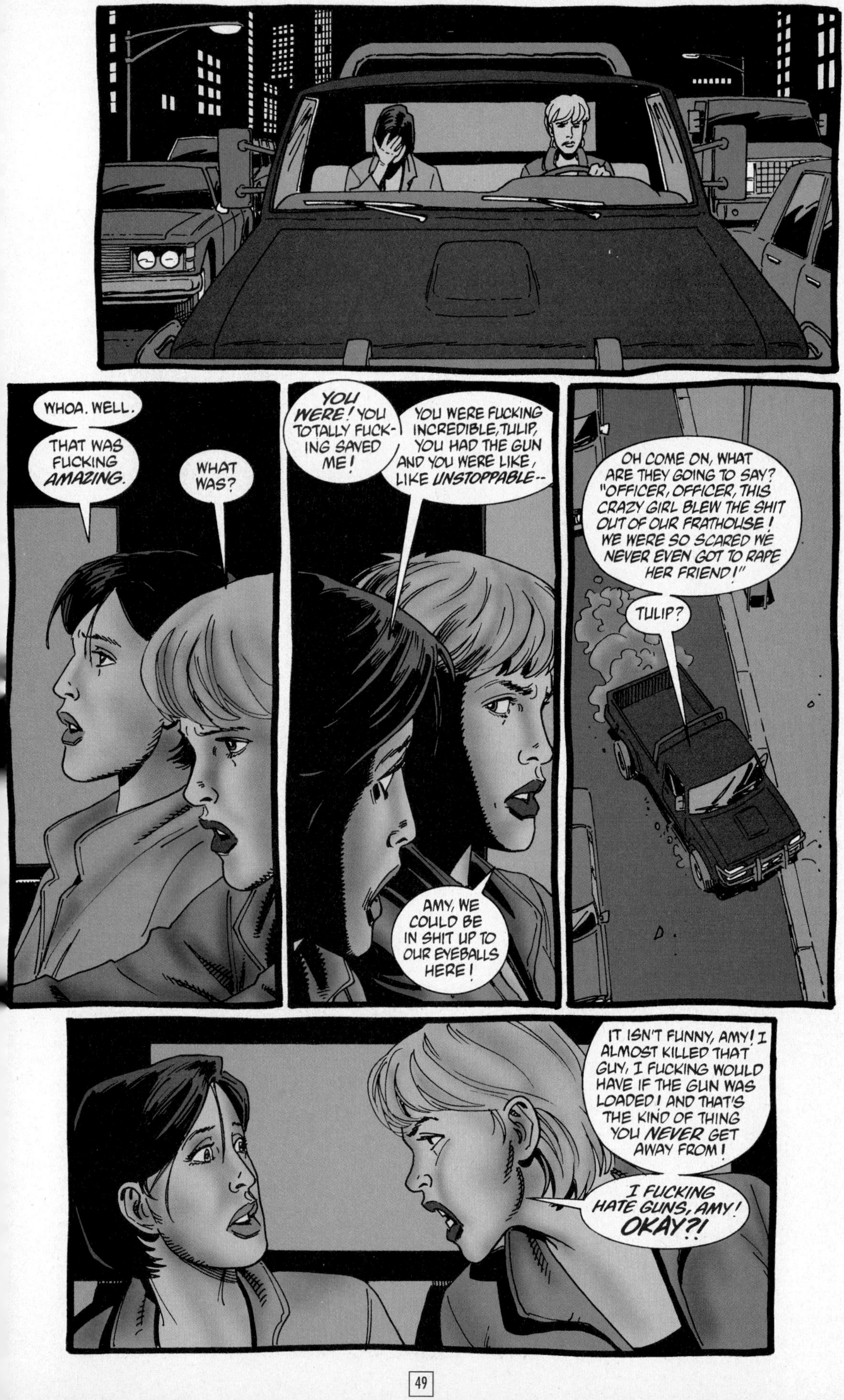

WHOA. WELL.
THAT WAS FUCKING AMAZING.
WHAT WAS?
YOU WERE! YOU TOTALLY FUCKING SAVED ME!
YOU WERE FUCKING INCREDIBLE, TULIP, YOU HAD THE GUN AND YOU WERE LIKE, LIKE UNSTOPPABLE--
AMY, WE COULD BE IN SHIT UP TO OUR EYEBALLS HERE!
OH COME ON, WHAT ARE THEY GOING TO SAY? "OFFICER, OFFICER, THIS CRAZY GIRL BLEW THE SHIT OUT OF OUR FRATHOUSE! WE WERE SO SCARED WE NEVER EVEN GOT TO RAPE HER FRIEND!"
TULIP?
IT ISN'T FUNNY, AMY! I ALMOST KILLED THAT GUY, I FUCKING WOULD HAVE IF THE GUN WAS LOADED! AND THAT'S THE KIND OF THING YOU NEVER GET AWAY FROM!
I FUCKING HATE GUNS, AMY! OKAY?!

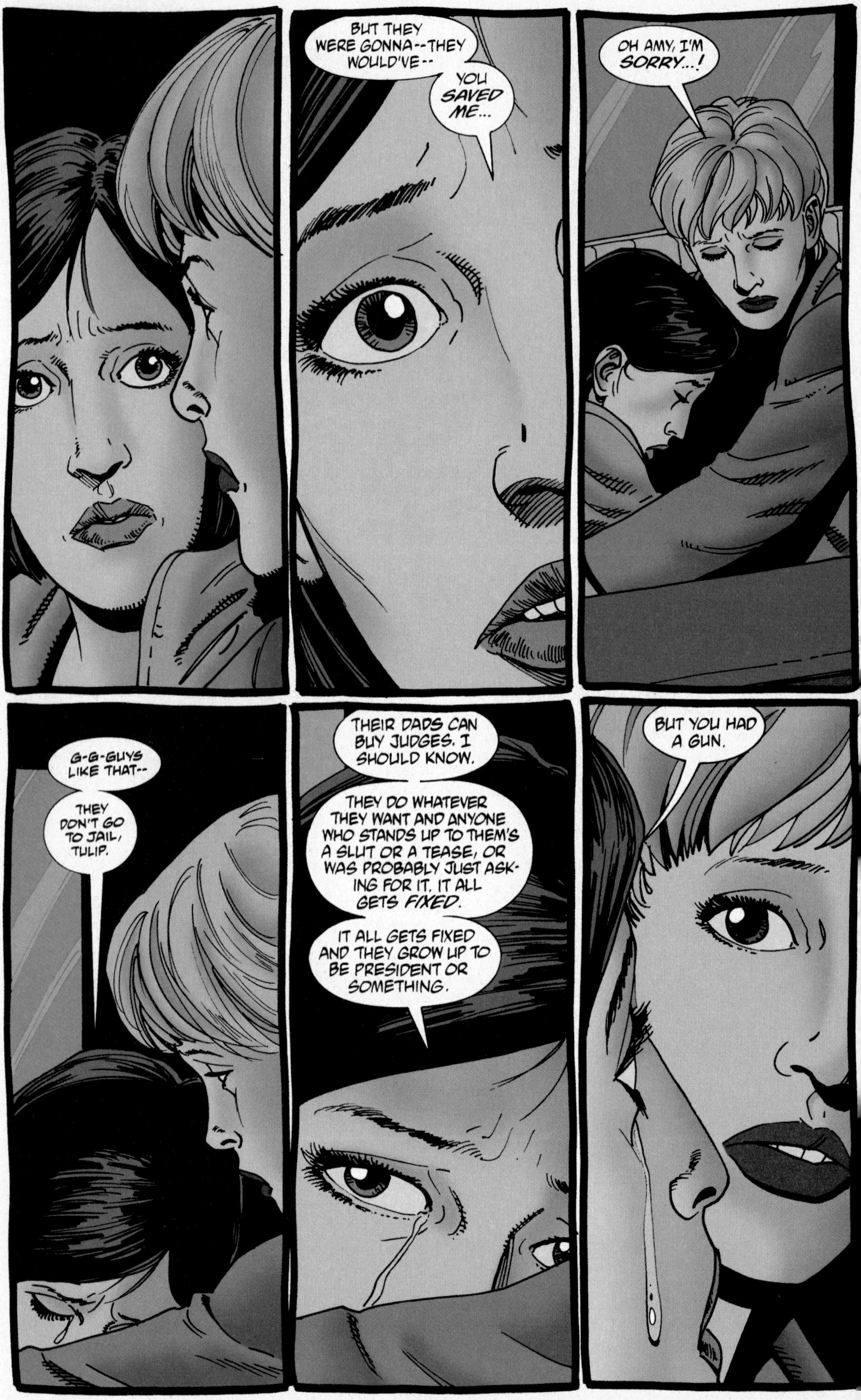
BUT THEY WERE GONNA--THEY WOULD'VE--
YOU SAVED ME...
OH AMY, I'M SORRY...!
G-G-GUYS LIKE THAT--
THEY DON'T GO TO JAIL, TULIP.
THEIR DADS CAN BUY JUDGES. I SHOULD KNOW.
THEY DO WHATEVER THEY WANT AND ANYONE WHO STANDS UP TO THEM'S A SLUT OR A TEASE, OR WAS PROBABLY JUST ASKING FOR IT. IT ALL GETS FIXED.
IT ALL GETS FIXED AND THEY GROW UP TO BE PRESIDENT OR SOMETHING.
BUT YOU HAD A GUN.

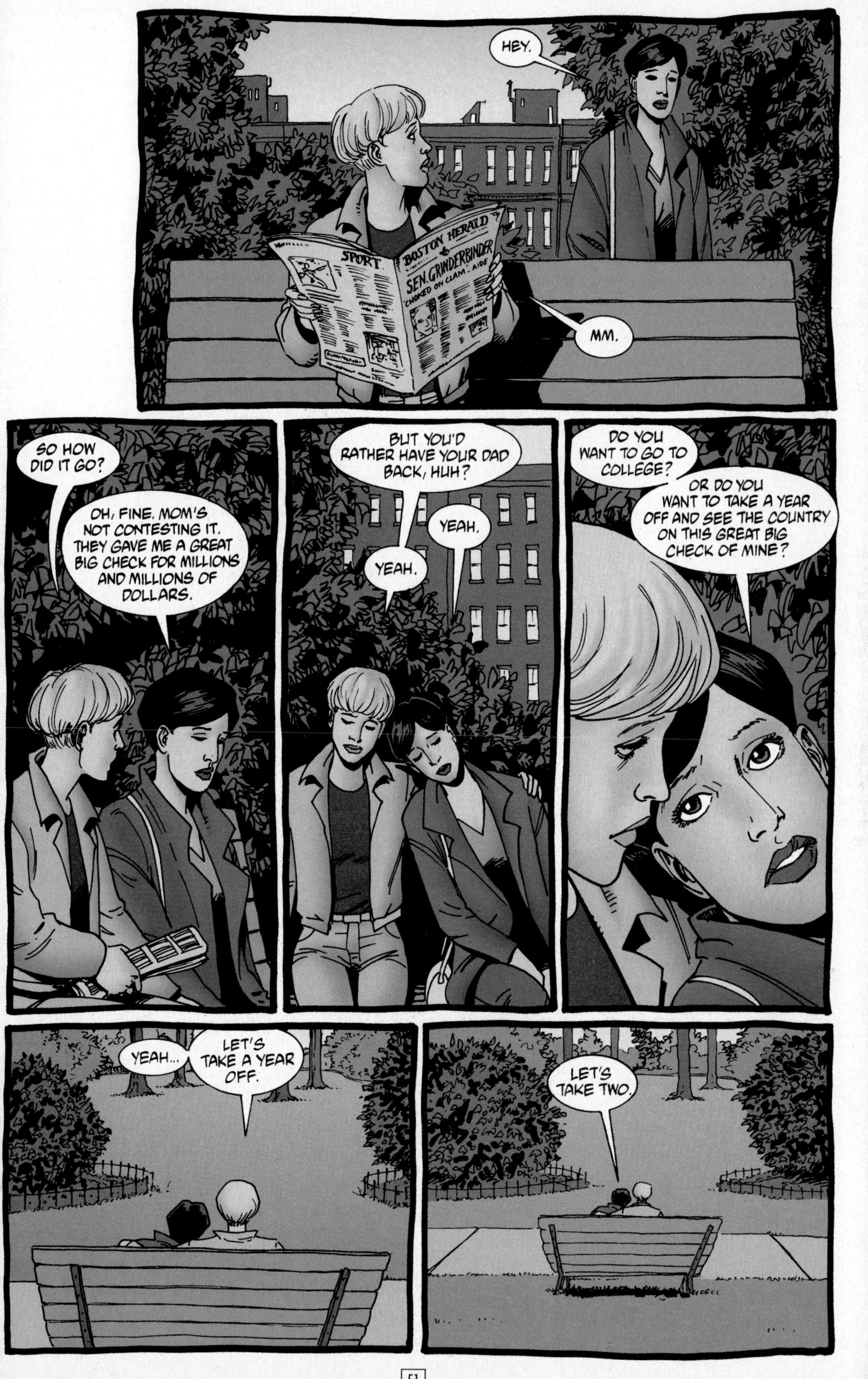
HEY.
SPORT
BOSTON HERALD
SEN. GRINDERBINDER
CHOKED ON CLAM - AIDE
MM.
SO HOW DID IT GO?
OH, FINE. MOM'S NOT CONTESTING IT. THEY GAVE ME A GREAT BIG CHECK FOR MILLIONS AND MILLIONS OF DOLLARS.
BUT YOU'D RATHER HAVE YOUR DAD BACK, HUH?
YEAH.
YEAH.
DO YOU WANT TO GO TO COLLEGE?
OR DO YOU WANT TO TAKE A YEAR OFF AND SEE THE COUNTRY ON THIS GREAT BIG CHECK OF MINE?
YEAH...
LET'S TAKE A YEAR OFF.
LET'S TAKE TWO.

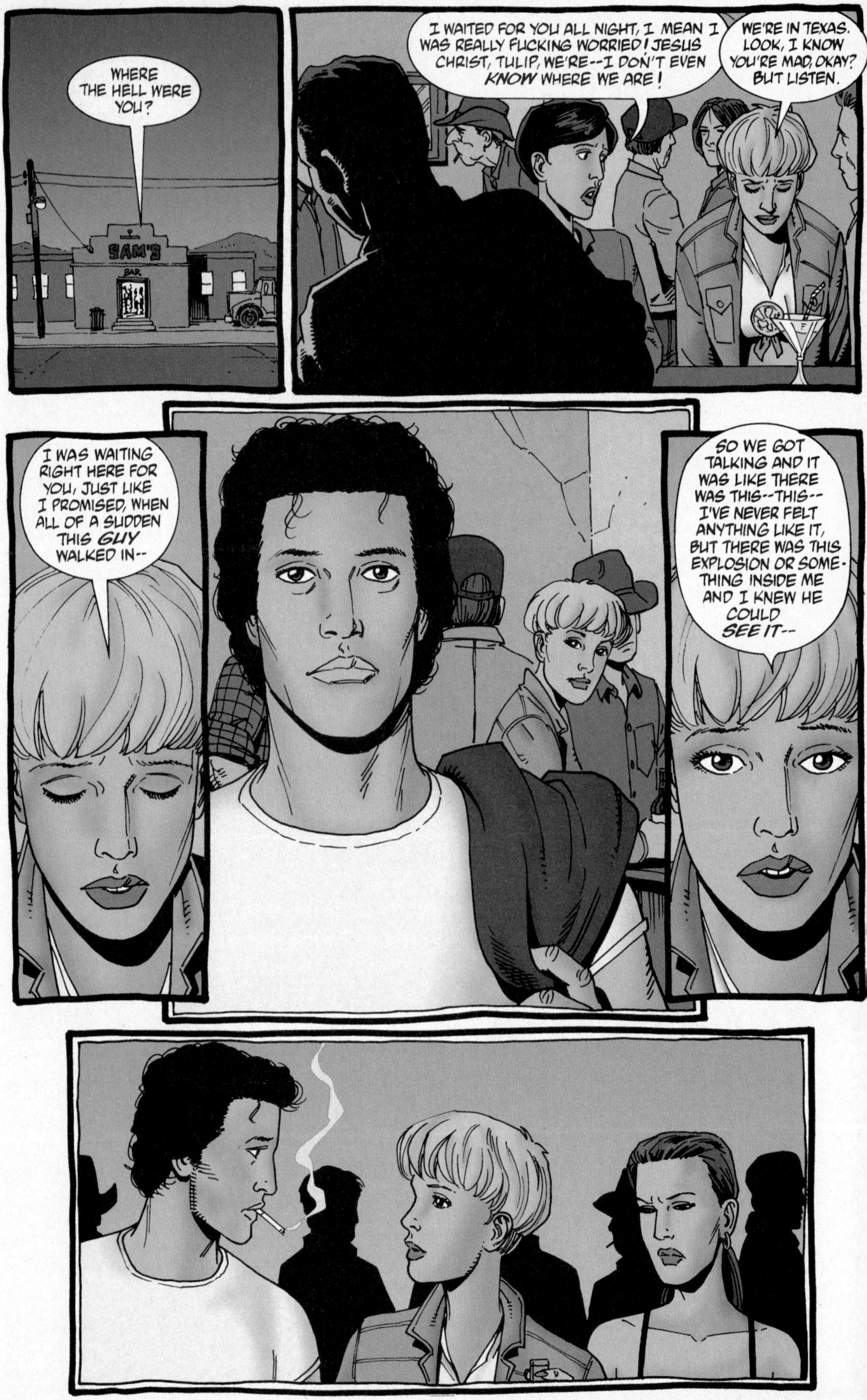
WHERE THE HELL WERE YOU?
SAM'S
BAR
I WAITED FOR YOU ALL NIGHT, I MEAN I WAS REALLY FUCKING WORRIED! JESUS CHRIST, TULIP, WE'RE--I DON'T EVEN KNOW WHERE WE ARE!
WE'RE IN TEXAS. LOOK, I KNOW YOU'RE MAD, OKAY? BUT LISTEN.
I WAS WAITING RIGHT HERE FOR YOU, JUST LIKE I PROMISED, WHEN ALL OF A SUDDEN THIS GUY WALKED IN--
SO WE GOT TALKING AND IT WAS LIKE THERE WAS THIS--THIS--I'VE NEVER FELT ANYTHING LIKE IT, BUT THERE WAS THIS EXPLOSION OR SOMETHING INSIDE ME AND I KNEW HE COULD SEE IT--

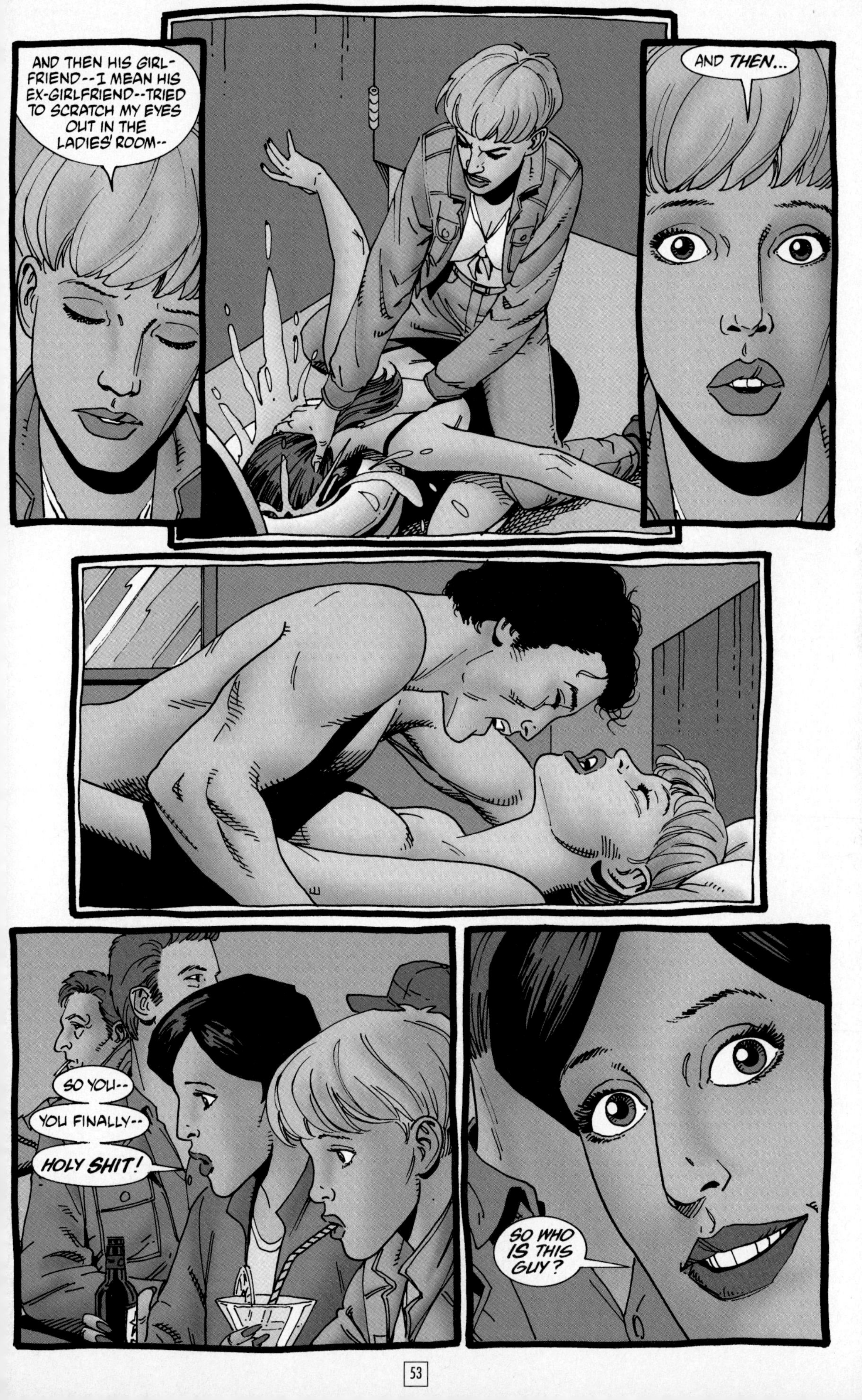
AND THEN HIS GIRL-FRIEND--I MEAN HIS EX-GIRLFRIEND--TRIED TO SCRATCH MY EYES OUT IN THE LADIES' ROOM--
AND THEN...
SO YOU--
YOU FINALLY--
HOLY SHIT!
SO WHO IS THIS GUY?

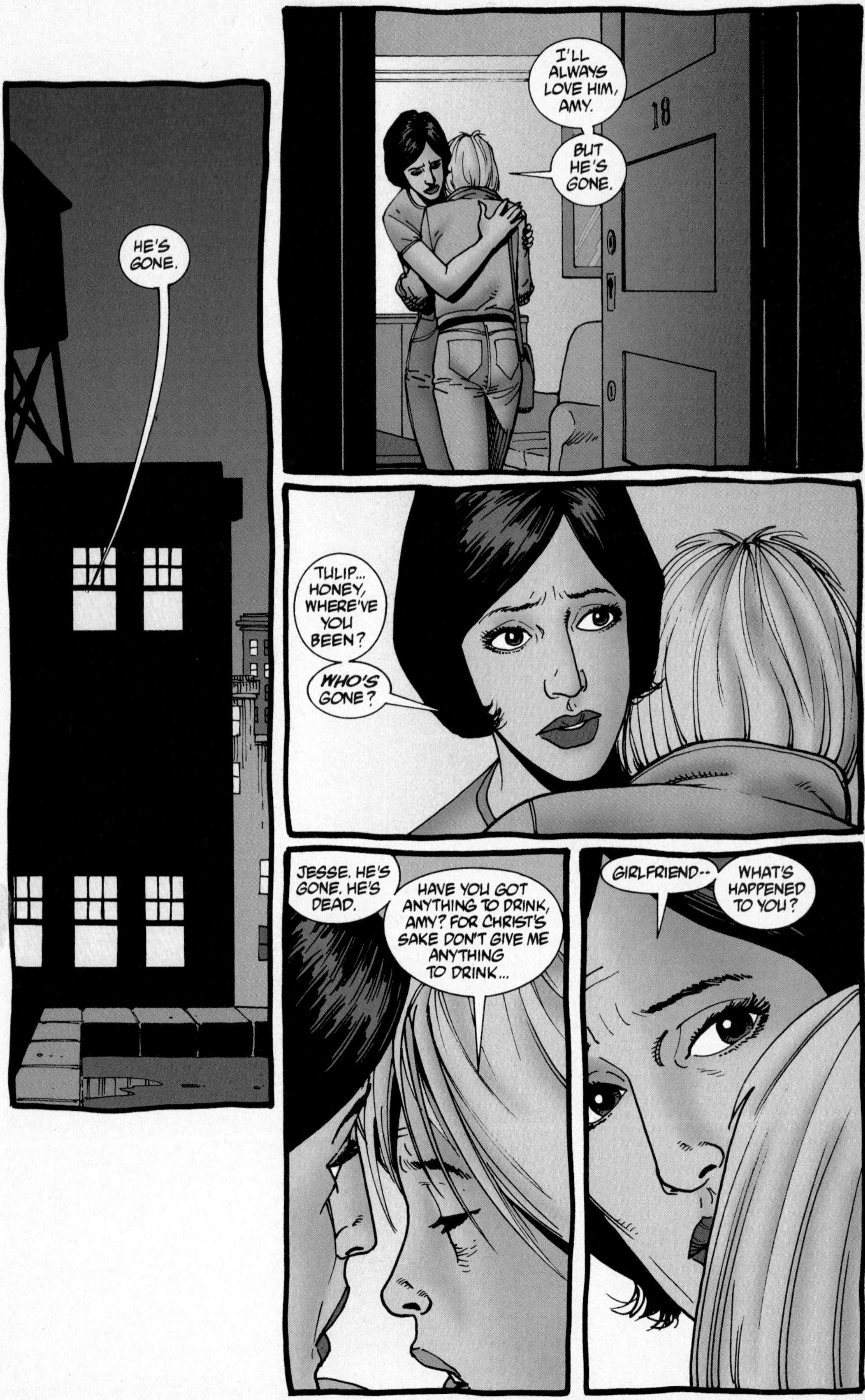
HE'S GONE.
I'LL ALWAYS LOVE HIM, AMY.
BUT HE'S GONE.
TULIP... HONEY, WHERE'VE YOU BEEN?
WHO'S GONE?
JESSE. HE'S GONE. HE'S DEAD.
HAVE YOU GOT ANYTHING TO DRINK, AMY? FOR CHRIST'S SAKE DON'T GIVE ME ANYTHING TO DRINK...
GIRLFRIEND--
WHAT'S HAPPENED TO YOU?

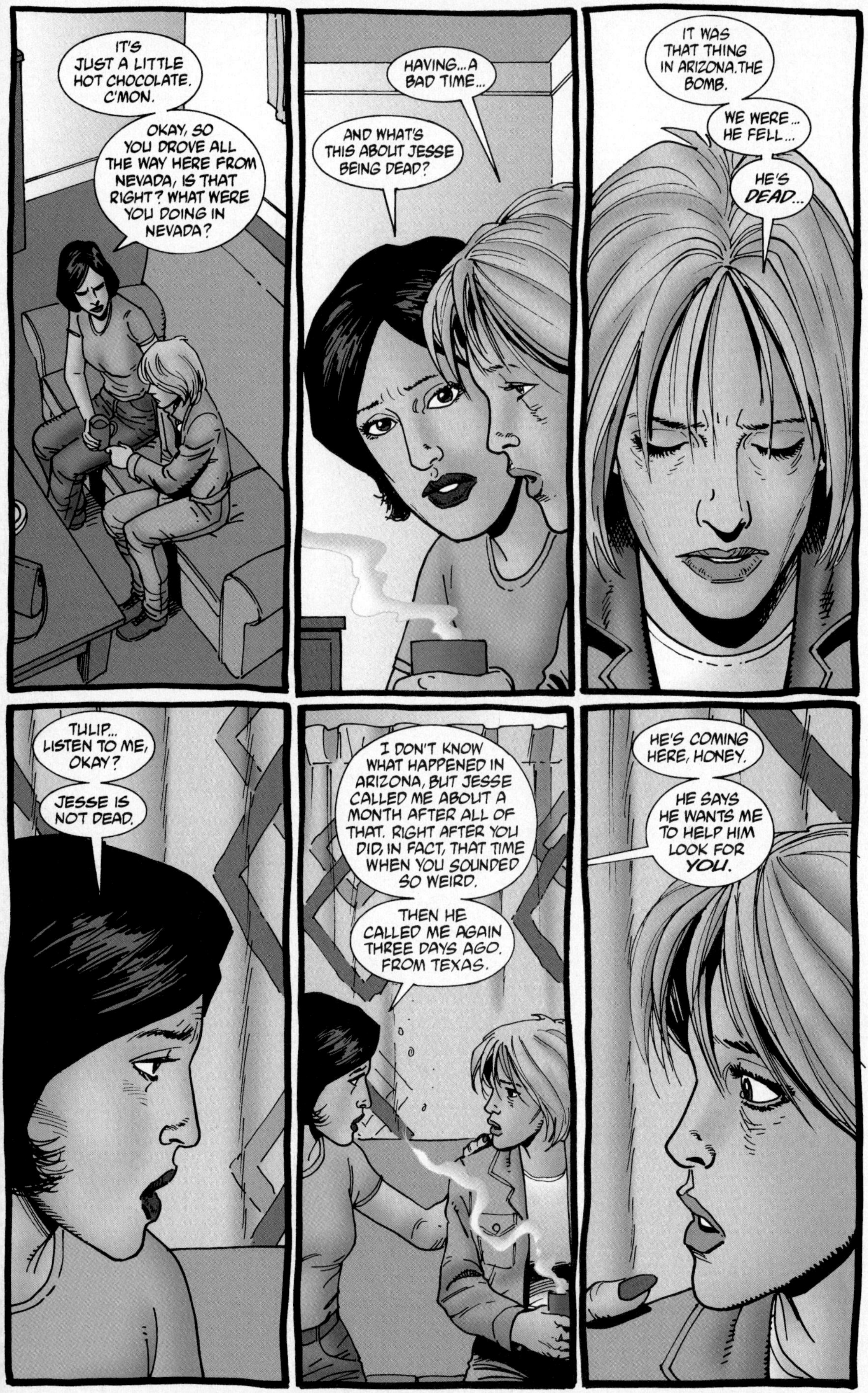
IT'S JUST A LITTLE HOT CHOCOLATE. C'MON.
OKAY, SO YOU DROVE ALL THE WAY HERE FROM NEVADA, IS THAT RIGHT? WHAT WERE YOU DOING IN NEVADA?
HAVING...A BAD TIME...
AND WHAT'S THIS ABOUT JESSE BEING DEAD?
IT WAS THAT THING IN ARIZONA. THE BOMB.
WE WERE... HE FELL...
HE'S DEAD...
TULIP... LISTEN TO ME, OKAY?
JESSE IS NOT DEAD.
I DON'T KNOW WHAT HAPPENED IN ARIZONA, BUT JESSE CALLED ME ABOUT A MONTH AFTER ALL OF THAT. RIGHT AFTER YOU DID, IN FACT, THAT TIME WHEN YOU SOUNDED SO WEIRD.
THEN HE CALLED ME AGAIN THREE DAYS AGO. FROM TEXAS.
HE'S COMING HERE, HONEY.
HE SAYS HE WANTS ME TO HELP HIM LOOK FOR YOU.

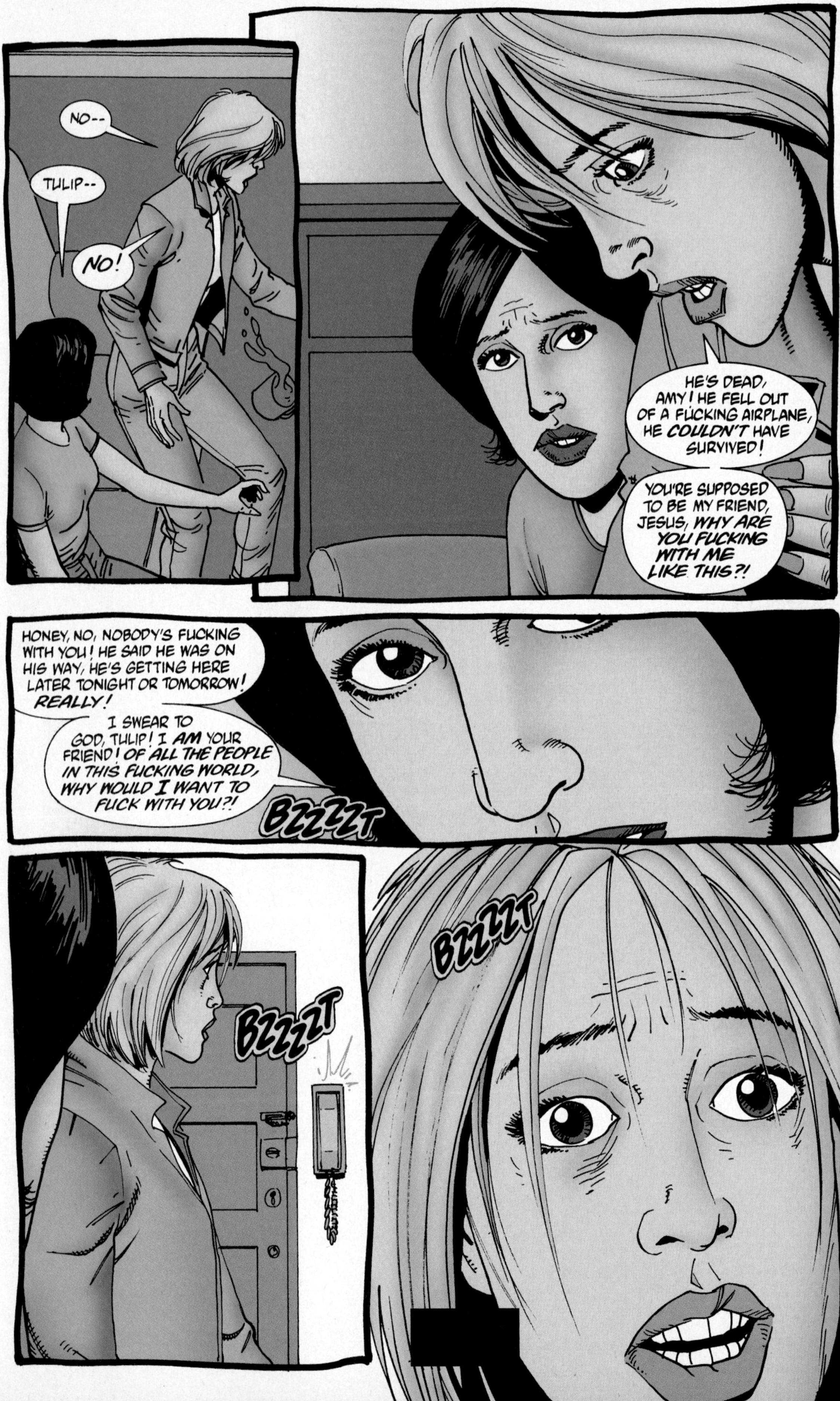
NO--
TULIP--
NO!
HE'S DEAD, AMY! HE FELL OUT OF A FUCKING AIRPLANE, HE COULDN'T HAVE SURVIVED!
YOU'RE SUPPOSED TO BE MY FRIEND, JESUS, WHY ARE YOU FUCKING WITH ME LIKE THIS?!
HONEY, NO, NOBODY'S FUCKING WITH YOU! HE SAID HE WAS ON HIS WAY, HE'S GETTING HERE LATER TONIGHT OR TOMORROW! REALLY!
I SWEAR TO GOD, TULIP! I AM YOUR FRIEND! OF ALL THE PEOPLE IN THIS FUCKING WORLD, WHY WOULD I WANT TO FUCK WITH YOU?!
BZZZZT
BZZZZT
BZZZZT

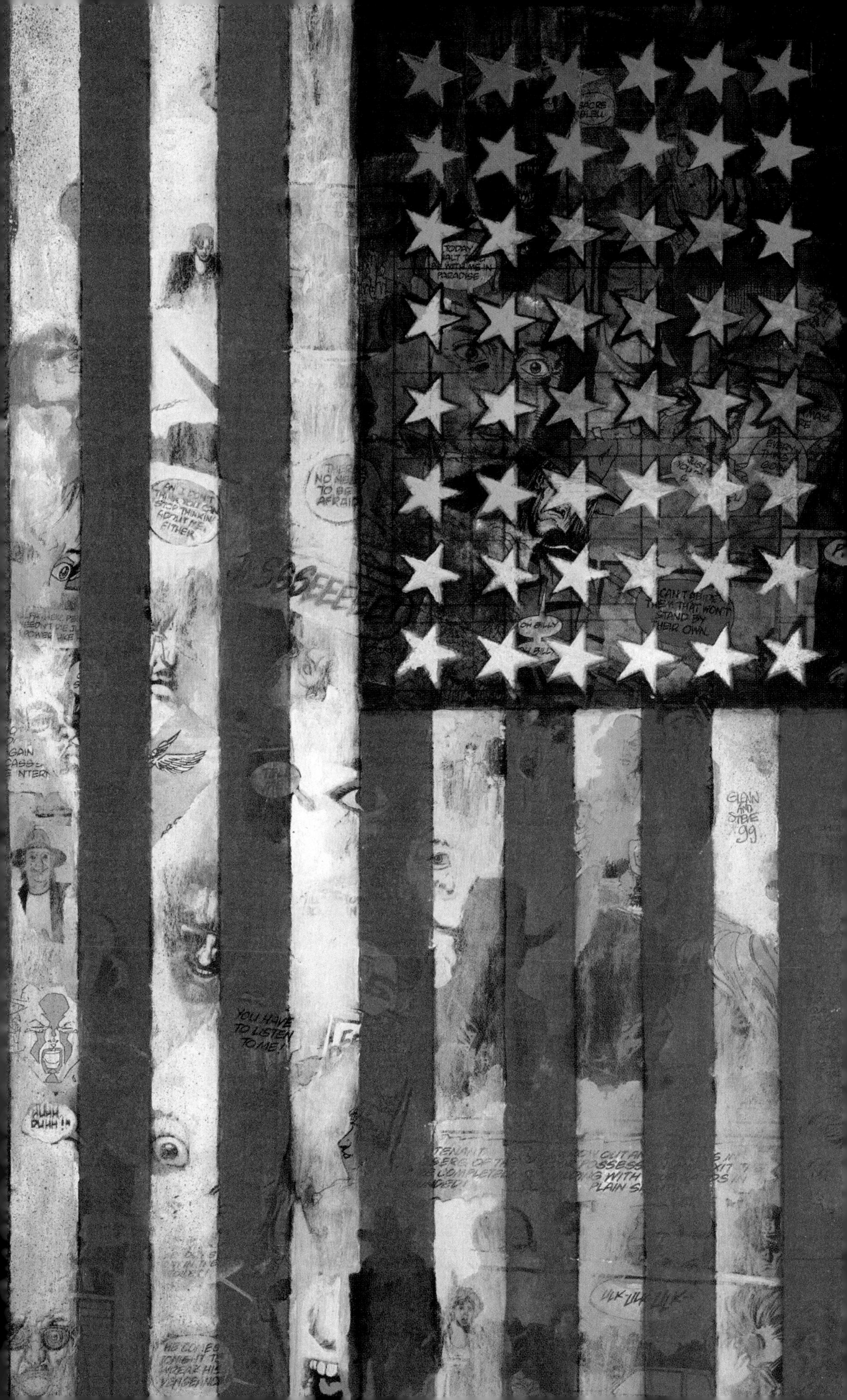
OH BILLY
YOU HAVE TO LISTEN TO ME!
DUHH DUHH!

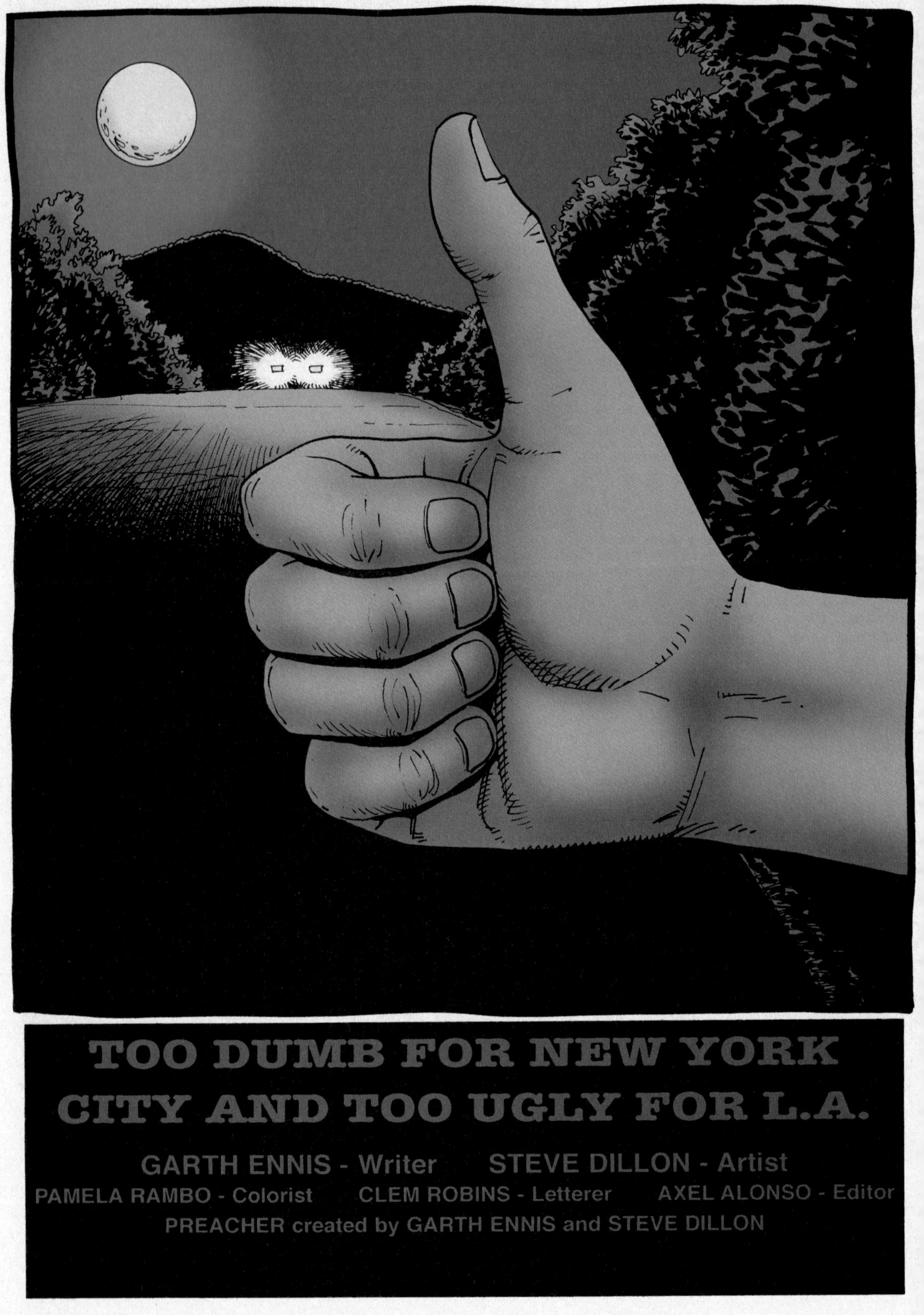

TOO DUMB FOR NEW YORK CITY AND TOO UGLY FOR L.A.

GARTH ENNIS - Writer   STEVE DILLON - Artist
PAMELA RAMBO - Colorist   CLEM ROBINS - Letterer   AXEL ALONSO - Editor
PREACHER created by GARTH ENNIS and STEVE DILLON

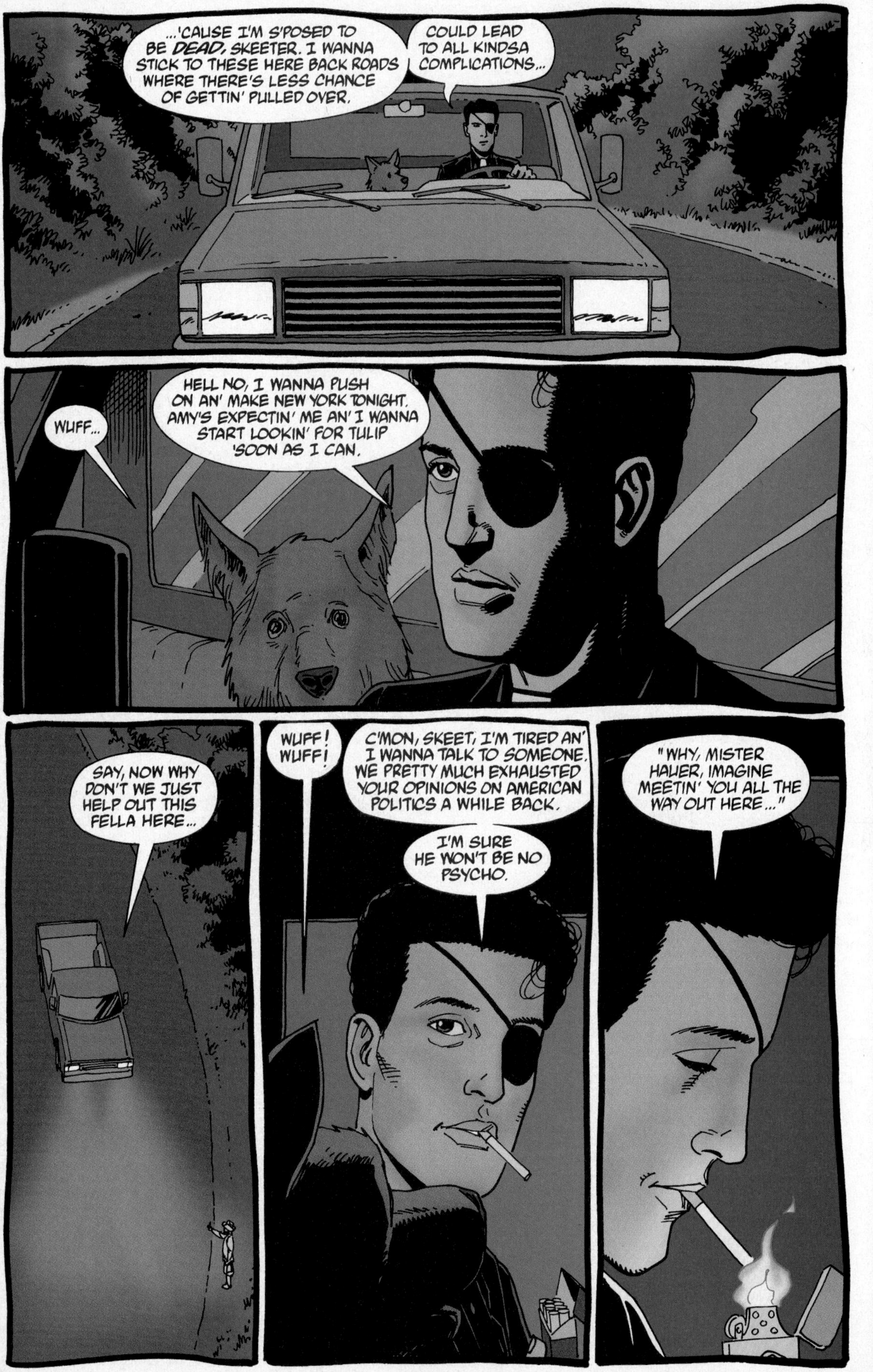
...'CAUSE I'M S'POSED TO BE DEAD, SKEETER. I WANNA STICK TO THESE HERE BACK ROADS WHERE THERE'S LESS CHANCE OF GETTIN' PULLED OVER.
COULD LEAD TO ALL KINDSA COMPLICATIONS...
WUFF...
HELL NO, I WANNA PUSH ON AN' MAKE NEW YORK TONIGHT. AMY'S EXPECTIN' ME AN' I WANNA START LOOKIN' FOR TULIP 'SOON AS I CAN.
SAY, NOW WHY DON'T WE JUST HELP OUT THIS FELLA HERE...
WUFF! WUFF!
C'MON, SKEET, I'M TIRED AN' I WANNA TALK TO SOMEONE. WE PRETTY MUCH EXHAUSTED YOUR OPINIONS ON AMERICAN POLITICS A WHILE BACK.
I'M SURE HE WON'T BE NO PSYCHO.
"WHY, MISTER HAUER, IMAGINE MEETIN' YOU ALL THE WAY OUT HERE..."

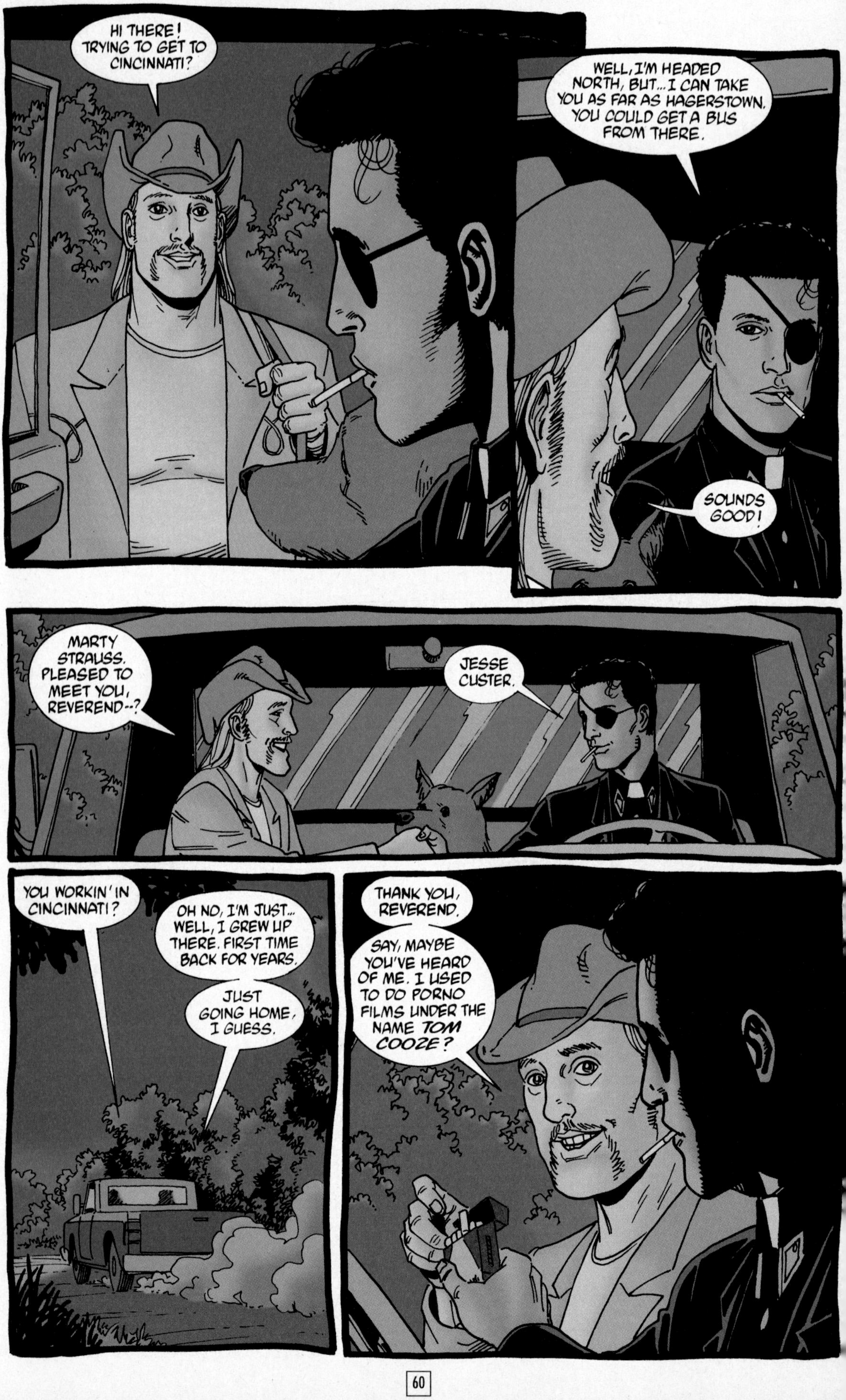
HI THERE! TRYING TO GET TO CINCINNATI?
WELL, I'M HEADED NORTH, BUT... I CAN TAKE YOU AS FAR AS HAGERSTOWN. YOU COULD GET A BUS FROM THERE.
SOUNDS GOOD!
MARTY STRAUSS. PLEASED TO MEET YOU, REVEREND--?
JESSE CUSTER.
YOU WORKIN' IN CINCINNATI?
OH NO, I'M JUST... WELL, I GREW UP THERE. FIRST TIME BACK FOR YEARS.
JUST GOING HOME, I GUESS.
THANK YOU, REVEREND.
SAY, MAYBE YOU'VE HEARD OF ME. I USED TO DO PORNO FILMS UNDER THE NAME *TOM COOZE*?

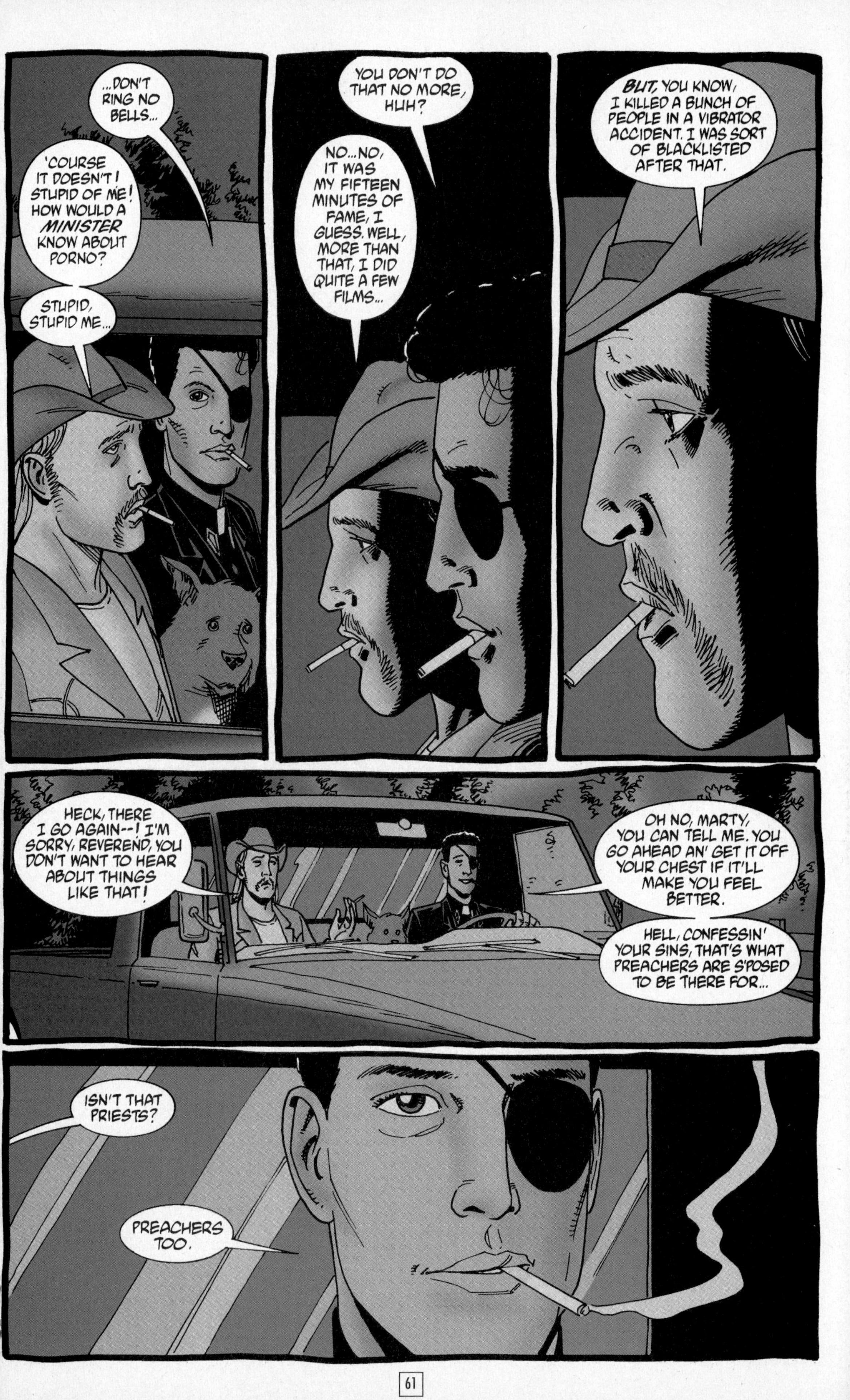
...DON'T RING NO BELLS...
'COURSE IT DOESN'T! STUPID OF ME! HOW WOULD A MINISTER KNOW ABOUT PORNO?
STUPID, STUPID ME...
YOU DON'T DO THAT NO MORE, HUH?
NO...NO, IT WAS MY FIFTEEN MINUTES OF FAME, I GUESS. WELL, MORE THAN THAT, I DID QUITE A FEW FILMS...
BUT, YOU KNOW, I KILLED A BUNCH OF PEOPLE IN A VIBRATOR ACCIDENT. I WAS SORT OF BLACKLISTED AFTER THAT.
HECK, THERE I GO AGAIN--! I'M SORRY, REVEREND, YOU DON'T WANT TO HEAR ABOUT THINGS LIKE THAT!
OH NO, MARTY, YOU CAN TELL ME. YOU GO AHEAD AN' GET IT OFF YOUR CHEST IF IT'LL MAKE YOU FEEL BETTER.
HELL, CONFESSIN' YOUR SINS, THAT'S WHAT PREACHERS ARE S'POSED TO BE THERE FOR...
ISN'T THAT PRIESTS?
PREACHERS TOO.

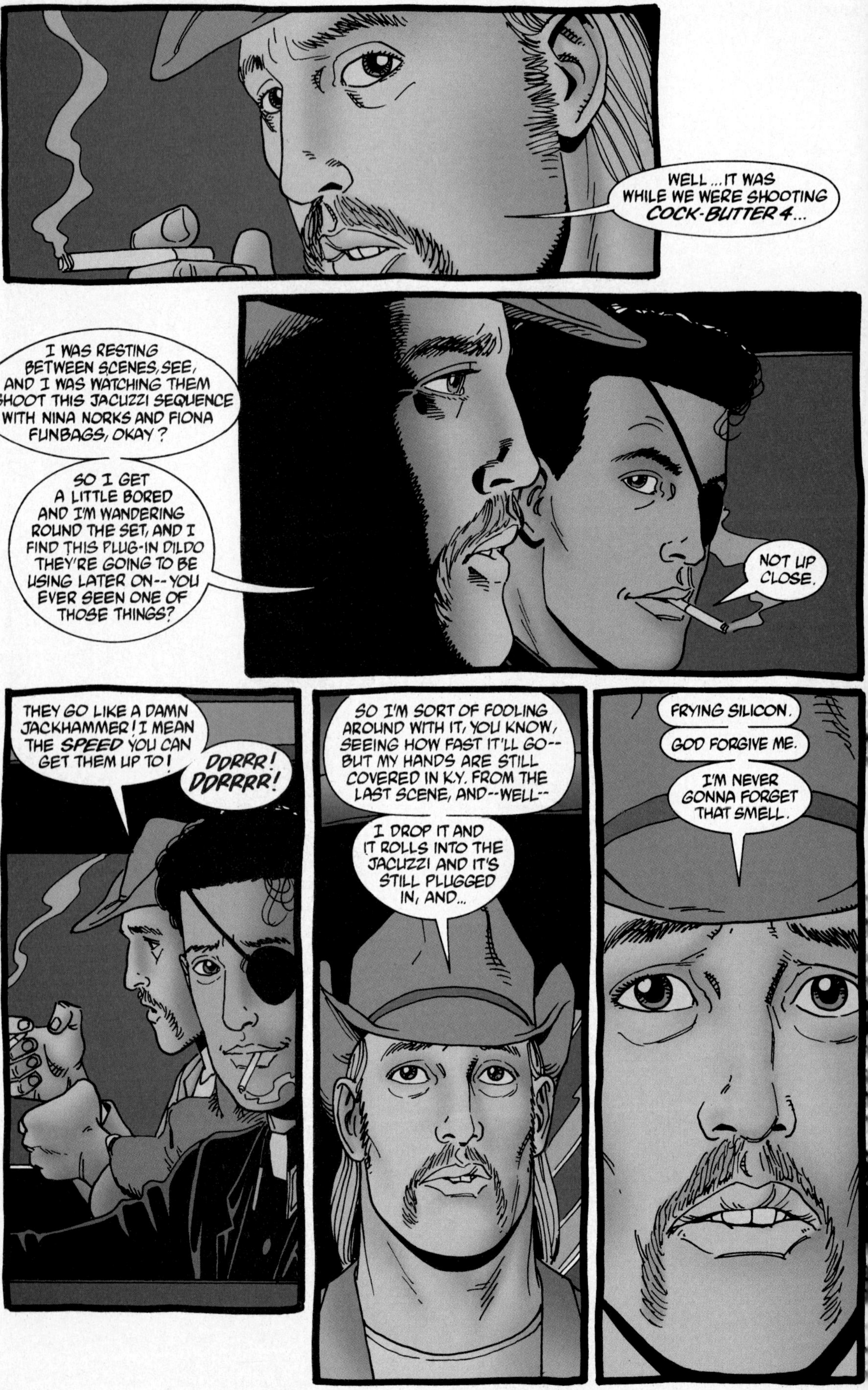

WELL ... IT WAS WHILE WE WERE SHOOTING COCK-BUTTER 4...
I WAS RESTING BETWEEN SCENES, SEE, AND I WAS WATCHING THEM SHOOT THIS JACUZZI SEQUENCE WITH NINA NORKS AND FIONA FUNBAGS, OKAY?
SO I GET A LITTLE BORED AND I'M WANDERING ROUND THE SET, AND I FIND THIS PLUG-IN DILDO THEY'RE GOING TO BE USING LATER ON--YOU EVER SEEN ONE OF THOSE THINGS?
NOT UP CLOSE.
THEY GO LIKE A DAMN JACKHAMMER! I MEAN THE SPEED YOU CAN GET THEM UP TO!
DDRRR! DDRRRR!
SO I'M SORT OF FOOLING AROUND WITH IT, YOU KNOW, SEEING HOW FAST IT'LL GO-- BUT MY HANDS ARE STILL COVERED IN K.Y. FROM THE LAST SCENE, AND--WELL--
I DROP IT AND IT ROLLS INTO THE JACUZZI AND IT'S STILL PLUGGED IN, AND...
FRYING SILICON.
GOD FORGIVE ME.
I'M NEVER GONNA FORGET THAT SMELL.

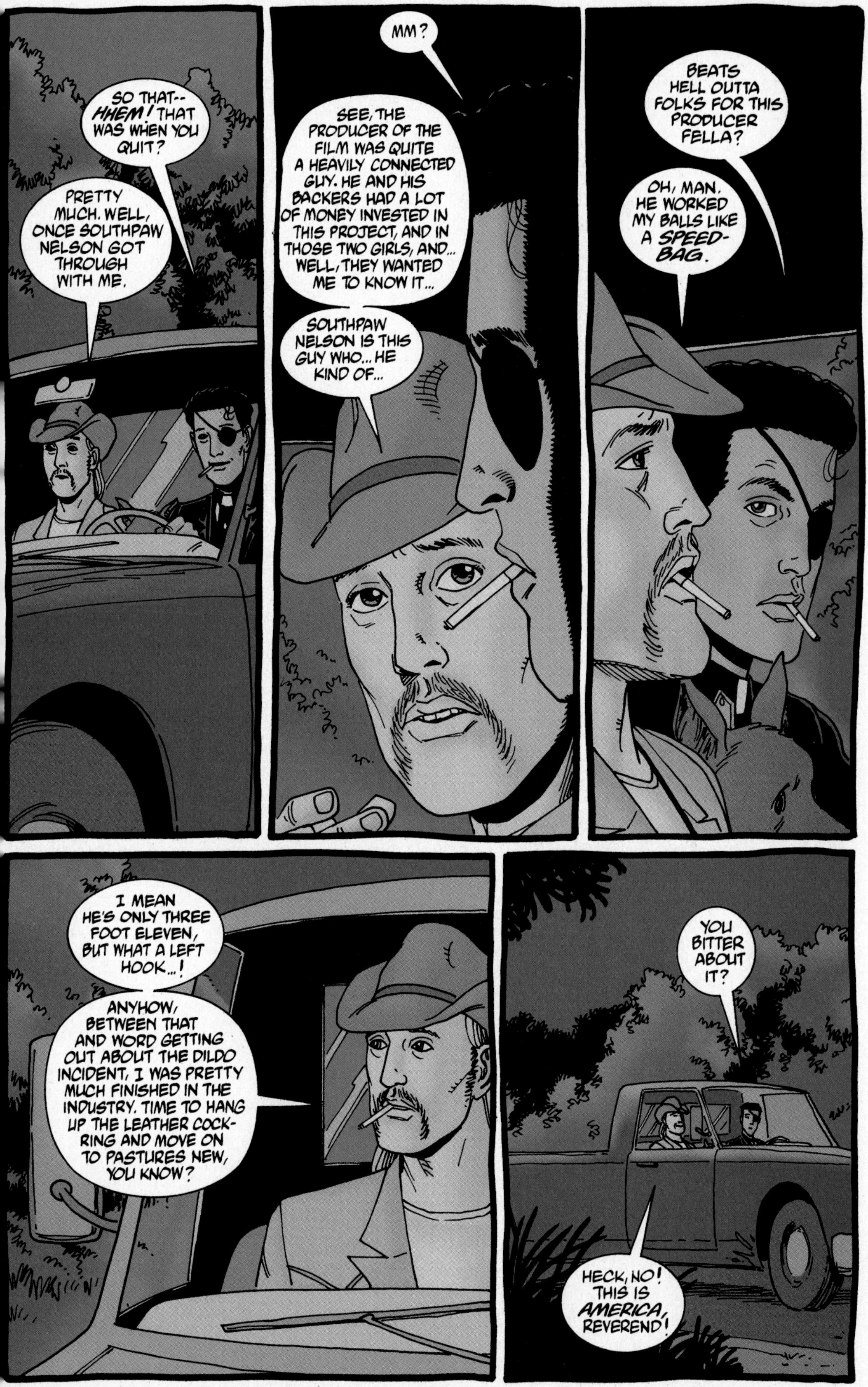
SO THAT-- HHEM! THAT WAS WHEN YOU QUIT?
PRETTY MUCH. WELL, ONCE SOUTHPAW NELSON GOT THROUGH WITH ME.
MM?
SEE, THE PRODUCER OF THE FILM WAS QUITE A HEAVILY CONNECTED GUY. HE AND HIS BACKERS HAD A LOT OF MONEY INVESTED IN THIS PROJECT, AND IN THOSE TWO GIRLS, AND... WELL, THEY WANTED ME TO KNOW IT...
SOUTHPAW NELSON IS THIS GUY WHO... HE KIND OF...
BEATS HELL OUTTA FOLKS FOR THIS PRODUCER FELLA?
OH, MAN. HE WORKED MY BALLS LIKE A SPEED-BAG.
I MEAN HE'S ONLY THREE FOOT ELEVEN, BUT WHAT A LEFT HOOK...!
ANYHOW, BETWEEN THAT AND WORD GETTING OUT ABOUT THE DILDO INCIDENT, I WAS PRETTY MUCH FINISHED IN THE INDUSTRY. TIME TO HANG UP THE LEATHER COCK-RING AND MOVE ON TO PASTURES NEW, YOU KNOW?
YOU BITTER ABOUT IT?
HECK, NO! THIS IS AMERICA, REVEREND!

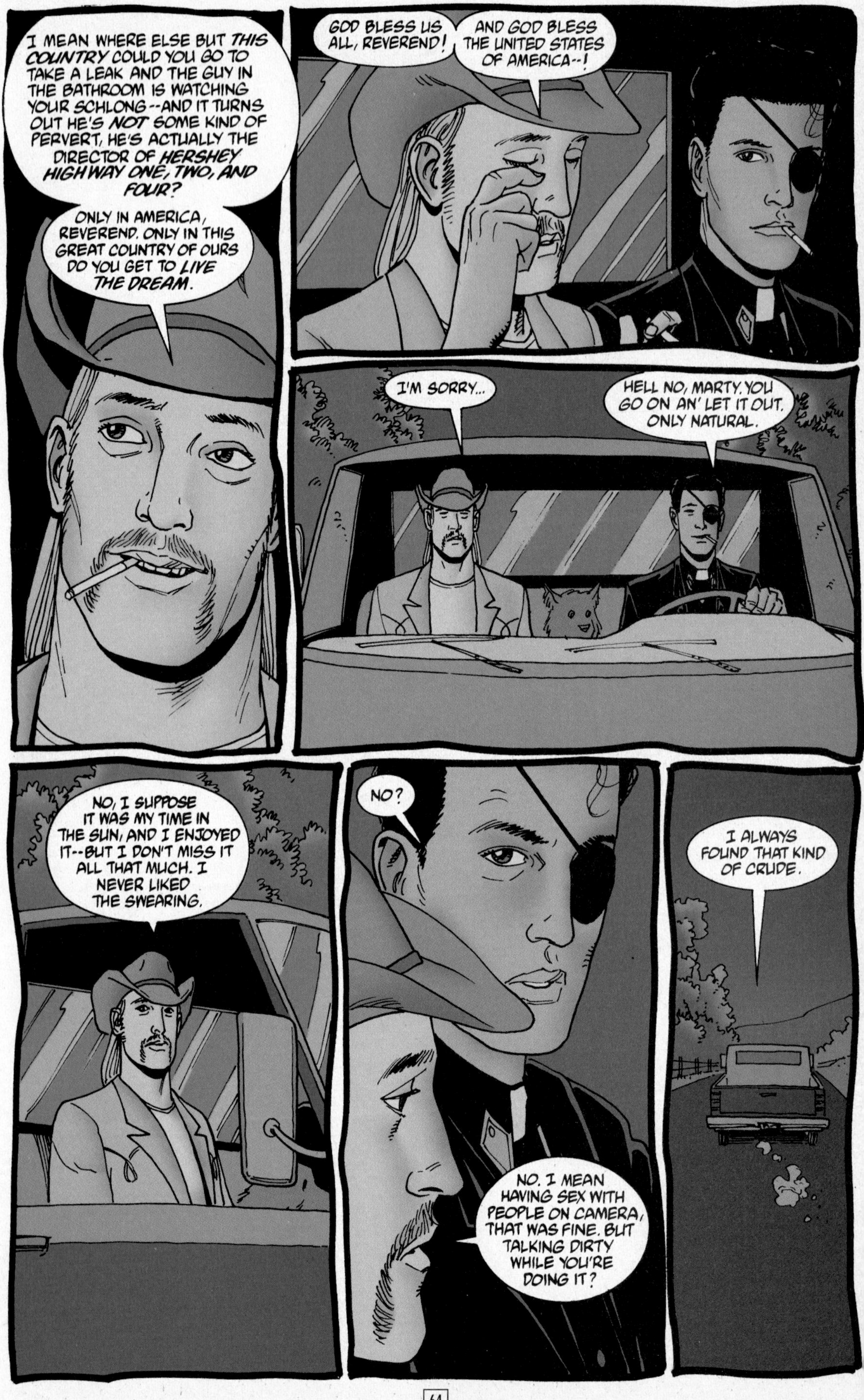
I MEAN WHERE ELSE BUT *THIS COUNTRY* COULD YOU GO TO TAKE A LEAK AND THE GUY IN THE BATHROOM IS WATCHING YOUR SCHLONG--AND IT TURNS OUT HE'S *NOT* SOME KIND OF PERVERT, HE'S ACTUALLY THE DIRECTOR OF *HERSHEY HIGHWAY ONE, TWO, AND FOUR?*
ONLY IN AMERICA, REVEREND. ONLY IN THIS GREAT COUNTRY OF OURS DO YOU GET TO *LIVE THE DREAM*.
GOD BLESS US ALL, REVEREND!
AND GOD BLESS THE UNITED STATES OF AMERICA--!
I'M SORRY...
HELL NO, MARTY. YOU GO ON AN' LET IT OUT. ONLY NATURAL.
NO, I SUPPOSE IT WAS MY TIME IN THE SUN, AND I ENJOYED IT--BUT I DON'T MISS IT ALL THAT MUCH. I NEVER LIKED THE SWEARING.
NO?
NO. I MEAN HAVING SEX WITH PEOPLE ON CAMERA, THAT WAS FINE. BUT TALKING DIRTY WHILE YOU'RE DOING IT?
I ALWAYS FOUND THAT KIND OF CRUDE.

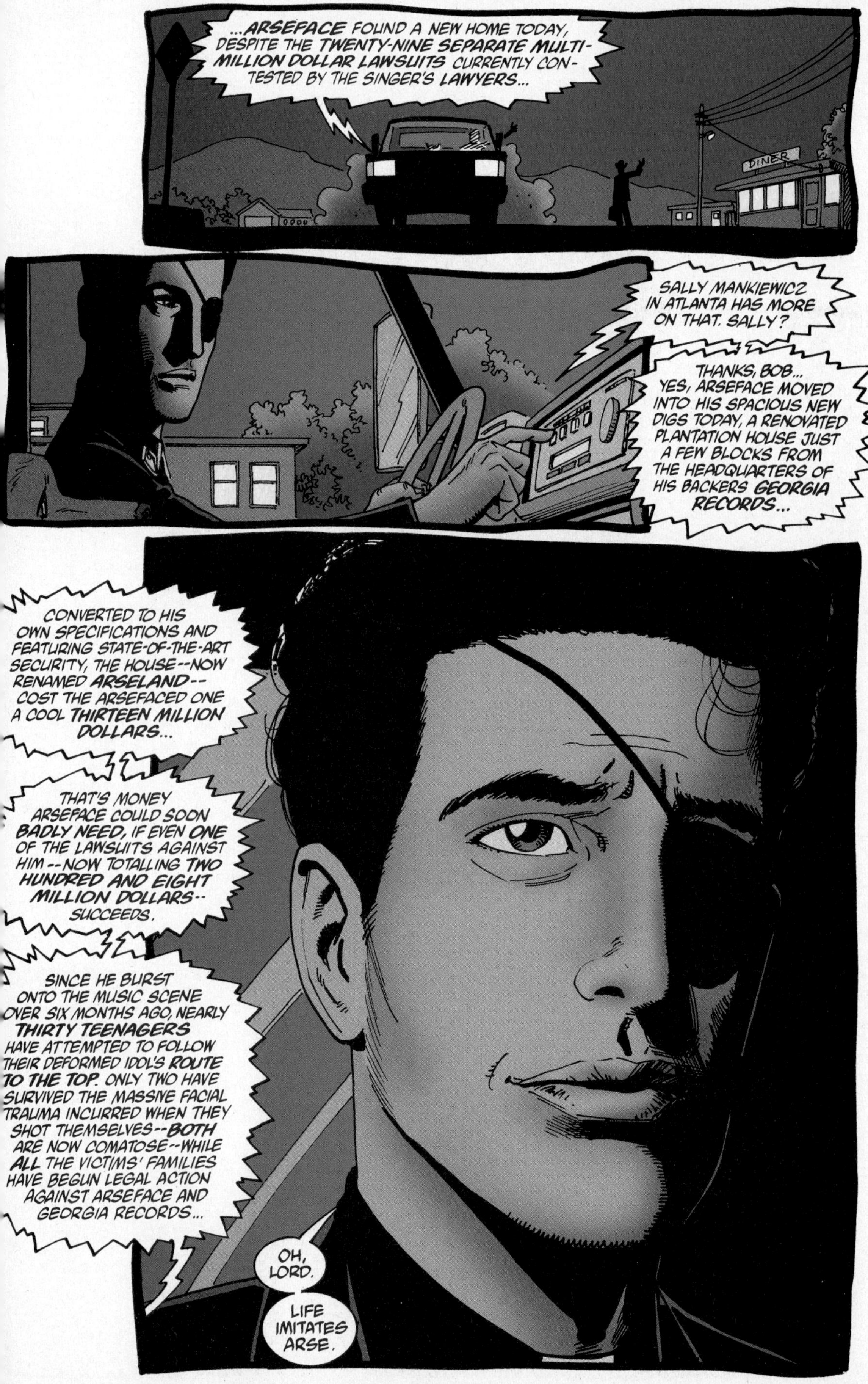
...ARSEFACE FOUND A NEW HOME TODAY, DESPITE THE TWENTY-NINE SEPARATE MULTI-MILLION DOLLAR LAWSUITS CURRENTLY CONTESTED BY THE SINGER'S LAWYERS...
DINER
SALLY MANKIEWICZ IN ATLANTA HAS MORE ON THAT. SALLY?
THANKS, BOB... YES, ARSEFACE MOVED INTO HIS SPACIOUS NEW DIGS TODAY, A RENOVATED PLANTATION HOUSE JUST A FEW BLOCKS FROM THE HEADQUARTERS OF HIS BACKERS GEORGIA RECORDS...
CONVERTED TO HIS OWN SPECIFICATIONS AND FEATURING STATE-OF-THE-ART SECURITY, THE HOUSE--NOW RENAMED ARSELAND--COST THE ARSEFACED ONE A COOL THIRTEEN MILLION DOLLARS...
THAT'S MONEY ARSEFACE COULD SOON BADLY NEED, IF EVEN ONE OF THE LAWSUITS AGAINST HIM--NOW TOTALLING TWO HUNDRED AND EIGHT MILLION DOLLARS--SUCCEEDS.
SINCE HE BURST ONTO THE MUSIC SCENE OVER SIX MONTHS AGO, NEARLY THIRTY TEENAGERS HAVE ATTEMPTED TO FOLLOW THEIR DEFORMED IDOL'S ROUTE TO THE TOP. ONLY TWO HAVE SURVIVED THE MASSIVE FACIAL TRAUMA INCURRED WHEN THEY SHOT THEMSELVES--BOTH ARE NOW COMATOSE--WHILE ALL THE VICTIMS' FAMILIES HAVE BEGUN LEGAL ACTION AGAINST ARSEFACE AND GEORGIA RECORDS...
OH, LORD.
LIFE IMITATES ARSE.

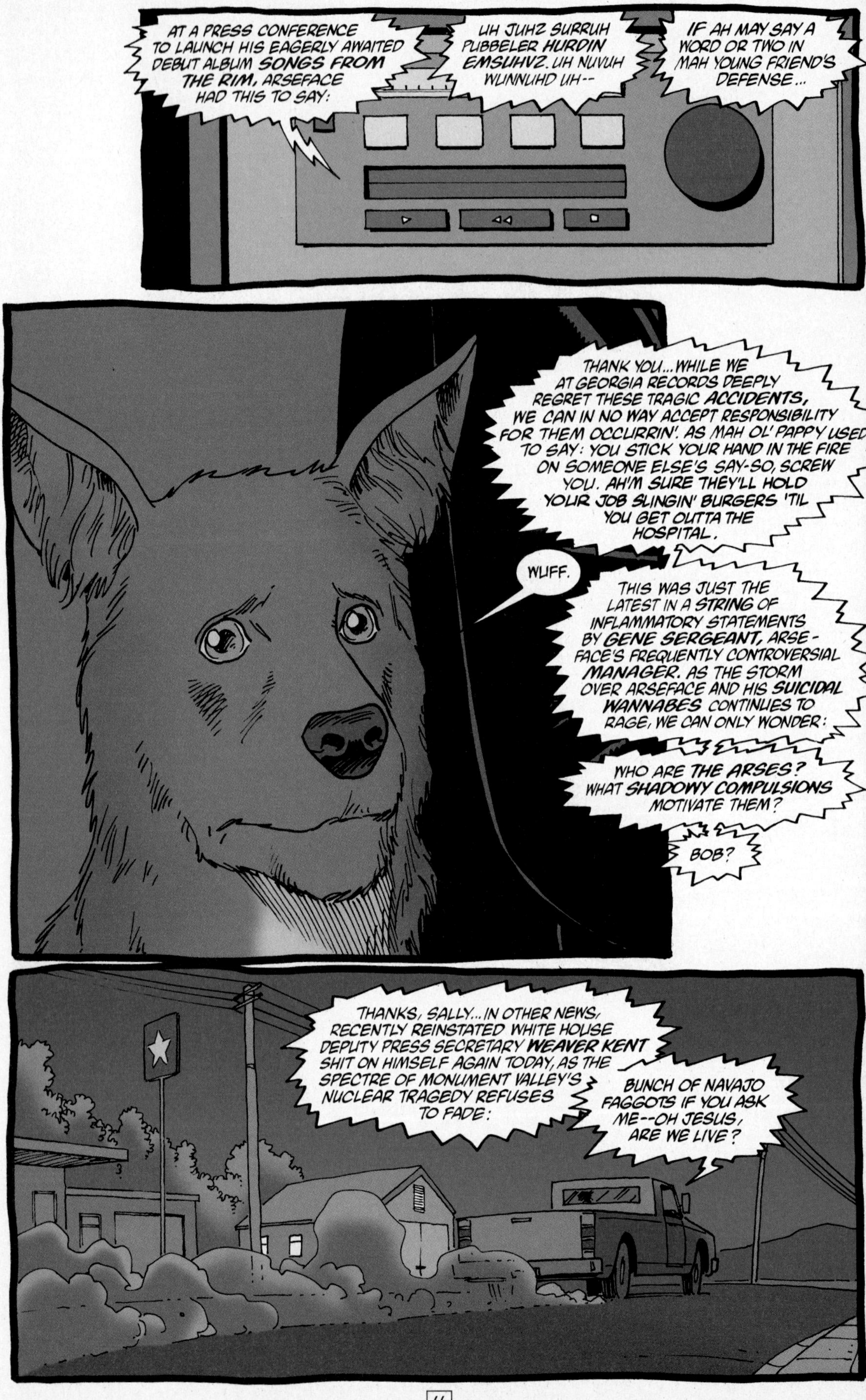

AT A PRESS CONFERENCE TO LAUNCH HIS EAGERLY AWAITED DEBUT ALBUM SONGS FROM THE RIM, ARSEFACE HAD THIS TO SAY:
UH JUHZ SURRUH PUBBELER HURDIN EMSUHVZ. UH NUVUH WUNNUHD UH--
IF AH MAY SAY A WORD OR TWO IN MAH YOUNG FRIEND'S DEFENSE...
THANK YOU... WHILE WE AT GEORGIA RECORDS DEEPLY REGRET THESE TRAGIC ACCIDENTS, WE CAN IN NO WAY ACCEPT RESPONSIBILITY FOR THEM OCCURRIN'. AS MAH OL' PAPPY USED TO SAY: YOU STICK YOUR HAND IN THE FIRE ON SOMEONE ELSE'S SAY-SO, SCREW YOU. AH'M SURE THEY'LL HOLD YOUR JOB SLINGIN' BURGERS 'TIL YOU GET OUTTA THE HOSPITAL.
WUFF.
THIS WAS JUST THE LATEST IN A STRING OF INFLAMMATORY STATEMENTS BY GENE SERGEANT, ARSE-FACE'S FREQUENTLY CONTROVERSIAL MANAGER. AS THE STORM OVER ARSEFACE AND HIS SUICIDAL WANNABES CONTINUES TO RAGE, WE CAN ONLY WONDER:
WHO ARE THE ARSES? WHAT SHADOWY COMPULSIONS MOTIVATE THEM?
BOB?
THANKS, SALLY... IN OTHER NEWS, RECENTLY REINSTATED WHITE HOUSE DEPUTY PRESS SECRETARY WEAVER KENT SHIT ON HIMSELF AGAIN TODAY, AS THE SPECTRE OF MONUMENT VALLEY'S NUCLEAR TRAGEDY REFUSES TO FADE:
BUNCH OF NAVAJO FAGGOTS IF YOU ASK ME--OH JESUS, ARE WE LIVE?

TFFF
TFFF

TFFF

TFFF
TFFF

BY 'ECK, FREDDY LAD, WE WERE FOOKIN' LUCKY TO GET OUT OF THERE ALIVE. IF IT 'ADN'T BEEN FOR ME TRADEMARK FAST-TALKIN' BANTER, WELL, I FOOKIN' DREAD TO THINK...

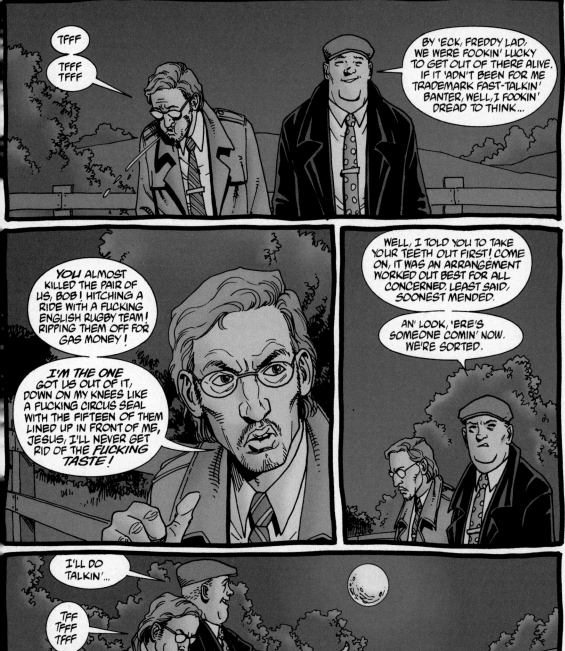

YOU ALMOST KILLED THE PAIR OF US, BOB! HITCHING A RIDE WITH A FUCKING ENGLISH RUGBY TEAM! RIPPING THEM OFF FOR GAS MONEY!

I'M THE ONE GOT US OUT OF IT, DOWN ON MY KNEES LIKE A FUCKING CIRCUS SEAL WITH THE FIFTEEN OF THEM LINED UP IN FRONT OF ME, JESUS, I'LL NEVER GET RID OF THE FUCKING TASTE!

WELL, I TOLD YOU TO TAKE YOUR TEETH OUT FIRST! COME ON, IT WAS AN ARRANGEMENT WORKED OUT BEST FOR ALL CONCERNED. LEAST SAID, SOONEST MENDED.

AN' LOOK, 'ERE'S SOMEONE COMIN' NOW. WE'RE SORTED.

I'LL DO TALKIN'...

TFF
TFFF
TFFF

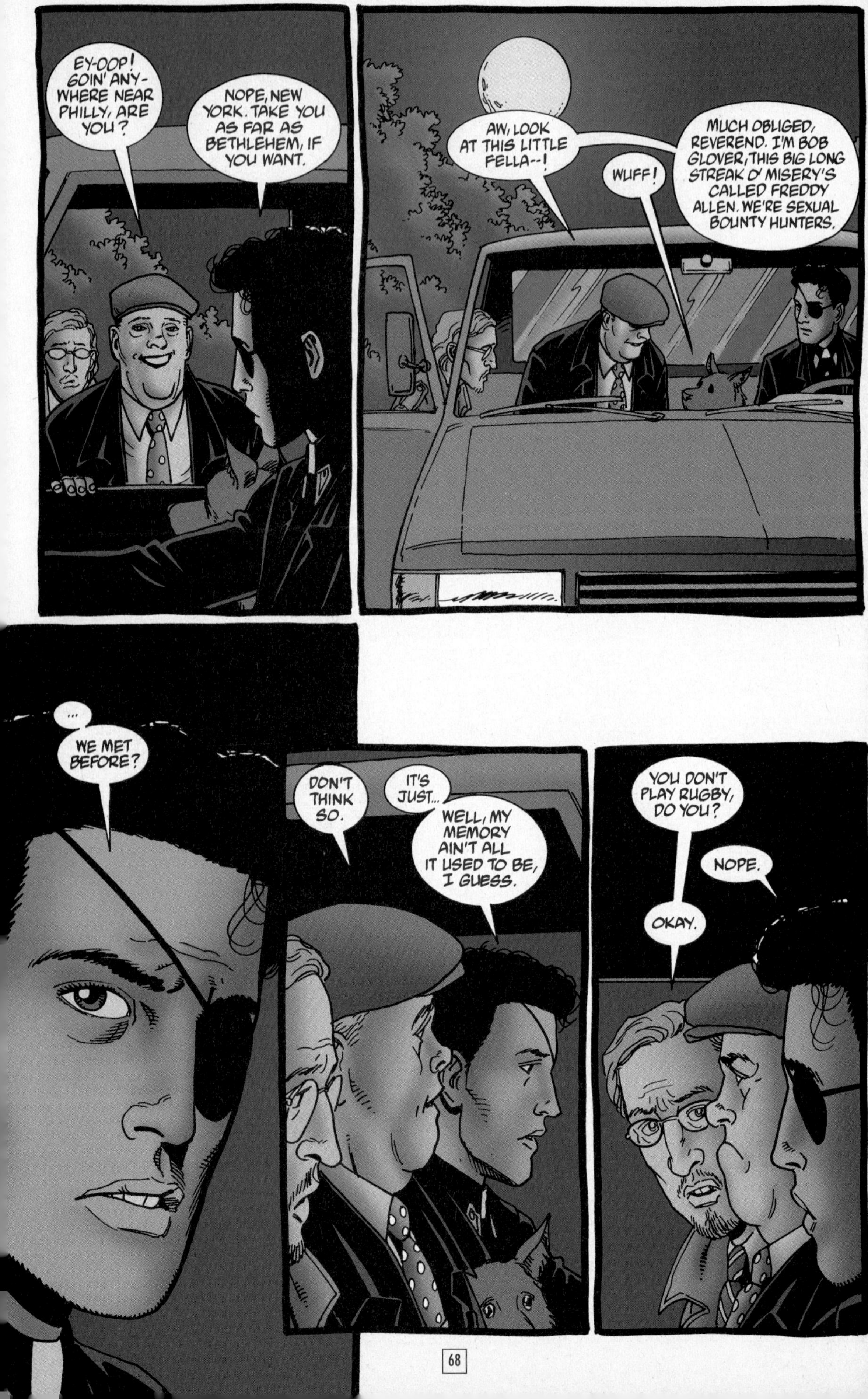
EY-OOP! GOIN' ANY-WHERE NEAR PHILLY, ARE YOU?
NOPE, NEW YORK. TAKE YOU AS FAR AS BETHLEHEM, IF YOU WANT.
AW, LOOK AT THIS LITTLE FELLA--!
WUFF!
MUCH OBLIGED, REVEREND. I'M BOB GLOVER, THIS BIG LONG STREAK O' MISERY'S CALLED FREDDY ALLEN. WE'RE SEXUAL BOUNTY HUNTERS.
...
WE MET BEFORE?
DON'T THINK SO.
IT'S JUST...
WELL, MY MEMORY AIN'T ALL IT USED TO BE, I GUESS.
YOU DON'T PLAY RUGBY, DO YOU?
NOPE.
OKAY.

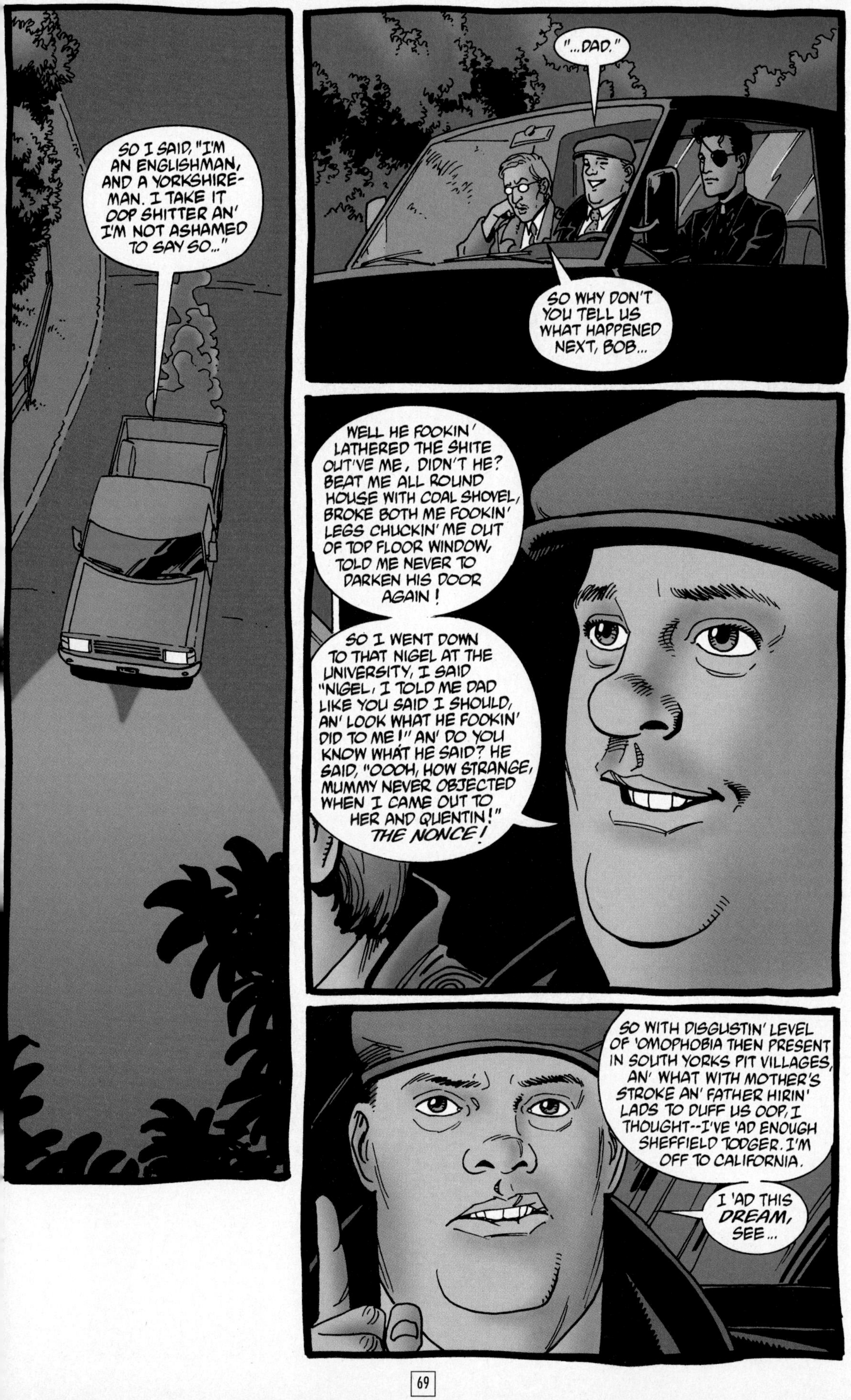
SO I SAID, "I'M AN ENGLISHMAN, AND A YORKSHIRE-MAN. I TAKE IT OOP SHITTER AN' I'M NOT ASHAMED TO SAY SO..."
"...DAD."
SO WHY DON'T YOU TELL US WHAT HAPPENED NEXT, BOB...
WELL HE FOOKIN' LATHERED THE SHITE OUT'VE ME, DIDN'T HE? BEAT ME ALL ROUND HOUSE WITH COAL SHOVEL, BROKE BOTH ME FOOKIN' LEGS CHUCKIN' ME OUT OF TOP FLOOR WINDOW, TOLD ME NEVER TO DARKEN HIS DOOR AGAIN!
SO I WENT DOWN TO THAT NIGEL AT THE UNIVERSITY, I SAID "NIGEL, I TOLD ME DAD LIKE YOU SAID I SHOULD, AN' LOOK WHAT HE FOOKIN' DID TO ME!" AN' DO YOU KNOW WHAT HE SAID? HE SAID, "OOOH, HOW STRANGE, MUMMY NEVER OBJECTED WHEN I CAME OUT TO HER AND QUENTIN!" THE NONCE!
SO WITH DISGUSTIN' LEVEL OF 'OMOPHOBIA THEN PRESENT IN SOUTH YORKS PIT VILLAGES, AN' WHAT WITH MOTHER'S STROKE AN' FATHER HIRIN' LADS TO DUFF US OOP, I THOUGHT--I'VE 'AD ENOUGH SHEFFIELD TODGER. I'M OFF TO CALIFORNIA.
I 'AD THIS DREAM, SEE...

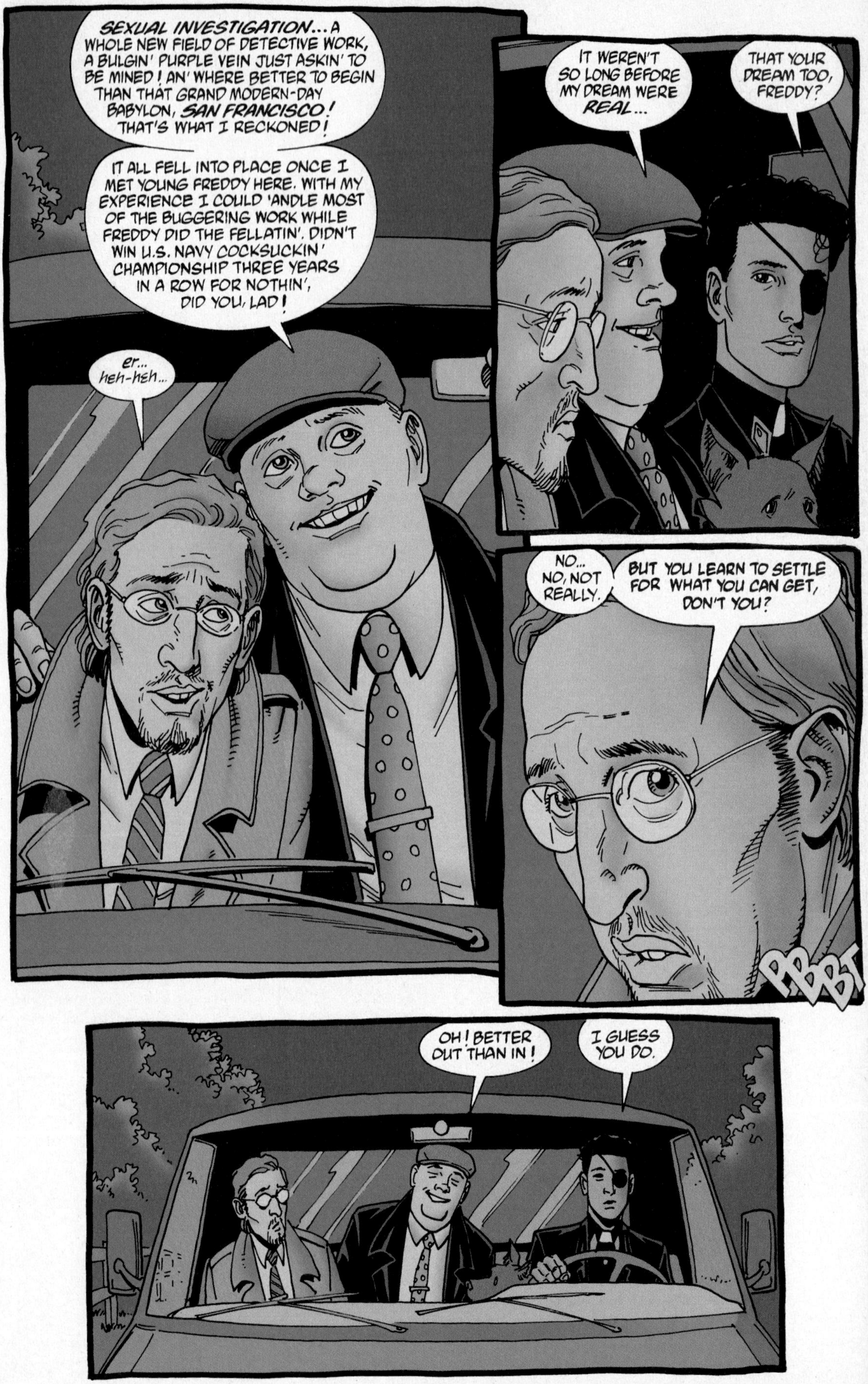
SEXUAL INVESTIGATION... A WHOLE NEW FIELD OF DETECTIVE WORK, A BULGIN' PURPLE VEIN JUST ASKIN' TO BE MINED! AN' WHERE BETTER TO BEGIN THAN THAT GRAND MODERN-DAY BABYLON, SAN FRANCISCO! THAT'S WHAT I RECKONED!
IT ALL FELL INTO PLACE ONCE I MET YOUNG FREDDY HERE. WITH MY EXPERIENCE I COULD 'ANDLE MOST OF THE BUGGERING WORK WHILE FREDDY DID THE FELLATIN'. DIDN'T WIN U.S. NAVY COCKSUCKIN' CHAMPIONSHIP THREE YEARS IN A ROW FOR NOTHIN', DID YOU, LAD!
er... heh-heh...
IT WEREN'T SO LONG BEFORE MY DREAM WERE REAL...
THAT YOUR DREAM TOO, FREDDY?
NO... NO, NOT REALLY.
BUT YOU LEARN TO SETTLE FOR WHAT YOU CAN GET, DON'T YOU?
PBBBT
OH! BETTER OUT THAN IN!
I GUESS YOU DO.
er...

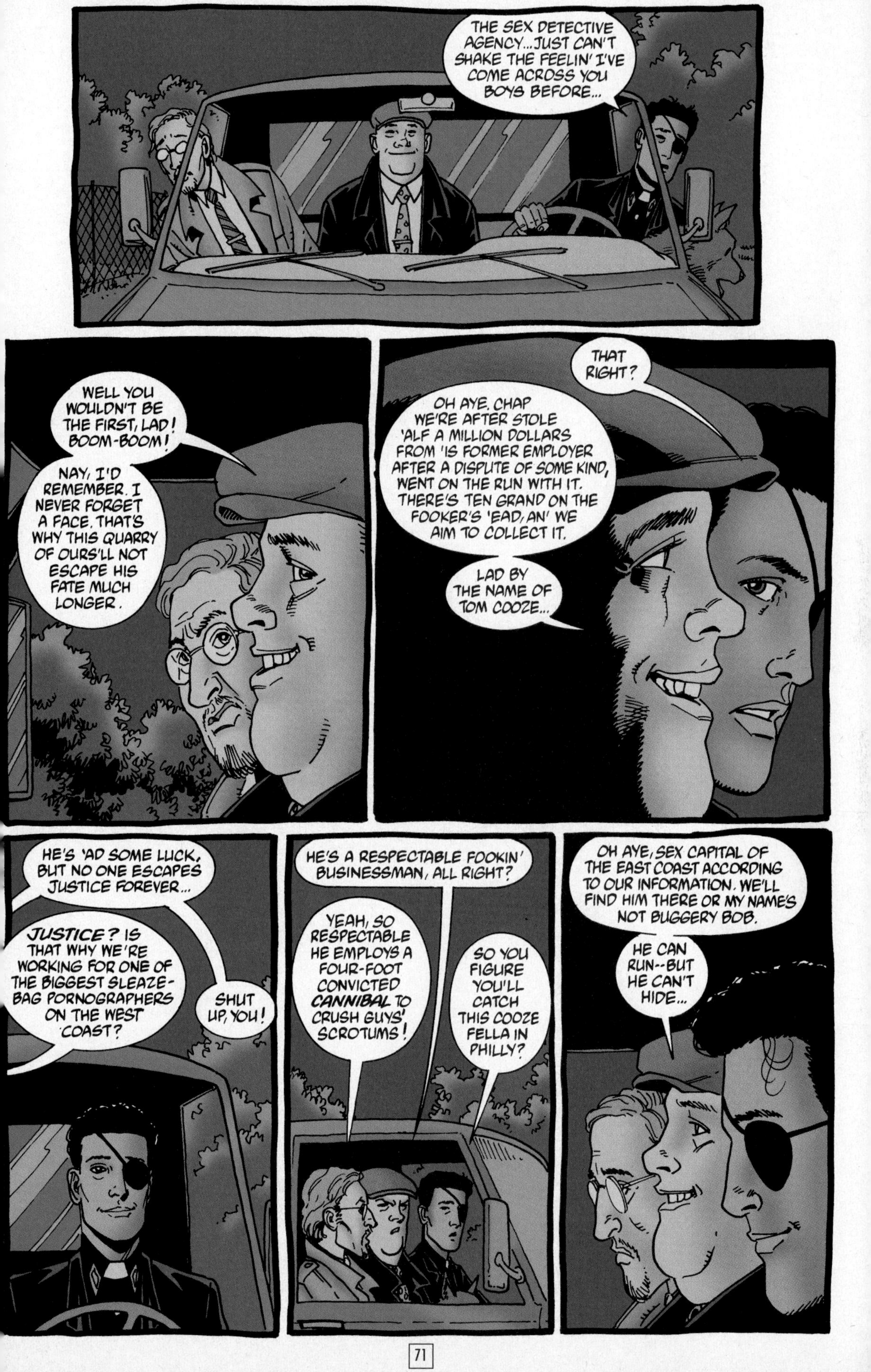
THE SEX DETECTIVE AGENCY...JUST CAN'T SHAKE THE FEELIN' I'VE COME ACROSS YOU BOYS BEFORE...
WELL YOU WOULDN'T BE THE FIRST, LAD! BOOM-BOOM!
NAY, I'D REMEMBER. I NEVER FORGET A FACE. THAT'S WHY THIS QUARRY OF OURS'LL NOT ESCAPE HIS FATE MUCH LONGER.
THAT RIGHT?
OH AYE. CHAP WE'RE AFTER STOLE 'ALF A MILLION DOLLARS FROM 'IS FORMER EMPLOYER AFTER A DISPUTE OF SOME KIND, WENT ON THE RUN WITH IT. THERE'S TEN GRAND ON THE FOOKER'S 'EAD, AN' WE AIM TO COLLECT IT.
LAD BY THE NAME OF TOM COOZE...
HE'S 'AD SOME LUCK, BUT NO ONE ESCAPES JUSTICE FOREVER...
JUSTICE? IS THAT WHY WE'RE WORKING FOR ONE OF THE BIGGEST SLEAZE-BAG PORNOGRAPHERS ON THE WEST COAST?
SHUT UP, YOU!
HE'S A RESPECTABLE FOOKIN' BUSINESSMAN, ALL RIGHT?
YEAH, SO RESPECTABLE HE EMPLOYS A FOUR-FOOT CONVICTED CANNIBAL TO CRUSH GUYS' SCROTUMS!
SO YOU FIGURE YOU'LL CATCH THIS COOZE FELLA IN PHILLY?
OH AYE, SEX CAPITAL OF THE EAST COAST ACCORDING TO OUR INFORMATION. WE'LL FIND HIM THERE OR MY NAME'S NOT BUGGERY BOB.
HE CAN RUN--BUT HE CAN'T HIDE...

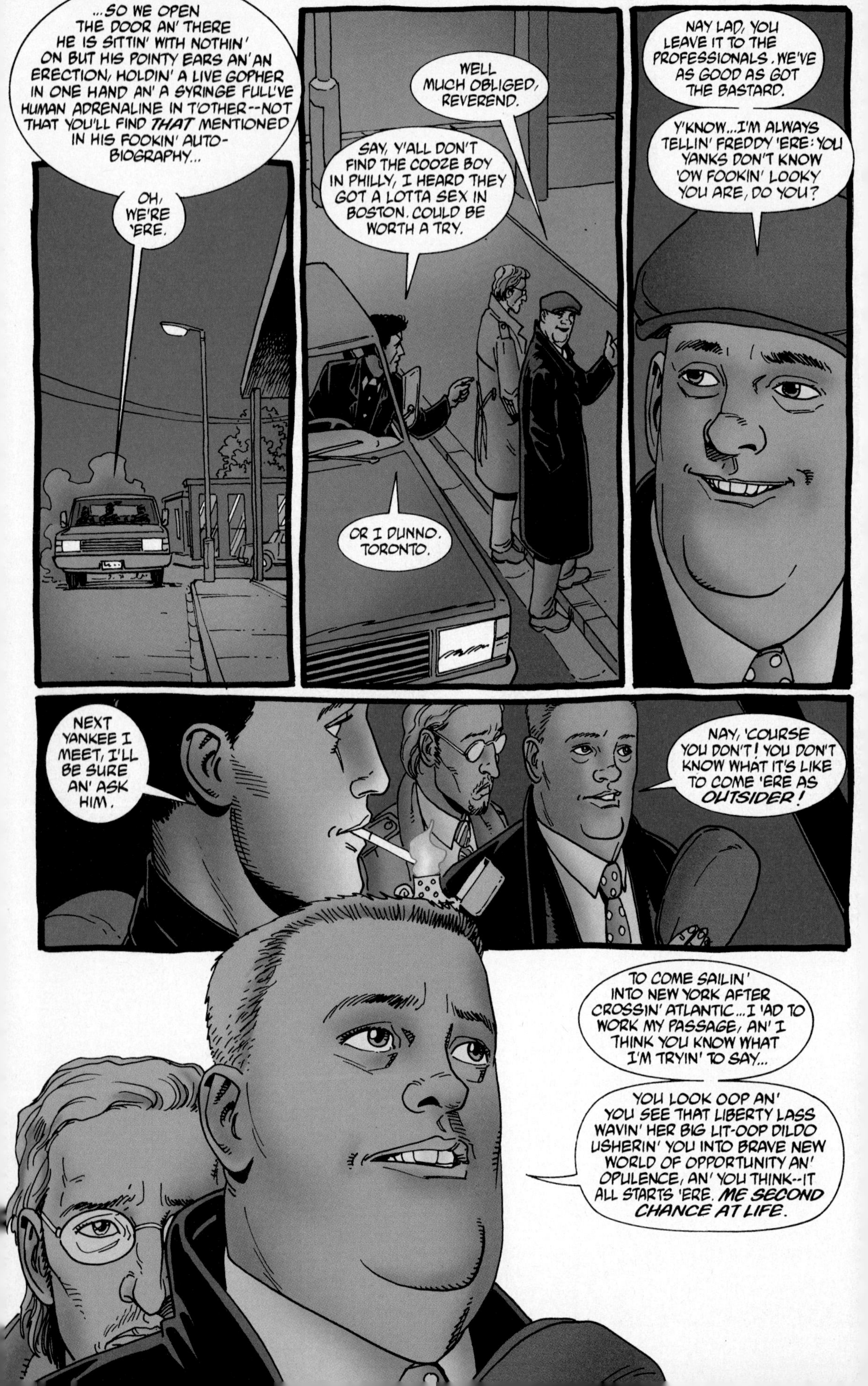
...SO WE OPEN THE DOOR AN' THERE HE IS SITTIN' WITH NOTHIN' ON BUT HIS POINTY EARS AN' AN ERECTION, HOLDIN' A LIVE GOPHER IN ONE HAND AN' A SYRINGE FULL'VE HUMAN ADRENALINE IN T'OTHER--NOT THAT YOU'LL FIND THAT MENTIONED IN HIS FOOKIN' AUTO-BIOGRAPHY...
OH, WE'RE 'ERE.
WELL MUCH OBLIGED, REVEREND.
SAY, Y'ALL DON'T FIND THE COOZE BOY IN PHILLY, I HEARD THEY GOT A LOTTA SEX IN BOSTON. COULD BE WORTH A TRY.
OR I DUNNO. TORONTO.
NAY LAD, YOU LEAVE IT TO THE PROFESSIONALS. WE'VE AS GOOD AS GOT THE BASTARD.
Y'KNOW...I'M ALWAYS TELLIN' FREDDY 'ERE: YOU YANKS DON'T KNOW 'OW FOOKIN' LOOKY YOU ARE, DO YOU?
NEXT YANKEE I MEET, I'LL BE SURE AN' ASK HIM.
NAY, 'COURSE YOU DON'T! YOU DON'T KNOW WHAT IT'S LIKE TO COME 'ERE AS OUTSIDER!
TO COME SAILIN' INTO NEW YORK AFTER CROSSIN' ATLANTIC...I 'AD TO WORK MY PASSAGE, AN' I THINK YOU KNOW WHAT I'M TRYIN' TO SAY...
YOU LOOK OOP AN' YOU SEE THAT LIBERTY LASS WAVIN' HER BIG LIT-OOP DILDO USHERIN' YOU INTO BRAVE NEW WORLD OF OPPORTUNITY AN' OPULENCE, AN' YOU THINK--IT ALL STARTS 'ERE. ME SECOND CHANCE AT LIFE.

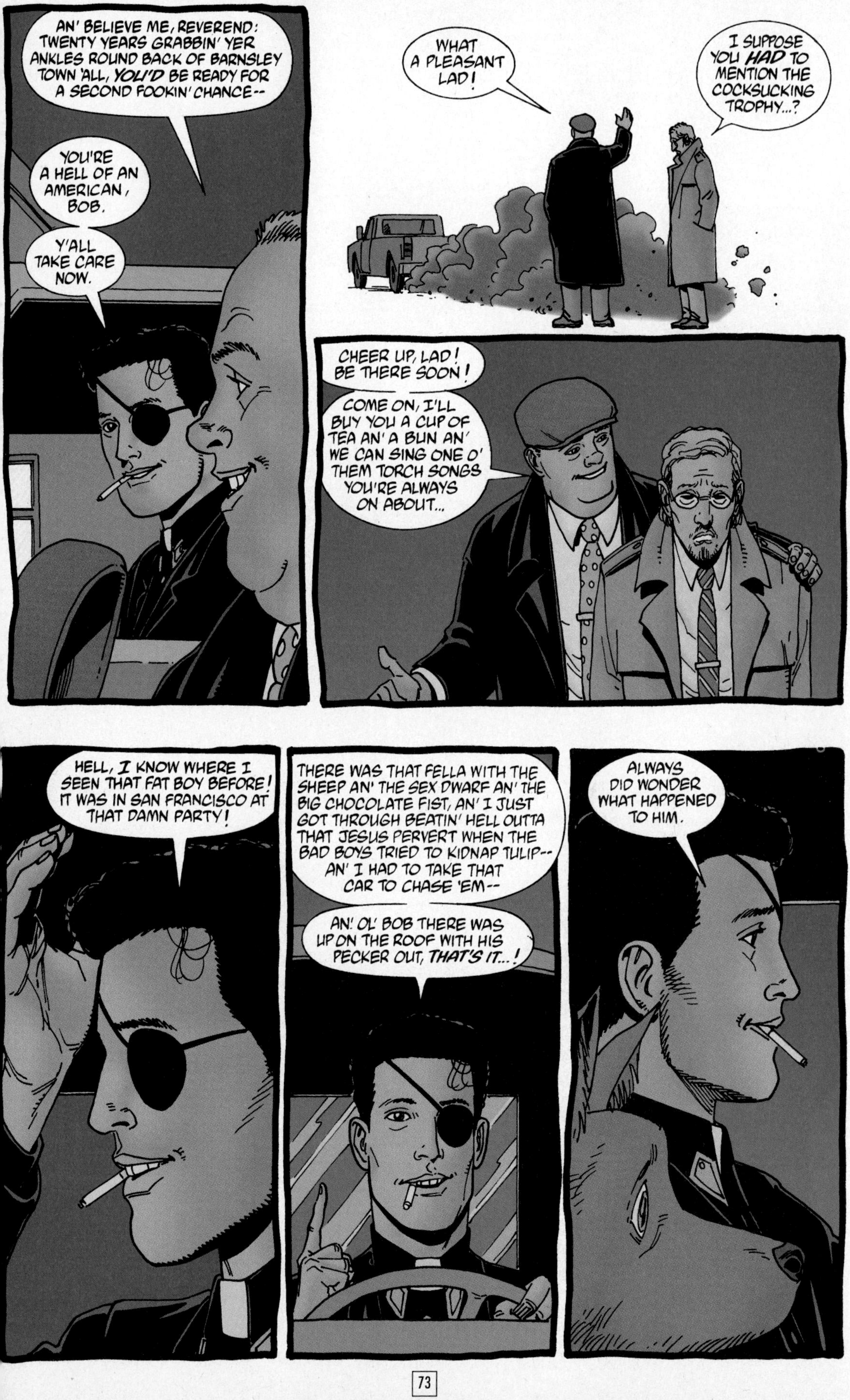
AN' BELIEVE ME, REVEREND: TWENTY YEARS GRABBIN' YER ANKLES ROUND BACK OF BARNSLEY TOWN 'ALL, *YOU'D* BE READY FOR A SECOND FOOKIN' CHANCE--
YOU'RE A HELL OF AN AMERICAN, BOB.
Y'ALL TAKE CARE NOW.
WHAT A PLEASANT LAD!
I SUPPOSE YOU *HAD* TO MENTION THE COCKSUCKING TROPHY...?
CHEER UP, LAD! BE THERE SOON!
COME ON, I'LL BUY YOU A CUP OF TEA AN' A BUN AN' WE CAN SING ONE O' THEM TORCH SONGS YOU'RE ALWAYS ON ABOUT...
HELL, *I* KNOW WHERE I SEEN THAT FAT BOY BEFORE! IT WAS IN SAN FRANCISCO AT THAT DAMN PARTY!
THERE WAS THAT FELLA WITH THE SHEEP AN' THE SEX DWARF AN' THE BIG CHOCOLATE FIST, AN' I JUST GOT THROUGH BEATIN' HELL OUTTA THAT JESUS PERVERT WHEN THE BAD BOYS TRIED TO KIDNAP TULIP-- AN' I HAD TO TAKE THAT CAR TO CHASE 'EM--
AN' OL' BOB THERE WAS UP ON THE ROOF WITH HIS PECKER OUT, *THAT'S IT...!*
ALWAYS DID WONDER WHAT HAPPENED TO HIM.

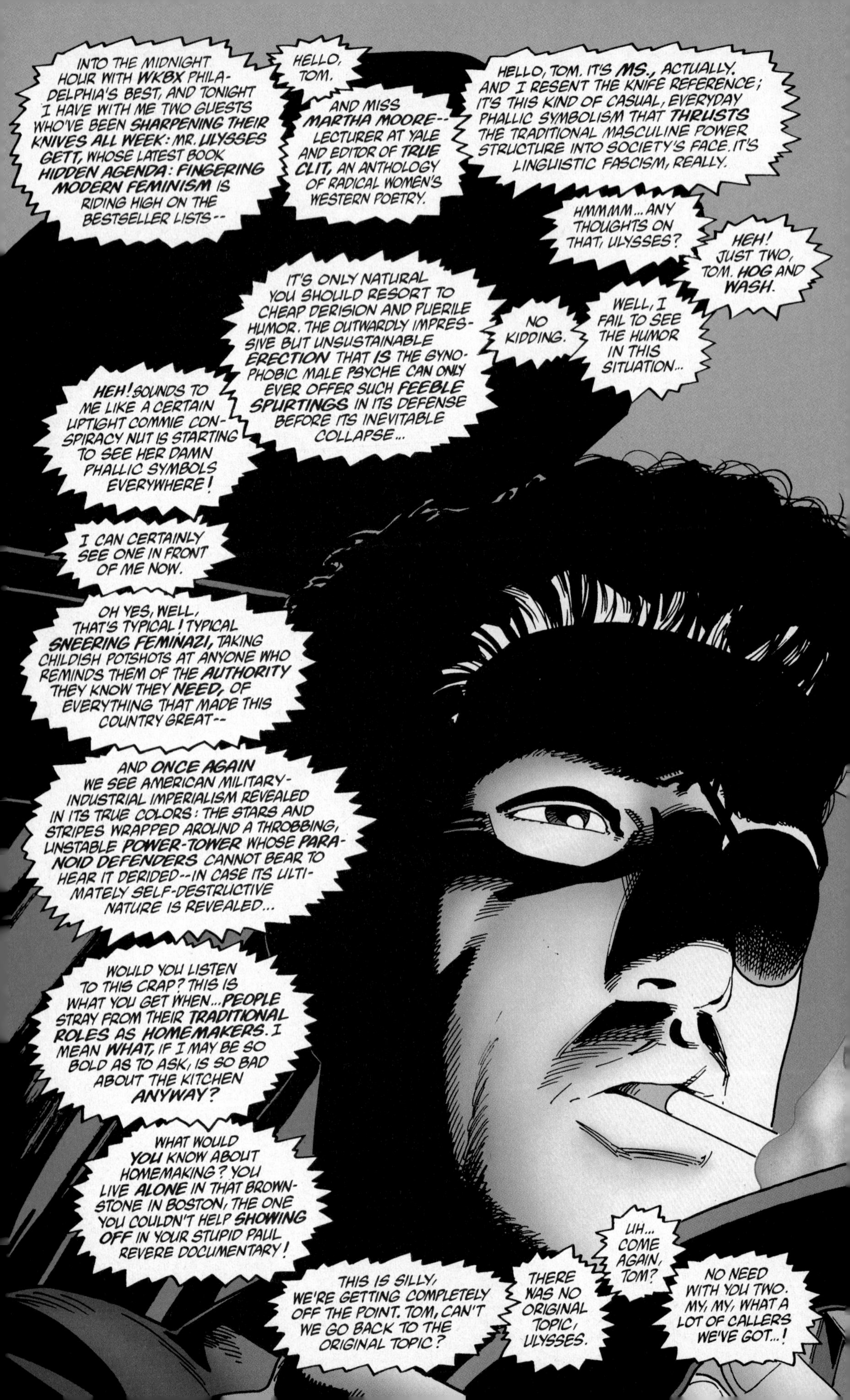
INTO THE MIDNIGHT HOUR WITH WKBX PHILADELPHIA'S BEST, AND TONIGHT I HAVE WITH ME TWO GUESTS WHO'VE BEEN SHARPENING THEIR KNIVES ALL WEEK: MR. ULYSSES GETT, WHOSE LATEST BOOK HIDDEN AGENDA: FINGERING MODERN FEMINISM IS RIDING HIGH ON THE BESTSELLER LISTS--
HELLO, TOM.
AND MISS MARTHA MOORE-- LECTURER AT YALE AND EDITOR OF TRUE CLIT, AN ANTHOLOGY OF RADICAL WOMEN'S WESTERN POETRY.
HELLO, TOM. IT'S MS., ACTUALLY. AND I RESENT THE KNIFE REFERENCE; IT'S THIS KIND OF CASUAL, EVERYDAY PHALLIC SYMBOLISM THAT THRUSTS THE TRADITIONAL MASCULINE POWER STRUCTURE INTO SOCIETY'S FACE. IT'S LINGUISTIC FASCISM, REALLY.
HMMMM... ANY THOUGHTS ON THAT, ULYSSES?
HEH! JUST TWO, TOM. HOG AND WASH.
IT'S ONLY NATURAL YOU SHOULD RESORT TO CHEAP DERISION AND PUERILE HUMOR. THE OUTWARDLY IMPRESSIVE BUT UNSUSTAINABLE ERECTION THAT IS THE GYNOPHOBIC MALE PSYCHE CAN ONLY EVER OFFER SUCH FEEBLE SPURTINGS IN ITS DEFENSE BEFORE ITS INEVITABLE COLLAPSE...
NO KIDDING.
WELL, I FAIL TO SEE THE HUMOR IN THIS SITUATION...
HEH! SOUNDS TO ME LIKE A CERTAIN UPTIGHT COMMIE CONSPIRACY NUT IS STARTING TO SEE HER DAMN PHALLIC SYMBOLS EVERYWHERE!
I CAN CERTAINLY SEE ONE IN FRONT OF ME NOW.
OH YES, WELL, THAT'S TYPICAL! TYPICAL SNEERING FEMINAZI, TAKING CHILDISH POTSHOTS AT ANYONE WHO REMINDS THEM OF THE AUTHORITY THEY KNOW THEY NEED, OF EVERYTHING THAT MADE THIS COUNTRY GREAT--
AND ONCE AGAIN WE SEE AMERICAN MILITARY-INDUSTRIAL IMPERIALISM REVEALED IN ITS TRUE COLORS: THE STARS AND STRIPES WRAPPED AROUND A THROBBING, UNSTABLE POWER-TOWER WHOSE PARANOID DEFENDERS CANNOT BEAR TO HEAR IT DERIDED--IN CASE ITS ULTIMATELY SELF-DESTRUCTIVE NATURE IS REVEALED...
WOULD YOU LISTEN TO THIS CRAP? THIS IS WHAT YOU GET WHEN...PEOPLE STRAY FROM THEIR TRADITIONAL ROLES AS HOMEMAKERS. I MEAN WHAT, IF I MAY BE SO BOLD AS TO ASK, IS SO BAD ABOUT THE KITCHEN ANYWAY?
WHAT WOULD YOU KNOW ABOUT HOMEMAKING? YOU LIVE ALONE IN THAT BROWNSTONE IN BOSTON, THE ONE YOU COULDN'T HELP SHOWING OFF IN YOUR STUPID PAUL REVERE DOCUMENTARY!
THIS IS SILLY, WE'RE GETTING COMPLETELY OFF THE POINT. TOM, CAN'T WE GO BACK TO THE ORIGINAL TOPIC?
THERE WAS NO ORIGINAL TOPIC, ULYSSES.
UH... COME AGAIN, TOM?
NO NEED WITH YOU TWO. MY, MY, WHAT A LOT OF CALLERS WE'VE GOT...!

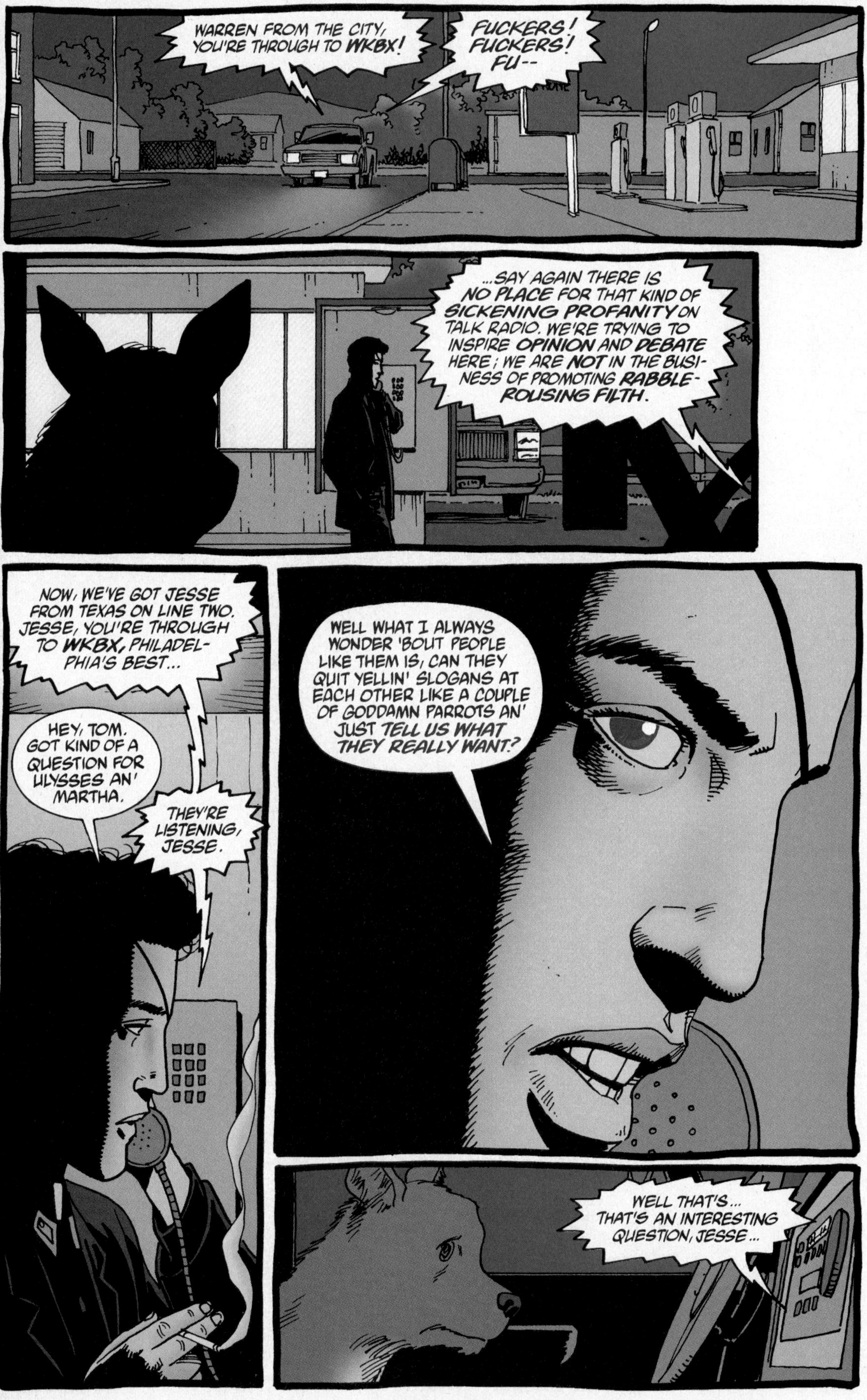
WARREN FROM THE CITY, YOU'RE THROUGH TO WKBX!
FUCKERS! FUCKERS! FU--
...SAY AGAIN THERE IS NO PLACE FOR THAT KIND OF SICKENING PROFANITY ON TALK RADIO. WE'RE TRYING TO INSPIRE OPINION AND DEBATE HERE; WE ARE NOT IN THE BUSINESS OF PROMOTING RABBLE-ROUSING FILTH.
NOW, WE'VE GOT JESSE FROM TEXAS ON LINE TWO. JESSE, YOU'RE THROUGH TO WKBX, PHILADELPHIA'S BEST...
HEY, TOM. GOT KIND OF A QUESTION FOR ULYSSES AN' MARTHA.
THEY'RE LISTENING, JESSE.
WELL WHAT I ALWAYS WONDER 'BOUT PEOPLE LIKE THEM IS, CAN THEY QUIT YELLIN' SLOGANS AT EACH OTHER LIKE A COUPLE OF GODDAMN PARROTS AN' JUST TELL US WHAT THEY REALLY WANT?
WELL THAT'S... THAT'S AN INTERESTING QUESTION, JESSE...

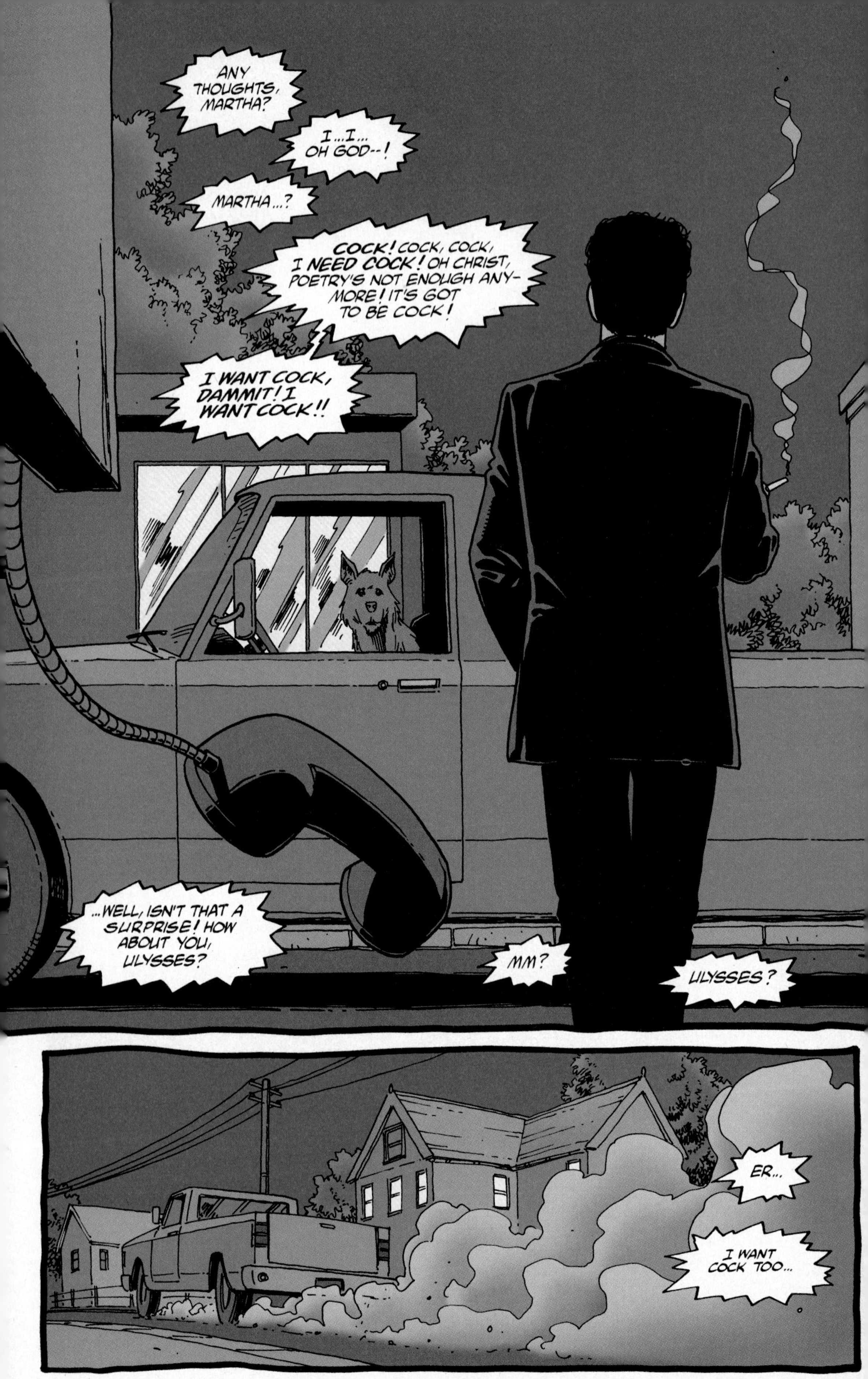
ANY THOUGHTS, MARTHA?
I...I... OH GOD--!
MARTHA...?
COCK! COCK, COCK, I NEED COCK! OH CHRIST, POETRY'S NOT ENOUGH ANYMORE! IT'S GOT TO BE COCK!
I WANT COCK, DAMMIT! I WANT COCK!!
...WELL, ISN'T THAT A SURPRISE! HOW ABOUT YOU, ULYSSES?
MM?
ULYSSES?
ER...
I WANT COCK TOO...

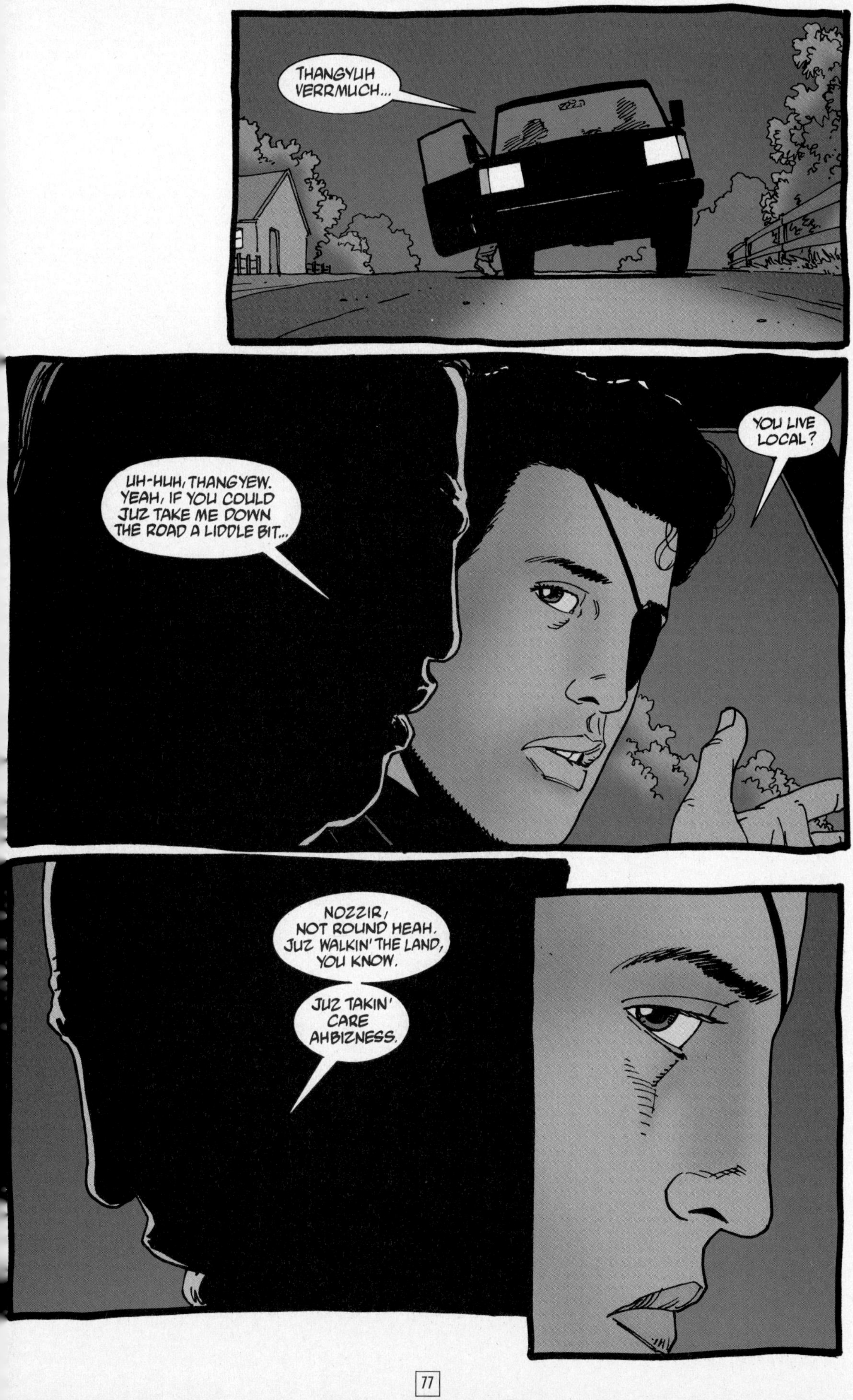
THANGYUH VERRMUCH...
YOU LIVE LOCAL?
UH-HUH, THANGYEW. YEAH, IF YOU COULD JUZ TAKE ME DOWN THE ROAD A LIDDLE BIT...
NOZZIR, NOT ROUND HEAH. JUZ WALKIN' THE LAND, YOU KNOW.
JUZ TAKIN' CARE AHBIZNESS.

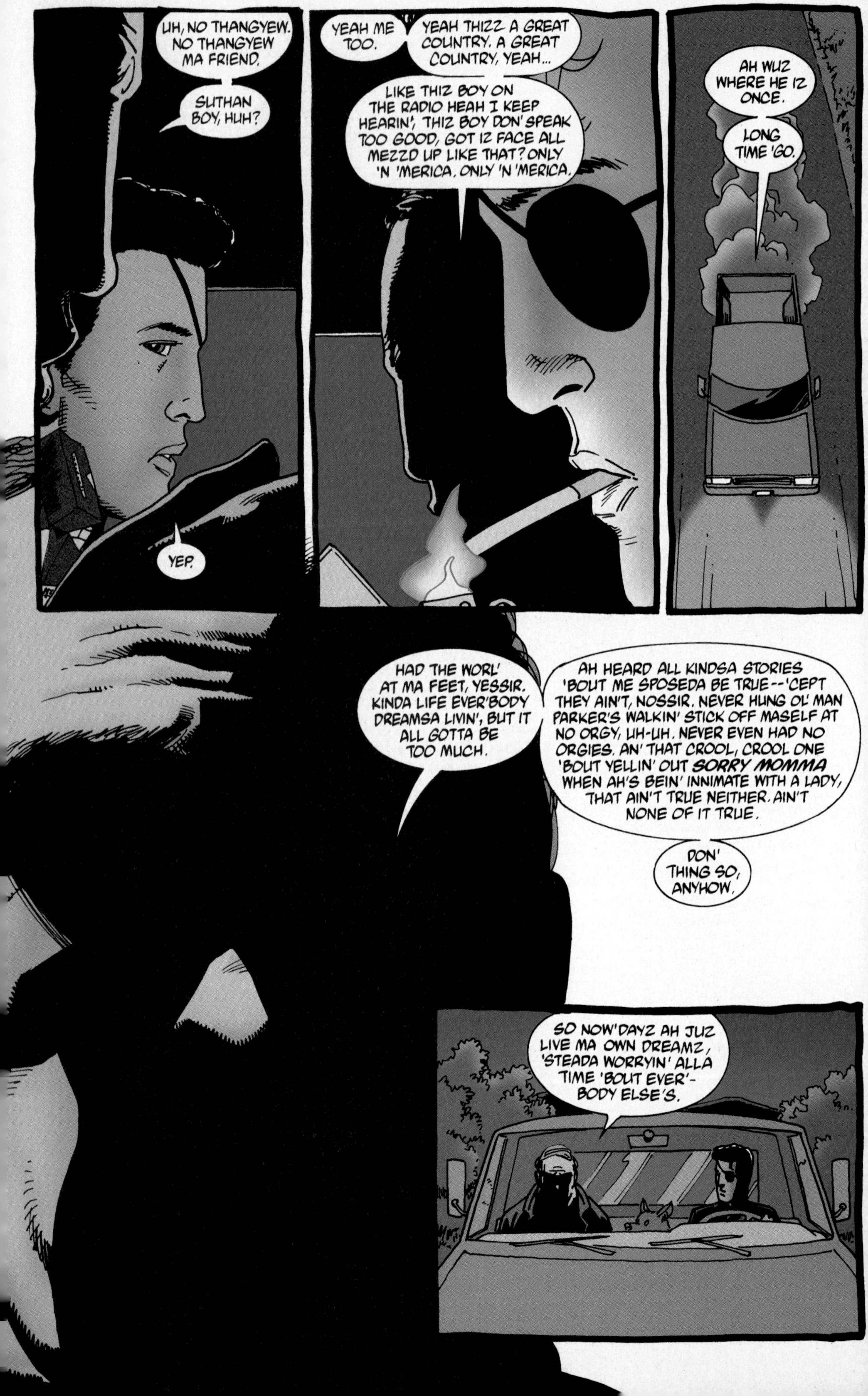
UH, NO THANGYEW. NO THANGYEW MA FRIEND.
SUTHAN BOY, HUH?
YEP.
YEAH ME TOO.
YEAH THIZZ A GREAT COUNTRY. A GREAT COUNTRY, YEAH...
LIKE THIZ BOY ON THE RADIO HEAH I KEEP HEARIN', THIZ BOY DON' SPEAK TOO GOOD, GOT IZ FACE ALL MEZZD UP LIKE THAT? ONLY 'N 'MERICA. ONLY 'N 'MERICA.
AH WUZ WHERE HE IZ ONCE.
LONG TIME 'GO.
HAD THE WORL' AT MA FEET, YESSIR. KINDA LIFE EVER'BODY DREAMSA LIVIN', BUT IT ALL GOTTA BE TOO MUCH.
AH HEARD ALL KINDSA STORIES 'BOUT ME SPOSEDA BE TRUE--'CEPT THEY AIN'T, NOSSIR. NEVER HUNG OL' MAN PARKER'S WALKIN' STICK OFF MASELF AT NO ORGY, UH-UH. NEVER EVEN HAD NO ORGIES. AN' THAT CROOL, CROOL ONE 'BOUT YELLIN' OUT SORRY MOMMA WHEN AH'S BEIN' INNIMATE WITH A LADY, THAT AIN'T TRUE NEITHER. AIN'T NONE OF IT TRUE.
DON' THING SO, ANYHOW.
SO NOW'DAYZ AH JUZ LIVE MA OWN DREAMZ, 'STEADA WORRYIN' ALLA TIME 'BOUT EVER'-BODY ELSE'S.

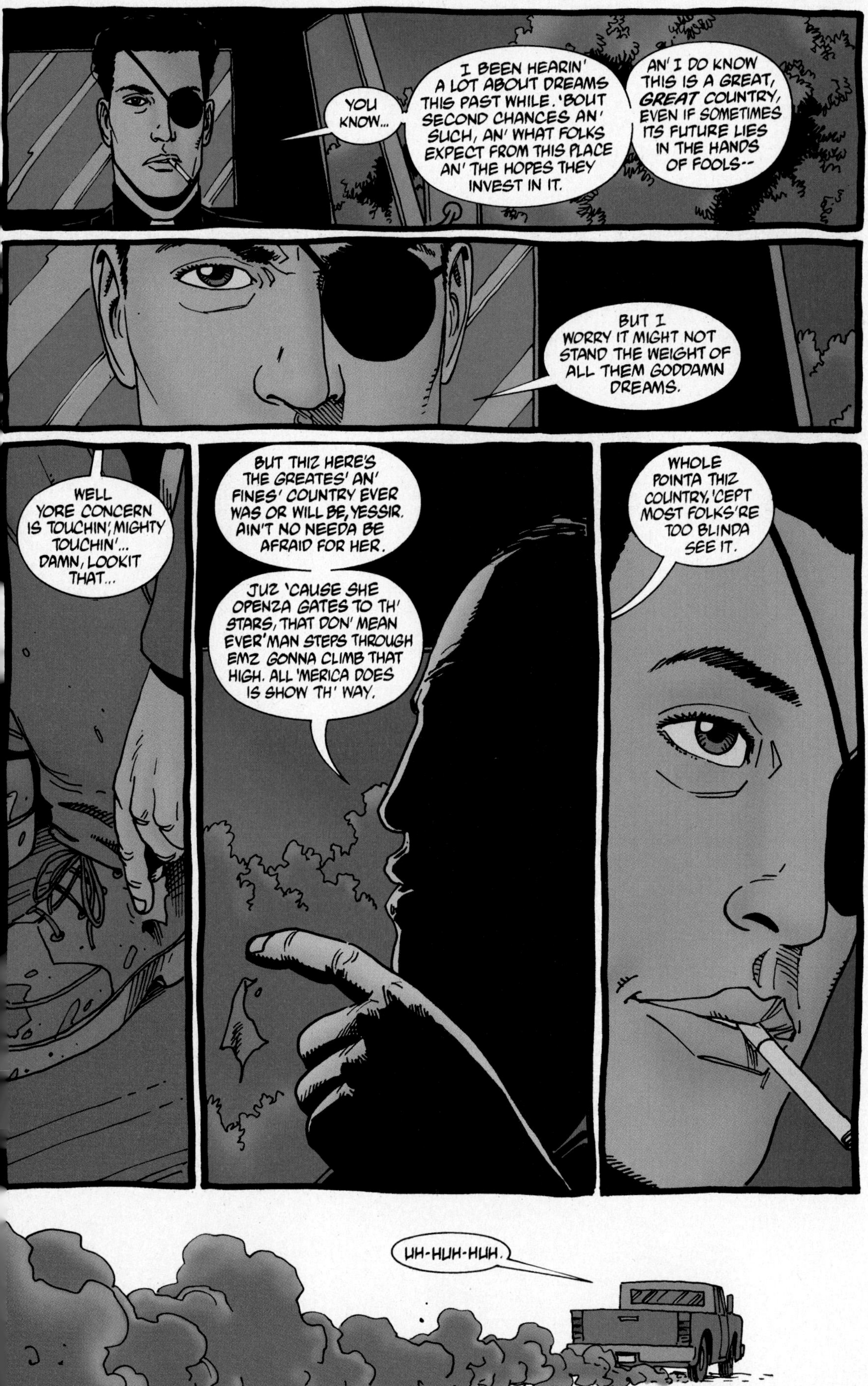
YOU KNOW...
I BEEN HEARIN' A LOT ABOUT DREAMS THIS PAST WHILE. 'BOUT SECOND CHANCES AN' SUCH, AN' WHAT FOLKS EXPECT FROM THIS PLACE AN' THE HOPES THEY INVEST IN IT.
AN' I DO KNOW THIS IS A GREAT, GREAT COUNTRY, EVEN IF SOMETIMES ITS FUTURE LIES IN THE HANDS OF FOOLS--
BUT I WORRY IT MIGHT NOT STAND THE WEIGHT OF ALL THEM GODDAMN DREAMS.
WELL YORE CONCERN IS TOUCHIN', MIGHTY TOUCHIN'... DAMN, LOOKIT THAT...
BUT THIZ HERE'S THE GREATES' AN' FINES' COUNTRY EVER WAS OR WILL BE, YESSIR. AIN'T NO NEEDA BE AFRAID FOR HER.
JUZ 'CAUSE SHE OPENZA GATES TO TH' STARS, THAT DON' MEAN EVER'MAN STEPS THROUGH EMZ GONNA CLIMB THAT HIGH. ALL 'MERICA DOES IS SHOW TH' WAY.
WHOLE POINTA THIZ COUNTRY, 'CEPT MOST FOLKS'RE TOO BLINDA SEE IT.
UH-HUH-HUH.

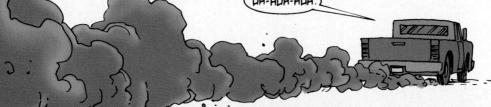

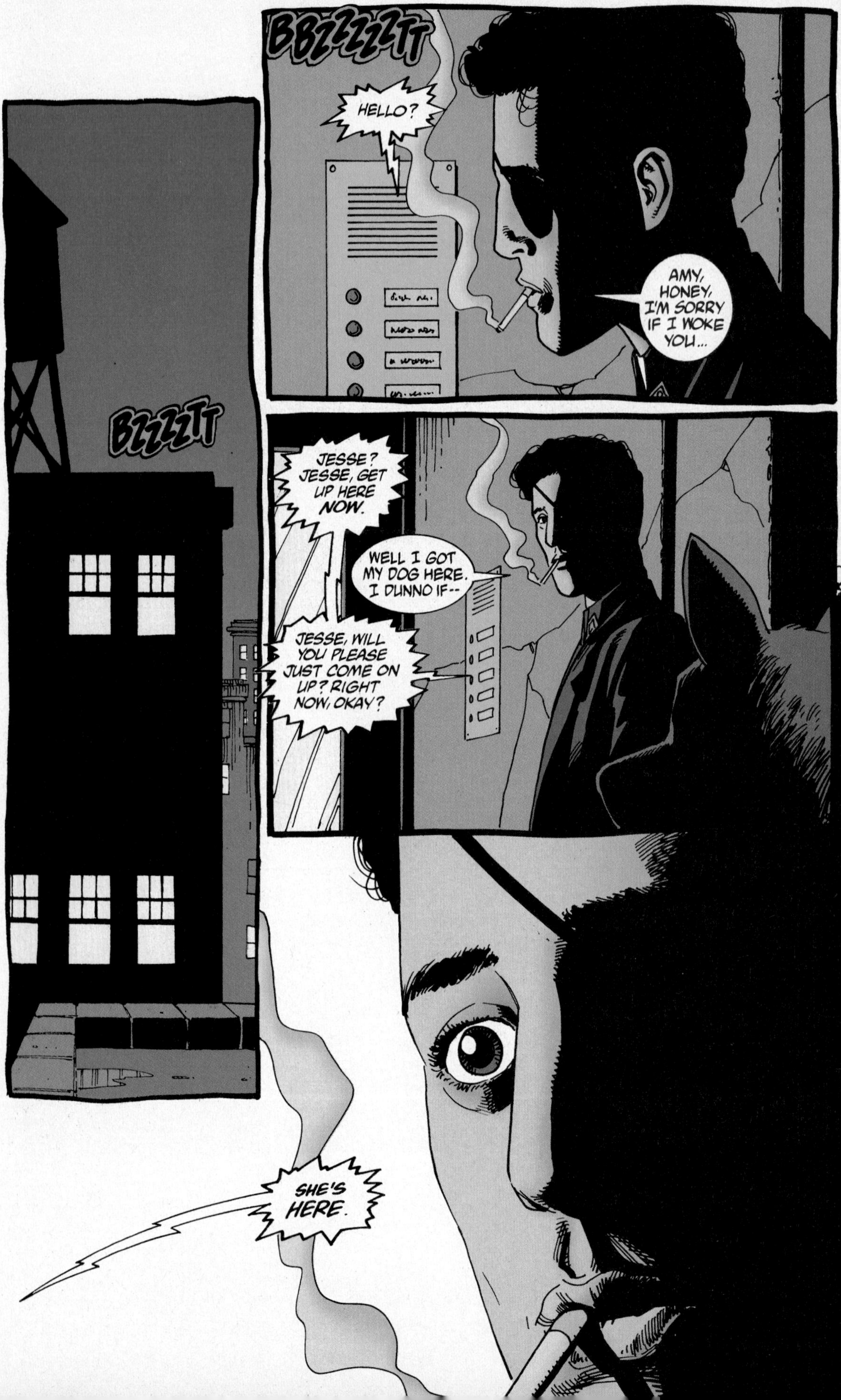
BBZZZZZTT
HELLO?
AMY, HONEY, I'M SORRY IF I WOKE YOU...
BZZZZTT
JESSE? JESSE, GET UP HERE NOW.
WELL I GOT MY DOG HERE. I DUNNO IF--
JESSE, WILL YOU PLEASE JUST COME ON UP? RIGHT NOW, OKAY?
SHE'S HERE.

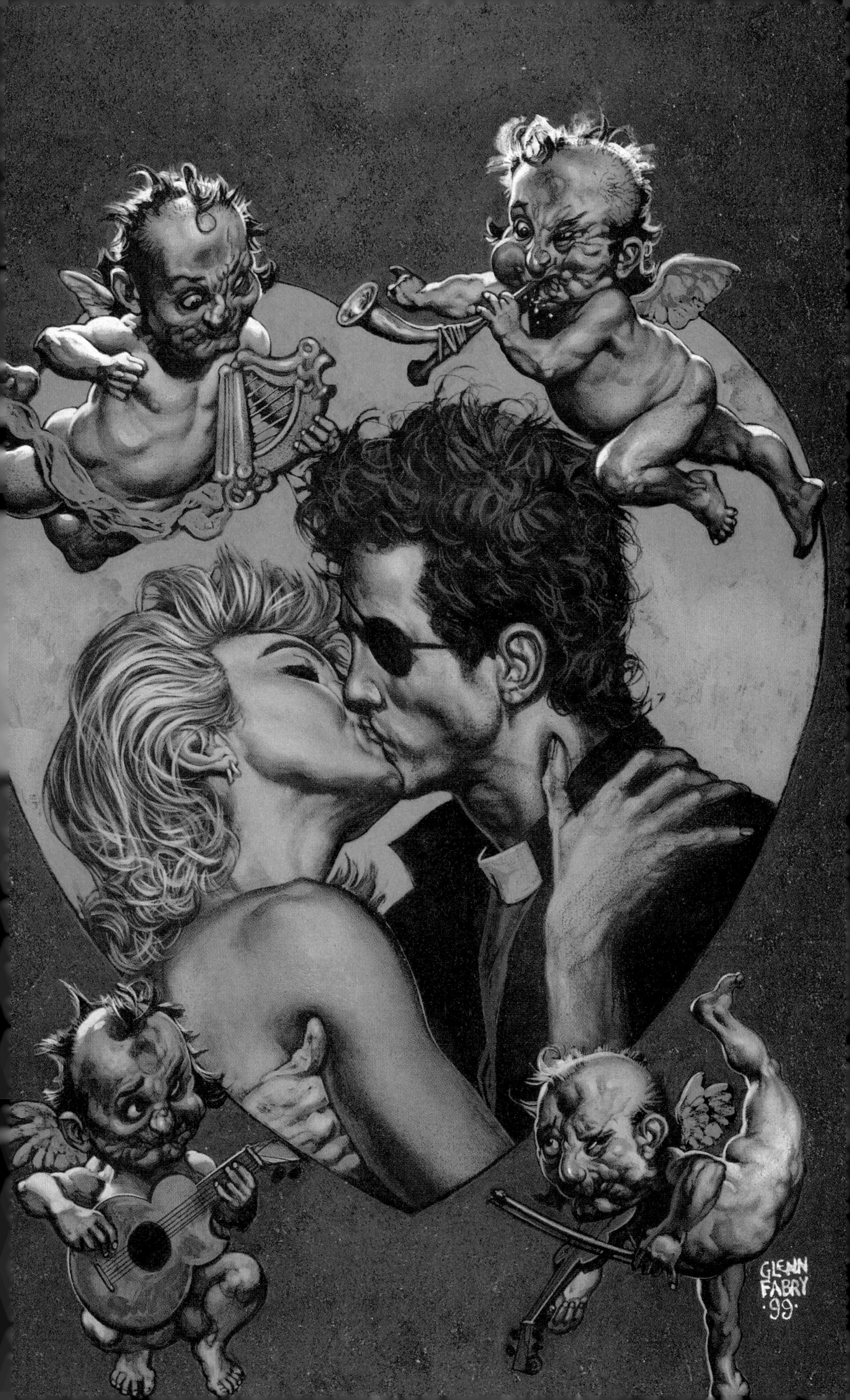
GLENN
FABRY
·99·

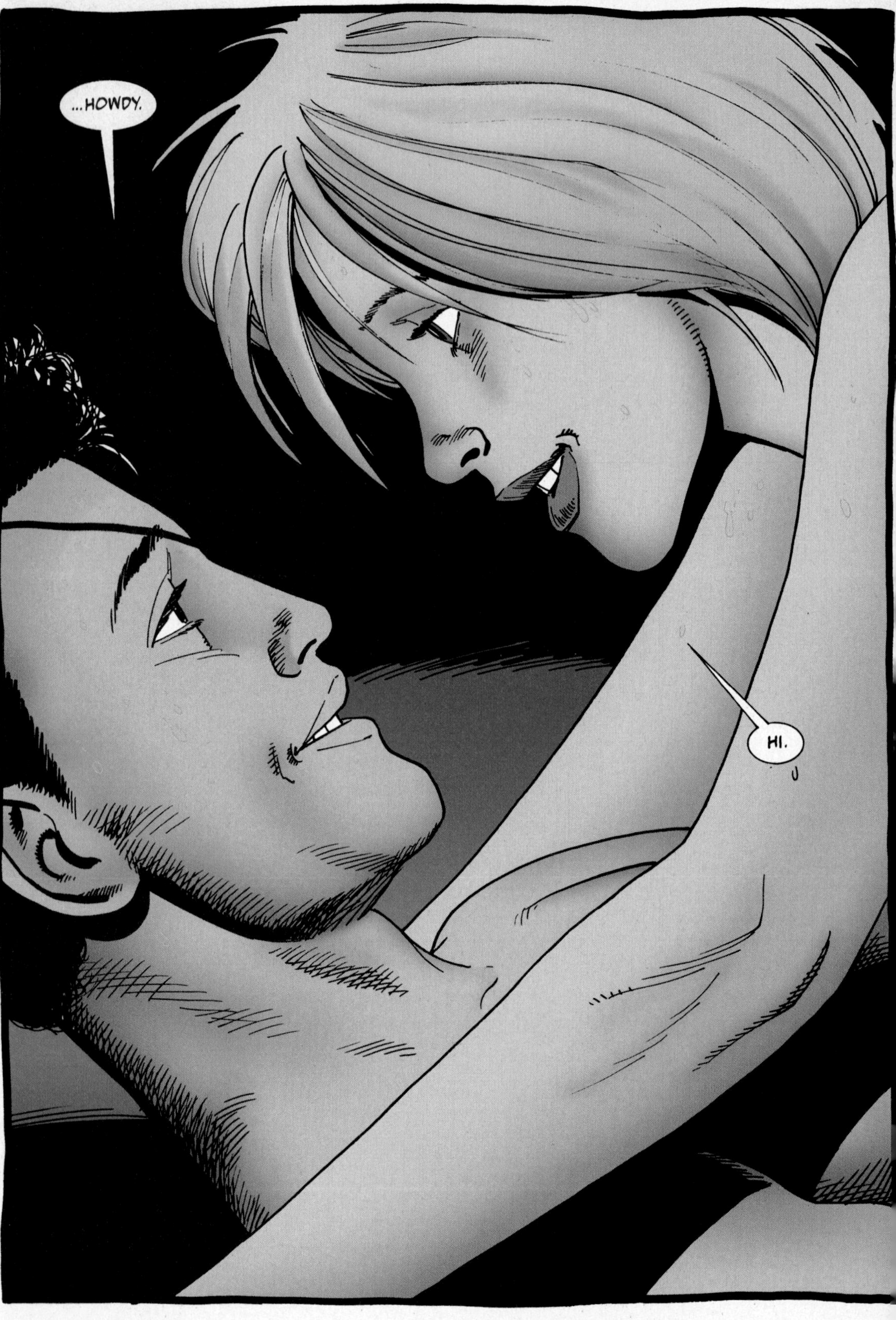
...HOWDY.
HI.

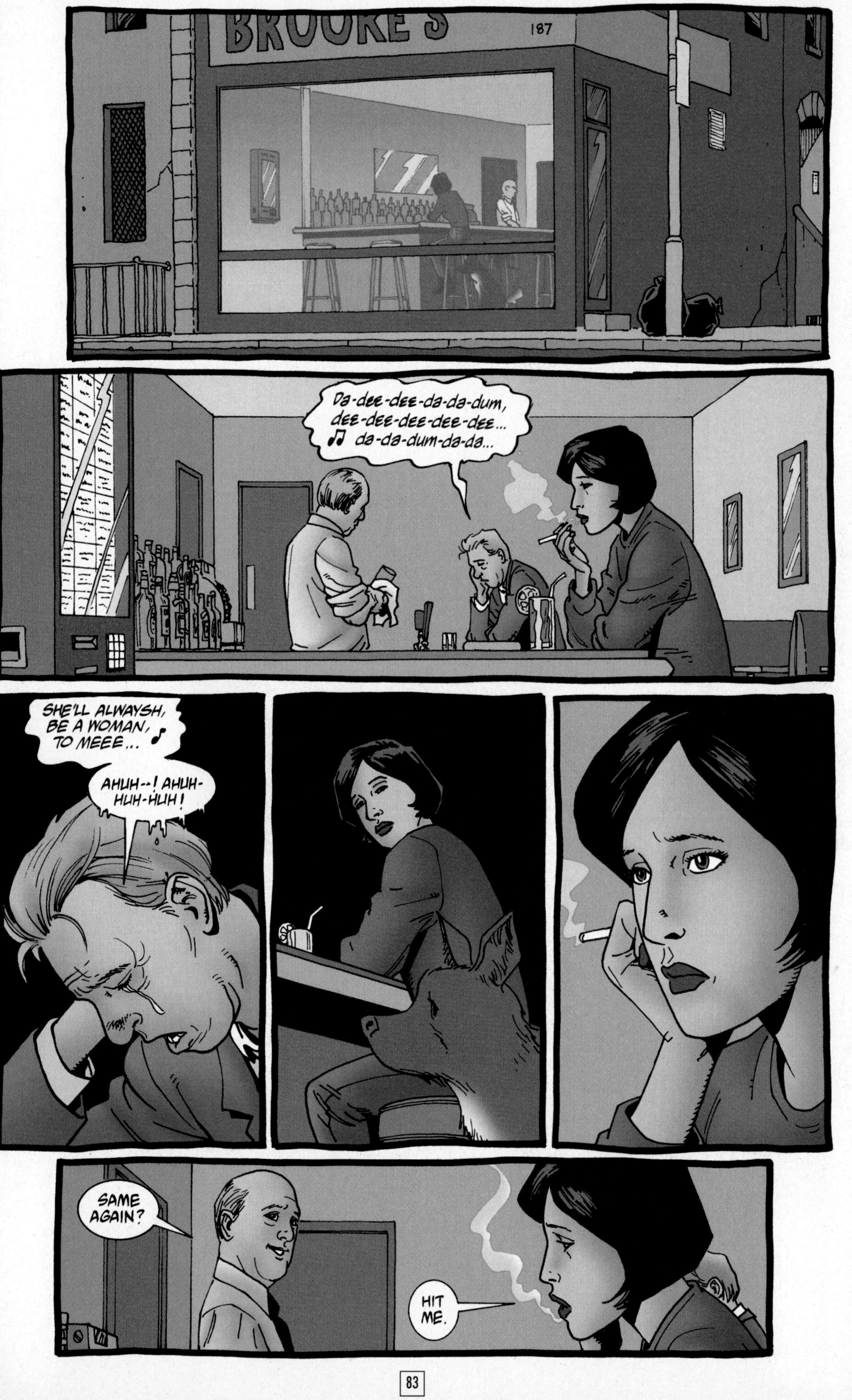
BROOKE'S
187
Da-dee-dee-da-da-dum, dee-dee-dee-dee-dee... ♫ da-da-dum-da-da...
SHE'LL ALWAYSH, BE A WOMAN, TO MEEE... ♪
AHUH--! AHUH-HUH-HUH!
SAME AGAIN?
HIT ME.

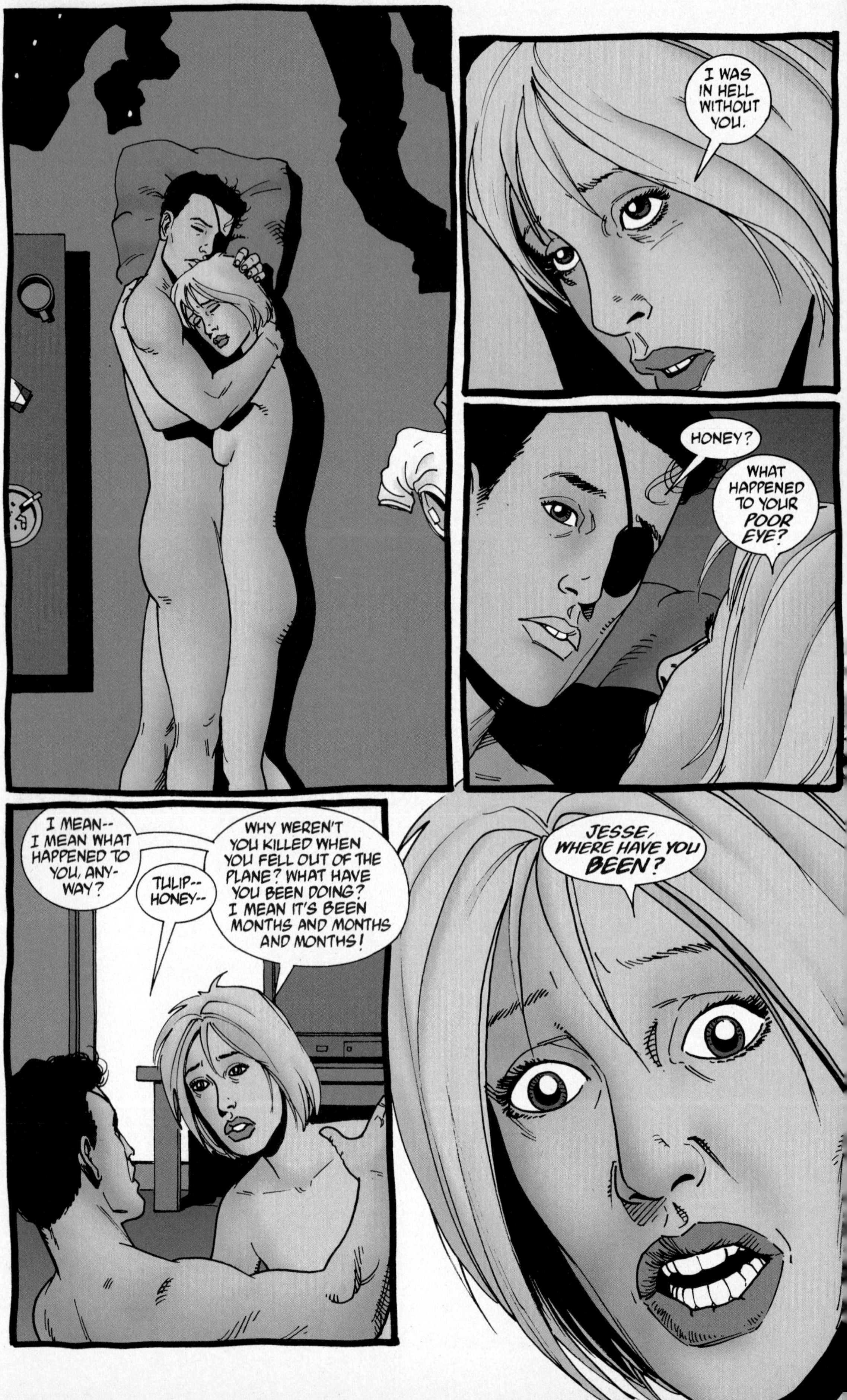
I WAS IN HELL WITHOUT YOU.
HONEY?
WHAT HAPPENED TO YOUR POOR EYE?
I MEAN-- I MEAN WHAT HAPPENED TO YOU, ANY-WAY?
WHY WEREN'T YOU KILLED WHEN YOU FELL OUT OF THE PLANE? WHAT HAVE YOU BEEN DOING? I MEAN IT'S BEEN MONTHS AND MONTHS AND MONTHS!
TULIP-- HONEY--
JESSE, WHERE HAVE YOU BEEN?

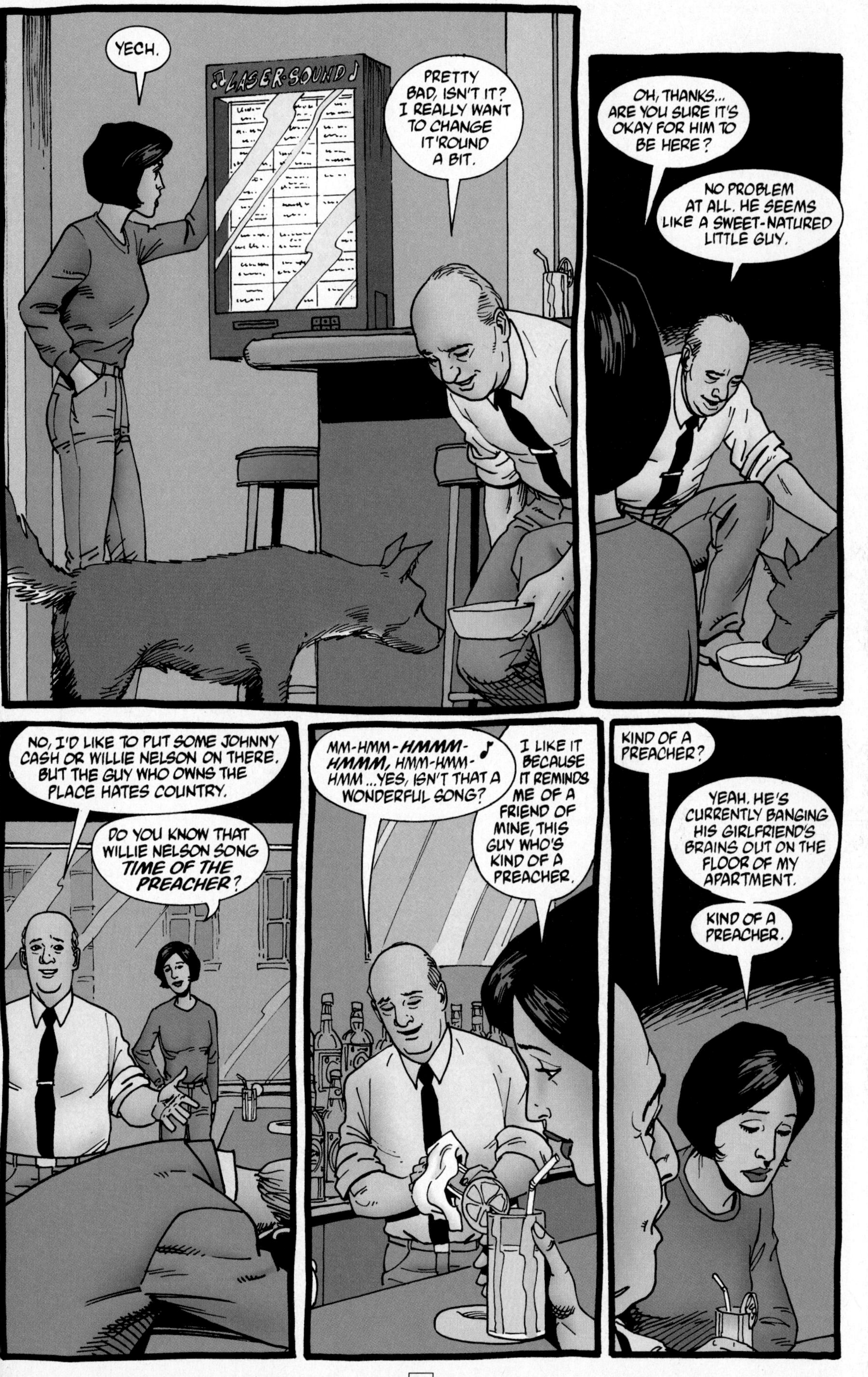
YECH.
LASER-SOUND
PRETTY BAD, ISN'T IT? I REALLY WANT TO CHANGE IT'ROUND A BIT.
OH, THANKS... ARE YOU SURE IT'S OKAY FOR HIM TO BE HERE?
NO PROBLEM AT ALL. HE SEEMS LIKE A SWEET-NATURED LITTLE GUY.
NO, I'D LIKE TO PUT SOME JOHNNY CASH OR WILLIE NELSON ON THERE. BUT THE GUY WHO OWNS THE PLACE HATES COUNTRY.
DO YOU KNOW THAT WILLIE NELSON SONG *TIME OF THE PREACHER*?
MM-HMM-*HMMM*-*HMMM*, HMM-HMM-HMM ...YES, ISN'T THAT A WONDERFUL SONG?
I LIKE IT BECAUSE IT REMINDS ME OF A FRIEND OF MINE, THIS GUY WHO'S KIND OF A PREACHER.
KIND OF A PREACHER?
YEAH, HE'S CURRENTLY BANGING HIS GIRLFRIEND'S BRAINS OUT ON THE FLOOR OF MY APARTMENT.
KIND OF A PREACHER.

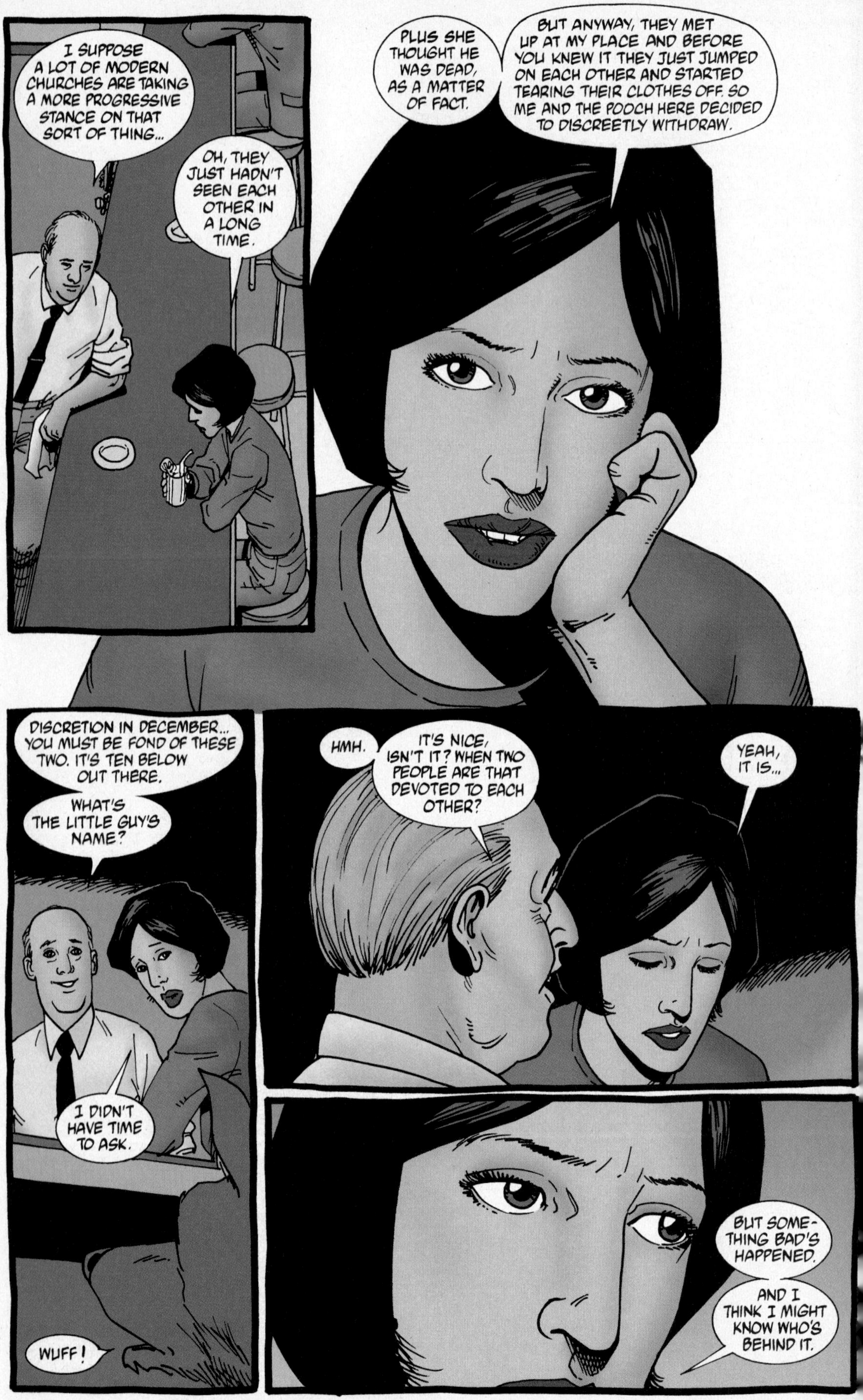
I SUPPOSE A LOT OF MODERN CHURCHES ARE TAKING A MORE PROGRESSIVE STANCE ON THAT SORT OF THING...
OH, THEY JUST HADN'T SEEN EACH OTHER IN A LONG TIME.
PLUS SHE THOUGHT HE WAS DEAD, AS A MATTER OF FACT.
BUT ANYWAY, THEY MET UP AT MY PLACE AND BEFORE YOU KNEW IT THEY JUST JUMPED ON EACH OTHER AND STARTED TEARING THEIR CLOTHES OFF. SO ME AND THE POOCH HERE DECIDED TO DISCREETLY WITHDRAW.
DISCRETION IN DECEMBER... YOU MUST BE FOND OF THESE TWO. IT'S TEN BELOW OUT THERE.
WHAT'S THE LITTLE GUY'S NAME?
I DIDN'T HAVE TIME TO ASK.
WUFF!
HMH.
IT'S NICE, ISN'T IT? WHEN TWO PEOPLE ARE THAT DEVOTED TO EACH OTHER?
YEAH, IT IS...
BUT SOME-THING BAD'S HAPPENED.
AND I THINK I MIGHT KNOW WHO'S BEHIND IT.

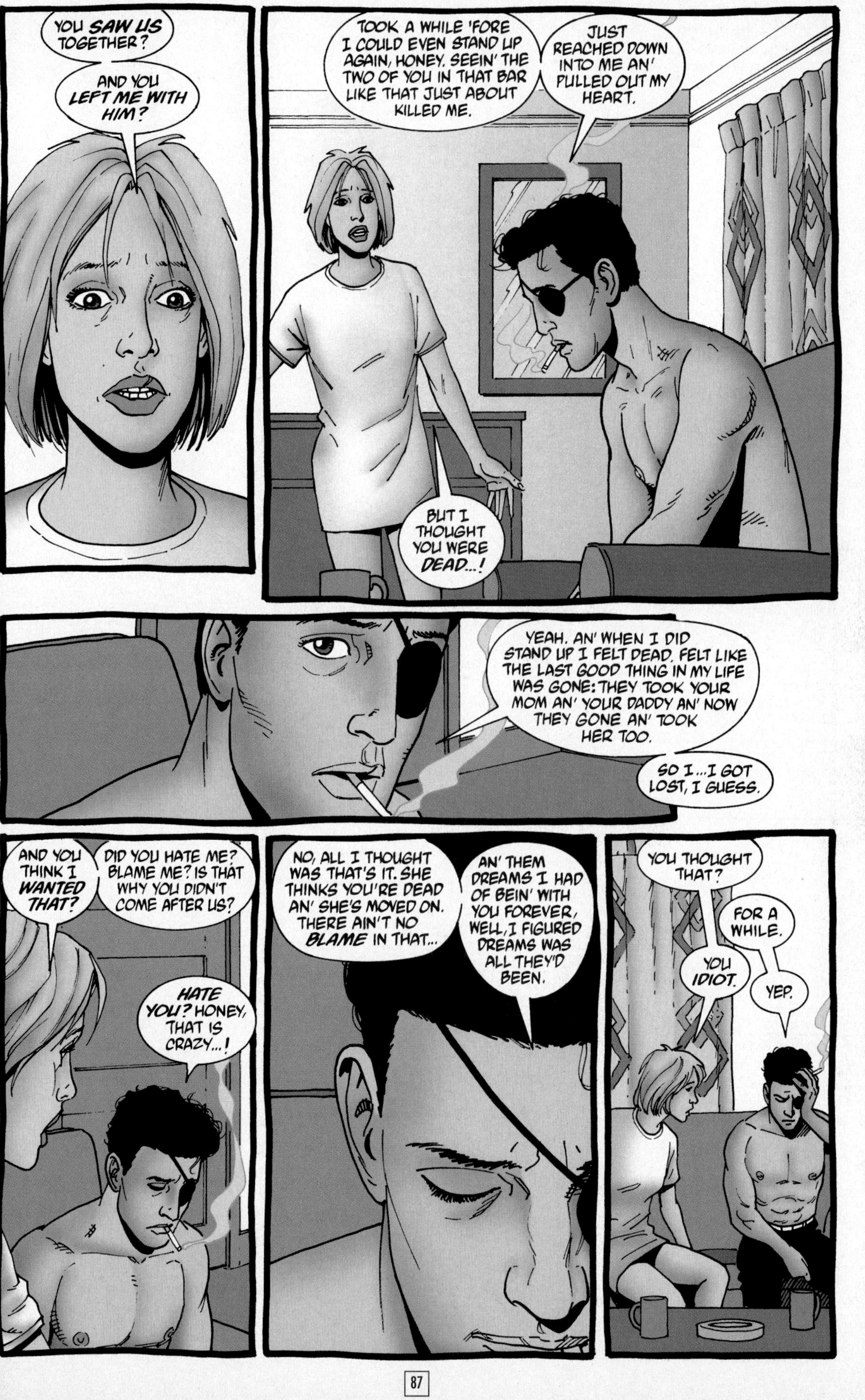
YOU SAW US TOGETHER?
AND YOU LEFT ME WITH HIM?
TOOK A WHILE 'FORE I COULD EVEN STAND UP AGAIN, HONEY. SEEIN' THE TWO OF YOU IN THAT BAR LIKE THAT JUST ABOUT KILLED ME.
JUST REACHED DOWN INTO ME AN' PULLED OUT MY HEART.
BUT I THOUGHT YOU WERE DEAD...!
YEAH. AN' WHEN I DID STAND UP I FELT DEAD. FELT LIKE THE LAST GOOD THING IN MY LIFE WAS GONE: THEY TOOK YOUR MOM AN' YOUR DADDY AN' NOW THEY GONE AN' TOOK HER TOO.
SO I...I GOT LOST, I GUESS.
AND YOU THINK I WANTED THAT?
DID YOU HATE ME? BLAME ME? IS THAT WHY YOU DIDN'T COME AFTER US?
HATE YOU? HONEY, THAT IS CRAZY...!
NO, ALL I THOUGHT WAS THAT'S IT. SHE THINKS YOU'RE DEAD AN' SHE'S MOVED ON. THERE AIN'T NO BLAME IN THAT...
AN' THEM DREAMS I HAD OF BEIN' WITH YOU FOREVER, WELL, I FIGURED DREAMS WAS ALL THEY'D BEEN.
YOU THOUGHT THAT?
FOR A WHILE.
YOU IDIOT.
YEP.

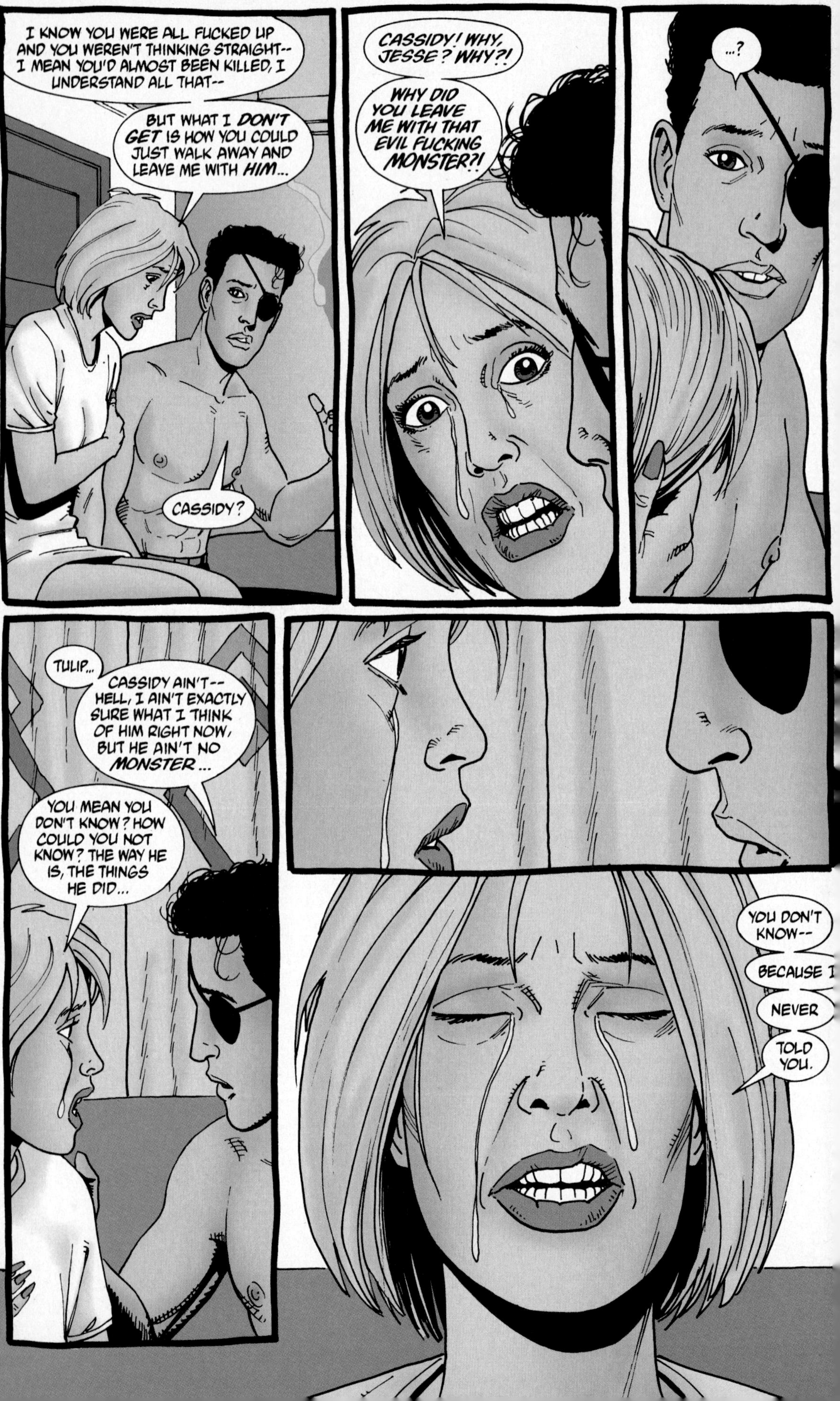
I KNOW YOU WERE ALL FUCKED UP AND YOU WEREN'T THINKING STRAIGHT-- I MEAN YOU'D ALMOST BEEN KILLED, I UNDERSTAND ALL THAT--
BUT WHAT I DON'T GET IS HOW YOU COULD JUST WALK AWAY AND LEAVE ME WITH HIM...
CASSIDY?
CASSIDY! WHY, JESSE? WHY?!
WHY DID YOU LEAVE ME WITH THAT EVIL FUCKING MONSTER?!
...?
TULIP...
CASSIDY AIN'T-- HELL, I AIN'T EXACTLY SURE WHAT I THINK OF HIM RIGHT NOW, BUT HE AIN'T NO MONSTER...
YOU MEAN YOU DON'T KNOW? HOW COULD YOU NOT KNOW? THE WAY HE IS, THE THINGS HE DID...
YOU DON'T KNOW--
BECAUSE I
NEVER
TOLD YOU.

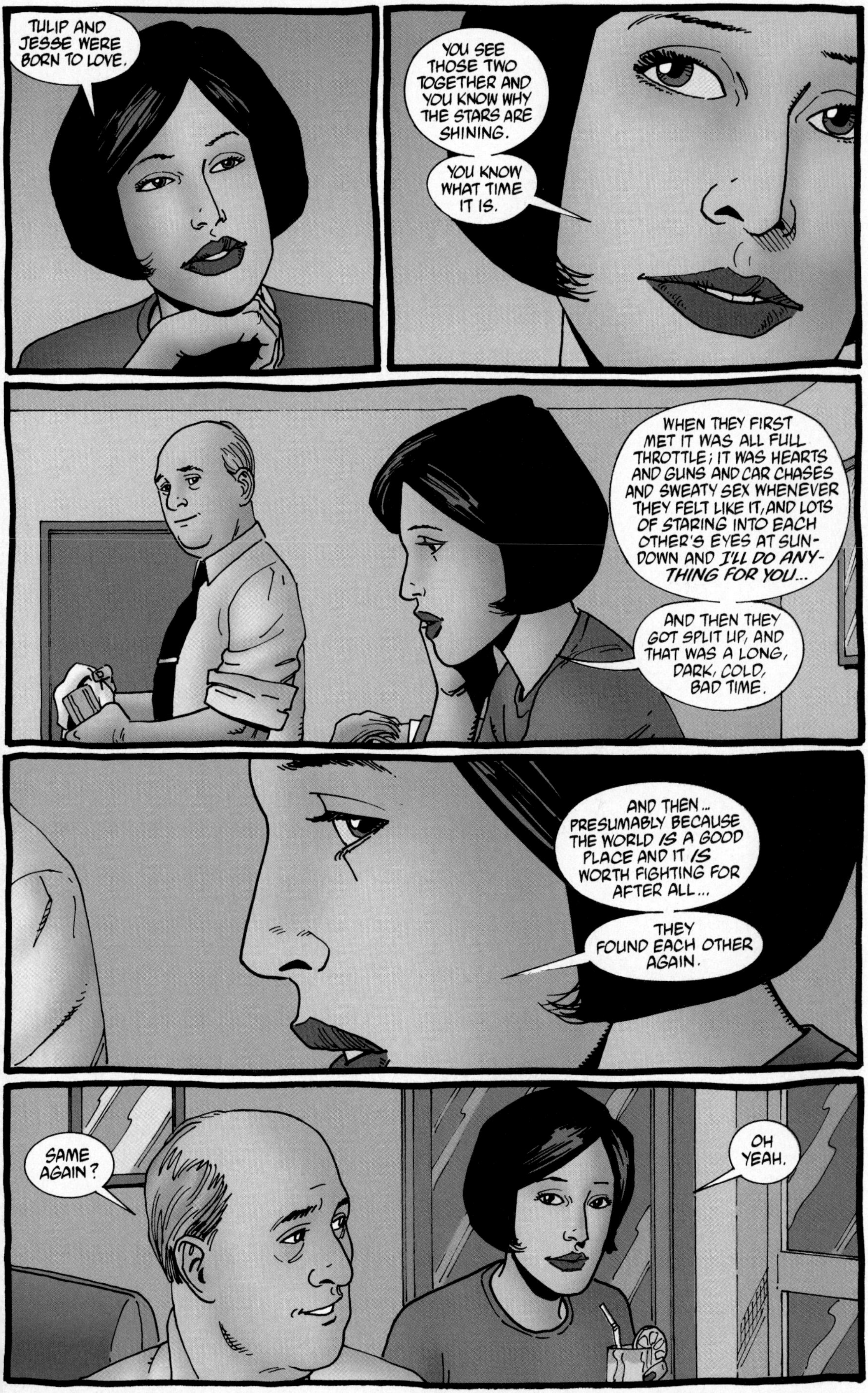
TULIP AND JESSE WERE BORN TO LOVE.
YOU SEE THOSE TWO TOGETHER AND YOU KNOW WHY THE STARS ARE SHINING.
YOU KNOW WHAT TIME IT IS.
WHEN THEY FIRST MET IT WAS ALL FULL THROTTLE; IT WAS HEARTS AND GUNS AND CAR CHASES AND SWEATY SEX WHENEVER THEY FELT LIKE IT, AND LOTS OF STARING INTO EACH OTHER'S EYES AT SUNDOWN AND *I'LL DO ANYTHING FOR YOU...*
AND THEN THEY GOT SPLIT UP, AND THAT WAS A LONG, DARK, COLD, BAD TIME.
AND THEN... PRESUMABLY BECAUSE THE WORLD *IS* A GOOD PLACE AND IT *IS* WORTH FIGHTING FOR AFTER ALL...
THEY FOUND EACH OTHER AGAIN.
SAME AGAIN?
OH YEAH.

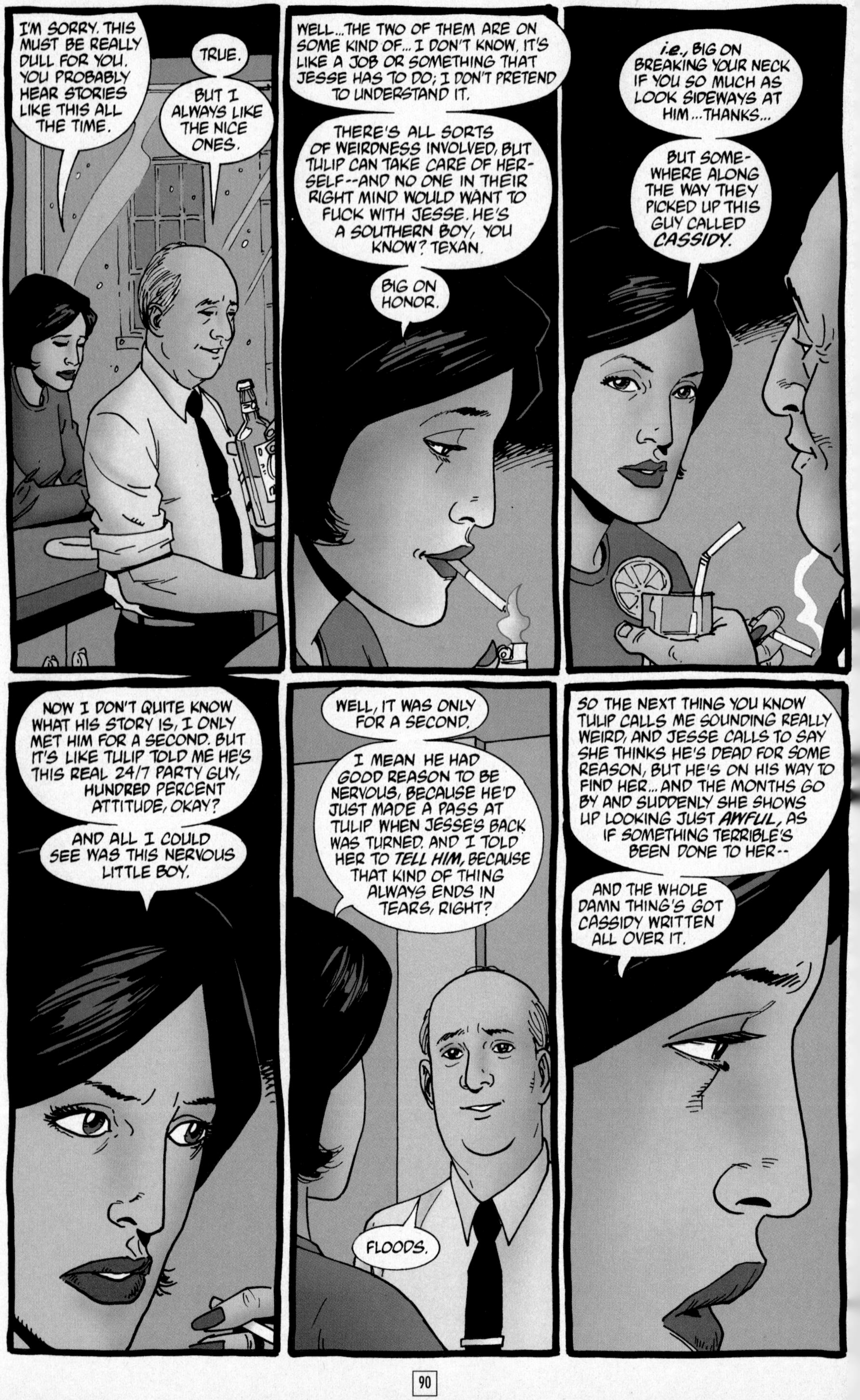
I'M SORRY. THIS MUST BE REALLY DULL FOR YOU. YOU PROBABLY HEAR STORIES LIKE THIS ALL THE TIME.
TRUE.
BUT I ALWAYS LIKE THE NICE ONES.
WELL...THE TWO OF THEM ARE ON SOME KIND OF... I DON'T KNOW, IT'S LIKE A JOB OR SOMETHING THAT JESSE HAS TO DO; I DON'T PRETEND TO UNDERSTAND IT.
THERE'S ALL SORTS OF WEIRDNESS INVOLVED, BUT TULIP CAN TAKE CARE OF HER-SELF--AND NO ONE IN THEIR RIGHT MIND WOULD WANT TO FUCK WITH JESSE. HE'S A SOUTHERN BOY, YOU KNOW? TEXAN.
BIG ON HONOR.
i.e., BIG ON BREAKING YOUR NECK IF YOU SO MUCH AS LOOK SIDEWAYS AT HIM...THANKS...
BUT SOME-WHERE ALONG THE WAY THEY PICKED UP THIS GUY CALLED CASSIDY.
NOW I DON'T QUITE KNOW WHAT HIS STORY IS, I ONLY MET HIM FOR A SECOND. BUT IT'S LIKE TULIP TOLD ME HE'S THIS REAL 24/7 PARTY GUY, HUNDRED PERCENT ATTITUDE, OKAY?
AND ALL I COULD SEE WAS THIS NERVOUS LITTLE BOY.
WELL, IT WAS ONLY FOR A SECOND.
I MEAN HE HAD GOOD REASON TO BE NERVOUS, BECAUSE HE'D JUST MADE A PASS AT TULIP WHEN JESSE'S BACK WAS TURNED. AND I TOLD HER TO TELL HIM, BECAUSE THAT KIND OF THING ALWAYS ENDS IN TEARS, RIGHT?
FLOODS.
SO THE NEXT THING YOU KNOW TULIP CALLS ME SOUNDING REALLY WEIRD, AND JESSE CALLS TO SAY SHE THINKS HE'S DEAD FOR SOME REASON, BUT HE'S ON HIS WAY TO FIND HER... AND THE MONTHS GO BY AND SUDDENLY SHE SHOWS UP LOOKING JUST AWFUL, AS IF SOMETHING TERRIBLE'S BEEN DONE TO HER--
AND THE WHOLE DAMN THING'S GOT CASSIDY WRITTEN ALL OVER IT.

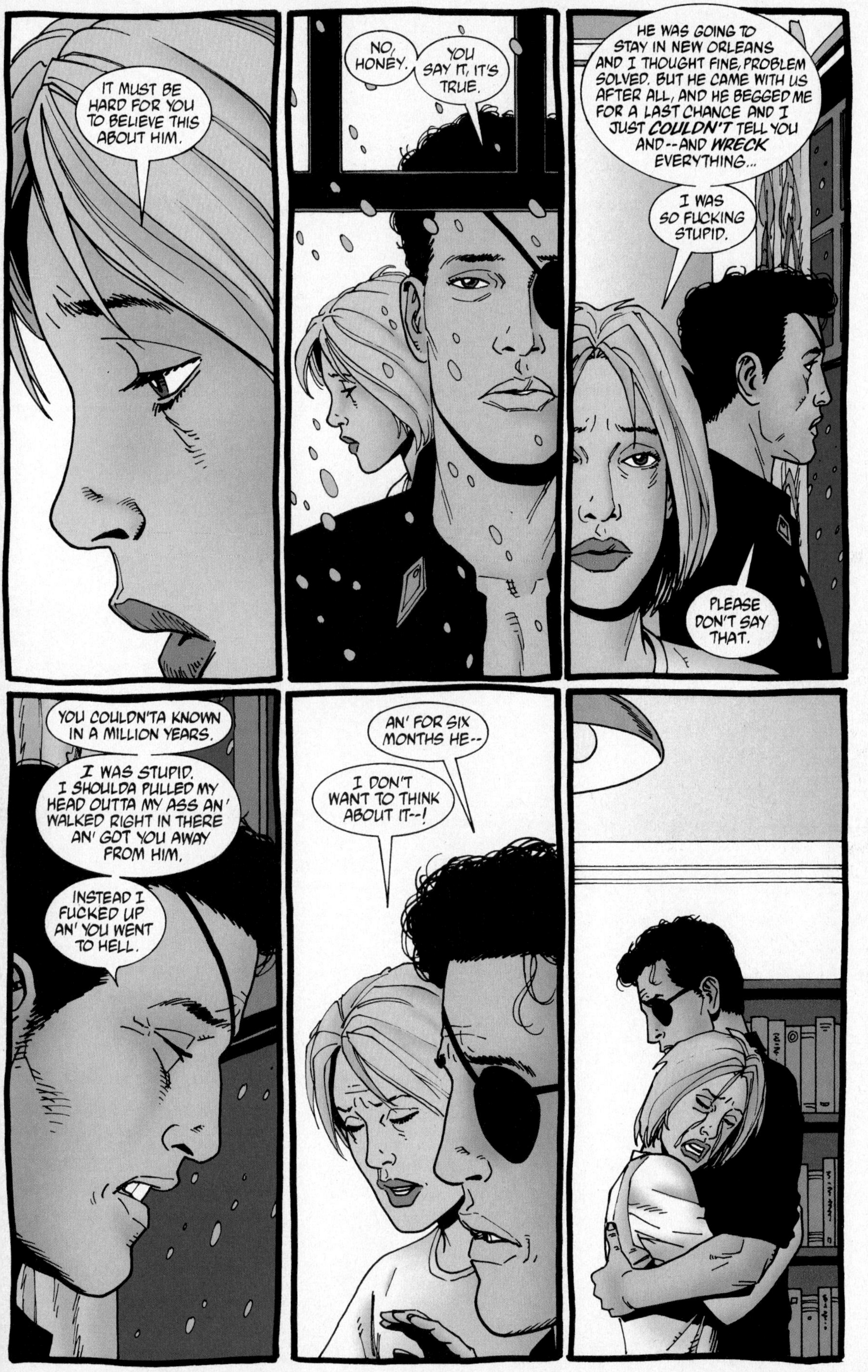
IT MUST BE HARD FOR YOU TO BELIEVE THIS ABOUT HIM.
NO, HONEY.
YOU SAY IT, IT'S TRUE.
HE WAS GOING TO STAY IN NEW ORLEANS AND I THOUGHT FINE, PROBLEM SOLVED. BUT HE CAME WITH US AFTER ALL, AND HE BEGGED ME FOR A LAST CHANCE AND I JUST COULDN'T TELL YOU AND--AND WRECK EVERYTHING...
I WAS SO FUCKING STUPID.
PLEASE DON'T SAY THAT.
YOU COULDN'TA KNOWN IN A MILLION YEARS.
I WAS STUPID. I SHOULDA PULLED MY HEAD OUTTA MY ASS AN' WALKED RIGHT IN THERE AN' GOT YOU AWAY FROM HIM.
INSTEAD I FUCKED UP AN' YOU WENT TO HELL.
AN' FOR SIX MONTHS HE--
I DON'T WANT TO THINK ABOUT IT--!

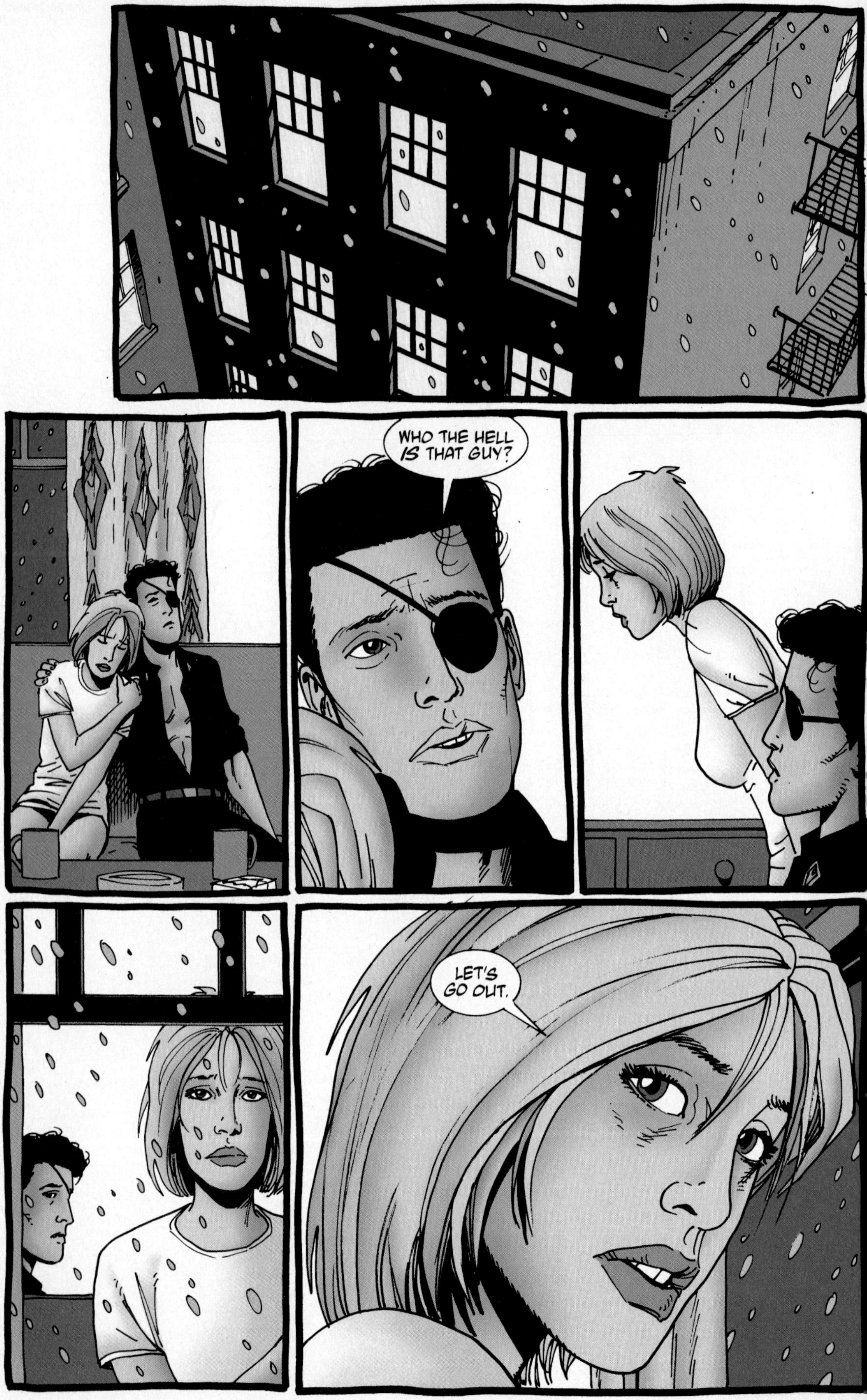
WHO THE HELL *IS* THAT GUY?
LET'S GO OUT.

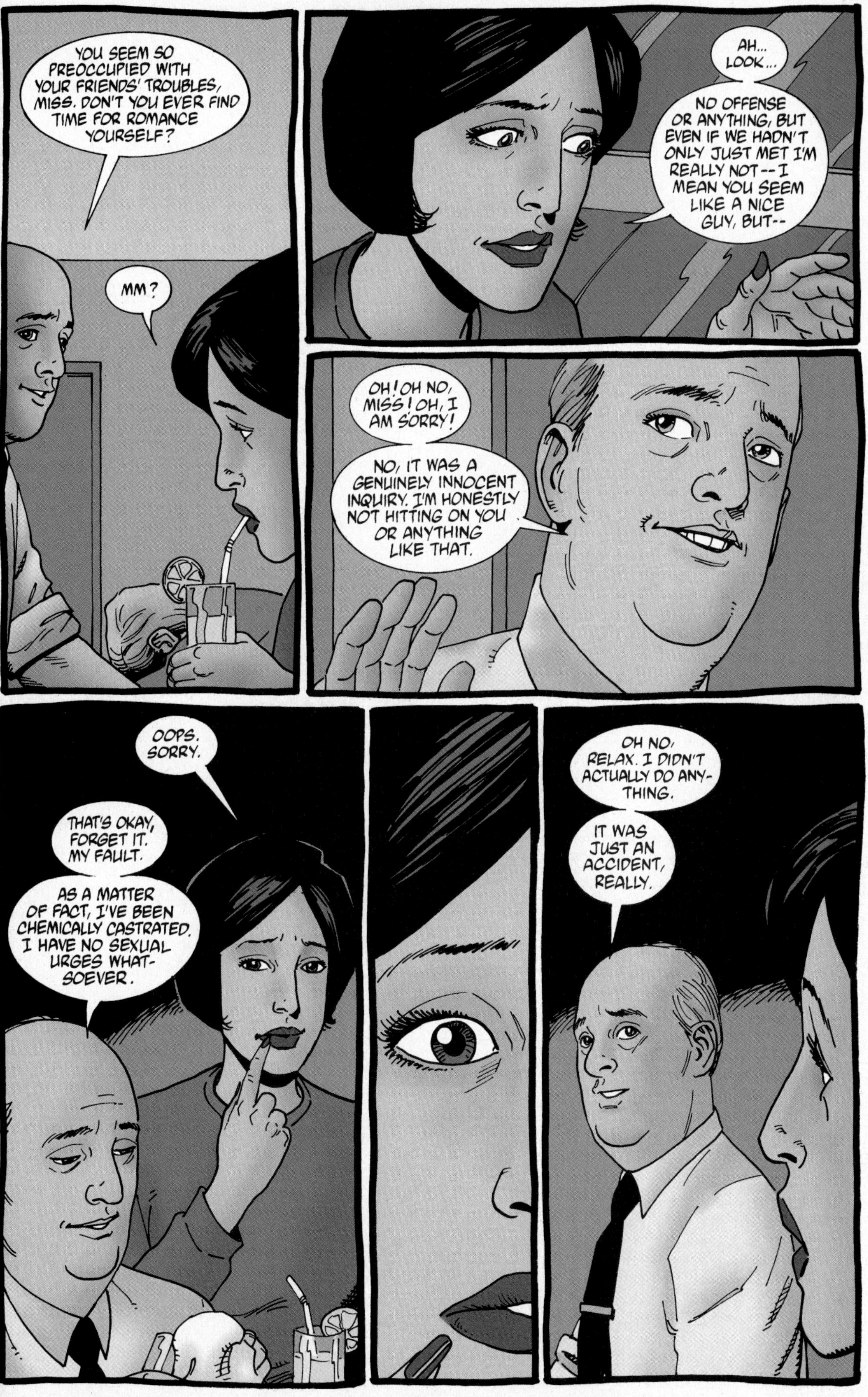
YOU SEEM SO PREOCCUPIED WITH YOUR FRIENDS' TROUBLES, MISS. DON'T YOU EVER FIND TIME FOR ROMANCE YOURSELF?
MM?
AH... LOOK...
NO OFFENSE OR ANYTHING, BUT EVEN IF WE HADN'T ONLY JUST MET I'M REALLY NOT -- I MEAN YOU SEEM LIKE A NICE GUY, BUT--
OH! OH NO, MISS! OH, I AM SORRY!
NO, IT WAS A GENUINELY INNOCENT INQUIRY. I'M HONESTLY NOT HITTING ON YOU OR ANYTHING LIKE THAT.
OOPS. SORRY.
THAT'S OKAY, FORGET IT. MY FAULT.
AS A MATTER OF FACT, I'VE BEEN CHEMICALLY CASTRATED. I HAVE NO SEXUAL URGES WHAT-SOEVER.
OH NO, RELAX. I DIDN'T ACTUALLY DO ANY-THING.
IT WAS JUST AN ACCIDENT, REALLY.

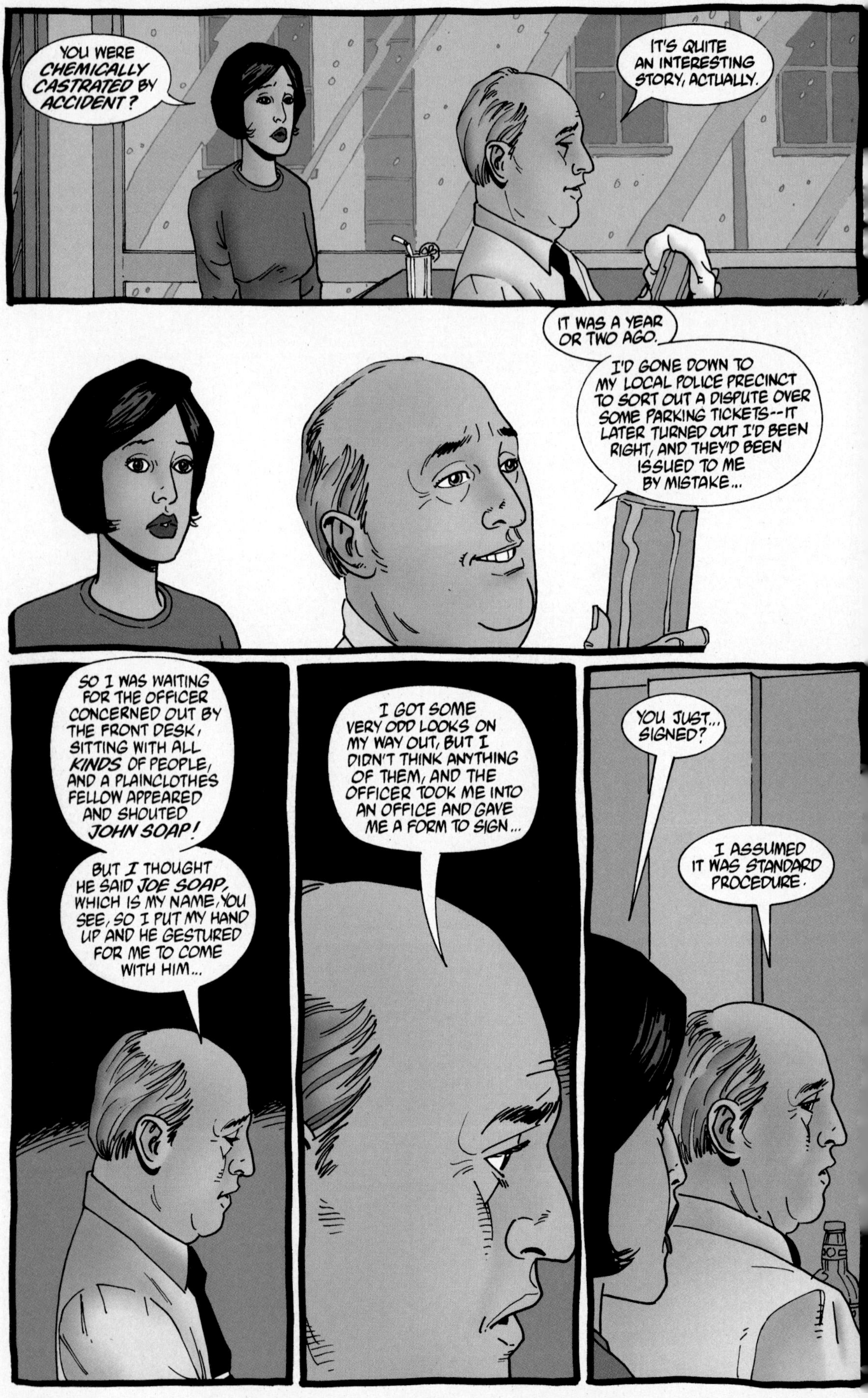
YOU WERE CHEMICALLY CASTRATED BY ACCIDENT?
IT'S QUITE AN INTERESTING STORY, ACTUALLY.
IT WAS A YEAR OR TWO AGO.
I'D GONE DOWN TO MY LOCAL POLICE PRECINCT TO SORT OUT A DISPUTE OVER SOME PARKING TICKETS--IT LATER TURNED OUT I'D BEEN RIGHT, AND THEY'D BEEN ISSUED TO ME BY MISTAKE...
SO I WAS WAITING FOR THE OFFICER CONCERNED OUT BY THE FRONT DESK, SITTING WITH ALL KINDS OF PEOPLE, AND A PLAINCLOTHES FELLOW APPEARED AND SHOUTED JOHN SOAP!
BUT I THOUGHT HE SAID JOE SOAP, WHICH IS MY NAME, YOU SEE, SO I PUT MY HAND UP AND HE GESTURED FOR ME TO COME WITH HIM...
I GOT SOME VERY ODD LOOKS ON MY WAY OUT, BUT I DIDN'T THINK ANYTHING OF THEM, AND THE OFFICER TOOK ME INTO AN OFFICE AND GAVE ME A FORM TO SIGN...
YOU JUST... SIGNED?
I ASSUMED IT WAS STANDARD PROCEDURE.

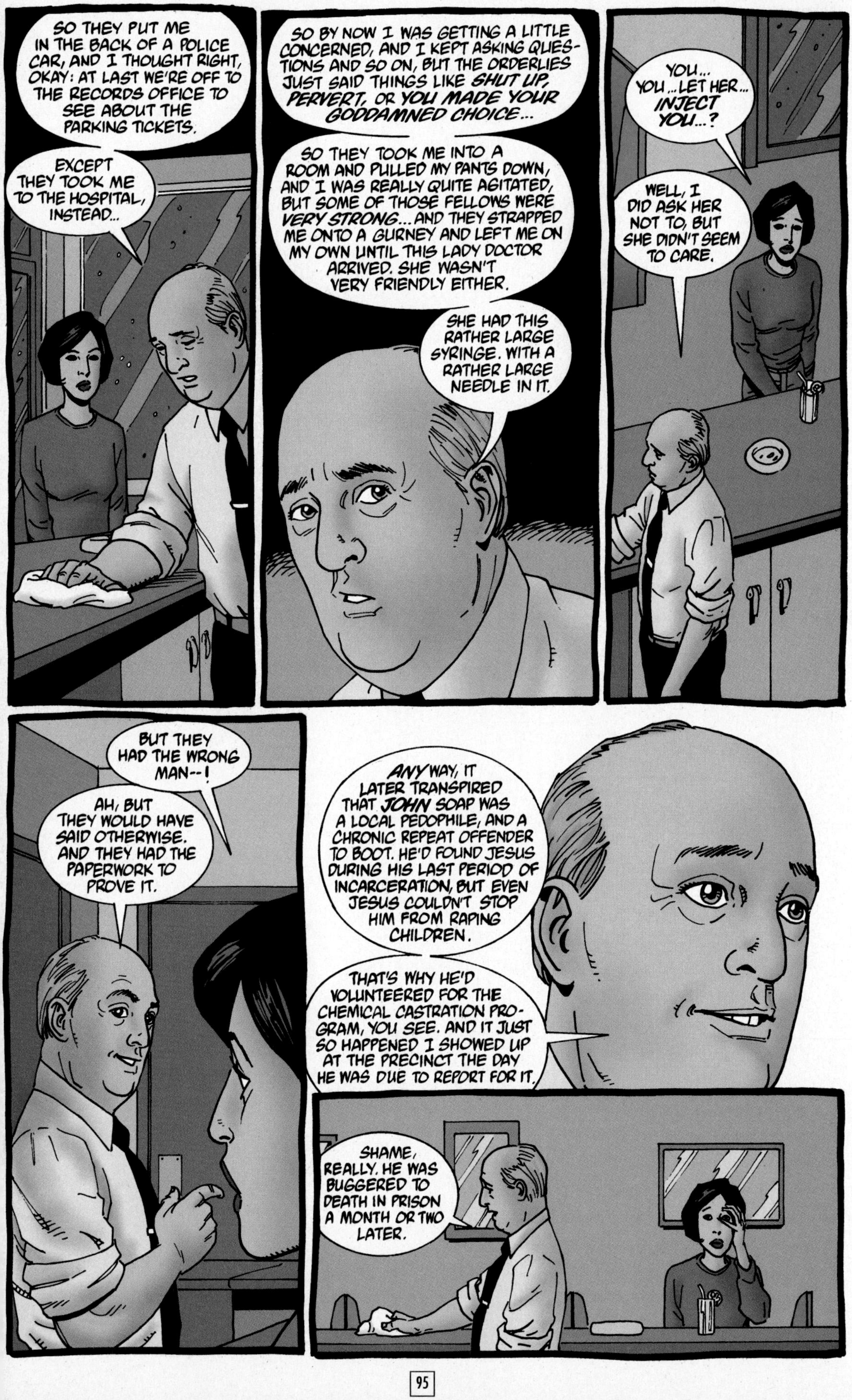
SO THEY PUT ME IN THE BACK OF A POLICE CAR, AND I THOUGHT RIGHT, OKAY: AT LAST WE'RE OFF TO THE RECORDS OFFICE TO SEE ABOUT THE PARKING TICKETS.
EXCEPT THEY TOOK ME TO THE HOSPITAL, INSTEAD...
SO BY NOW I WAS GETTING A LITTLE CONCERNED, AND I KEPT ASKING QUES-TIONS AND SO ON, BUT THE ORDERLIES JUST SAID THINGS LIKE SHUT UP, PERVERT, OR YOU MADE YOUR GODDAMNED CHOICE...
SO THEY TOOK ME INTO A ROOM AND PULLED MY PANTS DOWN, AND I WAS REALLY QUITE AGITATED, BUT SOME OF THOSE FELLOWS WERE VERY STRONG... AND THEY STRAPPED ME ONTO A GURNEY AND LEFT ME ON MY OWN UNTIL THIS LADY DOCTOR ARRIVED. SHE WASN'T VERY FRIENDLY EITHER.
SHE HAD THIS RATHER LARGE SYRINGE. WITH A RATHER LARGE NEEDLE IN IT.
YOU... YOU... LET HER... INJECT YOU...?
WELL, I DID ASK HER NOT TO, BUT SHE DIDN'T SEEM TO CARE.
BUT THEY HAD THE WRONG MAN--!
AH, BUT THEY WOULD HAVE SAID OTHERWISE. AND THEY HAD THE PAPERWORK TO PROVE IT.
ANYWAY, IT LATER TRANSPIRED THAT JOHN SOAP WAS A LOCAL PEDOPHILE, AND A CHRONIC REPEAT OFFENDER TO BOOT. HE'D FOUND JESUS DURING HIS LAST PERIOD OF INCARCERATION, BUT EVEN JESUS COULDN'T STOP HIM FROM RAPING CHILDREN.
THAT'S WHY HE'D VOLUNTEERED FOR THE CHEMICAL CASTRATION PRO-GRAM, YOU SEE. AND IT JUST SO HAPPENED I SHOWED UP AT THE PRECINCT THE DAY HE WAS DUE TO REPORT FOR IT.
SHAME, REALLY. HE WAS BUGGERED TO DEATH IN PRISON A MONTH OR TWO LATER.

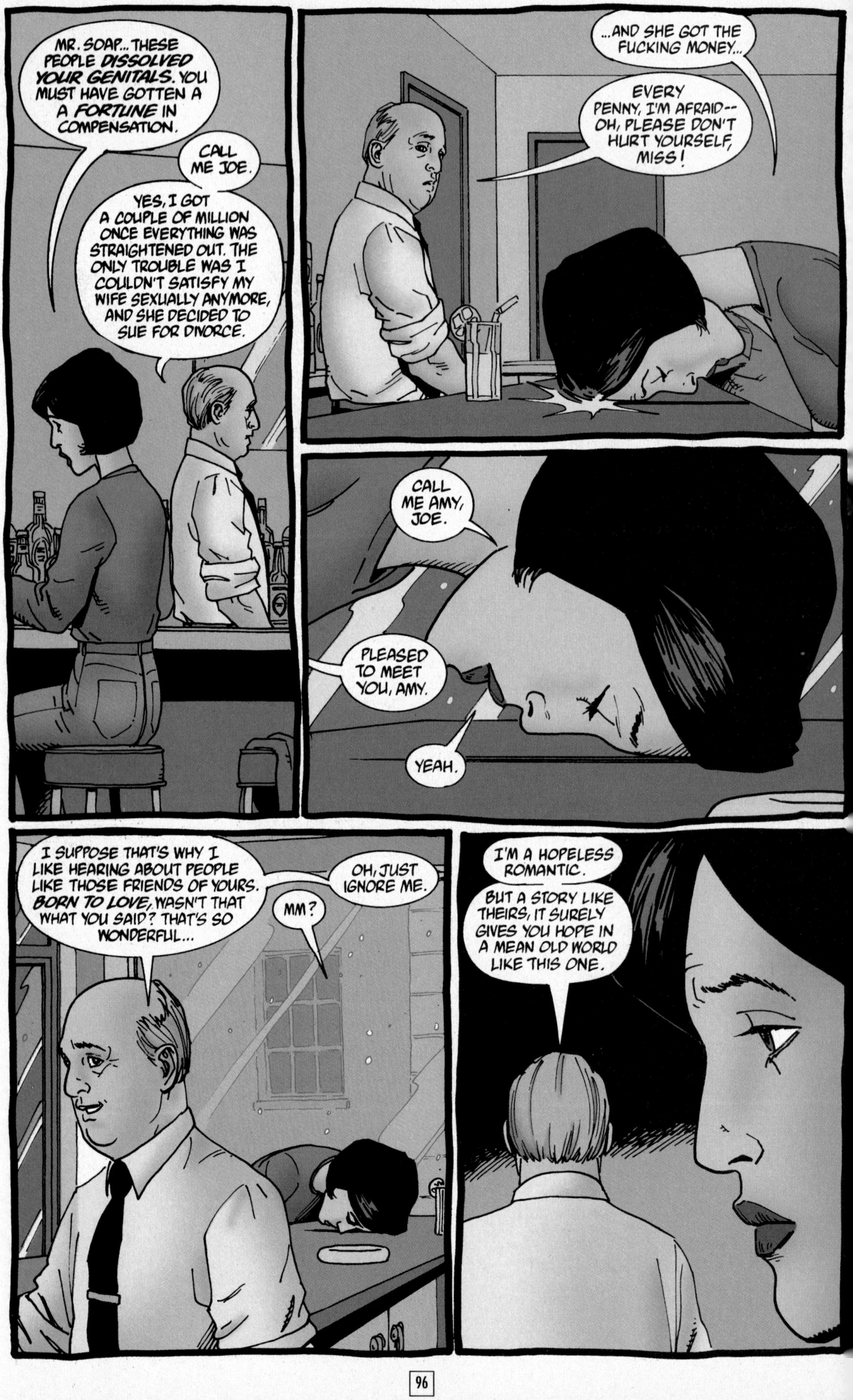
MR. SOAP... THESE PEOPLE DISSOLVED YOUR GENITALS. YOU MUST HAVE GOTTEN A A FORTUNE IN COMPENSATION.
CALL ME JOE.
YES, I GOT A COUPLE OF MILLION ONCE EVERYTHING WAS STRAIGHTENED OUT. THE ONLY TROUBLE WAS I COULDN'T SATISFY MY WIFE SEXUALLY ANYMORE, AND SHE DECIDED TO SUE FOR DIVORCE.
...AND SHE GOT THE FUCKING MONEY...
EVERY PENNY, I'M AFRAID-- OH, PLEASE DON'T HURT YOURSELF, MISS!
CALL ME AMY, JOE.
PLEASED TO MEET YOU, AMY.
YEAH.
I SUPPOSE THAT'S WHY I LIKE HEARING ABOUT PEOPLE LIKE THOSE FRIENDS OF YOURS. BORN TO LOVE, WASN'T THAT WHAT YOU SAID? THAT'S SO WONDERFUL...
OH, JUST IGNORE ME.
MM?
I'M A HOPELESS ROMANTIC.
BUT A STORY LIKE THEIRS, IT SURELY GIVES YOU HOPE IN A MEAN OLD WORLD LIKE THIS ONE.

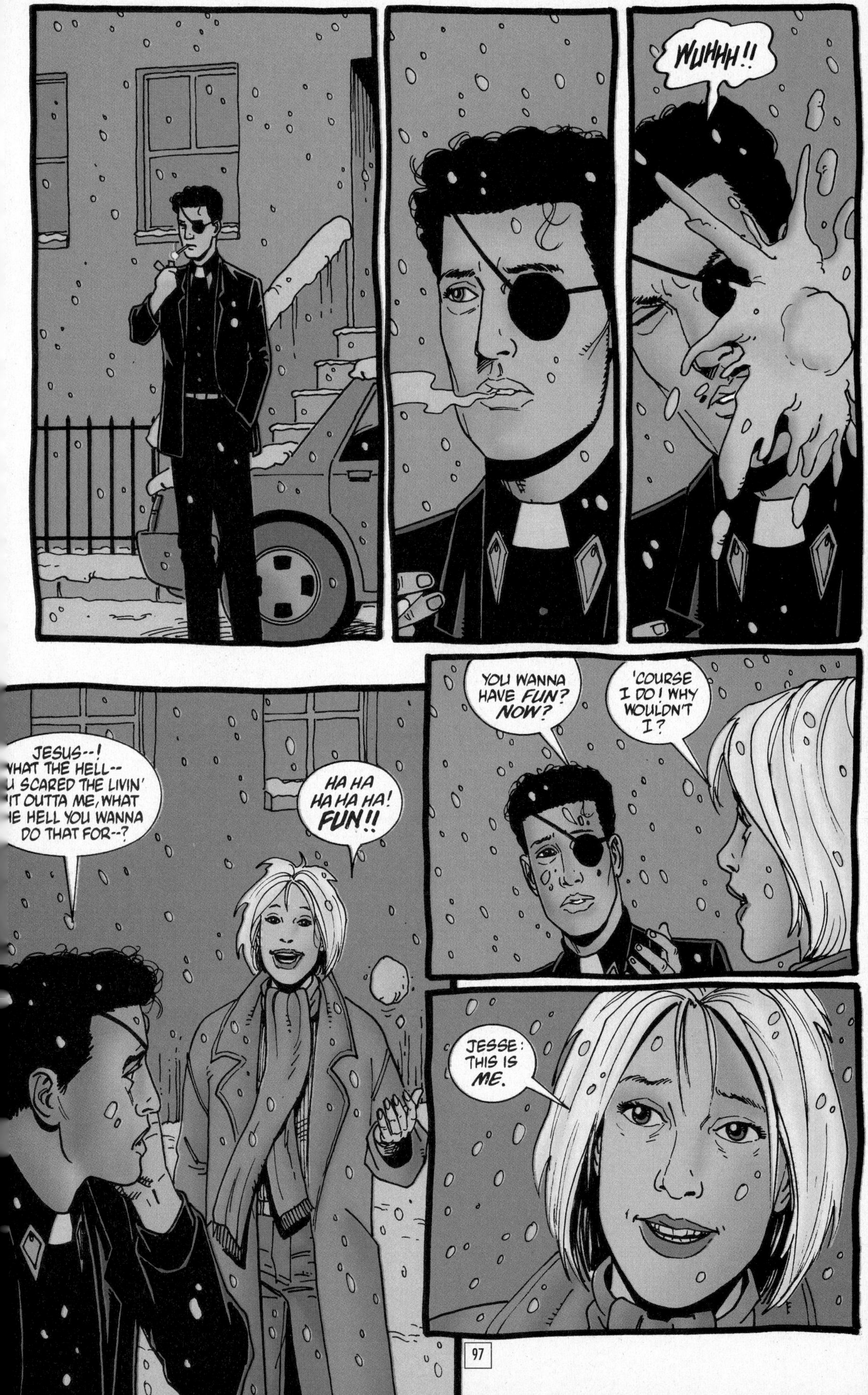
WUHHH!!
JESUS--! WHAT THE HELL-- U SCARED THE LIVIN' IT OUTTA ME, WHAT HE HELL YOU WANNA DO THAT FOR--?
HA HA HA HA HA! FUN!!
YOU WANNA HAVE FUN? NOW?
'COURSE I DO! WHY WOULDN'T I?
JESSE: THIS IS ME.

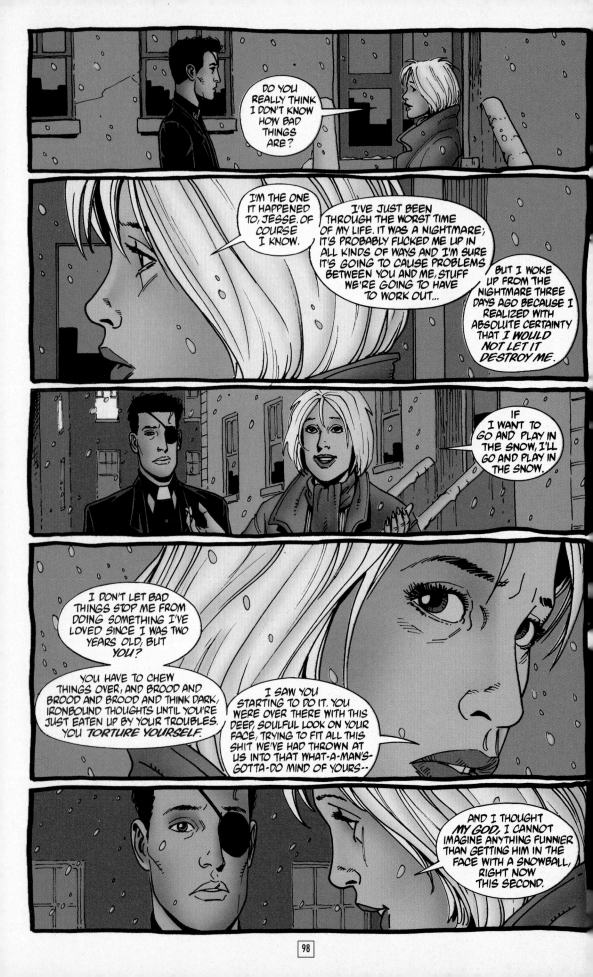

DO YOU REALLY THINK I DON'T KNOW HOW BAD THINGS ARE?

I'M THE ONE IT HAPPENED TO, JESSE, OF COURSE I KNOW.

I'VE JUST BEEN THROUGH THE WORST TIME OF MY LIFE. IT WAS A NIGHTMARE; IT'S PROBABLY FUCKED ME UP IN ALL KINDS OF WAYS AND I'M SURE IT'S GOING TO CAUSE PROBLEMS BETWEEN YOU AND ME, STUFF WE'RE GOING TO HAVE TO WORK OUT...

BUT I WOKE UP FROM THE NIGHTMARE THREE DAYS AGO BECAUSE I REALIZED WITH ABSOLUTE CERTAINTY THAT *I WOULD NOT LET IT DESTROY ME.*

IF I WANT TO GO AND PLAY IN THE SNOW, I'LL GO AND PLAY IN THE SNOW.

I DON'T LET BAD THINGS STOP ME FROM DOING SOMETHING I'VE LOVED SINCE I WAS TWO YEARS OLD, BUT *YOU?*

YOU HAVE TO CHEW THINGS OVER, AND BROOD AND BROOD AND BROOD AND THINK DARK, IRONBOUND THOUGHTS UNTIL YOU'RE JUST EATEN UP BY YOUR TROUBLES. YOU *TORTURE YOURSELF.*

I SAW YOU STARTING TO DO IT. YOU WERE OVER THERE WITH THIS DEEP, SOULFUL LOOK ON YOUR FACE, TRYING TO FIT ALL THIS SHIT WE'VE HAD THROWN AT US INTO THAT WHAT-A-MAN'S-GOTTA-DO MIND OF YOURS--

AND I THOUGHT *MY GOD,* I CANNOT IMAGINE ANYTHING FUNNIER THAN GETTING HIM IN THE FACE WITH A SNOWBALL, RIGHT NOW THIS SECOND.

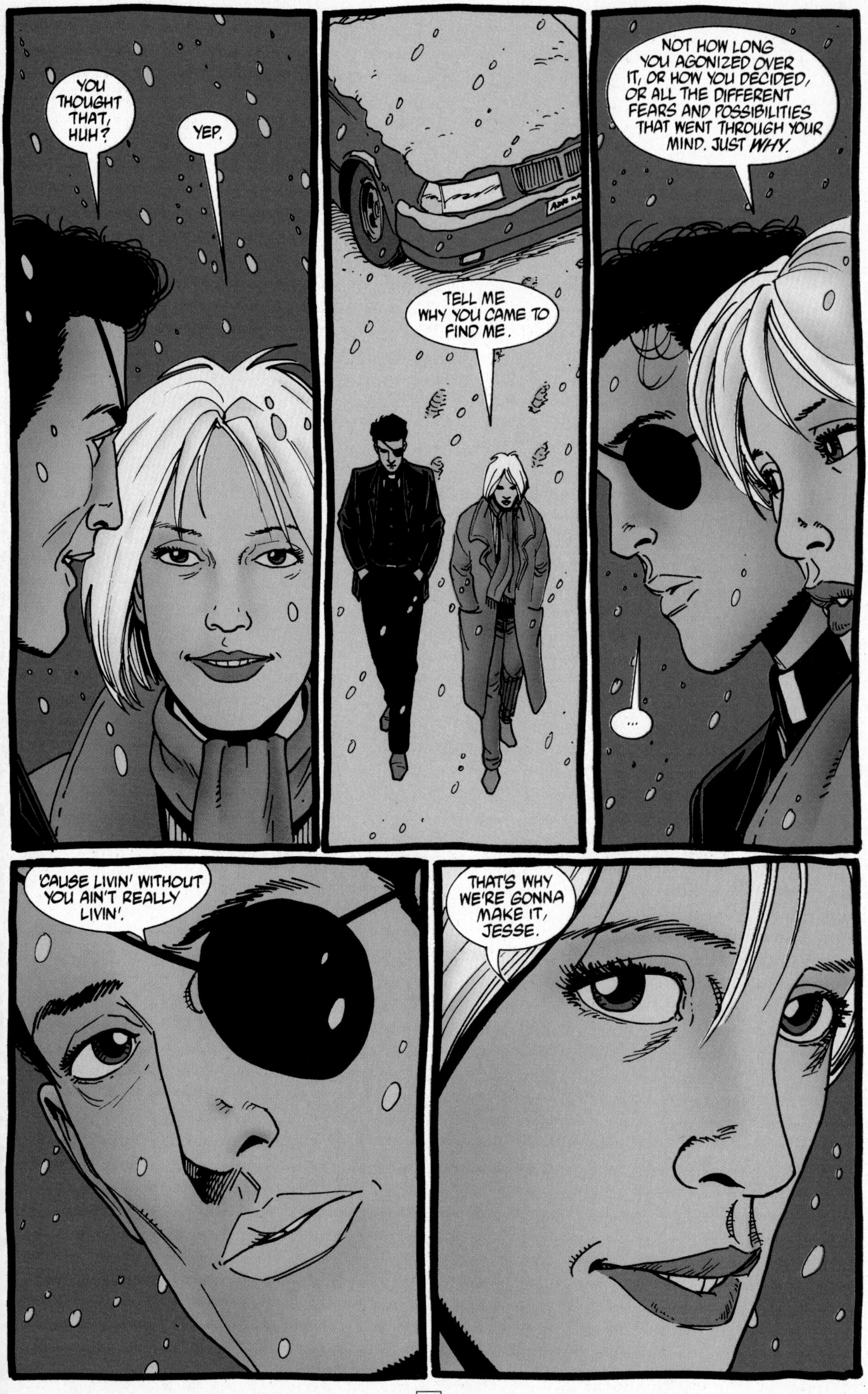
YOU THOUGHT THAT, HUH?
YEP.
TELL ME WHY YOU CAME TO FIND ME.
NOT HOW LONG YOU AGONIZED OVER IT, OR HOW YOU DECIDED, OR ALL THE DIFFERENT FEARS AND POSSIBILITIES THAT WENT THROUGH YOUR MIND. JUST *WHY*.
...
'CAUSE LIVIN' WITHOUT YOU AIN'T REALLY LIVIN'.
THAT'S WHY WE'RE GONNA MAKE IT, JESSE.

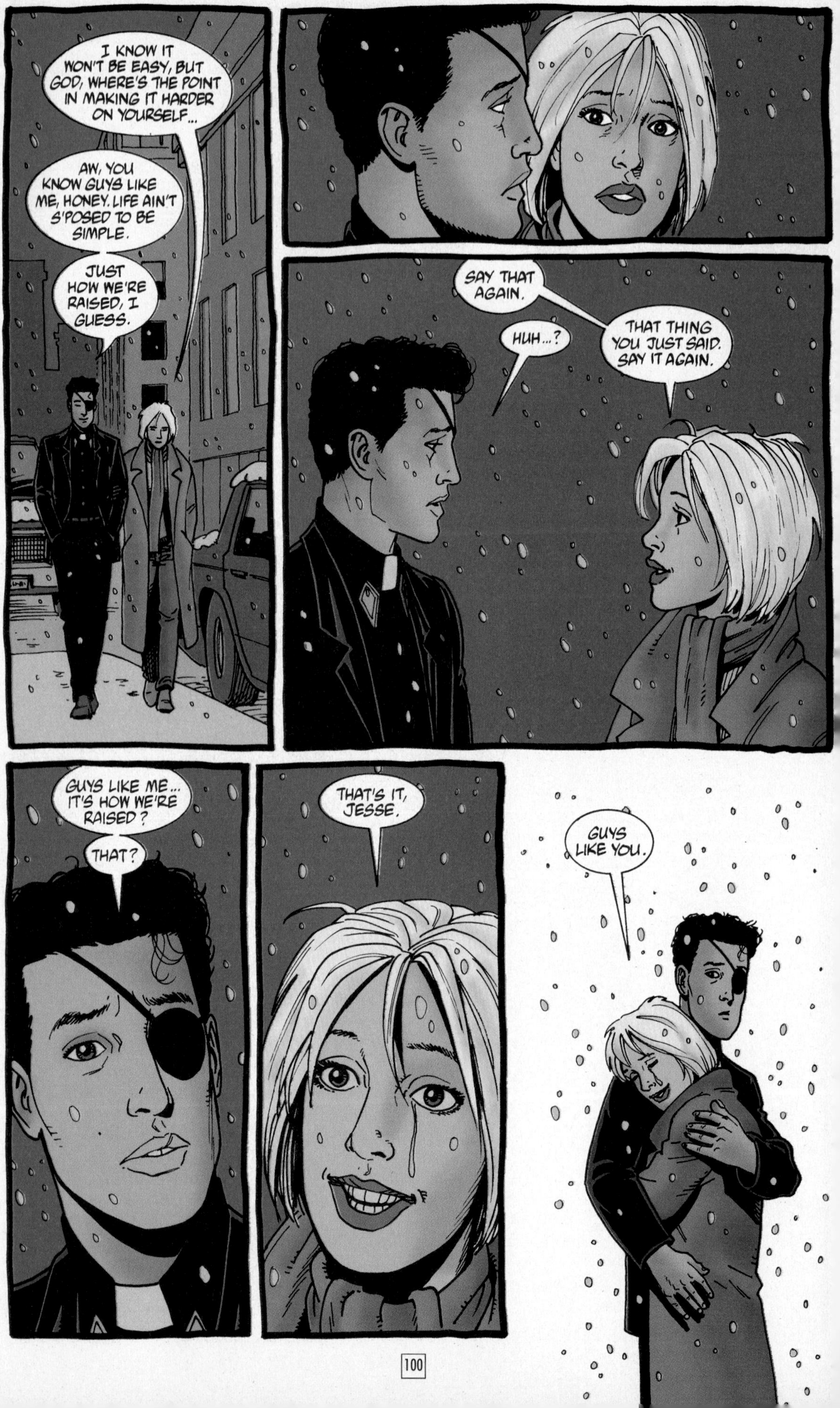
I KNOW IT WON'T BE EASY, BUT GOD, WHERE'S THE POINT IN MAKING IT HARDER ON YOURSELF...
AW, YOU KNOW GUYS LIKE ME, HONEY. LIFE AIN'T S'POSED TO BE SIMPLE.
JUST HOW WE'RE RAISED, I GUESS.
SAY THAT AGAIN.
HUH...?
THAT THING YOU JUST SAID. SAY IT AGAIN.
GUYS LIKE ME... IT'S HOW WE'RE RAISED?
THAT?
THAT'S IT, JESSE.
GUYS LIKE YOU.

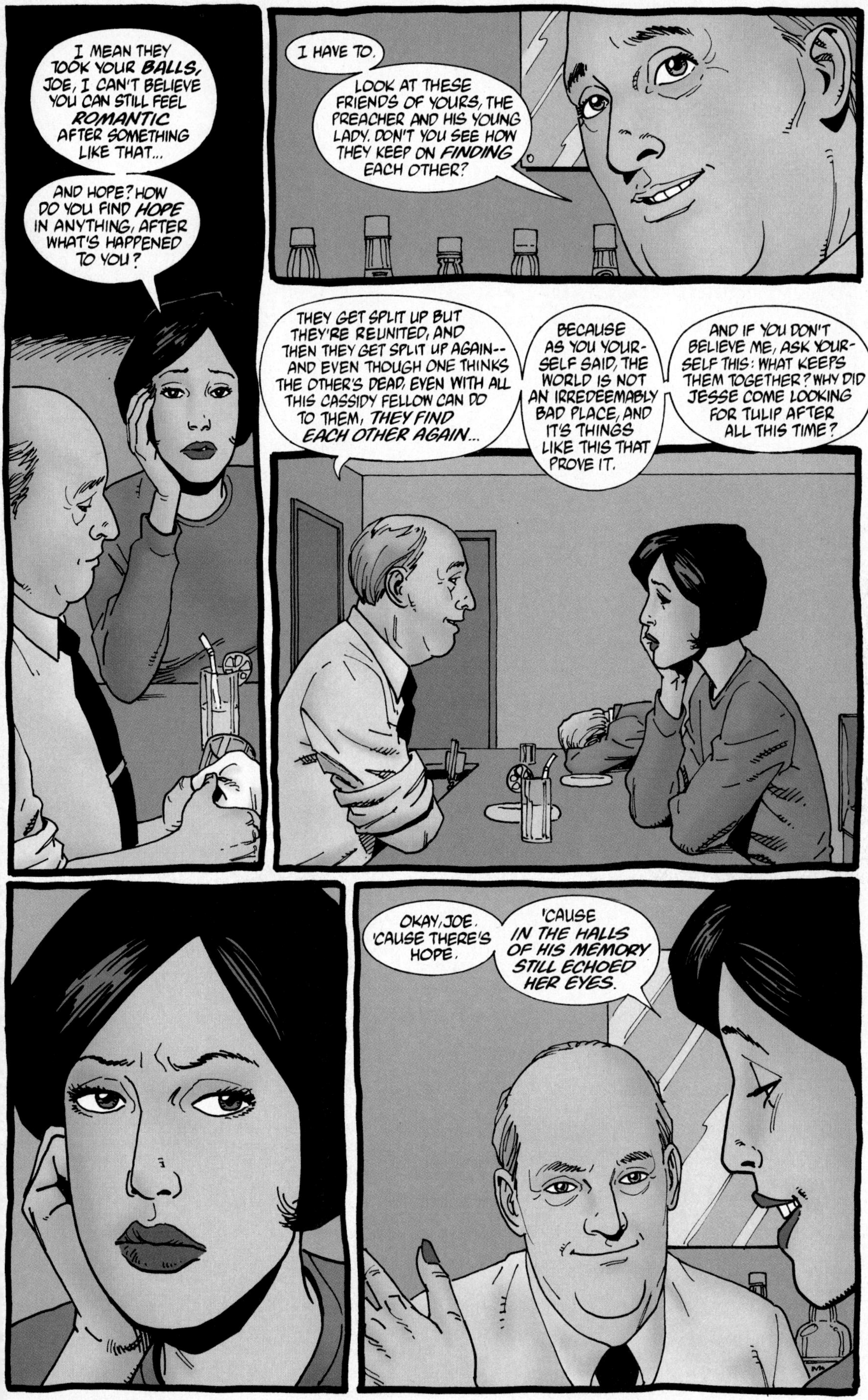

I MEAN THEY TOOK YOUR BALLS, JOE, I CAN'T BELIEVE YOU CAN STILL FEEL ROMANTIC AFTER SOMETHING LIKE THAT...
AND HOPE? HOW DO YOU FIND HOPE IN ANYTHING, AFTER WHAT'S HAPPENED TO YOU?
I HAVE TO.
LOOK AT THESE FRIENDS OF YOURS, THE PREACHER AND HIS YOUNG LADY. DON'T YOU SEE HOW THEY KEEP ON FINDING EACH OTHER?
THEY GET SPLIT UP BUT THEY'RE REUNITED, AND THEN THEY GET SPLIT UP AGAIN-- AND EVEN THOUGH ONE THINKS THE OTHER'S DEAD, EVEN WITH ALL THIS CASSIDY FELLOW CAN DO TO THEM, THEY FIND EACH OTHER AGAIN...
BECAUSE AS YOU YOURSELF SAID, THE WORLD IS NOT AN IRREDEEMABLY BAD PLACE, AND IT'S THINGS LIKE THIS THAT PROVE IT.
AND IF YOU DON'T BELIEVE ME, ASK YOURSELF THIS: WHAT KEEPS THEM TOGETHER? WHY DID JESSE COME LOOKING FOR TULIP AFTER ALL THIS TIME?
OKAY, JOE. 'CAUSE THERE'S HOPE.
'CAUSE IN THE HALLS OF HIS MEMORY STILL ECHOED HER EYES.

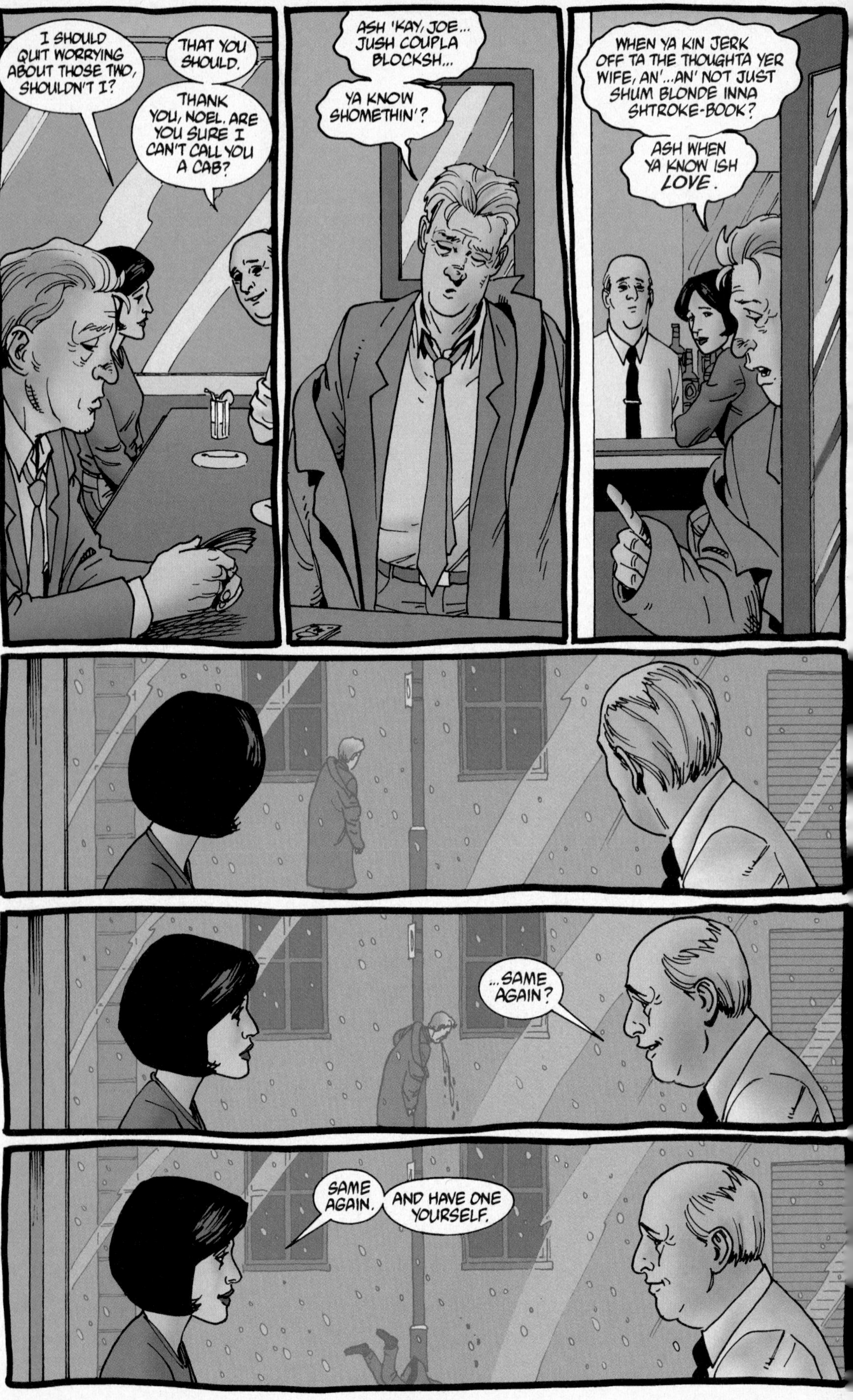

I SHOULD QUIT WORRYING ABOUT THOSE TWO, SHOULDN'T I?
THAT YOU SHOULD.
THANK YOU, NOEL. ARE YOU SURE I CAN'T CALL YOU A CAB?
ASH 'KAY, JOE... JUSH COUPLA BLOCKSH...
YA KNOW SHOMETHIN'?
WHEN YA KIN JERK OFF TA THE THOUGHTA YER WIFE, AN'...AN' NOT JUST SHUM BLONDE INNA SHTROKE-BOOK?
ASH WHEN YA KNOW ISH LOVE.
...SAME AGAIN?
SAME AGAIN.
AND HAVE ONE YOURSELF.

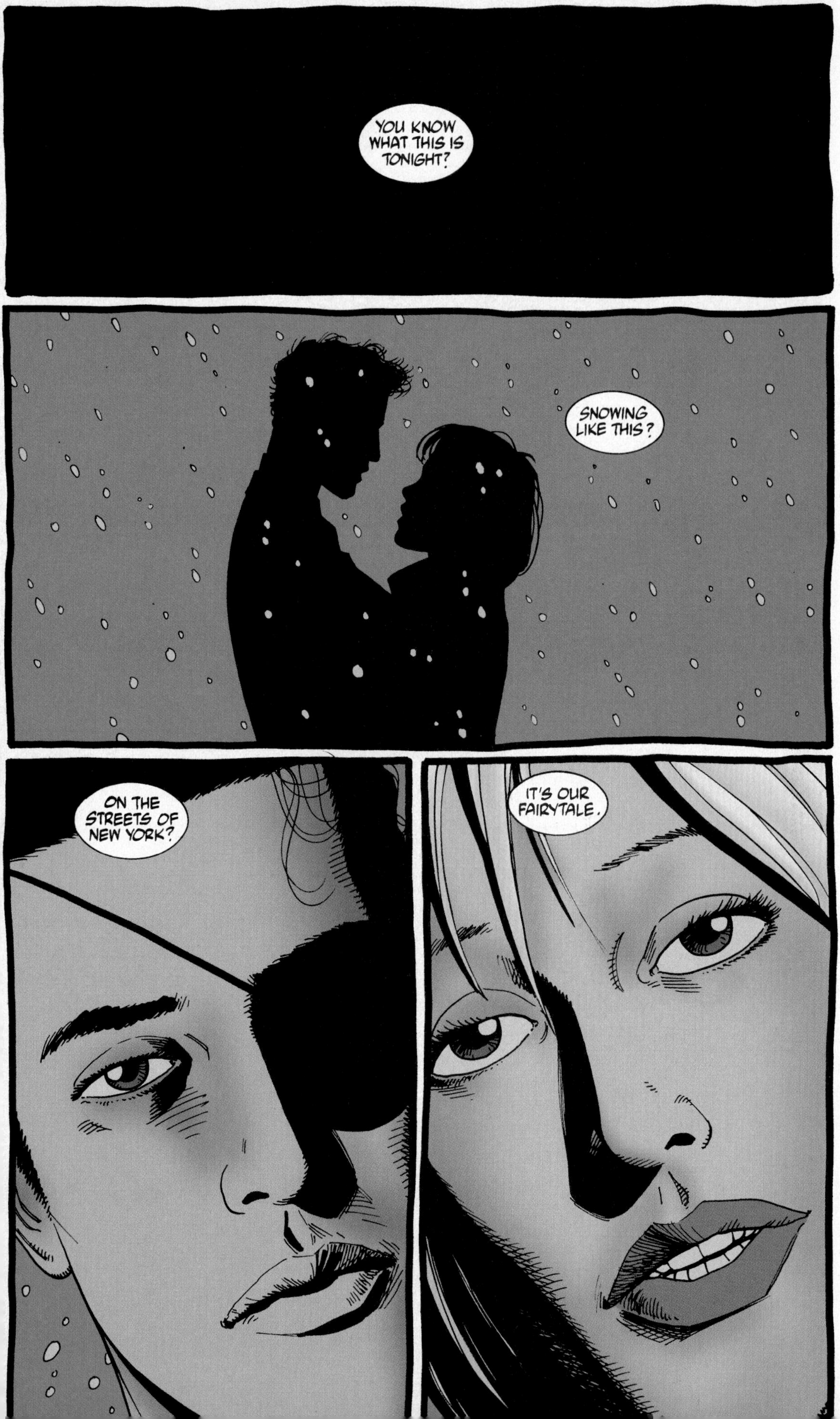
YOU KNOW WHAT THIS IS TONIGHT?
SNOWING LIKE THIS?
ON THE STREETS OF NEW YORK?
IT'S OUR FAIRYTALE.

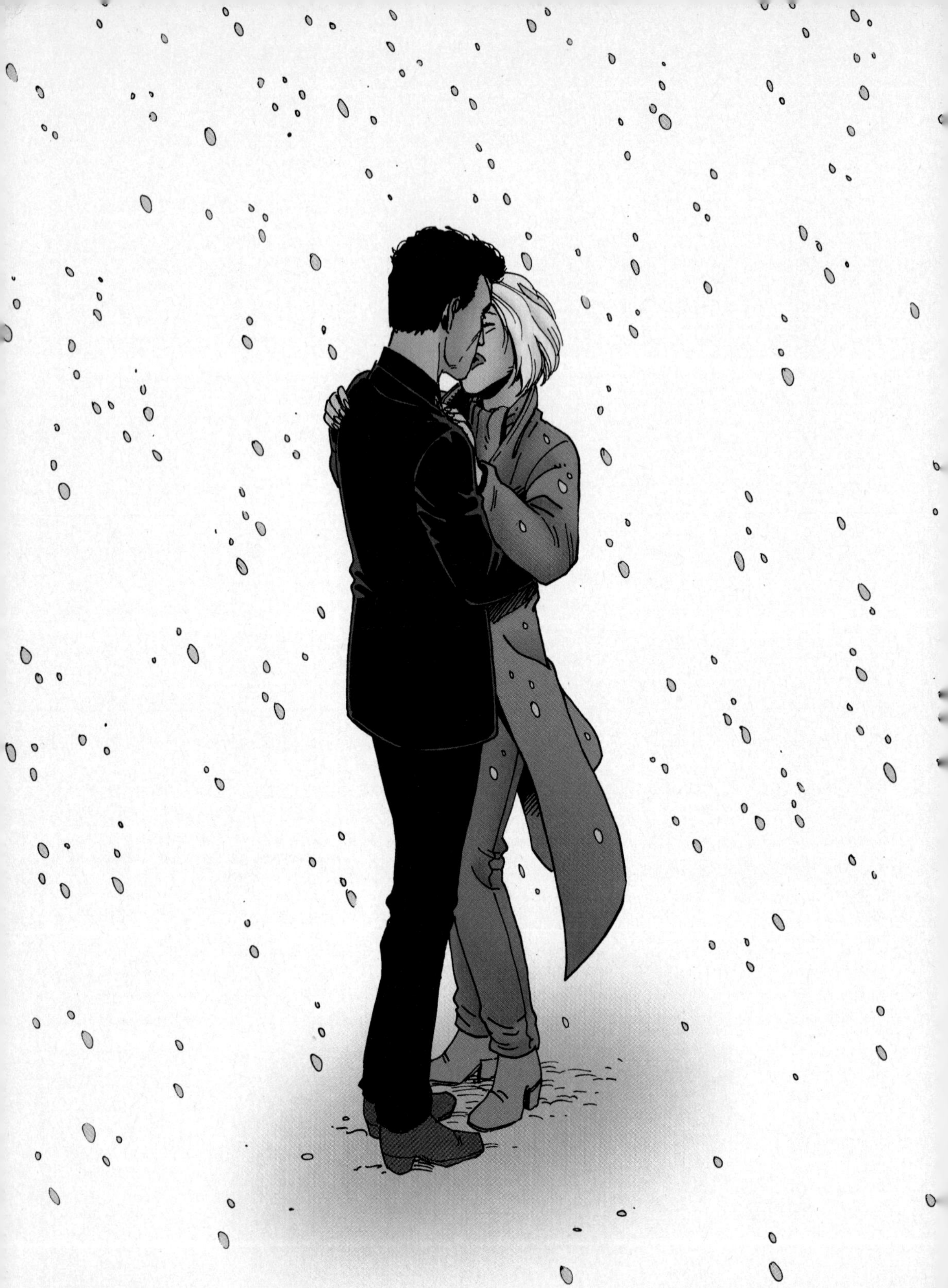

I BUILT MY DREAMS AROUND YOU

GARTH ENNIS - Writer STEVE DILLON - Artist

PAMELA RAMBO - Colorist CLEM ROBINS - Letterer AXEL ALONSO - Editor

PREACHER created by GARTH ENNIS and STEVE DILLON

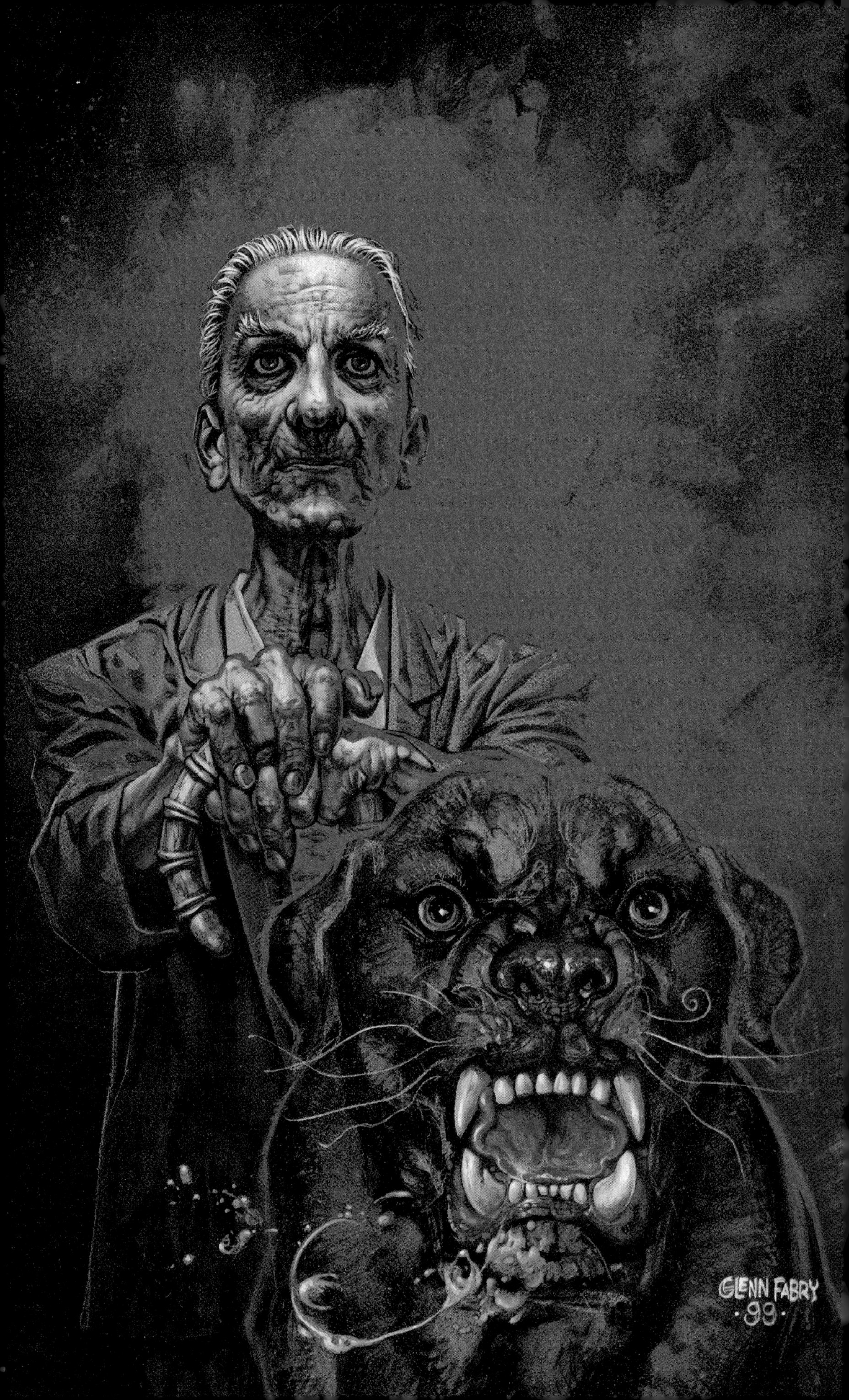
GLENN FABRY
·99·

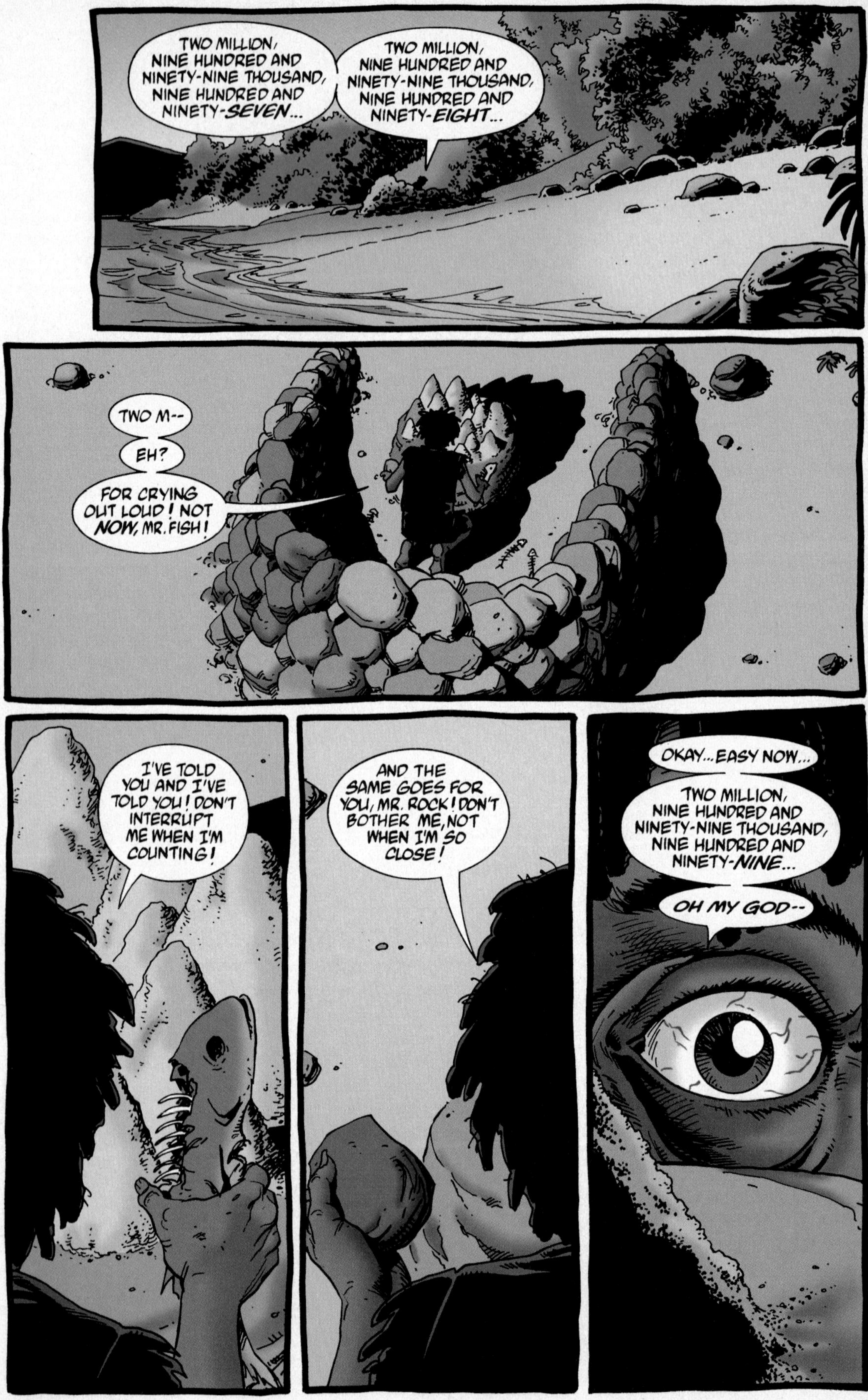
TWO MILLION, NINE HUNDRED AND NINETY-NINE THOUSAND, NINE HUNDRED AND NINETY-*SEVEN*...
TWO MILLION, NINE HUNDRED AND NINETY-NINE THOUSAND, NINE HUNDRED AND NINETY-*EIGHT*...
TWO M--
EH?
FOR CRYING OUT LOUD! NOT *NOW*, MR. FISH!
I'VE TOLD YOU AND I'VE TOLD YOU! DON'T INTERRUPT ME WHEN I'M COUNTING!
AND THE SAME GOES FOR YOU, MR. ROCK! DON'T BOTHER ME, NOT WHEN I'M SO CLOSE!
OKAY... EASY NOW...
TWO MILLION, NINE HUNDRED AND NINETY-NINE THOUSAND, NINE HUNDRED AND NINETY-*NINE*...
OH MY GOD--

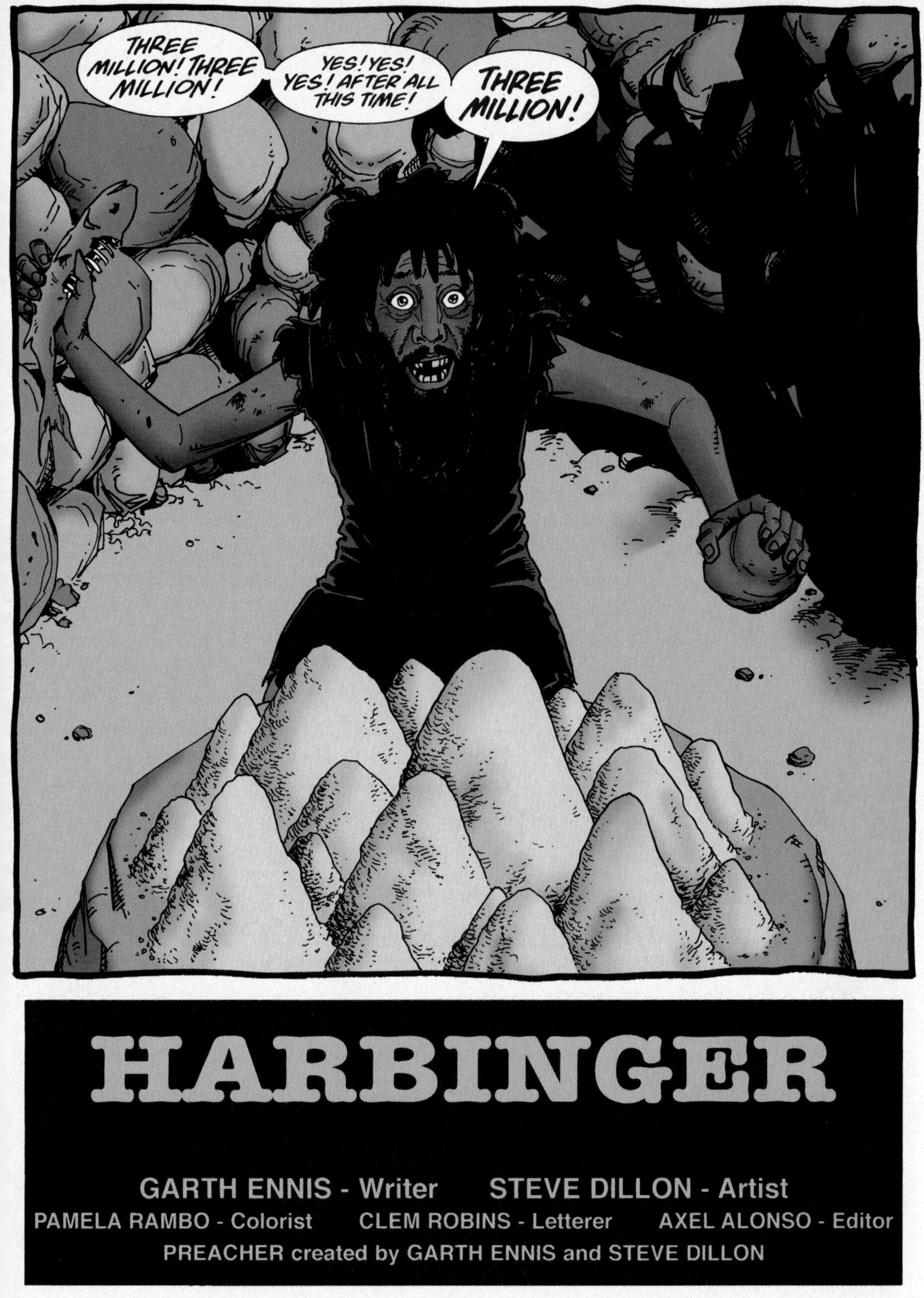
THREE MILLION! THREE MILLION!
YES! YES! YES! AFTER ALL THIS TIME!
THREE MILLION!

HARBINGER

GARTH ENNIS - Writer STEVE DILLON - Artist
PAMELA RAMBO - Colorist CLEM ROBINS - Letterer AXEL ALONSO - Editor
PREACHER created by GARTH ENNIS and STEVE DILLON

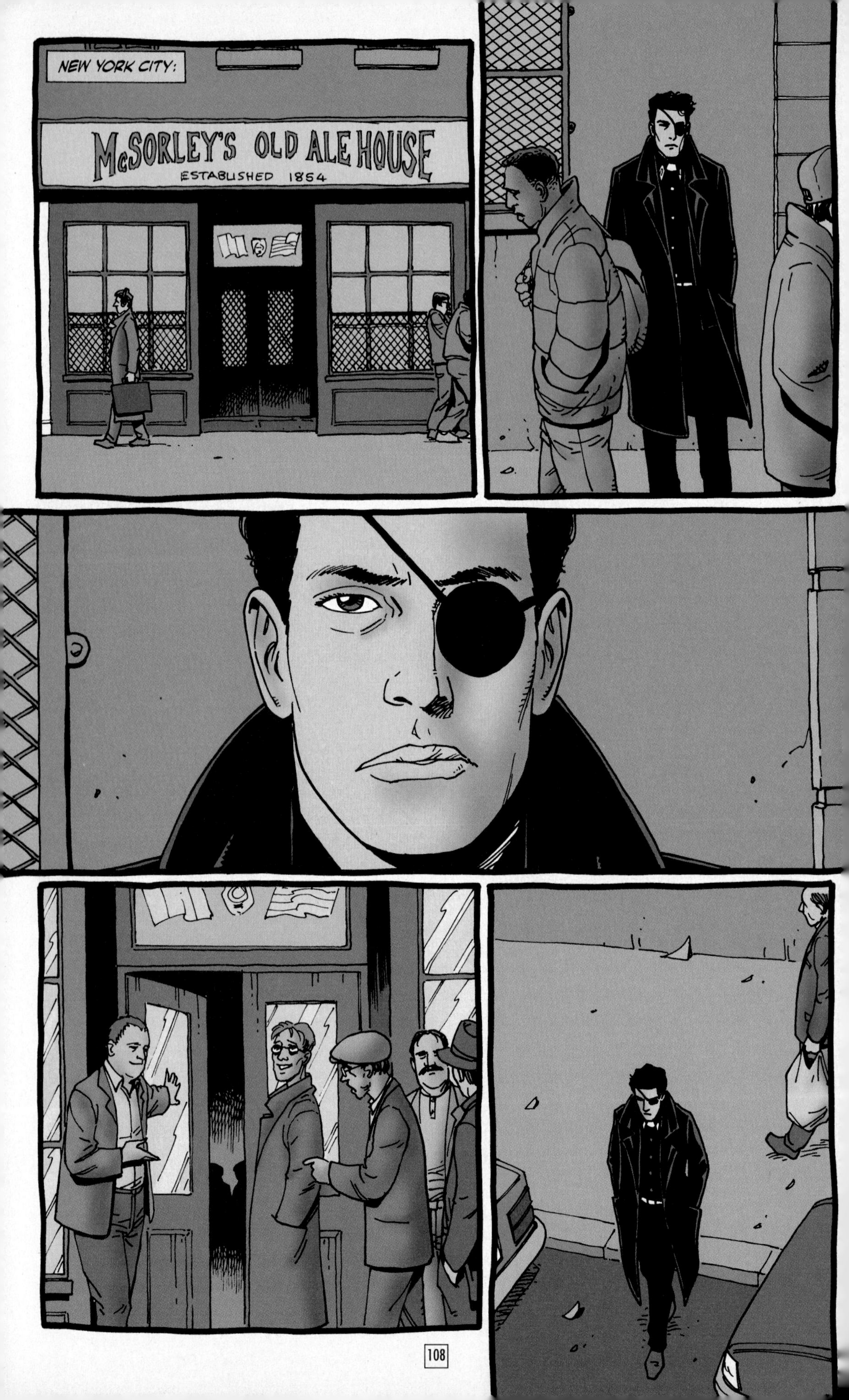
NEW YORK CITY:
McSORLEY'S OLD ALE HOUSE
ESTABLISHED 1854

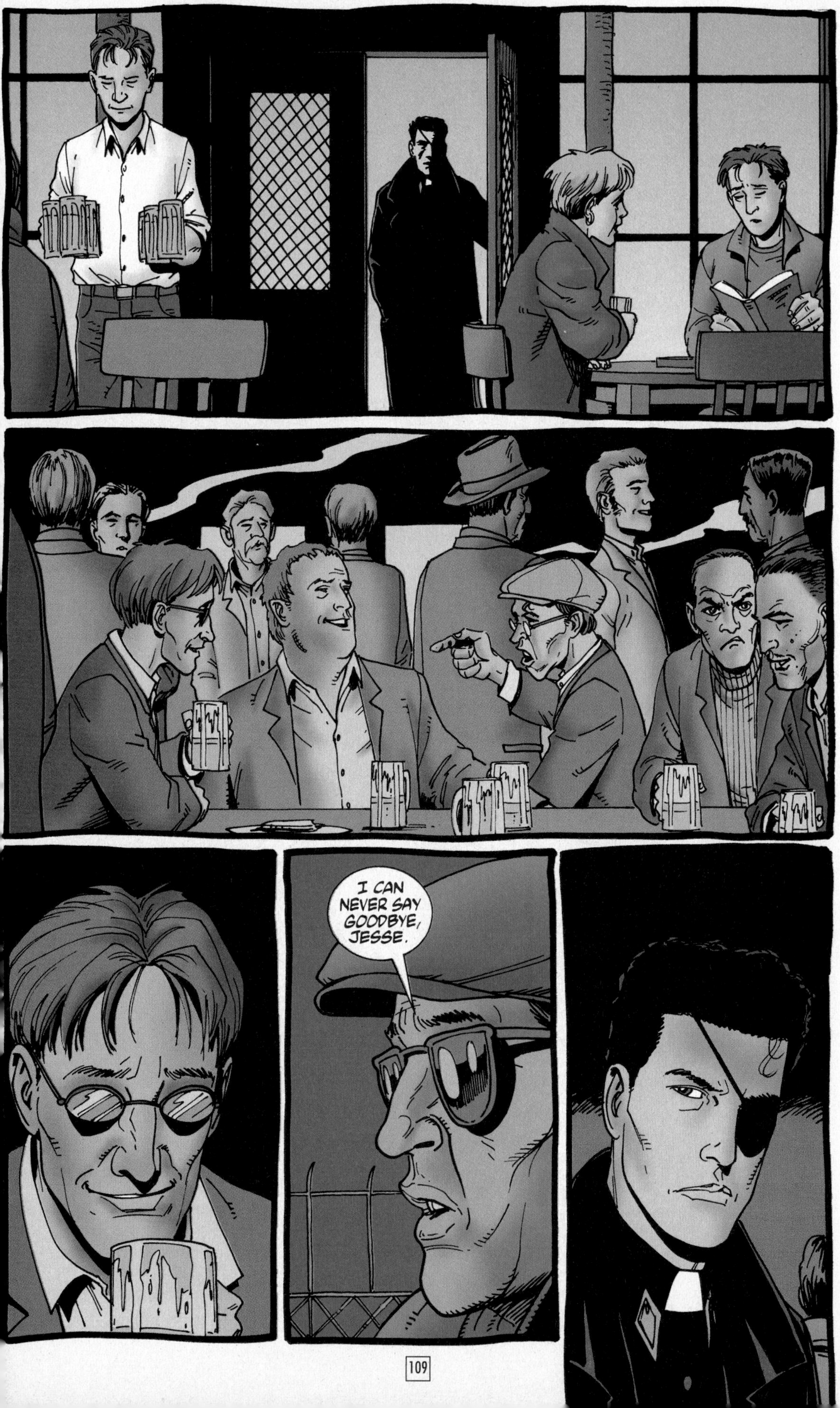
I CAN NEVER SAY GOODBYE, JESSE.

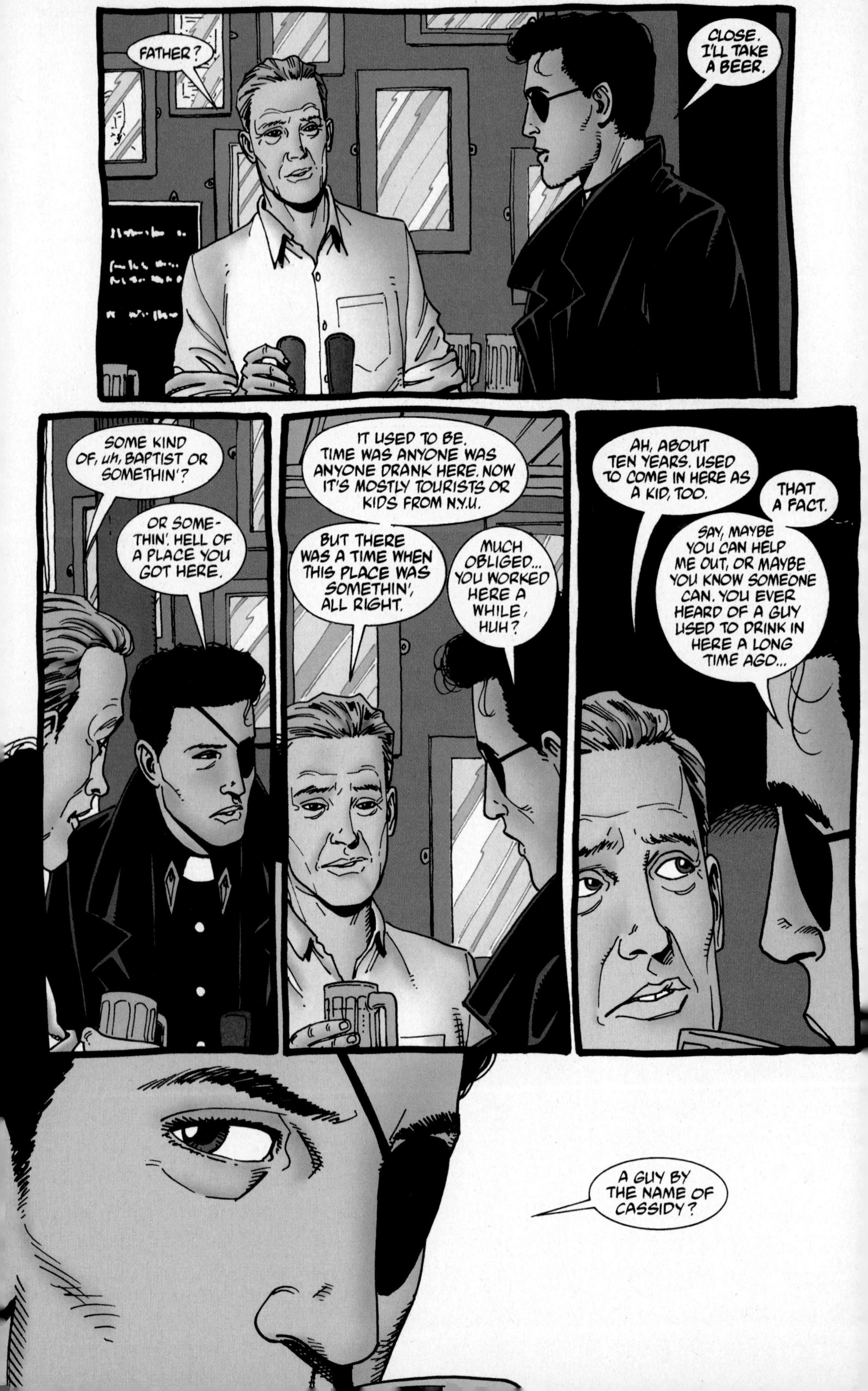
FATHER?
CLOSE. I'LL TAKE A BEER.
SOME KIND OF, uh, BAPTIST OR SOMETHIN'?
OR SOMETHIN'. HELL OF A PLACE YOU GOT HERE.
IT USED TO BE. TIME WAS ANYONE WAS ANYONE DRANK HERE. NOW IT'S MOSTLY TOURISTS OR KIDS FROM N.Y.U.
BUT THERE WAS A TIME WHEN THIS PLACE WAS SOMETHIN', ALL RIGHT.
MUCH OBLIGED... YOU WORKED HERE A WHILE, HUH?
AH, ABOUT TEN YEARS. USED TO COME IN HERE AS A KID, TOO.
THAT A FACT.
SAY, MAYBE YOU CAN HELP ME OUT, OR MAYBE YOU KNOW SOMEONE CAN. YOU EVER HEARD OF A GUY USED TO DRINK IN HERE A LONG TIME AGO...
A GUY BY THE NAME OF CASSIDY?

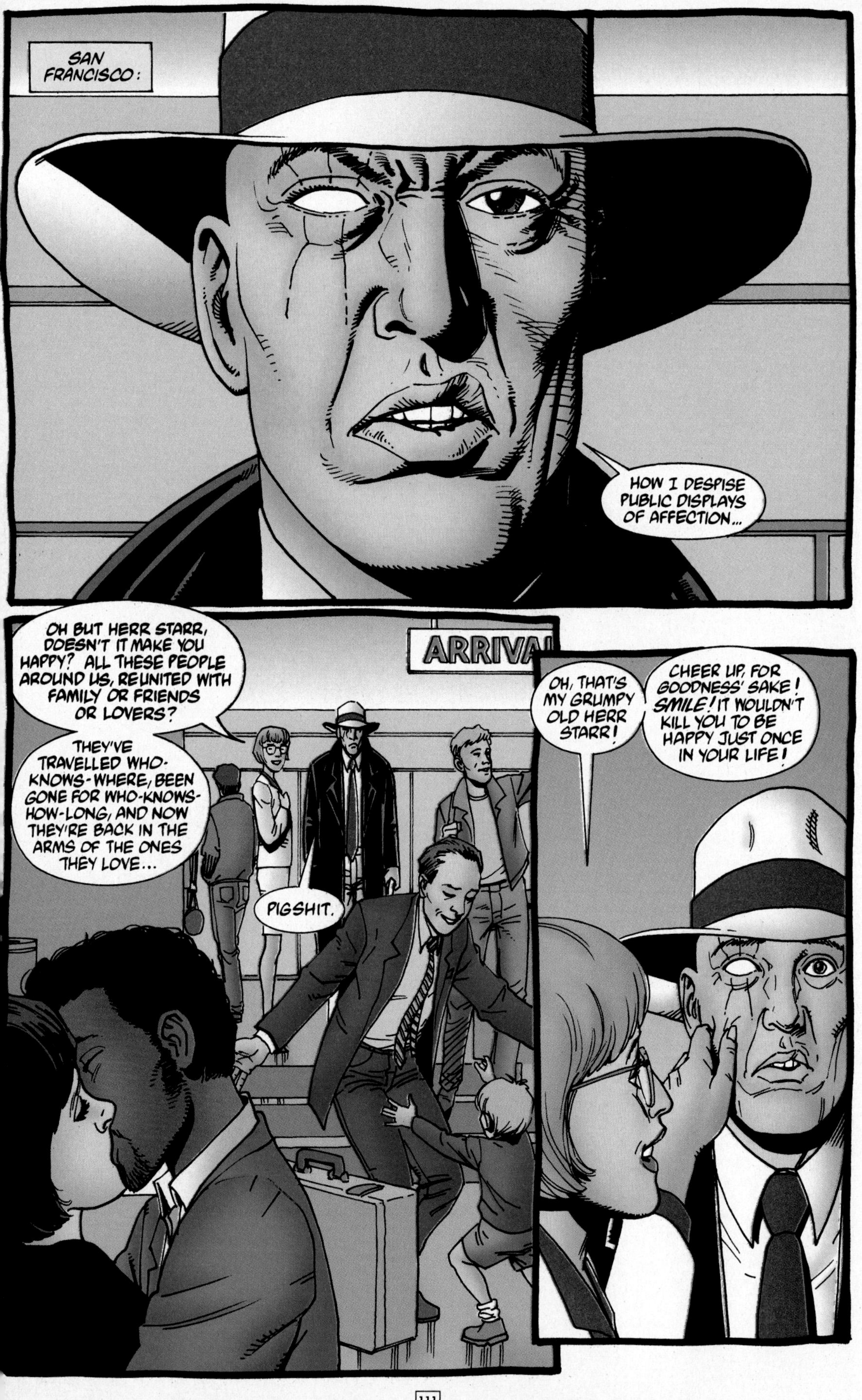
SAN FRANCISCO:
HOW I DESPISE PUBLIC DISPLAYS OF AFFECTION...
ARRIVA
OH BUT HERR STARR, DOESN'T IT MAKE YOU HAPPY? ALL THESE PEOPLE AROUND US, REUNITED WITH FAMILY OR FRIENDS OR LOVERS?
THEY'VE TRAVELLED WHO-KNOWS-WHERE, BEEN GONE FOR WHO-KNOWS-HOW-LONG, AND NOW THEY'RE BACK IN THE ARMS OF THE ONES THEY LOVE...
PIGSHIT.
OH, THAT'S MY GRUMPY OLD HERR STARR!
CHEER UP, FOR GOODNESS' SAKE! SMILE! IT WOULDN'T KILL YOU TO BE HAPPY JUST ONCE IN YOUR LIFE!

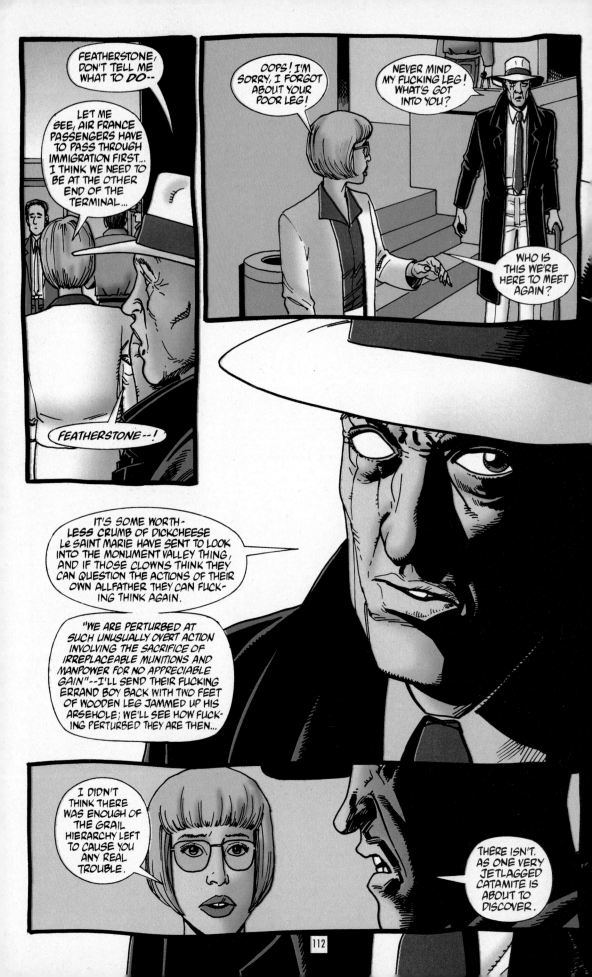

FEATHERSTONE, DON'T TELL ME WHAT TO *DO*--

LET ME SEE, AIR FRANCE PASSENGERS HAVE TO PASS THROUGH IMMIGRATION FIRST... I THINK WE NEED TO BE AT THE OTHER END OF THE TERMINAL...

FEATHERSTONE--!

OOPS! I'M SORRY, I FORGOT ABOUT YOUR POOR LEG!

NEVER MIND MY FUCKING LEG! WHAT'S GOT INTO YOU?

WHO IS THIS WE'RE HERE TO MEET AGAIN?

IT'S SOME WORTH-LESS CRUMB OF DICKCHEESE LE SAINT MARIE HAVE SENT TO LOOK INTO THE MONUMENT VALLEY THING, AND IF THOSE CLOWNS THINK THEY CAN QUESTION THE ACTIONS OF THEIR OWN ALLFATHER THEY CAN FUCK-ING THINK AGAIN.

"WE ARE PERTURBED AT SUCH UNUSUALLY OVERT ACTION INVOLVING THE SACRIFICE OF IRREPLACEABLE MUNITIONS AND MANPOWER FOR NO APPRECIABLE GAIN"--I'LL SEND THEIR FUCKING ERRAND BOY BACK WITH TWO FEET OF WOODEN LEG JAMMED UP HIS ARSEHOLE; WE'LL SEE HOW FUCK-ING PERTURBED THEY ARE THEN...

I DIDN'T THINK THERE WAS ENOUGH OF THE GRAIL HIERARCHY LEFT TO CAUSE YOU ANY REAL TROUBLE.

THERE ISN'T. AS ONE VERY JETLAGGED CATAMITE IS ABOUT TO DISCOVER.

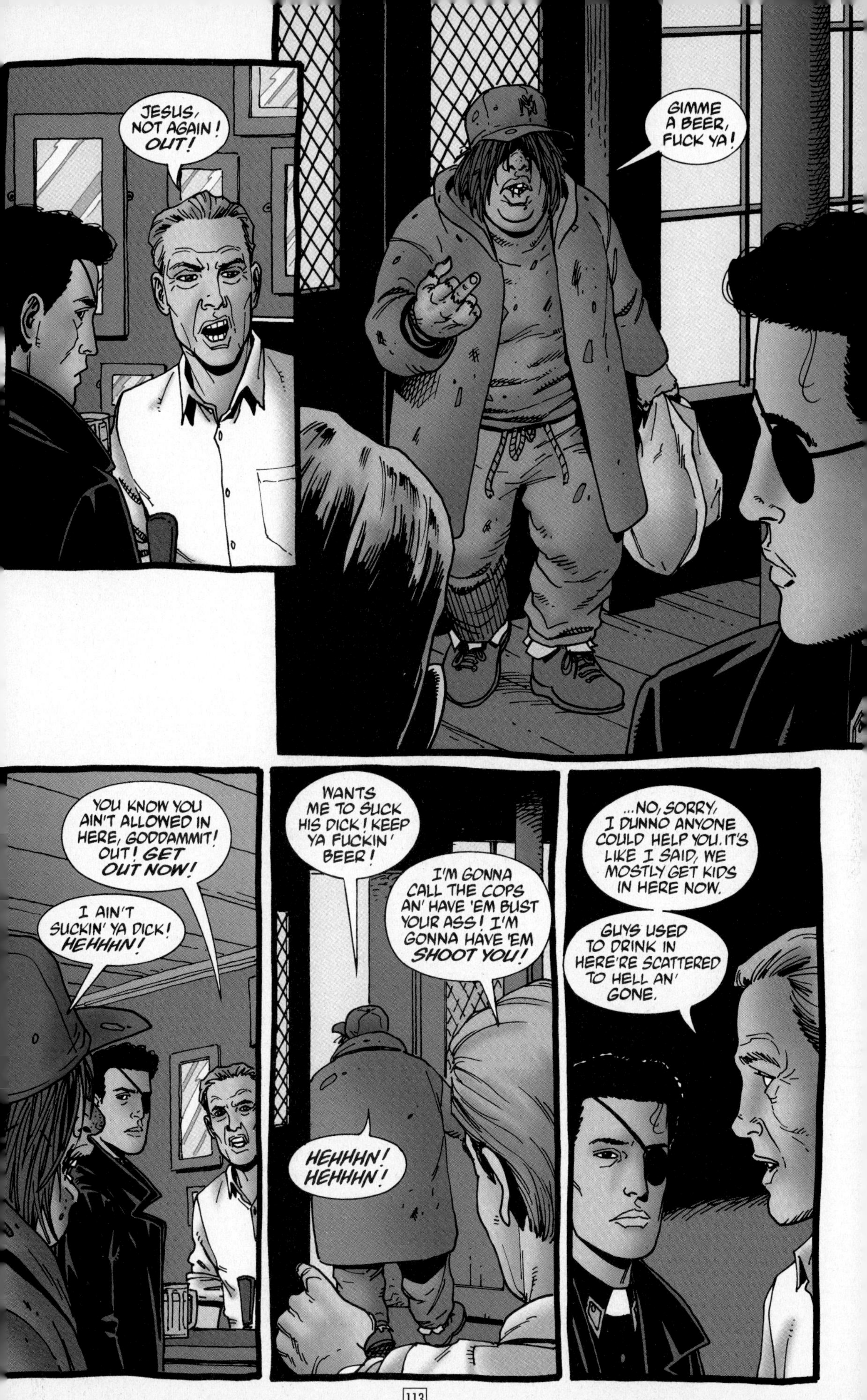
JESUS, NOT AGAIN! OUT!
GIMME A BEER, FUCK YA!
YOU KNOW YOU AIN'T ALLOWED IN HERE, GODDAMMIT! OUT! GET OUT NOW!
I AIN'T SUCKIN' YA DICK! HEHHHN!
WANTS ME TO SUCK HIS DICK! KEEP YA FUCKIN' BEER!
I'M GONNA CALL THE COPS AN' HAVE 'EM BUST YOUR ASS! I'M GONNA HAVE 'EM SHOOT YOU!
HEHHHN! HEHHHN!
...NO, SORRY, I DUNNO ANYONE COULD HELP YOU. IT'S LIKE I SAID, WE MOSTLY GET KIDS IN HERE NOW.
GUYS USED TO DRINK IN HERE'RE SCATTERED TO HELL AN' GONE.

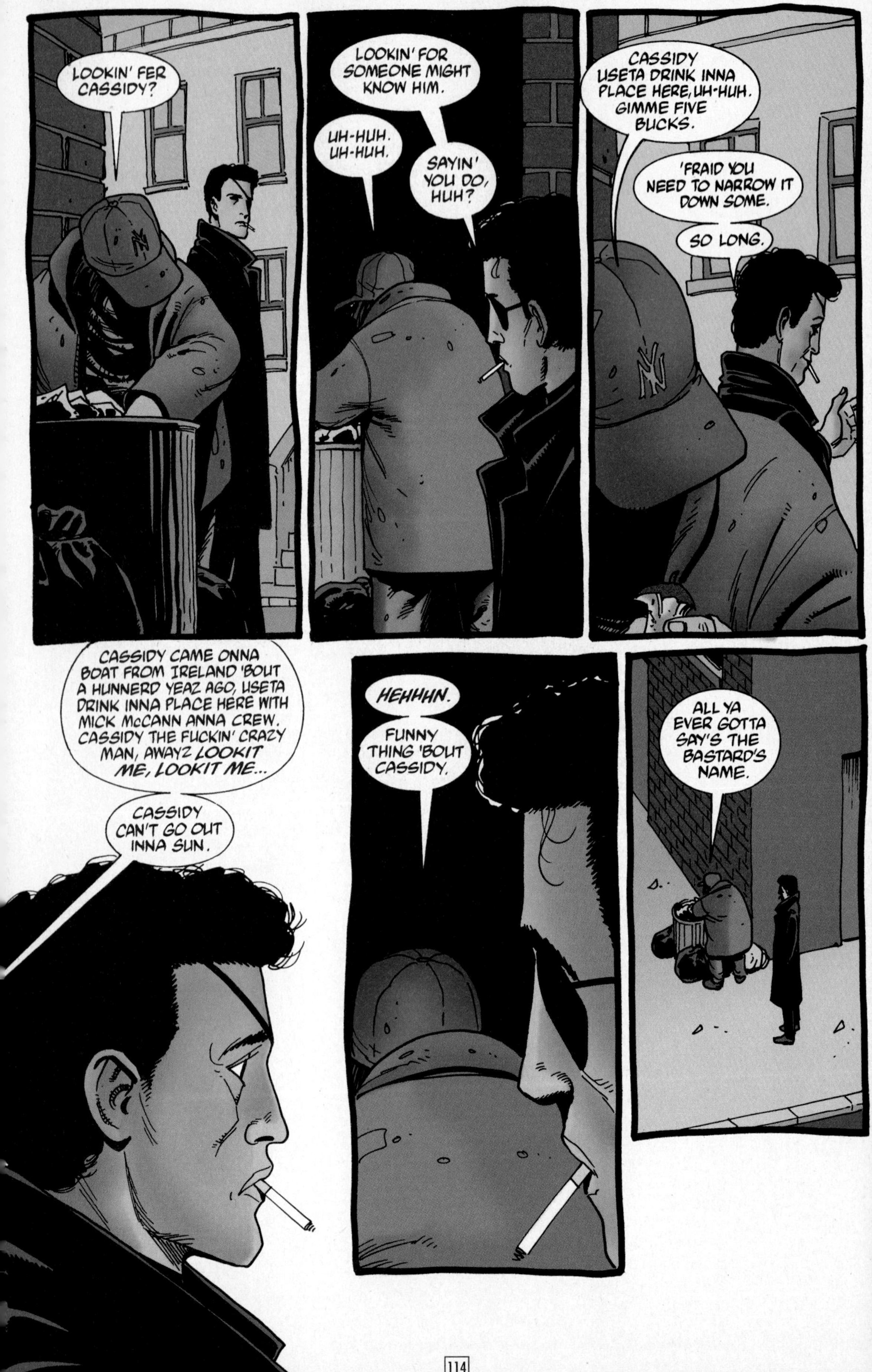
LOOKIN' FER CASSIDY?
LOOKIN' FOR SOMEONE MIGHT KNOW HIM.
UH-HUH. UH-HUH.
SAYIN' YOU DO, HUH?
CASSIDY USETA DRINK INNA PLACE HERE, UH-HUH. GIMME FIVE BUCKS.
'FRAID YOU NEED TO NARROW IT DOWN SOME.
SO LONG.
CASSIDY CAME ONNA BOAT FROM IRELAND 'BOUT A HUNNERD YEAZ AGO, USETA DRINK INNA PLACE HERE WITH MICK McCANN ANNA CREW. CASSIDY THE FUCKIN' CRAZY MAN, AWAYZ LOOKIT ME, LOOKIT ME...
CASSIDY CAN'T GO OUT INNA SUN.
HEHHHN.
FUNNY THING 'BOUT CASSIDY.
ALL YA EVER GOTTA SAY'S THE BASTARD'S NAME.

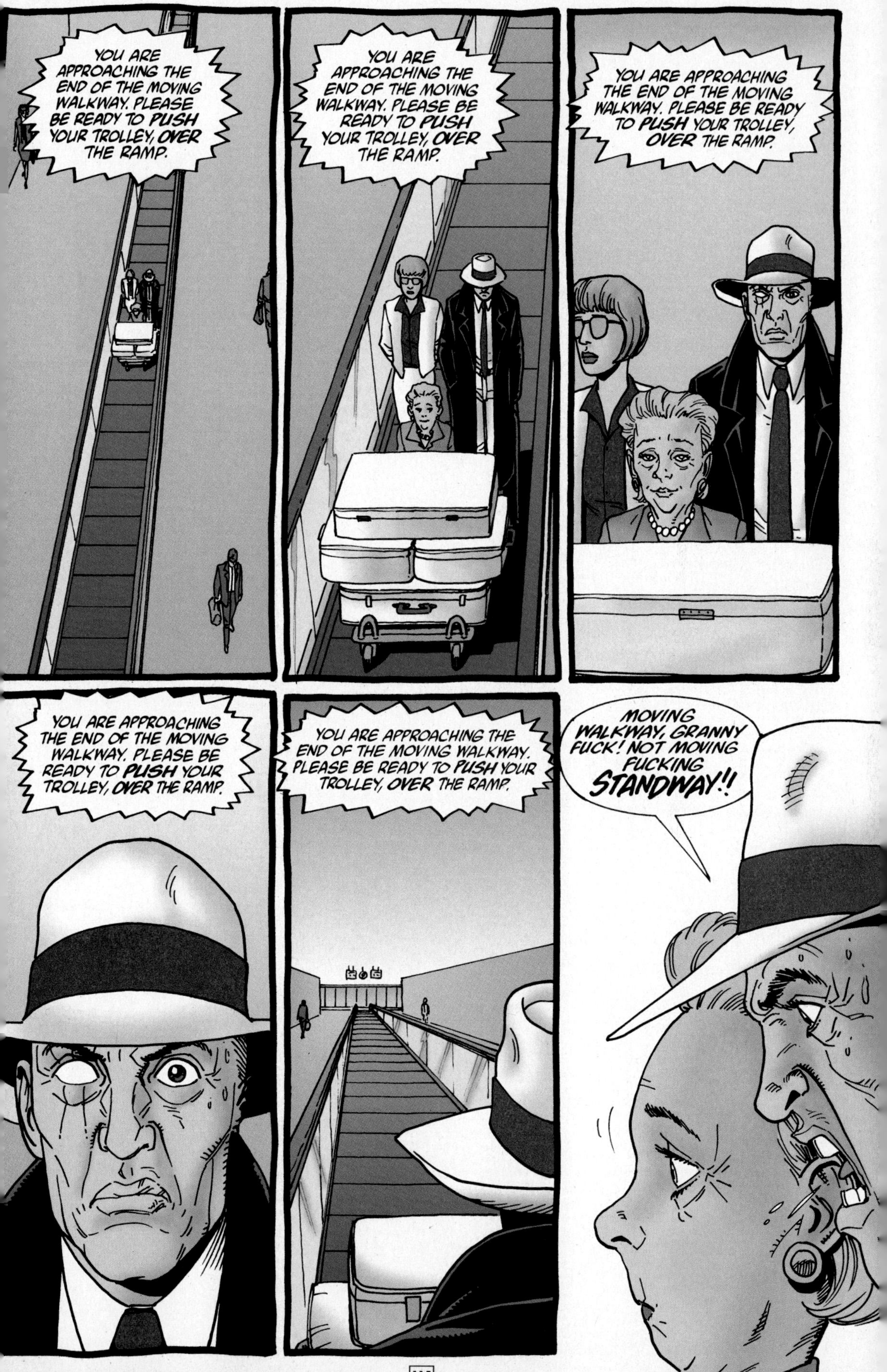
YOU ARE APPROACHING THE END OF THE MOVING WALKWAY. PLEASE BE READY TO PUSH YOUR TROLLEY, OVER THE RAMP.
YOU ARE APPROACHING THE END OF THE MOVING WALKWAY. PLEASE BE READY TO PUSH YOUR TROLLEY, OVER THE RAMP.
YOU ARE APPROACHING THE END OF THE MOVING WALKWAY. PLEASE BE READY TO PUSH YOUR TROLLEY, OVER THE RAMP.
YOU ARE APPROACHING THE END OF THE MOVING WALKWAY. PLEASE BE READY TO PUSH YOUR TROLLEY, OVER THE RAMP.
YOU ARE APPROACHING THE END OF THE MOVING WALKWAY. PLEASE BE READY TO PUSH YOUR TROLLEY, OVER THE RAMP.
MOVING WALKWAY, GRANNY FUCK! NOT MOVING FUCKING STANDWAY!!

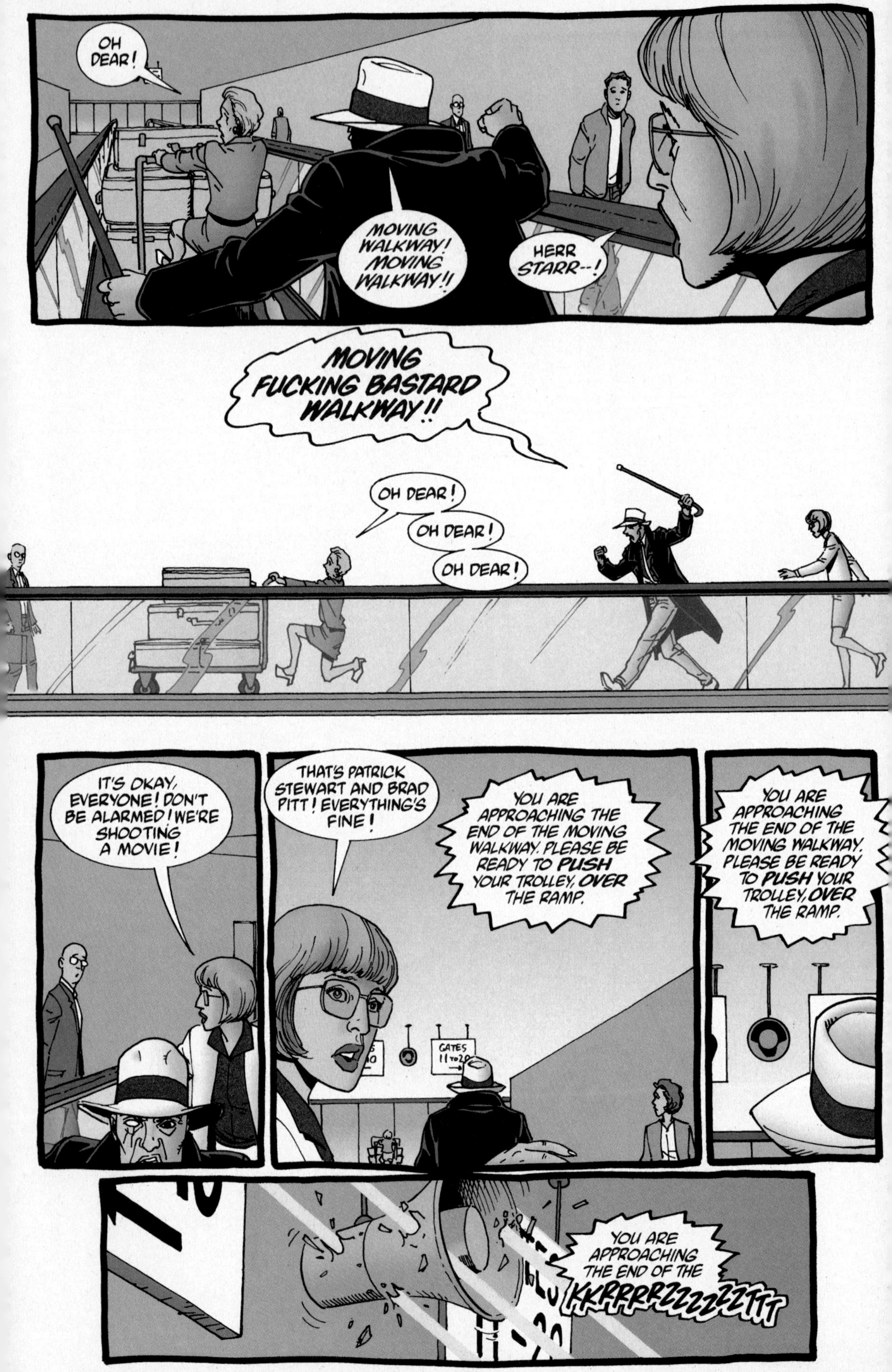
OH DEAR!
MOVING WALKWAY! MOVING WALKWAY!!
HERR STARR--!
MOVING FUCKING BASTARD WALKWAY!!
OH DEAR!
OH DEAR!
OH DEAR!
IT'S OKAY, EVERYONE! DON'T BE ALARMED! WE'RE SHOOTING A MOVIE!
THAT'S PATRICK STEWART AND BRAD PITT! EVERYTHING'S FINE!
YOU ARE APPROACHING THE END OF THE MOVING WALKWAY. PLEASE BE READY TO PUSH YOUR TROLLEY, OVER THE RAMP.
GATES 11 TO 20
YOU ARE APPROACHING THE END OF THE MOVING WALKWAY. PLEASE BE READY TO PUSH YOUR TROLLEY, OVER THE RAMP.
YOU ARE APPROACHING THE END OF THE KKRRRRZZZZZZTTT

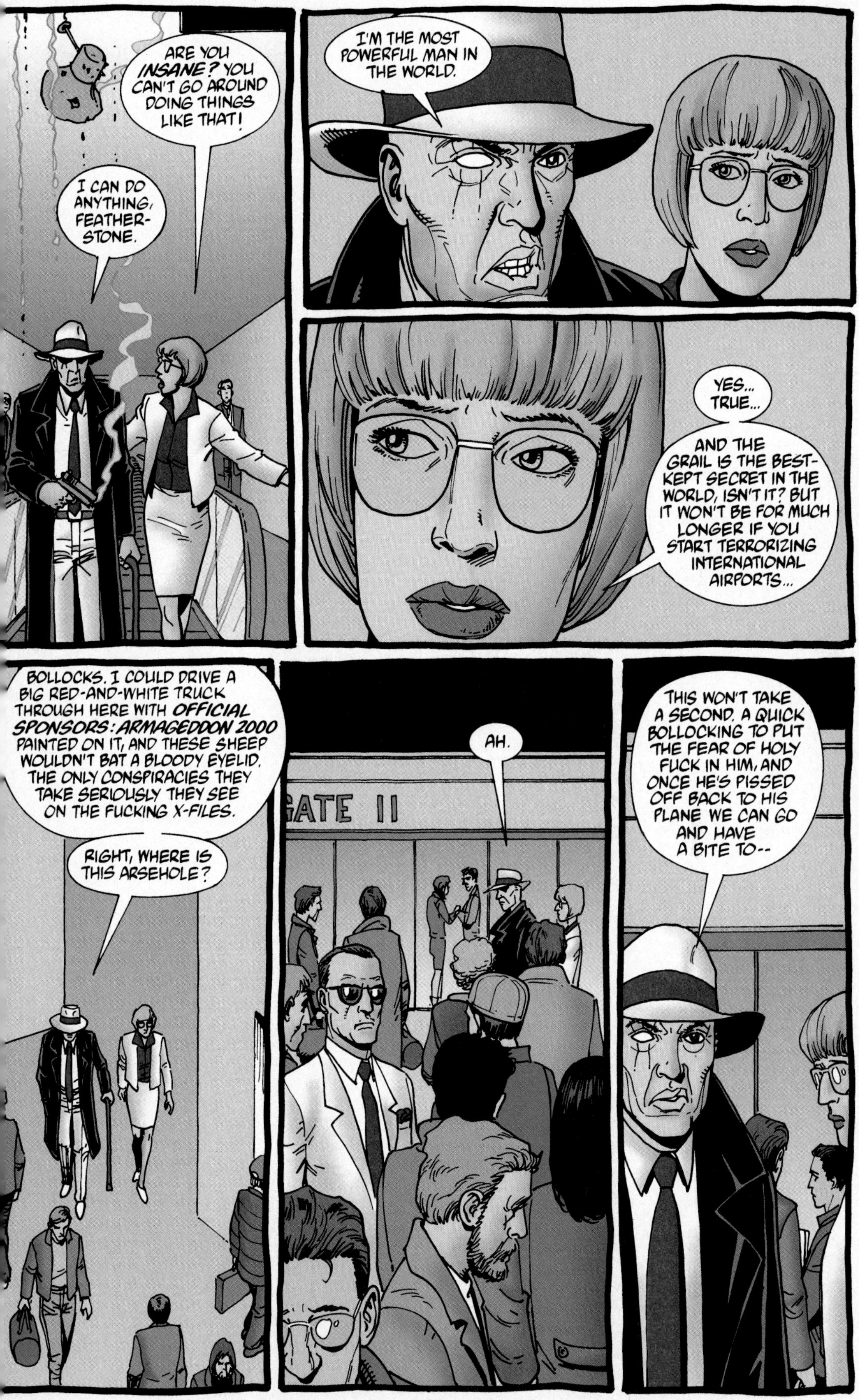
ARE YOU *INSANE?* YOU CAN'T GO AROUND DOING THINGS LIKE THAT!
I CAN DO ANYTHING, FEATHER-STONE.
I'M THE MOST POWERFUL MAN IN THE WORLD.
YES... TRUE...
AND THE GRAIL IS THE BEST-KEPT SECRET IN THE WORLD, ISN'T IT? BUT IT WON'T BE FOR MUCH LONGER IF YOU START TERRORIZING INTERNATIONAL AIRPORTS...
BOLLOCKS. I COULD DRIVE A BIG RED-AND-WHITE TRUCK THROUGH HERE WITH *OFFICIAL SPONSORS: ARMAGEDDON 2000* PAINTED ON IT, AND THESE SHEEP WOULDN'T BAT A BLOODY EYELID. THE ONLY CONSPIRACIES THEY TAKE SERIOUSLY THEY SEE ON THE FUCKING *X-FILES.*
RIGHT, WHERE IS THIS ARSEHOLE?
GATE 11
AH.
THIS WON'T TAKE A SECOND. A QUICK BOLLOCKING TO PUT THE FEAR OF HOLY FUCK IN HIM, AND ONCE HE'S PISSED OFF BACK TO HIS PLANE WE CAN GO AND HAVE A BITE TO--

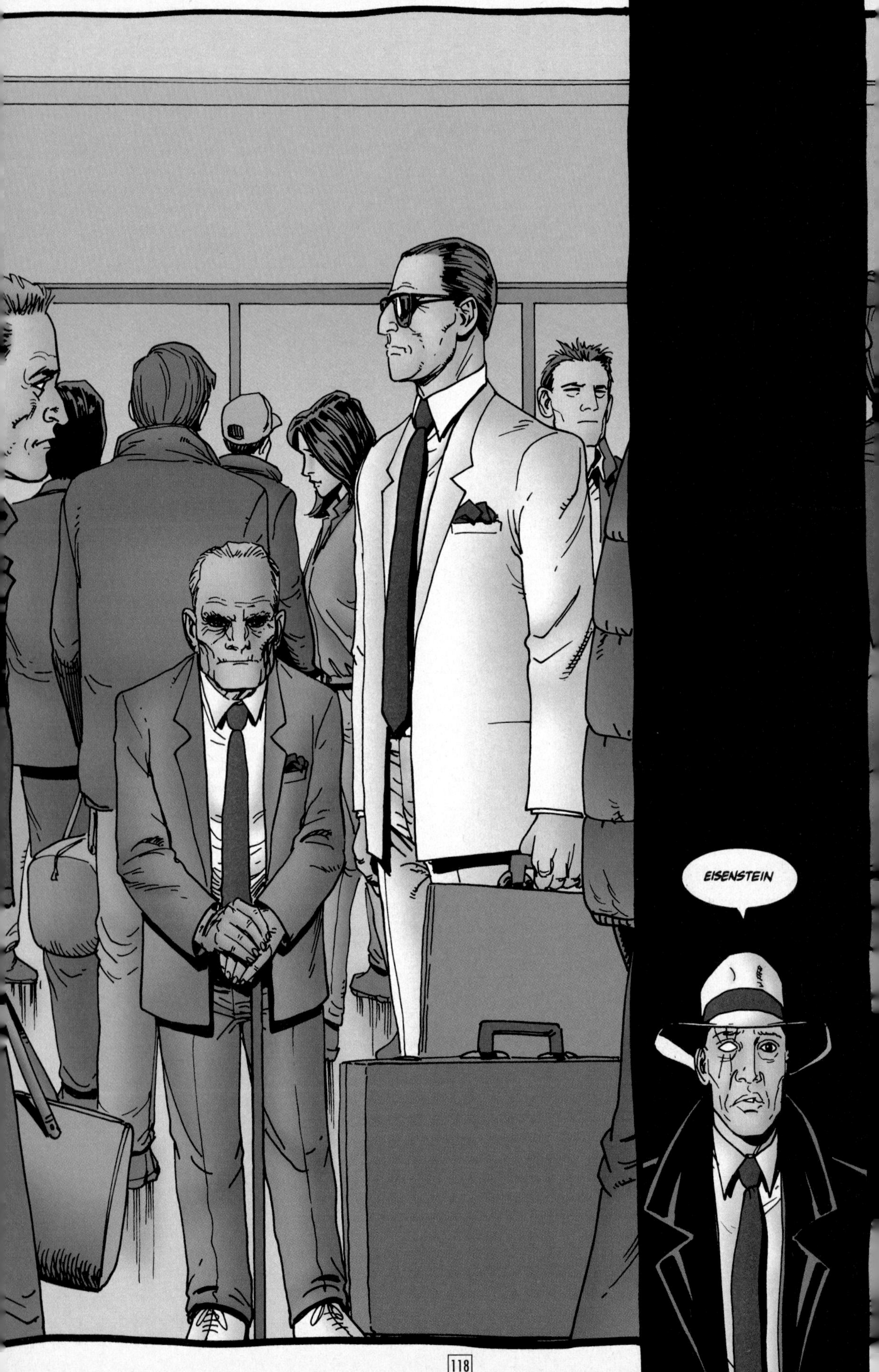
EISENSTEIN

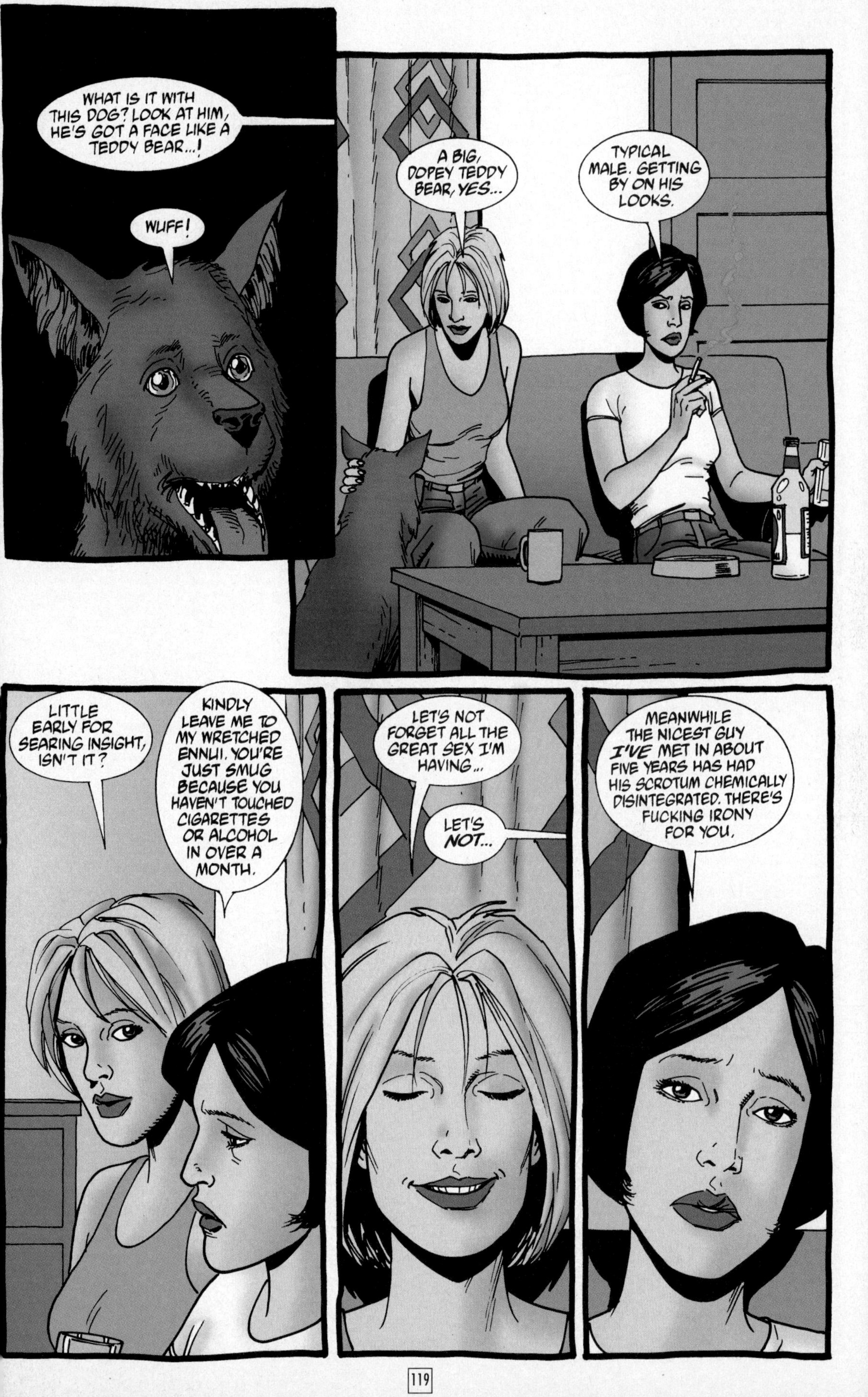
WHAT IS IT WITH THIS DOG? LOOK AT HIM, HE'S GOT A FACE LIKE A TEDDY BEAR...!
WUFF!
A BIG, DOPEY TEDDY BEAR, YES...
TYPICAL MALE. GETTING BY ON HIS LOOKS.
LITTLE EARLY FOR SEARING INSIGHT, ISN'T IT?
KINDLY LEAVE ME TO MY WRETCHED ENNUI. YOU'RE JUST SMUG BECAUSE YOU HAVEN'T TOUCHED CIGARETTES OR ALCOHOL IN OVER A MONTH.
LET'S NOT FORGET ALL THE GREAT SEX I'M HAVING...
LET'S NOT...
MEANWHILE THE NICEST GUY I'VE MET IN ABOUT FIVE YEARS HAS HAD HIS SCROTUM CHEMICALLY DISINTEGRATED. THERE'S FUCKING IRONY FOR YOU.

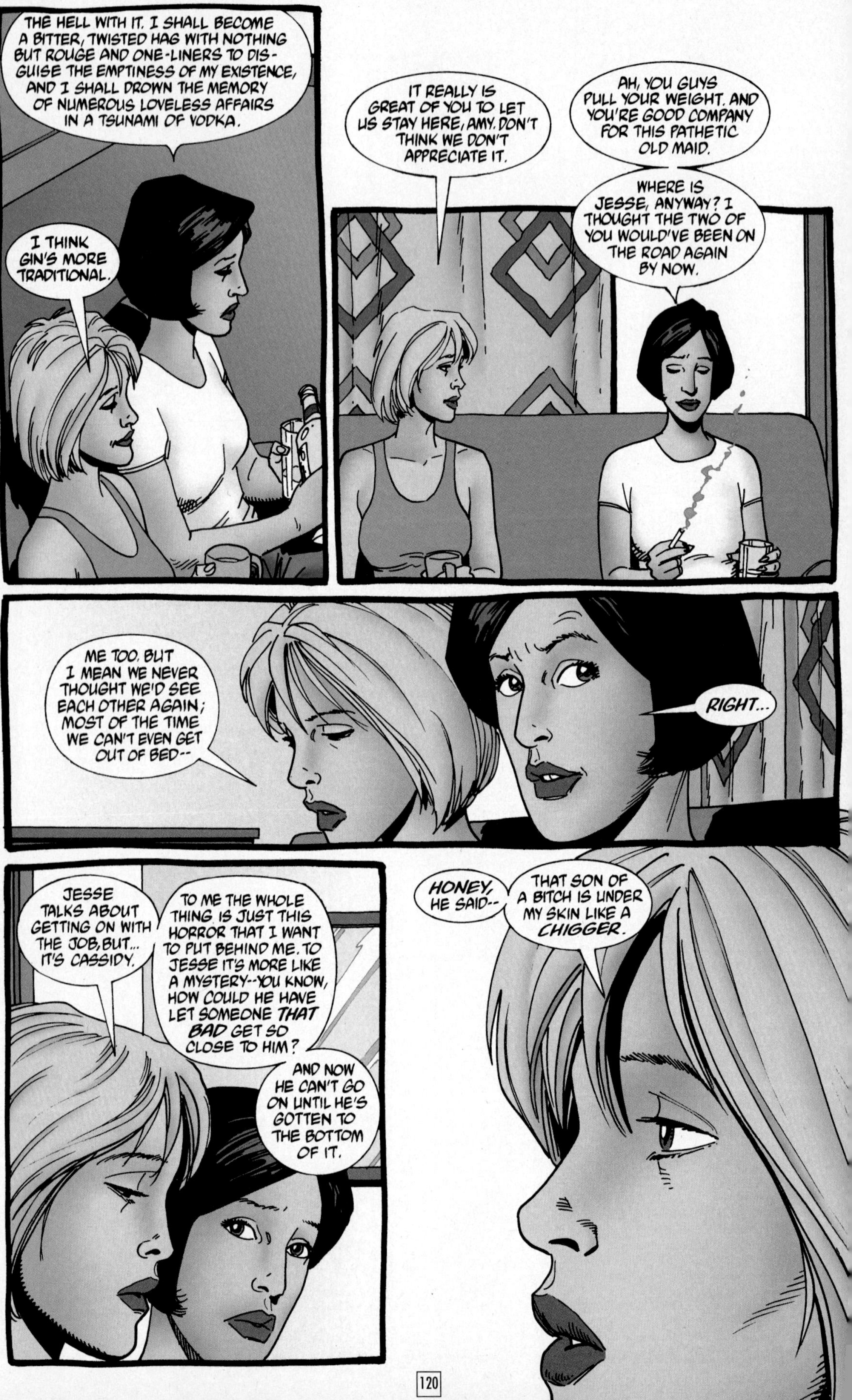
THE HELL WITH IT. I SHALL BECOME A BITTER, TWISTED HAG WITH NOTHING BUT ROUGE AND ONE-LINERS TO DISGUISE THE EMPTINESS OF MY EXISTENCE, AND I SHALL DROWN THE MEMORY OF NUMEROUS LOVELESS AFFAIRS IN A TSUNAMI OF VODKA.
I THINK GIN'S MORE TRADITIONAL.
IT REALLY IS GREAT OF YOU TO LET US STAY HERE, AMY. DON'T THINK WE DON'T APPRECIATE IT.
AH, YOU GUYS PULL YOUR WEIGHT. AND YOU'RE GOOD COMPANY FOR THIS PATHETIC OLD MAID.
WHERE IS JESSE, ANYWAY? I THOUGHT THE TWO OF YOU WOULD'VE BEEN ON THE ROAD AGAIN BY NOW.
ME TOO. BUT I MEAN WE NEVER THOUGHT WE'D SEE EACH OTHER AGAIN; MOST OF THE TIME WE CAN'T EVEN GET OUT OF BED--
RIGHT...
JESSE TALKS ABOUT GETTING ON WITH THE JOB, BUT... IT'S CASSIDY.
TO ME THE WHOLE THING IS JUST THIS HORROR THAT I WANT TO PUT BEHIND ME. TO JESSE IT'S MORE LIKE A MYSTERY--YOU KNOW, HOW COULD HE HAVE LET SOMEONE THAT BAD GET SO CLOSE TO HIM?
AND NOW HE CAN'T GO ON UNTIL HE'S GOTTEN TO THE BOTTOM OF IT.
HONEY, HE SAID--
THAT SON OF A BITCH IS UNDER MY SKIN LIKE A CHIGGER.

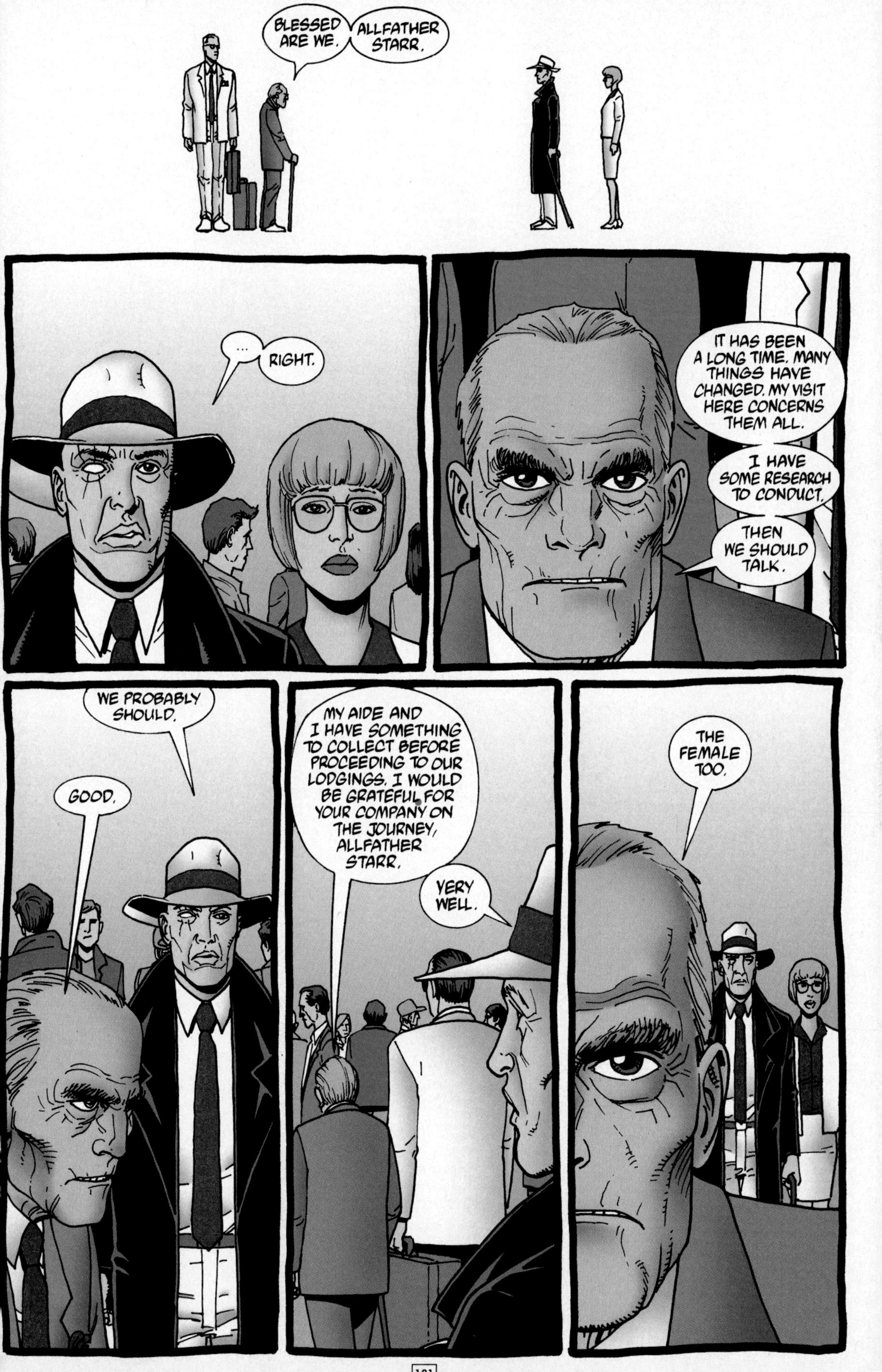
BLESSED ARE WE.
ALLFATHER STARR.
...
RIGHT.
IT HAS BEEN A LONG TIME. MANY THINGS HAVE CHANGED. MY VISIT HERE CONCERNS THEM ALL.
I HAVE SOME RESEARCH TO CONDUCT.
THEN WE SHOULD TALK.
WE PROBABLY SHOULD.
GOOD.
MY AIDE AND I HAVE SOMETHING TO COLLECT BEFORE PROCEEDING TO OUR LODGINGS. I WOULD BE GRATEFUL FOR YOUR COMPANY ON THE JOURNEY, ALLFATHER STARR.
VERY WELL.
THE FEMALE TOO.

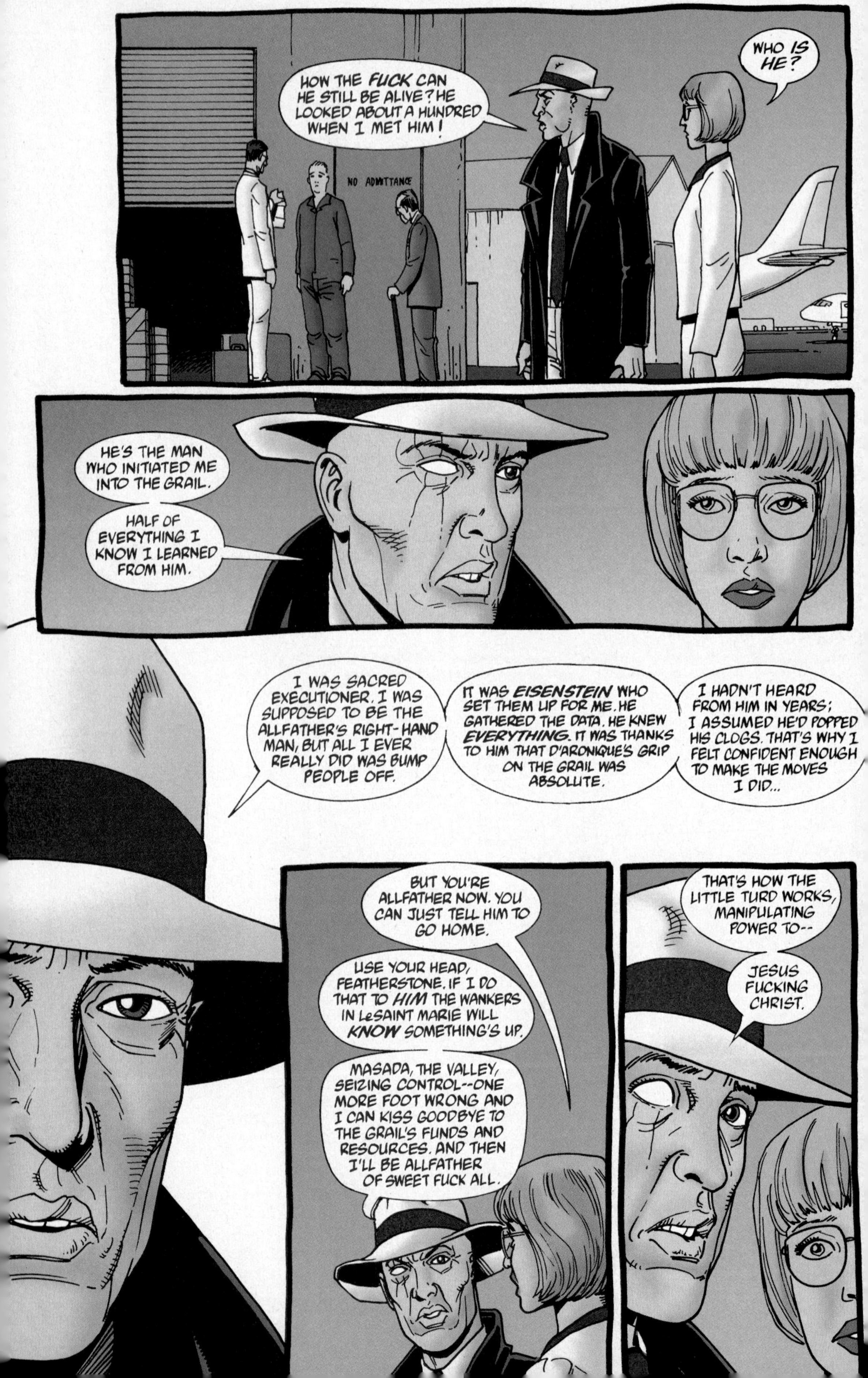
HOW THE FUCK CAN HE STILL BE ALIVE? HE LOOKED ABOUT A HUNDRED WHEN I MET HIM!
WHO IS HE?
NO ADMITTANCE
HE'S THE MAN WHO INITIATED ME INTO THE GRAIL.
HALF OF EVERYTHING I KNOW I LEARNED FROM HIM.
I WAS SACRED EXECUTIONER. I WAS SUPPOSED TO BE THE ALLFATHER'S RIGHT-HAND MAN, BUT ALL I EVER REALLY DID WAS BUMP PEOPLE OFF.
IT WAS EISENSTEIN WHO SET THEM UP FOR ME. HE GATHERED THE DATA. HE KNEW EVERYTHING. IT WAS THANKS TO HIM THAT D'ARONIQUE'S GRIP ON THE GRAIL WAS ABSOLUTE.
I HADN'T HEARD FROM HIM IN YEARS; I ASSUMED HE'D POPPED HIS CLOGS. THAT'S WHY I FELT CONFIDENT ENOUGH TO MAKE THE MOVES I DID...
BUT YOU'RE ALLFATHER NOW. YOU CAN JUST TELL HIM TO GO HOME.
USE YOUR HEAD, FEATHERSTONE. IF I DO THAT TO HIM THE WANKERS IN LeSAINT MARIE WILL KNOW SOMETHING'S UP.
MASADA, THE VALLEY, SEIZING CONTROL--ONE MORE FOOT WRONG AND I CAN KISS GOODBYE TO THE GRAIL'S FUNDS AND RESOURCES. AND THEN I'LL BE ALLFATHER OF SWEET FUCK ALL.
THAT'S HOW THE LITTLE TURD WORKS, MANIPULATING POWER TO--
JESUS FUCKING CHRIST.

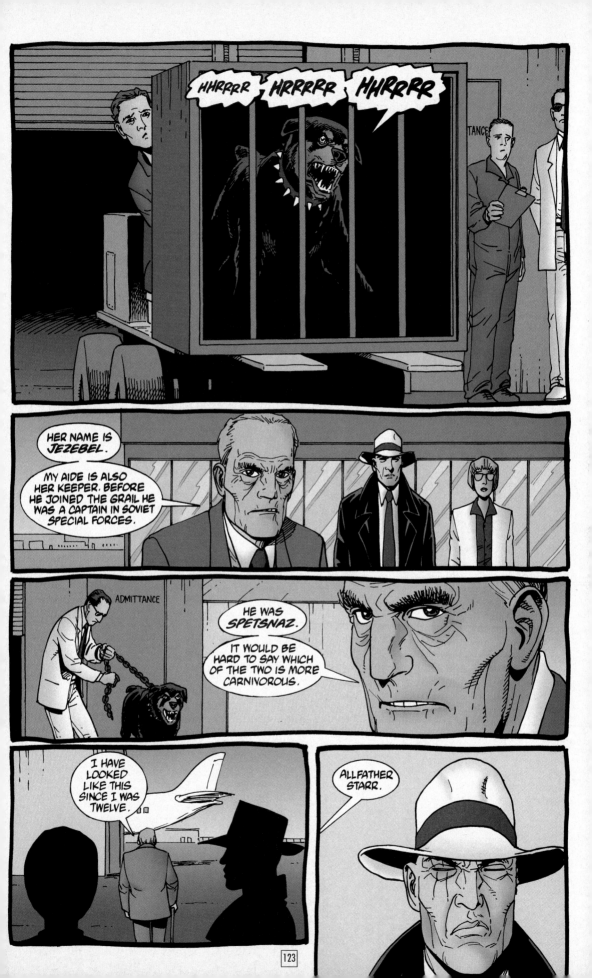

HHRRRR HRRRRR HHRRRR

TANCE

HER NAME IS JEZEBEL.

MY AIDE IS ALSO HER KEEPER. BEFORE HE JOINED THE GRAIL HE WAS A CAPTAIN IN SOVIET SPECIAL FORCES.

ADMITTANCE

HE WAS SPETSNAZ.

IT WOULD BE HARD TO SAY WHICH OF THE TWO IS MORE CARNIVOROUS.

I HAVE LOOKED LIKE THIS SINCE I WAS TWELVE.

ALLFATHER STARR.

123

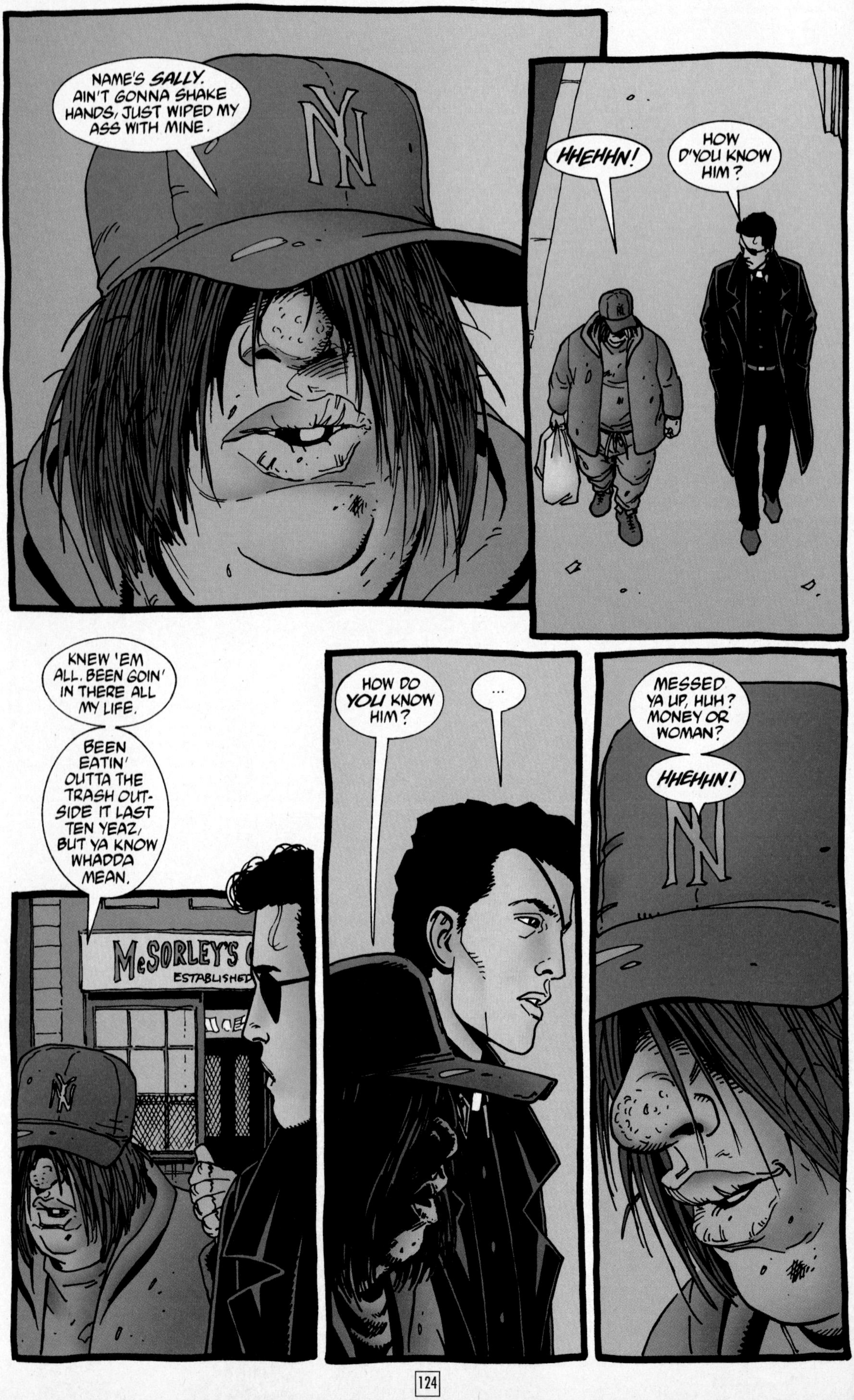
NAME'S SALLY. AIN'T GONNA SHAKE HANDS, JUST WIPED MY ASS WITH MINE.
HHEHHN!
HOW D'YOU KNOW HIM?
KNEW 'EM ALL. BEEN GOIN' IN THERE ALL MY LIFE.
BEEN EATIN' OUTTA THE TRASH OUTSIDE IT LAST TEN YEAZ, BUT YA KNOW WHADDA MEAN.
McSORLEY'S
ESTABLISHED
HOW DO YOU KNOW HIM?
...
MESSED YA UP, HUH? MONEY OR WOMAN?
HHEHHN!

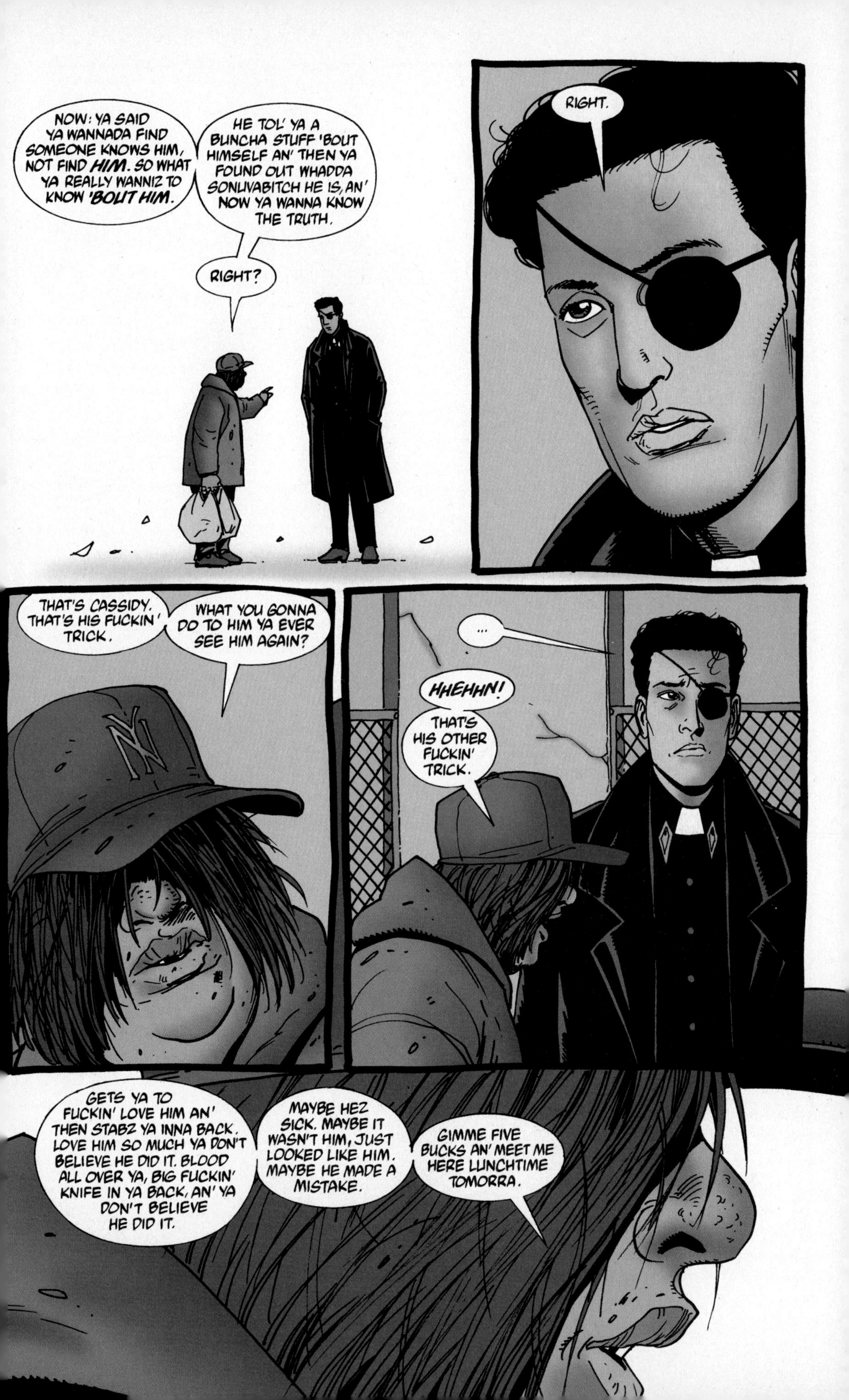
NOW: YA SAID YA WANNADA FIND SOMEONE KNOWS HIM, NOT FIND HIM. SO WHAT YA REALLY WANNIZ TO KNOW 'BOUT HIM.
HE TOL' YA A BUNCHA STUFF 'BOUT HIMSELF AN' THEN YA FOUND OUT WHADDA SONUVABITCH HE IS, AN' NOW YA WANNA KNOW THE TRUTH.
RIGHT?
RIGHT.
THAT'S CASSIDY. THAT'S HIS FUCKIN' TRICK.
WHAT YOU GONNA DO TO HIM YA EVER SEE HIM AGAIN?
...
HHEHHN!
THAT'S HIS OTHER FUCKIN' TRICK.
GETS YA TO FUCKIN' LOVE HIM AN' THEN STABZ YA INNA BACK. LOVE HIM SO MUCH YA DON'T BELIEVE HE DID IT. BLOOD ALL OVER YA, BIG FUCKIN' KNIFE IN YA BACK, AN' YA DON'T BELIEVE HE DID IT.
MAYBE HEZ SICK. MAYBE IT WASN'T HIM, JUST LOOKED LIKE HIM. MAYBE HE MADE A MISTAKE.
GIMME FIVE BUCKS AN' MEET ME HERE LUNCHTIME TOMORRA.

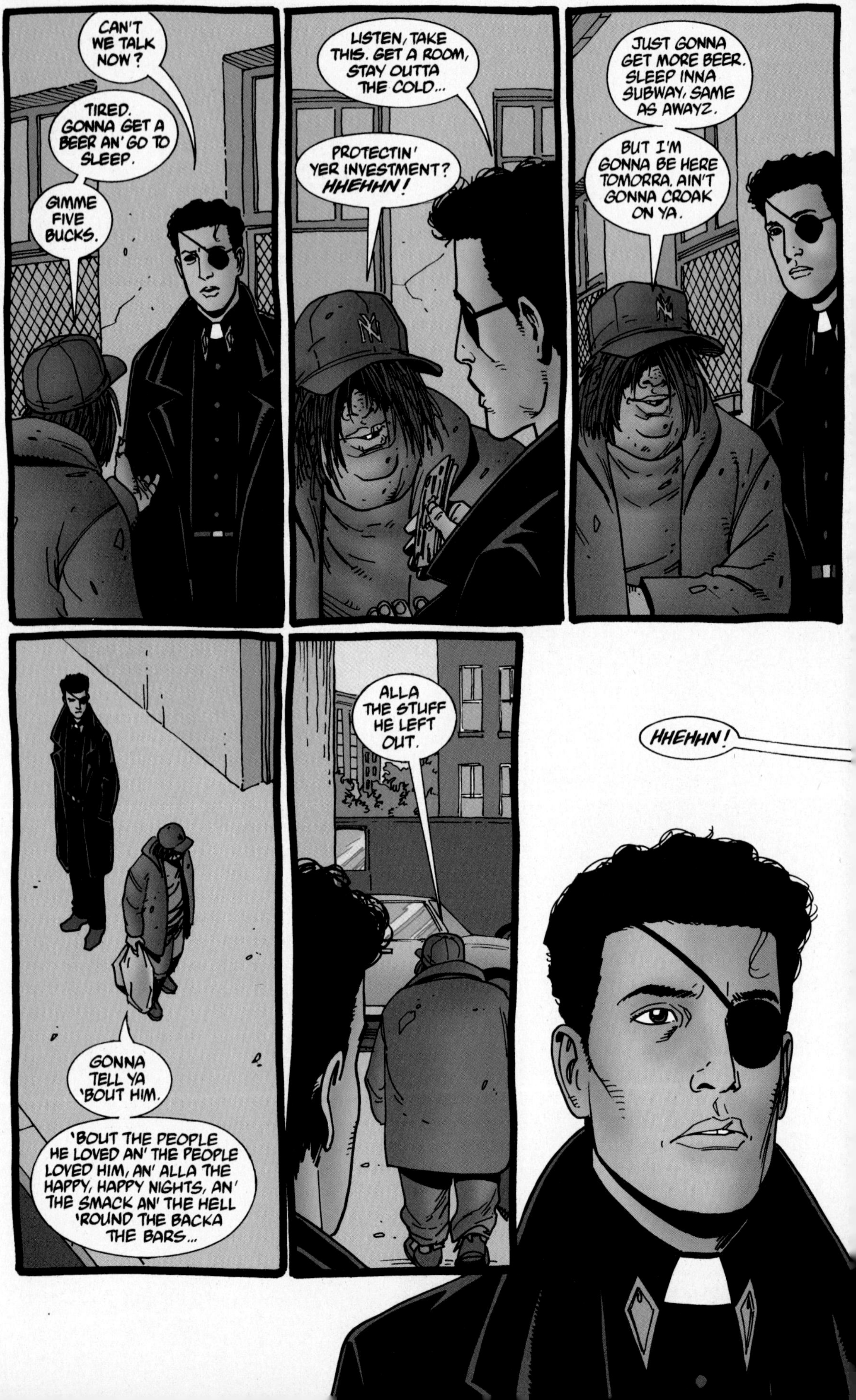
CAN'T WE TALK NOW?
TIRED. GONNA GET A BEER AN' GO TO SLEEP.
GIMME FIVE BUCKS.
LISTEN, TAKE THIS. GET A ROOM, STAY OUTTA THE COLD...
PROTECTIN' YER INVESTMENT? *HHEHHN!*
JUST GONNA GET MORE BEER. SLEEP INNA SUBWAY, SAME AS AWAYZ.
BUT I'M GONNA BE HERE TOMORRA. AIN'T GONNA CROAK ON YA.
GONNA TELL YA 'BOUT HIM.
'BOUT THE PEOPLE HE LOVED AN' THE PEOPLE LOVED HIM, AN' ALLA THE HAPPY, HAPPY NIGHTS, AN' THE SMACK AN' THE HELL 'ROUND THE BACKA THE BARS...
ALLA THE STUFF HE LEFT OUT.
HHEHHN!

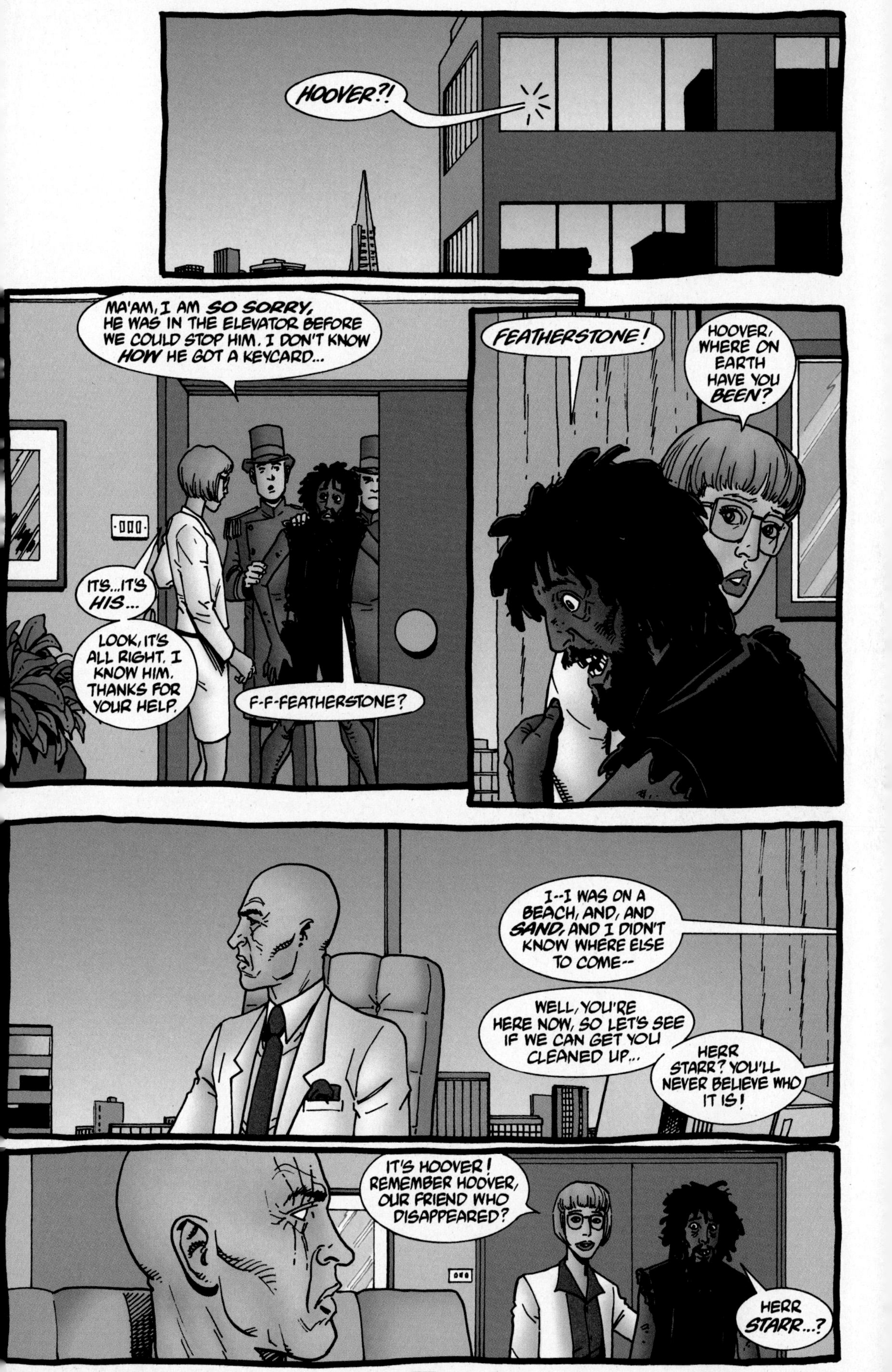
HOOVER?!
MA'AM, I AM SO SORRY, HE WAS IN THE ELEVATOR BEFORE WE COULD STOP HIM. I DON'T KNOW HOW HE GOT A KEYCARD...
IT'S...IT'S HIS...
LOOK, IT'S ALL RIGHT. I KNOW HIM. THANKS FOR YOUR HELP.
F-F-FEATHERSTONE?
FEATHERSTONE!
HOOVER, WHERE ON EARTH HAVE YOU BEEN?
I--I WAS ON A BEACH, AND, AND SAND, AND I DIDN'T KNOW WHERE ELSE TO COME--
WELL, YOU'RE HERE NOW, SO LET'S SEE IF WE CAN GET YOU CLEANED UP...
HERR STARR? YOU'LL NEVER BELIEVE WHO IT IS!
IT'S HOOVER! REMEMBER HOOVER, OUR FRIEND WHO DISAPPEARED?
HERR STARR...?

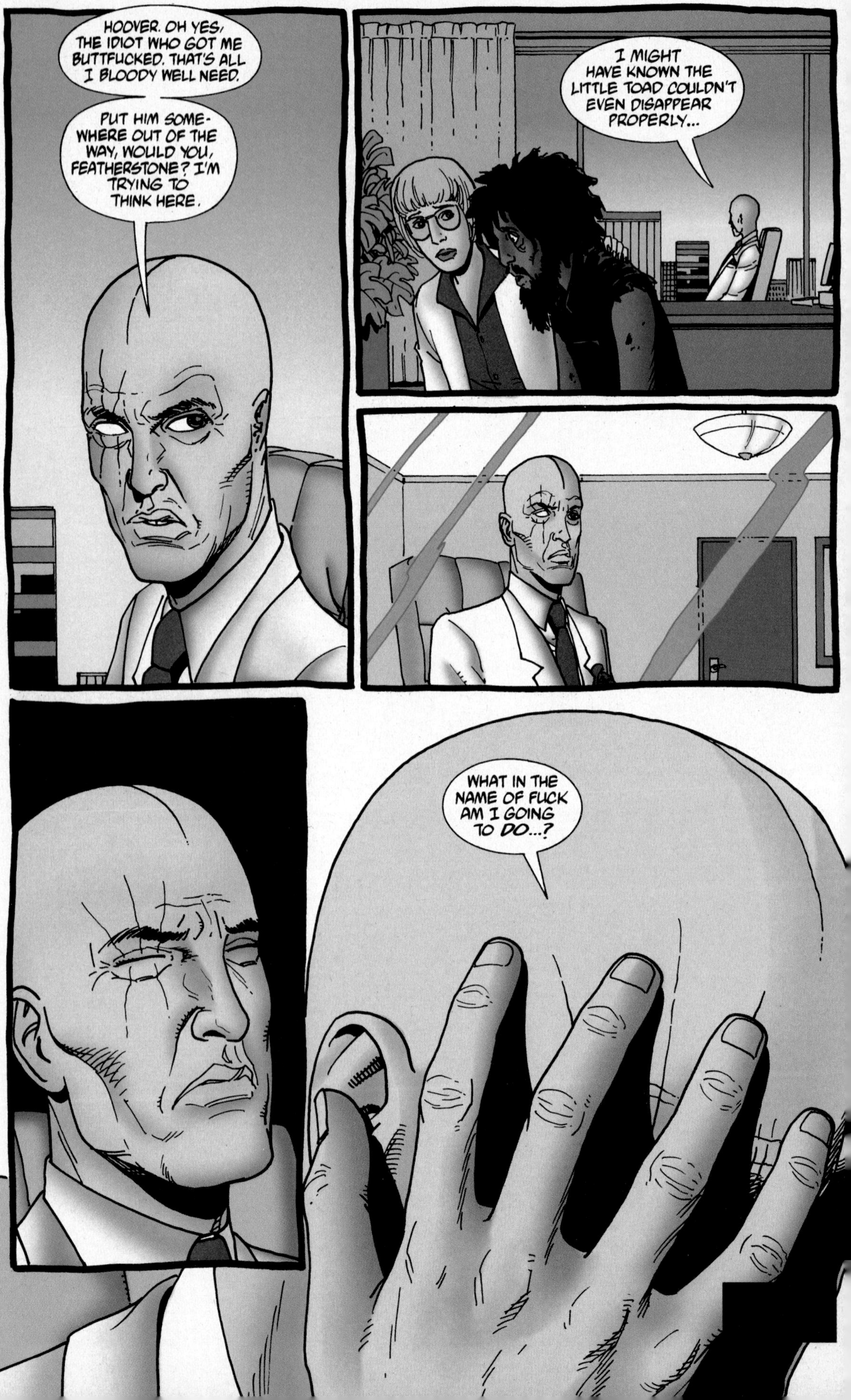
HOOVER. OH YES, THE IDIOT WHO GOT ME BUTTFUCKED. THAT'S ALL I BLOODY WELL NEED.
PUT HIM SOME-WHERE OUT OF THE WAY, WOULD YOU, FEATHERSTONE? I'M TRYING TO THINK HERE.
I MIGHT HAVE KNOWN THE LITTLE TOAD COULDN'T EVEN DISAPPEAR PROPERLY...
WHAT IN THE NAME OF FUCK AM I GOING TO *DO*...?

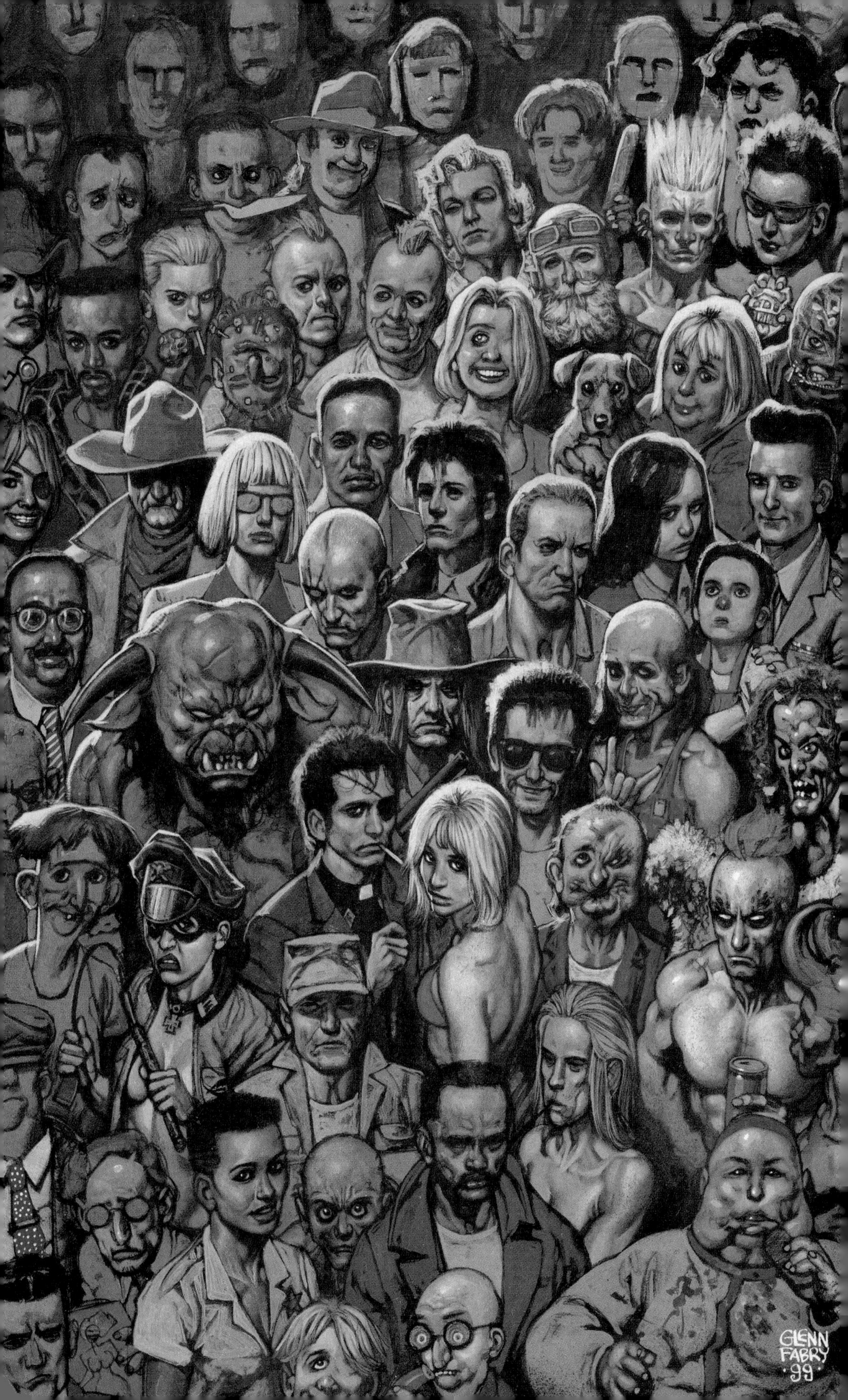
GLENN
FABRY
·99·

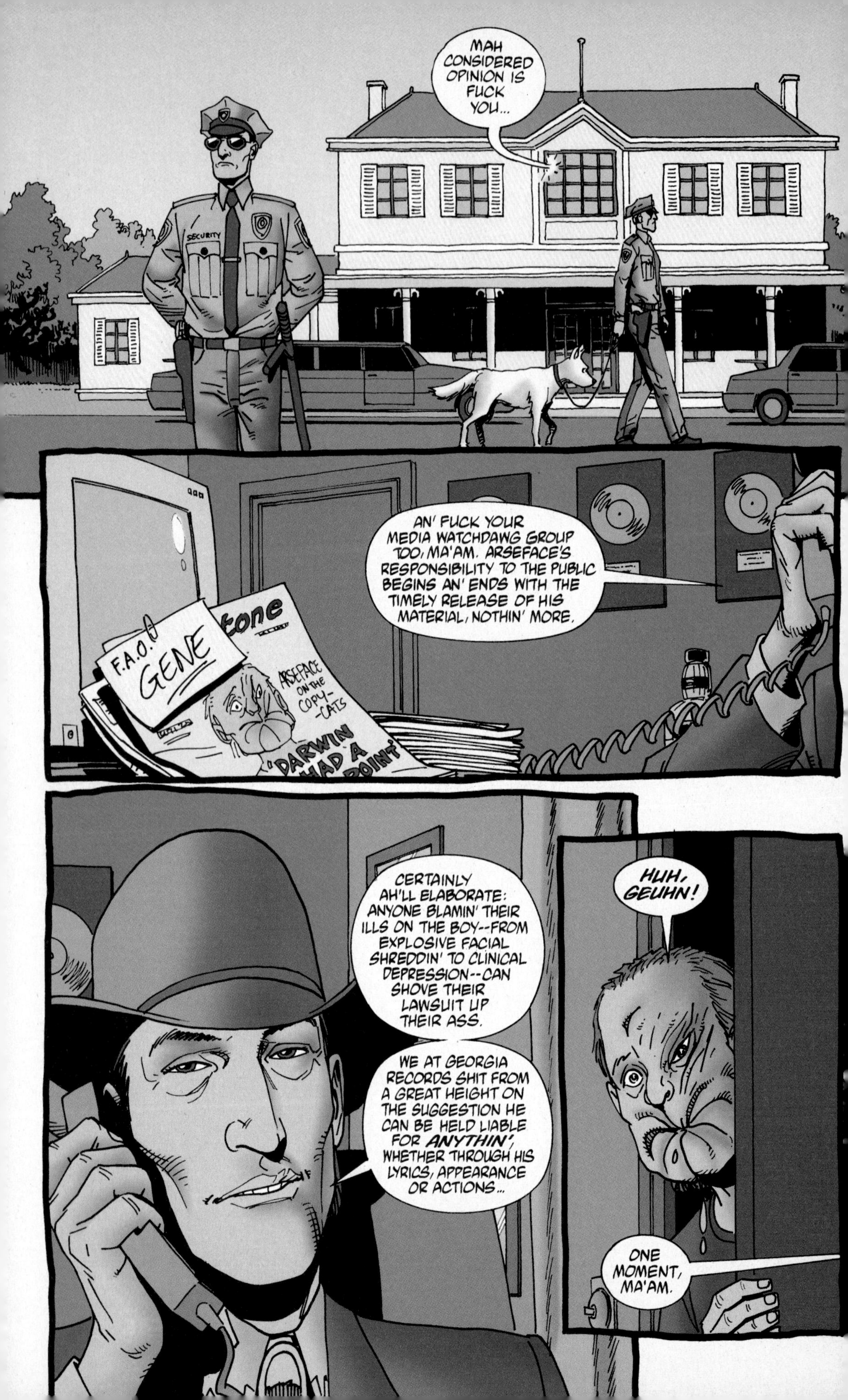
MAH CONSIDERED OPINION IS FUCK YOU...
SECURITY
AN' FUCK YOUR MEDIA WATCHDAWG GROUP TOO, MA'AM. ARSEFACE'S RESPONSIBILITY TO THE PUBLIC BEGINS AN' ENDS WITH THE TIMELY RELEASE OF HIS MATERIAL, NOTHIN' MORE.
F.A.O. GENE
tone
ARSEFACE ON THE COPY-CATS
DARWIN HAD A POINT
CERTAINLY AH'LL ELABORATE: ANYONE BLAMIN' THEIR ILLS ON THE BOY--FROM EXPLOSIVE FACIAL SHREDDIN' TO CLINICAL DEPRESSION--CAN SHOVE THEIR LAWSUIT UP THEIR ASS.
WE AT GEORGIA RECORDS SHIT FROM A GREAT HEIGHT ON THE SUGGESTION HE CAN BE HELD LIABLE FOR ***ANYTHIN'***, WHETHER THROUGH HIS LYRICS, APPEARANCE OR ACTIONS...
HUH, GEUHN!
ONE MOMENT, MA'AM.

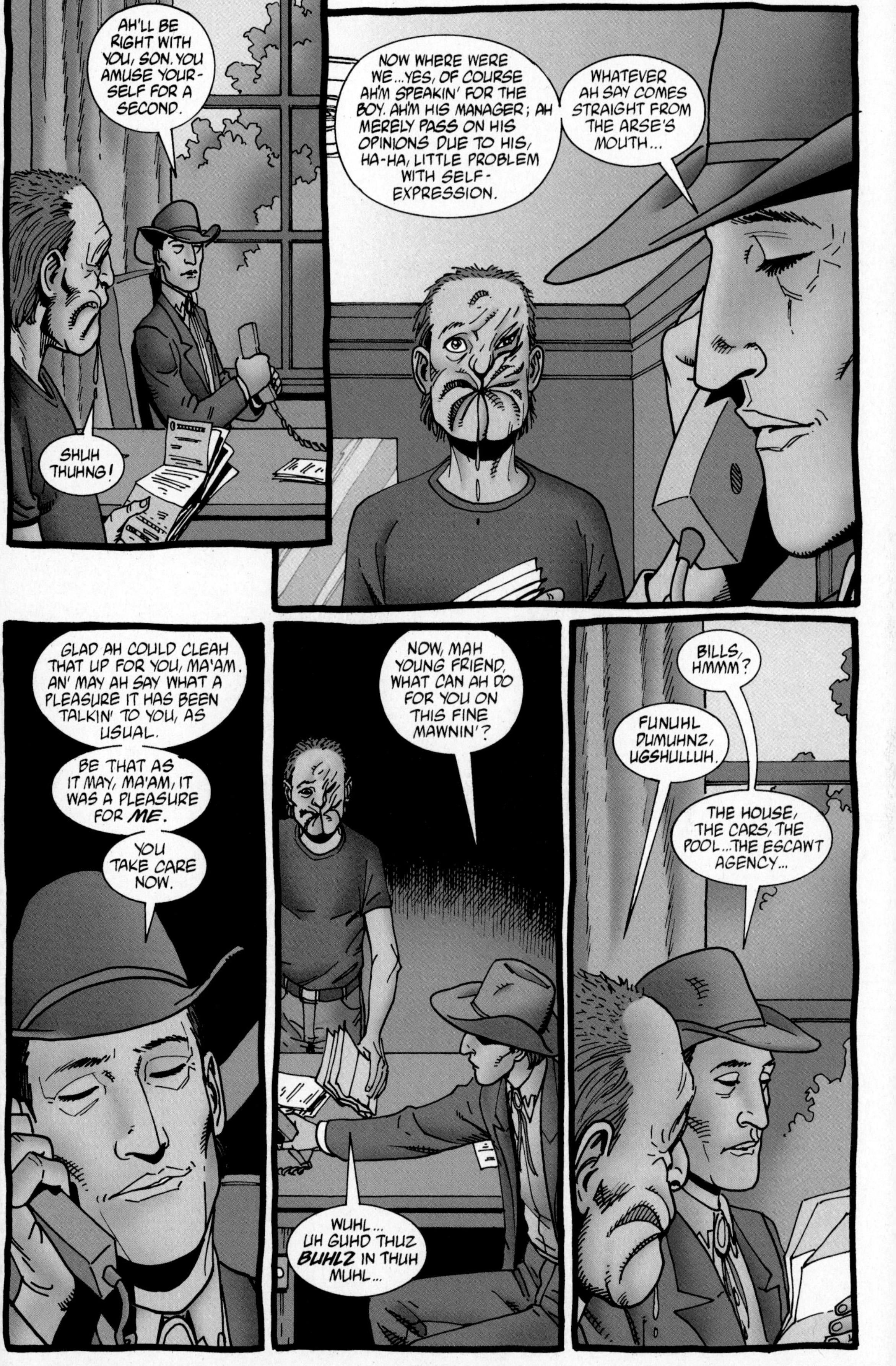
AH'LL BE RIGHT WITH YOU, SON. YOU AMUSE YOURSELF FOR A SECOND.
SHUH THUHNG!
NOW WHERE WERE WE...YES, OF COURSE AH'M SPEAKIN' FOR THE BOY. AH'M HIS MANAGER; AH MERELY PASS ON HIS OPINIONS DUE TO HIS, HA-HA, LITTLE PROBLEM WITH SELF-EXPRESSION.
WHATEVER AH SAY COMES STRAIGHT FROM THE ARSE'S MOUTH...
GLAD AH COULD CLEAH THAT UP FOR YOU, MA'AM. AN' MAY AH SAY WHAT A PLEASURE IT HAS BEEN TALKIN' TO YOU, AS USUAL.
BE THAT AS IT MAY, MA'AM, IT WAS A PLEASURE FOR ME.
YOU TAKE CARE NOW.
NOW, MAH YOUNG FRIEND, WHAT CAN AH DO FOR YOU ON THIS FINE MAWNIN'?
WUHL... UH GUHD THUZ BUHLZ IN THUH MUHL...
BILLS, HMMM?
FUNUHL DUMUHNZ, UGSHULLUH.
THE HOUSE, THE CARS, THE POOL...THE ESCAWT AGENCY...

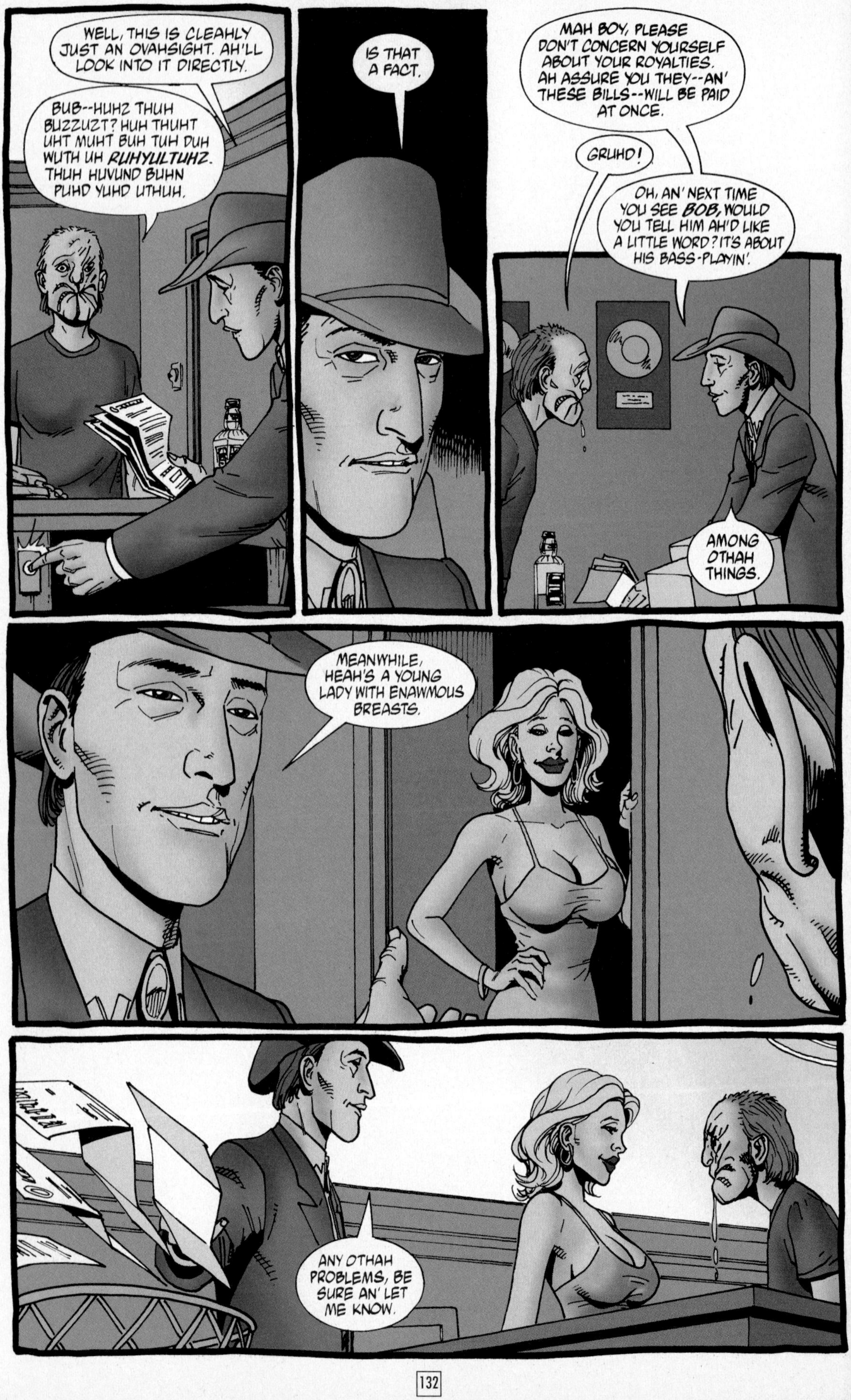
WELL, THIS IS CLEAHLY JUST AN OVAHSIGHT. AH'LL LOOK INTO IT DIRECTLY.
BUB--HUHZ THUH BUZZUZT? HUH THUHT UHT MUHT BUH TUH DUH WUTH UH RUHYULTUHZ. THUH HUVUND BUHN PUHD YUHD UTHUH.
IS THAT A FACT.
MAH BOY, PLEASE DON'T CONCERN YOURSELF ABOUT YOUR ROYALTIES. AH ASSURE YOU THEY--AN' THESE BILLS--WILL BE PAID AT ONCE.
GRUHD!
OH, AN' NEXT TIME YOU SEE BOB, WOULD YOU TELL HIM AH'D LIKE A LITTLE WORD? IT'S ABOUT HIS BASS-PLAYIN'.
AMONG OTHAH THINGS.
MEANWHILE, HEAH'S A YOUNG LADY WITH ENAWMOUS BREASTS.
ANY OTHAH PROBLEMS, BE SURE AN' LET ME KNOW.

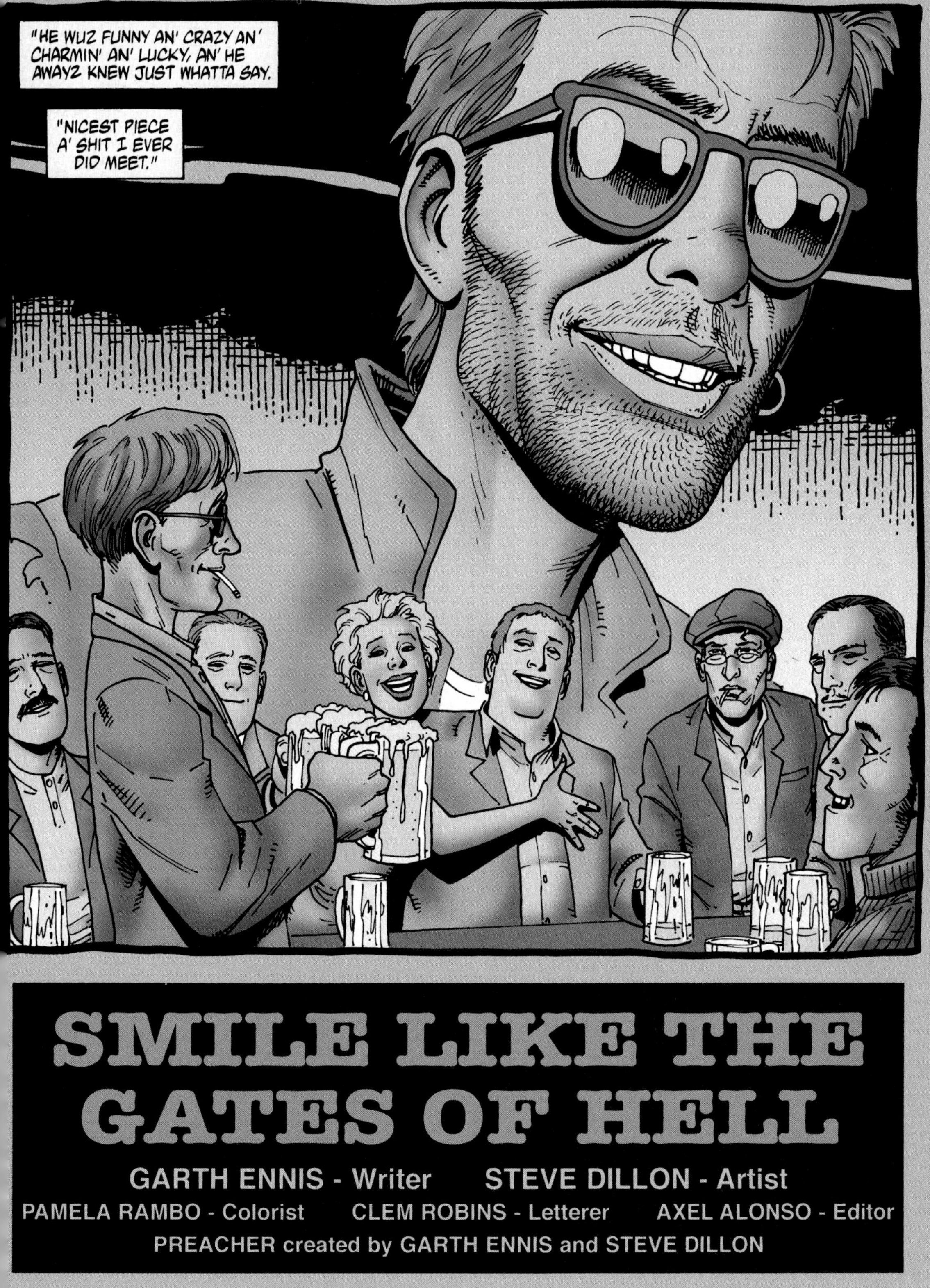
"HE WUZ FUNNY AN' CRAZY AN' CHARMIN' AN' LUCKY, AN' HE AWAYZ KNEW JUST WHATTA SAY.
"NICEST PIECE A' SHIT I EVER DID MEET."

SMILE LIKE THE GATES OF HELL

GARTH ENNIS - Writer STEVE DILLON - Artist

PAMELA RAMBO - Colorist CLEM ROBINS - Letterer AXEL ALONSO - Editor

PREACHER created by GARTH ENNIS and STEVE DILLON

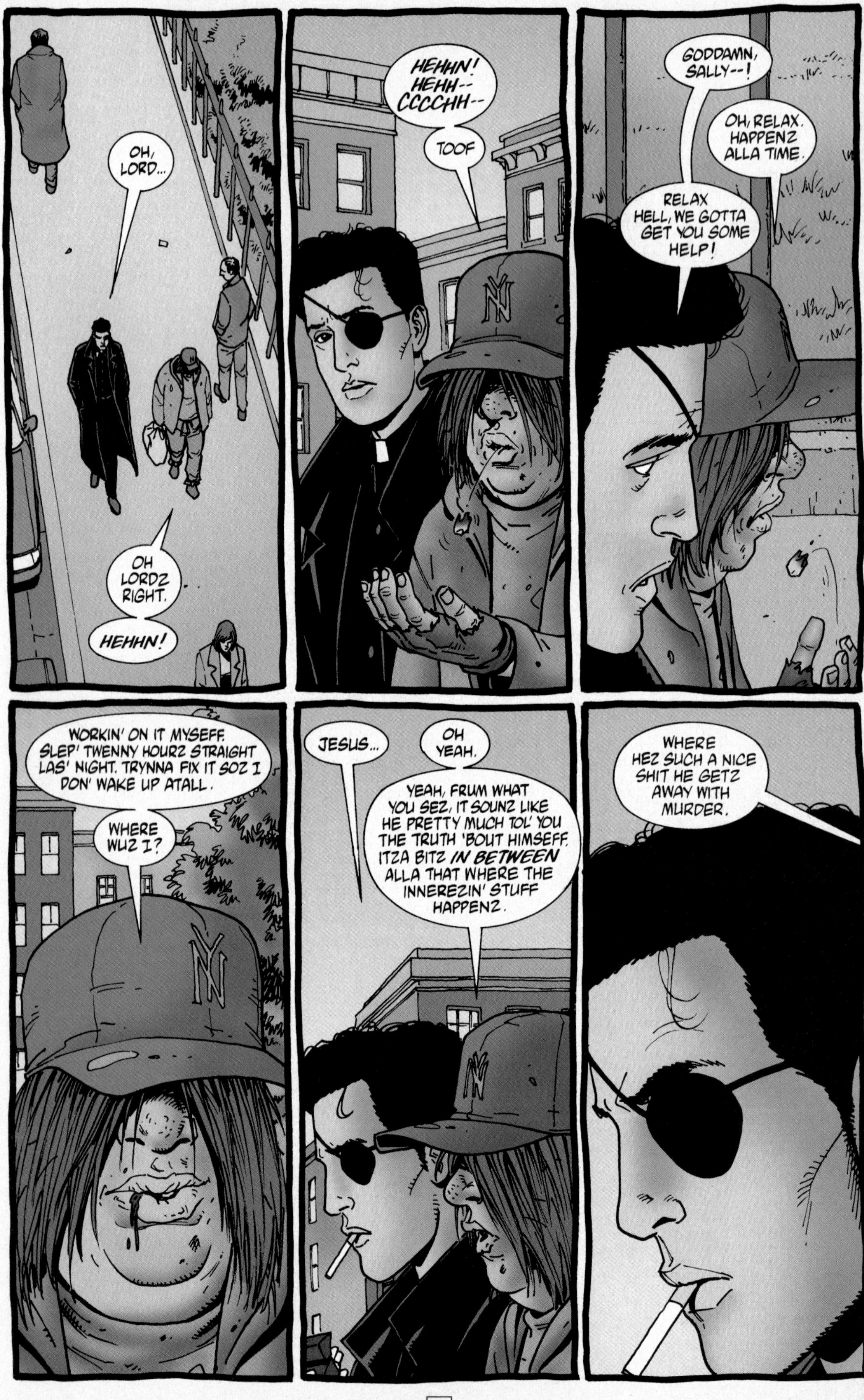
OH, LORD...
OH LORDZ RIGHT.
HEHHN!
HEHHN! HEHH-- CCCCHH--
TOOF
GODDAMN, SALLY--!
OH, RELAX. HAPPENZ ALLA TIME.
RELAX HELL, WE GOTTA GET YOU SOME HELP!
WORKIN' ON IT MYSEFF. SLEP' TWENNY HOURZ STRAIGHT LAS' NIGHT. TRYNNA FIX IT SOZ I DON' WAKE UP ATALL.
WHERE WUZ I?
JESUS...
OH YEAH.
YEAH, FRUM WHAT YOU SEZ, IT SOUNZ LIKE HE PRETTY MUCH TOL' YOU THE TRUTH 'BOUT HIMSEFF. ITZA BITZ IN BETWEEN ALLA THAT WHERE THE INNEREZIN' STUFF HAPPENZ.
WHERE HEZ SUCH A NICE SHIT HE GETZ AWAY WITH MURDER.

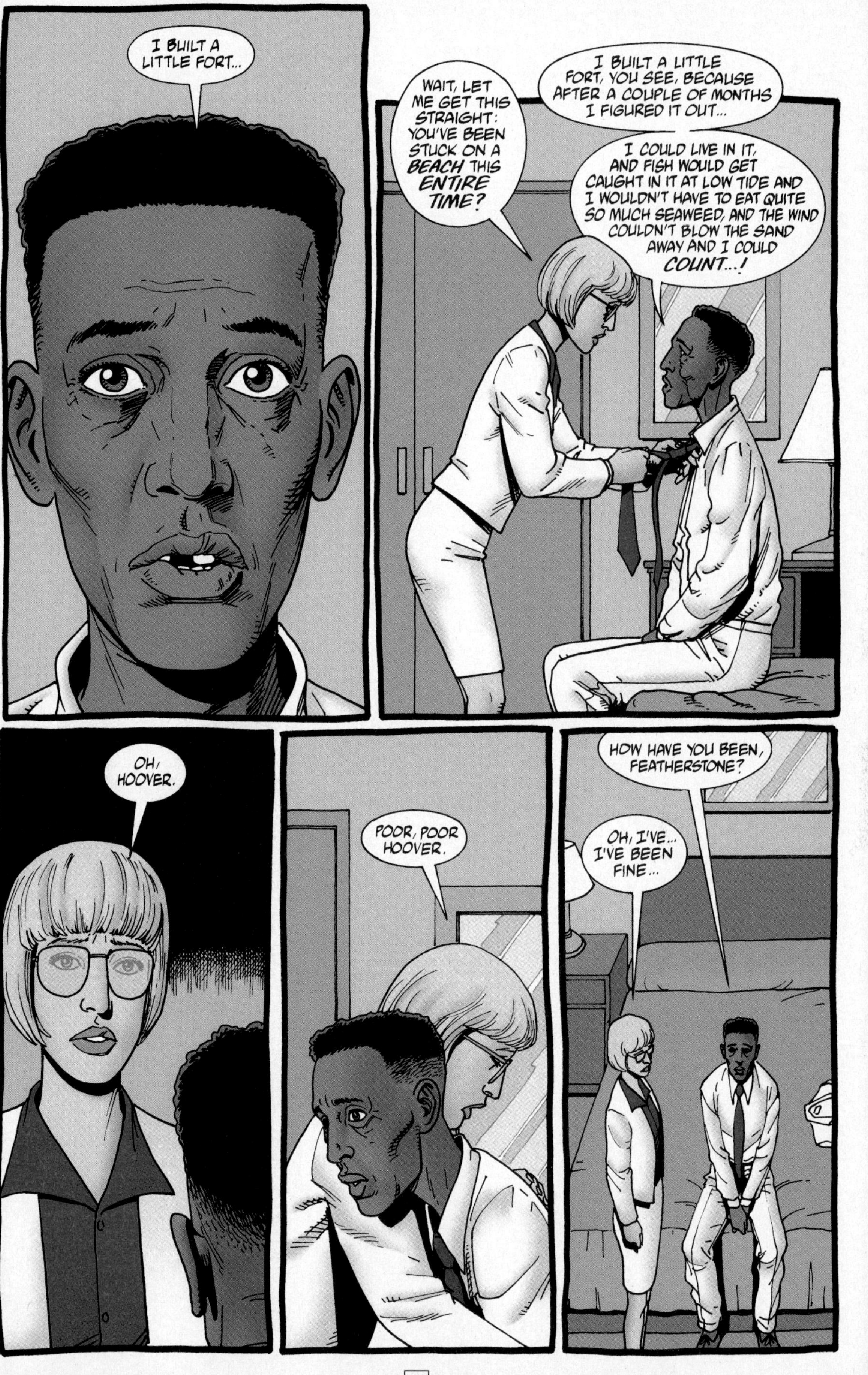
I BUILT A LITTLE FORT...
WAIT, LET ME GET THIS STRAIGHT: YOU'VE BEEN STUCK ON A BEACH THIS ENTIRE TIME?
I BUILT A LITTLE FORT, YOU SEE, BECAUSE AFTER A COUPLE OF MONTHS I FIGURED IT OUT...
I COULD LIVE IN IT, AND FISH WOULD GET CAUGHT IN IT AT LOW TIDE AND I WOULDN'T HAVE TO EAT QUITE SO MUCH SEAWEED, AND THE WIND COULDN'T BLOW THE SAND AWAY AND I COULD COUNT...!
OH, HOOVER.
POOR, POOR HOOVER.
HOW HAVE YOU BEEN, FEATHERSTONE?
OH, I'VE... I'VE BEEN FINE...

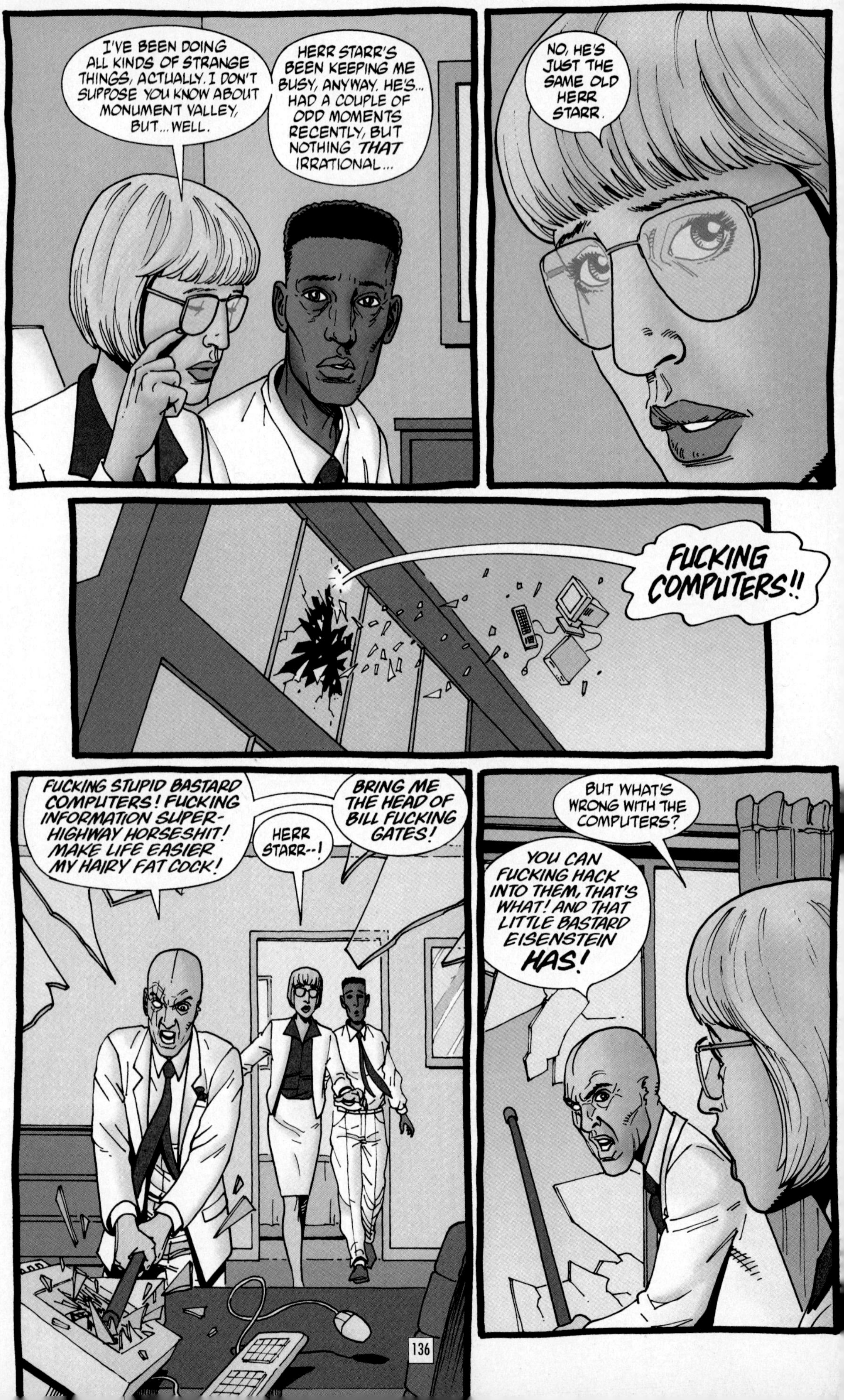
I'VE BEEN DOING ALL KINDS OF STRANGE THINGS, ACTUALLY. I DON'T SUPPOSE YOU KNOW ABOUT MONUMENT VALLEY, BUT... WELL.
HERR STARR'S BEEN KEEPING ME BUSY, ANYWAY. HE'S... HAD A COUPLE OF ODD MOMENTS RECENTLY, BUT NOTHING *THAT* IRRATIONAL...
NO, HE'S JUST THE SAME OLD HERR STARR.
FUCKING COMPUTERS!!
FUCKING STUPID BASTARD COMPUTERS! FUCKING INFORMATION SUPER-HIGHWAY HORSESHIT! MAKE LIFE EASIER MY HAIRY FAT COCK!
HERR STARR--!
BRING ME THE HEAD OF BILL FUCKING GATES!
BUT WHAT'S WRONG WITH THE COMPUTERS?
YOU CAN FUCKING HACK INTO THEM, THAT'S WHAT! AND THAT LITTLE BASTARD EISENSTEIN **HAS!**

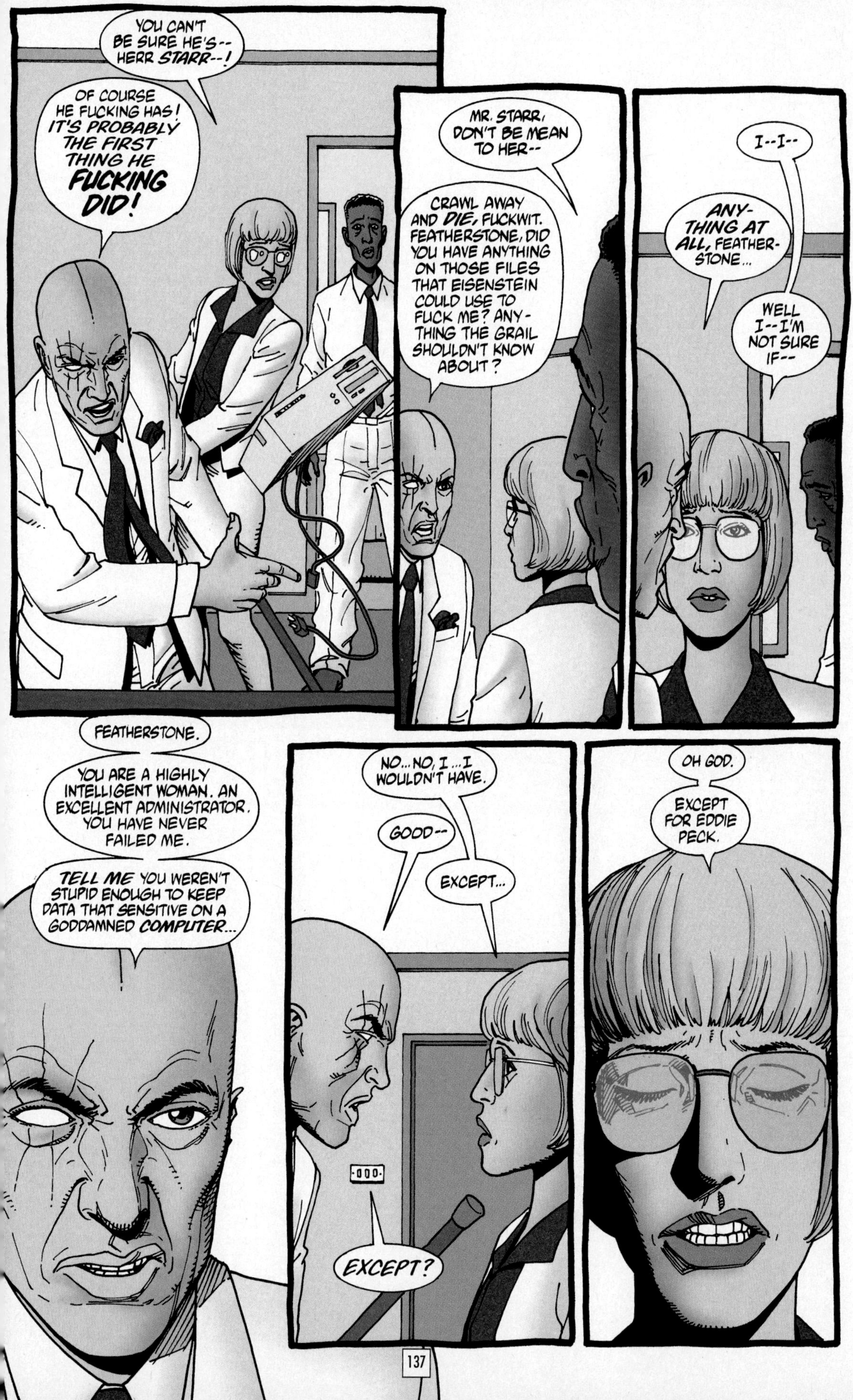

YOU CAN'T BE SURE HE'S-- HERR STARR--!
OF COURSE HE FUCKING HAS! IT'S PROBABLY THE FIRST THING HE FUCKING DID!
MR. STARR, DON'T BE MEAN TO HER--
CRAWL AWAY AND DIE, FUCKWIT. FEATHERSTONE, DID YOU HAVE ANYTHING ON THOSE FILES THAT EISENSTEIN COULD USE TO FUCK ME? ANY-THING THE GRAIL SHOULDN'T KNOW ABOUT?
I--I--
ANY-THING AT ALL, FEATHER-STONE...
WELL I--I'M NOT SURE IF--
FEATHERSTONE.
YOU ARE A HIGHLY INTELLIGENT WOMAN. AN EXCELLENT ADMINISTRATOR. YOU HAVE NEVER FAILED ME.
TELL ME YOU WEREN'T STUPID ENOUGH TO KEEP DATA THAT SENSITIVE ON A GODDAMNED COMPUTER...
NO...NO, I...I WOULDN'T HAVE.
GOOD--
EXCEPT...
EXCEPT?
OH GOD.
EXCEPT FOR EDDIE PECK.

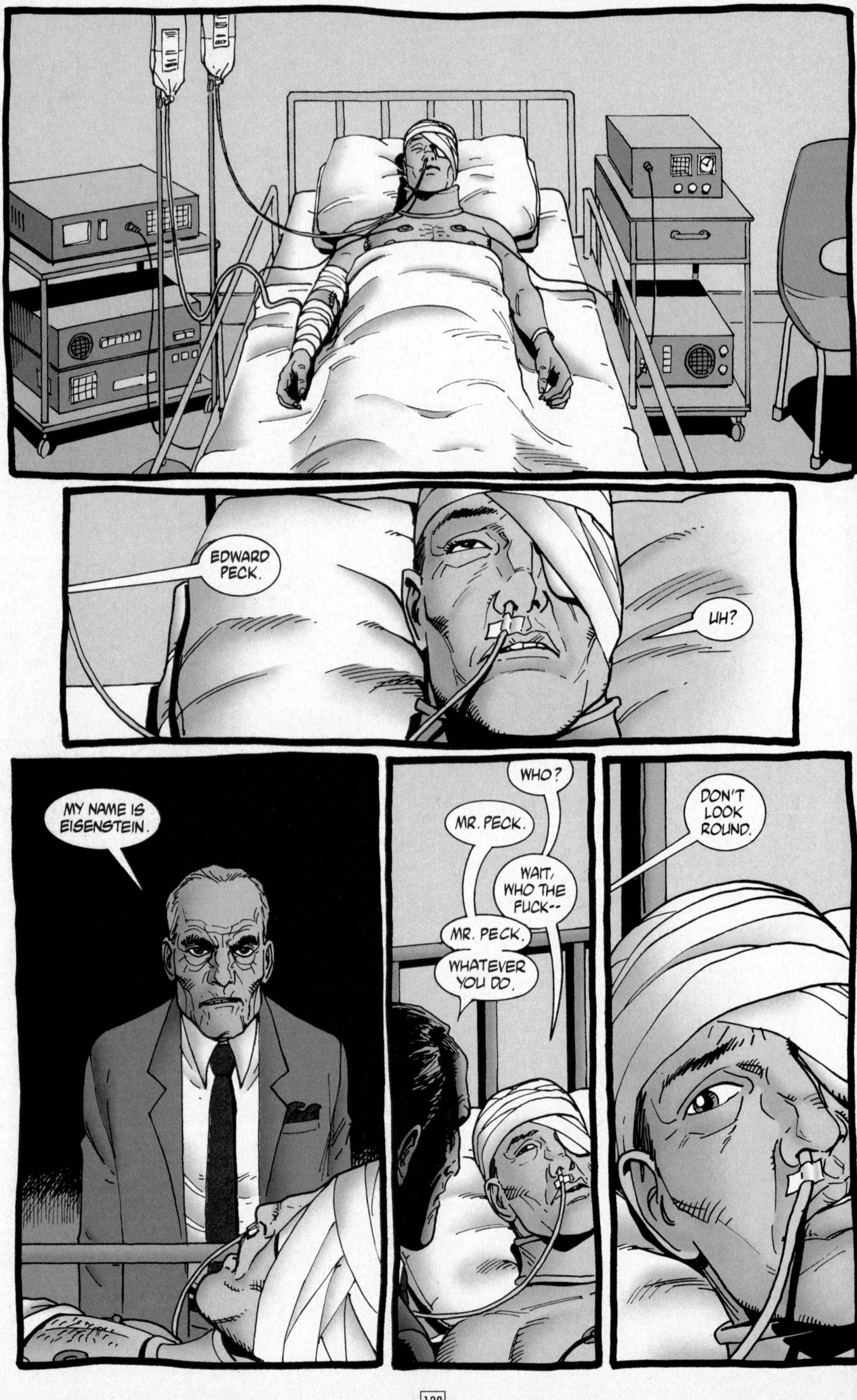
EDWARD PECK.
UH?
MY NAME IS EISENSTEIN.
WHO?
MR. PECK.
WAIT, WHO THE FUCK--
MR. PECK.
WHATEVER YOU DO.
DON'T LOOK ROUND.

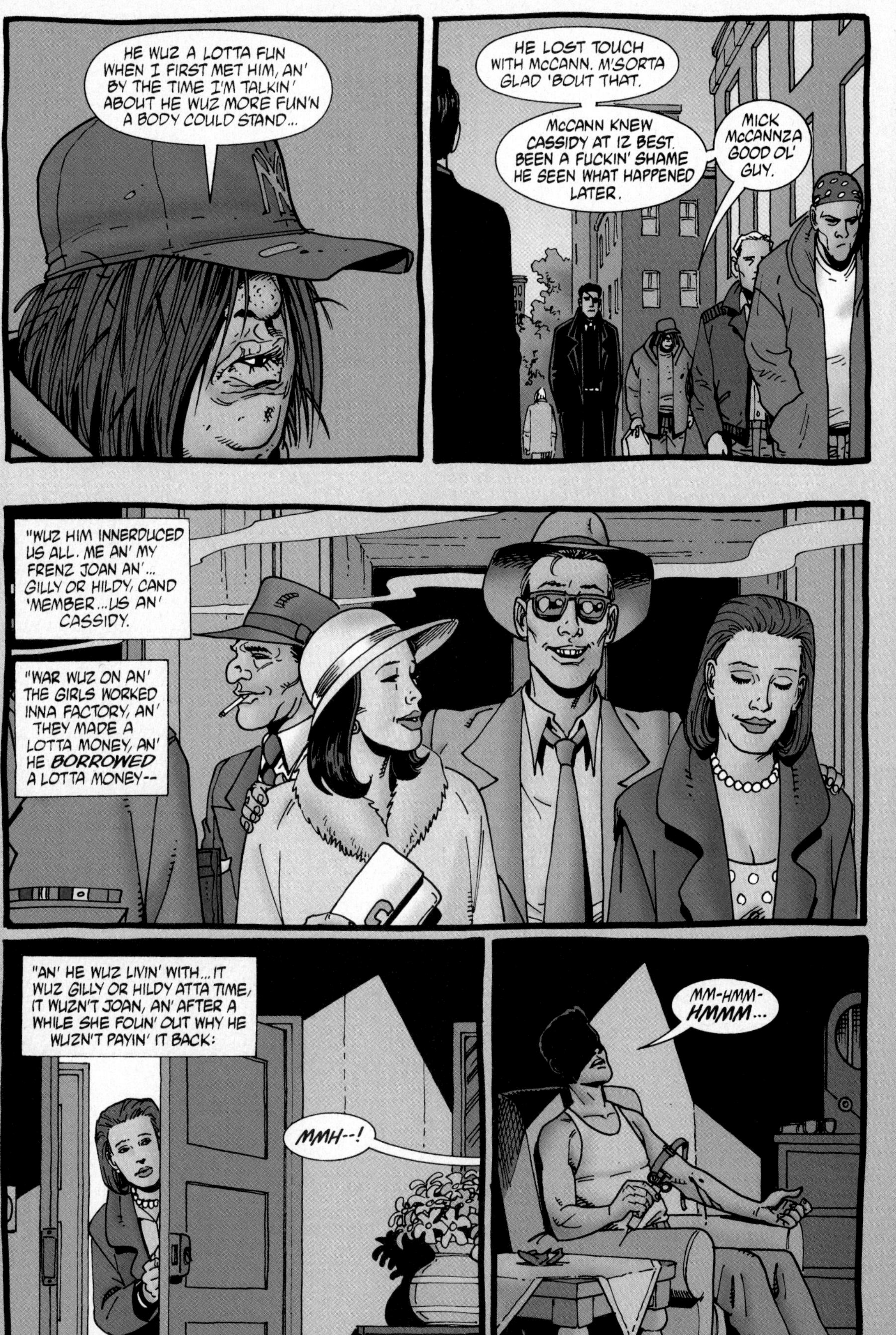
HE WUZ A LOTTA FUN WHEN I FIRST MET HIM, AN' BY THE TIME I'M TALKIN' ABOUT HE WUZ MORE FUN'N A BODY COULD STAND...
HE LOST TOUCH WITH McCANN. M'SORTA GLAD 'BOUT THAT.
McCANN KNEW CASSIDY AT IZ BEST. BEEN A FUCKIN' SHAME HE SEEN WHAT HAPPENED LATER.
MICK McCANNZA GOOD OL' GUY.
"WUZ HIM INNERDUCED US ALL. ME AN' MY FRENZ JOAN AN'... GILLY OR HILDY, CAND 'MEMBER...US AN' CASSIDY.
"WAR WUZ ON AN' THE GIRLS WORKED INNA FACTORY, AN' THEY MADE A LOTTA MONEY, AN' HE BORROWED A LOTTA MONEY--
"AN' HE WUZ LIVIN' WITH... IT WUZ GILLY OR HILDY ATTA TIME, IT WUZN'T JOAN, AN' AFTER A WHILE SHE FOUN' OUT WHY HE WUZN'T PAYIN' IT BACK:
MMH--!
MM-HMM-HMMM...

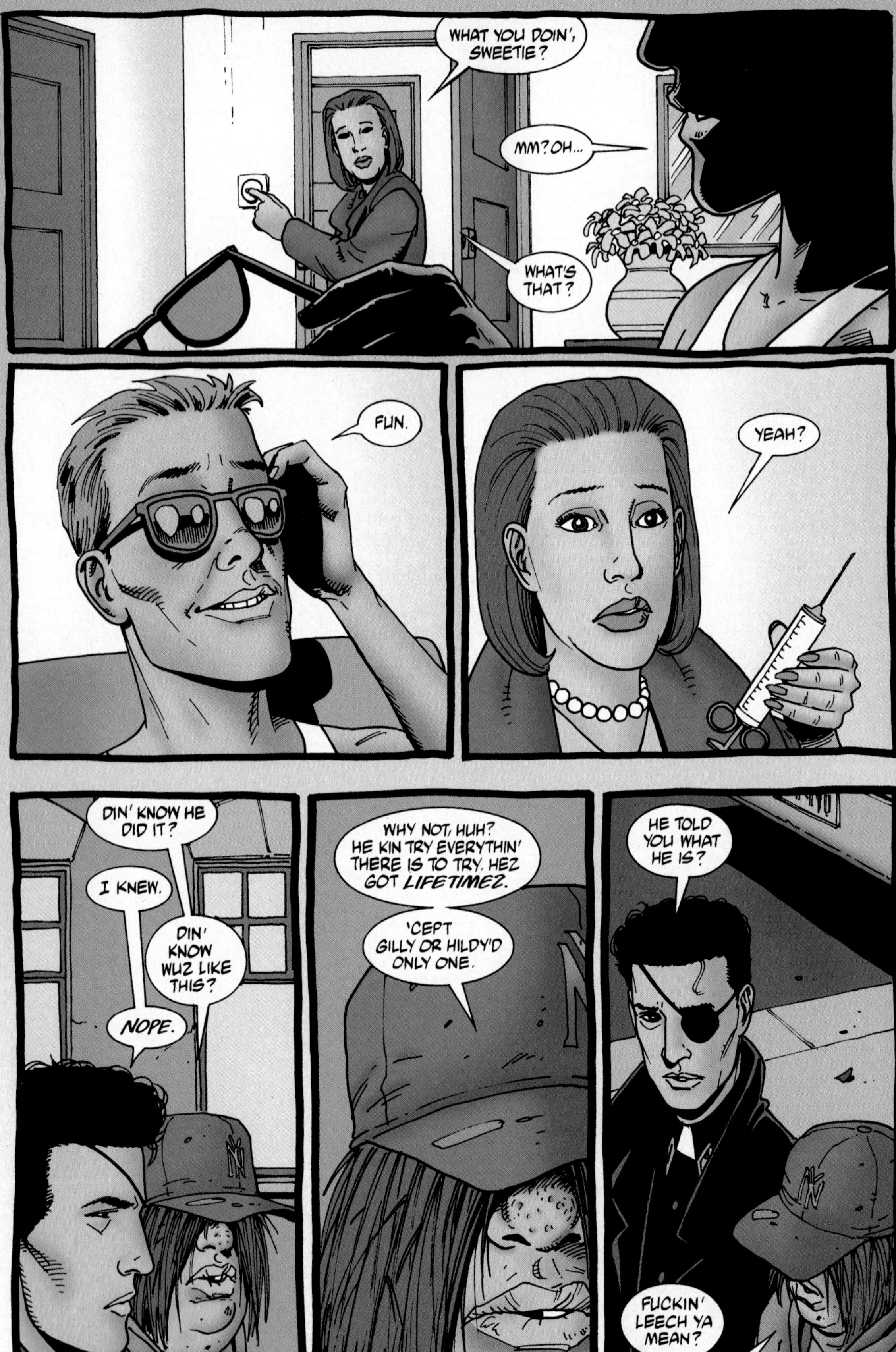
WHAT YOU DOIN', SWEETIE?
MM? OH...
WHAT'S THAT?
FUN.
YEAH?
DIN' KNOW HE DID IT?
I KNEW.
DIN' KNOW WUZ LIKE THIS?
NOPE.
WHY NOT, HUH? HE KIN TRY EVERYTHIN' THERE IS TO TRY. HEZ GOT LIFETIMEZ.
'CEPT GILLY OR HILDY'D ONLY ONE.
HE TOLD YOU WHAT HE IS?
FUCKIN' LEECH YA MEAN?
HEHHNN!

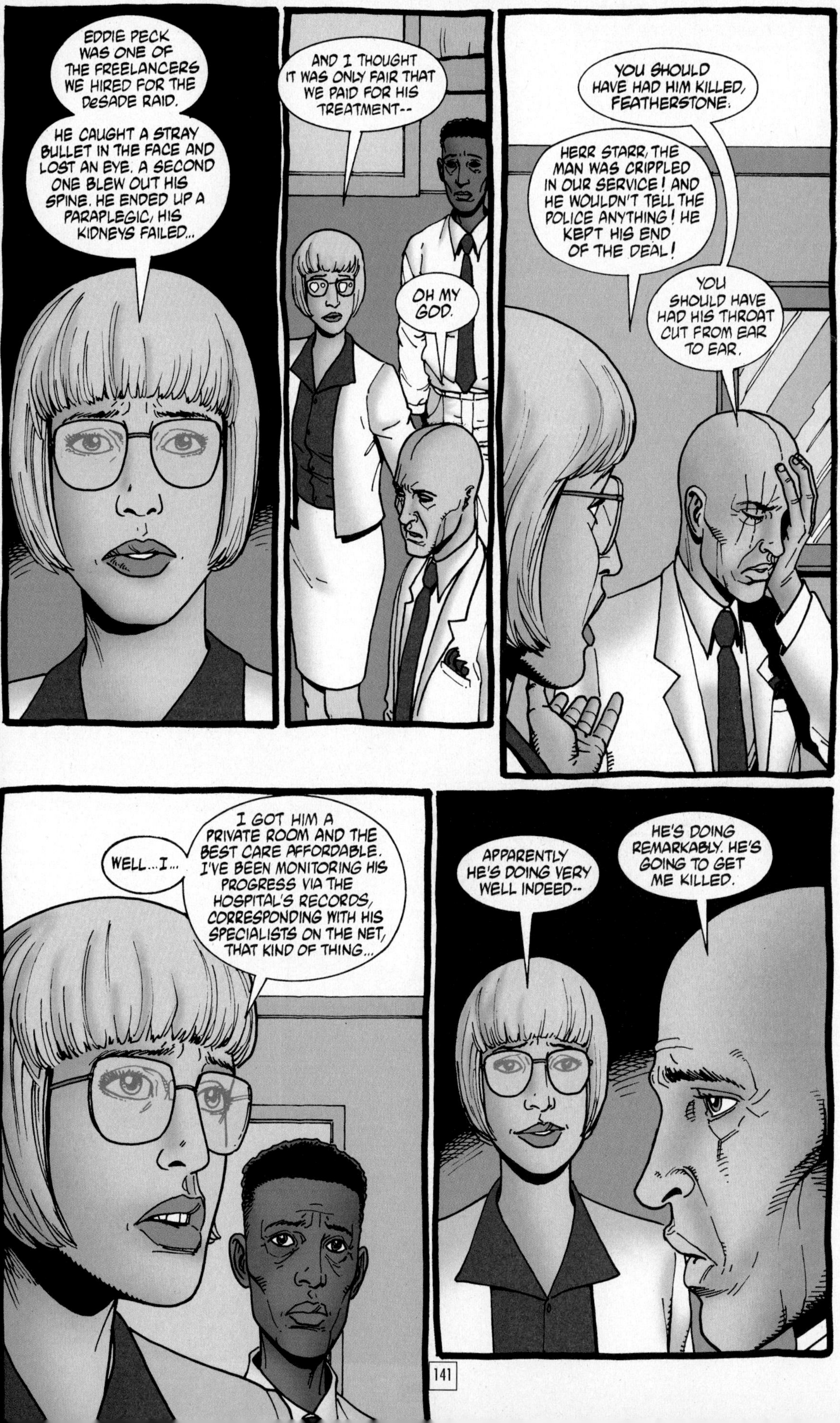
EDDIE PECK WAS ONE OF THE FREELANCERS WE HIRED FOR THE DeSADE RAID.
HE CAUGHT A STRAY BULLET IN THE FACE AND LOST AN EYE. A SECOND ONE BLEW OUT HIS SPINE. HE ENDED UP A PARAPLEGIC, HIS KIDNEYS FAILED...
AND I THOUGHT IT WAS ONLY FAIR THAT WE PAID FOR HIS TREATMENT--
OH MY GOD.
YOU SHOULD HAVE HAD HIM KILLED, FEATHERSTONE.
HERR STARR, THE MAN WAS CRIPPLED IN OUR SERVICE! AND HE WOULDN'T TELL THE POLICE ANYTHING! HE KEPT HIS END OF THE DEAL!
YOU SHOULD HAVE HAD HIS THROAT CUT FROM EAR TO EAR.
WELL...I...
I GOT HIM A PRIVATE ROOM AND THE BEST CARE AFFORDABLE. I'VE BEEN MONITORING HIS PROGRESS VIA THE HOSPITAL'S RECORDS, CORRESPONDING WITH HIS SPECIALISTS ON THE NET, THAT KIND OF THING...
APPARENTLY HE'S DOING VERY WELL INDEED--
HE'S DOING REMARKABLY. HE'S GOING TO GET ME KILLED.

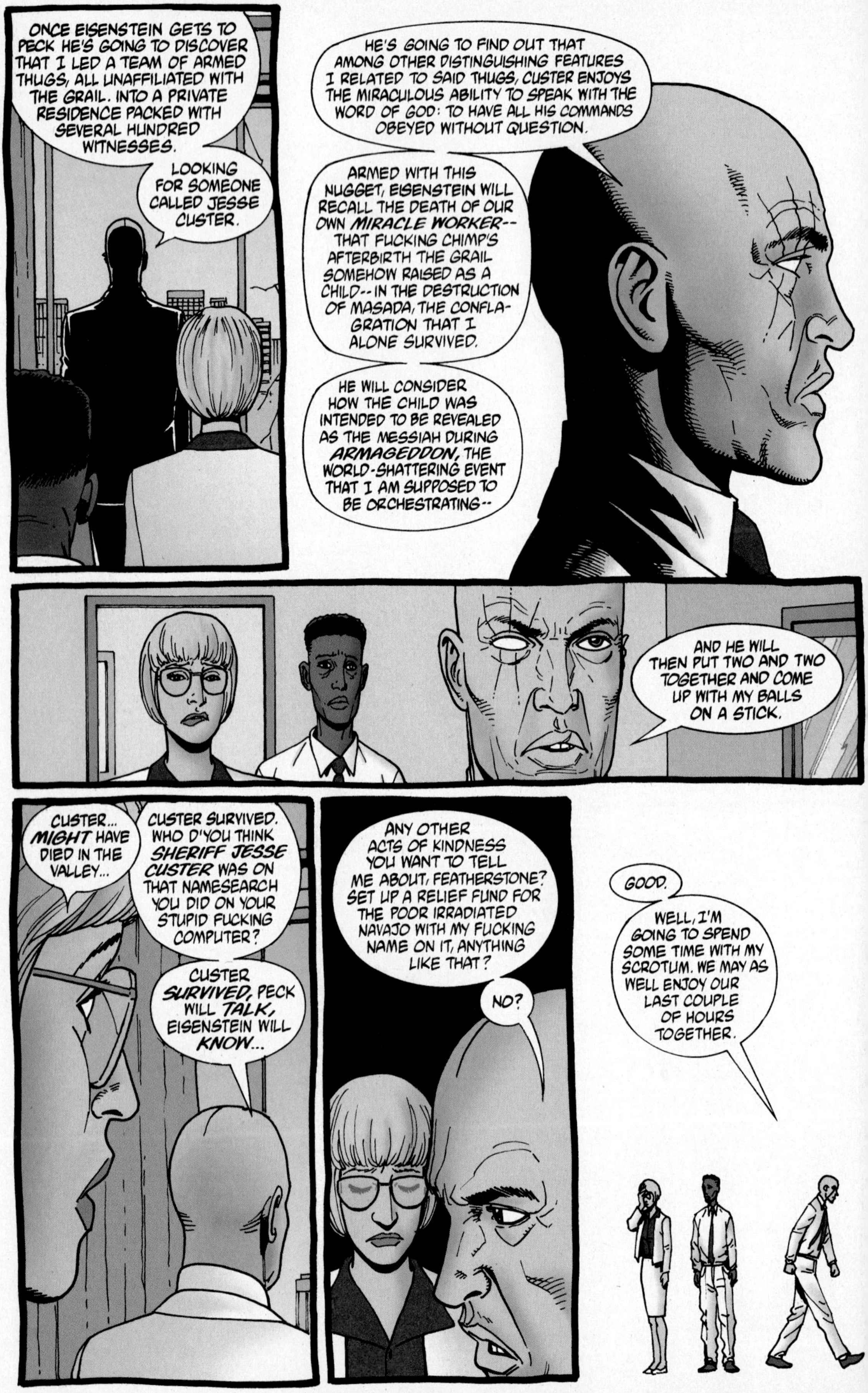
ONCE EISENSTEIN GETS TO PECK HE'S GOING TO DISCOVER THAT I LED A TEAM OF ARMED THUGS, ALL UNAFFILIATED WITH THE GRAIL, INTO A PRIVATE RESIDENCE PACKED WITH SEVERAL HUNDRED WITNESSES.
LOOKING FOR SOMEONE CALLED JESSE CUSTER.
HE'S GOING TO FIND OUT THAT AMONG OTHER DISTINGUISHING FEATURES I RELATED TO SAID THUGS, CUSTER ENJOYS THE MIRACULOUS ABILITY TO SPEAK WITH THE WORD OF GOD: TO HAVE ALL HIS COMMANDS OBEYED WITHOUT QUESTION.
ARMED WITH THIS NUGGET, EISENSTEIN WILL RECALL THE DEATH OF OUR OWN MIRACLE WORKER-- THAT FUCKING CHIMP'S AFTERBIRTH THE GRAIL SOMEHOW RAISED AS A CHILD--IN THE DESTRUCTION OF MASADA, THE CONFLAGRATION THAT I ALONE SURVIVED.
HE WILL CONSIDER HOW THE CHILD WAS INTENDED TO BE REVEALED AS THE MESSIAH DURING ARMAGEDDON, THE WORLD-SHATTERING EVENT THAT I AM SUPPOSED TO BE ORCHESTRATING--
AND HE WILL THEN PUT TWO AND TWO TOGETHER AND COME UP WITH MY BALLS ON A STICK.
CUSTER... MIGHT HAVE DIED IN THE VALLEY...
CUSTER SURVIVED. WHO D'YOU THINK SHERIFF JESSE CUSTER WAS ON THAT NAMESEARCH YOU DID ON YOUR STUPID FUCKING COMPUTER?
CUSTER SURVIVED, PECK WILL TALK, EISENSTEIN WILL KNOW...
ANY OTHER ACTS OF KINDNESS YOU WANT TO TELL ME ABOUT, FEATHERSTONE? SET UP A RELIEF FUND FOR THE POOR IRRADIATED NAVAJO WITH MY FUCKING NAME ON IT, ANYTHING LIKE THAT?
NO?
GOOD.
WELL, I'M GOING TO SPEND SOME TIME WITH MY SCROTUM. WE MAY AS WELL ENJOY OUR LAST COUPLE OF HOURS TOGETHER.

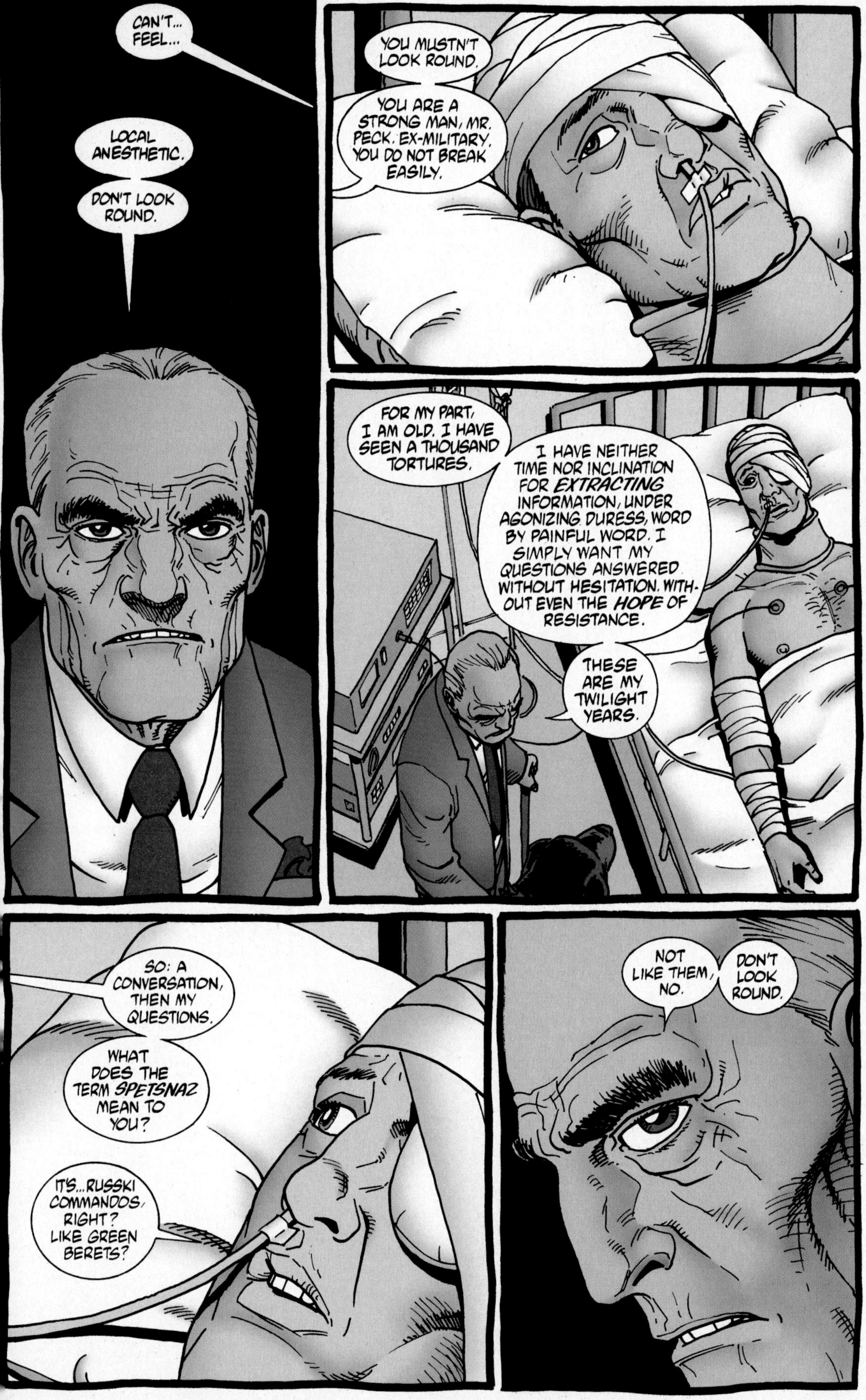
CAN'T... FEEL...
LOCAL ANESTHETIC.
DON'T LOOK ROUND.
YOU MUSTN'T LOOK ROUND.
YOU ARE A STRONG MAN, MR. PECK. EX-MILITARY. YOU DO NOT BREAK EASILY.
FOR MY PART, I AM OLD. I HAVE SEEN A THOUSAND TORTURES.
I HAVE NEITHER TIME NOR INCLINATION FOR *EXTRACTING* INFORMATION, UNDER AGONIZING DURESS, WORD BY PAINFUL WORD. I SIMPLY WANT MY QUESTIONS ANSWERED WITHOUT HESITATION. WITHOUT EVEN THE *HOPE* OF RESISTANCE.
THESE ARE MY TWILIGHT YEARS.
SO: A CONVERSATION, THEN MY QUESTIONS.
WHAT DOES THE TERM *SPETSNAZ* MEAN TO YOU?
IT'S...RUSSKI COMMANDOS, RIGHT? LIKE GREEN BERETS?
NOT LIKE THEM, NO.
DON'T LOOK ROUND.

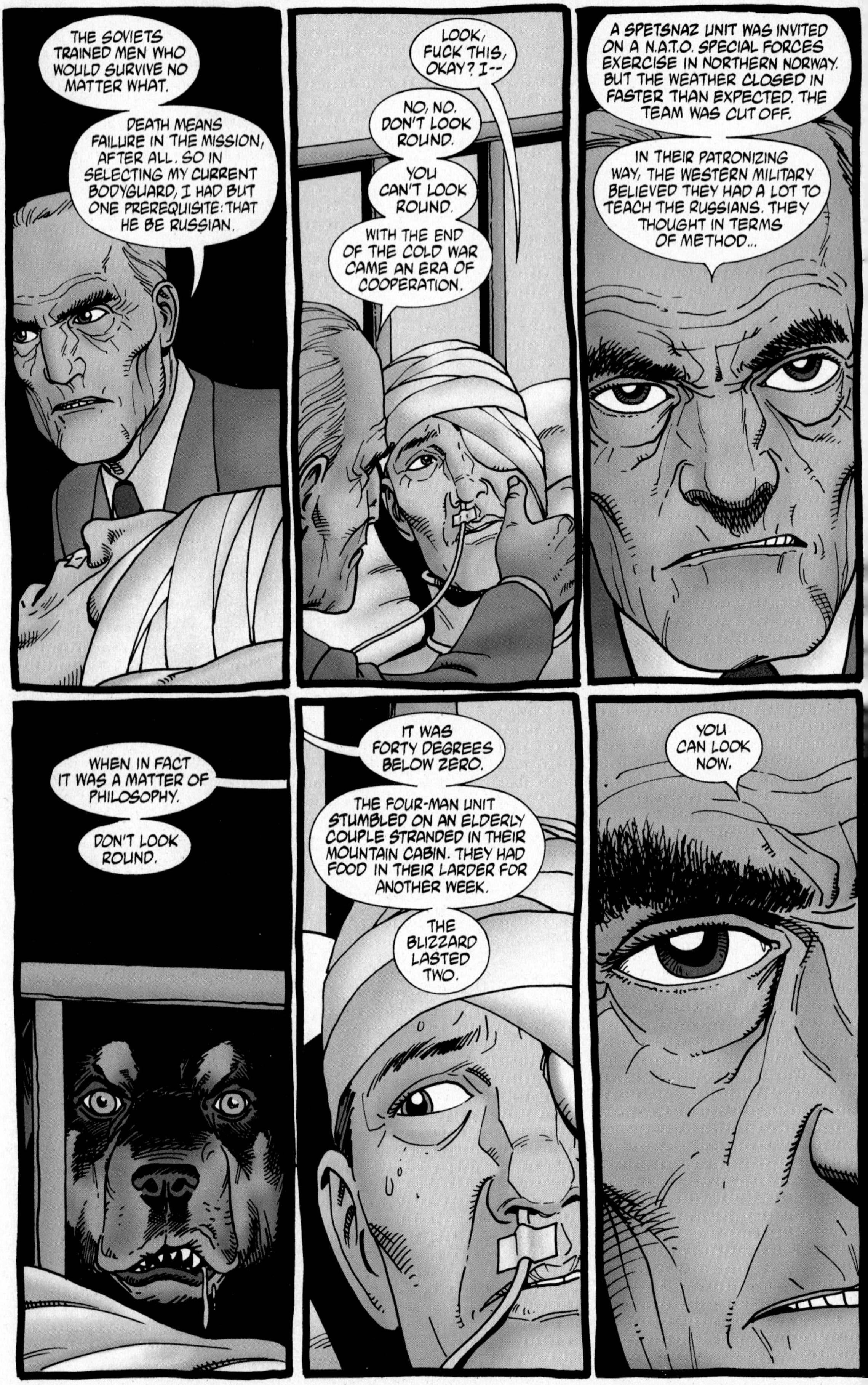
THE SOVIETS TRAINED MEN WHO WOULD SURVIVE NO MATTER WHAT.
DEATH MEANS FAILURE IN THE MISSION, AFTER ALL. SO IN SELECTING MY CURRENT BODYGUARD, I HAD BUT ONE PREREQUISITE: THAT HE BE RUSSIAN.
LOOK, FUCK THIS, OKAY? I--
NO, NO. DON'T LOOK ROUND.
YOU CAN'T LOOK ROUND.
WITH THE END OF THE COLD WAR CAME AN ERA OF COOPERATION.
A SPETSNAZ UNIT WAS INVITED ON A N.A.T.O. SPECIAL FORCES EXERCISE IN NORTHERN NORWAY. BUT THE WEATHER CLOSED IN FASTER THAN EXPECTED. THE TEAM WAS CUT OFF.
IN THEIR PATRONIZING WAY, THE WESTERN MILITARY BELIEVED THEY HAD A LOT TO TEACH THE RUSSIANS. THEY THOUGHT IN TERMS OF METHOD...
WHEN IN FACT IT WAS A MATTER OF PHILOSOPHY.
DON'T LOOK ROUND.
IT WAS FORTY DEGREES BELOW ZERO.
THE FOUR-MAN UNIT STUMBLED ON AN ELDERLY COUPLE STRANDED IN THEIR MOUNTAIN CABIN. THEY HAD FOOD IN THEIR LARDER FOR ANOTHER WEEK.
THE BLIZZARD LASTED TWO.
YOU CAN LOOK NOW.

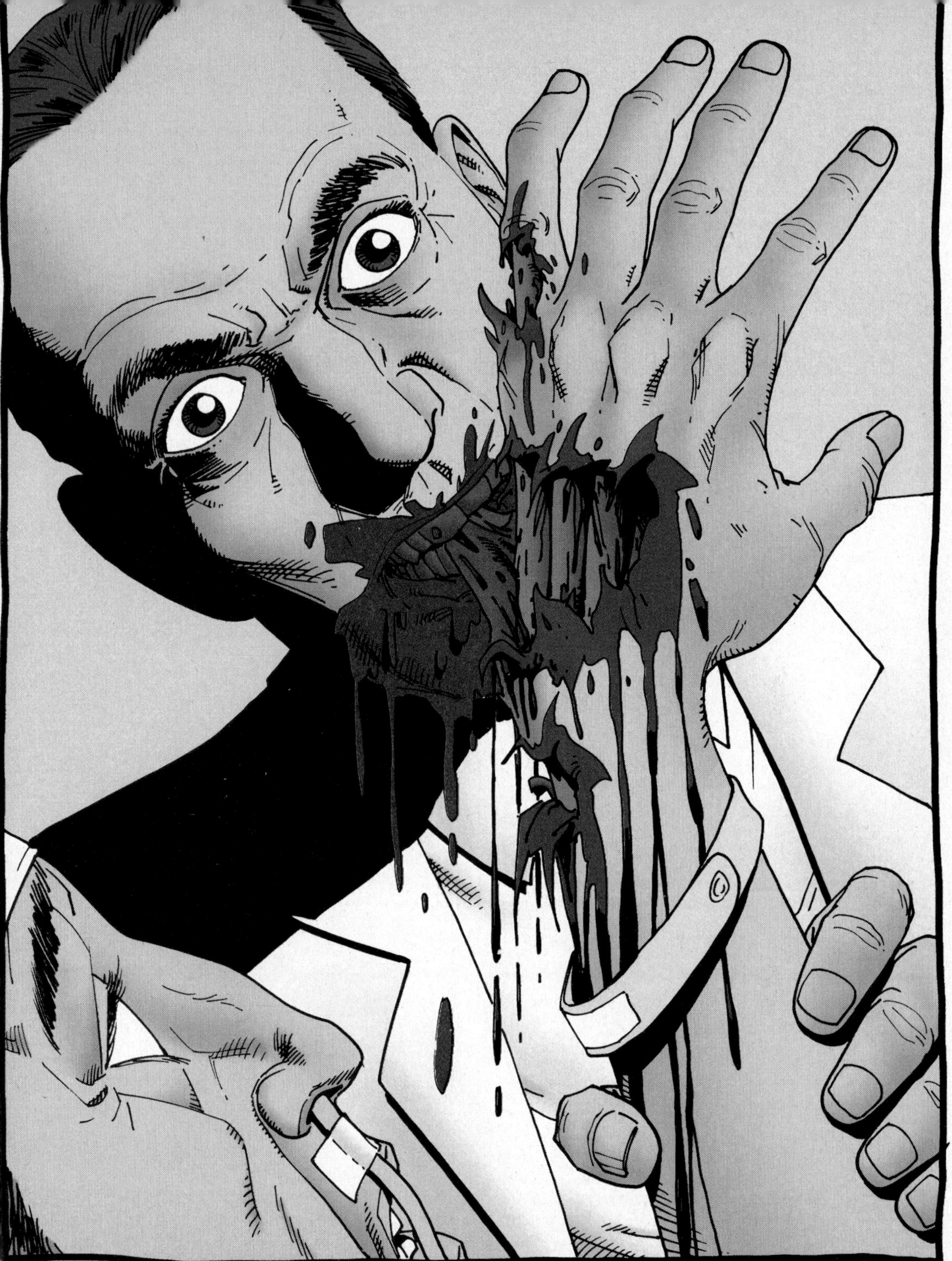

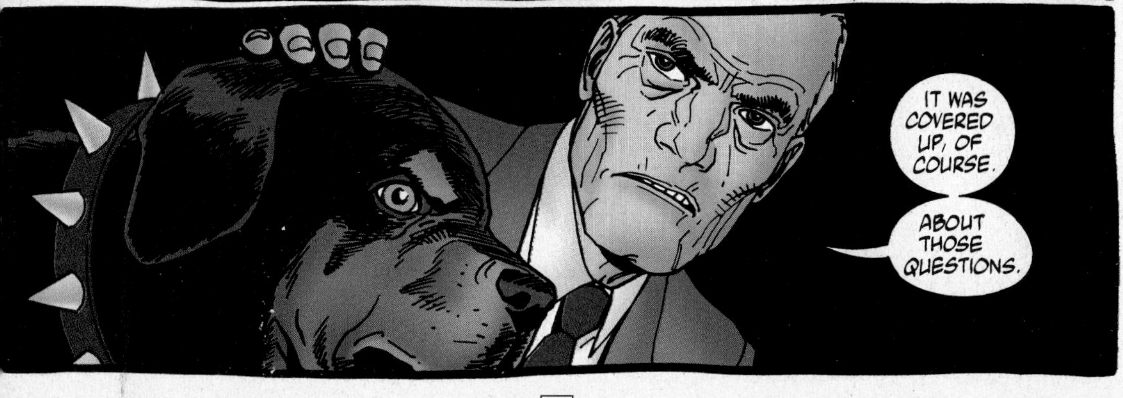
IT WAS COVERED UP, OF COURSE.
ABOUT THOSE QUESTIONS.

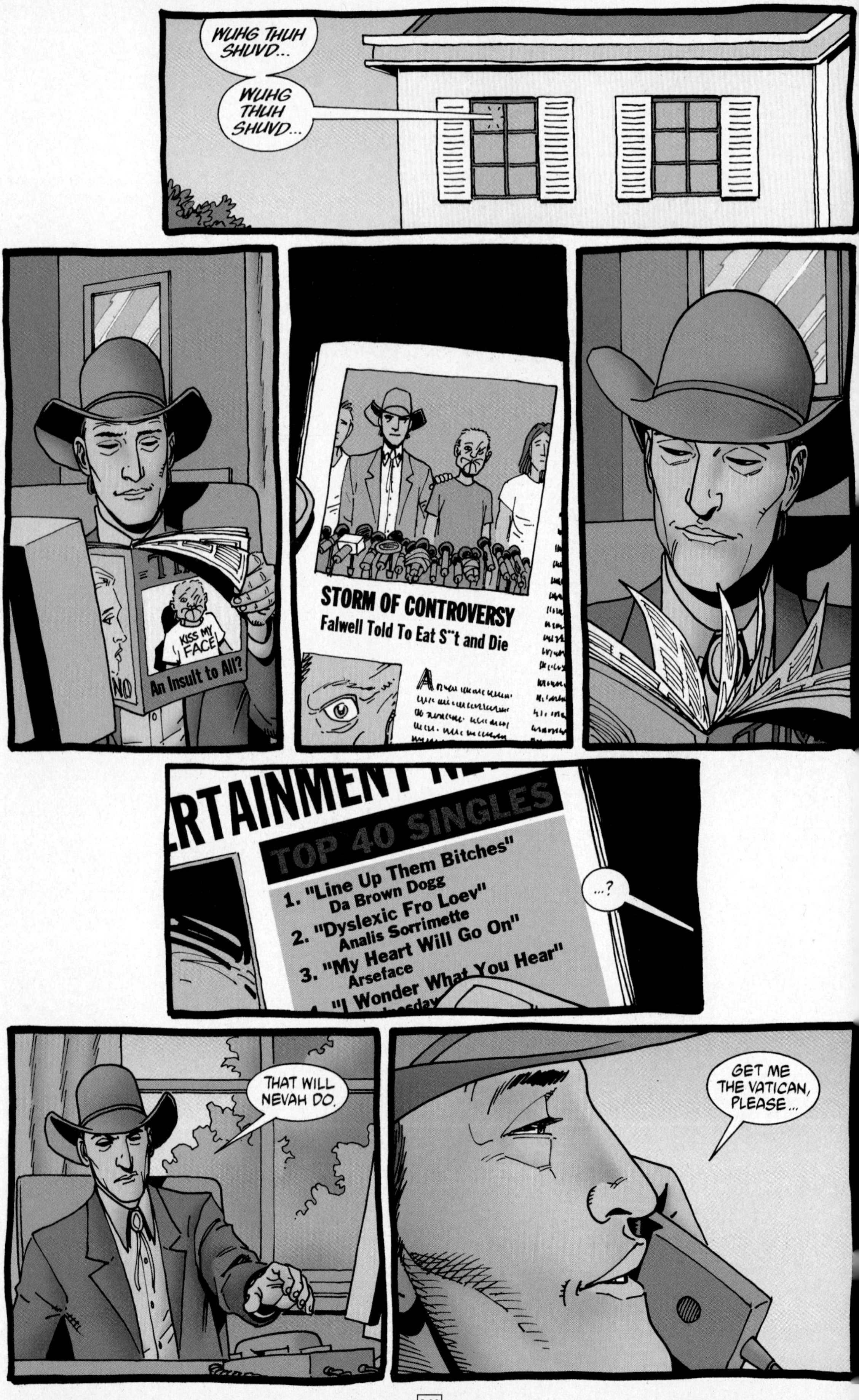

WUHG THUH SHUVD...
WUHG THUH SHUVD...
TIME
KISS MY FACE
An Insult to All?
NO
STORM OF CONTROVERSY
Falwell Told To Eat S**t and Die
ERTAINMENT NE
TOP 40 SINGLES
1. "Line Up Them Bitches" Da Brown Dogg
2. "Dyslexic Fro Loev" Analis Sorrimette
3. "My Heart Will Go On" Arseface
4. "I Wonder What You Hear"
...?
THAT WILL NEVAH DO.
GET ME THE VATICAN, PLEASE...

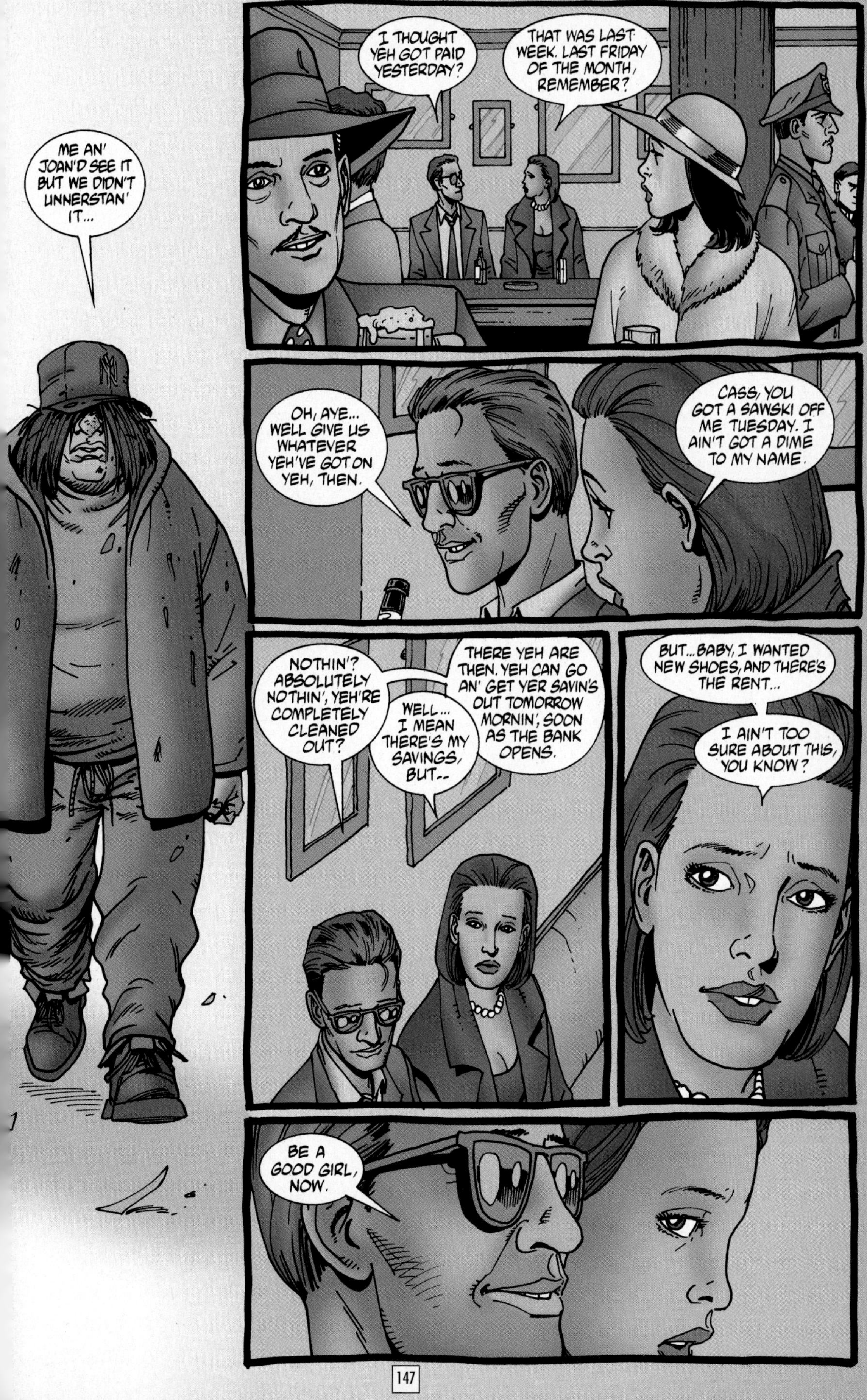
I THOUGHT YEH GOT PAID YESTERDAY?
THAT WAS LAST WEEK. LAST FRIDAY OF THE MONTH, REMEMBER?
ME AN' JOAN'D SEE IT BUT WE DIDN'T UNNERSTAN' IT...
OH, AYE... WELL GIVE US WHATEVER YEH'VE GOT ON YEH, THEN.
CASS, YOU GOT A SAWSKI OFF ME TUESDAY. I AIN'T GOT A DIME TO MY NAME.
NOTHIN'? ABSOLUTELY NOTHIN', YEH'RE COMPLETELY CLEANED OUT?
WELL... I MEAN THERE'S MY SAVINGS, BUT--
THERE YEH ARE THEN. YEH CAN GO AN' GET YER SAVIN'S OUT TOMORROW MORNIN', SOON AS THE BANK OPENS.
BUT... BABY, I WANTED NEW SHOES, AND THERE'S THE RENT...
I AIN'T TOO SURE ABOUT THIS, YOU KNOW?
BE A GOOD GIRL, NOW.

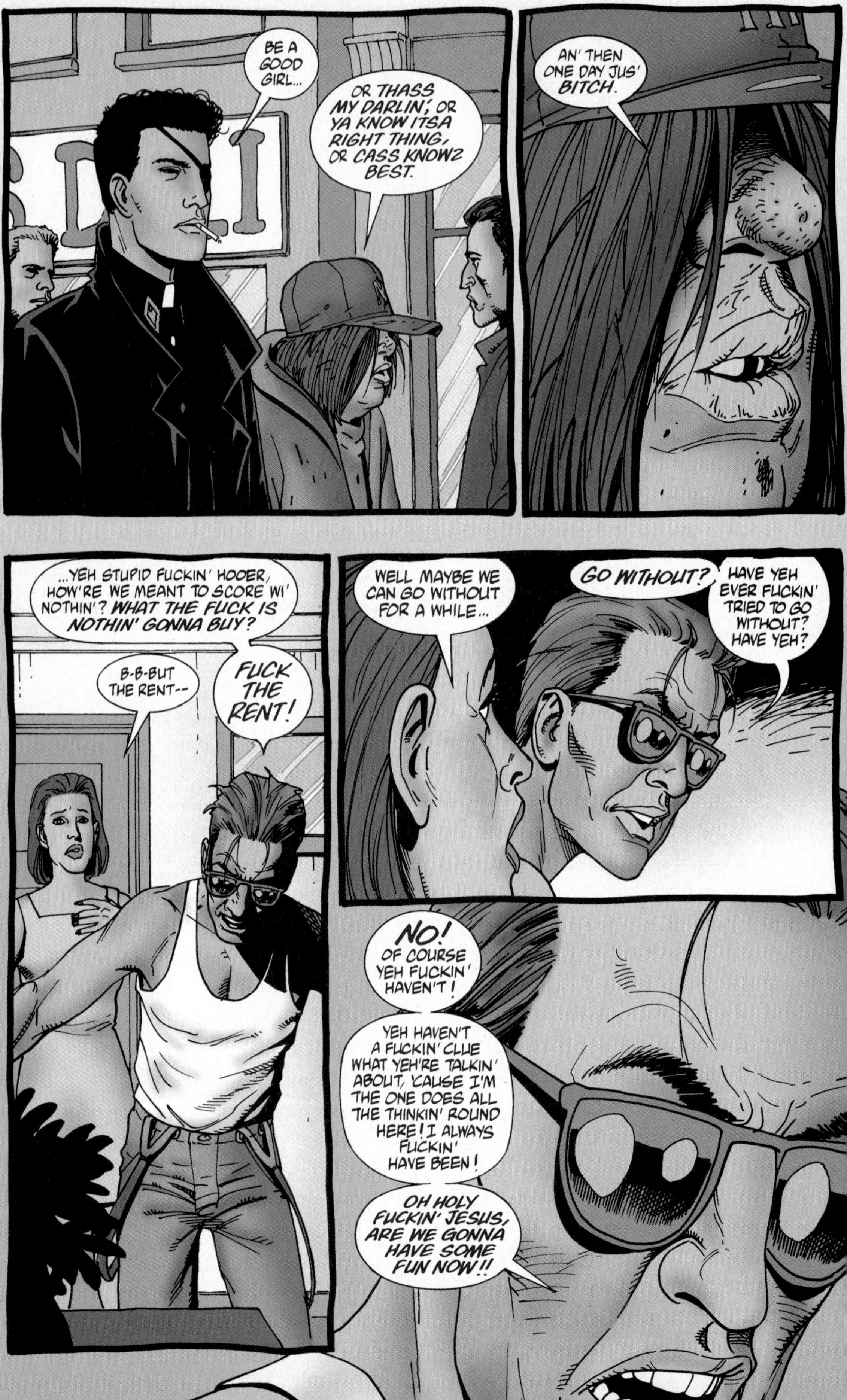

BE A GOOD GIRL...
OR THASS MY DARLIN', OR YA KNOW ITSA RIGHT THING, OR CASS KNOWZ BEST.
AN' THEN ONE DAY JUS' BITCH.
...YEH STUPID FUCKIN' HOOER, HOW'RE WE MEANT TO SCORE WI' NOTHIN'? WHAT THE FUCK IS NOTHIN' GONNA BUY?
B-B-BUT THE RENT--
FUCK THE RENT!
WELL MAYBE WE CAN GO WITHOUT FOR A WHILE...
GO WITHOUT?
HAVE YEH EVER FUCKIN' TRIED TO GO WITHOUT? HAVE YEH?
NO! OF COURSE YEH FUCKIN' HAVEN'T!
YEH HAVEN'T A FUCKIN' CLUE WHAT YEH'RE TALKIN' ABOUT, 'CAUSE I'M THE ONE DOES ALL THE THINKIN' ROUND HERE! I ALWAYS FUCKIN' HAVE BEEN!
OH HOLY FUCKIN' JESUS, ARE WE GONNA HAVE SOME FUN NOW!!

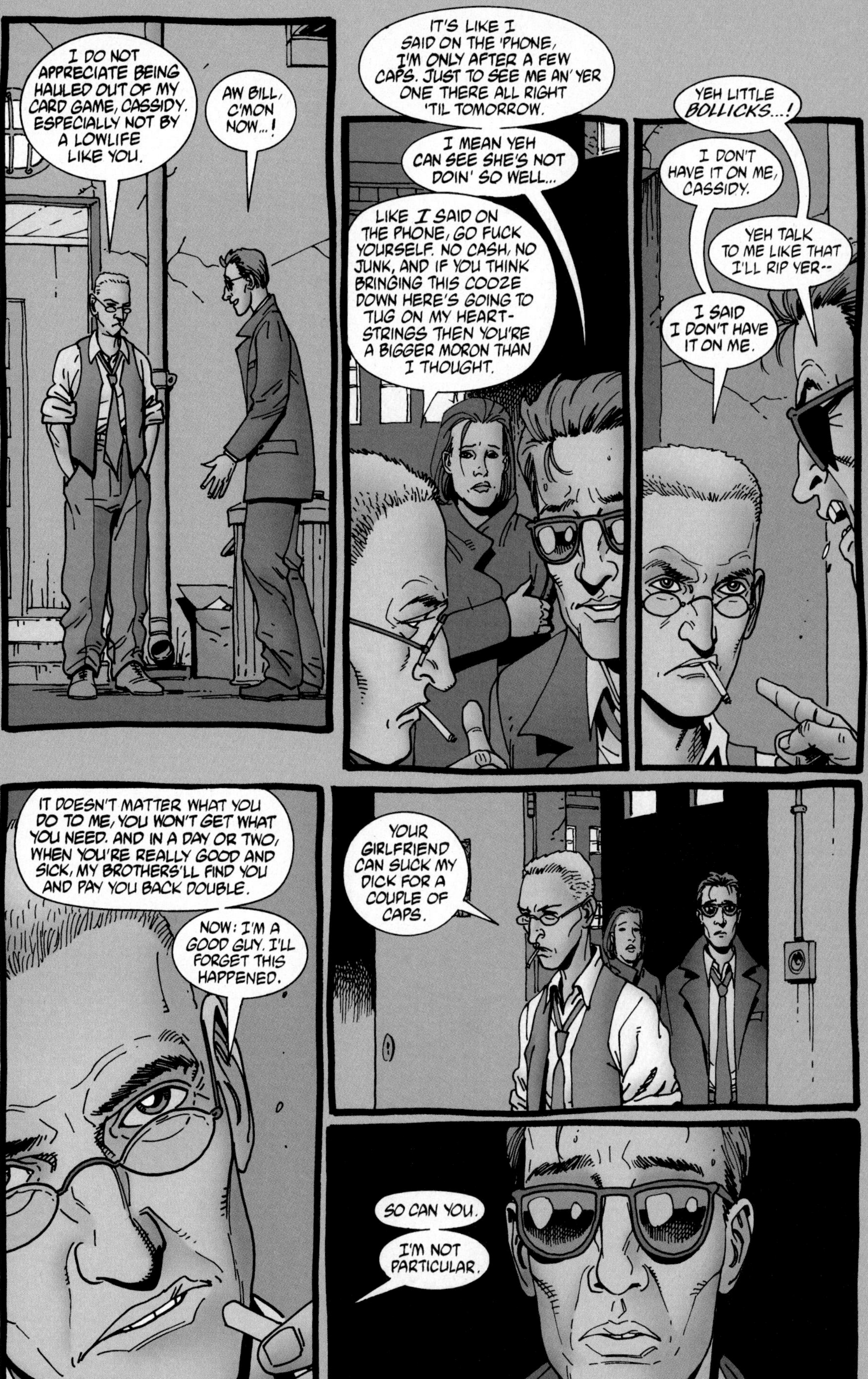
I DO NOT APPRECIATE BEING HAULED OUT OF MY CARD GAME, CASSIDY. ESPECIALLY NOT BY A LOWLIFE LIKE YOU.
AW BILL, C'MON NOW...!
IT'S LIKE I SAID ON THE 'PHONE, I'M ONLY AFTER A FEW CAPS. JUST TO SEE ME AN' YER ONE THERE ALL RIGHT 'TIL TOMORROW.
I MEAN YEH CAN SEE SHE'S NOT DOIN' SO WELL...
LIKE I SAID ON THE PHONE, GO FUCK YOURSELF. NO CASH, NO JUNK, AND IF YOU THINK BRINGING THIS COOZE DOWN HERE'S GOING TO TUG ON MY HEART-STRINGS THEN YOU'RE A BIGGER MORON THAN I THOUGHT.
YEH LITTLE BOLLICKS...!
I DON'T HAVE IT ON ME, CASSIDY.
YEH TALK TO ME LIKE THAT I'LL RIP YER--
I SAID I DON'T HAVE IT ON ME.
IT DOESN'T MATTER WHAT YOU DO TO ME, YOU WON'T GET WHAT YOU NEED. AND IN A DAY OR TWO, WHEN YOU'RE REALLY GOOD AND SICK, MY BROTHERS'LL FIND YOU AND PAY YOU BACK DOUBLE.
NOW: I'M A GOOD GUY. I'LL FORGET THIS HAPPENED.
YOUR GIRLFRIEND CAN SUCK MY DICK FOR A COUPLE OF CAPS.
SO CAN YOU.
I'M NOT PARTICULAR.

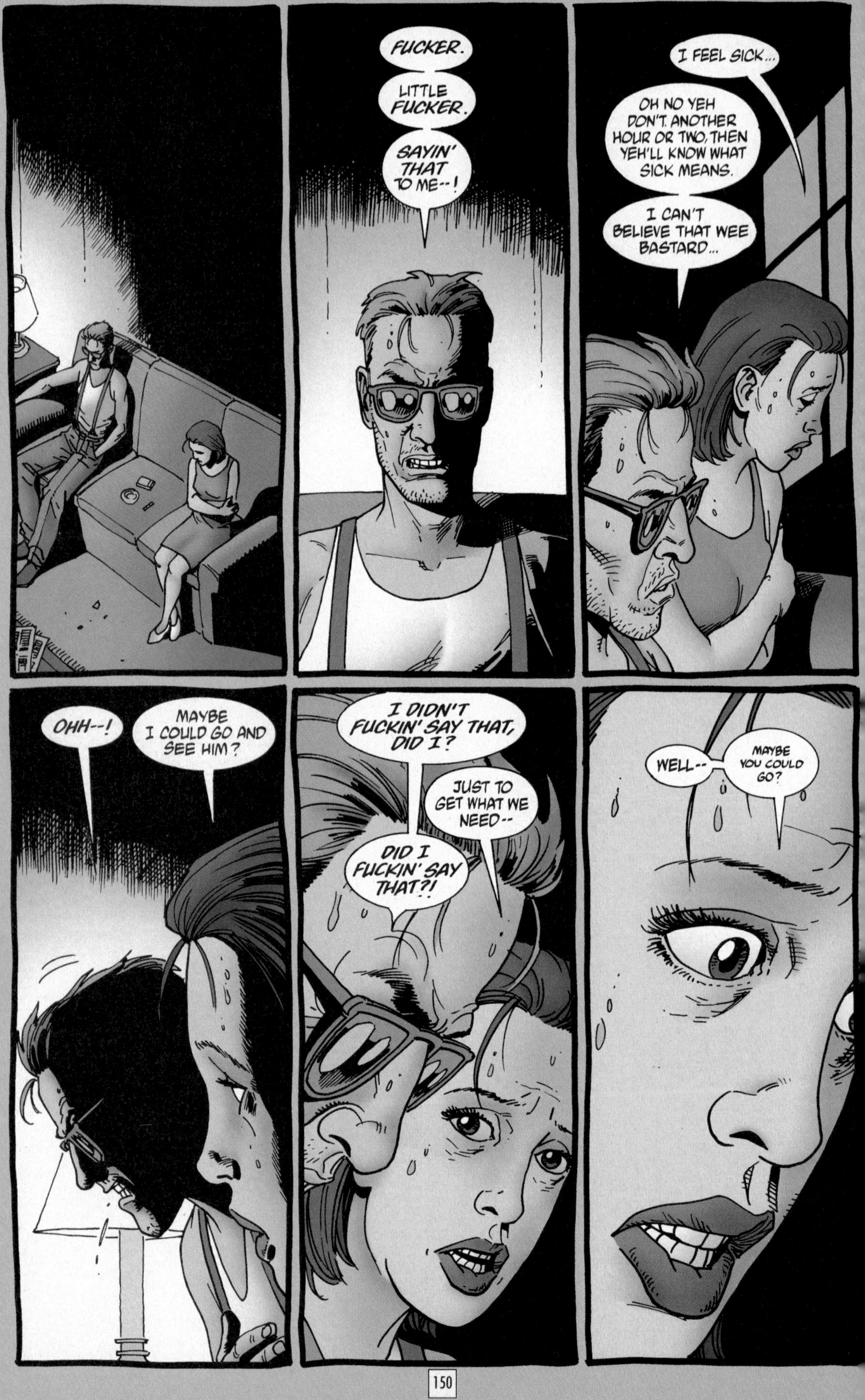
FUCKER.
LITTLE FUCKER.
SAYIN' THAT TO ME--!
I FEEL SICK...
OH NO YEH DON'T. ANOTHER HOUR OR TWO, THEN YEH'LL KNOW WHAT SICK MEANS.
I CAN'T BELIEVE THAT WEE BASTARD...
OHH--!
MAYBE I COULD GO AND SEE HIM?
I DIDN'T FUCKIN' SAY THAT, DID I?
JUST TO GET WHAT WE NEED--
DID I FUCKIN' SAY THAT?!
WELL--
MAYBE YOU COULD GO?

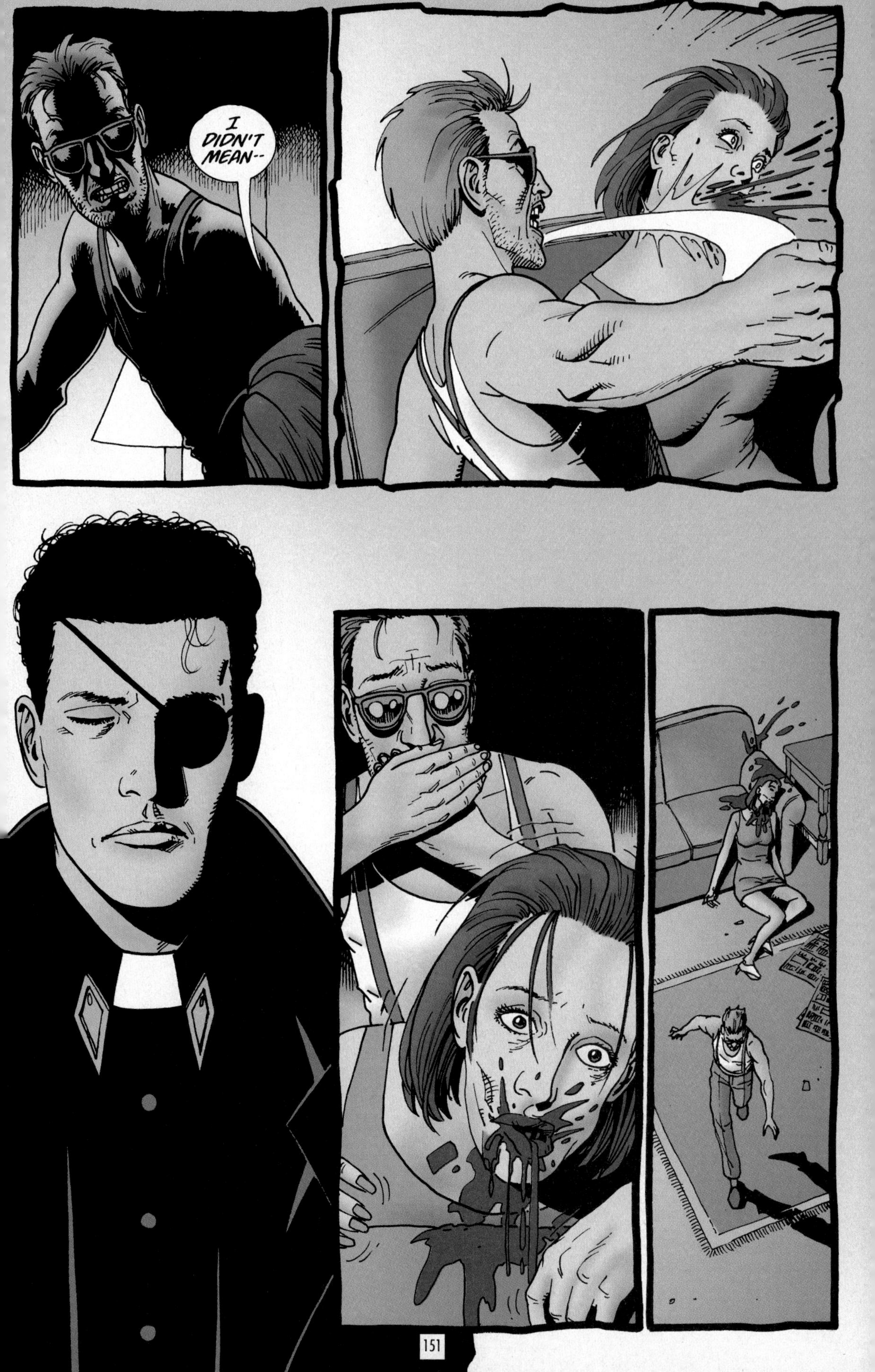
I DIDN'T MEAN--

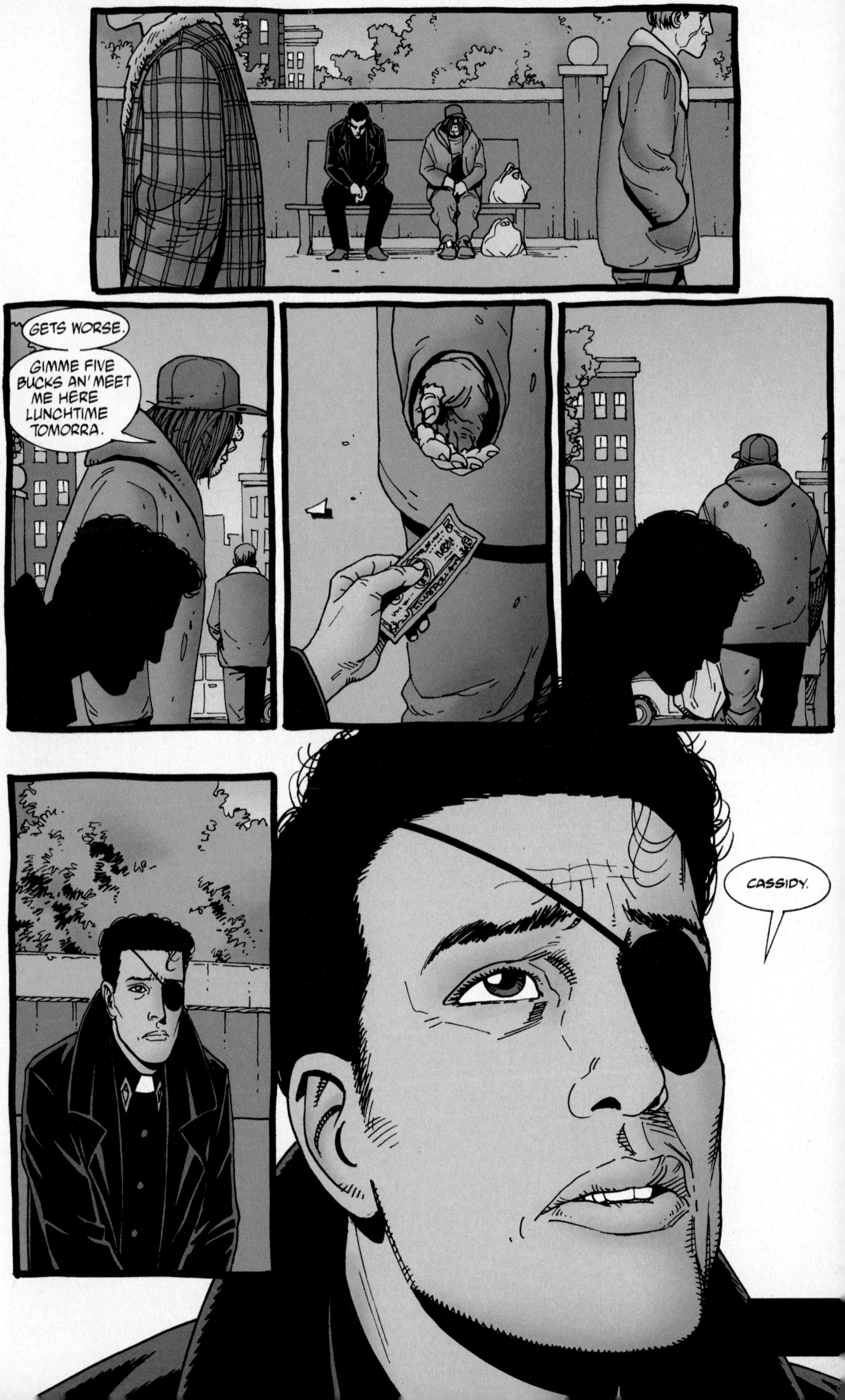
GETS WORSE.
GIMME FIVE BUCKS AN' MEET ME HERE LUNCHTIME TOMORRA.
CASSIDY.

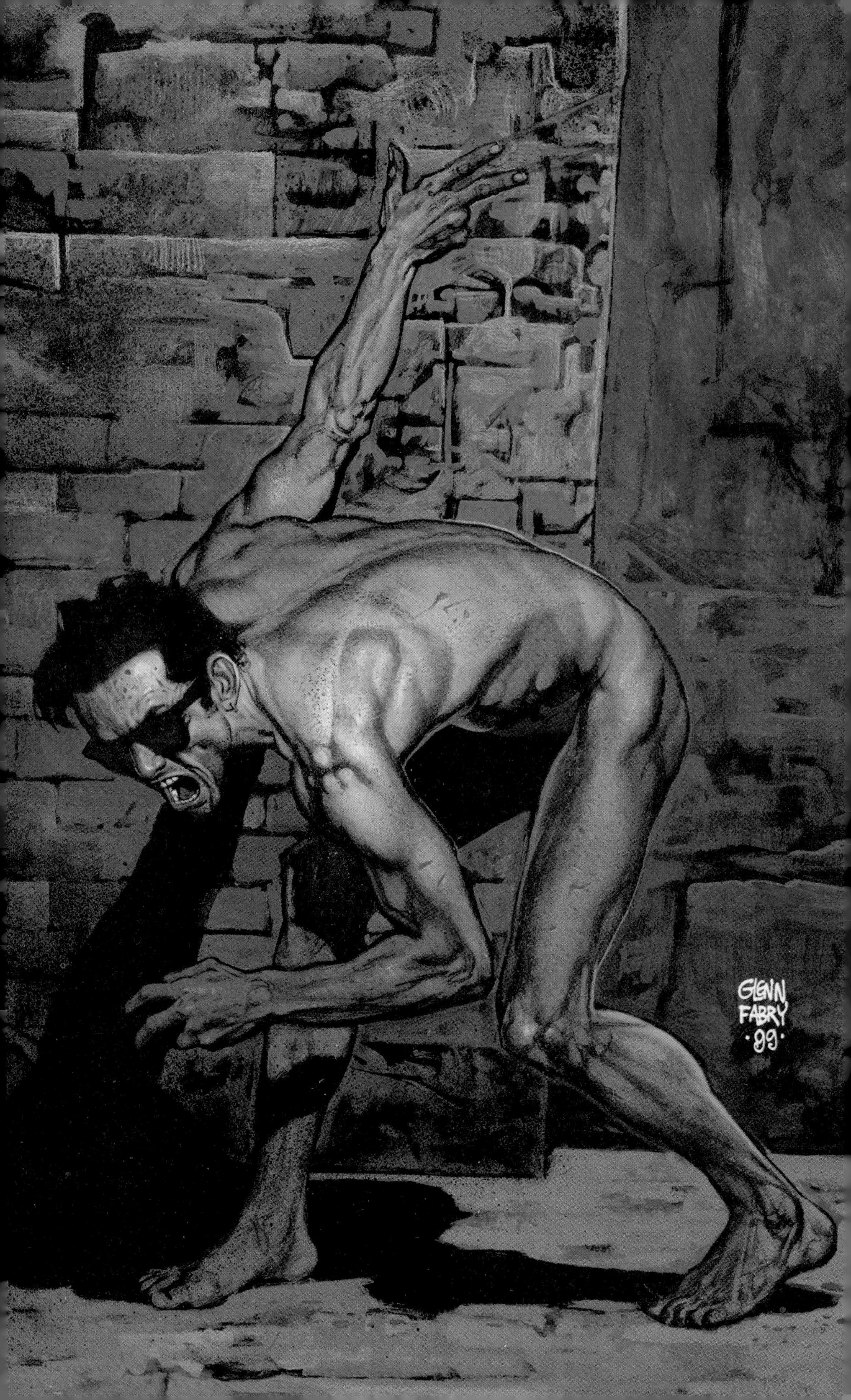
GLENN
FABRY
·99·

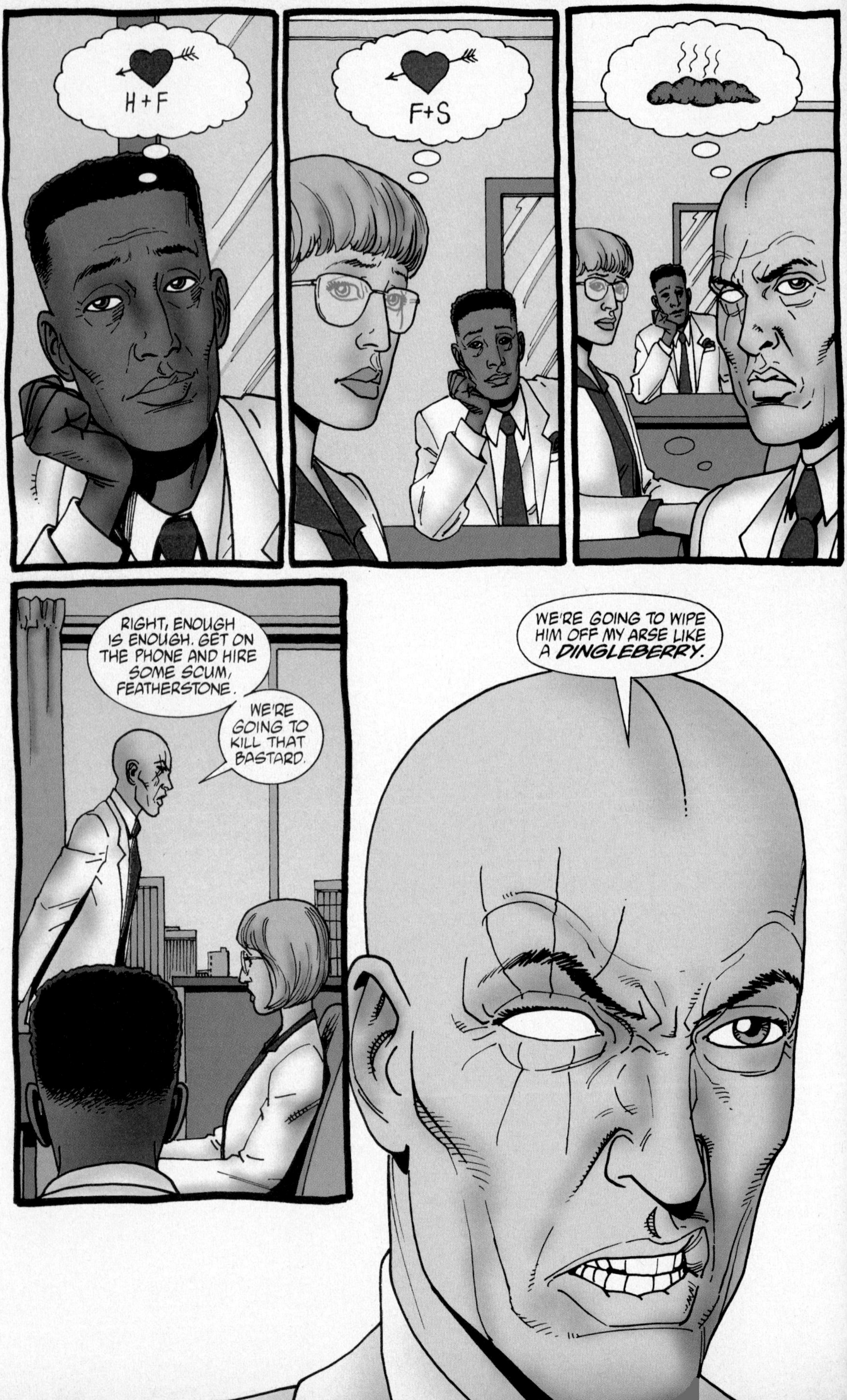
H + F
F+S
RIGHT, ENOUGH IS ENOUGH. GET ON THE PHONE AND HIRE SOME SCUM, FEATHERSTONE.
WE'RE GOING TO KILL THAT BASTARD.
WE'RE GOING TO WIPE HIM OFF MY ARSE LIKE A DINGLEBERRY.

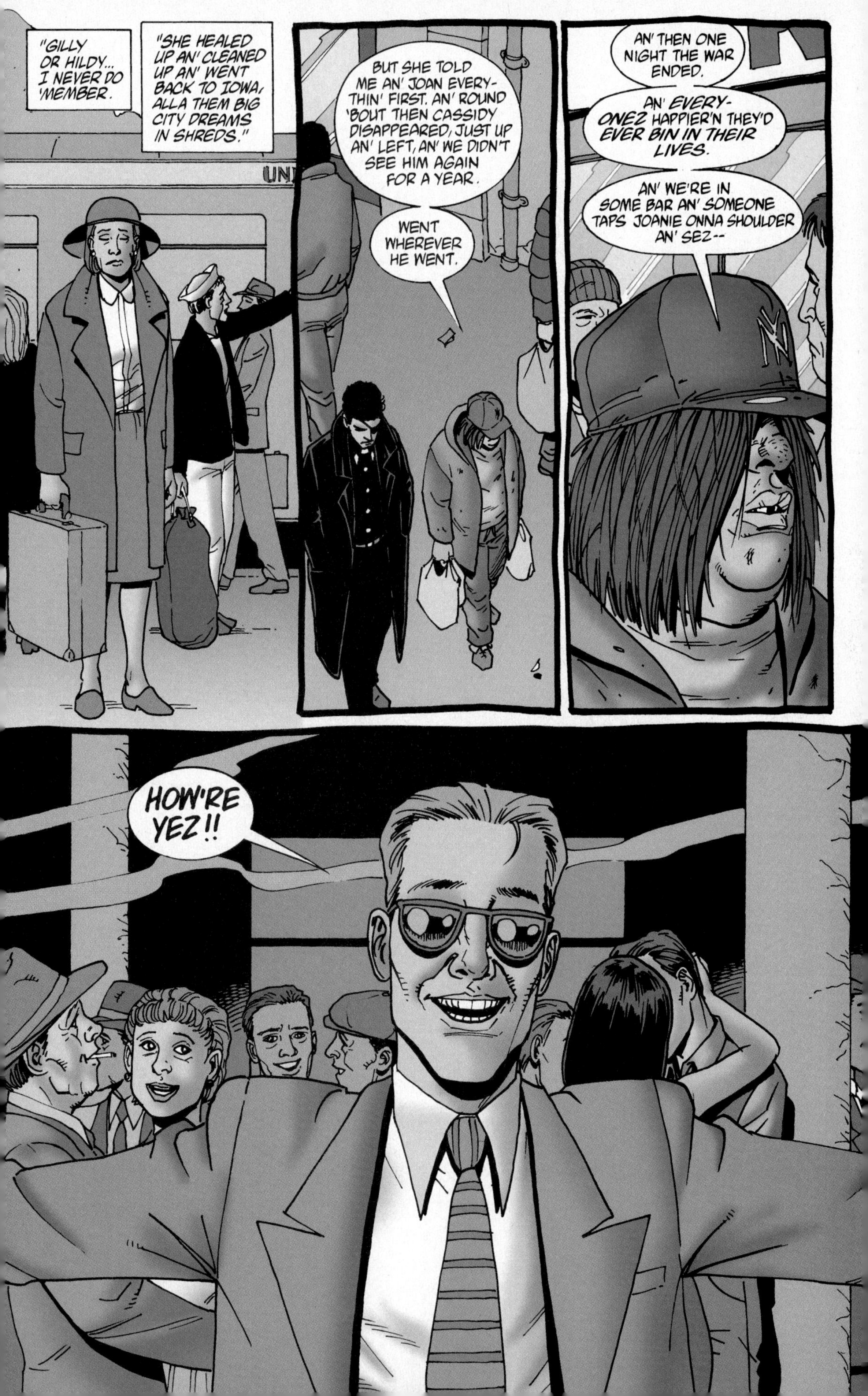
"GILLY OR HILDY... I NEVER DO 'MEMBER.
"SHE HEALED UP AN' CLEANED UP AN' WENT BACK TO IOWA, ALLA THEM BIG CITY DREAMS IN SHREDS."
BUT SHE TOLD ME AN' JOAN EVERY-THIN' FIRST. AN' ROUND 'BOUT THEN CASSIDY DISAPPEARED, JUST UP AN' LEFT, AN' WE DIDN'T SEE HIM AGAIN FOR A YEAR.
WENT WHEREVER HE WENT.
AN' THEN ONE NIGHT THE WAR ENDED.
AN' EVERY-ONEZ HAPPIER'N THEY'D EVER BIN IN THEIR LIVES.
AN' WE'RE IN SOME BAR AN' SOMEONE TAPS JOANIE ONNA SHOULDER AN' SEZ--
HOW'RE YEZ!!

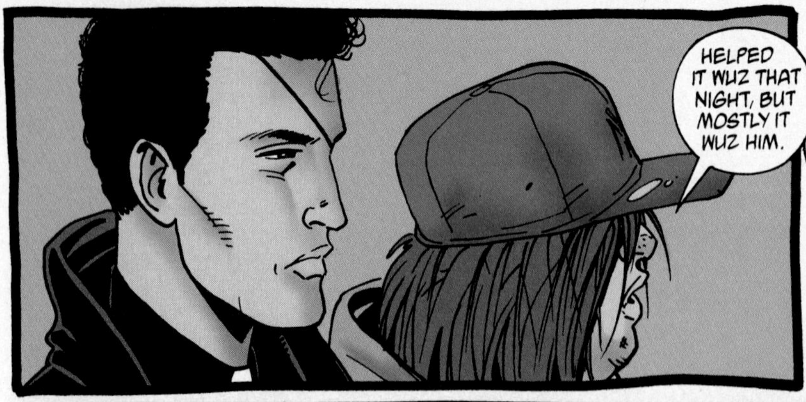
HELPED IT WUZ THAT NIGHT, BUT MOSTLY IT WUZ HIM.
HIM AT HIS BEST, YA KNOW, AN' HE'D MONEY TO BURN AN' WE HELPED HIM BURN IT... AN' A COUPLE WEEKS WENT BY AN' JOANIE SAID TO ME--GILLY OR HILDY, SHE MUSTA BIN MAKIN' IT UP. WHAT WITHA SMACK AN' ALL.
SO PRETTY SOON ONE THING LED TO 'NOTHER.

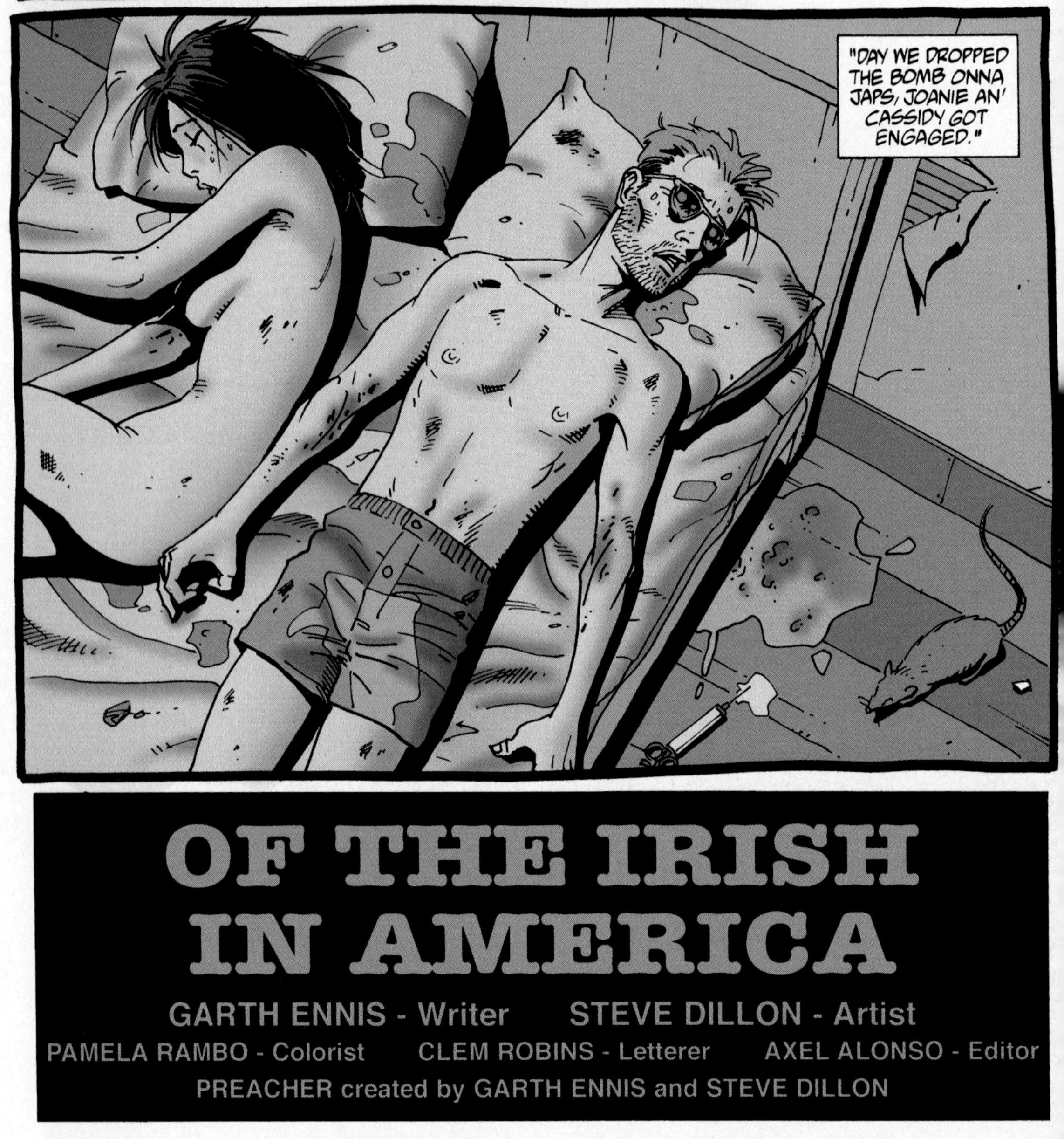
"DAY WE DROPPED THE BOMB ONNA JAPS, JOANIE AN' CASSIDY GOT ENGAGED."

OF THE IRISH IN AMERICA

GARTH ENNIS - Writer STEVE DILLON - Artist

PAMELA RAMBO - Colorist CLEM ROBINS - Letterer AXEL ALONSO - Editor

PREACHER created by GARTH ENNIS and STEVE DILLON

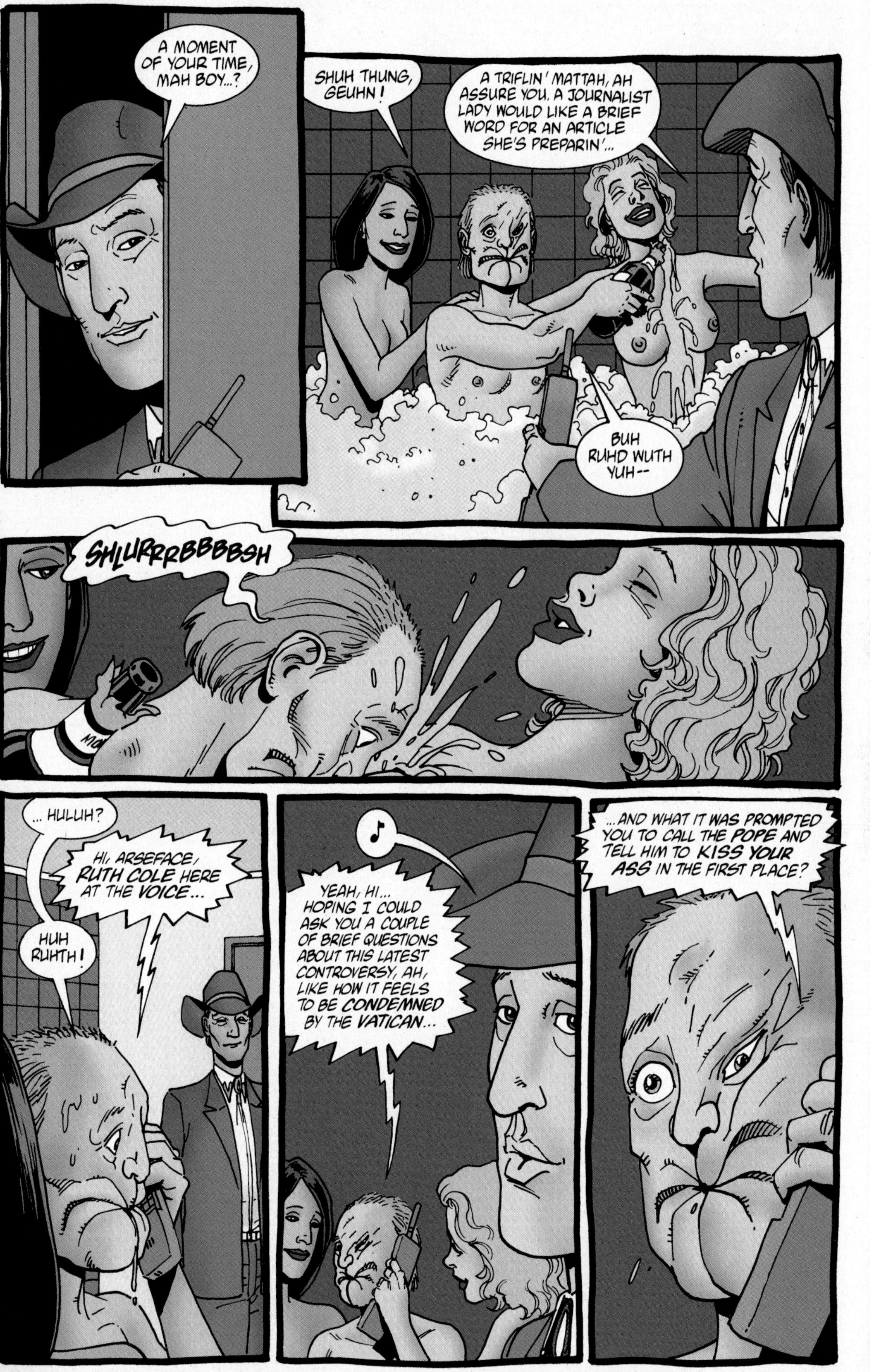
A MOMENT OF YOUR TIME, MAH BOY...?
SHUH THUNG, GEUHN!
A TRIFLIN' MATTAH, AH ASSURE YOU. A JOURNALIST LADY WOULD LIKE A BRIEF WORD FOR AN ARTICLE SHE'S PREPARIN'...
BUH RUHD WUTH YUH--
SHLURRRBBBBSH
... HULUH?
HI, ARSEFACE, **RUTH COLE** HERE AT THE **VOICE**...
HUH RUHTH!
♪
YEAH, HI... HOPING I COULD ASK YOU A COUPLE OF BRIEF QUESTIONS ABOUT THIS LATEST CONTROVERSY, AH, LIKE HOW IT FEELS TO BE **CONDEMNED** BY THE **VATICAN**...
...AND WHAT IT WAS PROMPTED YOU TO CALL THE **POPE** AND TELL HIM TO **KISS YOUR ASS** IN THE FIRST PLACE?

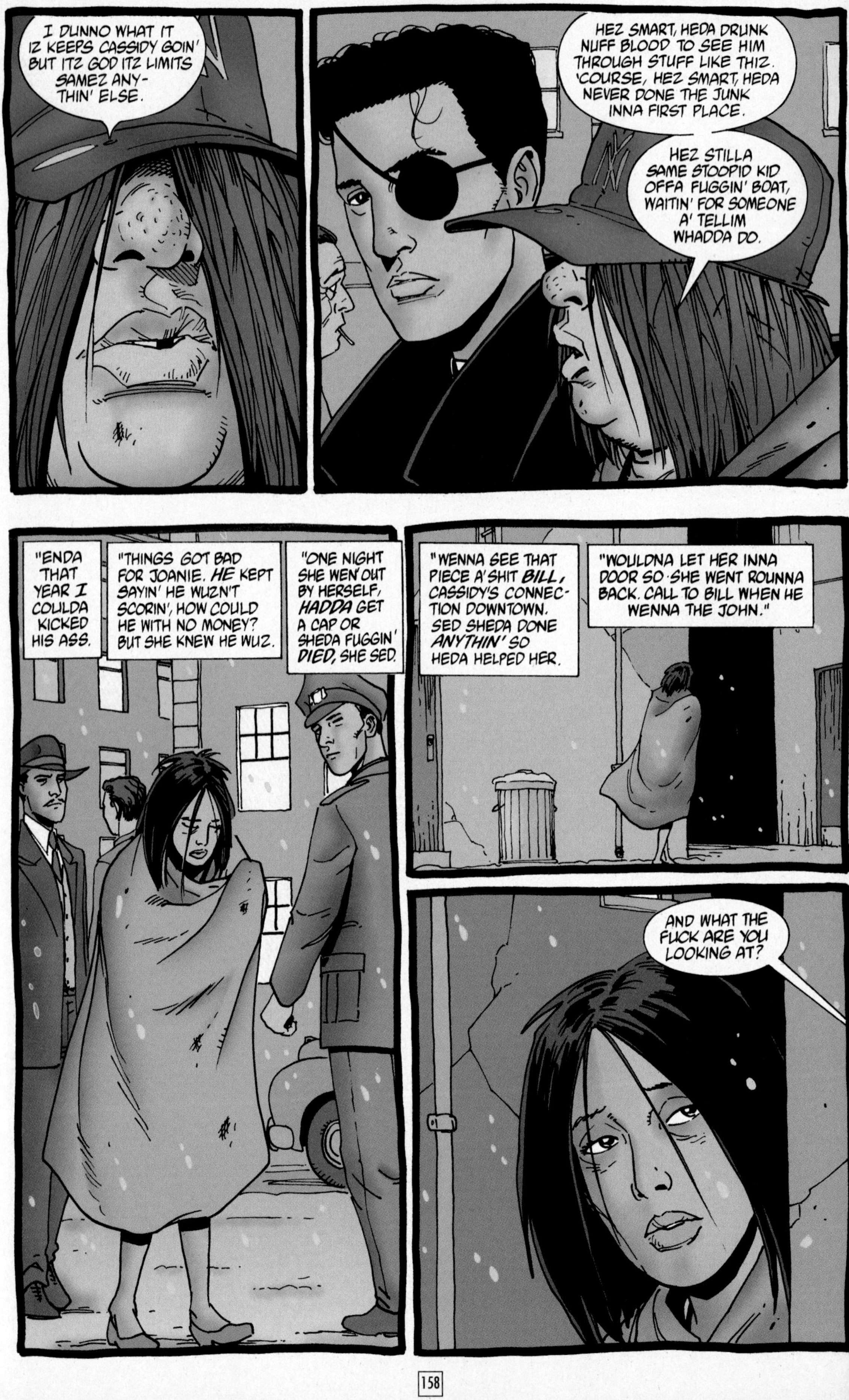
I DUNNO WHAT IT IZ KEEPS CASSIDY GOIN' BUT ITZ GOD ITZ LIMITS SAMEZ ANYTHIN' ELSE.
HEZ SMART, HEDA DRUNK NUFF BLOOD TO SEE HIM THROUGH STUFF LIKE THIZ. 'COURSE, HEZ SMART, HEDA NEVER DONE THE JUNK INNA FIRST PLACE.
HEZ STILLA SAME STOOPID KID OFFA FUGGIN' BOAT, WAITIN' FOR SOMEONE A' TELLIM WHADDA DO.
"ENDA THAT YEAR *I* COULDA KICKED HIS ASS.
"THINGS GOT BAD FOR JOANIE. *HE* KEPT SAYIN' HE WUZN'T SCORIN', HOW COULD HE WITH NO MONEY? BUT SHE KNEW HE WUZ.
"ONE NIGHT SHE WEN' OUT BY HERSELF, *HADDA* GET A CAP OR SHEDA FUGGIN' *DIED,* SHE SED.
"WENNA SEE THAT PIECE A'SHIT *BILL,* CASSIDY'S CONNECTION DOWNTOWN. SED SHEDA DONE *ANYTHIN'* SO HEDA HELPED HER.
"WOULDNA LET HER INNA DOOR SO SHE WENT ROUNNA BACK. CALL TO BILL WHEN HE WENNA THE JOHN."
AND WHAT THE FUCK ARE YOU LOOKING AT?

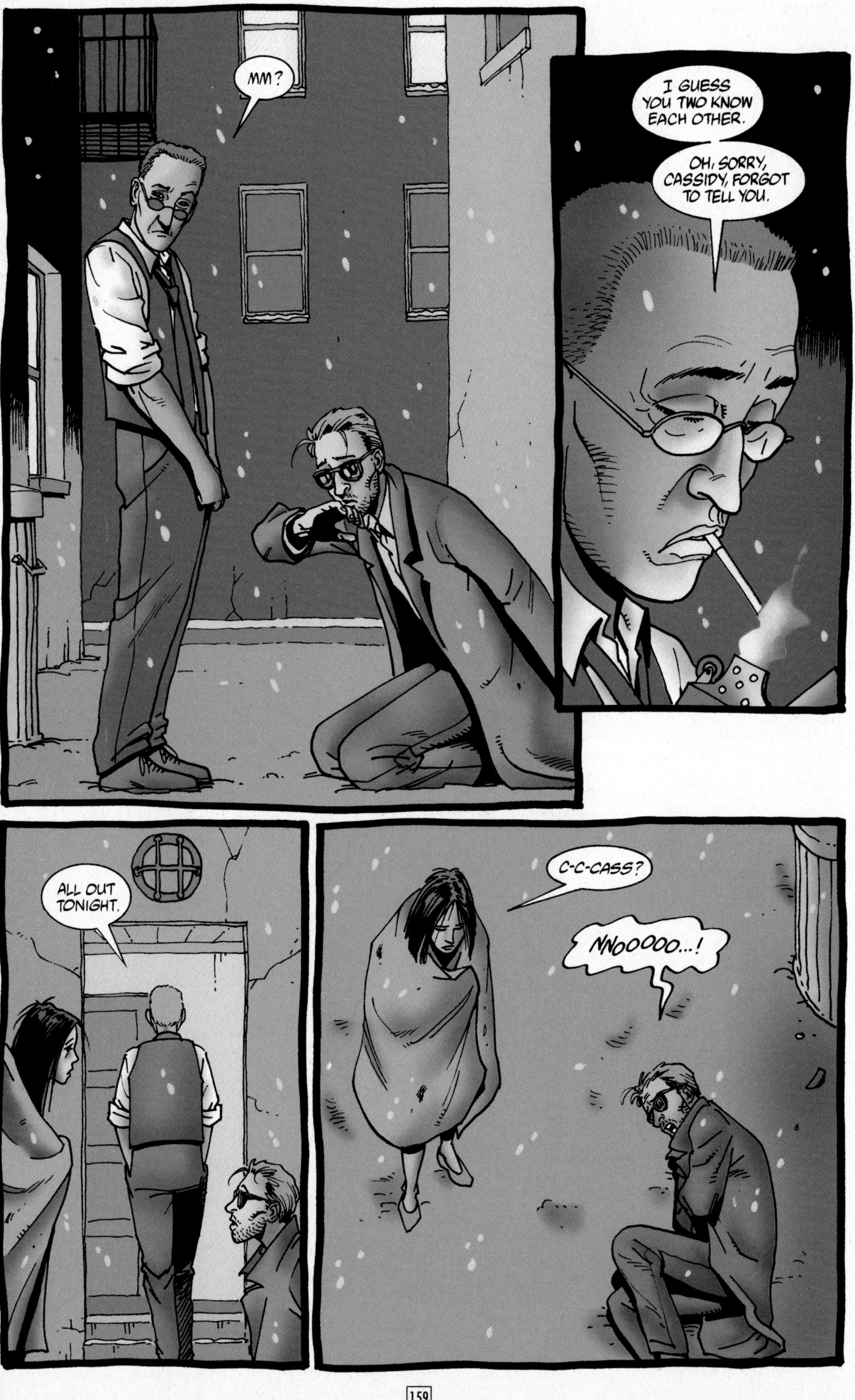
MM?
I GUESS YOU TWO KNOW EACH OTHER.
OH, SORRY, CASSIDY, FORGOT TO TELL YOU.
ALL OUT TONIGHT.
C-C-CASS?
NNOOOOO...!

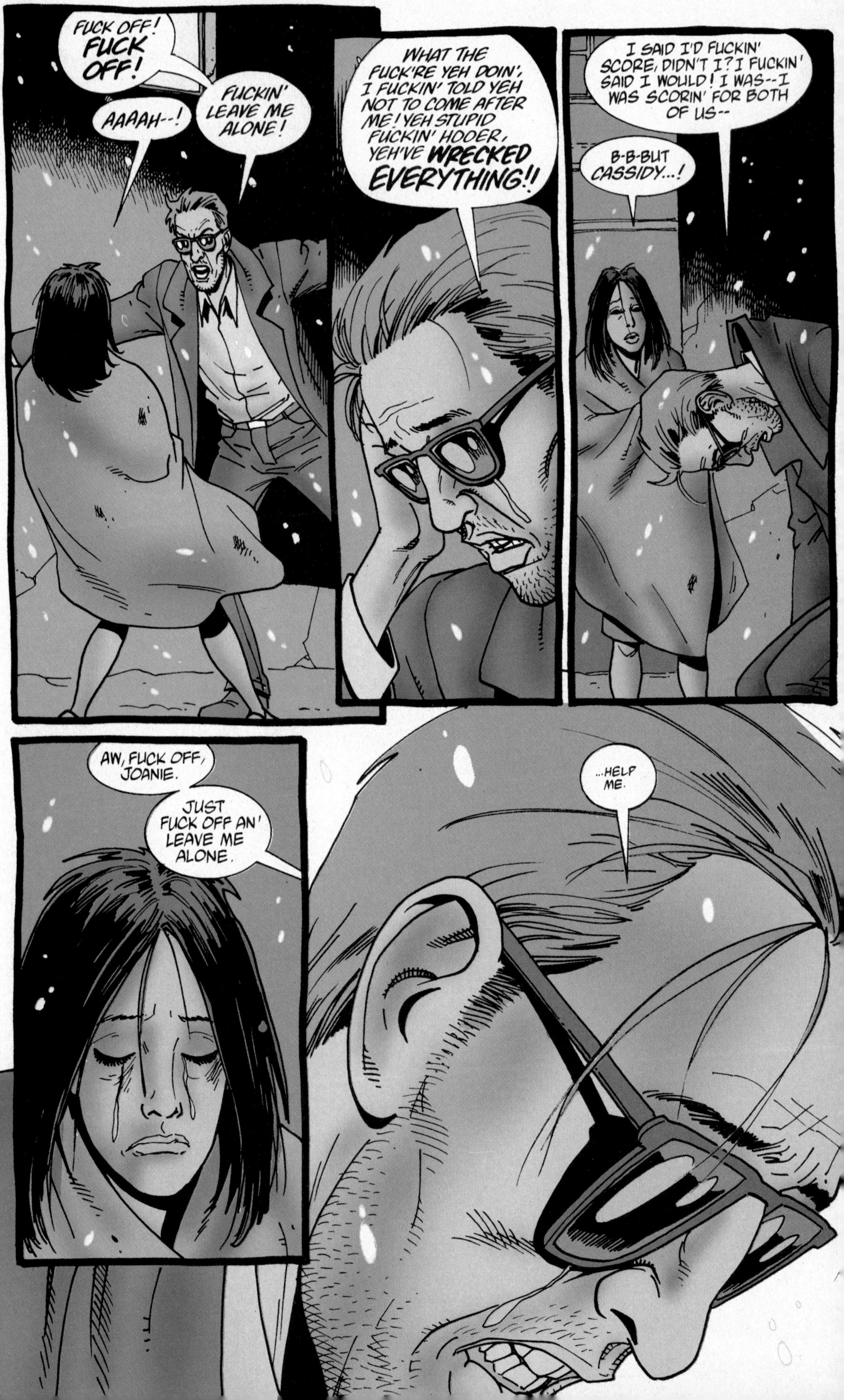
FUCK OFF! FUCK OFF!
AAAAH--!
FUCKIN' LEAVE ME ALONE!
WHAT THE FUCK'RE YEH DOIN', I FUCKIN' TOLD YEH NOT TO COME AFTER ME! YEH STUPID FUCKIN' HOOER, YEH'VE WRECKED EVERYTHING!!
I SAID I'D FUCKIN' SCORE, DIDN'T I? I FUCKIN' SAID I WOULD! I WAS--I WAS SCORIN' FOR BOTH OF US--
B-B-BUT CASSIDY...!
AW, FUCK OFF, JOANIE.
JUST FUCK OFF AN' LEAVE ME ALONE.
...HELP ME.

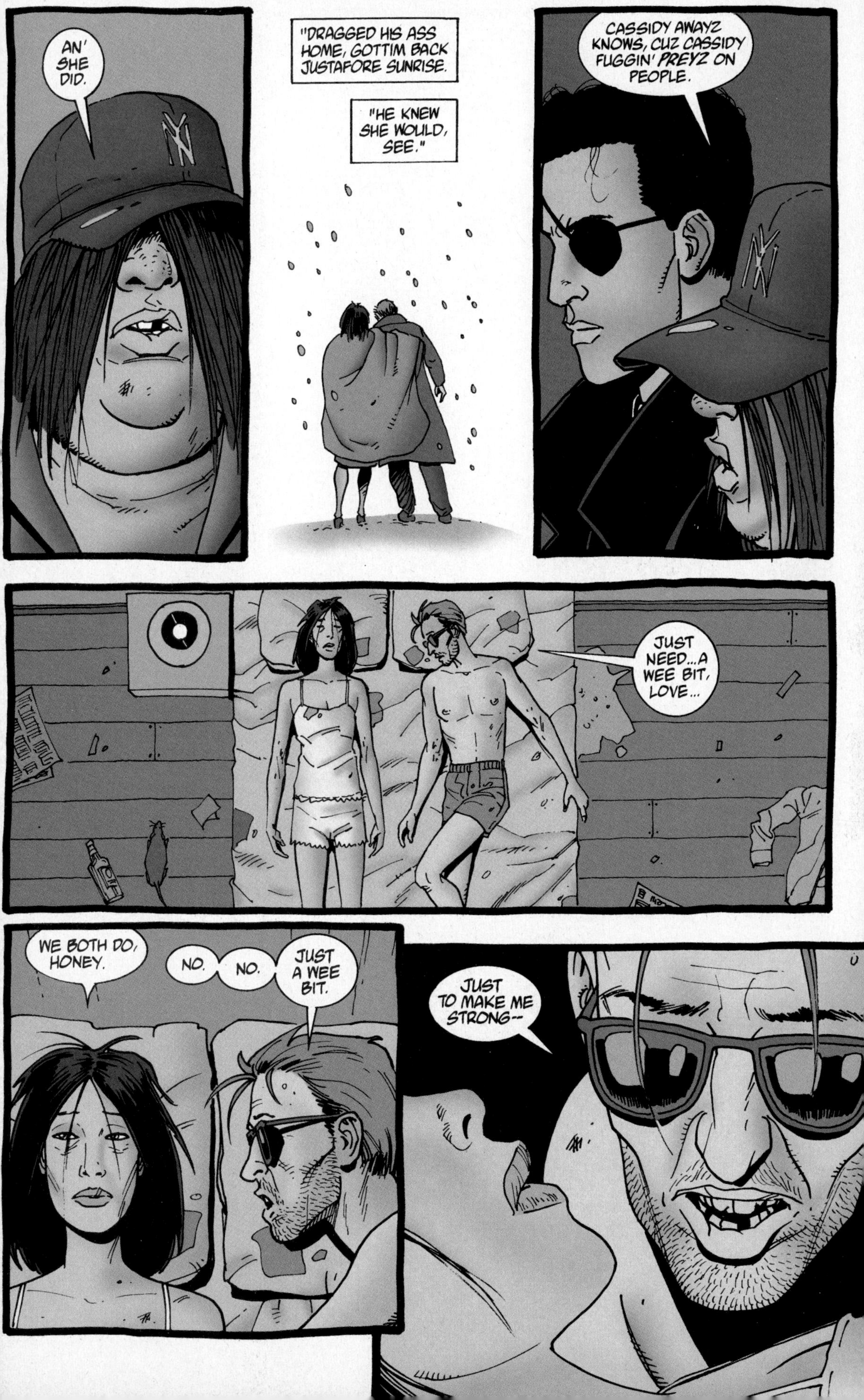
AN' SHE DID.
"DRAGGED HIS ASS HOME, GOTTIM BACK JUSTAFORE SUNRISE.
"HE KNEW SHE WOULD, SEE."
CASSIDY AWAYZ KNOWS, CUZ CASSIDY FUGGIN' PREYZ ON PEOPLE.
JUST NEED...A WEE BIT, LOVE...
WE BOTH DO, HONEY.
NO.
NO.
JUST A WEE BIT.
JUST TO MAKE ME STRONG--

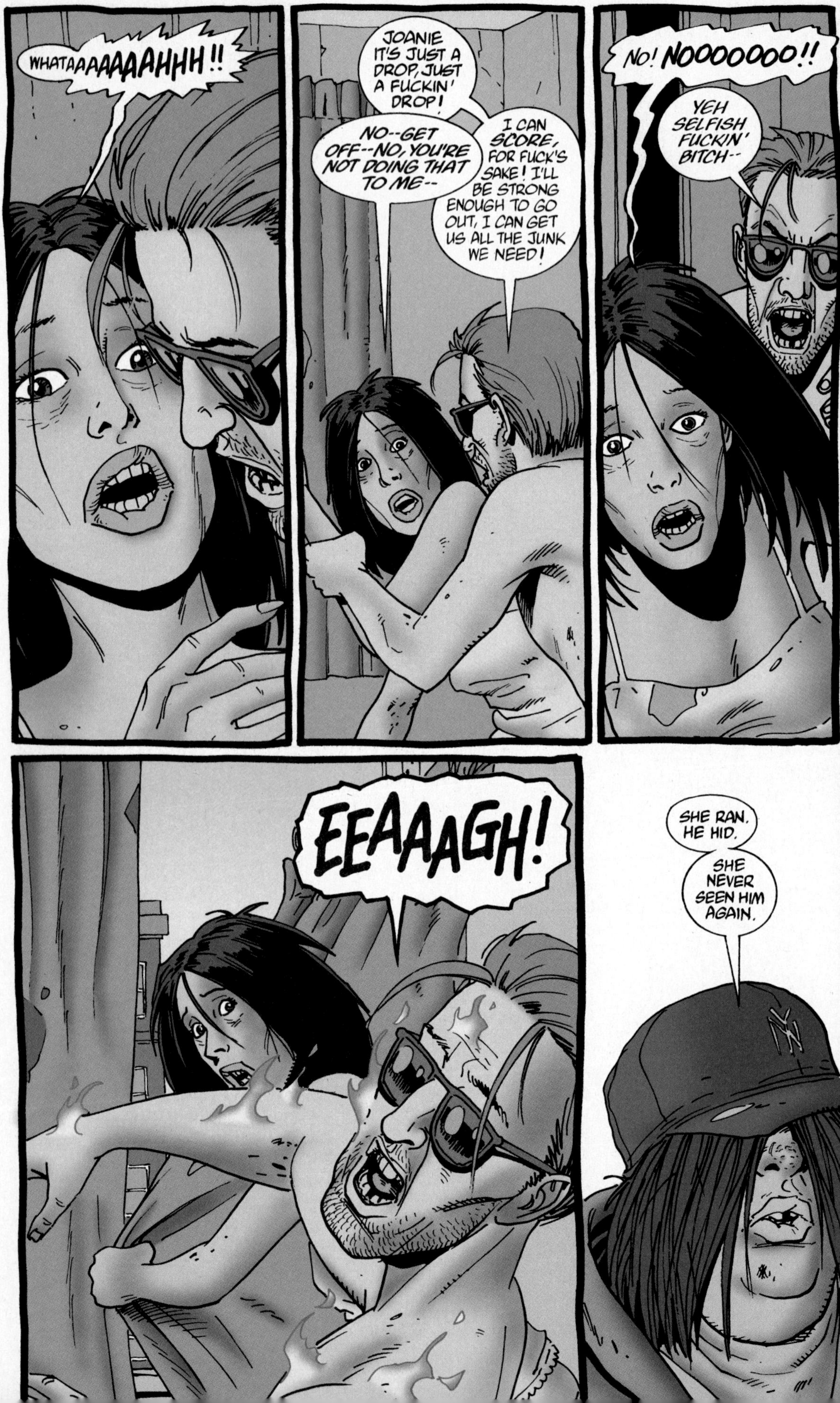
WHATAAAAAAAHHH!!
JOANIE IT'S JUST A DROP, JUST A FUCKIN' DROP!
NO--GET OFF--NO, YOU'RE NOT DOING THAT TO ME--
I CAN SCORE, FOR FUCK'S SAKE! I'LL BE STRONG ENOUGH TO GO OUT, I CAN GET US ALL THE JUNK WE NEED!
NO! NOOOOOOO!!
YEH SELFISH FUCKIN' BITCH--
EEAAAGH!
SHE RAN. HE HID.
SHE NEVER SEEN HIM AGAIN.

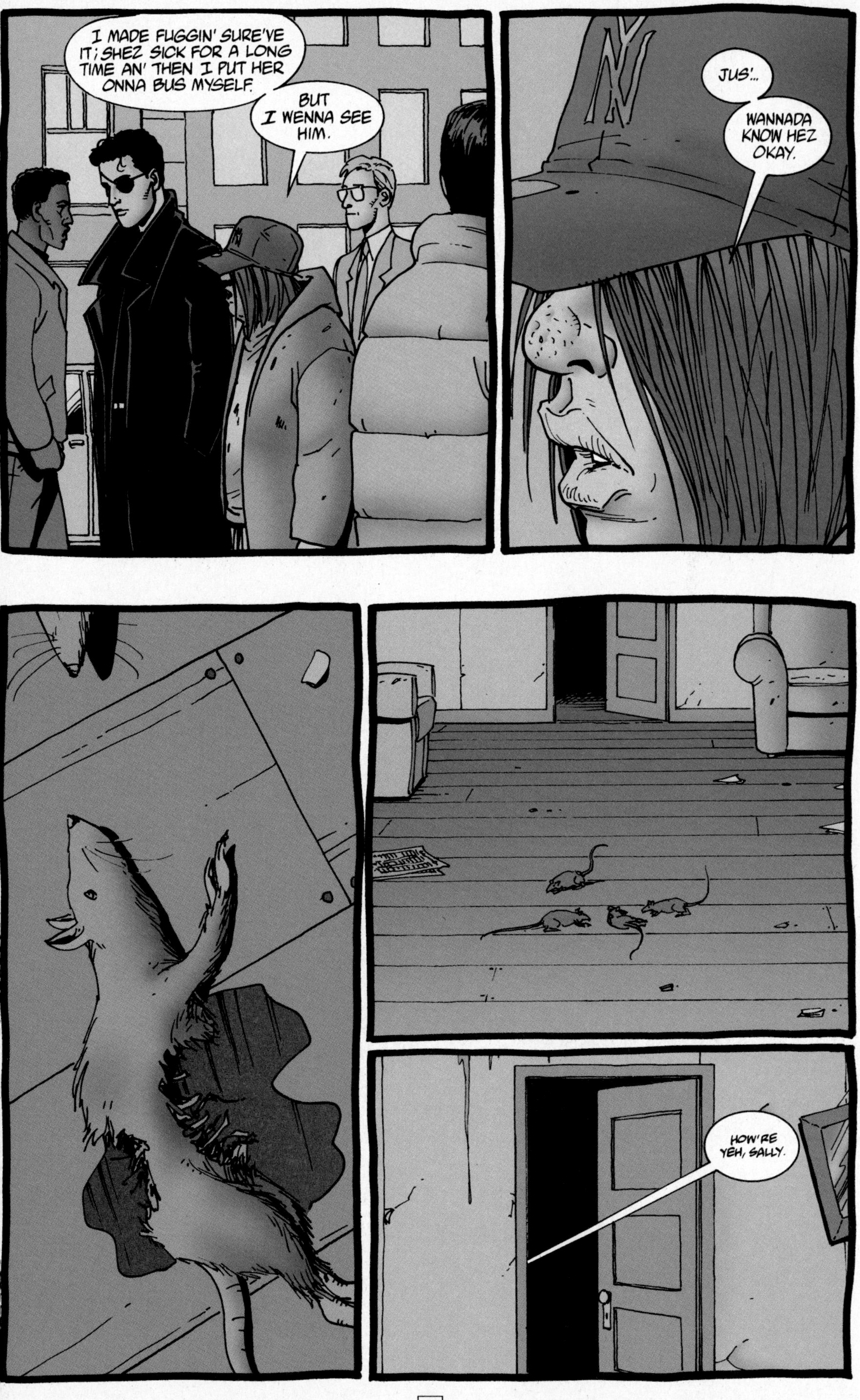
I MADE FUGGIN' SURE'VE IT; SHEZ SICK FOR A LONG TIME AN' THEN I PUT HER ONNA BUS MYSELF.
BUT I WENNA SEE HIM.
JUS'...
WANNADA KNOW HEZ OKAY.
HOW'RE YEH, SALLY.

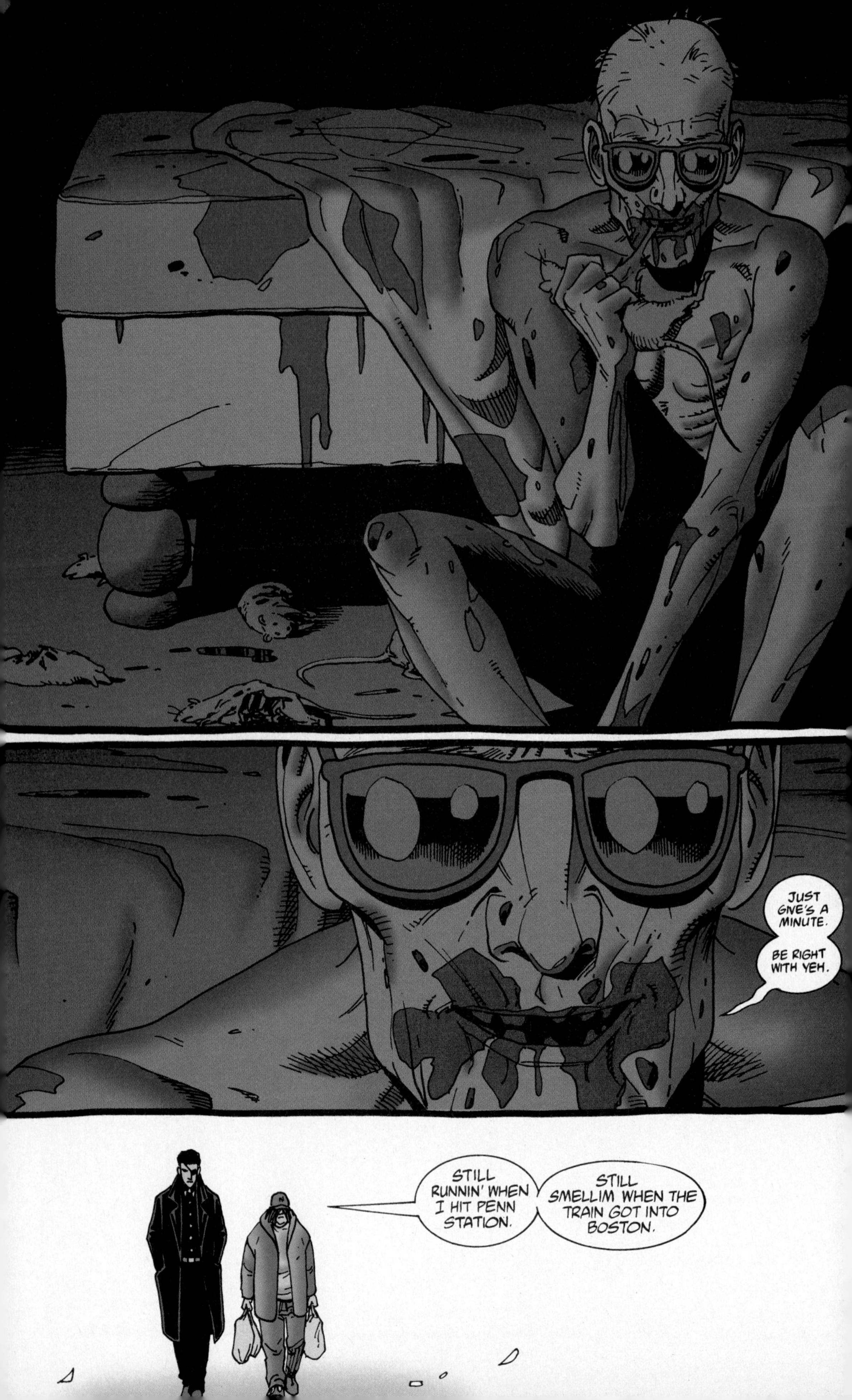
JUST GIVE'S A MINUTE.
BE RIGHT WITH YEH.
STILL RUNNIN' WHEN I HIT PENN STATION.
STILL SMELLIM WHEN THE TRAIN GOT INTO BOSTON.

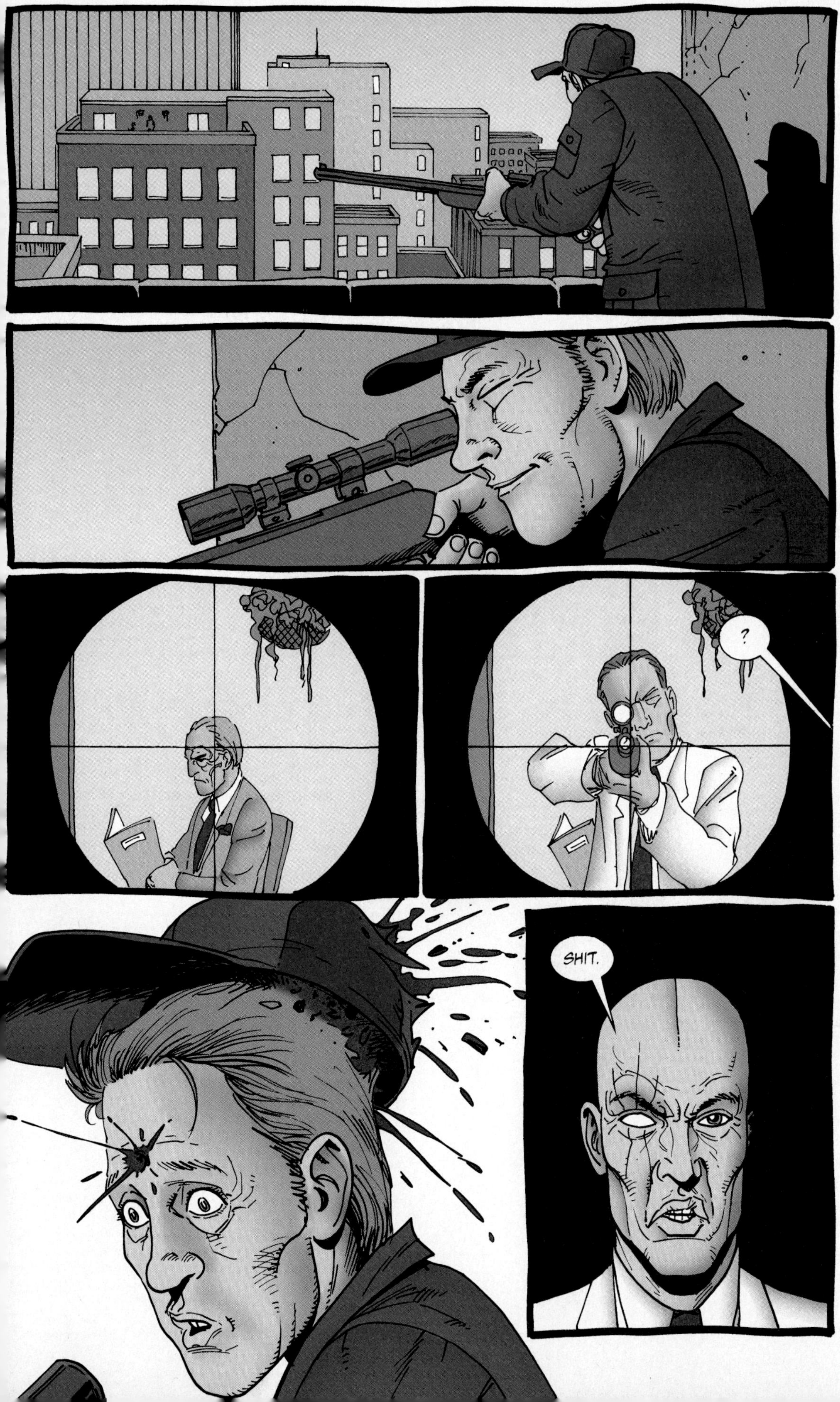
?
SHIT.

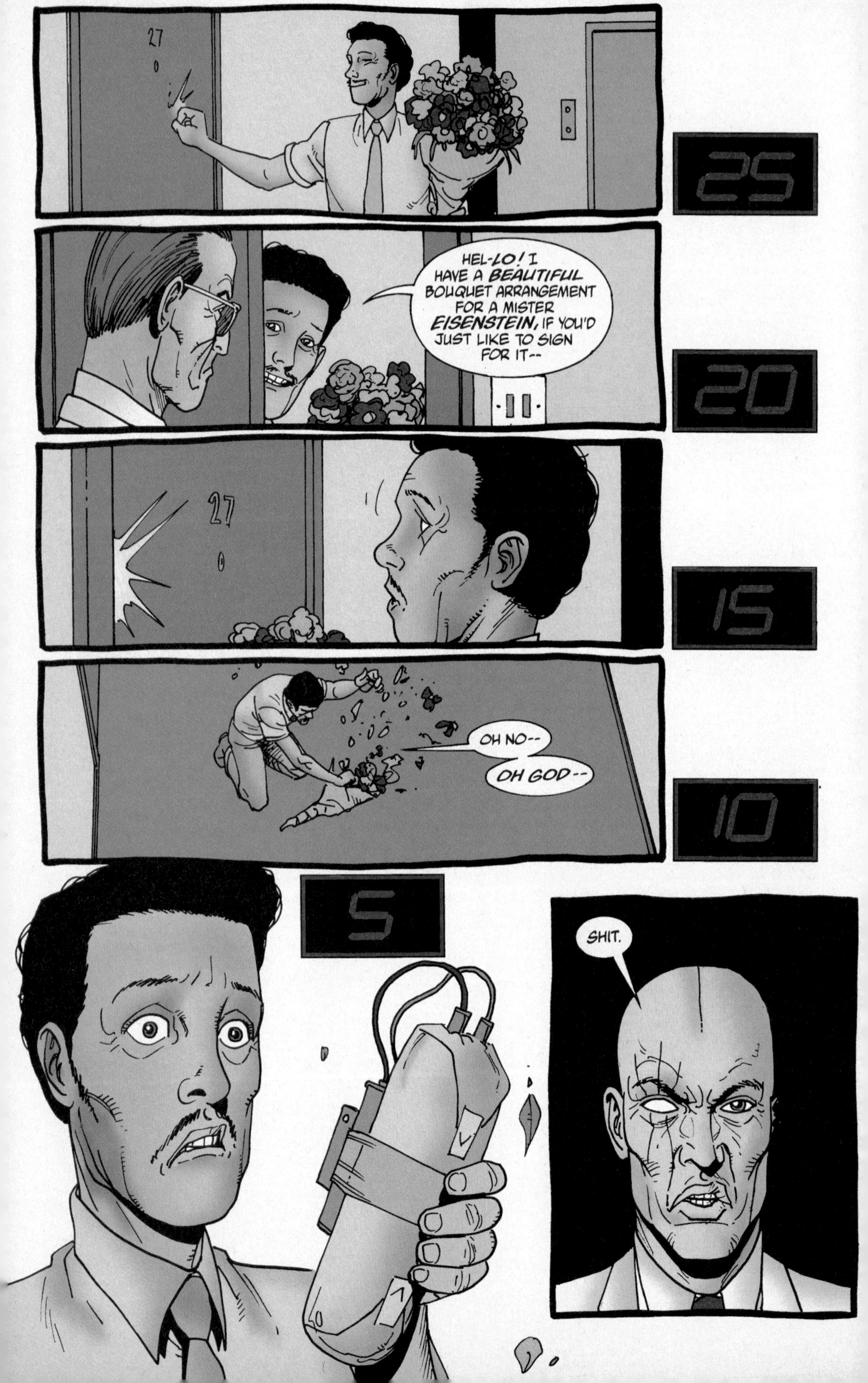
27
25
HEL-LO! I HAVE A BEAUTIFUL BOUQUET ARRANGEMENT FOR A MISTER EISENSTEIN, IF YOU'D JUST LIKE TO SIGN FOR IT--
20
27
15
OH NO--
OH GOD--
10
5
SHIT.

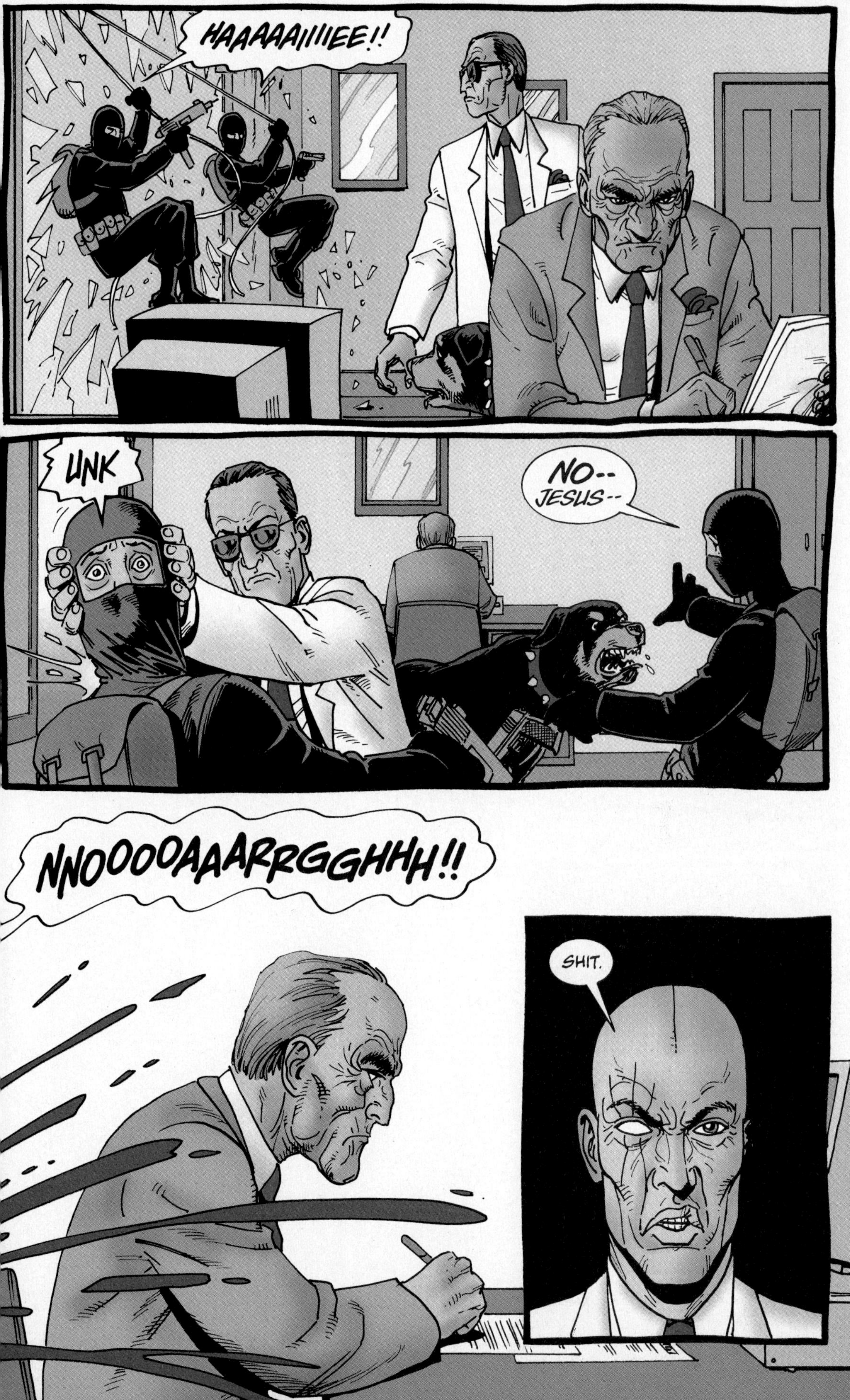
HAAAAAIIIIEE!!
UNK
NO--
JESUS--
NNOOOOAAARRGGHHH!!
SHIT.

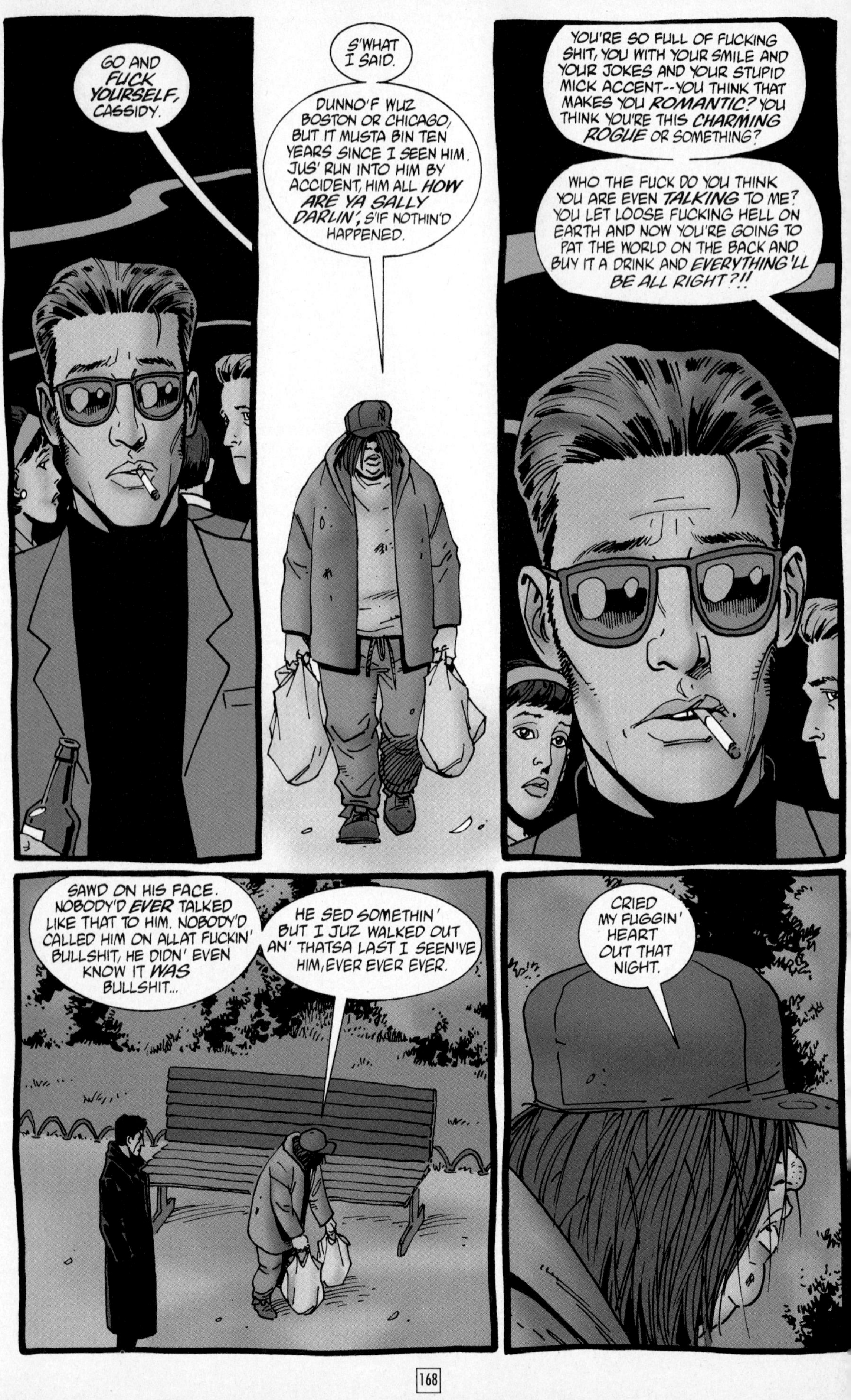
GO AND FUCK YOURSELF, CASSIDY.
S'WHAT I SAID.
DUNNO'F WUZ BOSTON OR CHICAGO, BUT IT MUSTA BIN TEN YEARS SINCE I SEEN HIM. JUS' RUN INTO HIM BY ACCIDENT, HIM ALL HOW ARE YA SALLY DARLIN', S'IF NOTHIN'D HAPPENED.
YOU'RE SO FULL OF FUCKING SHIT, YOU WITH YOUR SMILE AND YOUR JOKES AND YOUR STUPID MICK ACCENT--YOU THINK THAT MAKES YOU ROMANTIC? YOU THINK YOU'RE THIS CHARMING ROGUE OR SOMETHING?
WHO THE FUCK DO YOU THINK YOU ARE EVEN TALKING TO ME? YOU LET LOOSE FUCKING HELL ON EARTH AND NOW YOU'RE GOING TO PAT THE WORLD ON THE BACK AND BUY IT A DRINK AND EVERYTHING'LL BE ALL RIGHT?!!
SAWD ON HIS FACE. NOBODY'D EVER TALKED LIKE THAT TO HIM. NOBODY'D CALLED HIM ON ALLAT FUCKIN' BULLSHIT, HE DIDN' EVEN KNOW IT WAS BULLSHIT...
HE SED SOMETHIN' BUT I JUZ WALKED OUT AN' THATSA LAST I SEEN'VE HIM, EVER EVER EVER.
CRIED MY FUGGIN' HEART OUT THAT NIGHT.

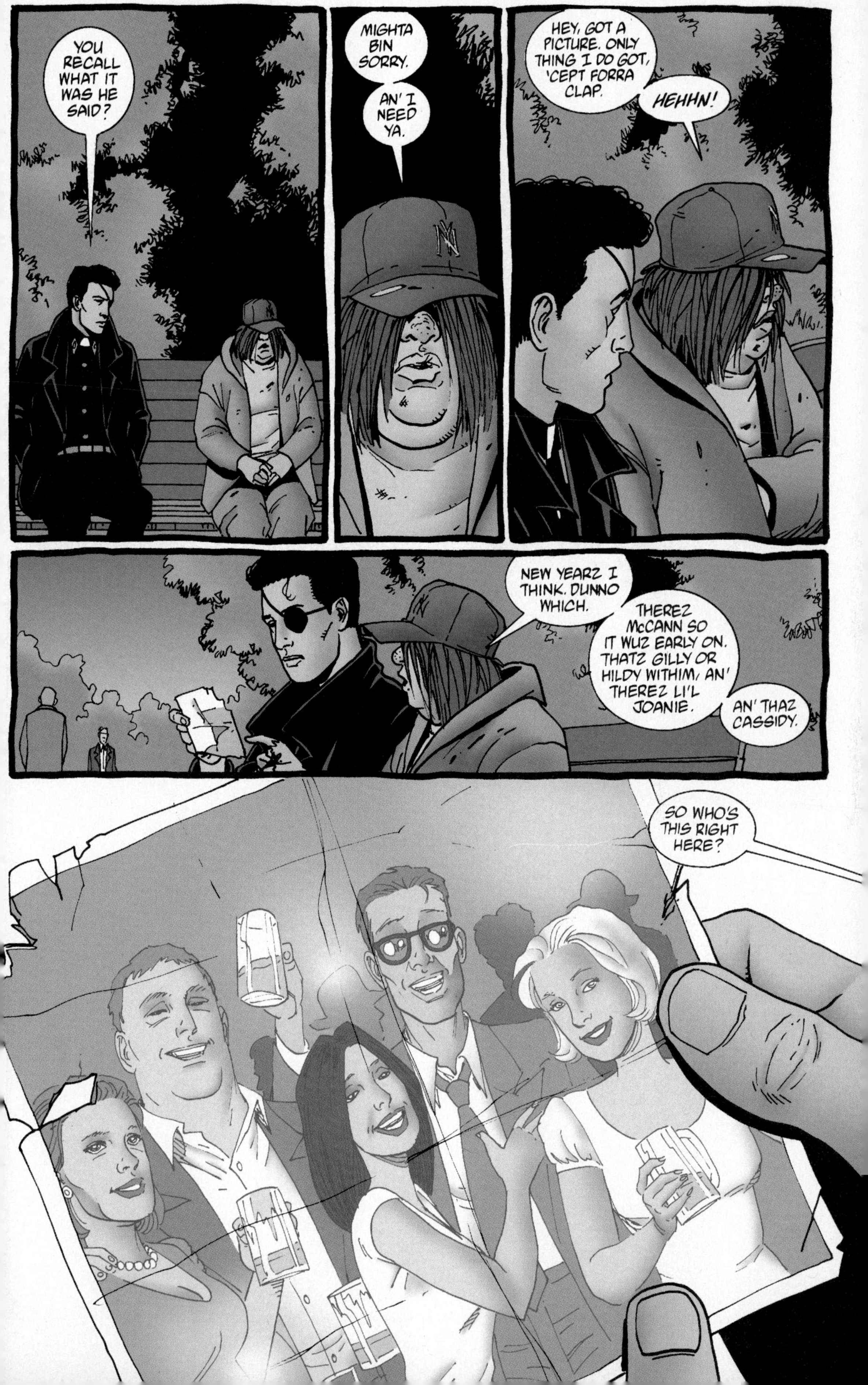
YOU RECALL WHAT IT WAS HE SAID?
MIGHTA BIN SORRY.
AN' I NEED YA.
HEY, GOT A PICTURE. ONLY THING I DO GOT, 'CEPT FORRA CLAP.
HEHHN!
NEW YEARZ I THINK. DUNNO WHICH.
THEREZ McCANN SO IT WUZ EARLY ON. THATZ GILLY OR HILDY WITHIM, AN' THEREZ LI'L JOANIE.
AN' THAZ CASSIDY.
SO WHO'S THIS RIGHT HERE?

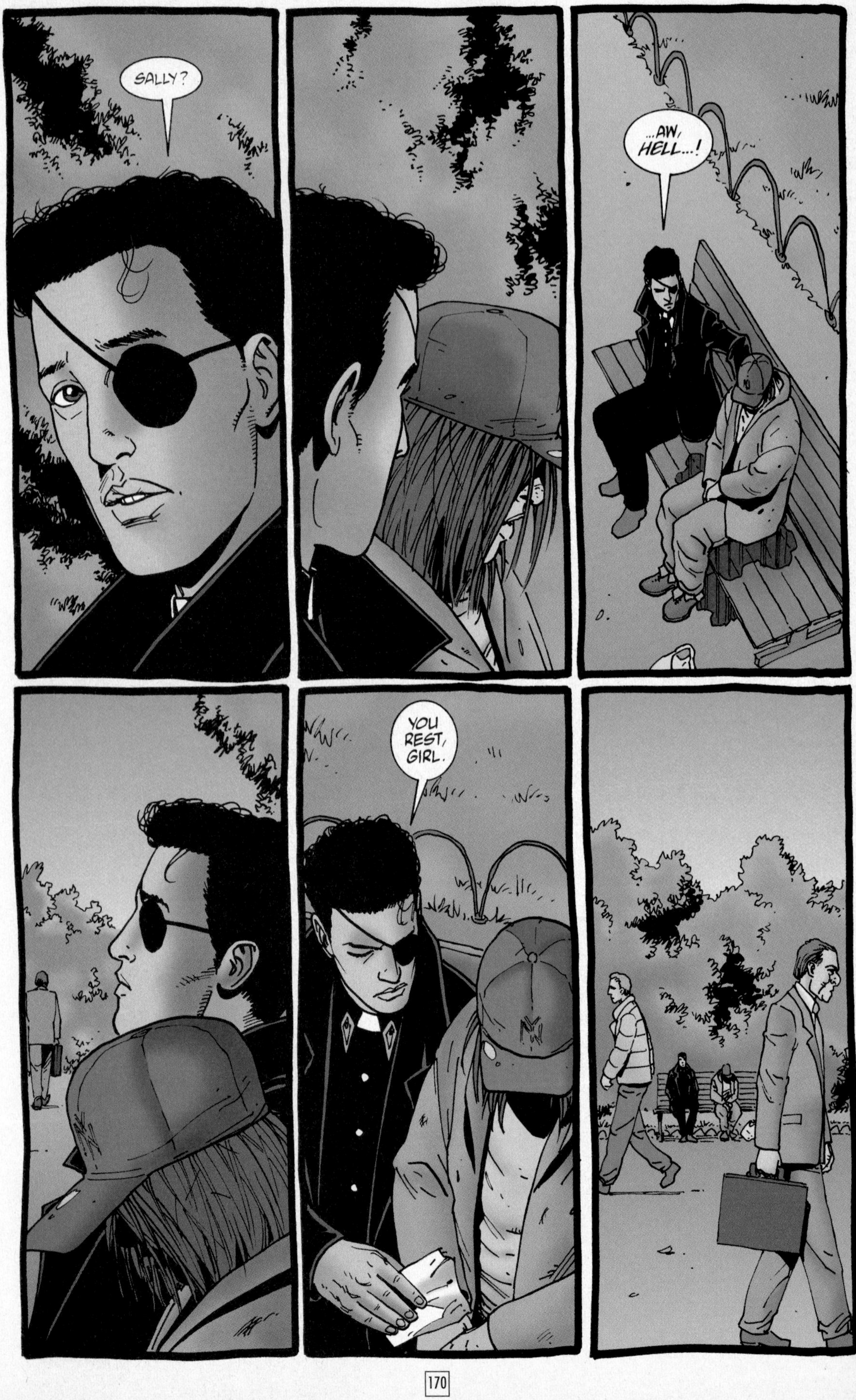
SALLY?
...AW, HELL...!
YOU REST, GIRL.

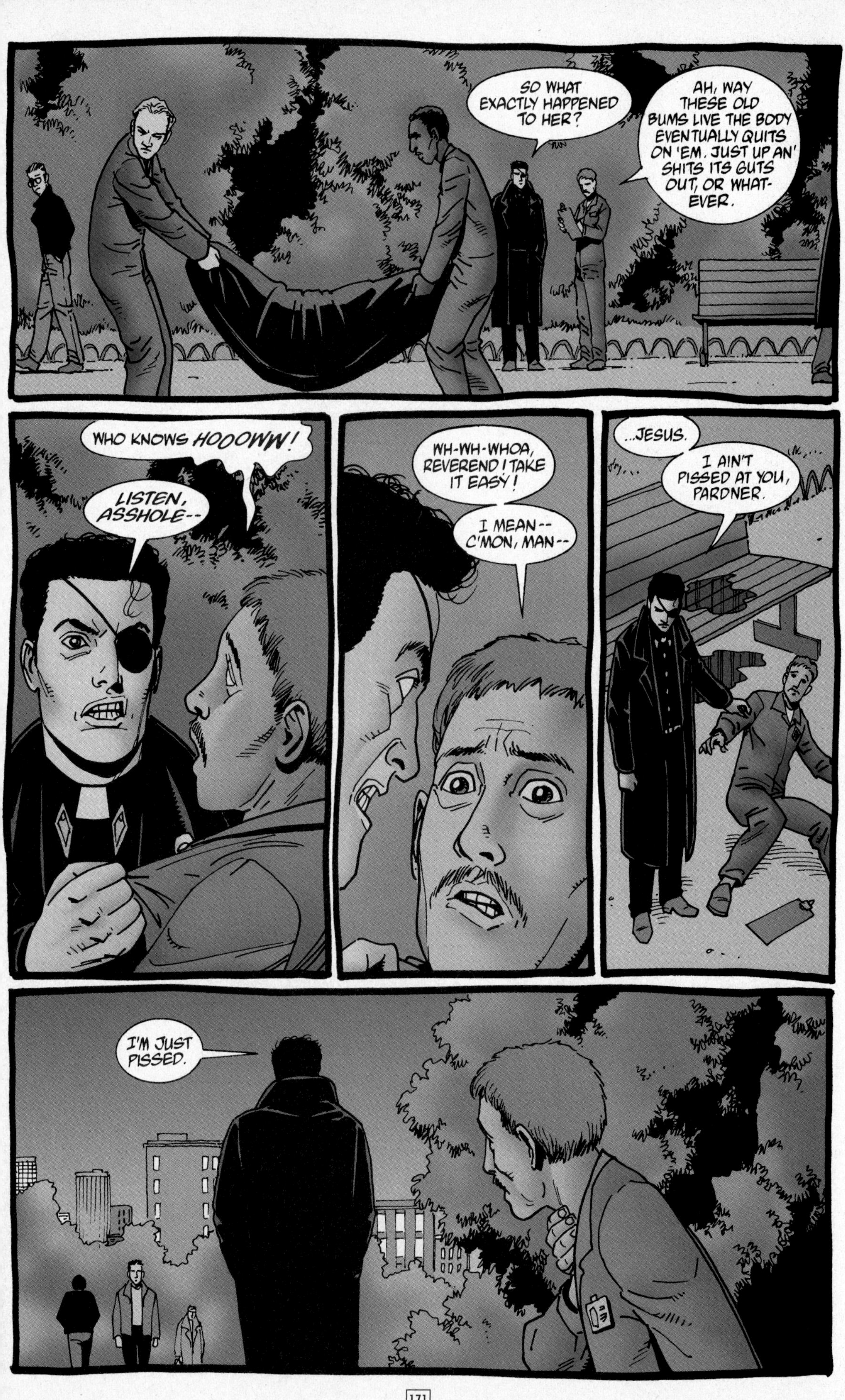
SO WHAT EXACTLY HAPPENED TO HER?
AH, WAY THESE OLD BUMS LIVE THE BODY EVENTUALLY QUITS ON 'EM. JUST UP AN' SHITS ITS GUTS OUT, OR WHAT-EVER.
WHO KNOWS HOOOWW!
LISTEN, ASSHOLE--
WH-WH-WHOA, REVEREND! TAKE IT EASY!
I MEAN-- C'MON, MAN--
...JESUS.
I AIN'T PISSED AT YOU, PARDNER.
I'M JUST PISSED.

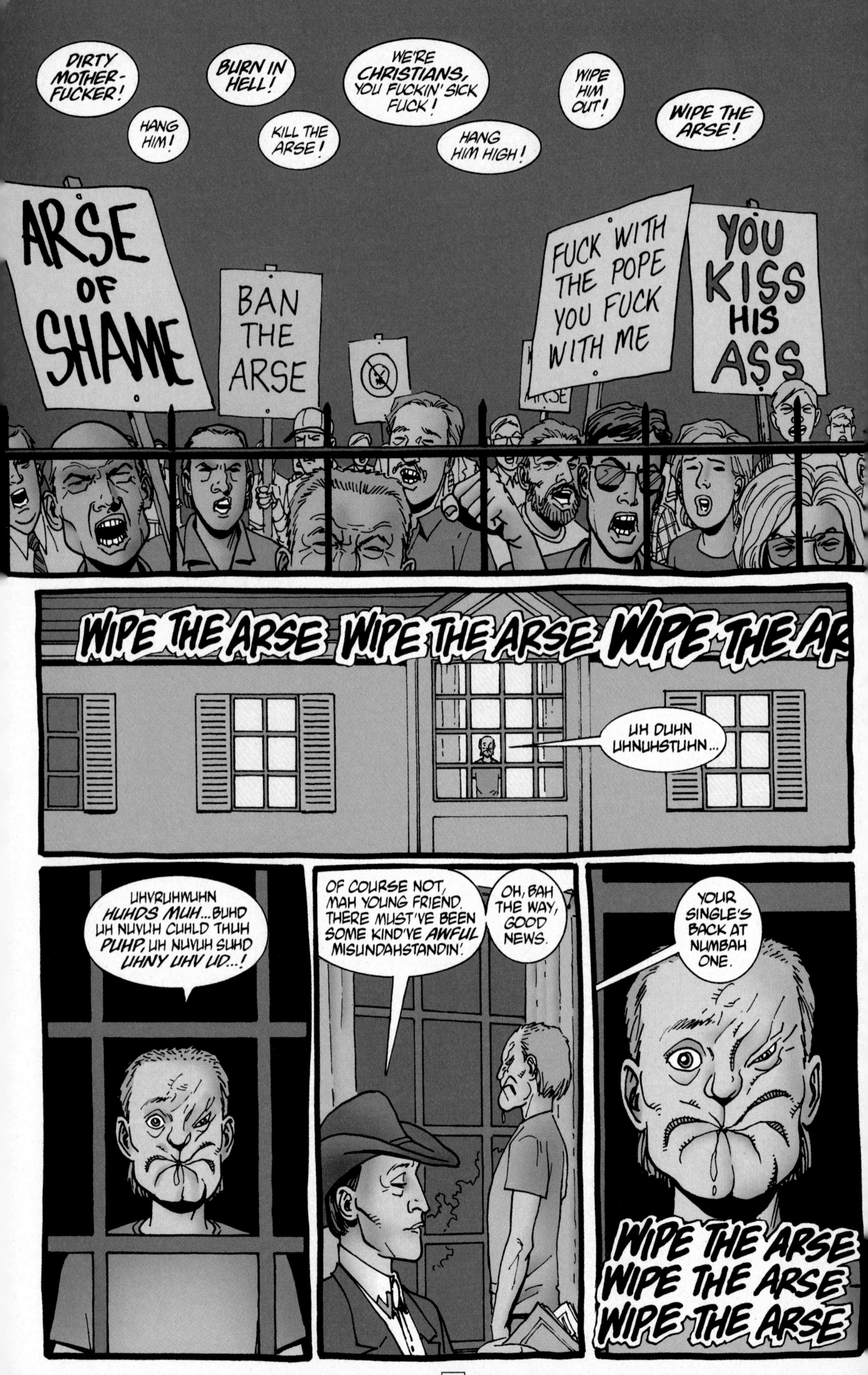
DIRTY MOTHER-FUCKER!
HANG HIM!
BURN IN HELL!
KILL THE ARSE!
WE'RE CHRISTIANS, YOU FUCKIN' SICK FUCK!
HANG HIM HIGH!
WIPE HIM OUT!
WIPE THE ARSE!
ARSE OF SHAME
BAN THE ARSE
FUCK WITH THE POPE YOU FUCK WITH ME
YOU KISS HIS ASS
WIPE THE ARSE WIPE THE ARSE WIPE THE AR
UH DUHN UHNUHSTUHN...
UHVRUHWUHN HUHDS MUH...BUHD UH NUVUH CUHLD THUH PUHP, UH NUVUH SUHD UHNY UHV UD...!
OF COURSE NOT, MAH YOUNG FRIEND. THERE MUST'VE BEEN SOME KIND'VE AWFUL MISUNDAHSTANDIN'.
OH, BAH THE WAY, GOOD NEWS.
YOUR SINGLE'S BACK AT NUMBAH ONE.
WIPE THE ARSE
WIPE THE ARSE
WIPE THE ARSE

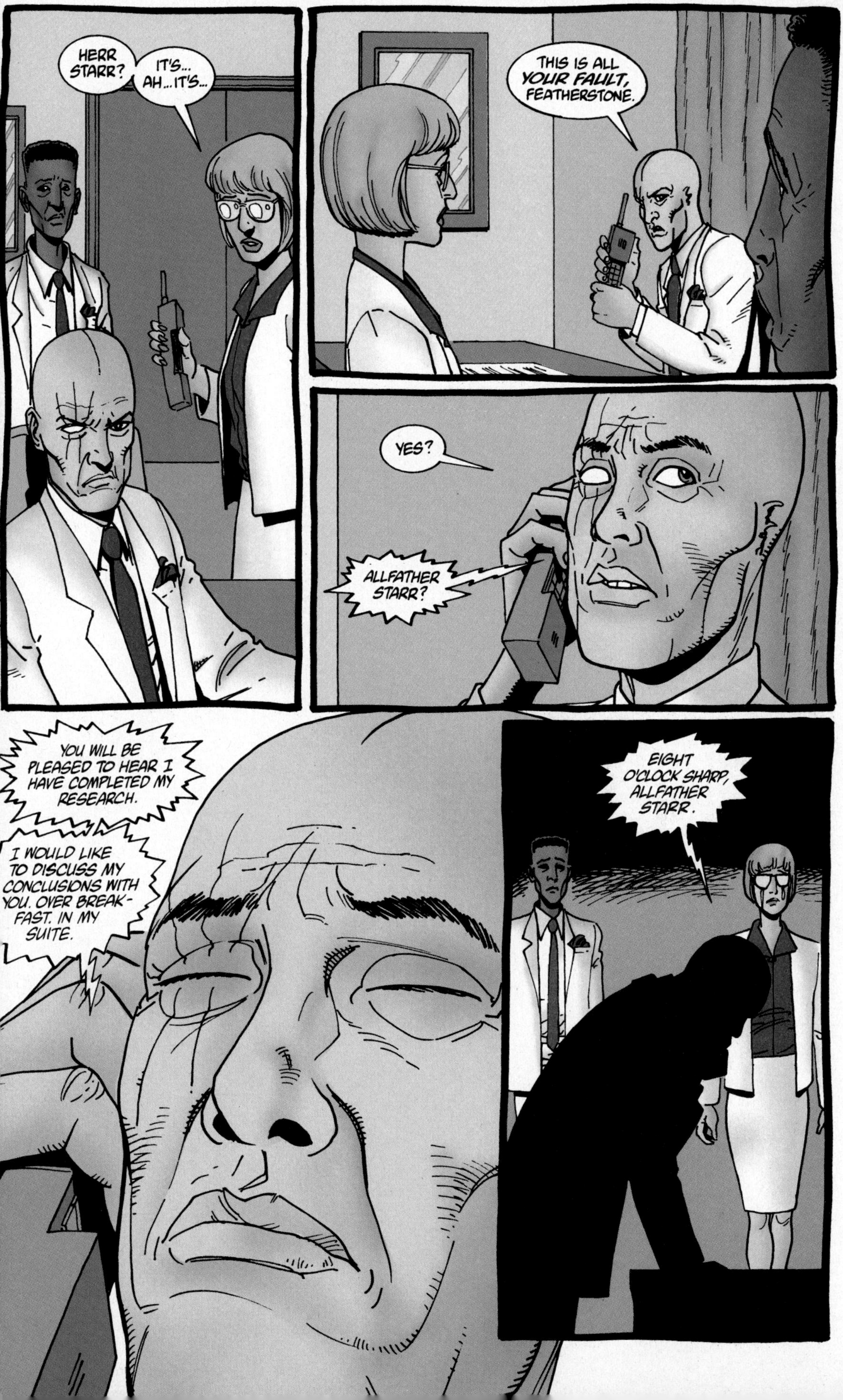
HERR STARR?
IT'S... AH...IT'S...
THIS IS ALL YOUR FAULT, FEATHERSTONE.
YES?
ALLFATHER STARR?
YOU WILL BE PLEASED TO HEAR I HAVE COMPLETED MY RESEARCH.
I WOULD LIKE TO DISCUSS MY CONCLUSIONS WITH YOU. OVER BREAK-FAST. IN MY SUITE.
EIGHT O'CLOCK SHARP, ALLFATHER STARR.

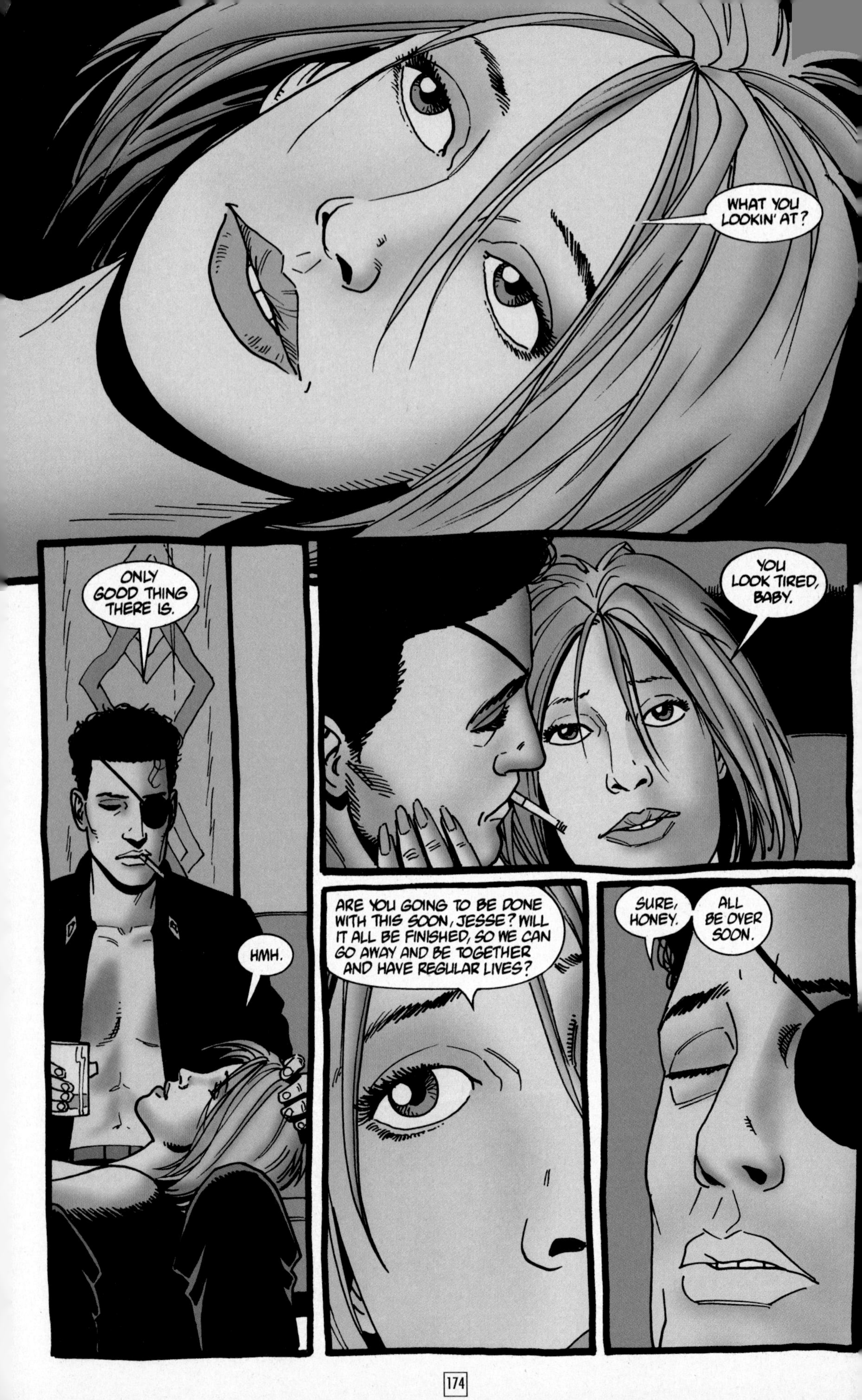
WHAT YOU LOOKIN' AT?
ONLY GOOD THING THERE IS.
YOU LOOK TIRED, BABY.
HMH.
ARE YOU GOING TO BE DONE WITH THIS SOON, JESSE? WILL IT ALL BE FINISHED, SO WE CAN GO AWAY AND BE TOGETHER AND HAVE REGULAR LIVES?
SURE, HONEY.
ALL BE OVER SOON.

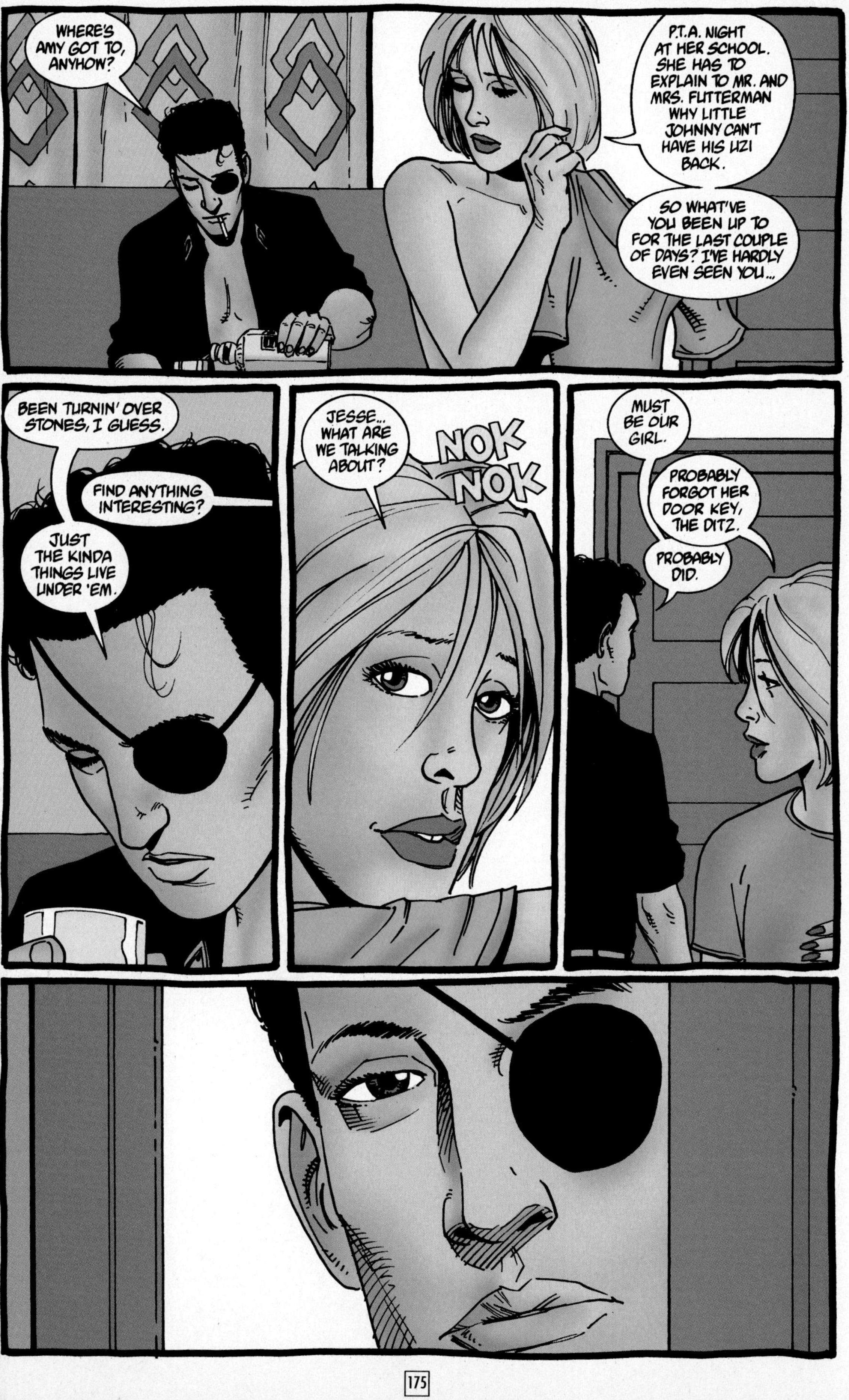
WHERE'S AMY GOT TO, ANYHOW?
P.T.A. NIGHT AT HER SCHOOL. SHE HAS TO EXPLAIN TO MR. AND MRS. FLUTTERMAN WHY LITTLE JOHNNY CAN'T HAVE HIS UZI BACK.
SO WHAT'VE YOU BEEN UP TO FOR THE LAST COUPLE OF DAYS? I'VE HARDLY EVEN SEEN YOU...
BEEN TURNIN' OVER STONES, I GUESS.
FIND ANYTHING INTERESTING?
JUST THE KINDA THINGS LIVE UNDER 'EM.
JESSE... WHAT ARE WE TALKING ABOUT?
NOK NOK
MUST BE OUR GIRL.
PROBABLY FORGOT HER DOOR KEY, THE DITZ.
PROBABLY DID.

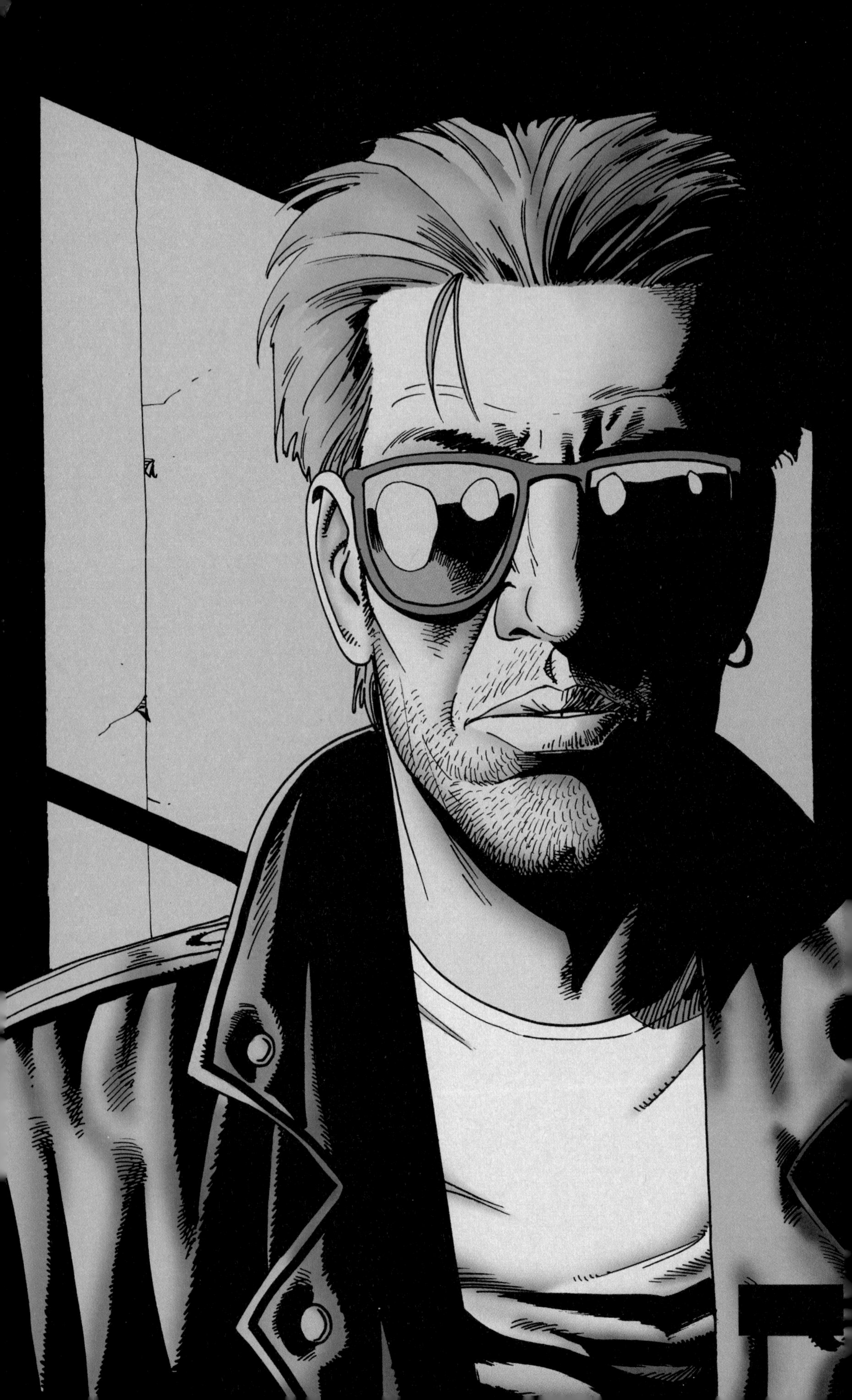

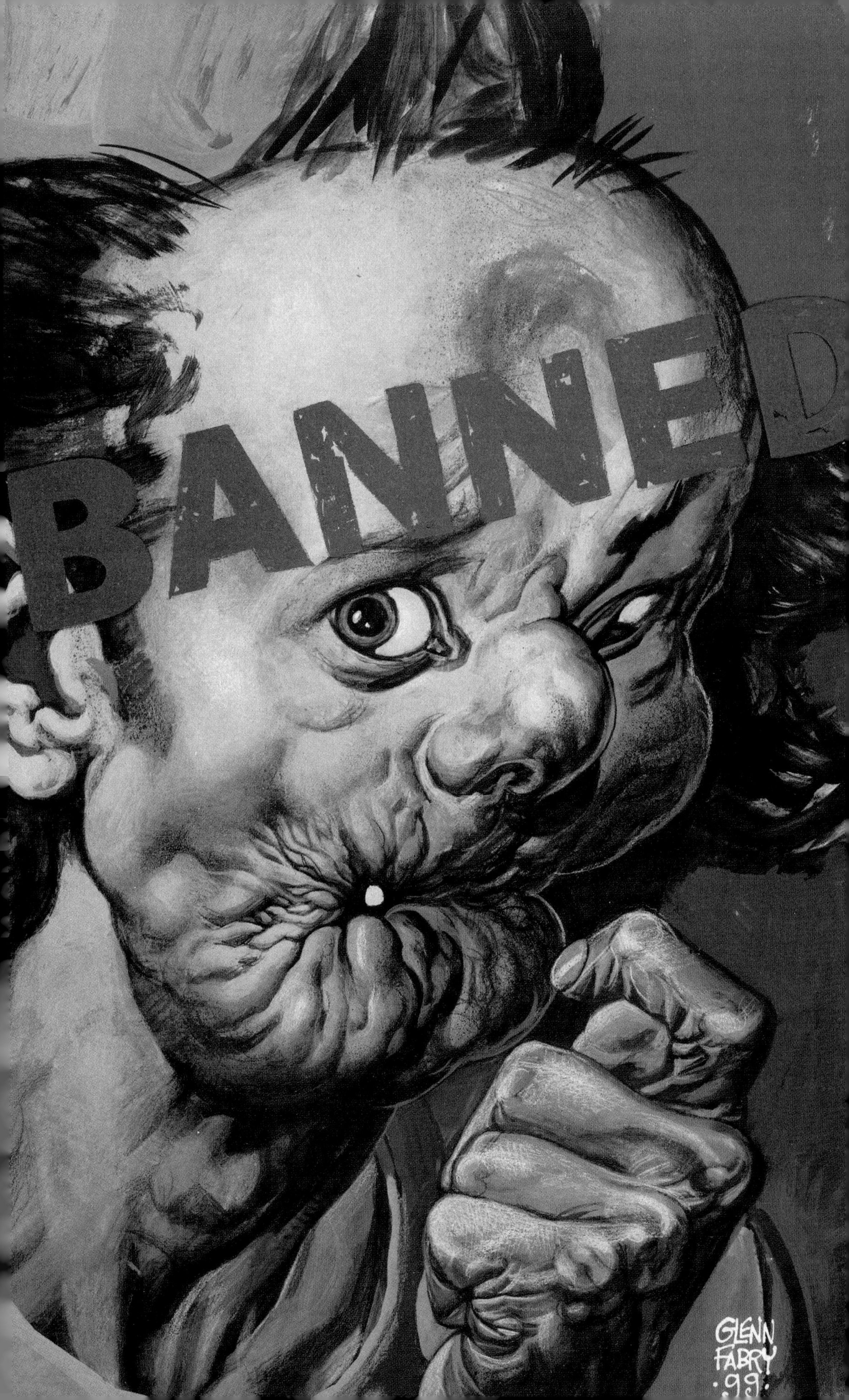
BANNED
GLENN FABRY 99

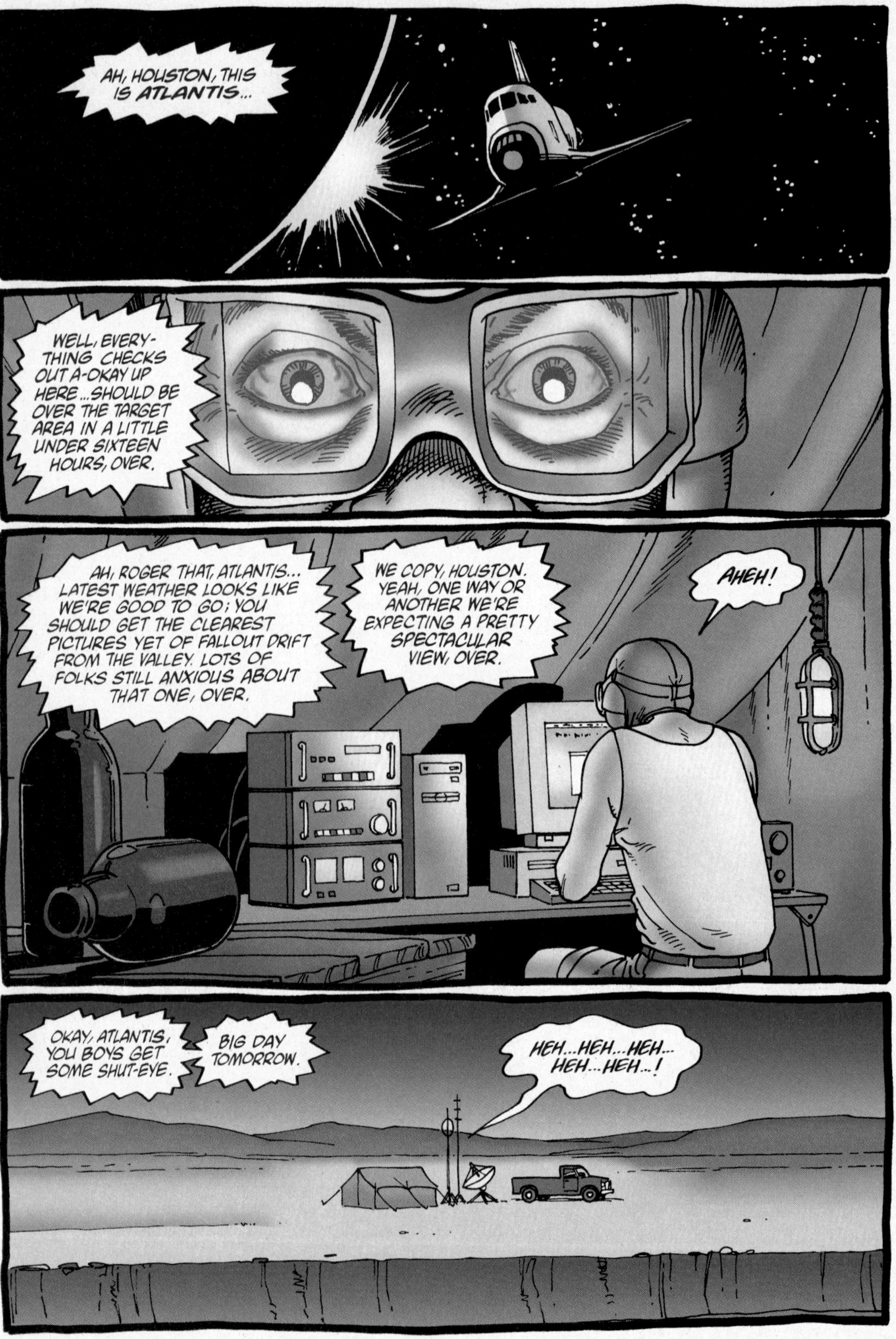
AH, HOUSTON, THIS IS ATLANTIS...
WELL, EVERY-THING CHECKS OUT A-OKAY UP HERE...SHOULD BE OVER THE TARGET AREA IN A LITTLE UNDER SIXTEEN HOURS, OVER.
AH, ROGER THAT, ATLANTIS... LATEST WEATHER LOOKS LIKE WE'RE GOOD TO GO; YOU SHOULD GET THE CLEAREST PICTURES YET OF FALLOUT DRIFT FROM THE VALLEY. LOTS OF FOLKS STILL ANXIOUS ABOUT THAT ONE, OVER.
WE COPY, HOUSTON. YEAH, ONE WAY OR ANOTHER WE'RE EXPECTING A PRETTY SPECTACULAR VIEW, OVER.
AHEH!
OKAY, ATLANTIS, YOU BOYS GET SOME SHUT-EYE.
BIG DAY TOMORROW.
HEH...HEH...HEH... HEH...HEH...!

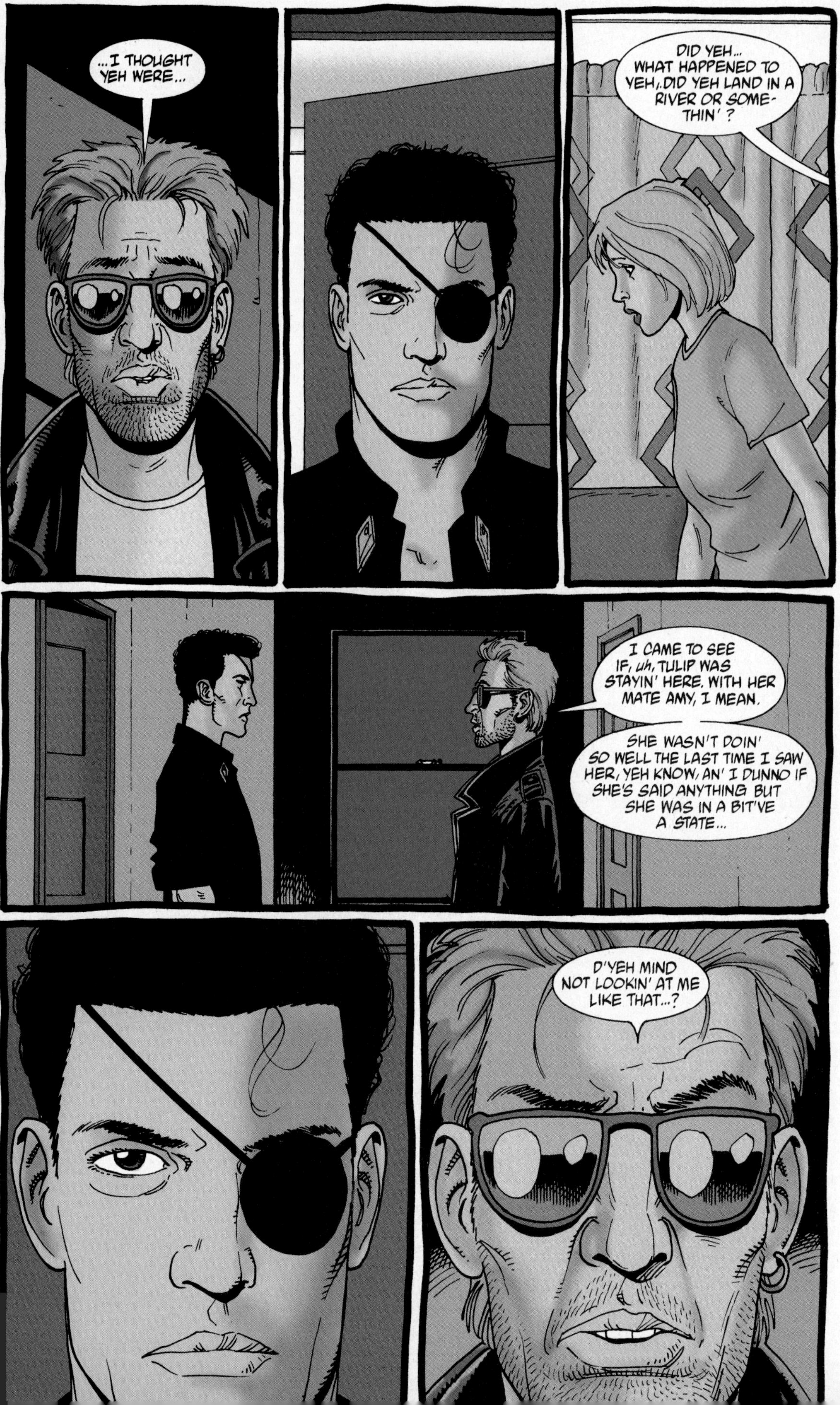
...I THOUGHT YEH WERE...
DID YEH... WHAT HAPPENED TO YEH, DID YEH LAND IN A RIVER OR SOMETHIN'?
I CAME TO SEE IF, uh, TULIP WAS STAYIN' HERE. WITH HER MATE AMY, I MEAN.
SHE WASN'T DOIN' SO WELL THE LAST TIME I SAW HER, YEH KNOW, AN' I DUNNO IF SHE'S SAID ANYTHING BUT SHE WAS IN A BIT'VE A STATE...
D'YEH MIND NOT LOOKIN' AT ME LIKE THAT...?

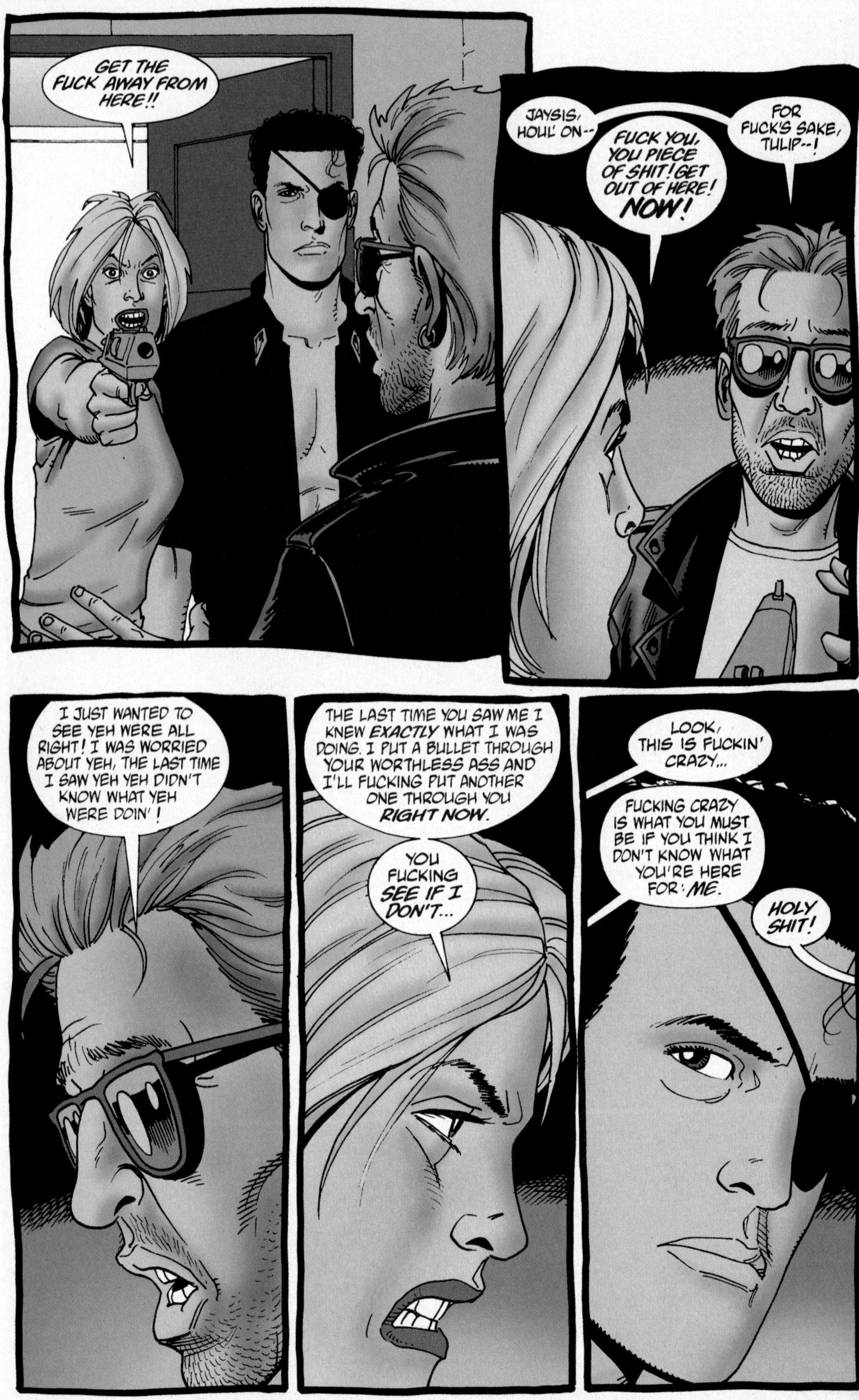
GET THE FUCK AWAY FROM HERE!!
JAYSIS, HOUL' ON--
FUCK YOU, YOU PIECE OF SHIT! GET OUT OF HERE! NOW!
FOR FUCK'S SAKE, TULIP--!
I JUST WANTED TO SEE YEH WERE ALL RIGHT! I WAS WORRIED ABOUT YEH, THE LAST TIME I SAW YEH YEH DIDN'T KNOW WHAT YEH WERE DOIN'!
THE LAST TIME YOU SAW ME I KNEW EXACTLY WHAT I WAS DOING. I PUT A BULLET THROUGH YOUR WORTHLESS ASS AND I'LL FUCKING PUT ANOTHER ONE THROUGH YOU RIGHT NOW.
YOU FUCKING SEE IF I DON'T...
LOOK, THIS IS FUCKIN' CRAZY...
FUCKING CRAZY IS WHAT YOU MUST BE IF YOU THINK I DON'T KNOW WHAT YOU'RE HERE FOR: ME.
HOLY SHIT!

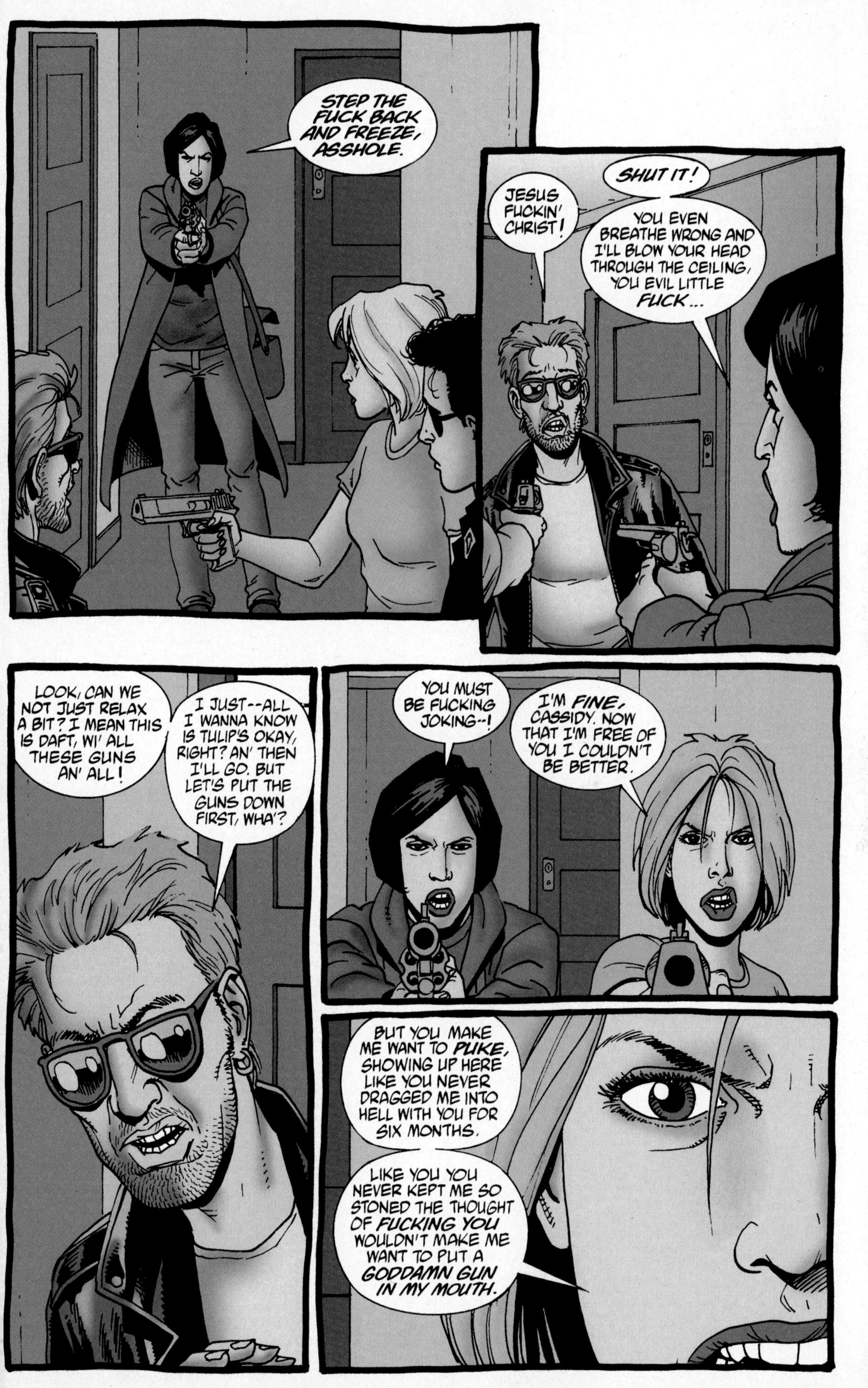
STEP THE FUCK BACK AND FREEZE, ASSHOLE.
JESUS FUCKIN' CHRIST!
SHUT IT!
YOU EVEN BREATHE WRONG AND I'LL BLOW YOUR HEAD THROUGH THE CEILING, YOU EVIL LITTLE FUCK...
LOOK, CAN WE NOT JUST RELAX A BIT? I MEAN THIS IS DAFT, WI' ALL THESE GUNS AN' ALL!
I JUST--ALL I WANNA KNOW IS TULIP'S OKAY, RIGHT? AN' THEN I'LL GO. BUT LET'S PUT THE GUNS DOWN FIRST, WHA'?
YOU MUST BE FUCKING JOKING--!
I'M FINE, CASSIDY. NOW THAT I'M FREE OF YOU I COULDN'T BE BETTER.
BUT YOU MAKE ME WANT TO PUKE, SHOWING UP HERE LIKE YOU NEVER DRAGGED ME INTO HELL WITH YOU FOR SIX MONTHS.
LIKE YOU YOU NEVER KEPT ME SO STONED THE THOUGHT OF FUCKING YOU WOULDN'T MAKE ME WANT TO PUT A GODDAMN GUN IN MY MOUTH.

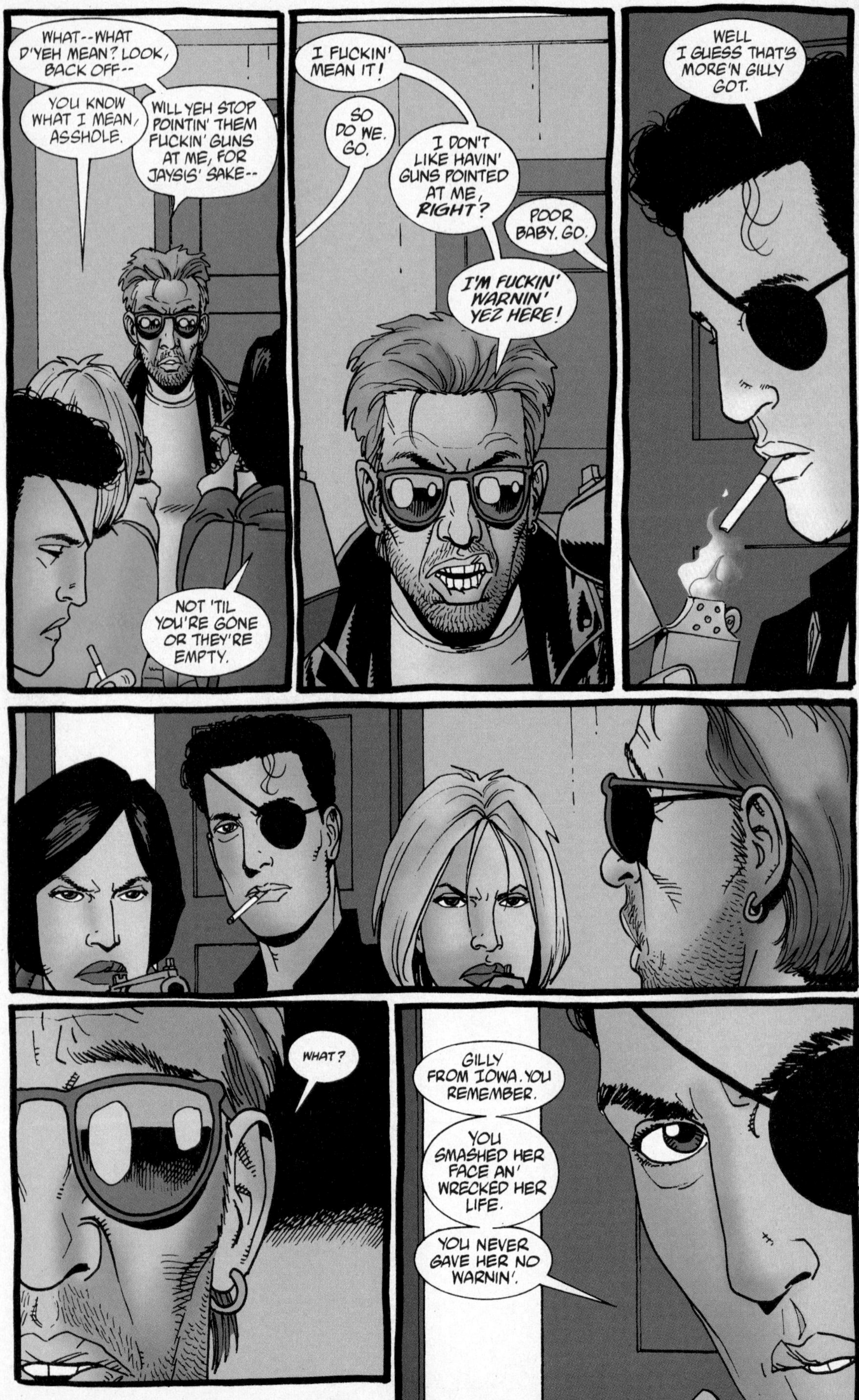
WHAT--WHAT D'YEH MEAN? LOOK, BACK OFF--
YOU KNOW WHAT I MEAN, ASSHOLE.
WILL YEH STOP POINTIN' THEM FUCKIN' GUNS AT ME, FOR JAYSIS' SAKE--
NOT 'TIL YOU'RE GONE OR THEY'RE EMPTY.
I FUCKIN' MEAN IT!
SO DO WE. GO.
I DON'T LIKE HAVIN' GUNS POINTED AT ME, RIGHT?
POOR BABY. GO.
I'M FUCKIN' WARNIN' YEZ HERE!
WELL I GUESS THAT'S MORE'N GILLY GOT.
WHAT?
GILLY FROM IOWA. YOU REMEMBER.
YOU SMASHED HER FACE AN' WRECKED HER LIFE.
YOU NEVER GAVE HER NO WARNIN'.

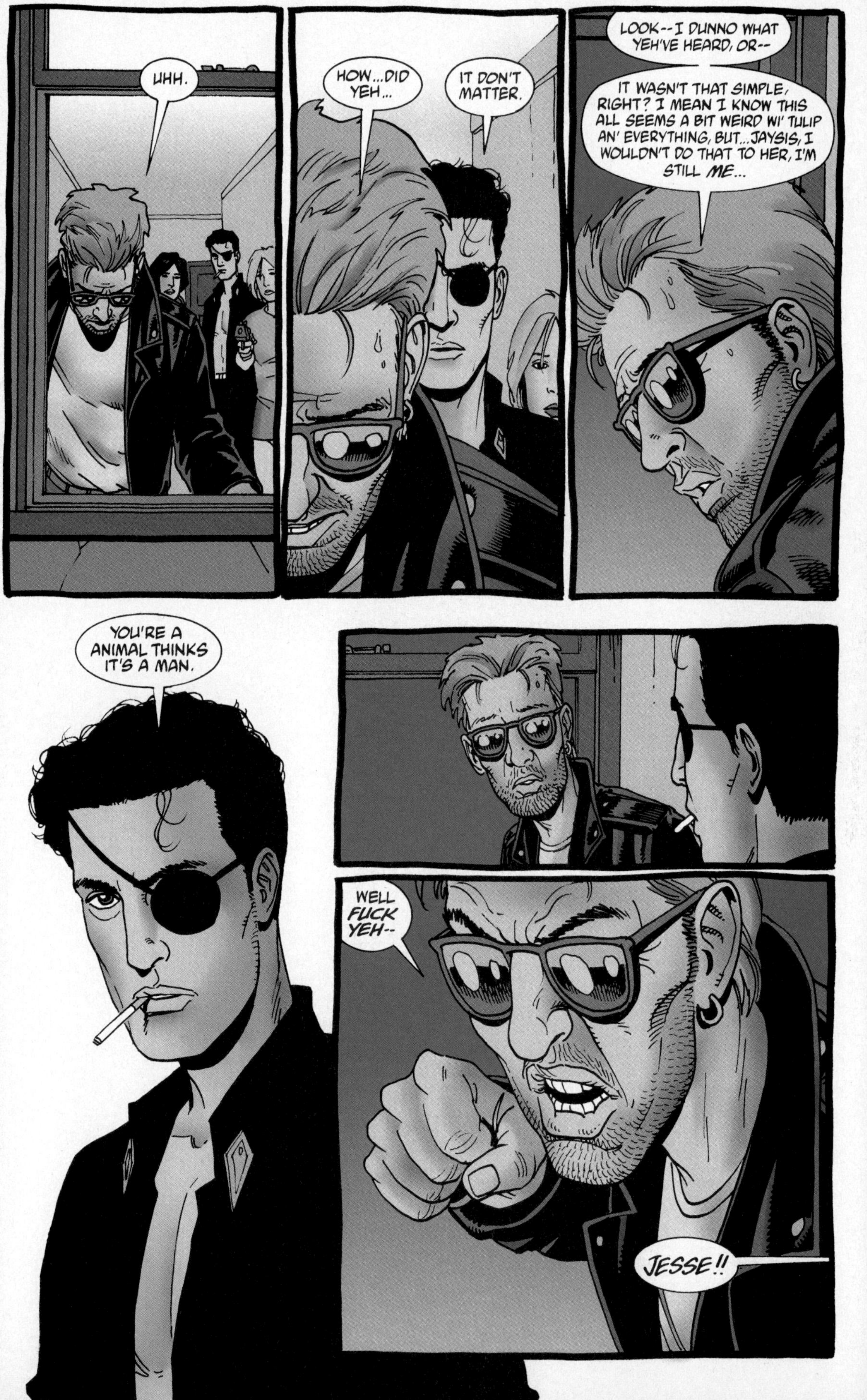
UHH.
HOW...DID YEH...
IT DON'T MATTER.
LOOK--I DUNNO WHAT YEH'VE HEARD, OR--
IT WASN'T THAT SIMPLE, RIGHT? I MEAN I KNOW THIS ALL SEEMS A BIT WEIRD WI' TULIP AN' EVERYTHING, BUT...JAYSIS, I WOULDN'T DO THAT TO HER, I'M STILL *ME*...
YOU'RE A ANIMAL THINKS IT'S A MAN.
WELL *FUCK* YEH--
JESSE!!

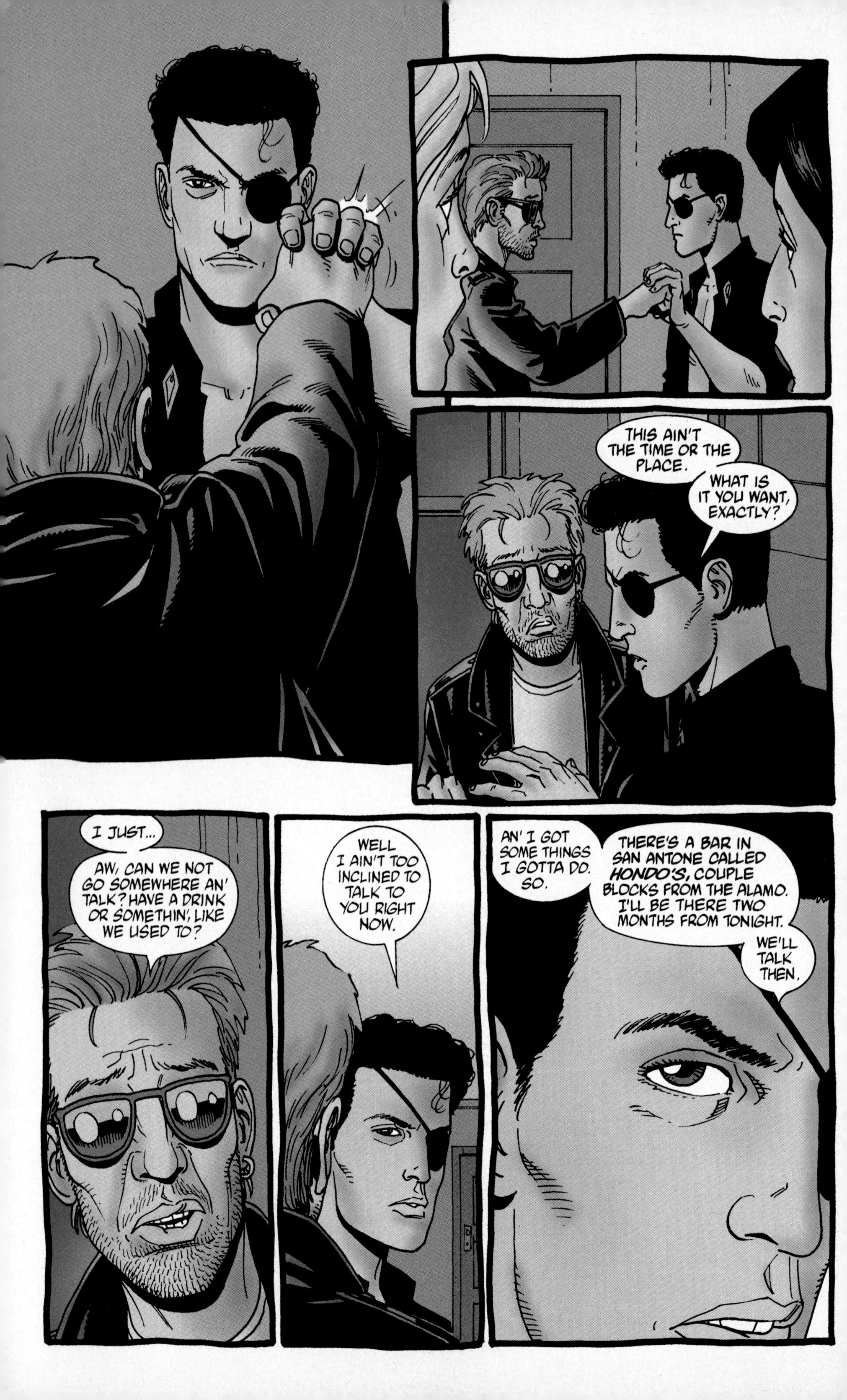
THIS AIN'T THE TIME OR THE PLACE.
WHAT IS IT YOU WANT, EXACTLY?
I JUST...
AW, CAN WE NOT GO SOMEWHERE AN' TALK? HAVE A DRINK OR SOMETHIN', LIKE WE USED TO?
WELL I AIN'T TOO INCLINED TO TALK TO YOU RIGHT NOW.
AN' I GOT SOME THINGS I GOTTA DO. SO.
THERE'S A BAR IN SAN ANTONE CALLED HONDO'S, COUPLE BLOCKS FROM THE ALAMO. I'LL BE THERE TWO MONTHS FROM TONIGHT.
WE'LL TALK THEN.

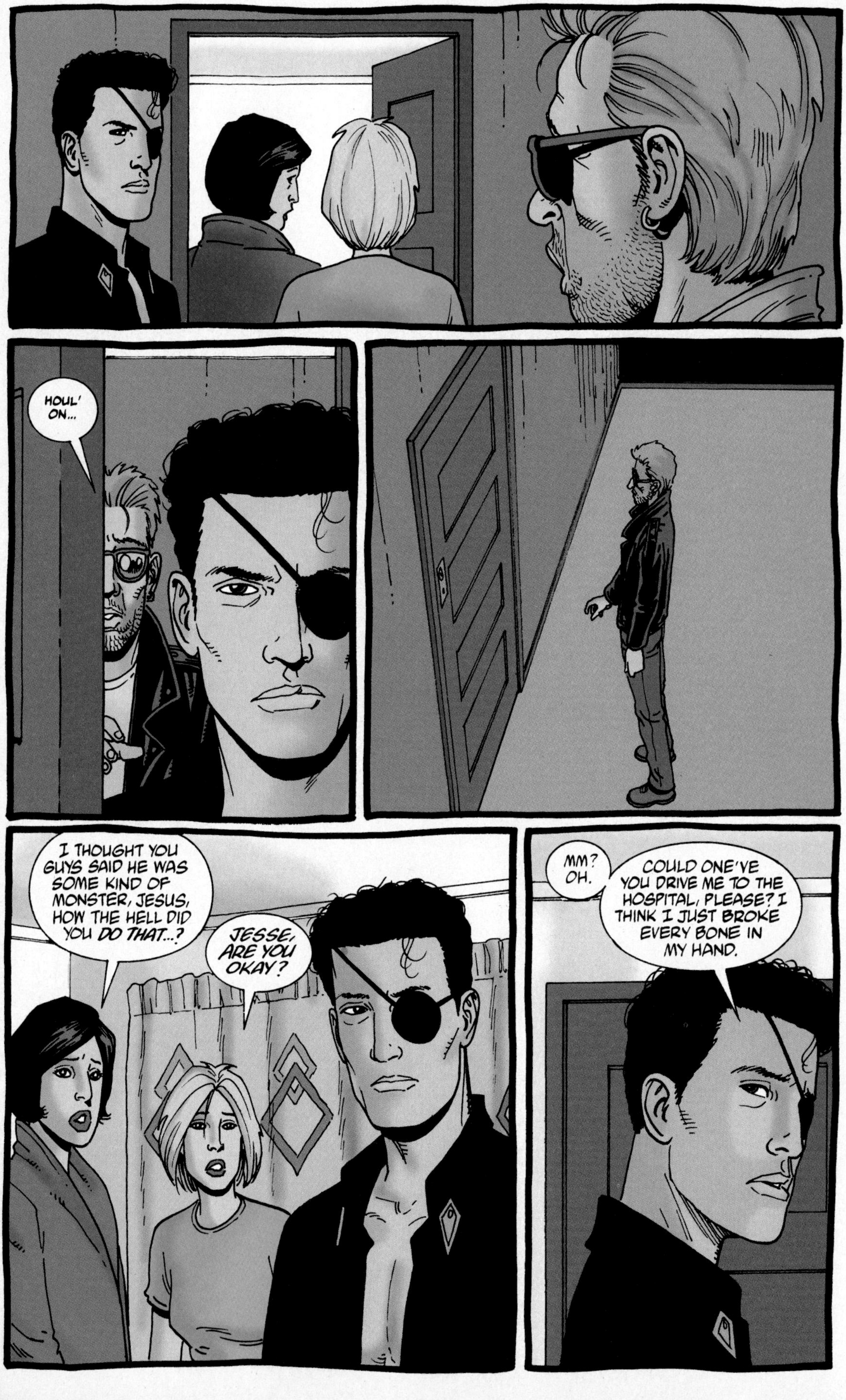
HOUL' ON...
I THOUGHT YOU GUYS SAID HE WAS SOME KIND OF MONSTER, JESUS, HOW THE HELL DID YOU *DO THAT*...?
JESSE, ARE YOU OKAY?
MM? OH.
COULD ONE'VE YOU DRIVE ME TO THE HOSPITAL, PLEASE? I THINK I JUST BROKE EVERY BONE IN MY HAND.

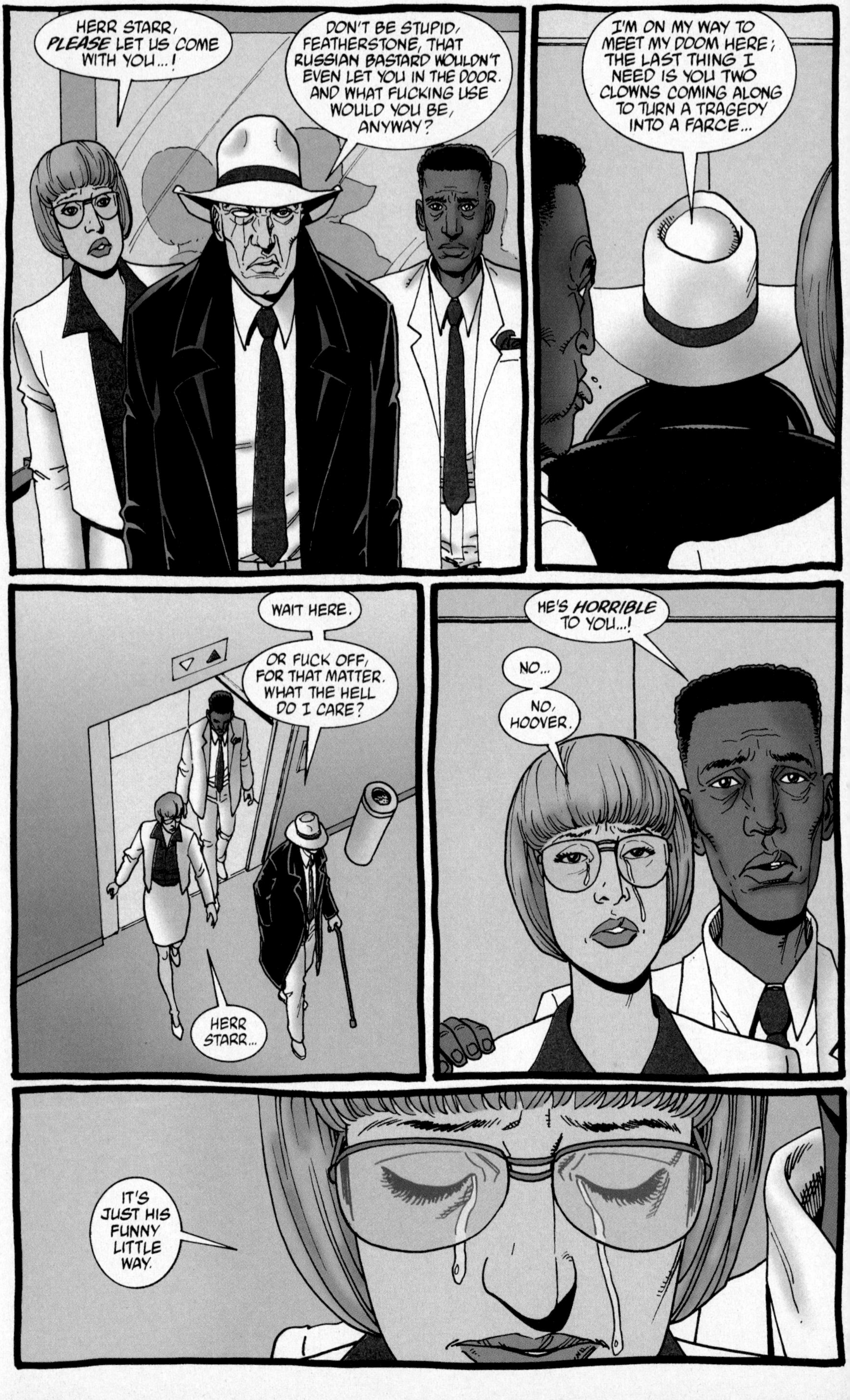
HERR STARR, *PLEASE* LET US COME WITH YOU...!
DON'T BE STUPID, FEATHERSTONE, THAT RUSSIAN BASTARD WOULDN'T EVEN LET YOU IN THE DOOR. AND WHAT FUCKING USE WOULD YOU BE, ANYWAY?
I'M ON MY WAY TO MEET MY DOOM HERE; THE LAST THING I NEED IS YOU TWO CLOWNS COMING ALONG TO TURN A TRAGEDY INTO A FARCE...
WAIT HERE.
OR FUCK OFF, FOR THAT MATTER. WHAT THE HELL DO I CARE?
HERR STARR...
HE'S *HORRIBLE* TO YOU...!
NO...
NO, HOOVER.
IT'S JUST HIS FUNNY LITTLE WAY.

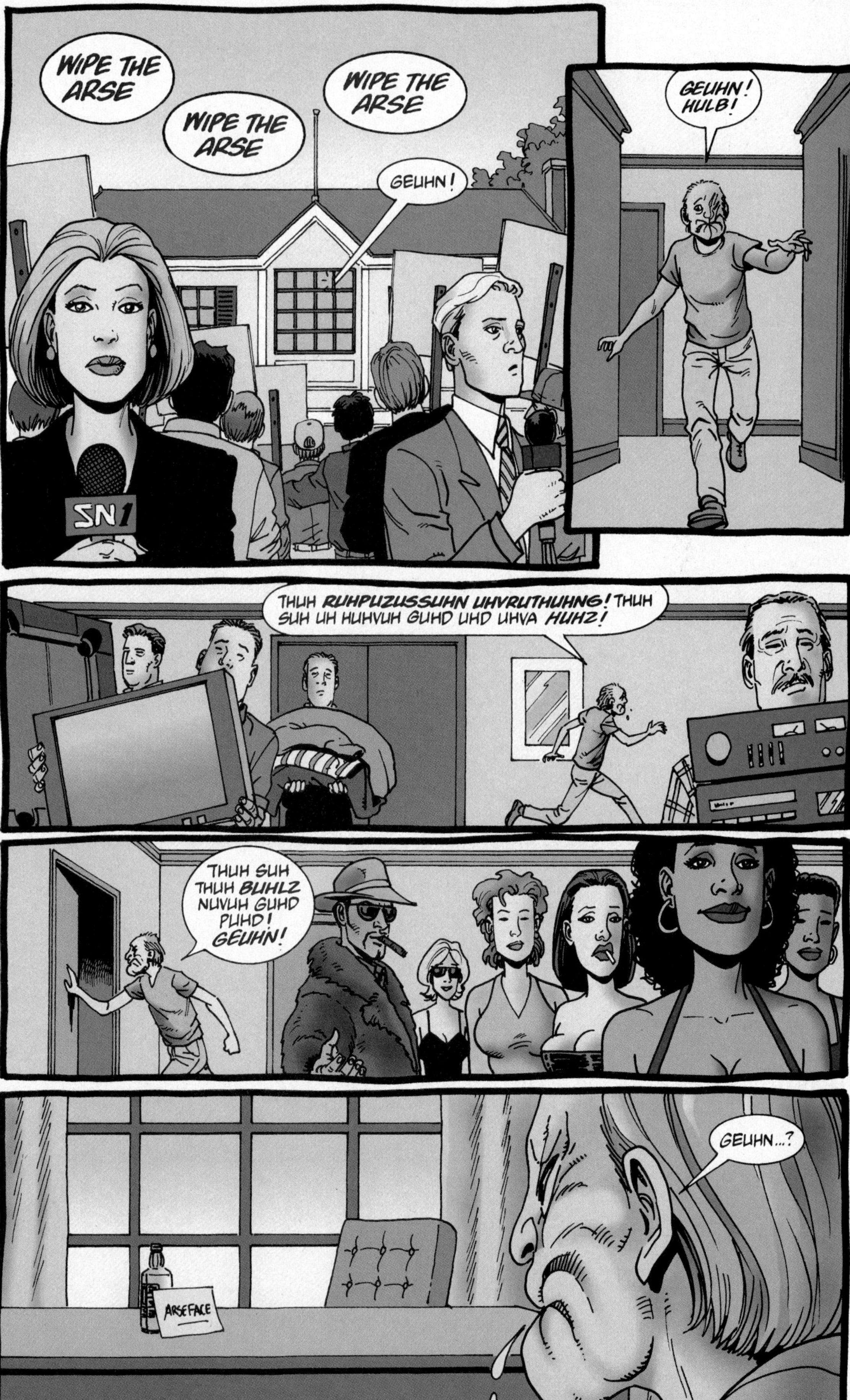
WIPE THE ARSE
WIPE THE ARSE
WIPE THE ARSE
GEUHN!
SN1
GEUHN! HULB!
THUH RUHPUZUSSUHN UHVRUTHUHNG! THUH SUH UH HUHVUH GUHD UHD UHVA HUHZ!
THUH SUH THUH BUHLZ NUVUH GUHD PUHD! GEUHN!
ARSEFACE
GEUHN...?

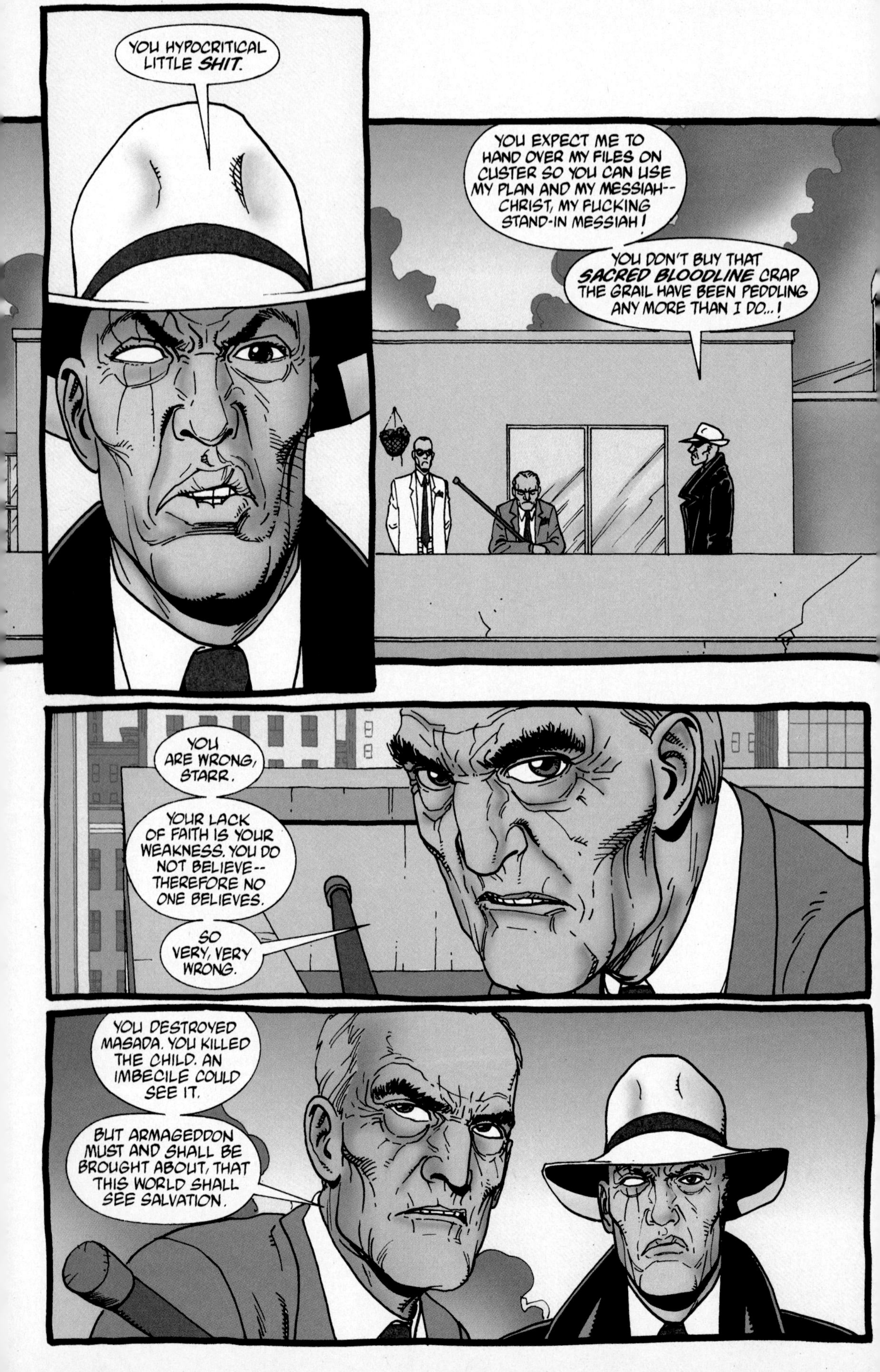
YOU HYPOCRITICAL LITTLE SHIT.
YOU EXPECT ME TO HAND OVER MY FILES ON CUSTER SO YOU CAN USE MY PLAN AND MY MESSIAH-- CHRIST, MY FUCKING STAND-IN MESSIAH!
YOU DON'T BUY THAT SACRED BLOODLINE CRAP THE GRAIL HAVE BEEN PEDDLING ANY MORE THAN I DO...!
YOU ARE WRONG, STARR.
YOUR LACK OF FAITH IS YOUR WEAKNESS. YOU DO NOT BELIEVE-- THEREFORE NO ONE BELIEVES.
SO VERY, VERY WRONG.
YOU DESTROYED MASADA. YOU KILLED THE CHILD. AN IMBECILE COULD SEE IT.
BUT ARMAGEDDON MUST AND SHALL BE BROUGHT ABOUT, THAT THIS WORLD SHALL SEE SALVATION.

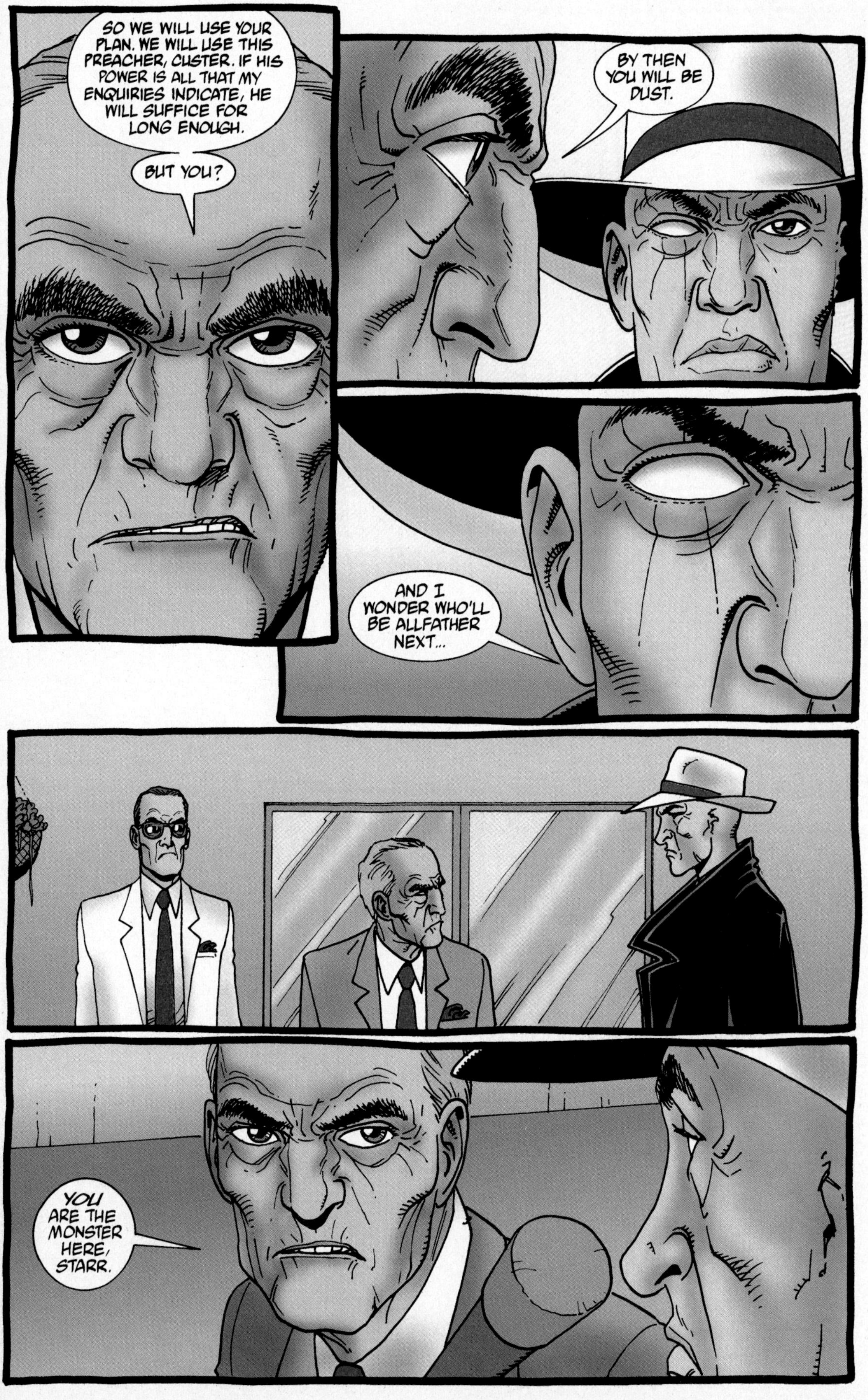
SO WE WILL USE YOUR PLAN. WE WILL USE THIS PREACHER, CUSTER. IF HIS POWER IS ALL THAT MY ENQUIRIES INDICATE, HE WILL SUFFICE FOR LONG ENOUGH.
BUT YOU?
BY THEN YOU WILL BE DUST.
AND I WONDER WHO'LL BE ALLFATHER NEXT...
YOU ARE THE MONSTER HERE, STARR.

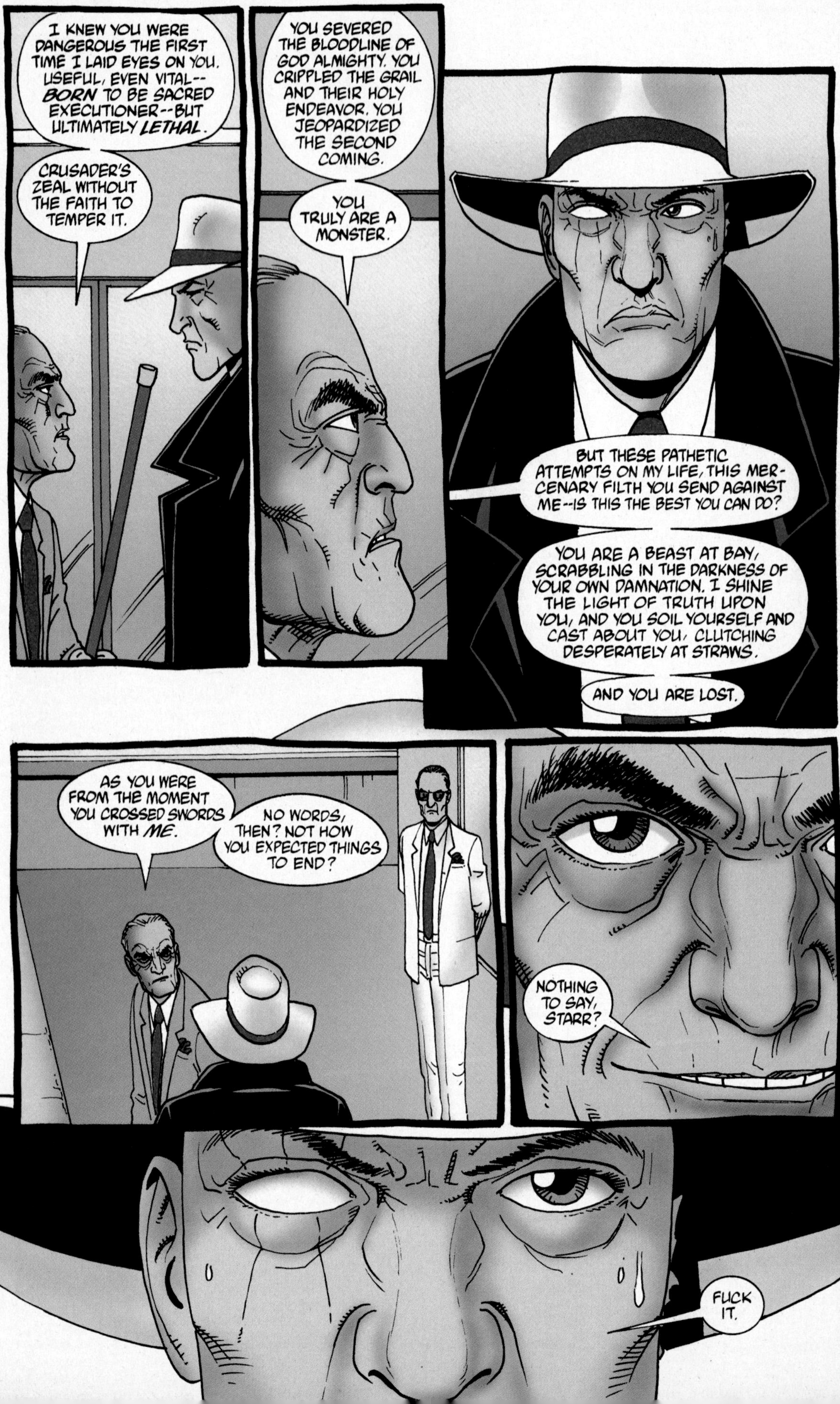
I KNEW YOU WERE DANGEROUS THE FIRST TIME I LAID EYES ON YOU. USEFUL, EVEN VITAL-- BORN TO BE SACRED EXECUTIONER--BUT ULTIMATELY LETHAL.
CRUSADER'S ZEAL WITHOUT THE FAITH TO TEMPER IT.
YOU SEVERED THE BLOODLINE OF GOD ALMIGHTY. YOU CRIPPLED THE GRAIL AND THEIR HOLY ENDEAVOR. YOU JEOPARDIZED THE SECOND COMING.
YOU TRULY ARE A MONSTER.
BUT THESE PATHETIC ATTEMPTS ON MY LIFE, THIS MER-CENARY FILTH YOU SEND AGAINST ME--IS THIS THE BEST YOU CAN DO?
YOU ARE A BEAST AT BAY, SCRABBLING IN THE DARKNESS OF YOUR OWN DAMNATION. I SHINE THE LIGHT OF TRUTH UPON YOU, AND YOU SOIL YOURSELF AND CAST ABOUT YOU, CLUTCHING DESPERATELY AT STRAWS.
AND YOU ARE LOST.
AS YOU WERE FROM THE MOMENT YOU CROSSED SWORDS WITH ME.
NO WORDS, THEN? NOT HOW YOU EXPECTED THINGS TO END?
NOTHING TO SAY, STARR?
FUCK IT.

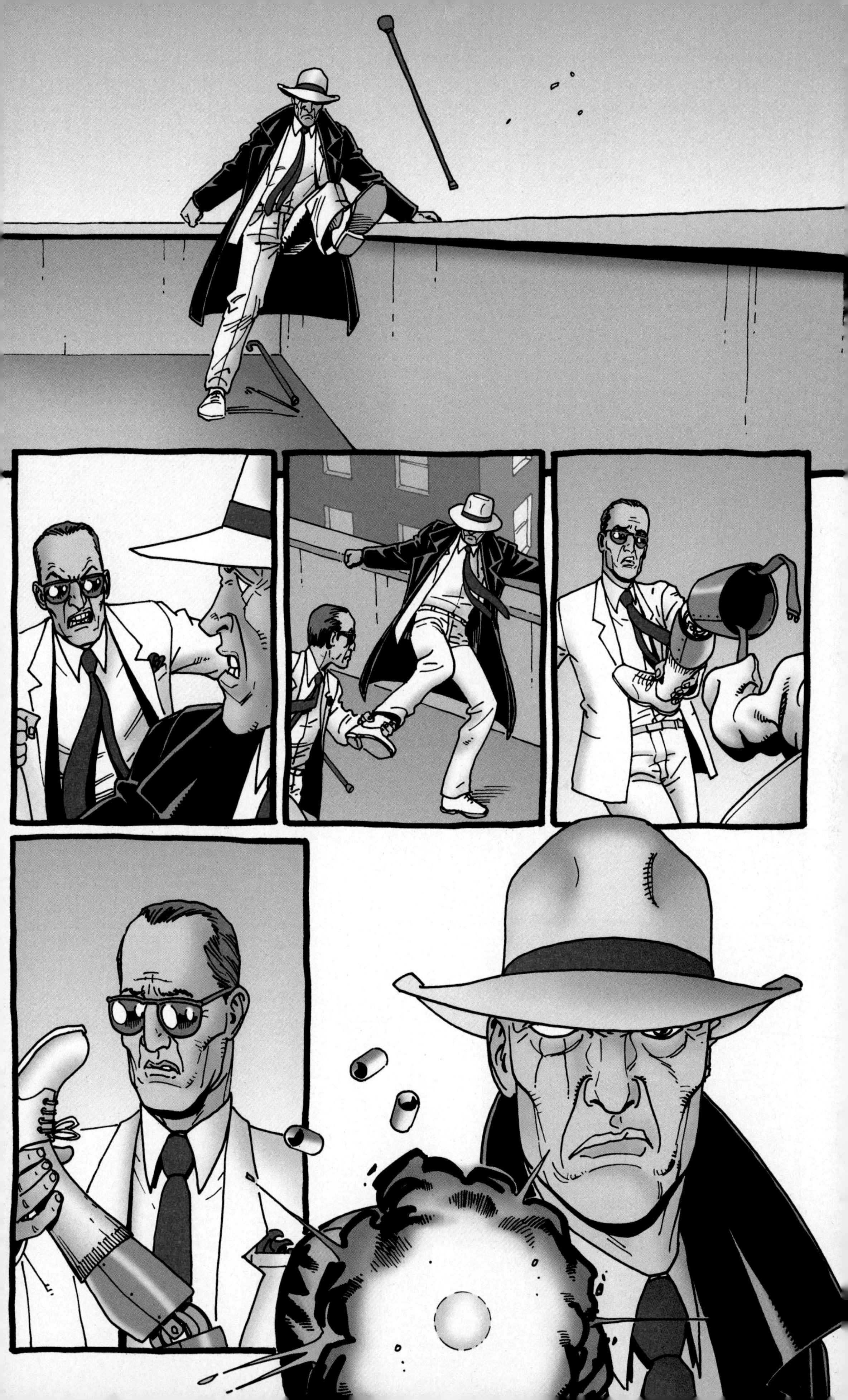

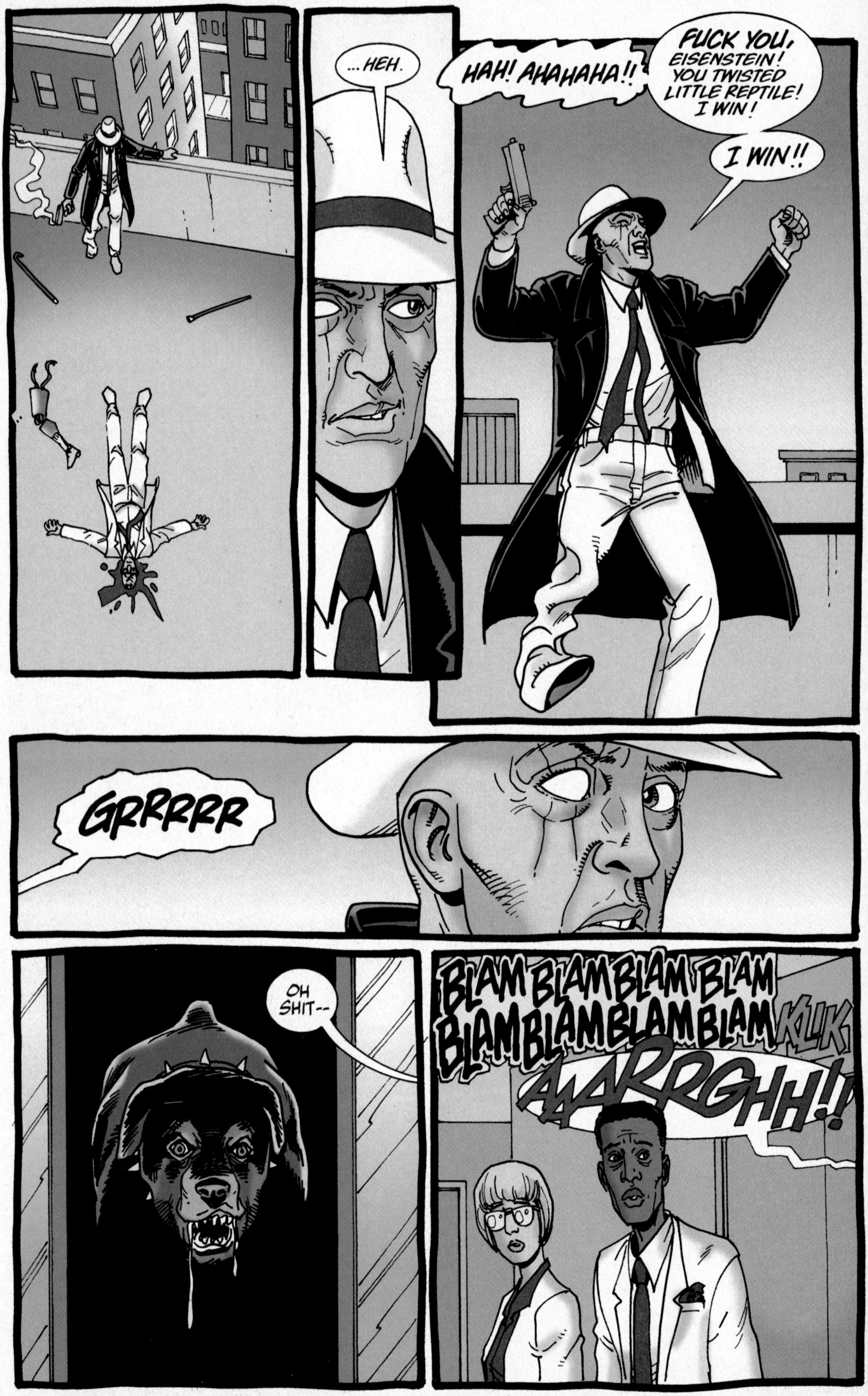
...HEH.
HAH! AHAHAHA!!
FUCK YOU, EISENSTEIN! YOU TWISTED LITTLE REPTILE! I WIN!
I WIN!!
GRRRRR
OH SHIT--
BLAM BLAM BLAM BLAM
BLAM BLAM BLAM BLAM KLIK
AARRGHH!!

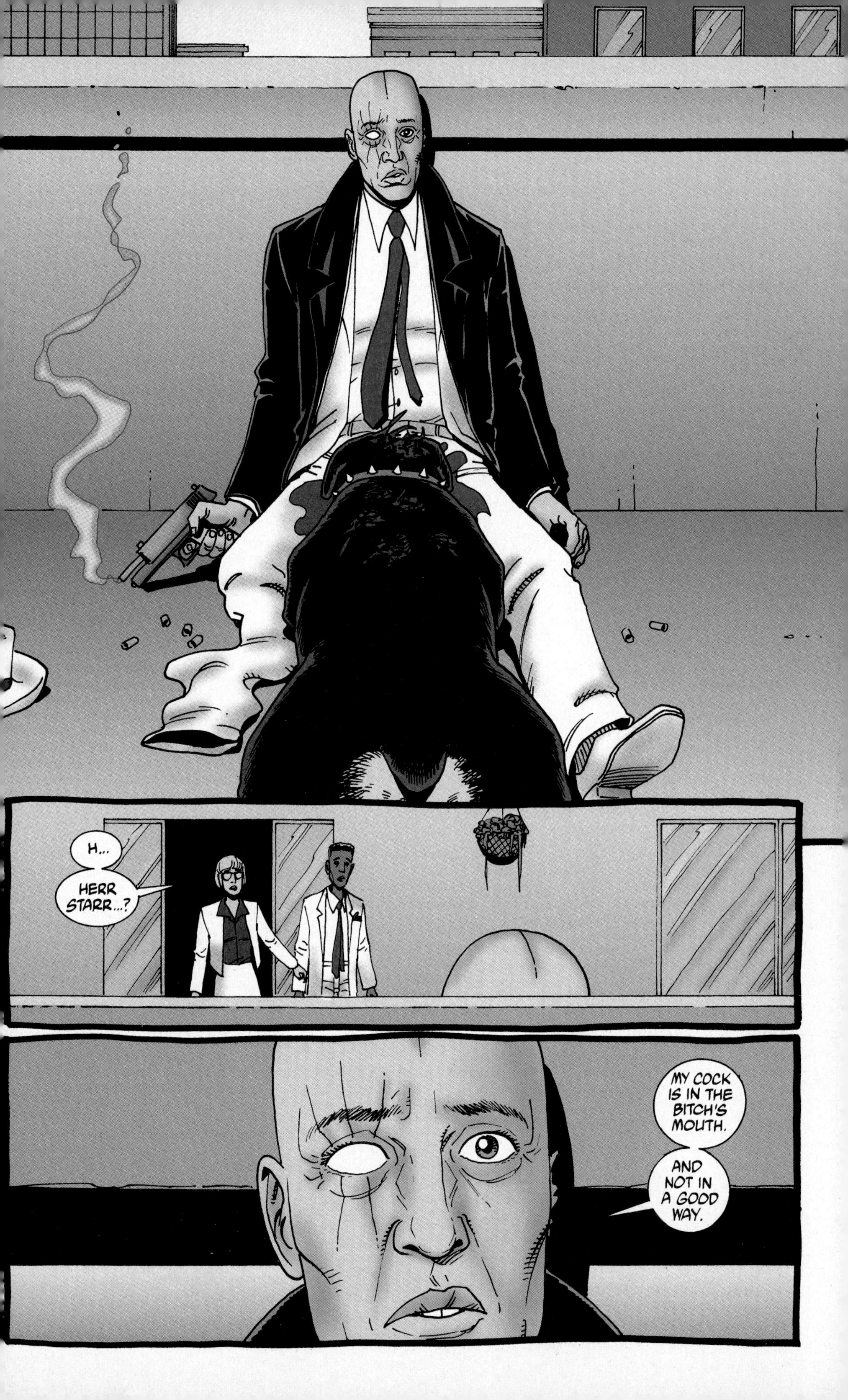
H...
HERR STARR...?
MY COCK IS IN THE BITCH'S MOUTH.
AND NOT IN A GOOD WAY.

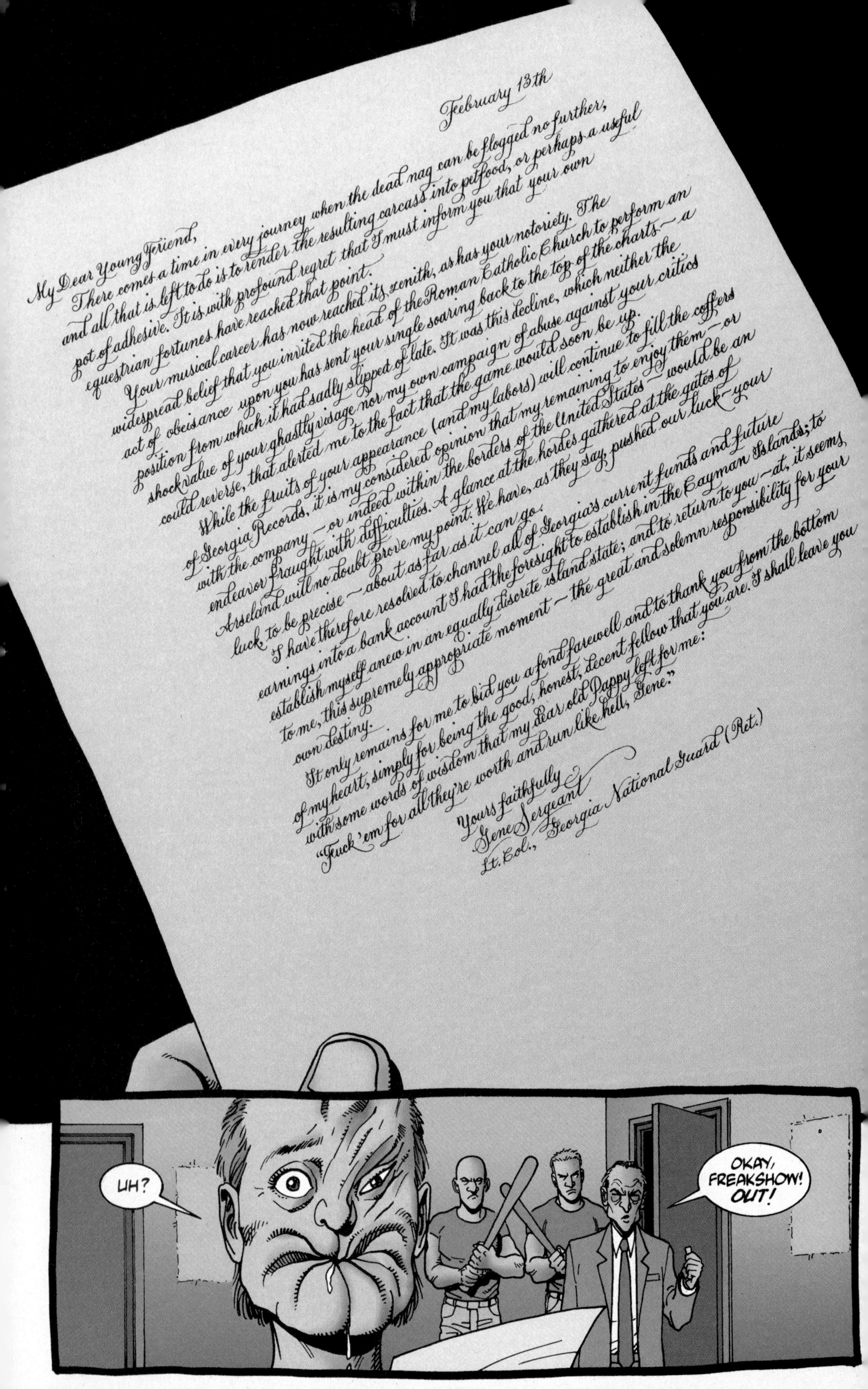
February 13th
My Dear Young Friend,
There comes a time in every journey when the dead nag can be flogged no further, and all that is left to do is to render the resulting carcass into petfood, or perhaps a useful pot of adhesive. It is with profound regret that I must inform you that your own equestrian fortunes have reached that point.
Your musical career has now reached its zenith, as has your notoriety. The widespread belief that you invited the head of the Roman Catholic Church to perform an act of obeisance upon you has sent your single soaring back to the top of the charts—a position from which it had sadly slipped of late. It was this decline, which neither the shock value of your ghastly visage nor my own campaign of abuse against your critics could reverse, that alerted me to the fact that the game would soon be up.
While the fruits of your appearance (and my labors) will continue to fill the coffers of Georgia Records, it is my considered opinion that my remaining to enjoy them—or with the company—or indeed within the borders of the United States—would be an endeavor fraught with difficulties. A glance at the hordes gathered at the gates of Arseland will no doubt prove my point. We have, as they say, pushed our luck—your luck, to be precise—about as far as it can go.
I have therefore resolved to channel all of Georgia's current funds and future earnings into a bank account I had the foresight to establish in the Cayman Islands; to establish myself anew in an equally discrete island state; and to return to you—at, it seems to me, this supremely appropriate moment—the great and solemn responsibility for your own destiny.
It only remains for me to bid you a fond farewell and to thank you from the bottom of my heart, simply for being the good, honest, decent fellow that you are. I shall leave you with some words of wisdom that my dear old Pappy left for me:
"Fuck 'em for all they're worth and run like hell, Gene."
Yours faithfully
Gene Sergeant
Lt. Col., Georgia National Guard (Ret.)
UH?
OKAY, FREAKSHOW! OUT!

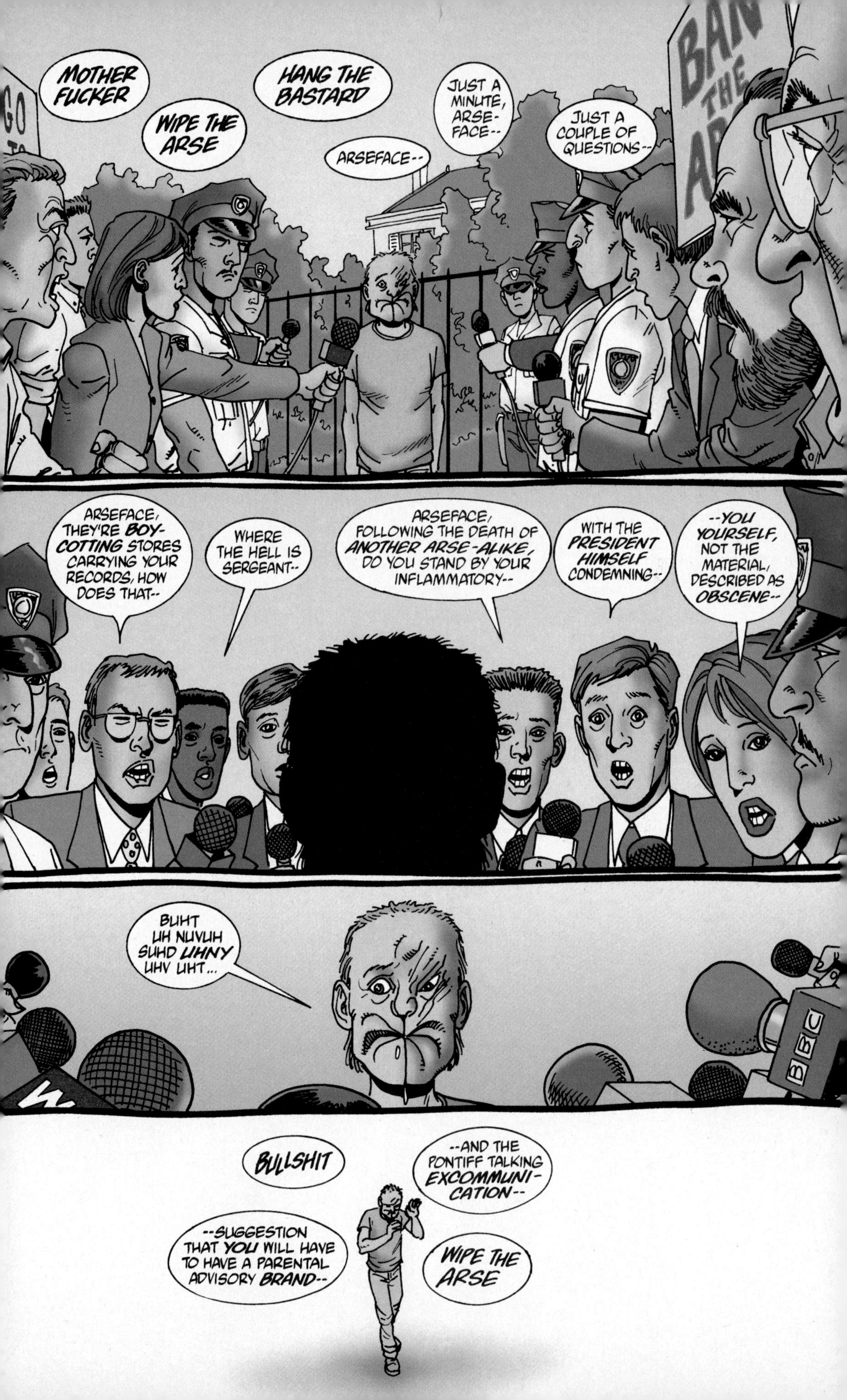
MOTHER FUCKER
WIPE THE ARSE
HANG THE BASTARD
ARSEFACE--
JUST A MINUTE, ARSE-FACE--
JUST A COUPLE OF QUESTIONS--
BAN THE AR
GO TO
ARSEFACE, THEY'RE BOY-COTTING STORES CARRYING YOUR RECORDS, HOW DOES THAT--
WHERE THE HELL IS SERGEANT--
ARSEFACE, FOLLOWING THE DEATH OF ANOTHER ARSE-ALIKE, DO YOU STAND BY YOUR INFLAMMATORY--
WITH THE PRESIDENT HIMSELF CONDEMNING--
--YOU YOURSELF, NOT THE MATERIAL, DESCRIBED AS OBSCENE--
BUHT UH NUVUH SUHD UHNY UHV UHT...
BBC
BULLSHIT
--AND THE PONTIFF TALKING EXCOMMUNI-CATION--
--SUGGESTION THAT YOU WILL HAVE TO HAVE A PARENTAL ADVISORY BRAND--
WIPE THE ARSE

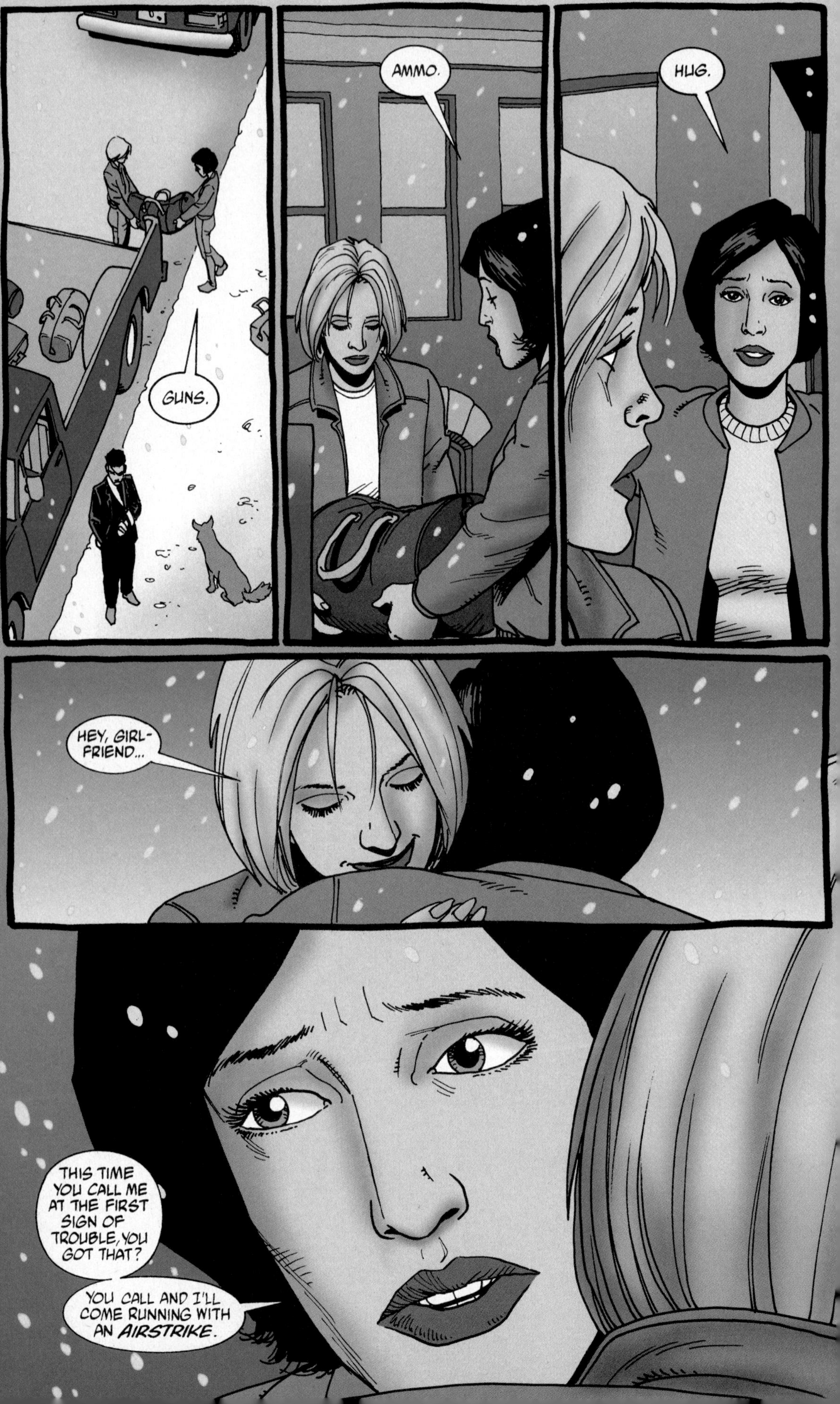
GUNS.
AMMO.
HUG.
HEY, GIRL-FRIEND...
THIS TIME YOU CALL ME AT THE FIRST SIGN OF TROUBLE, YOU GOT THAT?
YOU CALL AND I'LL COME RUNNING WITH AN *AIRSTRIKE*.

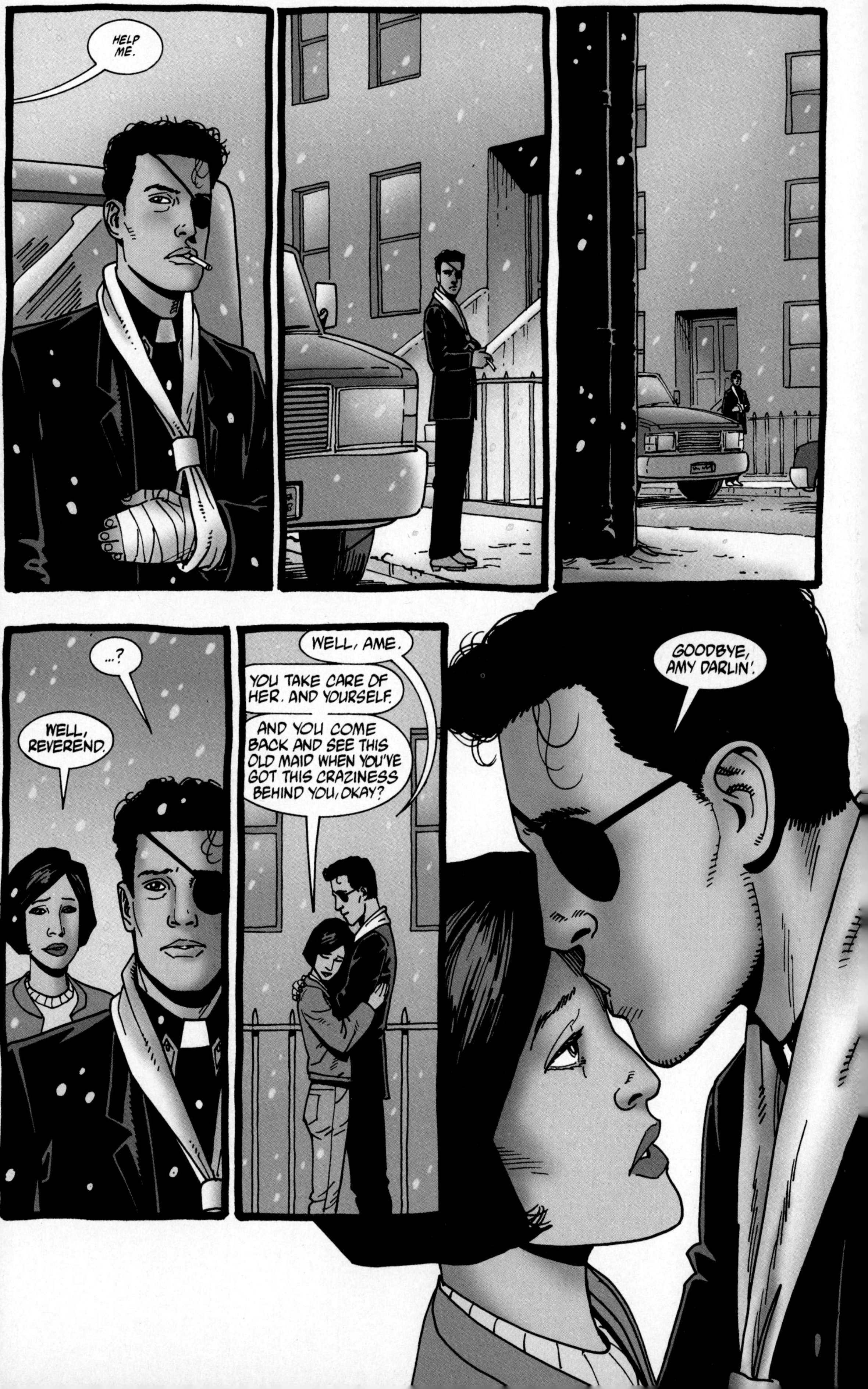
HELP ME.
...?
WELL, REVEREND.
WELL, AME.
YOU TAKE CARE OF HER. AND YOURSELF.
AND YOU COME BACK AND SEE THIS OLD MAID WHEN YOU'VE GOT THIS CRAZINESS BEHIND YOU, OKAY?
GOODBYE, AMY DARLIN'.

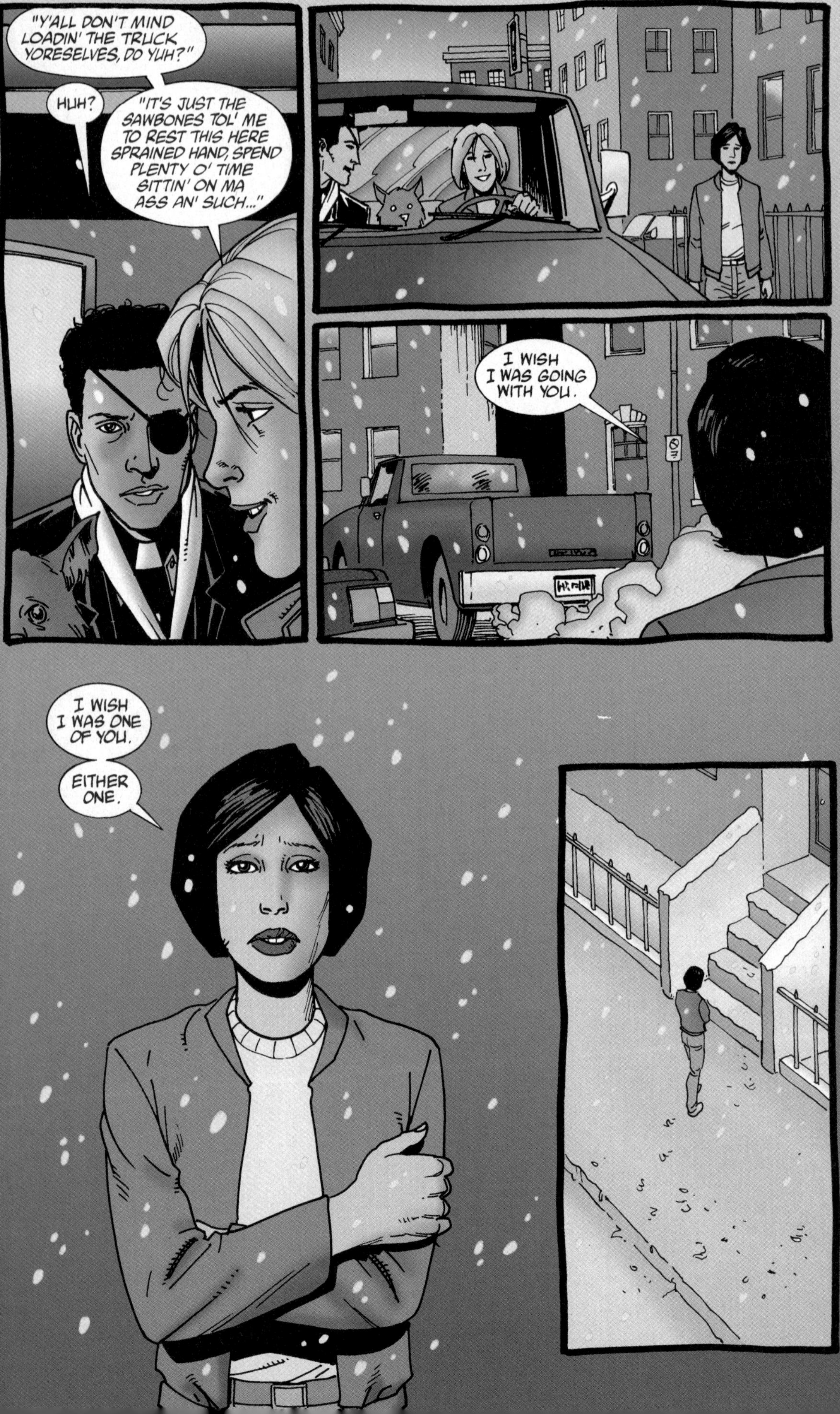
"Y'ALL DON'T MIND LOADIN' THE TRUCK YORESELVES, DO YUH?"
HUH?
"IT'S JUST THE SAWBONES TOL' ME TO REST THIS HERE SPRAINED HAND, SPEND PLENTY O' TIME SITTIN' ON MA ASS AN' SUCH..."
I WISH I WAS GOING WITH YOU.
I WISH I WAS ONE OF YOU.
EITHER ONE.

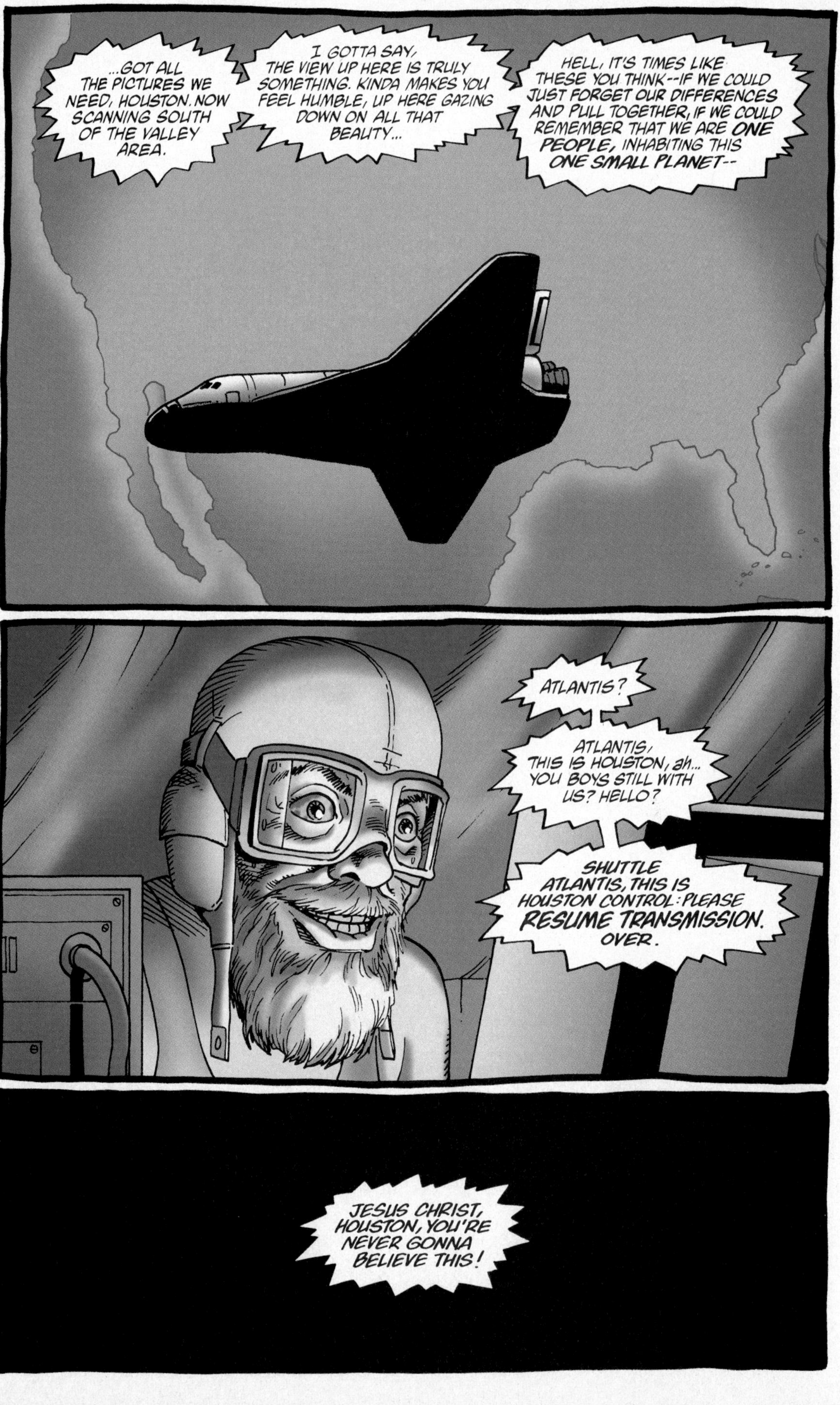
...GOT ALL THE PICTURES WE NEED, HOUSTON. NOW SCANNING SOUTH OF THE VALLEY AREA.
I GOTTA SAY, THE VIEW UP HERE IS TRULY SOMETHING. KINDA MAKES YOU FEEL HUMBLE, UP HERE GAZING DOWN ON ALL THAT BEAUTY...
HELL, IT'S TIMES LIKE THESE YOU THINK--IF WE COULD JUST FORGET OUR DIFFERENCES AND PULL TOGETHER, IF WE COULD REMEMBER THAT WE ARE ONE PEOPLE, INHABITING THIS ONE SMALL PLANET--
ATLANTIS?
ATLANTIS, THIS IS HOUSTON, ah... YOU BOYS STILL WITH US? HELLO?
SHUTTLE ATLANTIS, THIS IS HOUSTON CONTROL: PLEASE RESUME TRANSMISSION. OVER.
JESUS CHRIST, HOUSTON, YOU'RE NEVER GONNA BELIEVE THIS!

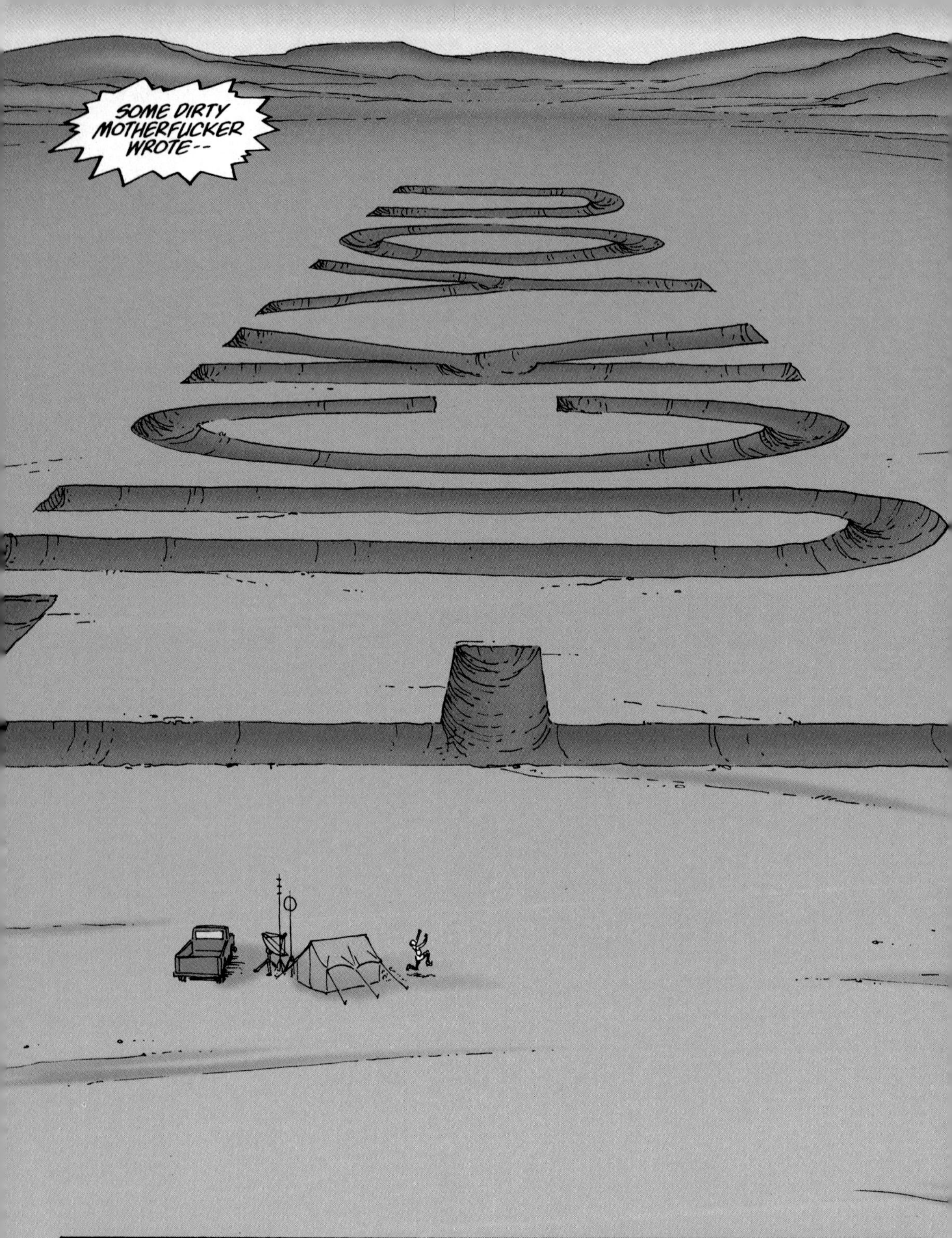
SOME DIRTY MOTHERFUCKER WROTE--

DOT THE I'S AND CROSS THE T'S

GARTH ENNIS - Writer STEVE DILLON - Artist
PAMELA RAMBO - Colorist (pages 2-8) • PATRICIA MULVILHILL - Colorist (pages 1,9-23)
CLEM ROBINS - Letter • AXEL ALONSO - Editor
PREACHER created by GARTH ENNIS and STEVE DILLON

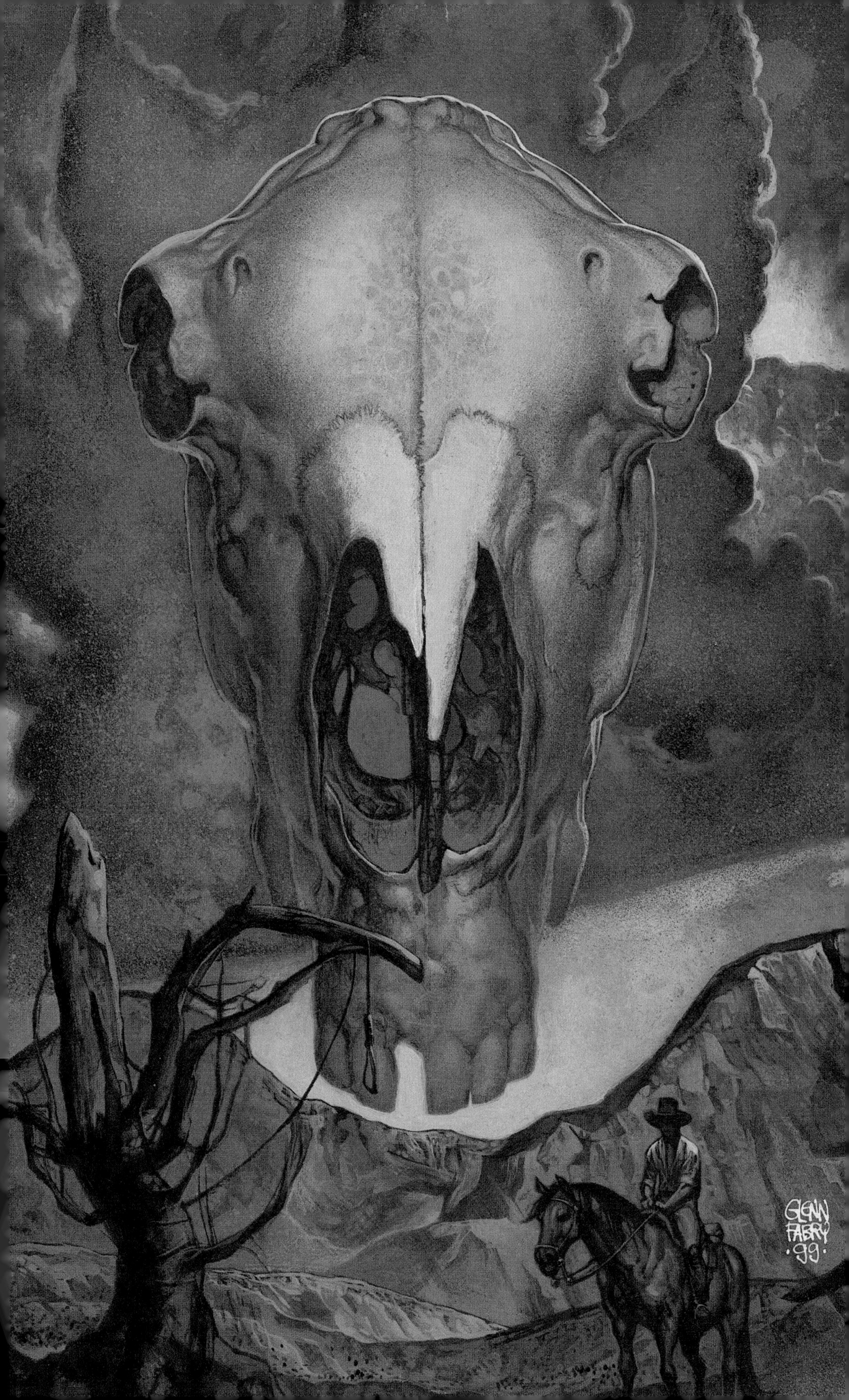
GLENN
FABRY
·99·

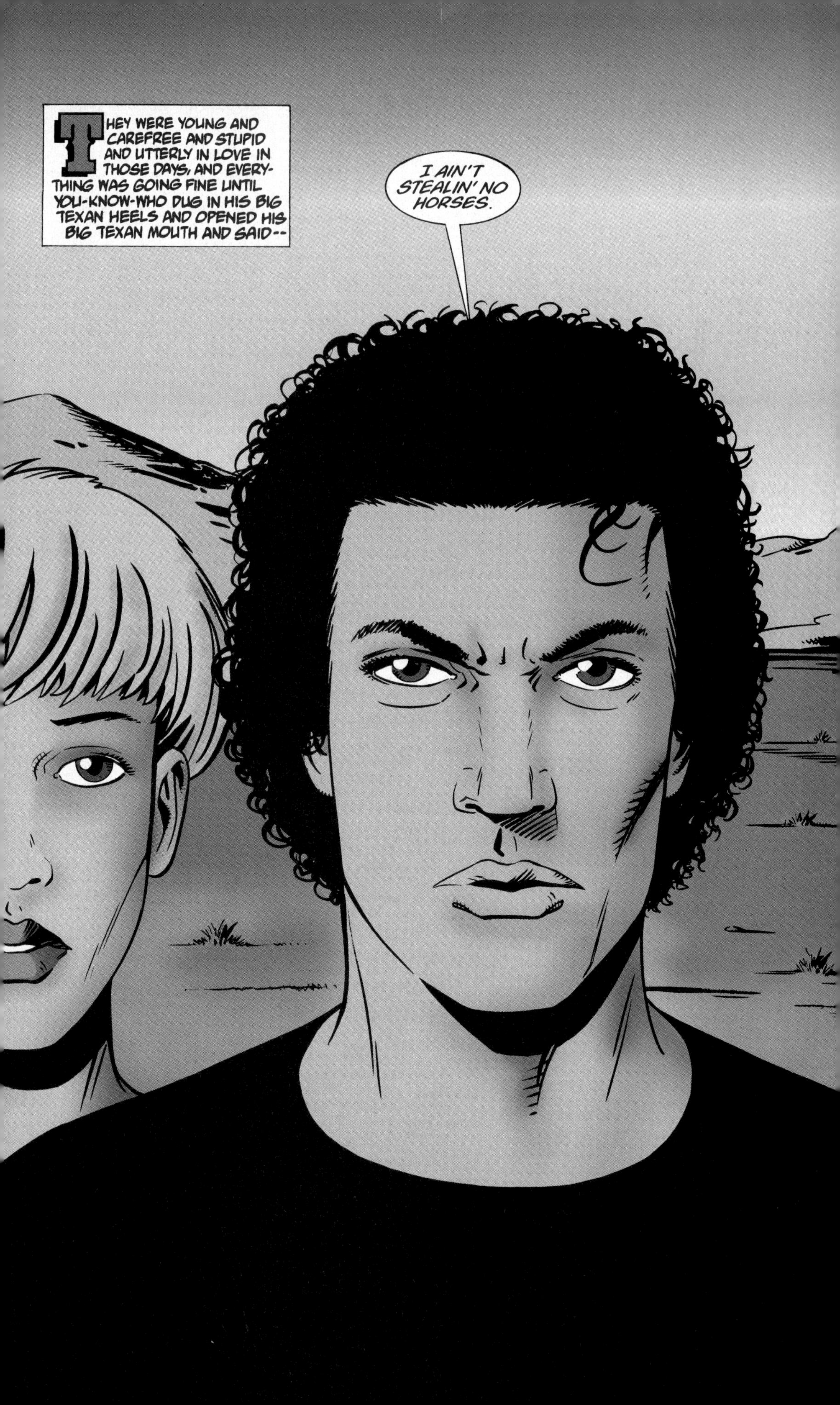
THEY WERE YOUNG AND CAREFREE AND STUPID AND UTTERLY IN LOVE IN THOSE DAYS, AND EVERY-THING WAS GOING FINE UNTIL YOU-KNOW-WHO DUG IN HIS BIG TEXAN HEELS AND OPENED HIS BIG TEXAN MOUTH AND SAID--
I AIN'T STEALIN' NO HORSES.

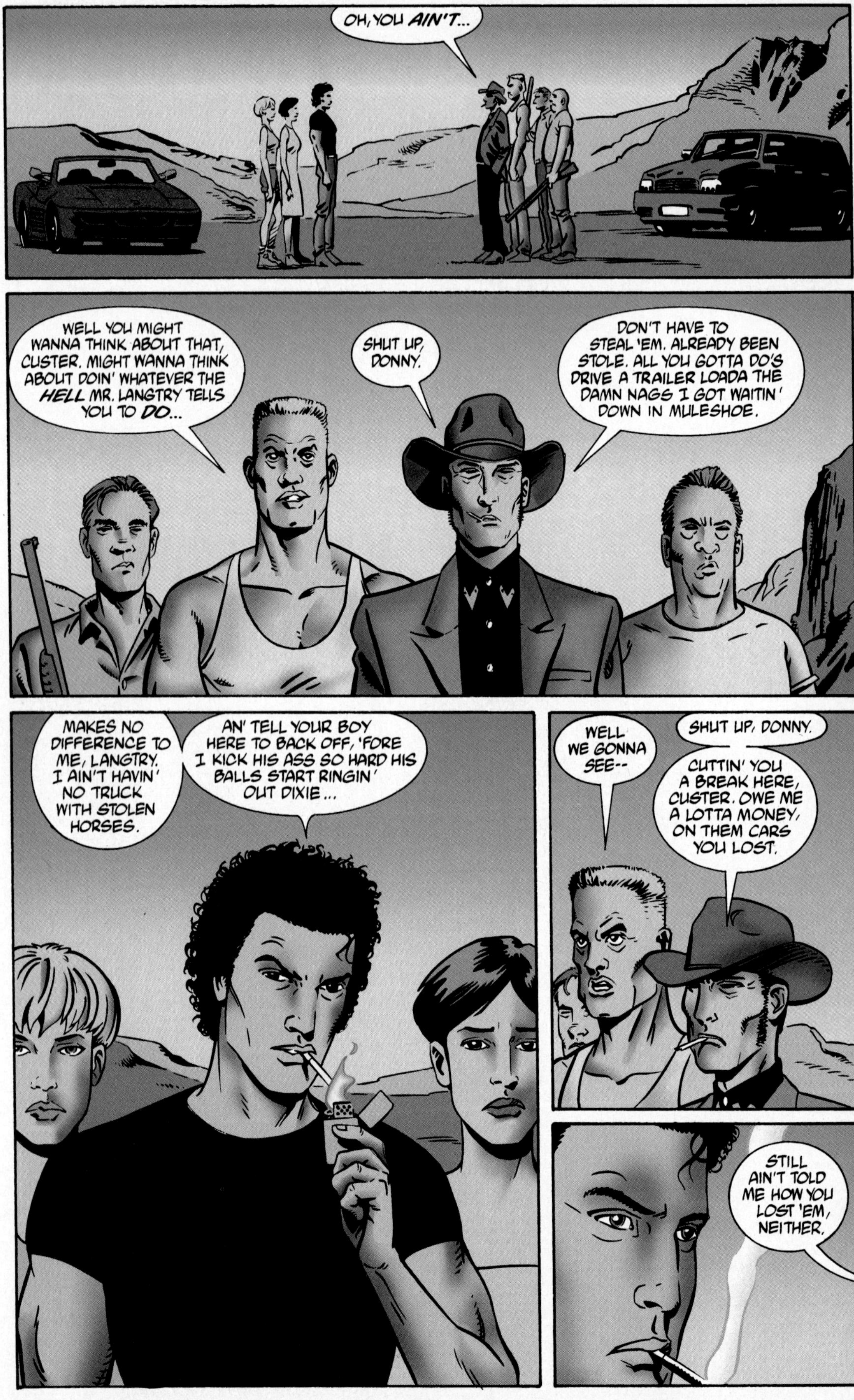
OH, YOU AIN'T...
WELL YOU MIGHT WANNA THINK ABOUT THAT, CUSTER. MIGHT WANNA THINK ABOUT DOIN' WHATEVER THE HELL MR. LANGTRY TELLS YOU TO DO...
SHUT UP, DONNY.
DON'T HAVE TO STEAL 'EM. ALREADY BEEN STOLE. ALL YOU GOTTA DO'S DRIVE A TRAILER LOADA THE DAMN NAGS I GOT WAITIN' DOWN IN MULESHOE.
MAKES NO DIFFERENCE TO ME, LANGTRY. I AIN'T HAVIN' NO TRUCK WITH STOLEN HORSES.
AN' TELL YOUR BOY HERE TO BACK OFF, 'FORE I KICK HIS ASS SO HARD HIS BALLS START RINGIN' OUT DIXIE...
WELL WE GONNA SEE--
SHUT UP, DONNY.
CUTTIN' YOU A BREAK HERE, CUSTER. OWE ME A LOTTA MONEY, ON THEM CARS YOU LOST.
STILL AIN'T TOLD ME HOW YOU LOST 'EM, NEITHER.

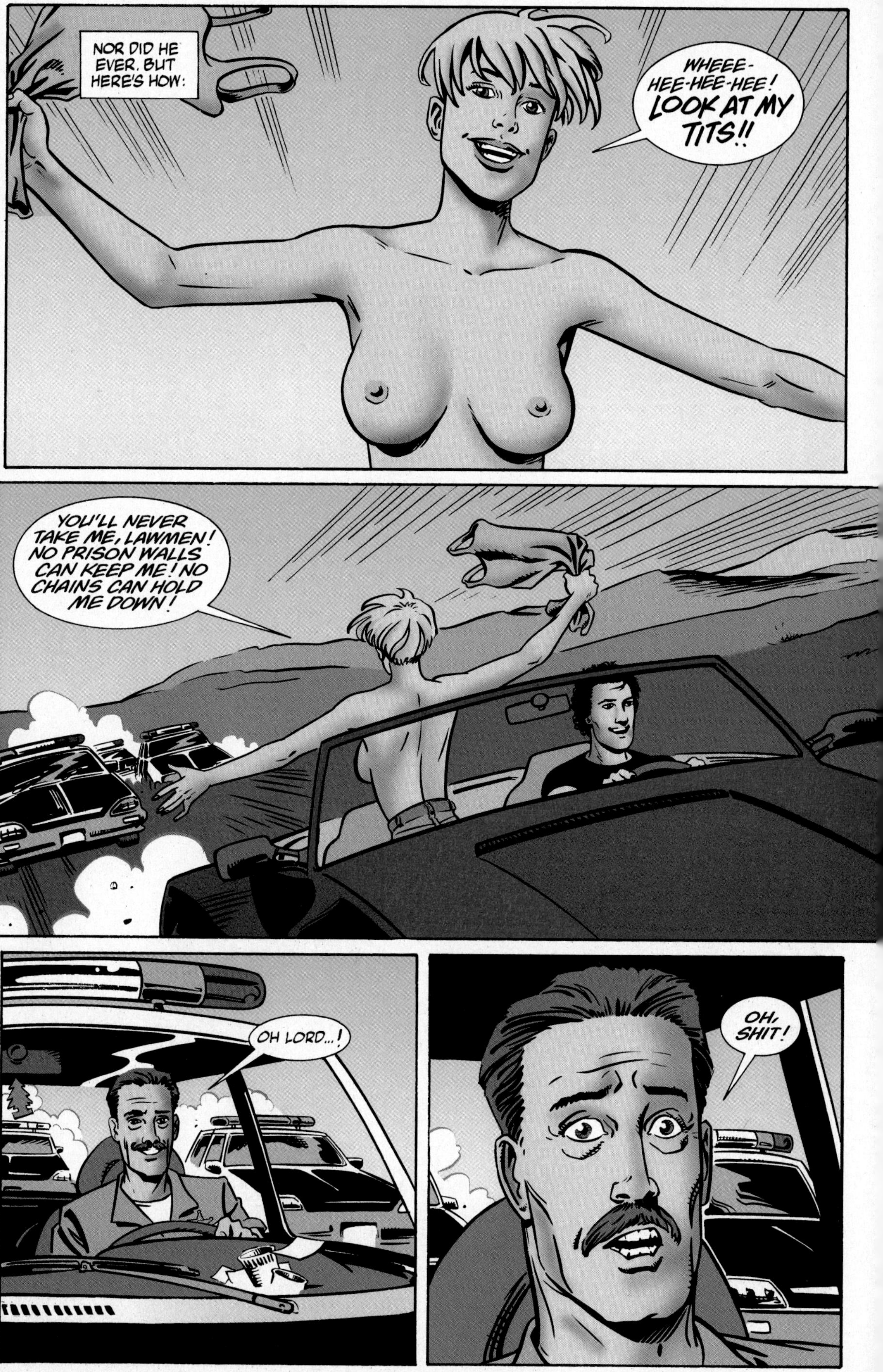
NOR DID HE EVER. BUT HERE'S HOW:
WHEEE-HEE-HEE-HEE! LOOK AT MY TITS!!
YOU'LL NEVER TAKE ME, LAWMEN! NO PRISON WALLS CAN KEEP ME! NO CHAINS CAN HOLD ME DOWN!
OH LORD...!
OH, SHIT!

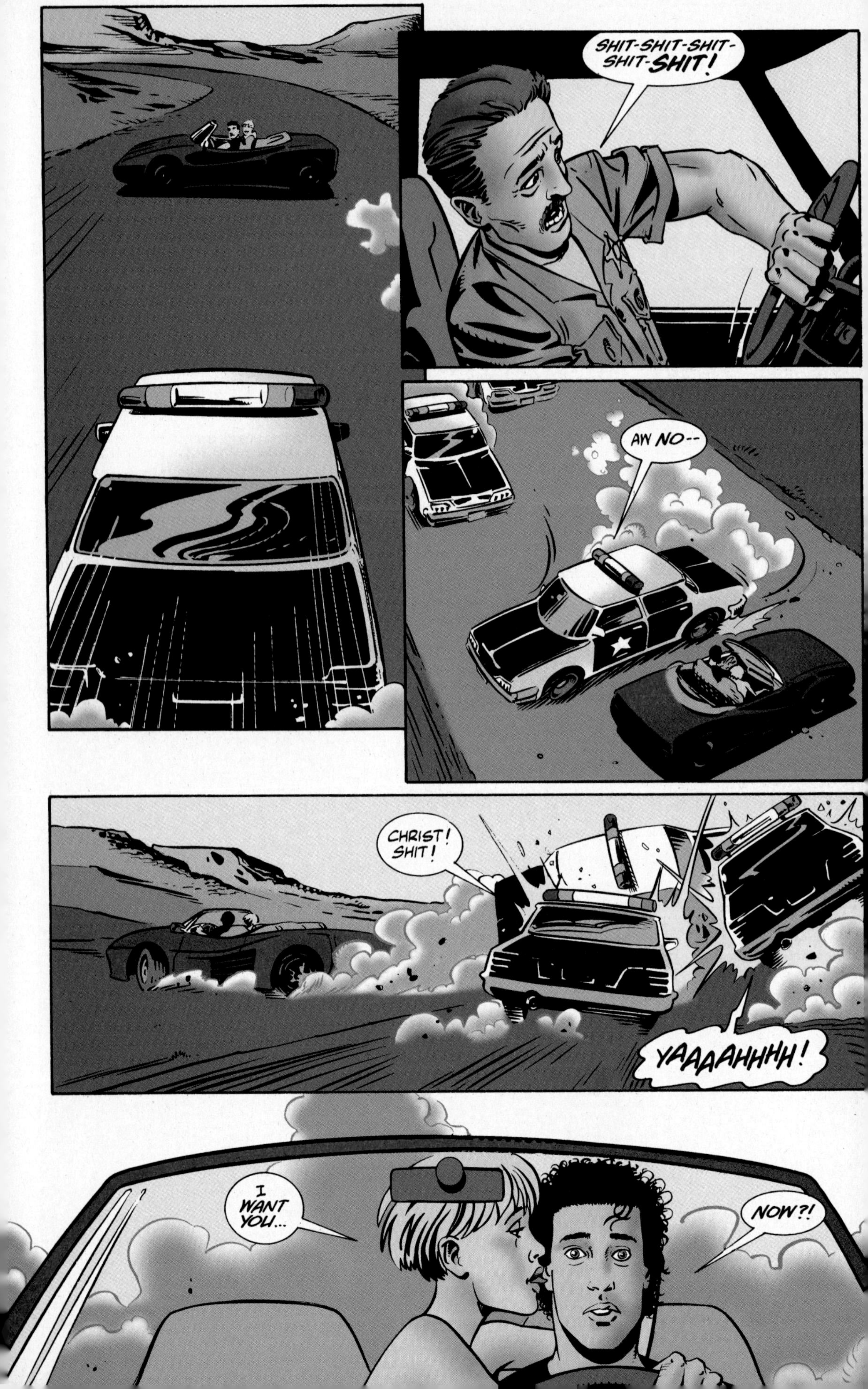
SHIT-SHIT-SHIT-
SHIT-SHIT!
AW NO--
CHRIST!
SHIT!
YAAAAHHHH!
I WANT YOU...
NOW?!

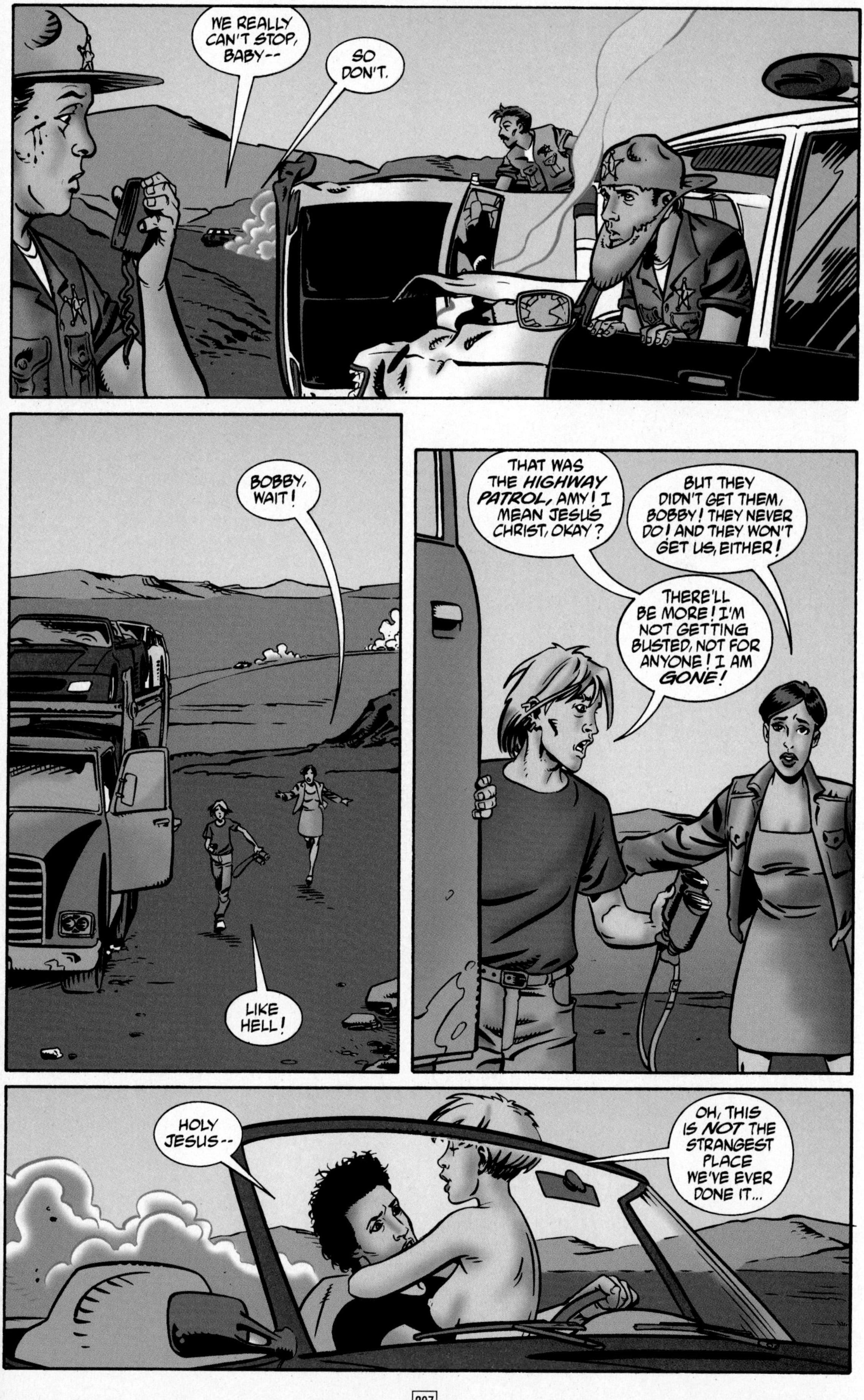
WE REALLY CAN'T STOP, BABY--
SO DON'T.
BOBBY, WAIT!
LIKE HELL!
THAT WAS THE HIGHWAY PATROL, AMY! I MEAN JESUS CHRIST, OKAY?
BUT THEY DIDN'T GET THEM, BOBBY! THEY NEVER DO! AND THEY WON'T GET US, EITHER!
THERE'LL BE MORE! I'M NOT GETTING BUSTED, NOT FOR ANYONE! I AM GONE!
HOLY JESUS--
OH, THIS IS NOT THE STRANGEST PLACE WE'VE EVER DONE IT...

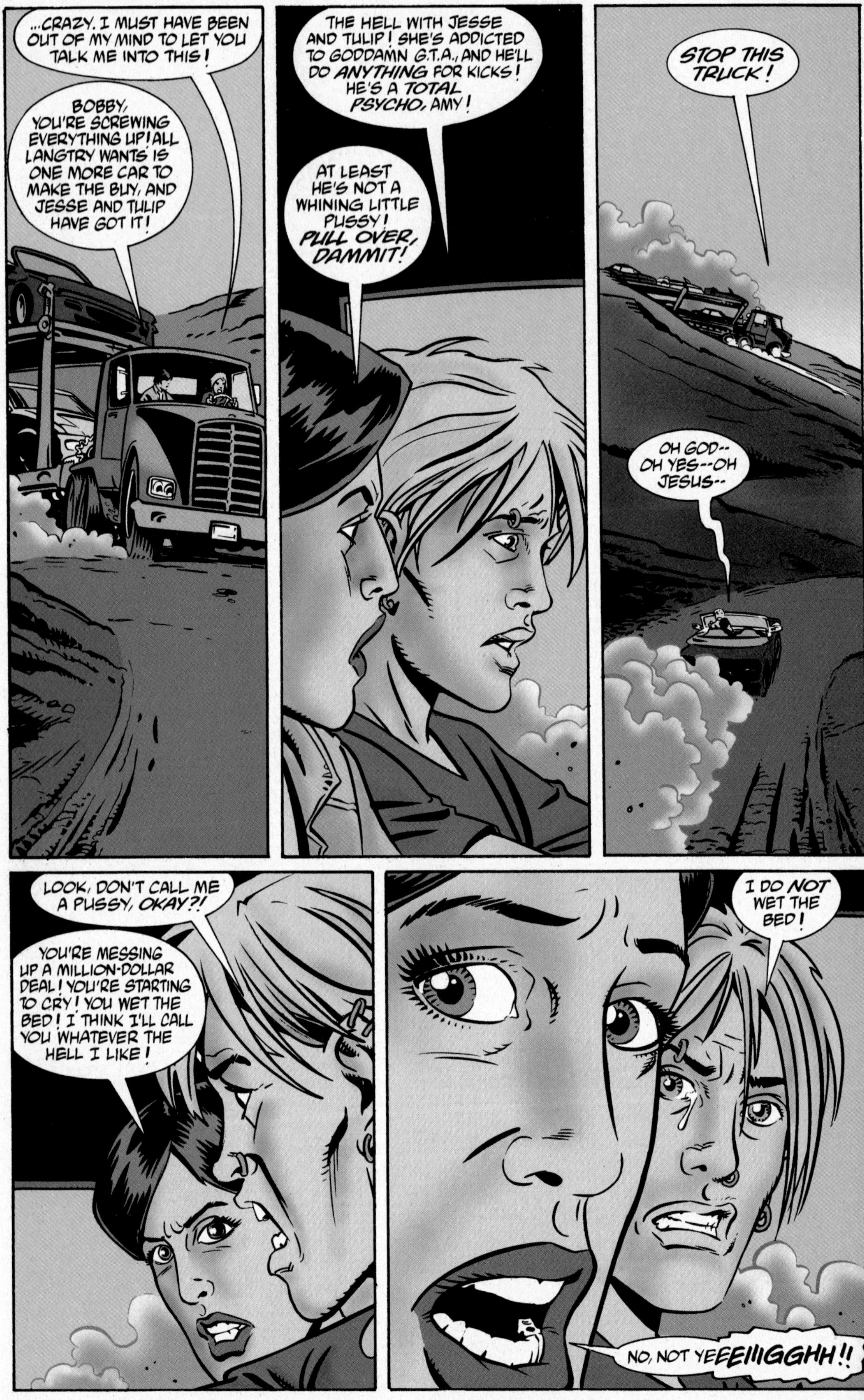
...CRAZY. I MUST HAVE BEEN OUT OF MY MIND TO LET YOU TALK ME INTO THIS!
BOBBY, YOU'RE SCREWING EVERYTHING UP! ALL LANGTRY WANTS IS ONE MORE CAR TO MAKE THE BUY, AND JESSE AND TULIP HAVE GOT IT!
THE HELL WITH JESSE AND TULIP! SHE'S ADDICTED TO GODDAMN G.T.A., AND HE'LL DO ANYTHING FOR KICKS! HE'S A TOTAL PSYCHO, AMY!
AT LEAST HE'S NOT A WHINING LITTLE PUSSY! PULL OVER, DAMMIT!
STOP THIS TRUCK!
OH GOD-- OH YES--OH JESUS--
LOOK, DON'T CALL ME A PUSSY, OKAY?!
YOU'RE MESSING UP A MILLION-DOLLAR DEAL! YOU'RE STARTING TO CRY! YOU WET THE BED! I THINK I'LL CALL YOU WHATEVER THE HELL I LIKE!
I DO NOT WET THE BED!
NO, NOT YEEEIIIGGHH!!

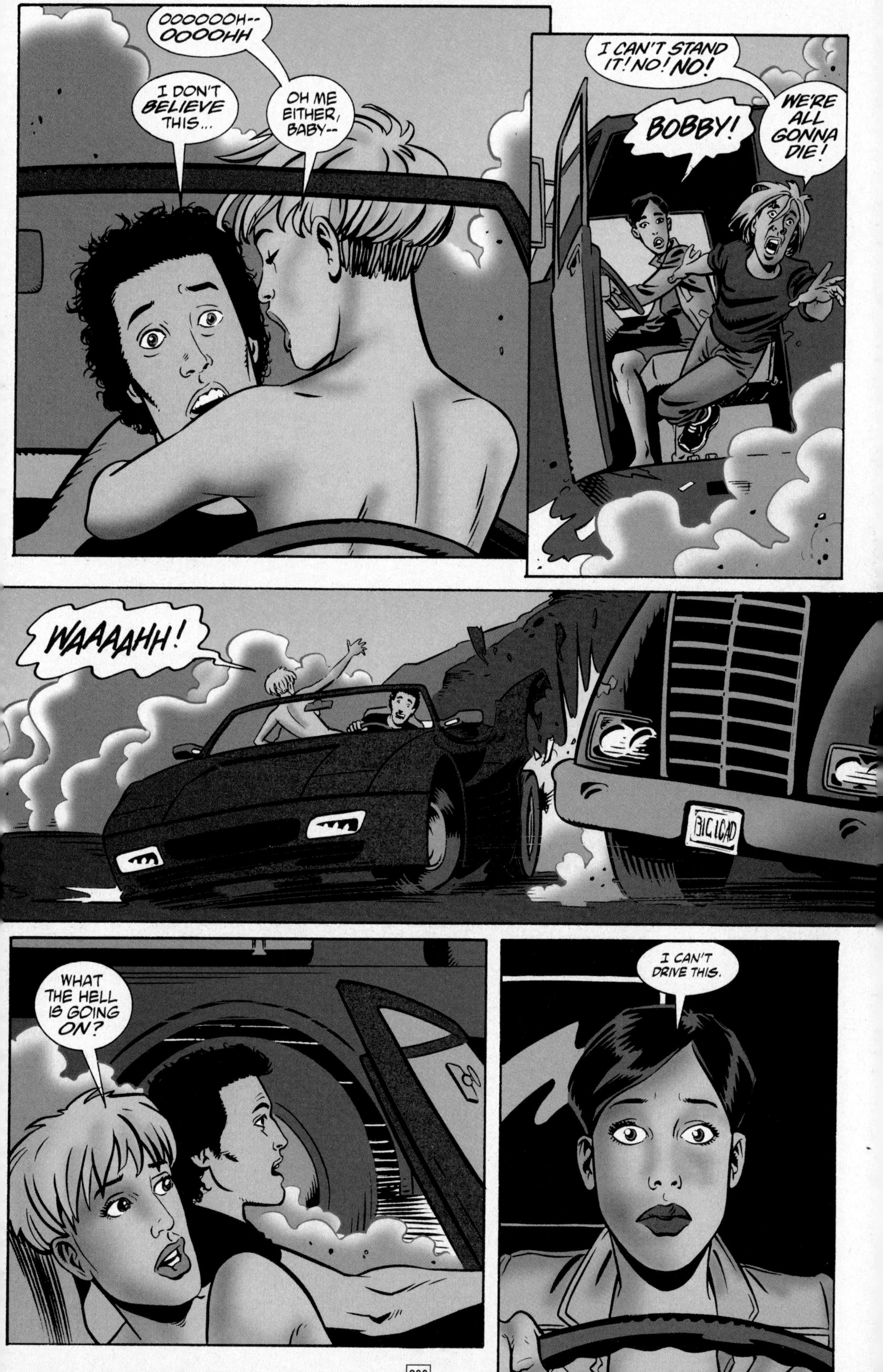
OOOOOOH--
OOOOHH
I DON'T BELIEVE THIS...
OH ME EITHER, BABY--
I CAN'T STAND IT! NO! NO!
BOBBY!
WE'RE ALL GONNA DIE!
WAAAAHH!
BIG LOAD
WHAT THE HELL IS GOING ON?
I CAN'T DRIVE THIS.

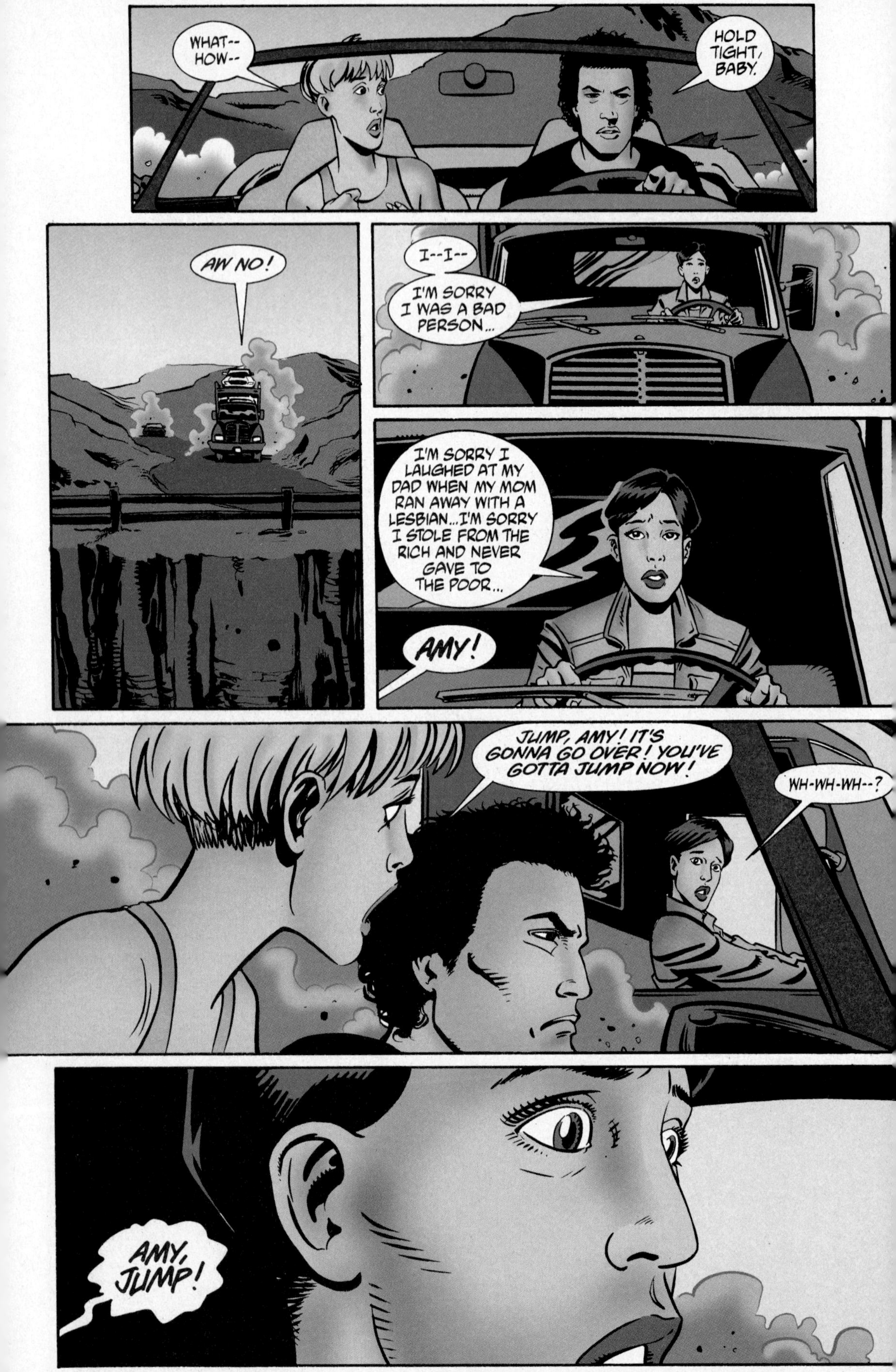
WHAT--
HOW--
HOLD TIGHT, BABY.
AW NO!
I--I--
I'M SORRY I WAS A BAD PERSON...
I'M SORRY I LAUGHED AT MY DAD WHEN MY MOM RAN AWAY WITH A LESBIAN...I'M SORRY I STOLE FROM THE RICH AND NEVER GAVE TO THE POOR...
AMY!
JUMP, AMY! IT'S GONNA GO OVER! YOU'VE GOTTA JUMP NOW!
WH-WH-WH--?
AMY, JUMP!

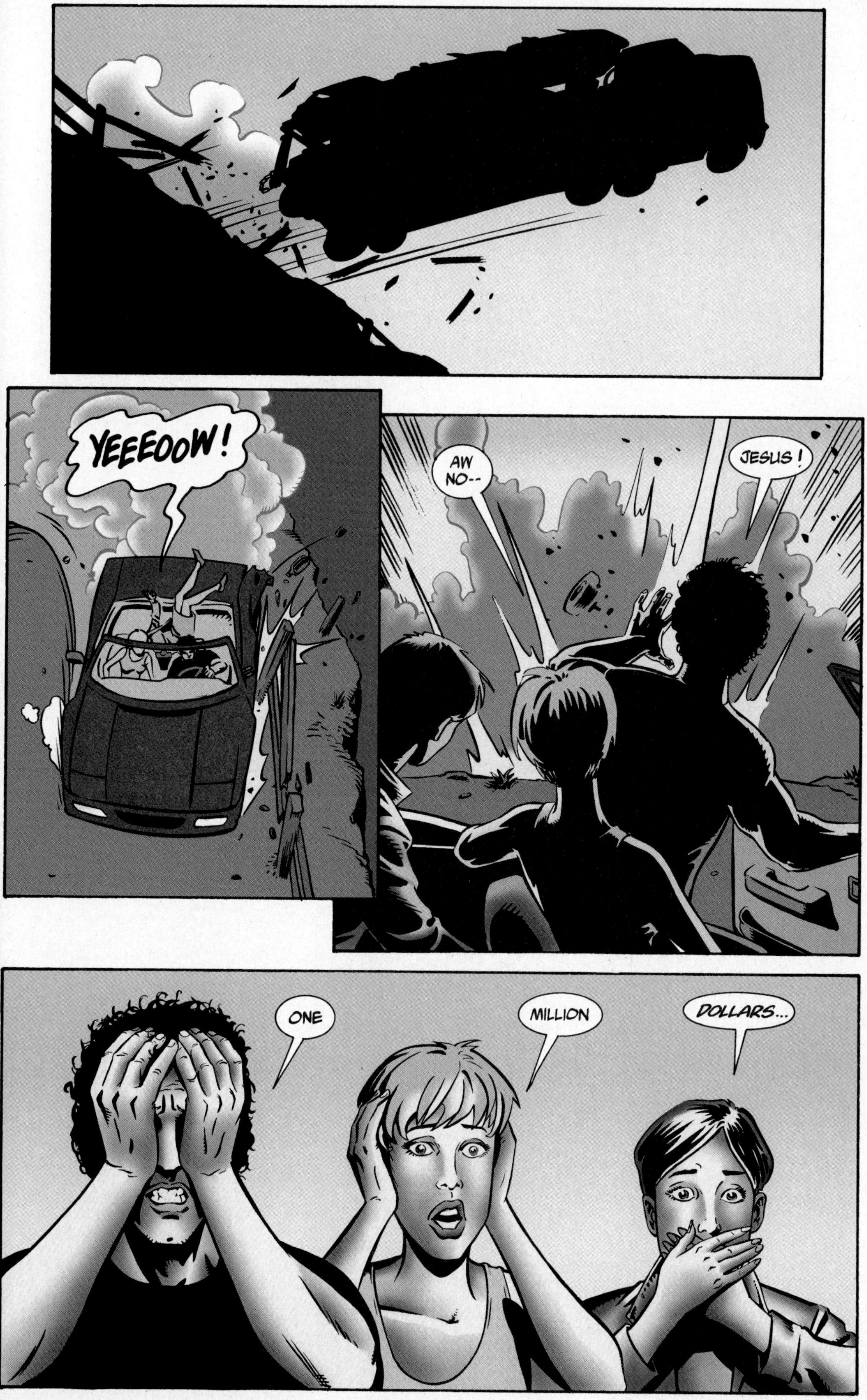
YEEEOOW!
AW NO--
JESUS!
ONE
MILLION
DOLLARS...

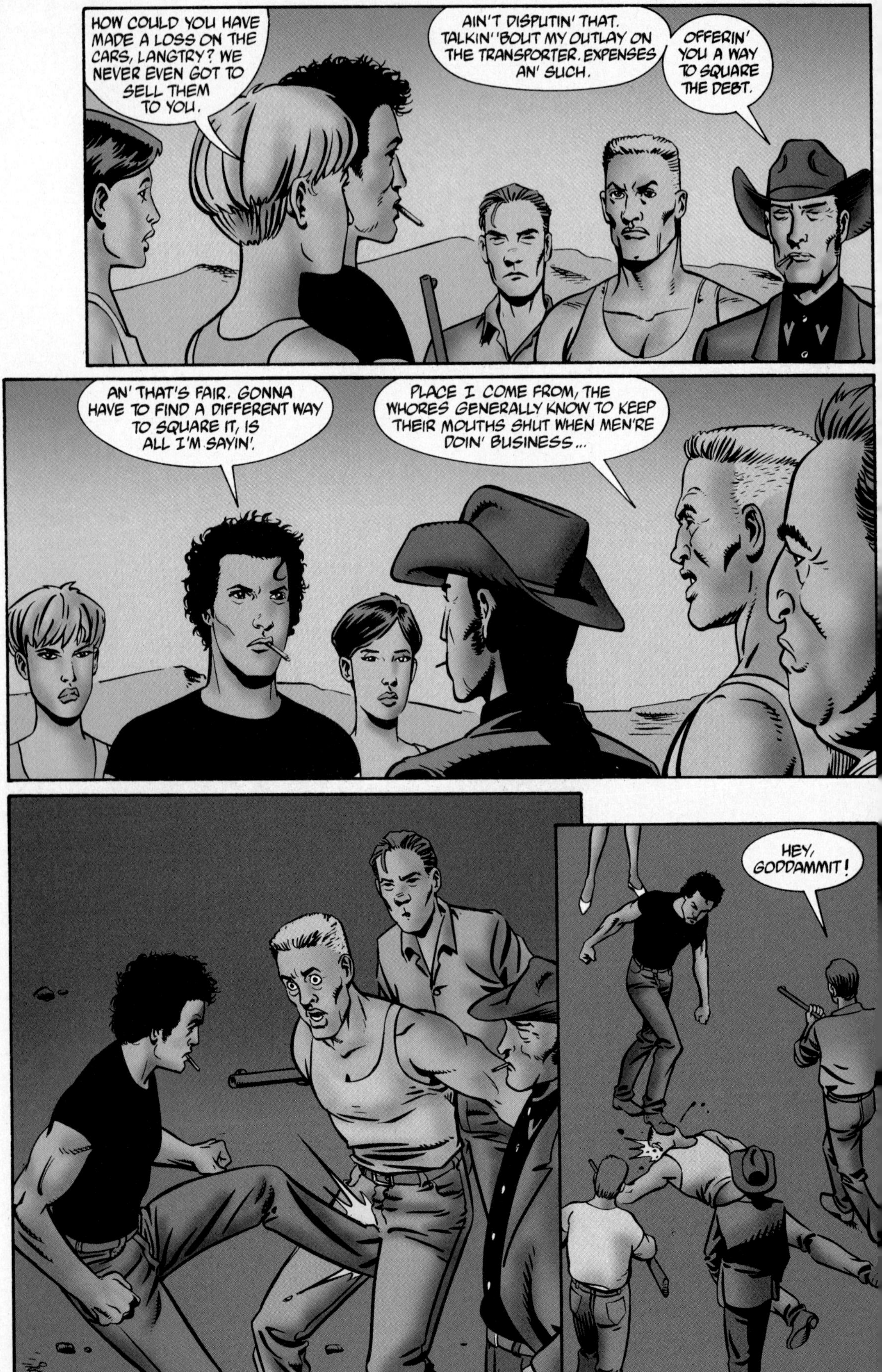
HOW COULD YOU HAVE MADE A LOSS ON THE CARS, LANGTRY? WE NEVER EVEN GOT TO SELL THEM TO YOU.
AIN'T DISPUTIN' THAT. TALKIN' 'BOUT MY OUTLAY ON THE TRANSPORTER. EXPENSES AN' SUCH.
OFFERIN' YOU A WAY TO SQUARE THE DEBT.
AN' THAT'S FAIR. GONNA HAVE TO FIND A DIFFERENT WAY TO SQUARE IT, IS ALL I'M SAYIN'.
PLACE I COME FROM, THE WHORES GENERALLY KNOW TO KEEP THEIR MOUTHS SHUT WHEN MEN'RE DOIN' BUSINESS...
HEY, GODDAMMIT!

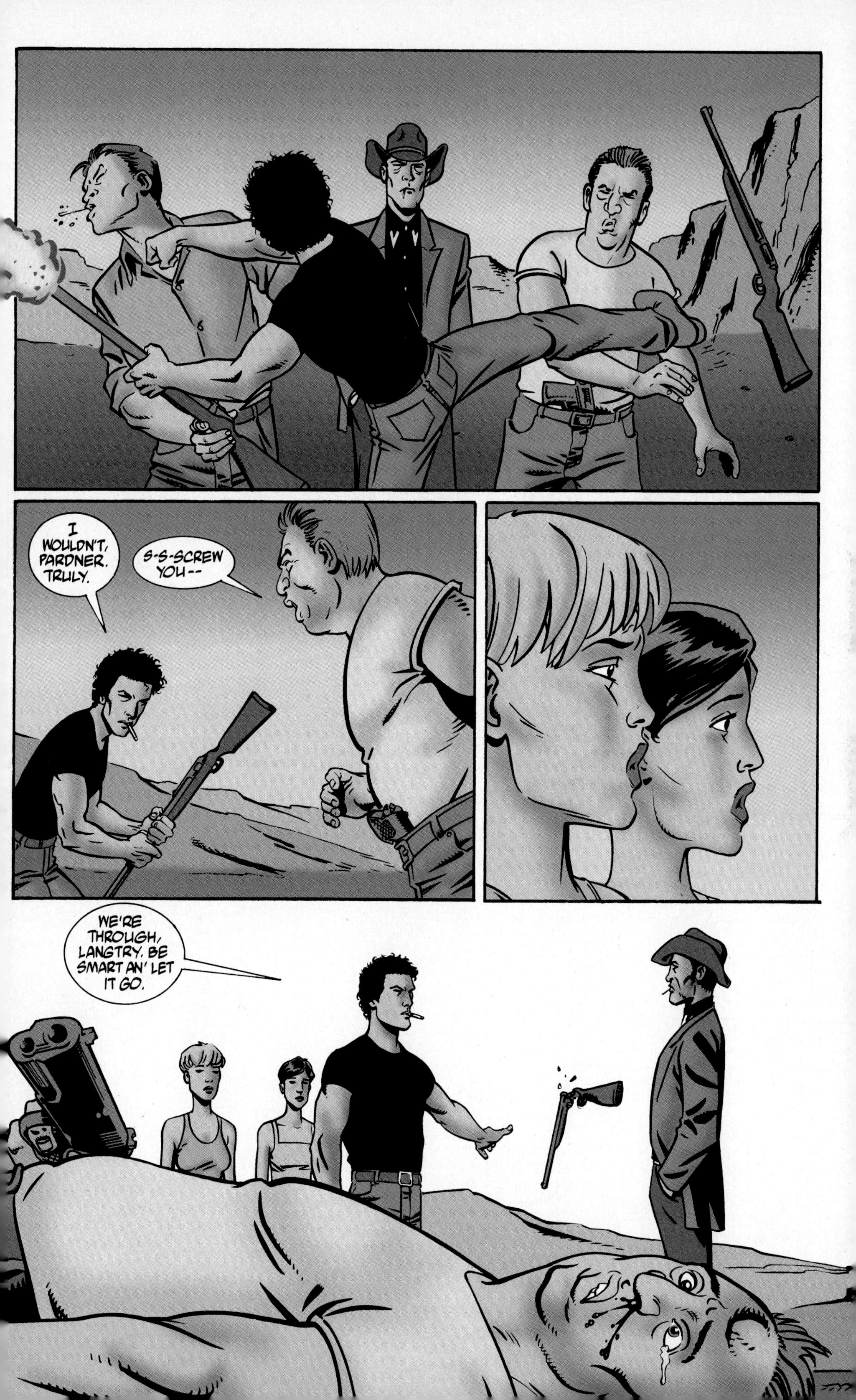
I WOULDN'T, PARDNER. TRULY.
S-S-SCREW YOU--
WE'RE THROUGH, LANGTRY. BE SMART AN' LET IT GO.

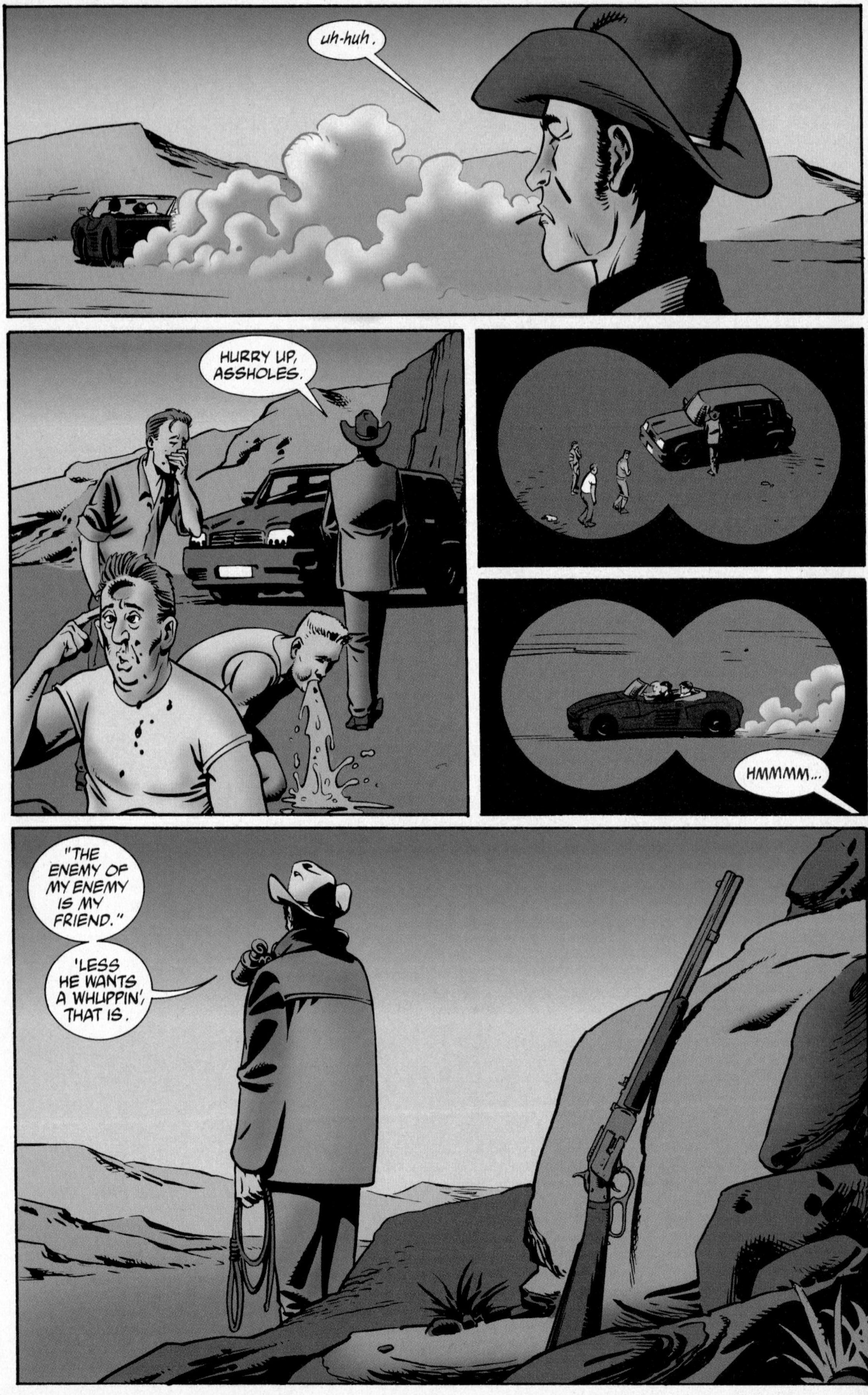
uh-huh.
HURRY UP, ASSHOLES.
HMMMM...
"THE ENEMY OF MY ENEMY IS MY FRIEND."
'LESS HE WANTS A WHUPPIN', THAT IS.

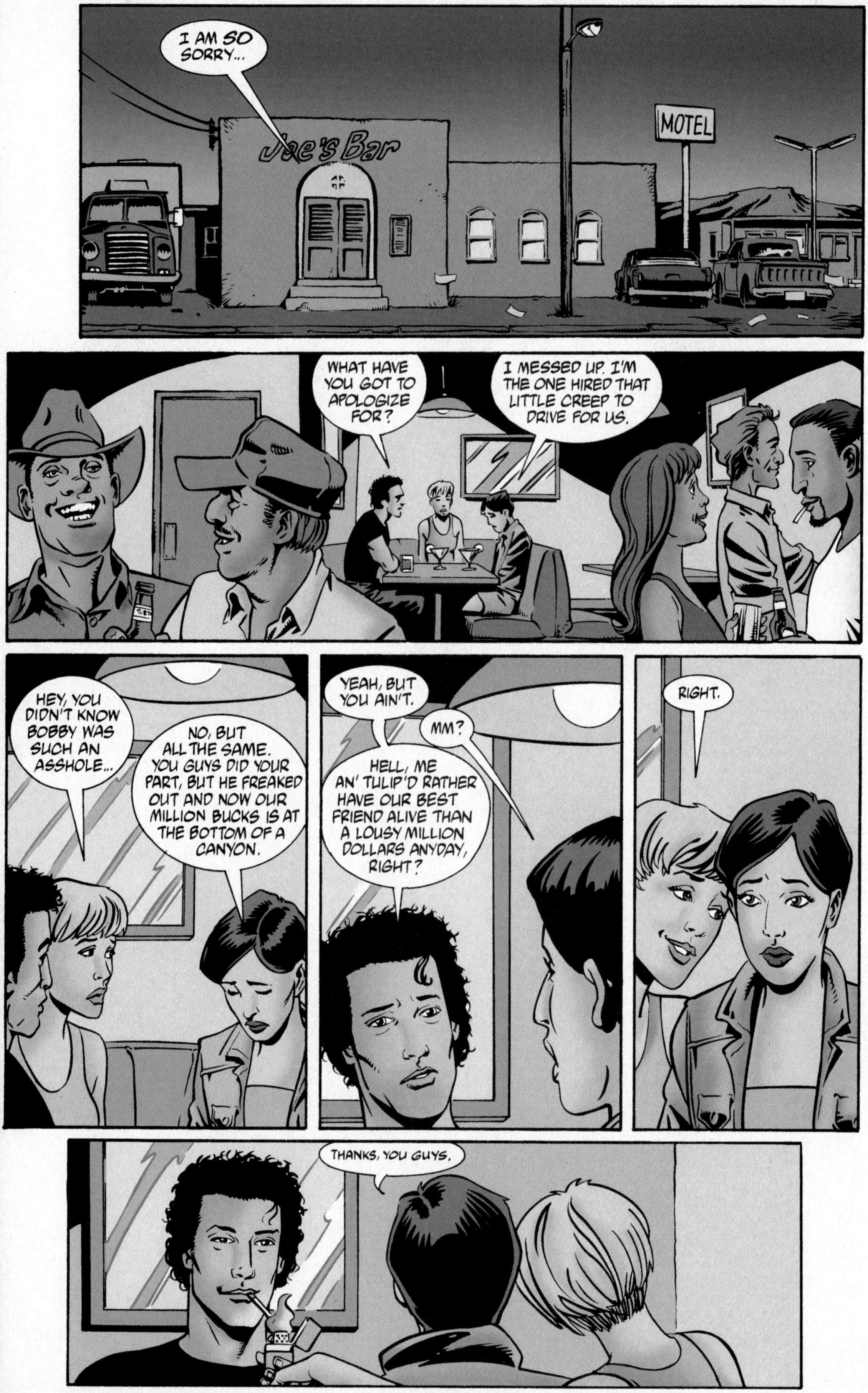
I AM SO SORRY...
Joe's Bar
MOTEL
WHAT HAVE YOU GOT TO APOLOGIZE FOR?
I MESSED UP. I'M THE ONE HIRED THAT LITTLE CREEP TO DRIVE FOR US.
HEY, YOU DIDN'T KNOW BOBBY WAS SUCH AN ASSHOLE...
NO, BUT ALL THE SAME. YOU GUYS DID YOUR PART, BUT HE FREAKED OUT AND NOW OUR MILLION BUCKS IS AT THE BOTTOM OF A CANYON.
YEAH, BUT YOU AIN'T.
MM?
HELL, ME AN' TULIP'D RATHER HAVE OUR BEST FRIEND ALIVE THAN A LOUSY MILLION DOLLARS ANYDAY, RIGHT?
RIGHT.
THANKS, YOU GUYS.

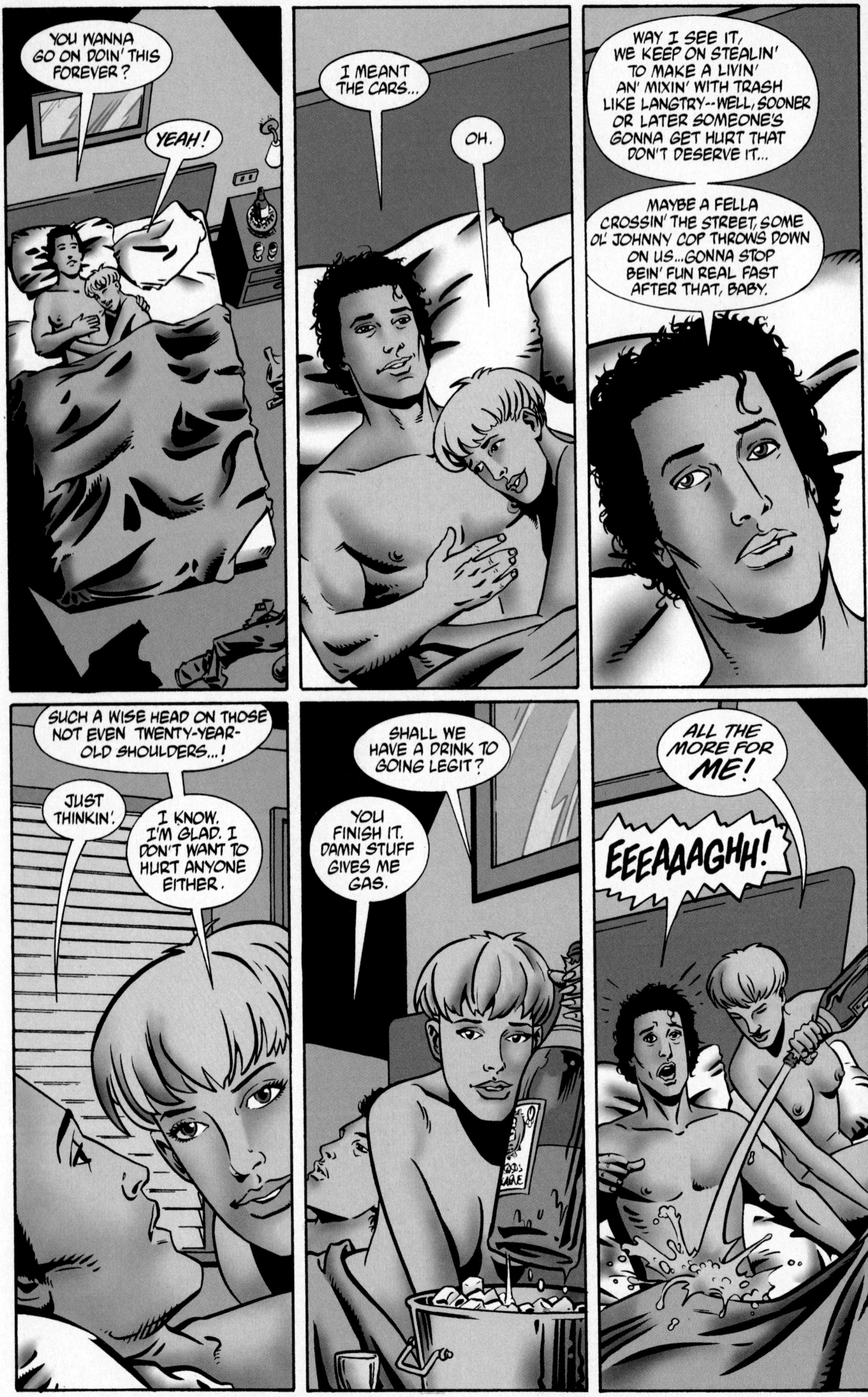
YOU WANNA GO ON DOIN' THIS FOREVER?
YEAH!
I MEANT THE CARS...
OH.
WAY I SEE IT, WE KEEP ON STEALIN' TO MAKE A LIVIN' AN' MIXIN' WITH TRASH LIKE LANGTRY--WELL, SOONER OR LATER SOMEONE'S GONNA GET HURT THAT DON'T DESERVE IT...
MAYBE A FELLA CROSSIN' THE STREET, SOME OL' JOHNNY COP THROWS DOWN ON US...GONNA STOP BEIN' FUN REAL FAST AFTER THAT, BABY.
SUCH A WISE HEAD ON THOSE NOT EVEN TWENTY-YEAR-OLD SHOULDERS...!
JUST THINKIN'.
I KNOW. I'M GLAD. I DON'T WANT TO HURT ANYONE EITHER.
SHALL WE HAVE A DRINK TO GOING LEGIT?
YOU FINISH IT. DAMN STUFF GIVES ME GAS.
ALL THE MORE FOR ME!
EEEAAAGHH!

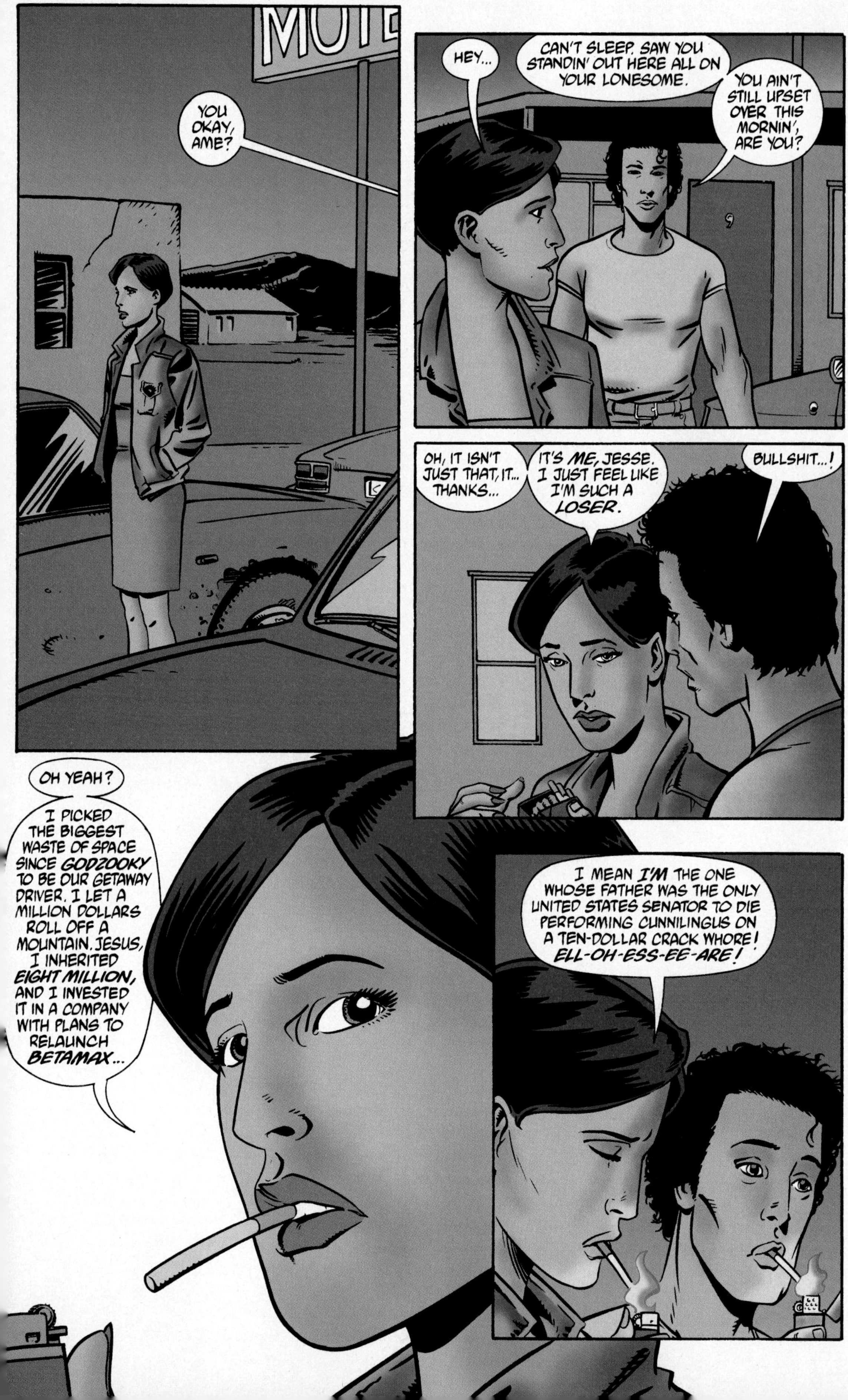
MOTE
YOU OKAY, AME?
HEY...
CAN'T SLEEP. SAW YOU STANDIN' OUT HERE ALL ON YOUR LONESOME.
YOU AIN'T STILL UPSET OVER THIS MORNIN', ARE YOU?
OH, IT ISN'T JUST THAT, IT... THANKS...
IT'S ME, JESSE. I JUST FEEL LIKE I'M SUCH A LOSER.
BULLSHIT...!
OH YEAH?
I PICKED THE BIGGEST WASTE OF SPACE SINCE GODZOOKY TO BE OUR GETAWAY DRIVER. I LET A MILLION DOLLARS ROLL OFF A MOUNTAIN. JESUS, I INHERITED EIGHT MILLION, AND I INVESTED IT IN A COMPANY WITH PLANS TO RELAUNCH BETAMAX...
I MEAN I'M THE ONE WHOSE FATHER WAS THE ONLY UNITED STATES SENATOR TO DIE PERFORMING CUNNILINGUS ON A TEN-DOLLAR CRACK WHORE! ELL-OH-ESS-EE-ARE!

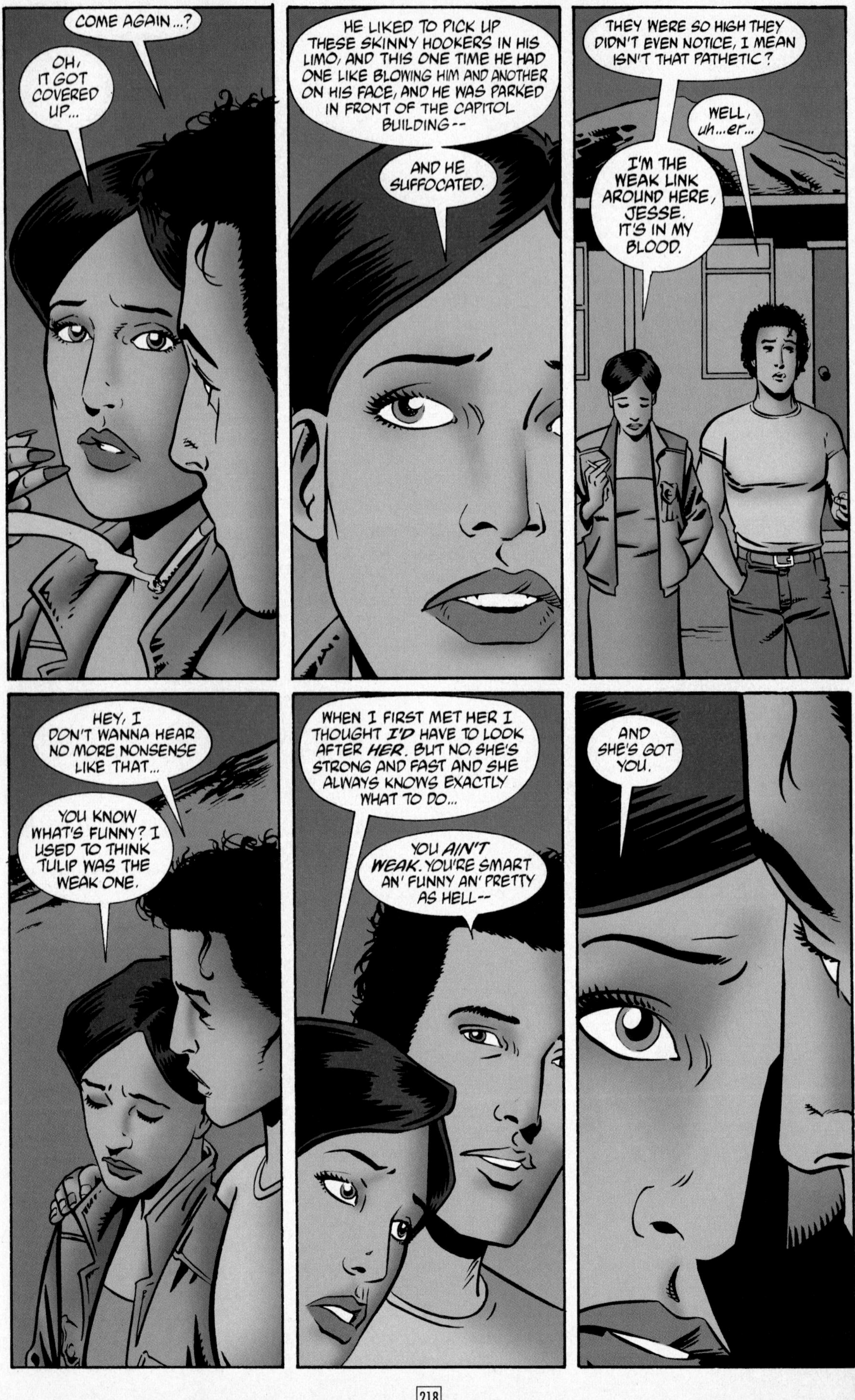
COME AGAIN...?
OH, IT GOT COVERED UP...
HE LIKED TO PICK UP THESE SKINNY HOOKERS IN HIS LIMO, AND THIS ONE TIME HE HAD ONE LIKE BLOWING HIM AND ANOTHER ON HIS FACE, AND HE WAS PARKED IN FRONT OF THE CAPITOL BUILDING--
AND HE SUFFOCATED.
THEY WERE SO HIGH THEY DIDN'T EVEN NOTICE, I MEAN ISN'T THAT PATHETIC?
WELL, uh...er...
I'M THE WEAK LINK AROUND HERE, JESSE. IT'S IN MY BLOOD.
HEY, I DON'T WANNA HEAR NO MORE NONSENSE LIKE THAT...
YOU KNOW WHAT'S FUNNY? I USED TO THINK TULIP WAS THE WEAK ONE.
WHEN I FIRST MET HER I THOUGHT *I'D* HAVE TO LOOK AFTER *HER*. BUT NO, SHE'S STRONG AND FAST AND SHE ALWAYS KNOWS EXACTLY WHAT TO DO...
YOU *AIN'T WEAK*. YOU'RE SMART AN' FUNNY AN' PRETTY AS HELL--
AND SHE'S GOT YOU.

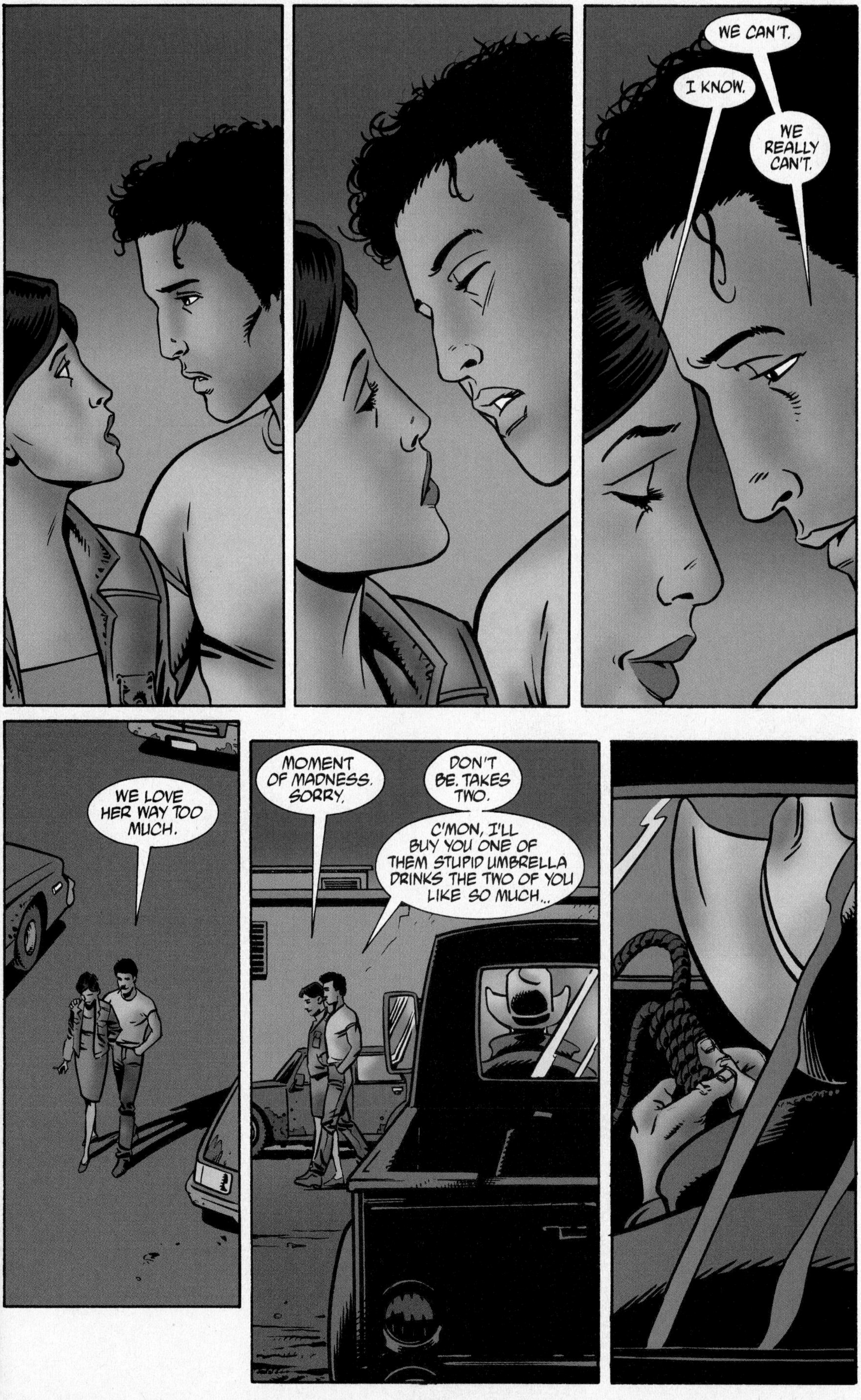
WE CAN'T.
I KNOW.
WE REALLY CAN'T.
WE LOVE HER WAY TOO MUCH.
MOMENT OF MADNESS. SORRY.
DON'T BE. TAKES TWO.
C'MON, I'LL BUY YOU ONE OF THEM STUPID UMBRELLA DRINKS THE TWO OF YOU LIKE SO MUCH...

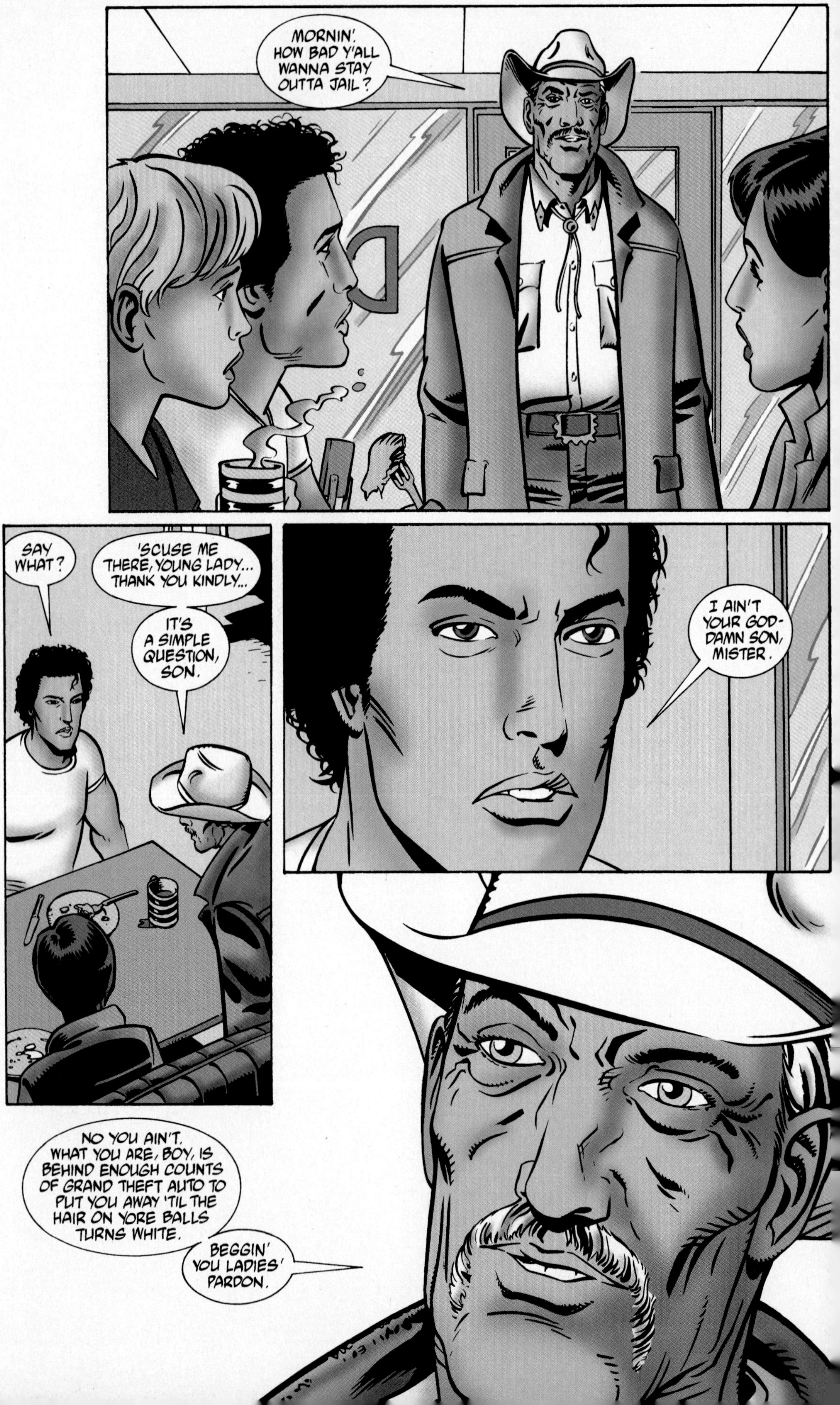
MORNIN'. HOW BAD Y'ALL WANNA STAY OUTTA JAIL?
SAY WHAT?
'SCUSE ME THERE, YOUNG LADY... THANK YOU KINDLY...
IT'S A SIMPLE QUESTION, SON.
I AIN'T YOUR GOD-DAMN SON, MISTER.
NO YOU AIN'T. WHAT YOU ARE, BOY, IS BEHIND ENOUGH COUNTS OF GRAND THEFT AUTO TO PUT YOU AWAY 'TIL THE HAIR ON YORE BALLS TURNS WHITE.
BEGGIN' YOU LADIES' PARDON.

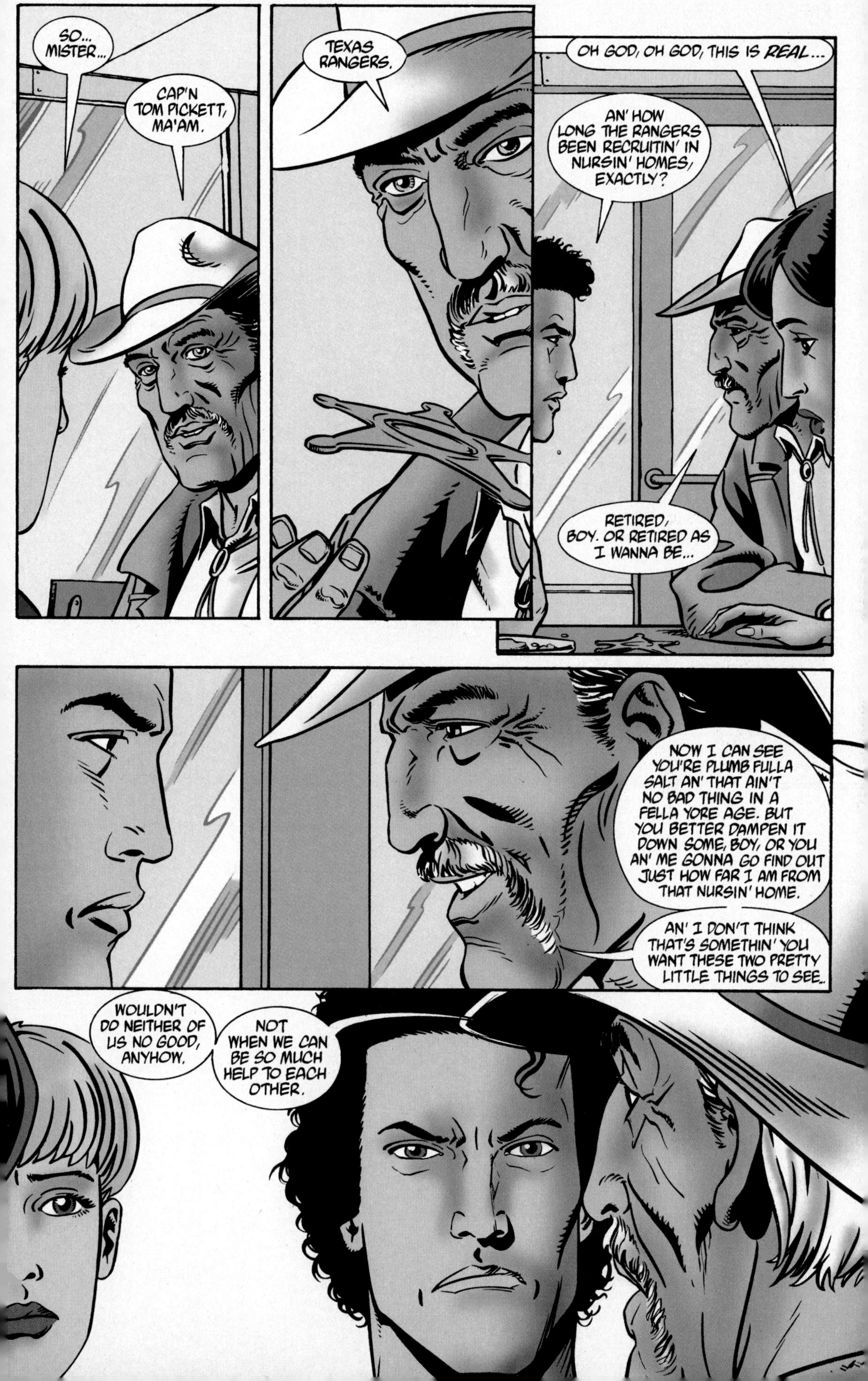
SO... MISTER...
CAP'N TOM PICKETT, MA'AM.
TEXAS RANGERS.
OH GOD, OH GOD, THIS IS *REAL*...
AN' HOW LONG THE RANGERS BEEN RECRUITIN' IN NURSIN' HOMES, EXACTLY?
RETIRED, BOY. OR RETIRED AS I WANNA BE...
NOW I CAN SEE YOU'RE PLUMB FULLA SALT AN' THAT AIN'T NO BAD THING IN A FELLA YORE AGE. BUT YOU BETTER DAMPEN IT DOWN SOME, BOY, OR YOU AN' ME GONNA GO FIND OUT JUST HOW FAR I AM FROM THAT NURSIN' HOME.
AN' I DON'T THINK THAT'S SOMETHIN' YOU WANT THESE TWO PRETTY LITTLE THINGS TO SEE..
WOULDN'T DO NEITHER OF US NO GOOD, ANYHOW.
NOT WHEN WE CAN BE SO MUCH HELP TO EACH OTHER.

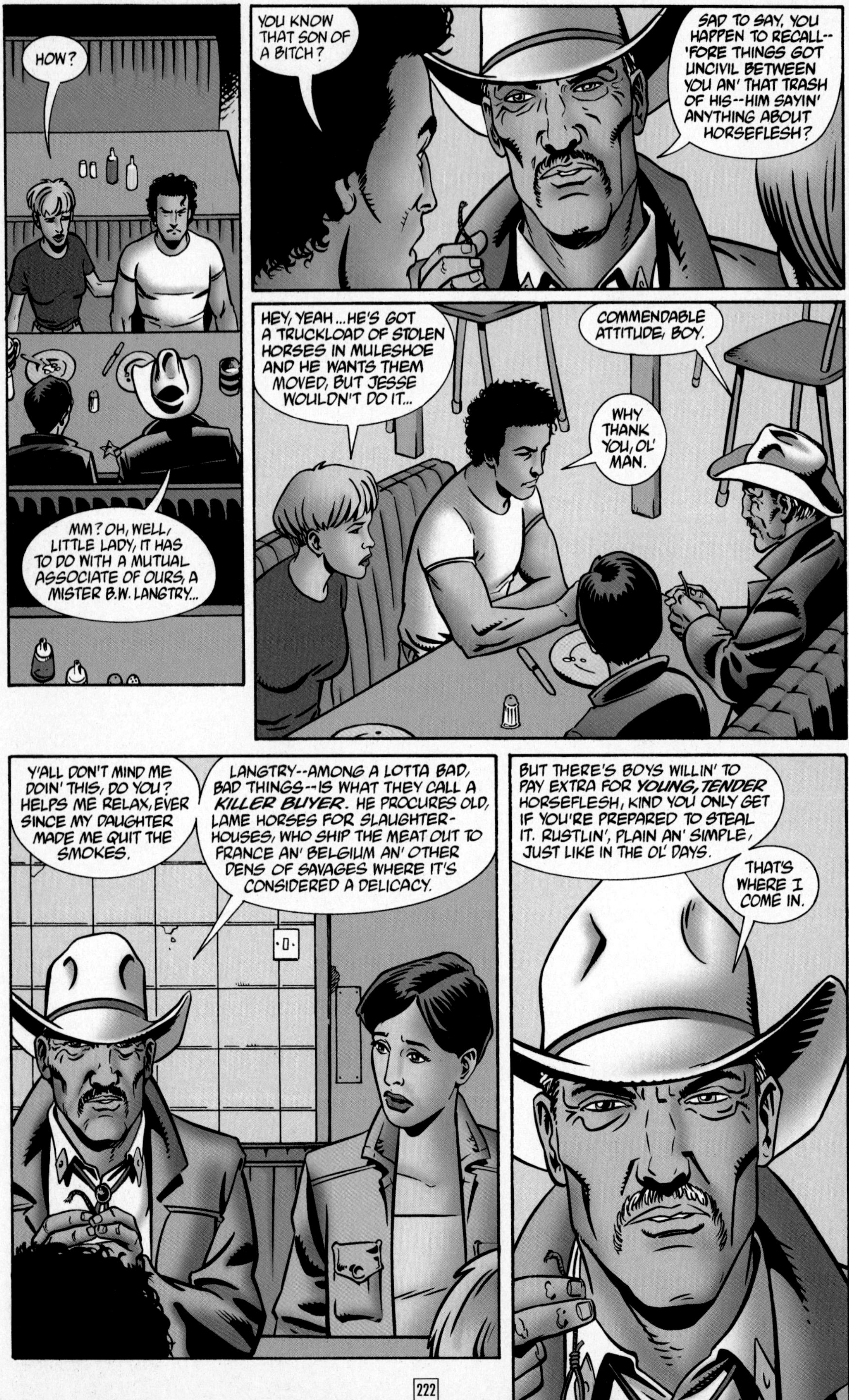
HOW?
MM? OH, WELL, LITTLE LADY, IT HAS TO DO WITH A MUTUAL ASSOCIATE OF OURS, A MISTER B.W. LANGTRY...
YOU KNOW THAT SON OF A BITCH?
SAD TO SAY. YOU HAPPEN TO RECALL--'FORE THINGS GOT UNCIVIL BETWEEN YOU AN' THAT TRASH OF HIS--HIM SAYIN' ANYTHING ABOUT HORSEFLESH?
HEY, YEAH ...HE'S GOT A TRUCKLOAD OF STOLEN HORSES IN MULESHOE AND HE WANTS THEM MOVED, BUT JESSE WOULDN'T DO IT...
COMMENDABLE ATTITUDE, BOY.
WHY THANK YOU, OL' MAN.
Y'ALL DON'T MIND ME DOIN' THIS, DO YOU? HELPS ME RELAX, EVER SINCE MY DAUGHTER MADE ME QUIT THE SMOKES.
LANGTRY--AMONG A LOTTA BAD, BAD THINGS--IS WHAT THEY CALL A KILLER BUYER. HE PROCURES OLD, LAME HORSES FOR SLAUGHTER-HOUSES, WHO SHIP THE MEAT OUT TO FRANCE AN' BELGIUM AN' OTHER DENS OF SAVAGES WHERE IT'S CONSIDERED A DELICACY.
BUT THERE'S BOYS WILLIN' TO PAY EXTRA FOR YOUNG, TENDER HORSEFLESH, KIND YOU ONLY GET IF YOU'RE PREPARED TO STEAL IT. RUSTLIN', PLAIN AN' SIMPLE, JUST LIKE IN THE OL' DAYS.
THAT'S WHERE I COME IN.

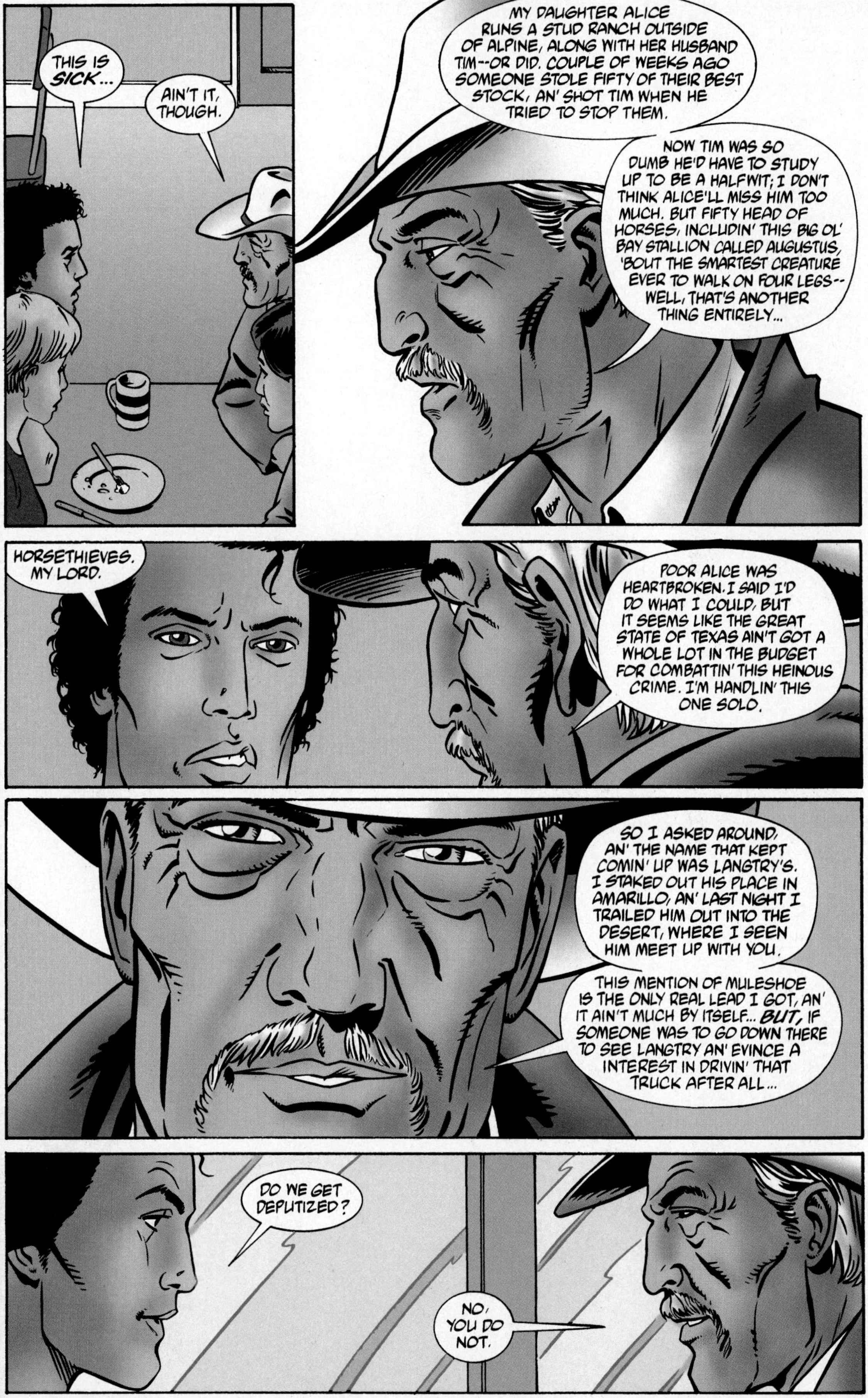
THIS IS SICK...
AIN'T IT, THOUGH.
MY DAUGHTER ALICE RUNS A STUD RANCH OUTSIDE OF ALPINE, ALONG WITH HER HUSBAND TIM--OR DID. COUPLE OF WEEKS AGO SOMEONE STOLE FIFTY OF THEIR BEST STOCK, AN' SHOT TIM WHEN HE TRIED TO STOP THEM.
NOW TIM WAS SO DUMB HE'D HAVE TO STUDY UP TO BE A HALFWIT; I DON'T THINK ALICE'LL MISS HIM TOO MUCH. BUT FIFTY HEAD OF HORSES, INCLUDIN' THIS BIG OL' BAY STALLION CALLED AUGUSTUS, 'BOUT THE SMARTEST CREATURE EVER TO WALK ON FOUR LEGS--WELL, THAT'S ANOTHER THING ENTIRELY...
HORSETHIEVES. MY LORD.
POOR ALICE WAS HEARTBROKEN. I SAID I'D DO WHAT I COULD, BUT IT SEEMS LIKE THE GREAT STATE OF TEXAS AIN'T GOT A WHOLE LOT IN THE BUDGET FOR COMBATTIN' THIS HEINOUS CRIME. I'M HANDLIN' THIS ONE SOLO.
SO I ASKED AROUND, AN' THE NAME THAT KEPT COMIN' UP WAS LANGTRY'S. I STAKED OUT HIS PLACE IN AMARILLO, AN' LAST NIGHT I TRAILED HIM OUT INTO THE DESERT, WHERE I SEEN HIM MEET UP WITH YOU.
THIS MENTION OF MULESHOE IS THE ONLY REAL LEAD I GOT, AN' IT AIN'T MUCH BY ITSELF... BUT, IF SOMEONE WAS TO GO DOWN THERE TO SEE LANGTRY AN' EVINCE A INTEREST IN DRIVIN' THAT TRUCK AFTER ALL...
DO WE GET DEPUTIZED?
NO, YOU DO NOT.

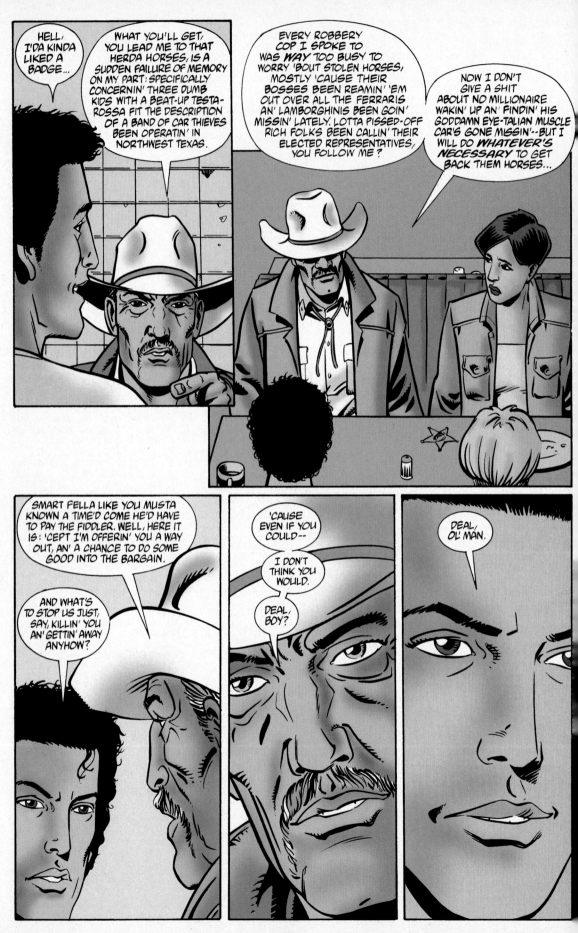

HELL, I'DA KINDA LIKED A BADGE...

WHAT YOU'LL GET, YOU LEAD ME TO THAT HERDA HORSES, IS A SUDDEN FAILURE OF MEMORY ON MY PART: SPECIFICALLY CONCERNIN' THREE DUMB KIDS WITH A BEAT-UP TESTA-ROSSA FIT THE DESCRIPTION OF A BAND OF CAR THIEVES BEEN OPERATIN' IN NORTHWEST TEXAS.

EVERY ROBBERY COP I SPOKE TO WAS *WAY* TOO BUSY TO WORRY 'BOUT STOLEN HORSES, MOSTLY 'CAUSE THEIR BOSSES BEEN REAMIN' 'EM OUT OVER ALL THE FERRARIS AN' LAMBORGHINIS BEEN GOIN' MISSIN' LATELY. LOTTA PISSED-OFF RICH FOLKS BEEN CALLIN' THEIR ELECTED REPRESENTATIVES, YOU FOLLOW ME?

NOW I DON'T GIVE A SHIT ABOUT NO MILLIONAIRE WAKIN' UP AN' FINDIN' HIS GODDAMN EYE-TALIAN MUSCLE CAR'S GONE MISSIN'--BUT I WILL DO *WHATEVER'S NECESSARY* TO GET BACK THEM HORSES...

SMART FELLA LIKE YOU MUSTA KNOWN A TIME'D COME HE'D HAVE TO PAY THE FIDDLER. WELL, HERE IT IS: 'CEPT I'M OFFERIN' YOU A WAY OUT, AN' A CHANCE TO DO SOME GOOD INTO THE BARGAIN.

AND WHAT'S TO STOP US JUST, SAY, KILLIN' YOU AN' GETTIN' AWAY ANYHOW?

'CAUSE EVEN IF YOU COULD--

I DON'T THINK YOU WOULD.

DEAL, BOY?

DEAL, OL' MAN.

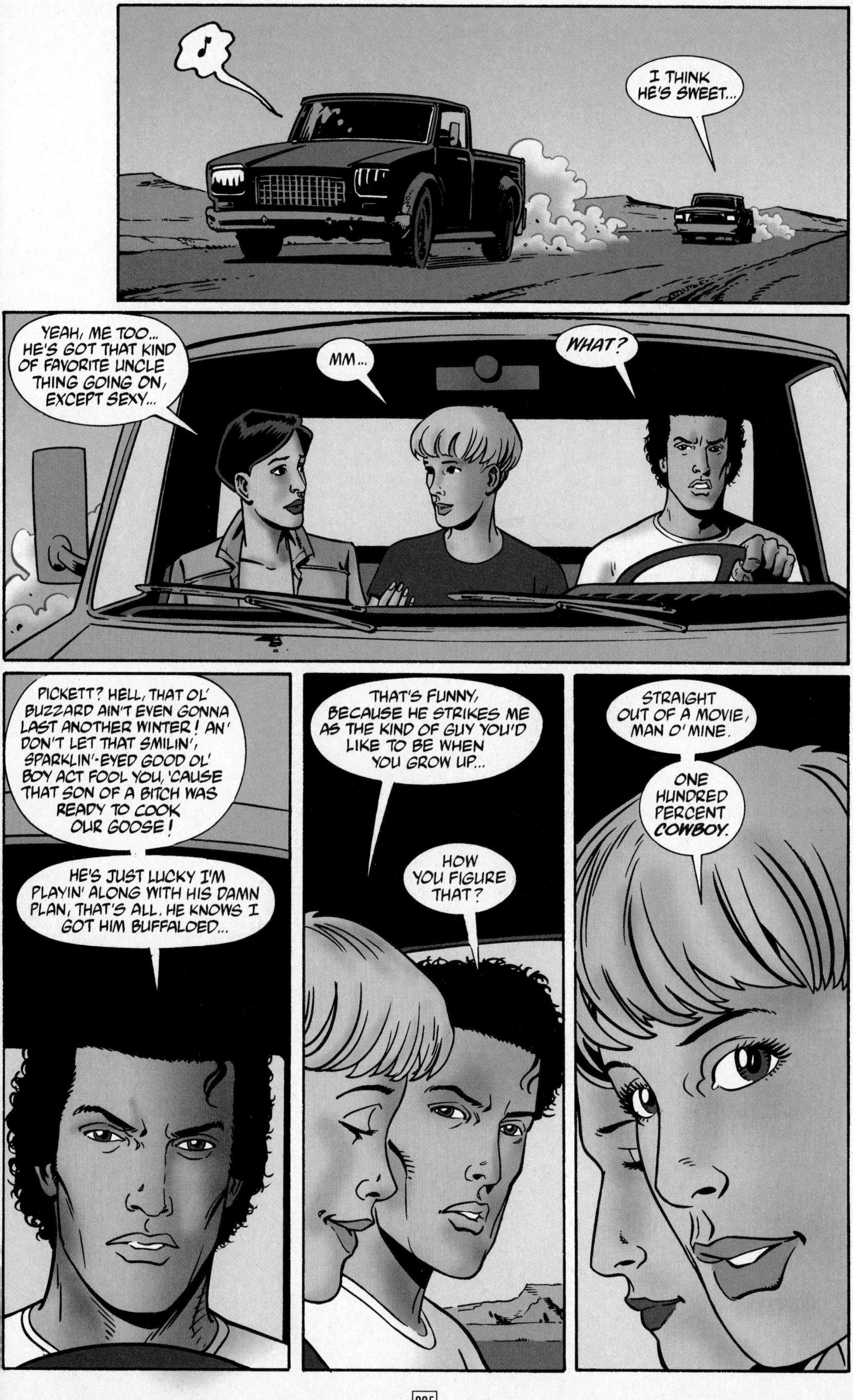
♪
I THINK HE'S SWEET...
YEAH, ME TOO... HE'S GOT THAT KIND OF FAVORITE UNCLE THING GOING ON, EXCEPT SEXY...
MM...
WHAT?
PICKETT? HELL, THAT OL' BUZZARD AIN'T EVEN GONNA LAST ANOTHER WINTER! AN' DON'T LET THAT SMILIN', SPARKLIN'-EYED GOOD OL' BOY ACT FOOL YOU, 'CAUSE THAT SON OF A BITCH WAS READY TO COOK OUR GOOSE!
HE'S JUST LUCKY I'M PLAYIN' ALONG WITH HIS DAMN PLAN, THAT'S ALL. HE KNOWS I GOT HIM BUFFALOED...
THAT'S FUNNY, BECAUSE HE STRIKES ME AS THE KIND OF GUY YOU'D LIKE TO BE WHEN YOU GROW UP...
HOW YOU FIGURE THAT?
STRAIGHT OUT OF A MOVIE, MAN O' MINE.
ONE HUNDRED PERCENT COWBOY.

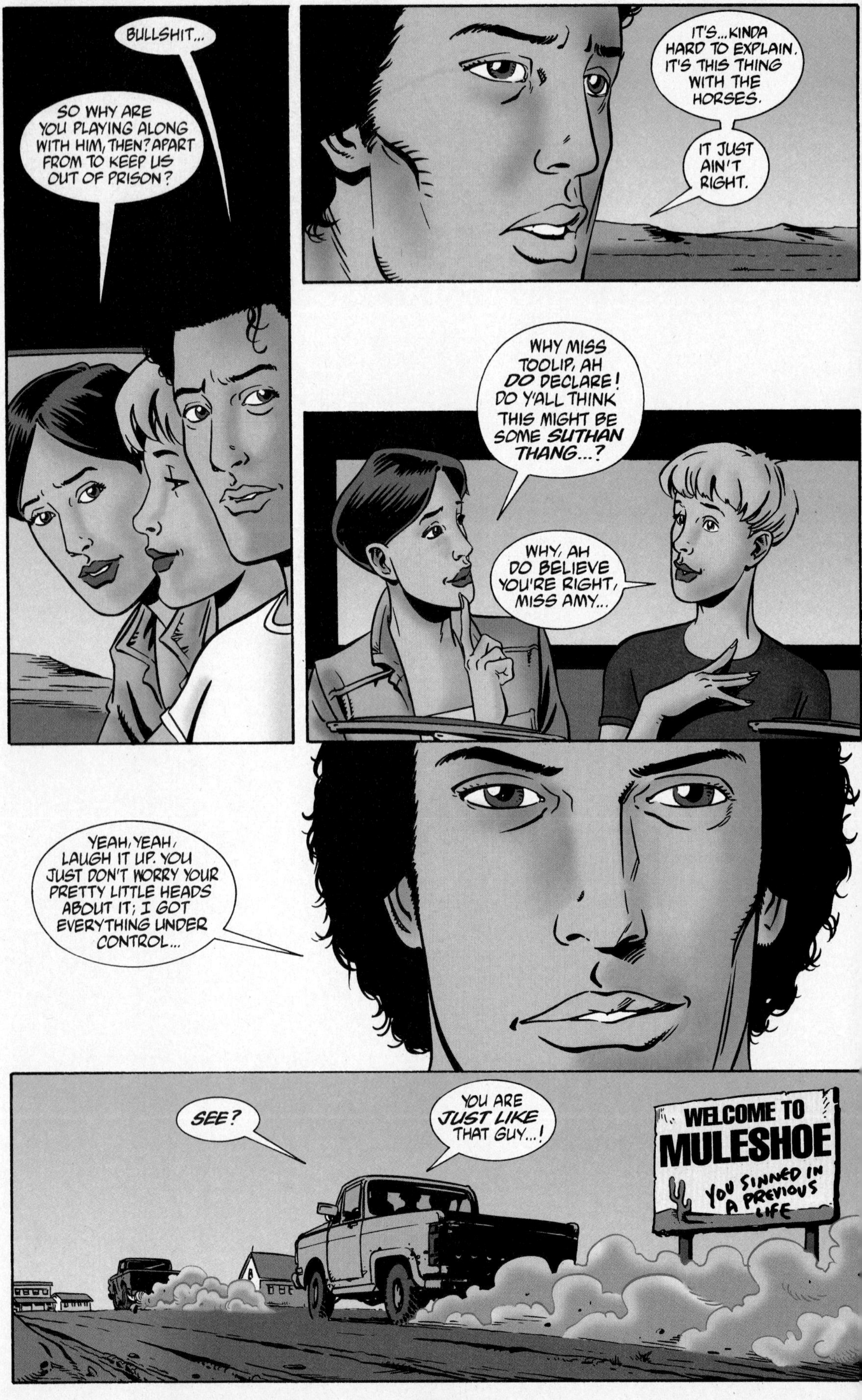

BULLSHIT...
SO WHY ARE YOU PLAYING ALONG WITH HIM, THEN? APART FROM TO KEEP US OUT OF PRISON?
IT'S...KINDA HARD TO EXPLAIN. IT'S THIS THING WITH THE HORSES.
IT JUST AIN'T RIGHT.
WHY MISS TOOLIP, AH *DO* DECLARE! DO Y'ALL THINK THIS MIGHT BE SOME *SUTHAN THANG*...?
WHY, AH DO BELIEVE YOU'RE RIGHT, MISS AMY...
YEAH, YEAH, LAUGH IT UP. YOU JUST DON'T WORRY YOUR PRETTY LITTLE HEADS ABOUT IT; I GOT EVERYTHING UNDER CONTROL...
SEE?
YOU ARE *JUST LIKE* THAT GUY...!
WELCOME TO
MULESHOE
YOU SINNED IN A PREVIOUS LIFE

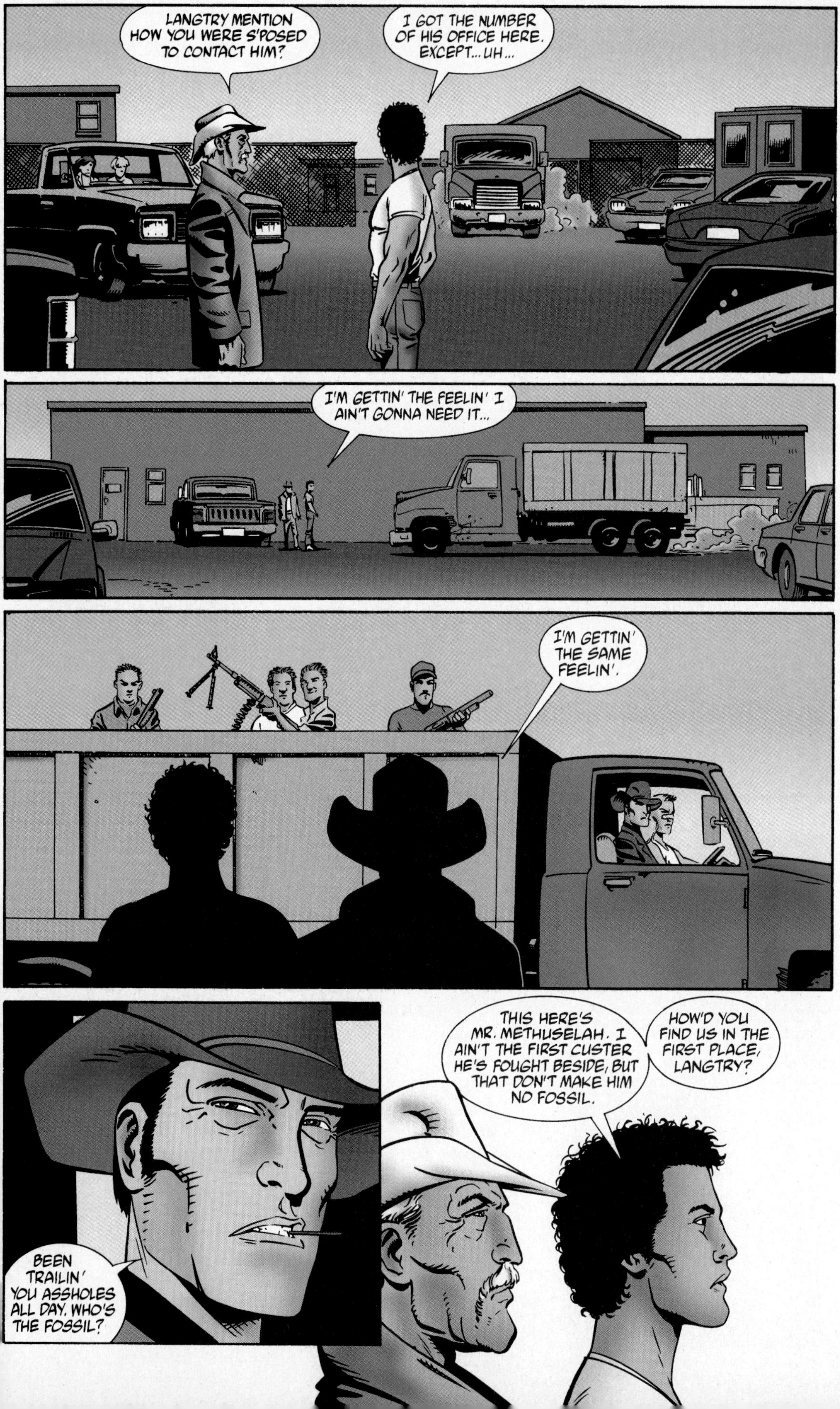
LANGTRY MENTION HOW YOU WERE S'POSED TO CONTACT HIM?
I GOT THE NUMBER OF HIS OFFICE HERE. EXCEPT... UH...
I'M GETTIN' THE FEELIN' I AIN'T GONNA NEED IT...
I'M GETTIN' THE SAME FEELIN'.
THIS HERE'S MR. METHUSELAH. I AIN'T THE FIRST CUSTER HE'S FOUGHT BESIDE, BUT THAT DON'T MAKE HIM NO FOSSIL.
HOW'D YOU FIND US IN THE FIRST PLACE, LANGTRY?
BEEN TRAILIN' YOU ASSHOLES ALL DAY. WHO'S THE FOSSIL?

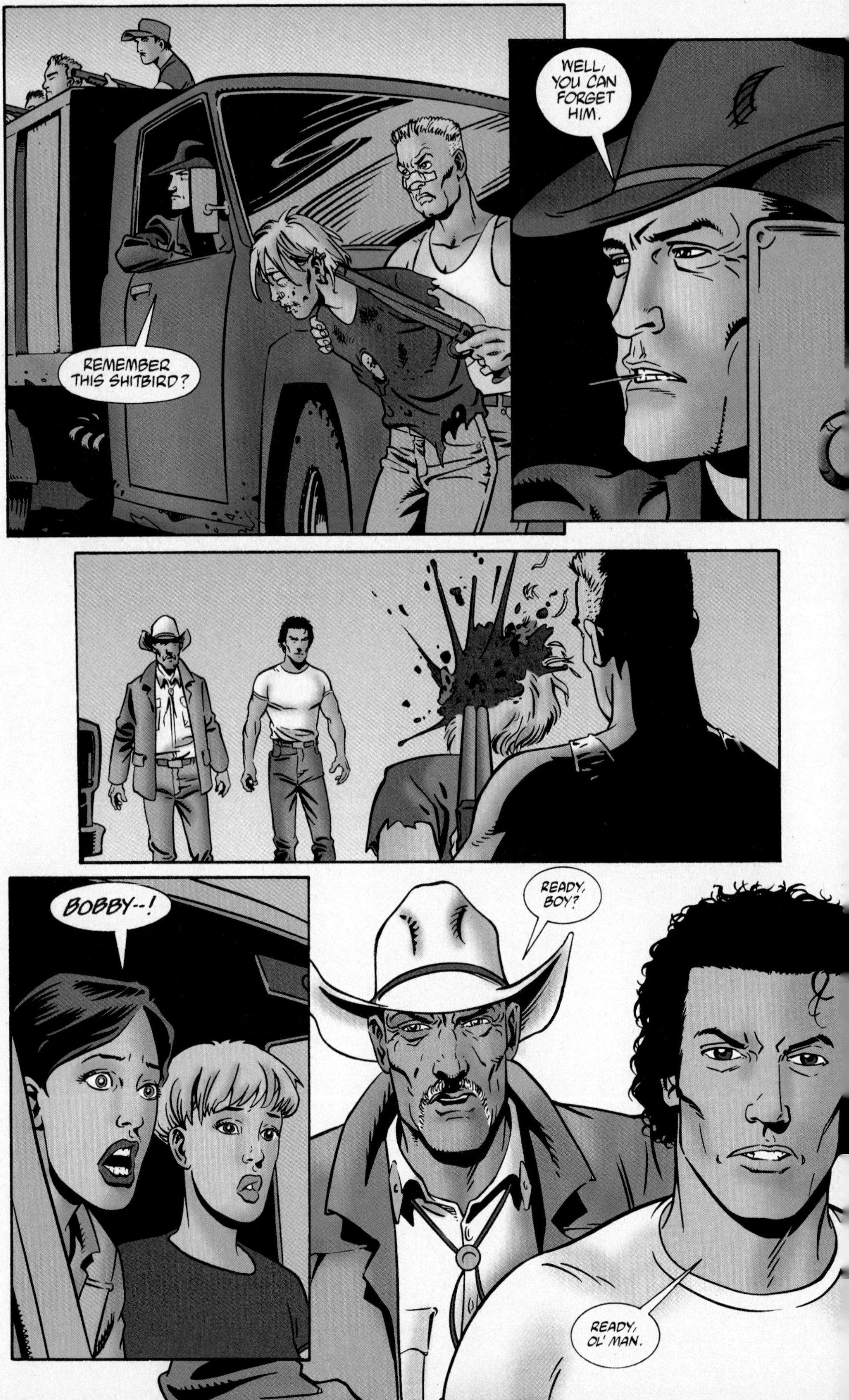
REMEMBER THIS SHITBIRD?
WELL, YOU CAN FORGET HIM.
BOBBY--!
READY, BOY?
READY, OL' MAN.

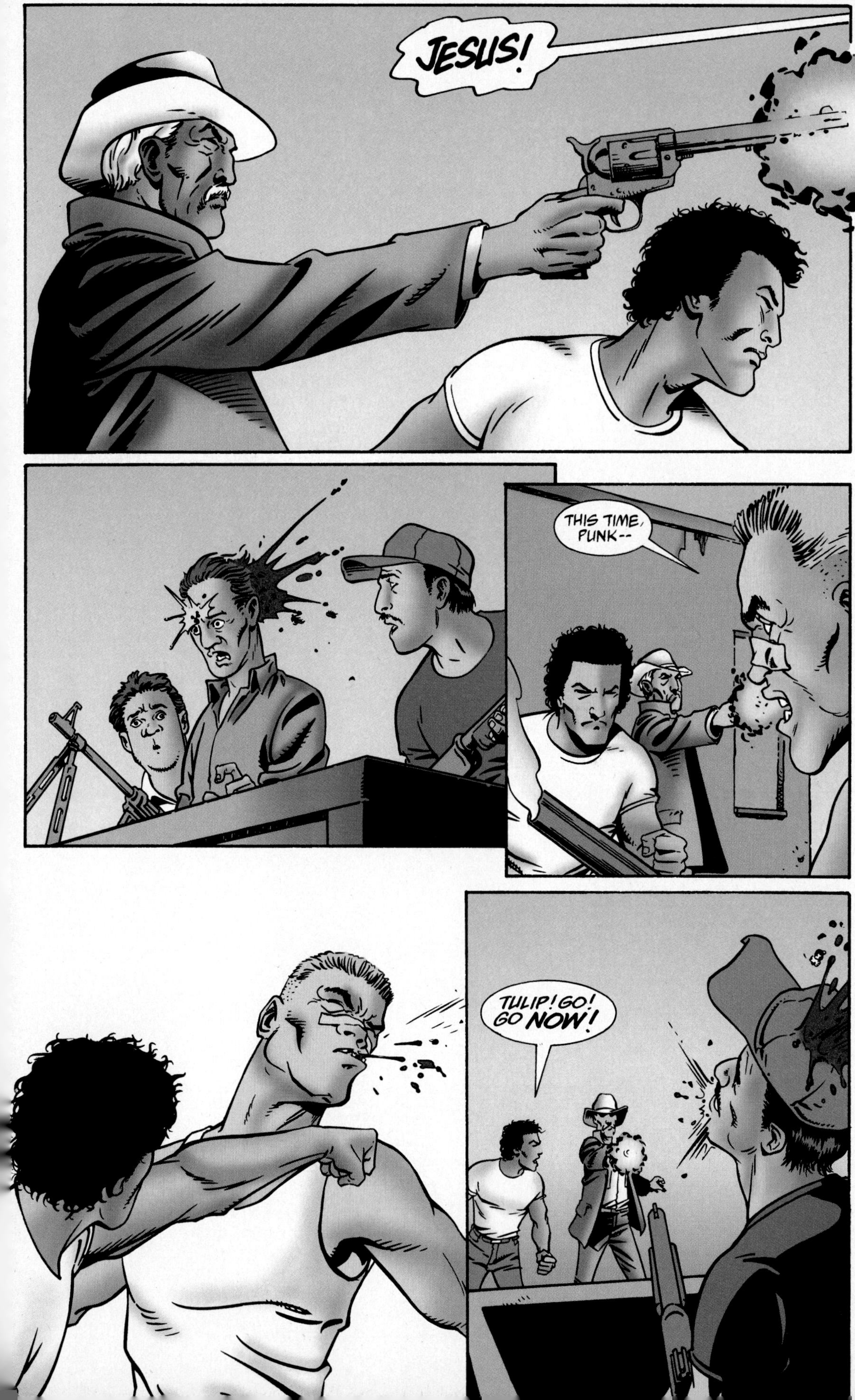
JESUS!
THIS TIME, PUNK--
TULIP! GO! GO NOW!

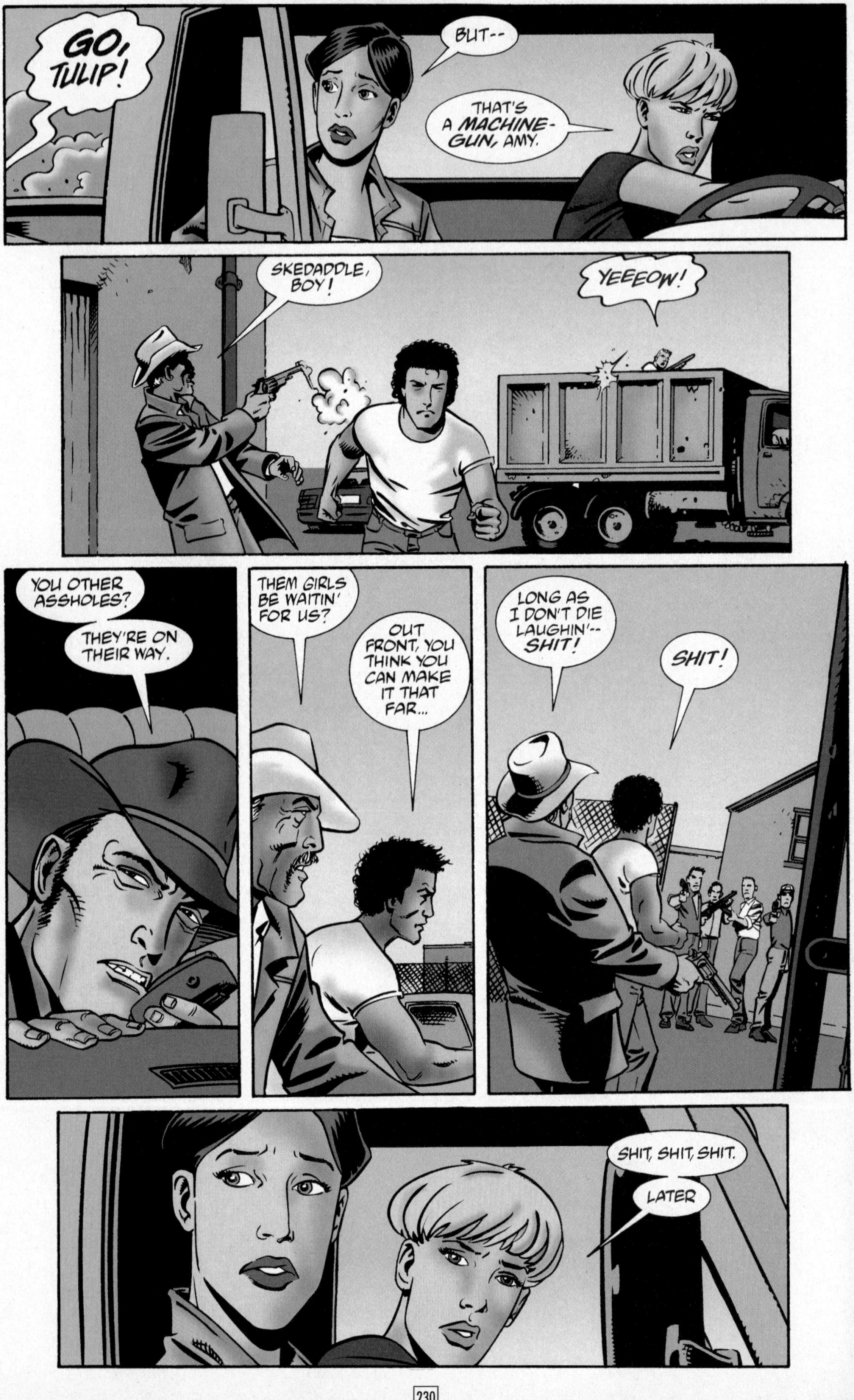
GO, TULIP!
BUT--
THAT'S A MACHINE-GUN, AMY.
SKEDADDLE, BOY!
YEEEOW!
YOU OTHER ASSHOLES?
THEY'RE ON THEIR WAY.
THEM GIRLS BE WAITIN' FOR US?
OUT FRONT, YOU THINK YOU CAN MAKE IT THAT FAR...
LONG AS I DON'T DIE LAUGHIN'-- SHIT!
SHIT!
SHIT, SHIT, SHIT.
LATER

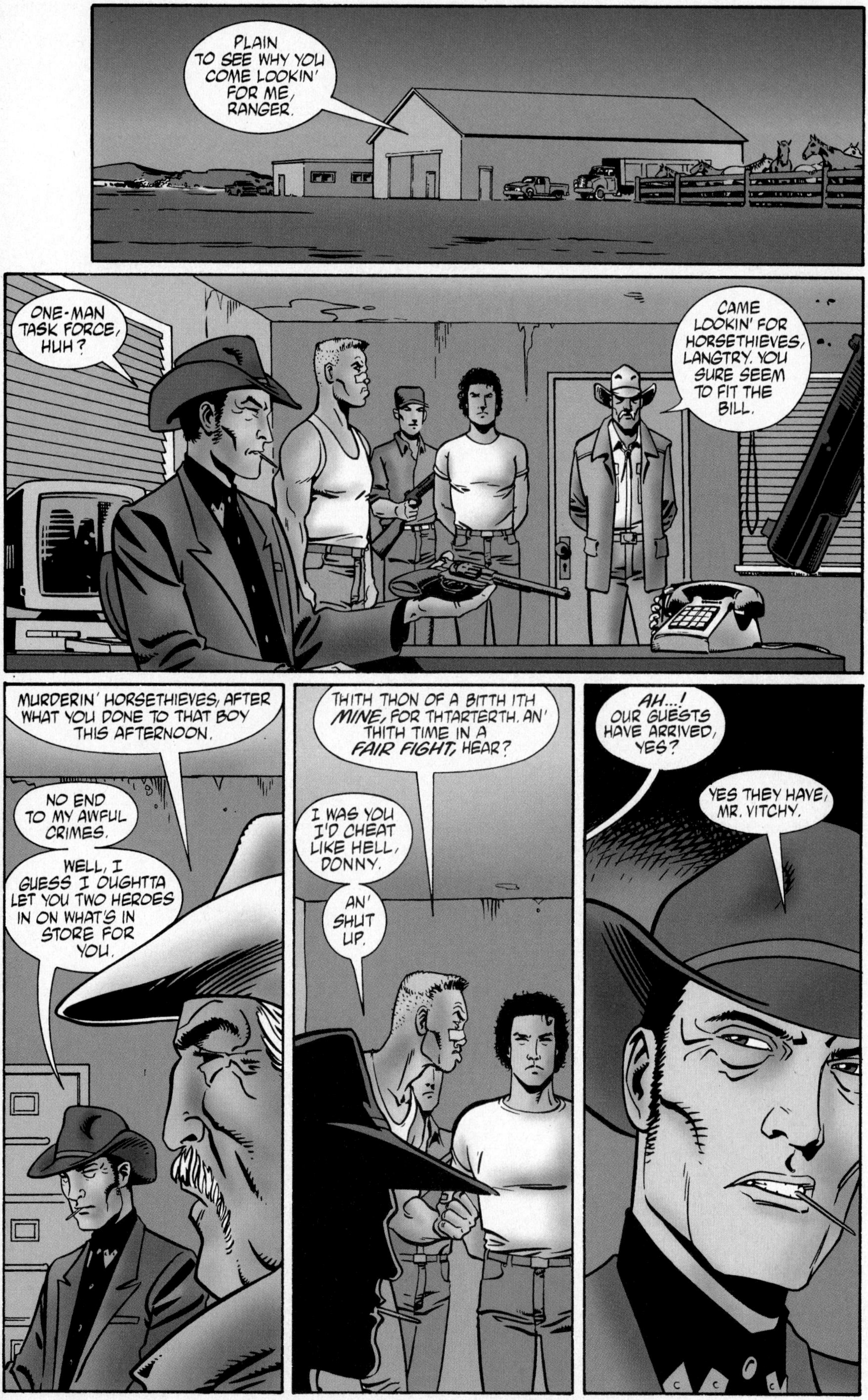
PLAIN TO SEE WHY YOU COME LOOKIN' FOR ME, RANGER.
ONE-MAN TASK FORCE, HUH?
CAME LOOKIN' FOR HORSETHIEVES, LANGTRY. YOU SURE SEEM TO FIT THE BILL.
MURDERIN' HORSETHIEVES, AFTER WHAT YOU DONE TO THAT BOY THIS AFTERNOON.
NO END TO MY AWFUL CRIMES.
WELL, I GUESS I OUGHTTA LET YOU TWO HEROES IN ON WHAT'S IN STORE FOR YOU.
THITH THON OF A BITTH ITH MINE, FOR THTARTERTH. AN' THITH TIME IN A FAIR FIGHT, HEAR?
I WAS YOU I'D CHEAT LIKE HELL, DONNY.
AN' SHUT UP.
AH...! OUR GUESTS HAVE ARRIVED, YES?
YES THEY HAVE, MR. VITCHY.

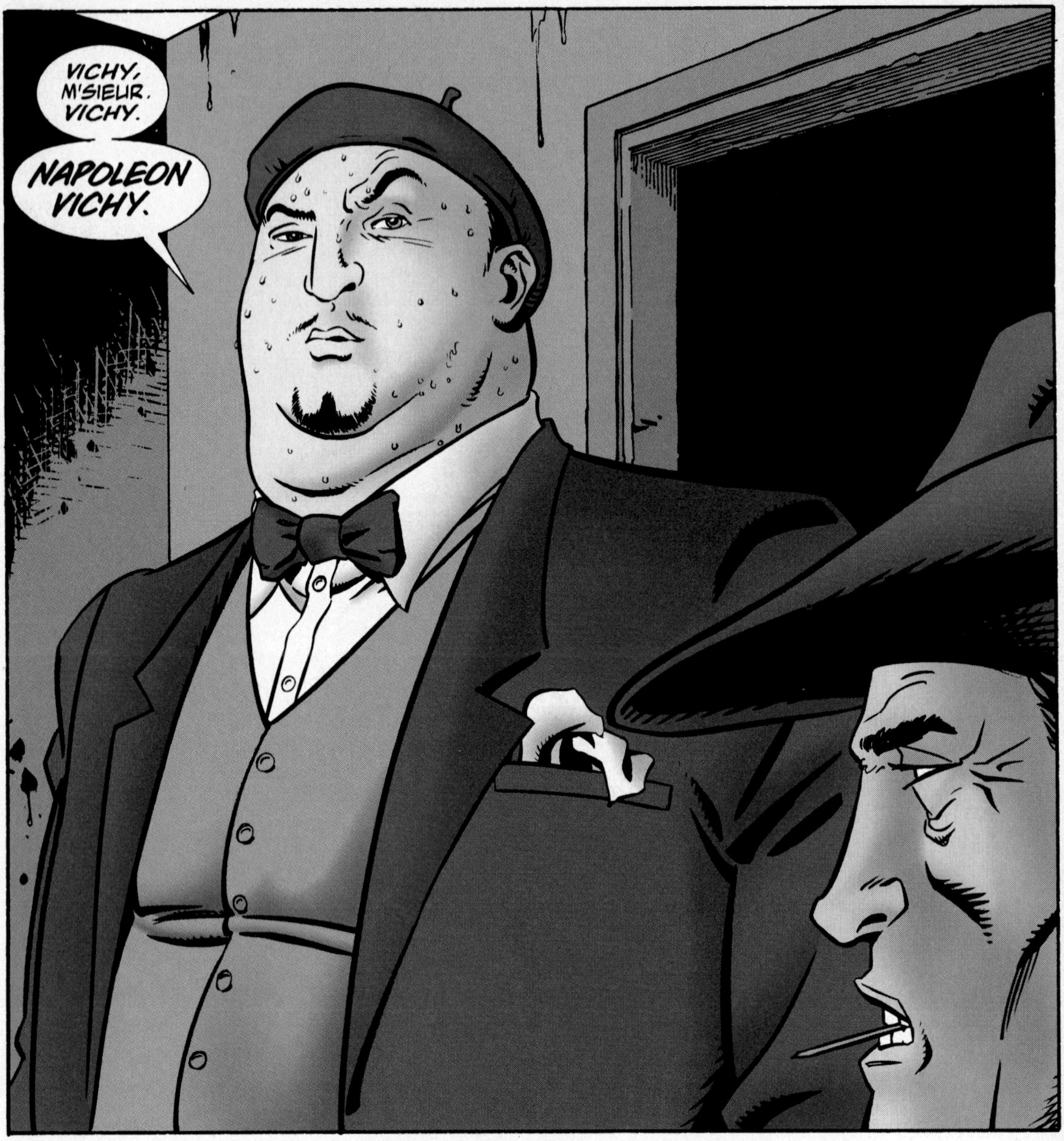
VICHY, M'SIEUR. VICHY.
NAPOLEON VICHY.

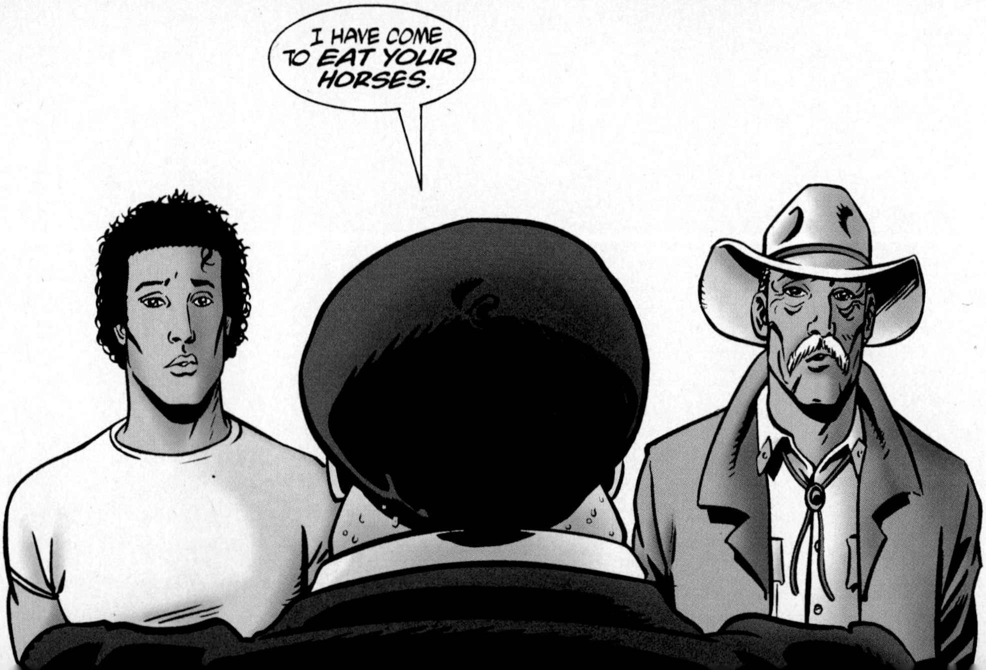
I HAVE COME TO EAT YOUR HORSES.

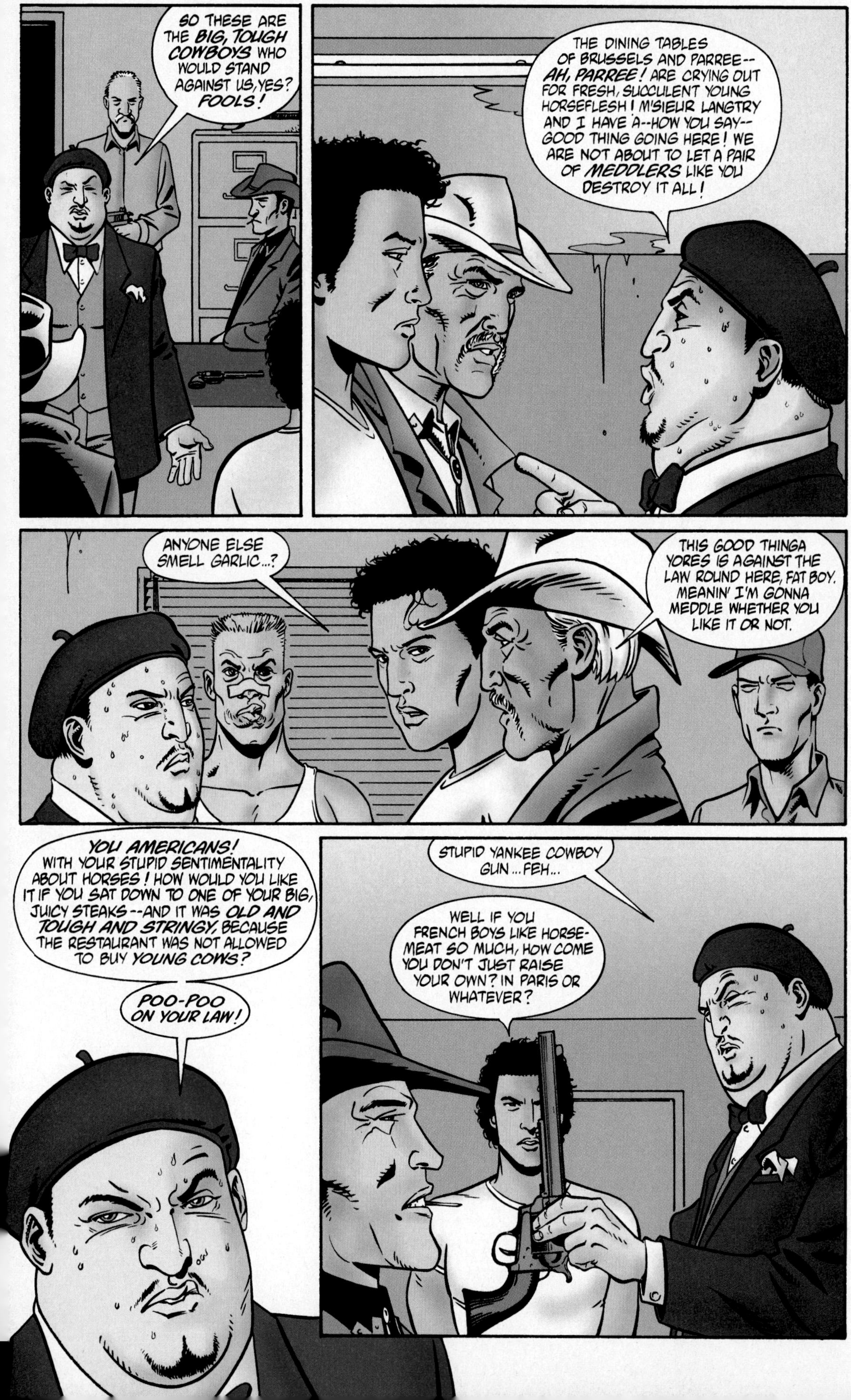
SO THESE ARE THE BIG, TOUGH COWBOYS WHO WOULD STAND AGAINST US, YES? FOOLS!
THE DINING TABLES OF BRUSSELS AND PARREE-- AH, PARREE! ARE CRYING OUT FOR FRESH, SUCCULENT YOUNG HORSEFLESH! M'SIEUR LANGTRY AND I HAVE A--HOW YOU SAY-- GOOD THING GOING HERE! WE ARE NOT ABOUT TO LET A PAIR OF MEDDLERS LIKE YOU DESTROY IT ALL!
ANYONE ELSE SMELL GARLIC...?
THIS GOOD THINGA YORES IS AGAINST THE LAW ROUND HERE, FAT BOY. MEANIN' I'M GONNA MEDDLE WHETHER YOU LIKE IT OR NOT.
YOU AMERICANS! WITH YOUR STUPID SENTIMENTALITY ABOUT HORSES! HOW WOULD YOU LIKE IT IF YOU SAT DOWN TO ONE OF YOUR BIG, JUICY STEAKS --AND IT WAS OLD AND TOUGH AND STRINGY, BECAUSE THE RESTAURANT WAS NOT ALLOWED TO BUY YOUNG COWS?
POO-POO ON YOUR LAW!
STUPID YANKEE COWBOY GUN ...FEH...
WELL IF YOU FRENCH BOYS LIKE HORSE-MEAT SO MUCH, HOW COME YOU DON'T JUST RAISE YOUR OWN? IN PARIS OR WHATEVER?

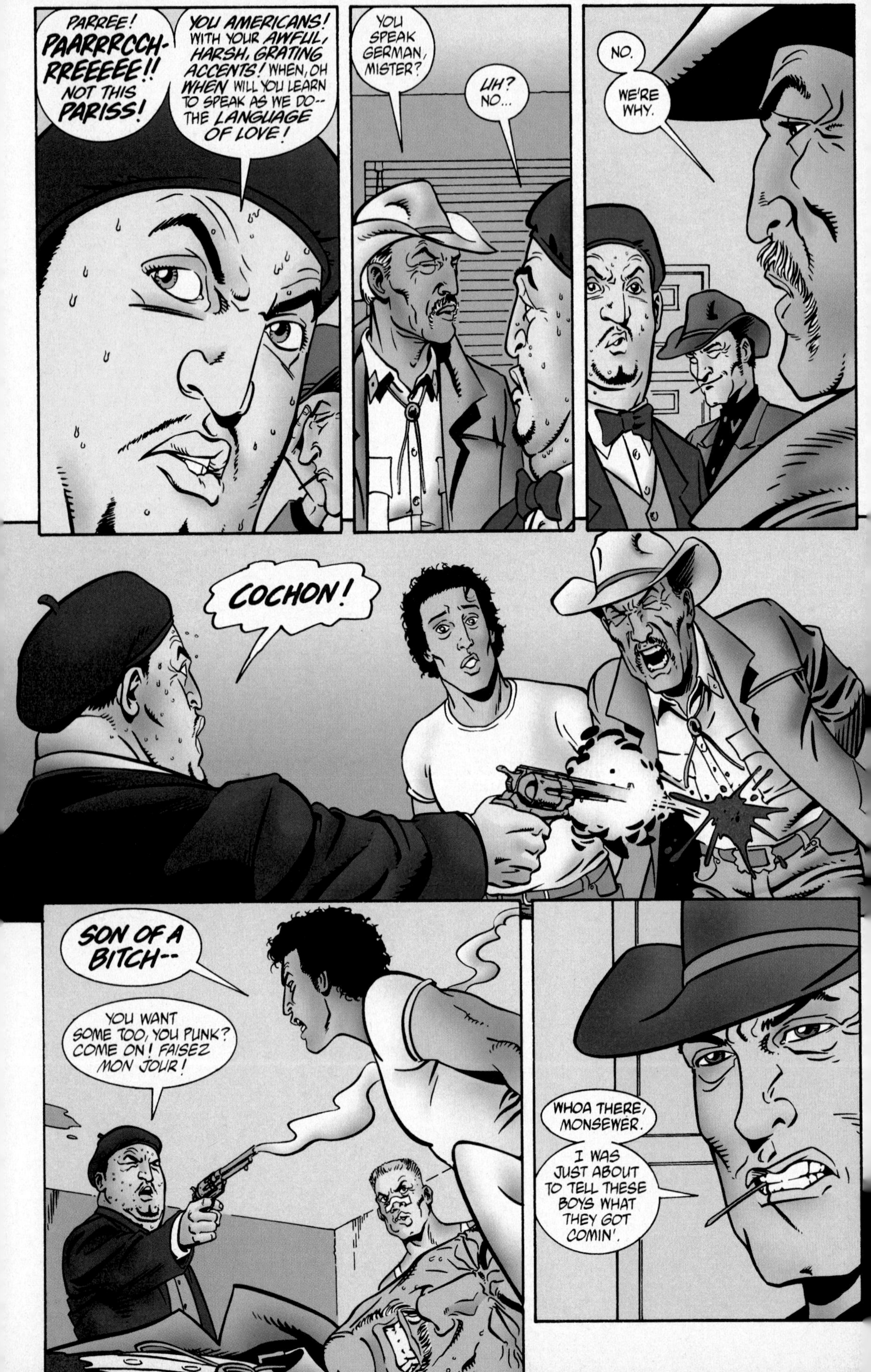
PARREE! PAARRRCCH-RREEEEE!! NOT THIS PARISS!
YOU AMERICANS! WITH YOUR AWFUL, HARSH, GRATING ACCENTS! WHEN, OH WHEN WILL YOU LEARN TO SPEAK AS WE DO-- THE LANGUAGE OF LOVE!
YOU SPEAK GERMAN, MISTER?
UH? NO...
NO.
WE'RE WHY.
COCHON!
SON OF A BITCH--
YOU WANT SOME TOO, YOU PUNK? COME ON! FAISEZ MON JOUR!
WHOA THERE, MONSEWER.
I WAS JUST ABOUT TO TELL THESE BOYS WHAT THEY GOT COMIN'.

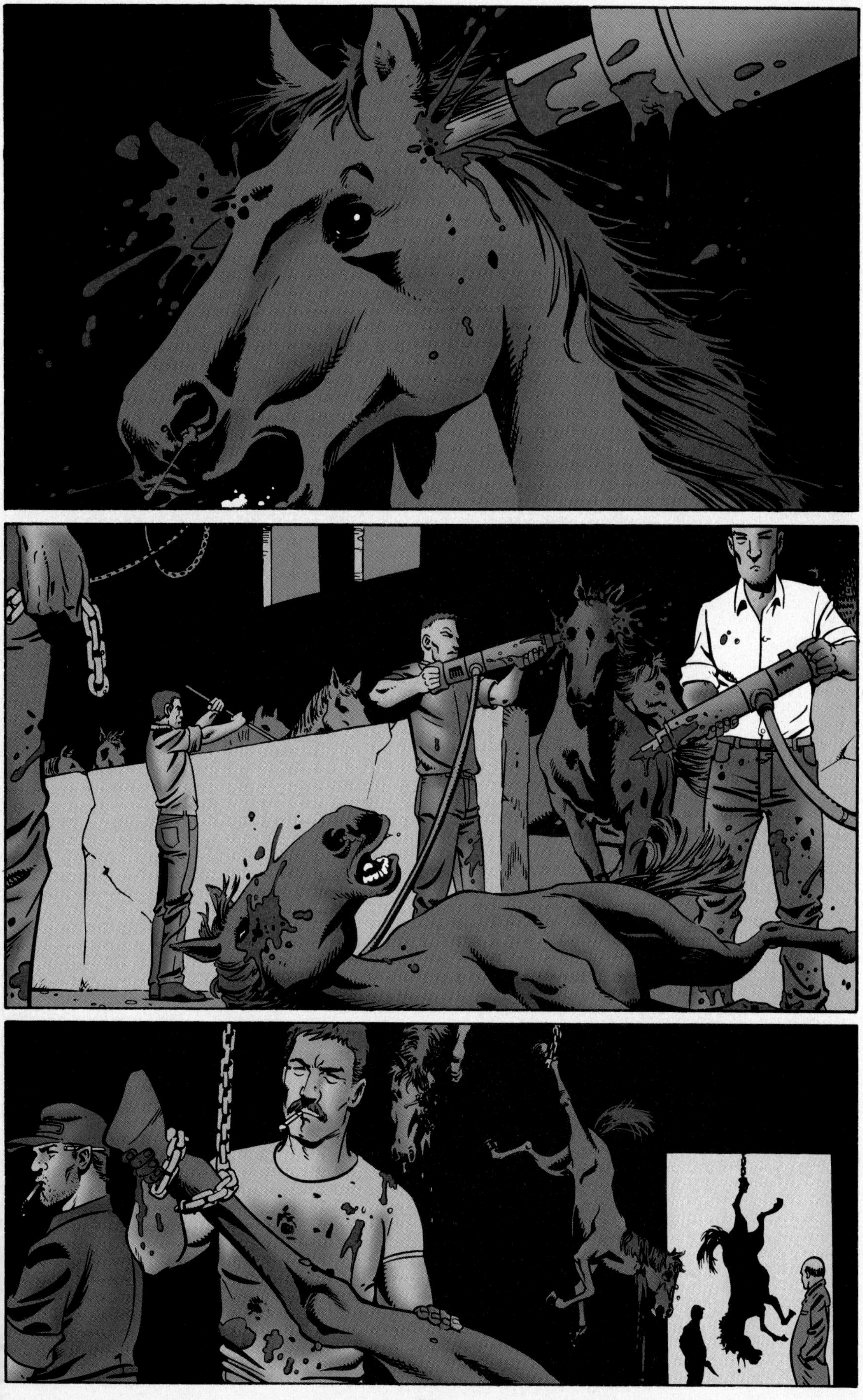

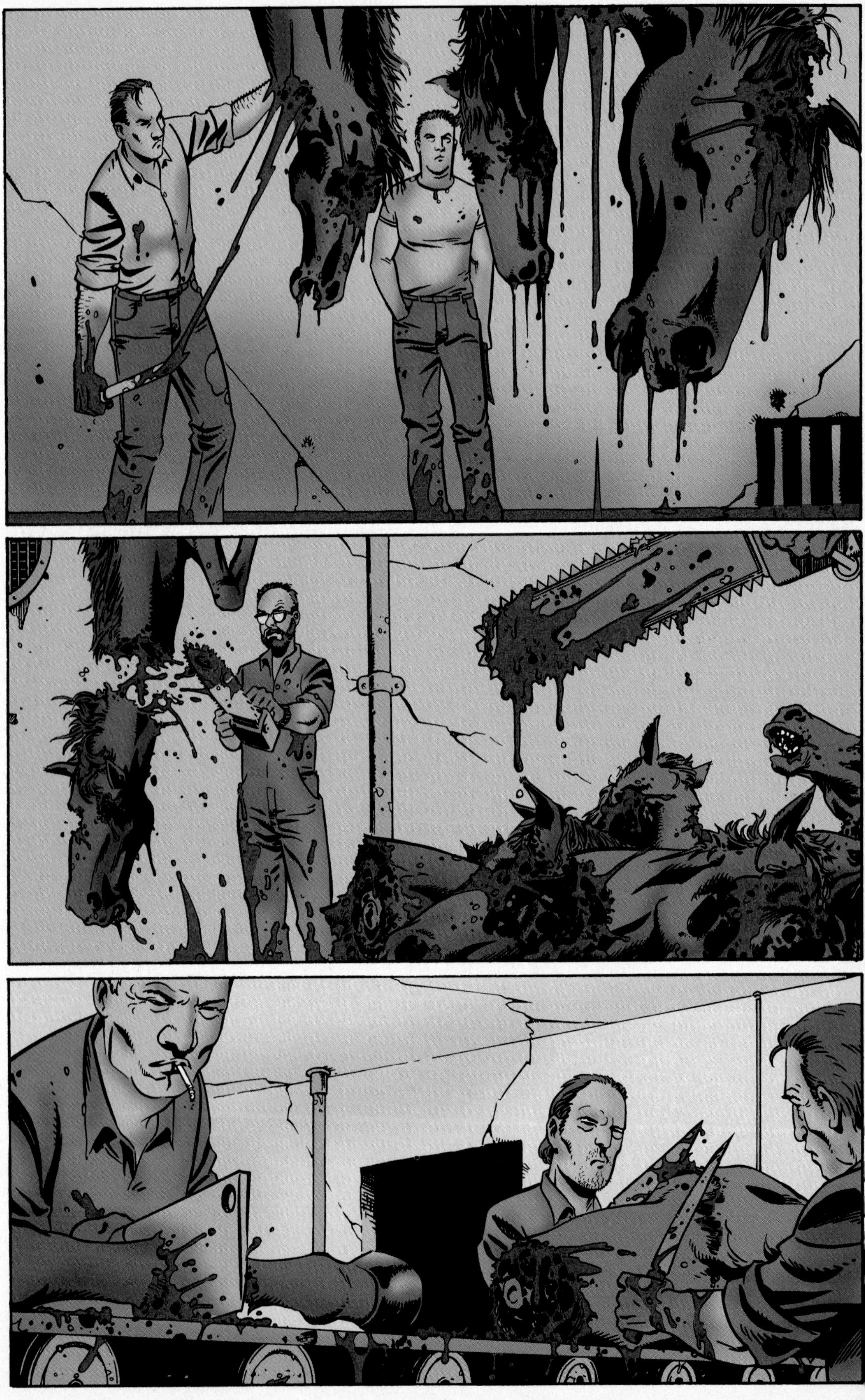

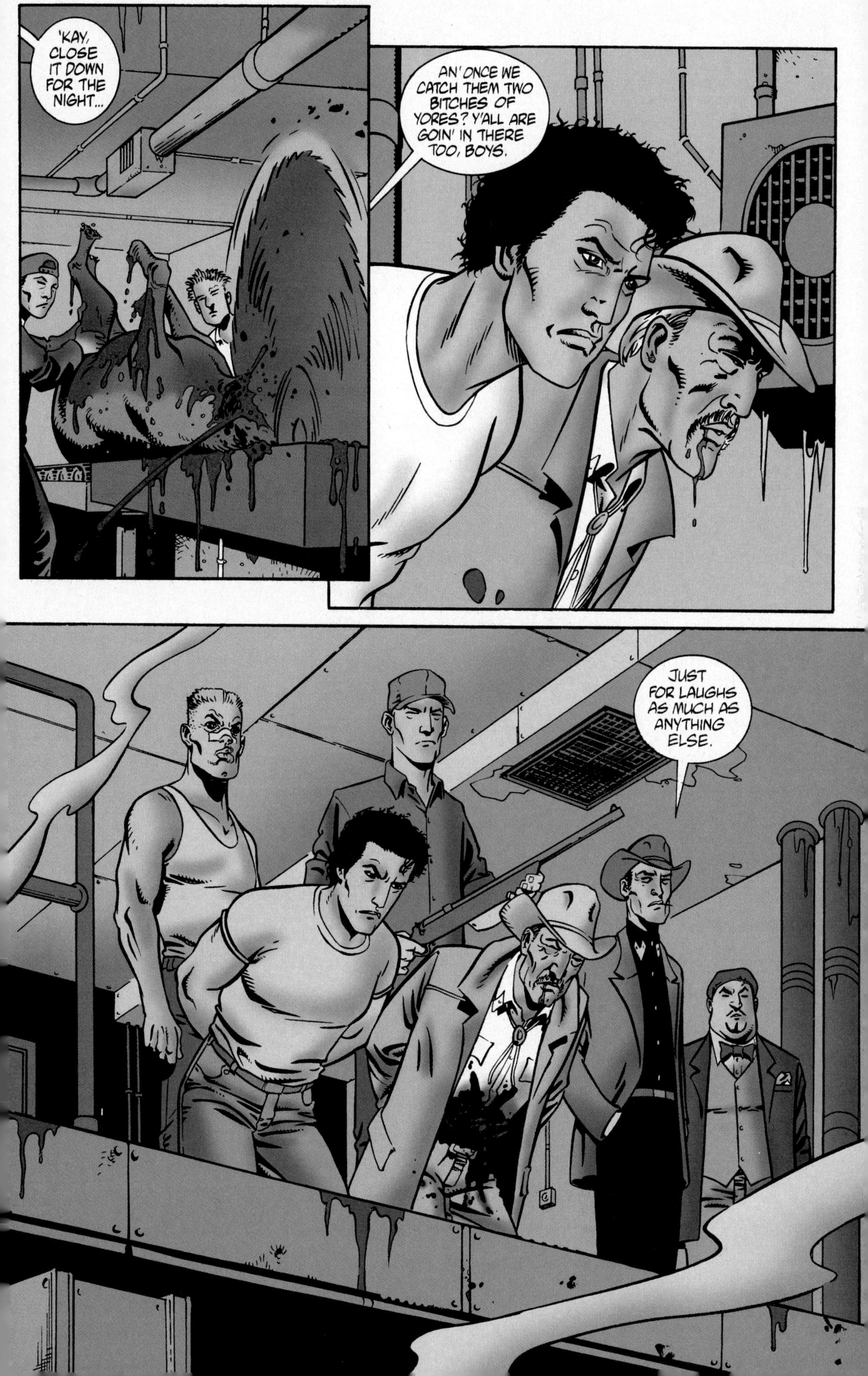
'KAY, CLOSE IT DOWN FOR THE NIGHT...
AN' ONCE WE CATCH THEM TWO BITCHES OF YORES? Y'ALL ARE GOIN' IN THERE TOO, BOYS.
JUST FOR LAUGHS AS MUCH AS ANYTHING ELSE.

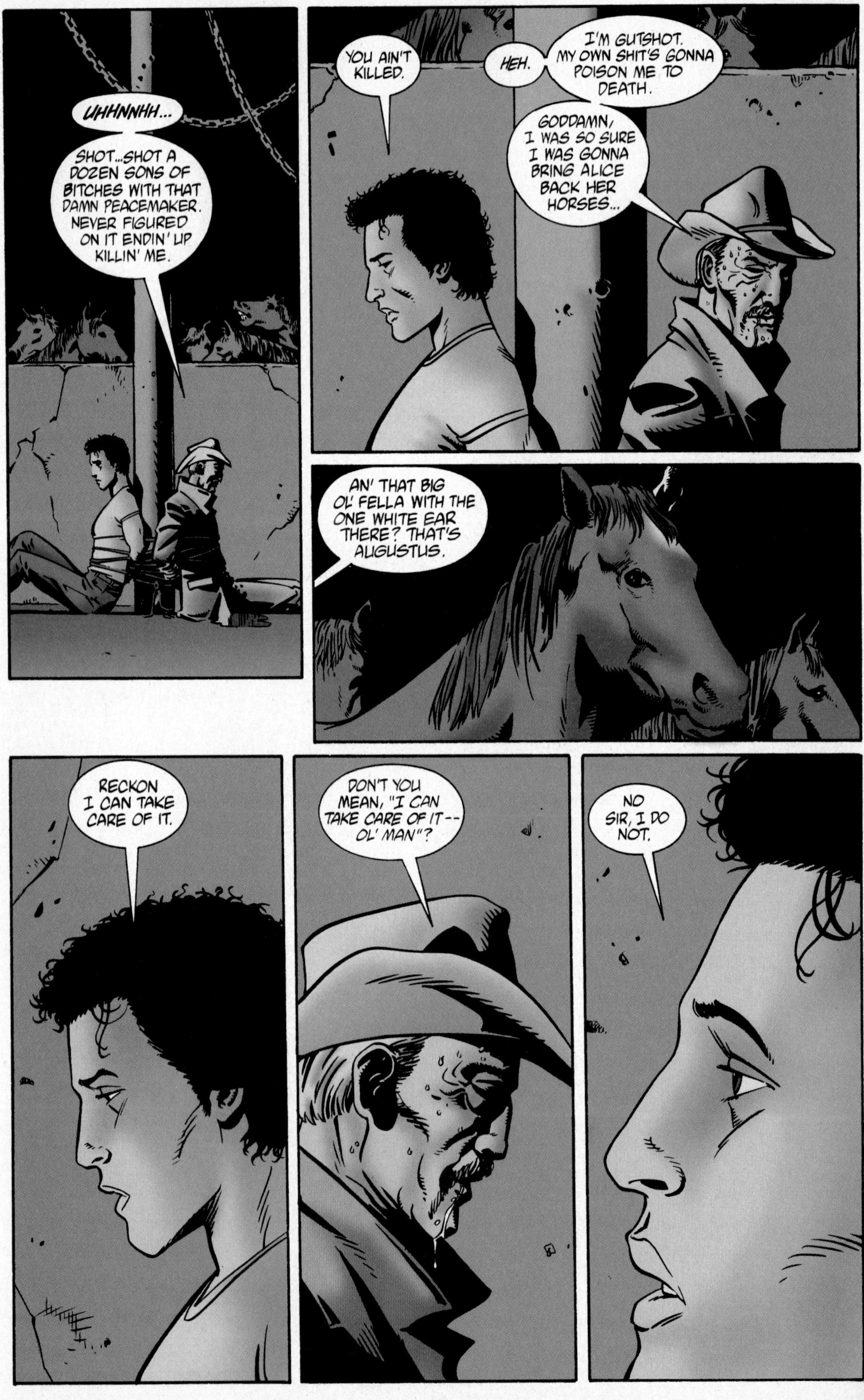
UHHNNHH...
SHOT...SHOT A DOZEN SONS OF BITCHES WITH THAT DAMN PEACEMAKER. NEVER FIGURED ON IT ENDIN' UP KILLIN' ME.
YOU AIN'T KILLED.
HEH.
I'M GUTSHOT. MY OWN SHIT'S GONNA POISON ME TO DEATH.
GODDAMN, I WAS SO SURE I WAS GONNA BRING ALICE BACK HER HORSES...
AN' THAT BIG OL' FELLA WITH THE ONE WHITE EAR THERE? THAT'S AUGUSTUS.
RECKON I CAN TAKE CARE OF IT.
DON'T YOU MEAN, "I CAN TAKE CARE OF IT--OL' MAN"?
NO SIR, I DO NOT.

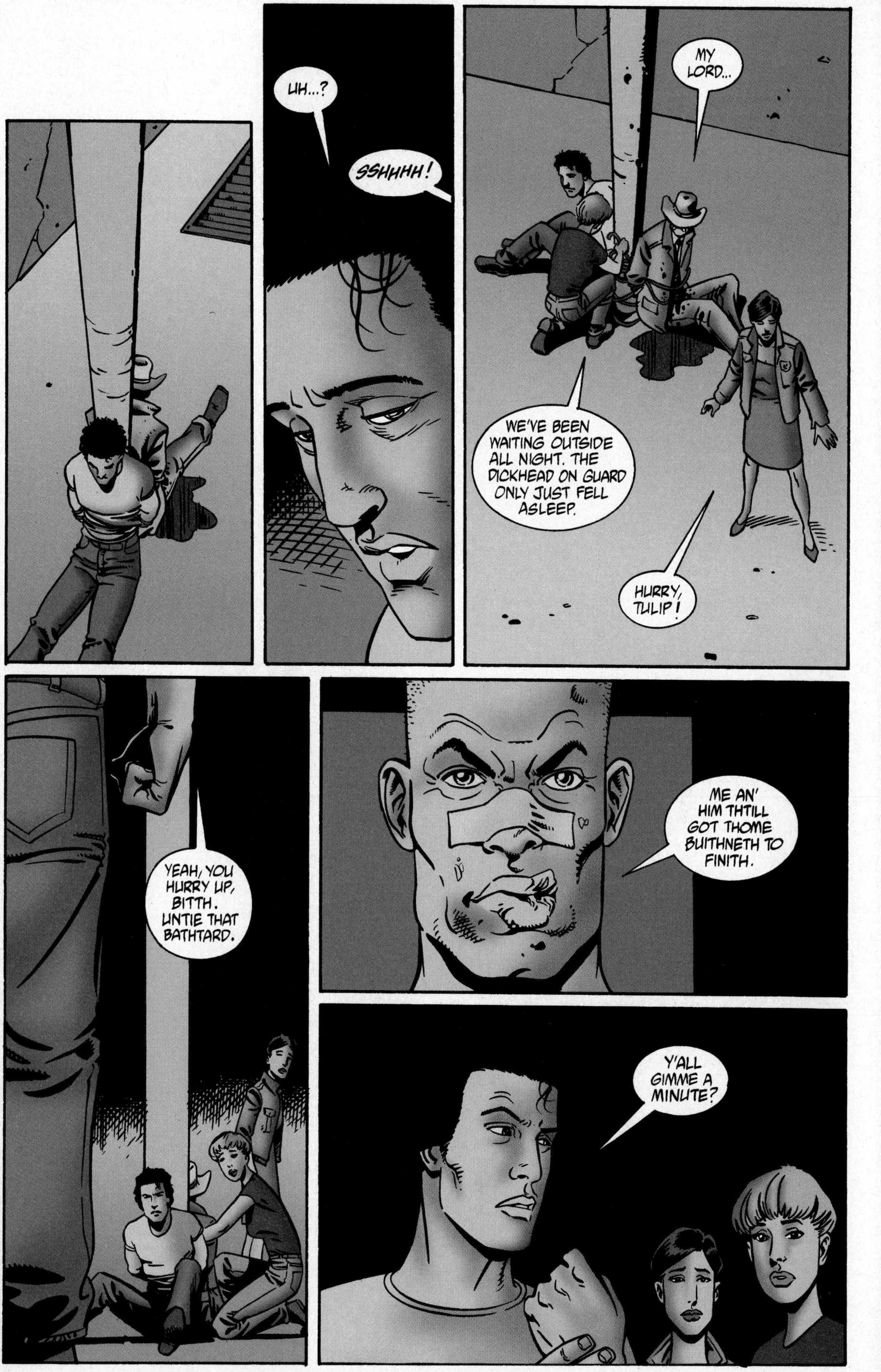
UH...?
SSHHHH!
MY LORD...
WE'VE BEEN WAITING OUTSIDE ALL NIGHT. THE DICKHEAD ON GUARD ONLY JUST FELL ASLEEP.
HURRY, TULIP!
YEAH, YOU HURRY UP, BITTH. UNTIE THAT BATHTARD.
ME AN' HIM THTILL GOT THOME BUITHNETH TO FINITH.
Y'ALL GIMME A MINUTE?

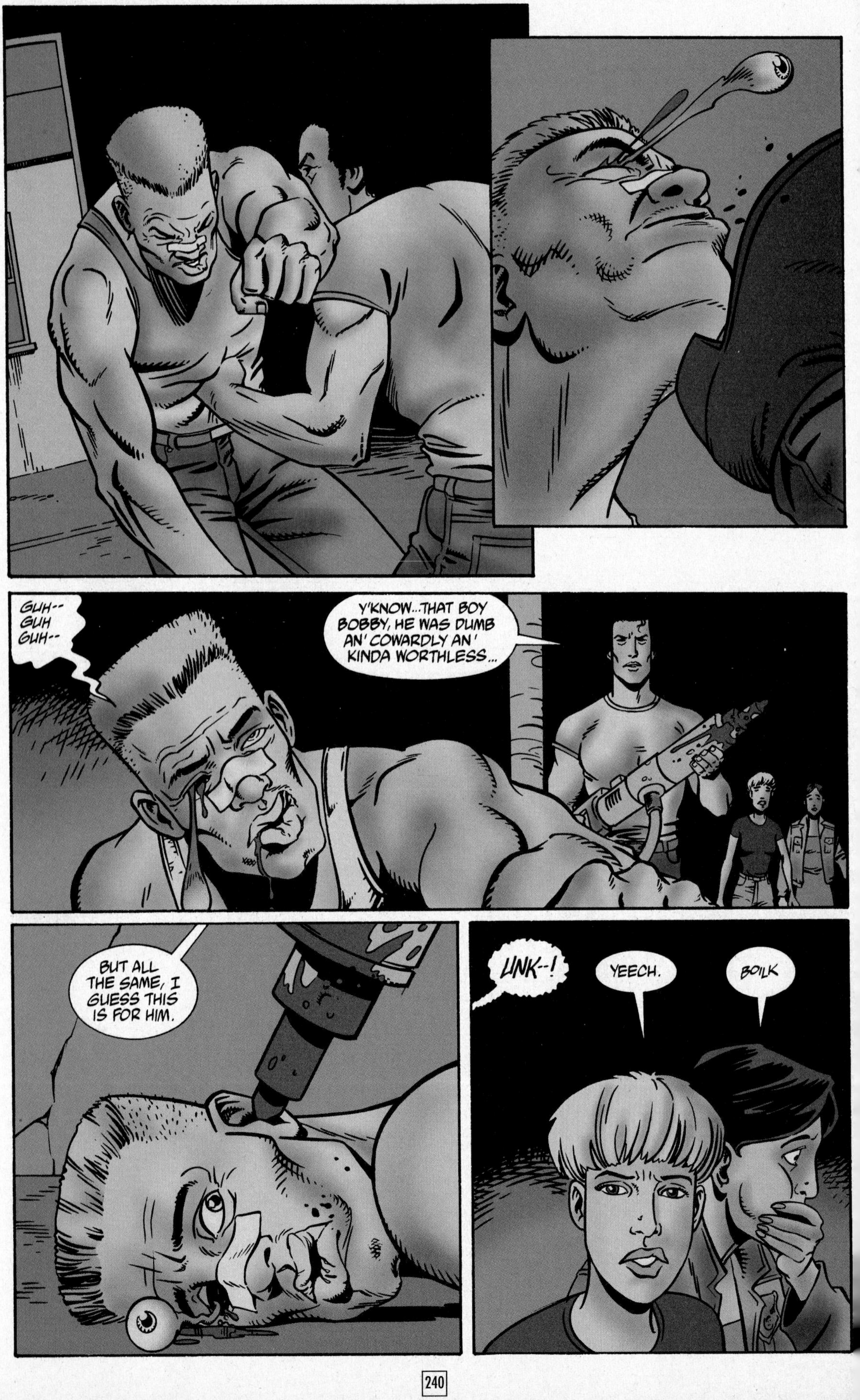
GUH--
GUH GUH--
Y'KNOW...THAT BOY BOBBY, HE WAS DUMB AN' COWARDLY AN' KINDA WORTHLESS...
BUT ALL THE SAME, I GUESS THIS IS FOR HIM.
UNK--!
YEECH.
BOILK

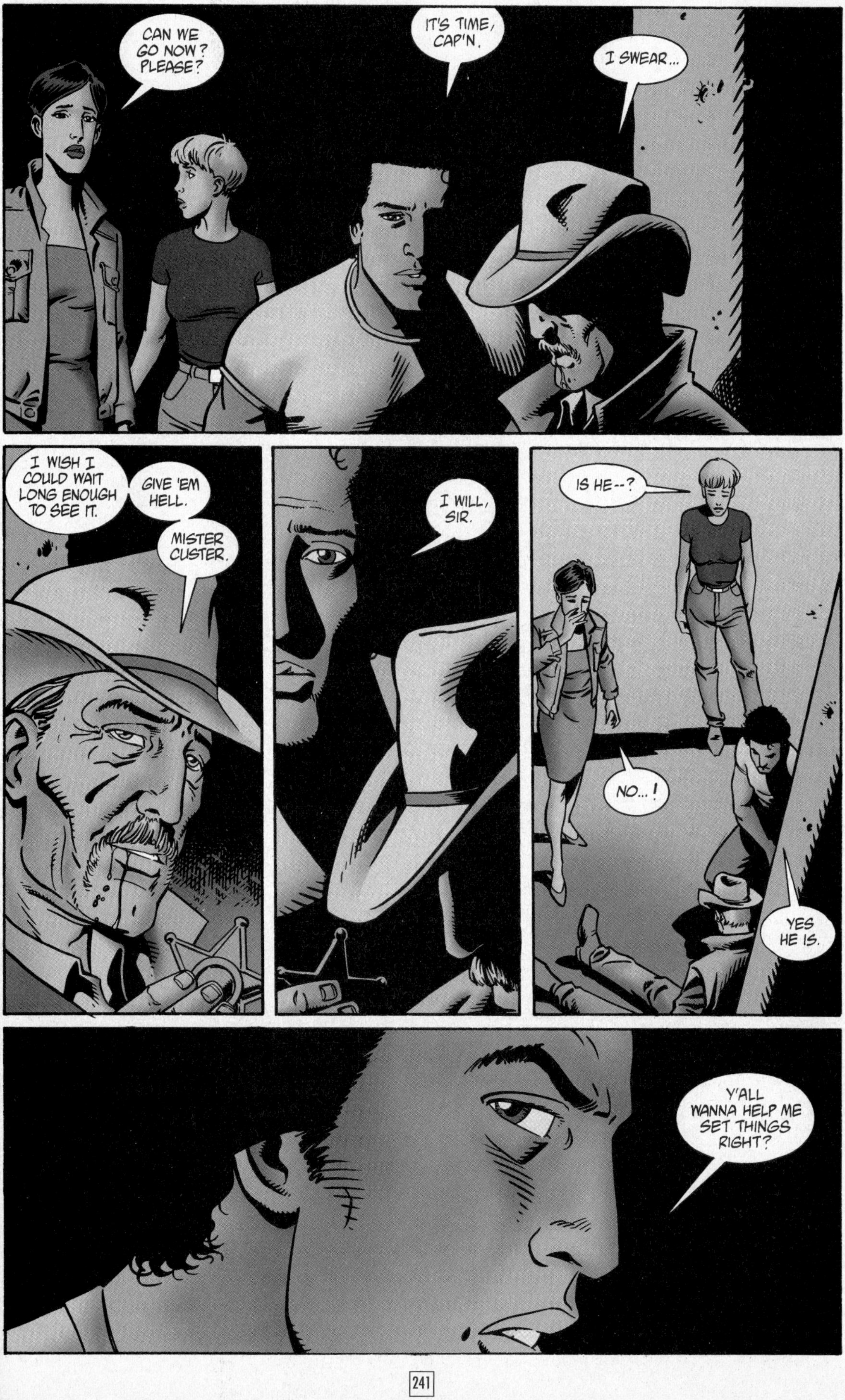
CAN WE GO NOW? PLEASE?
IT'S TIME, CAP'N.
I SWEAR...
I WISH I COULD WAIT LONG ENOUGH TO SEE IT.
GIVE 'EM HELL.
MISTER CUSTER.
I WILL, SIR.
IS HE--?
NO...!
YES HE IS.
Y'ALL WANNA HELP ME SET THINGS RIGHT?

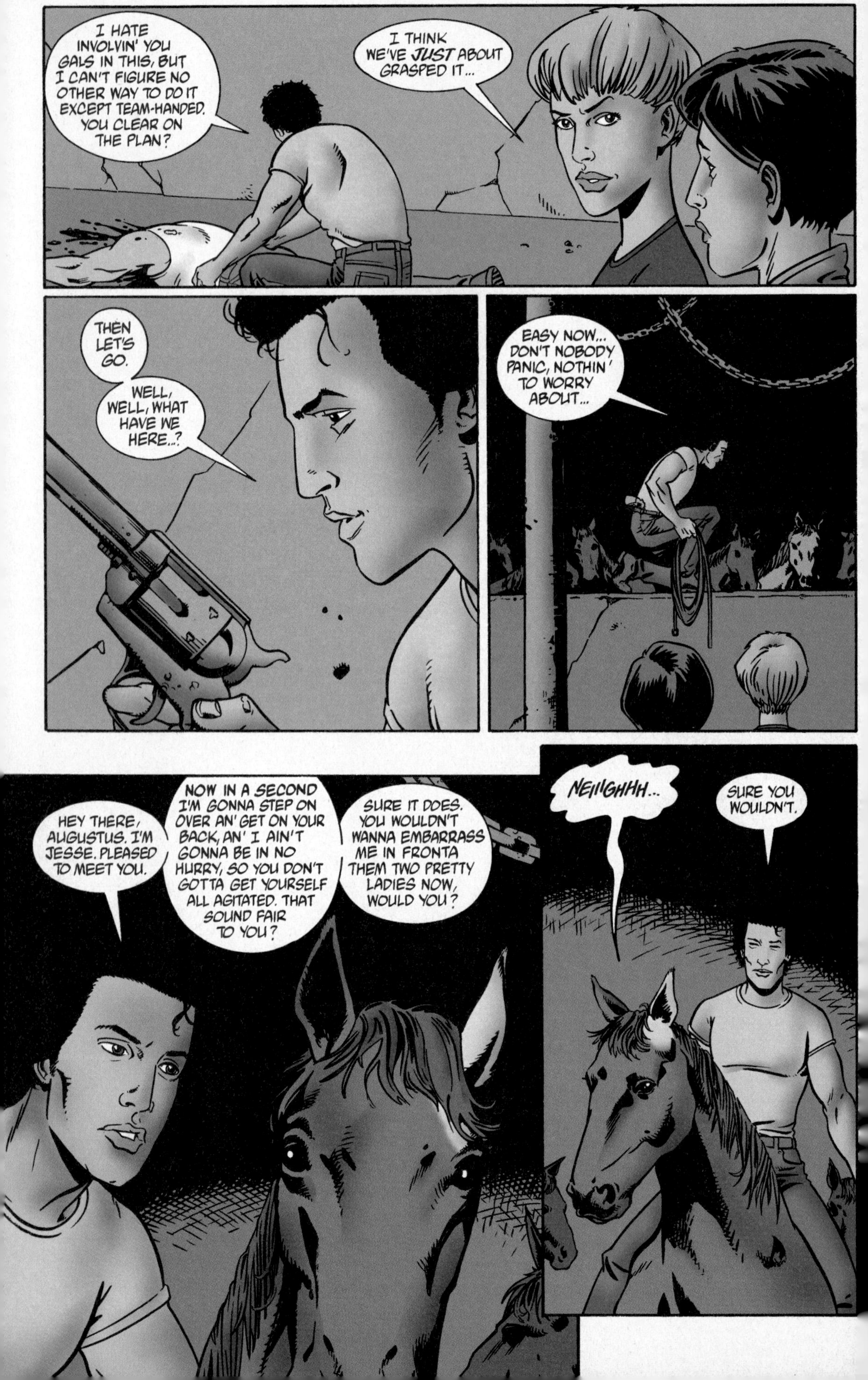
I HATE INVOLVIN' YOU GALS IN THIS, BUT I CAN'T FIGURE NO OTHER WAY TO DO IT EXCEPT TEAM-HANDED. YOU CLEAR ON THE PLAN?
I THINK WE'VE JUST ABOUT GRASPED IT...
THEN LET'S GO.
WELL, WELL, WHAT HAVE WE HERE...?
EASY NOW... DON'T NOBODY PANIC, NOTHIN' TO WORRY ABOUT...
HEY THERE, AUGUSTUS. I'M JESSE. PLEASED TO MEET YOU.
NOW IN A SECOND I'M GONNA STEP ON OVER AN' GET ON YOUR BACK, AN' I AIN'T GONNA BE IN NO HURRY, SO YOU DON'T GOTTA GET YOURSELF ALL AGITATED. THAT SOUND FAIR TO YOU?
SURE IT DOES. YOU WOULDN'T WANNA EMBARRASS ME IN FRONTA THEM TWO PRETTY LADIES NOW, WOULD YOU?
NEIIGHHH...
SURE YOU WOULDN'T.

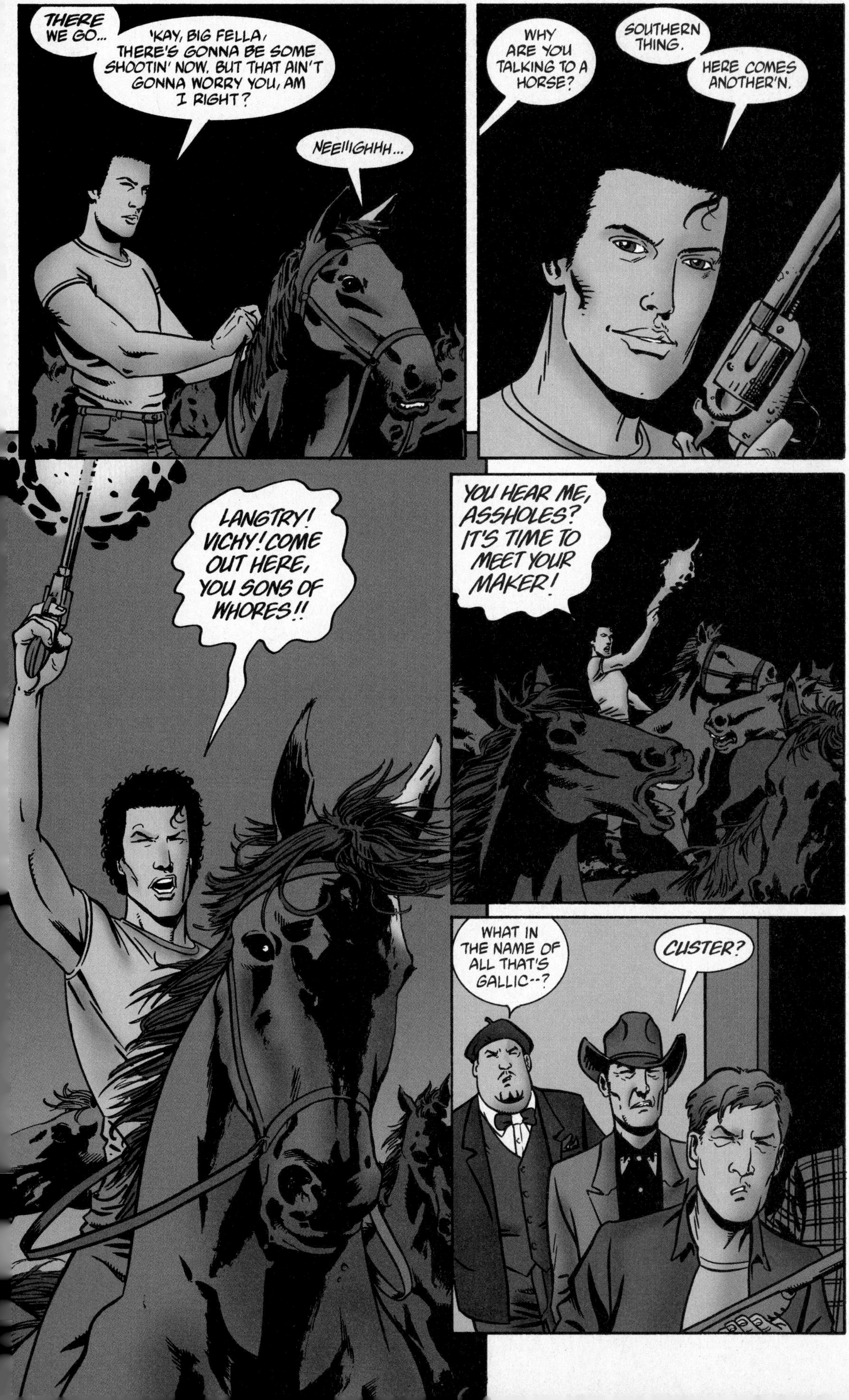
THERE WE GO...
'KAY, BIG FELLA, THERE'S GONNA BE SOME SHOOTIN' NOW. BUT THAT AIN'T GONNA WORRY YOU, AM I RIGHT?
NEEIIIGHHH...
WHY ARE YOU TALKING TO A HORSE?
SOUTHERN THING.
HERE COMES ANOTHER'N.
LANGTRY! VICHY! COME OUT HERE, YOU SONS OF WHORES!!
YOU HEAR ME, ASSHOLES? IT'S TIME TO MEET YOUR MAKER!
WHAT IN THE NAME OF ALL THAT'S GALLIC--?
CUSTER?

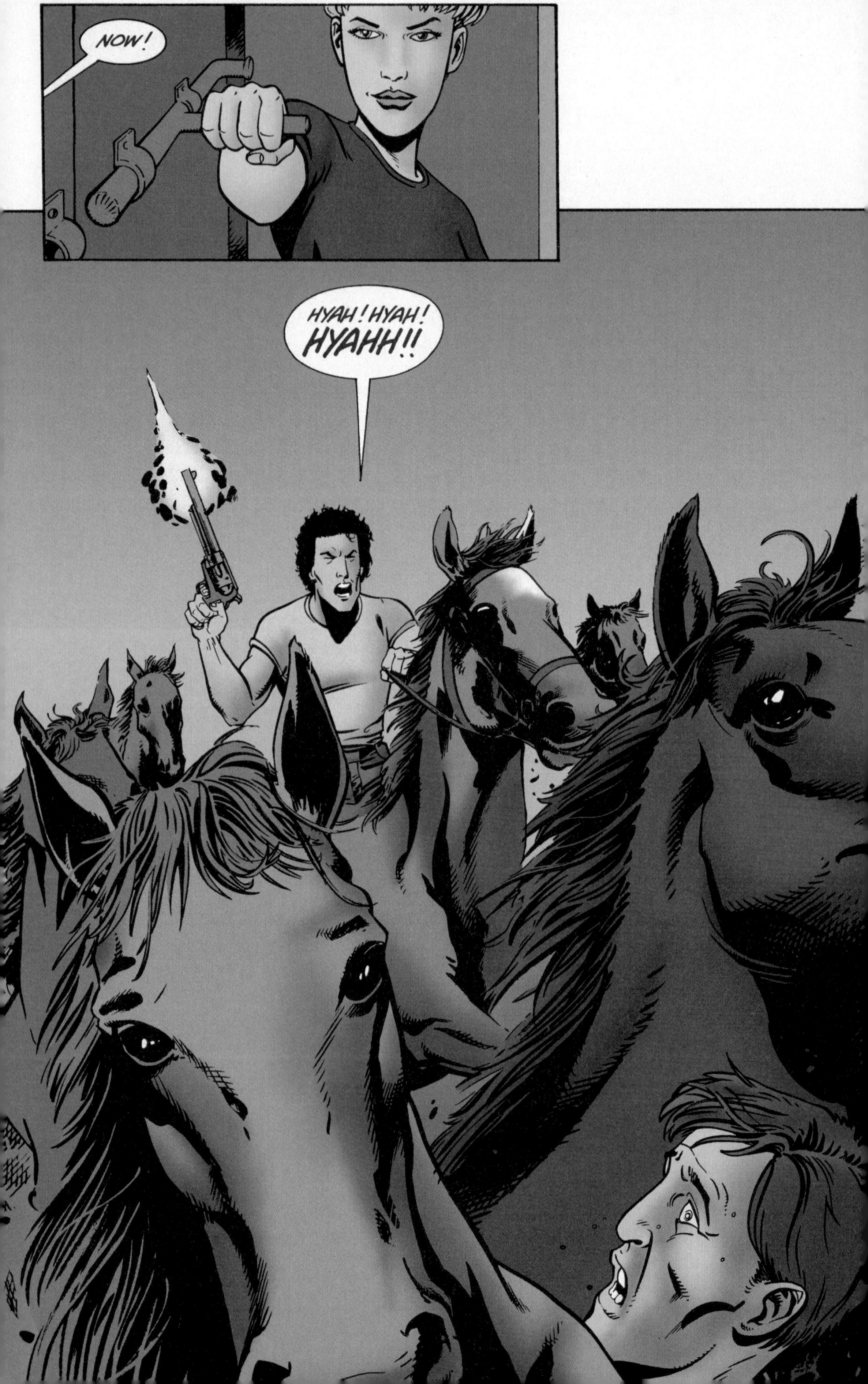
NOW!
HYAH! HYAH! HYAHH!!

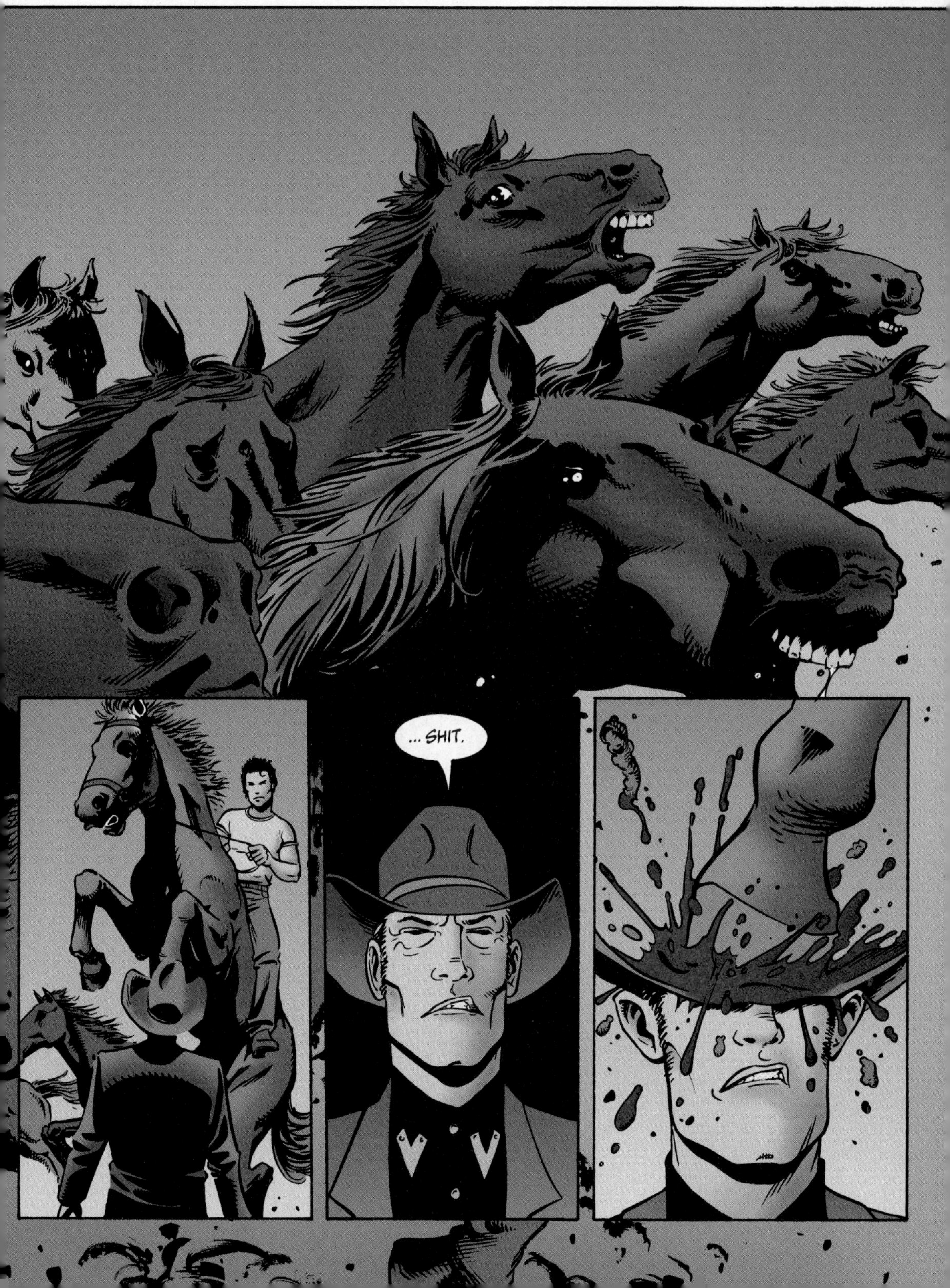
... SHIT.

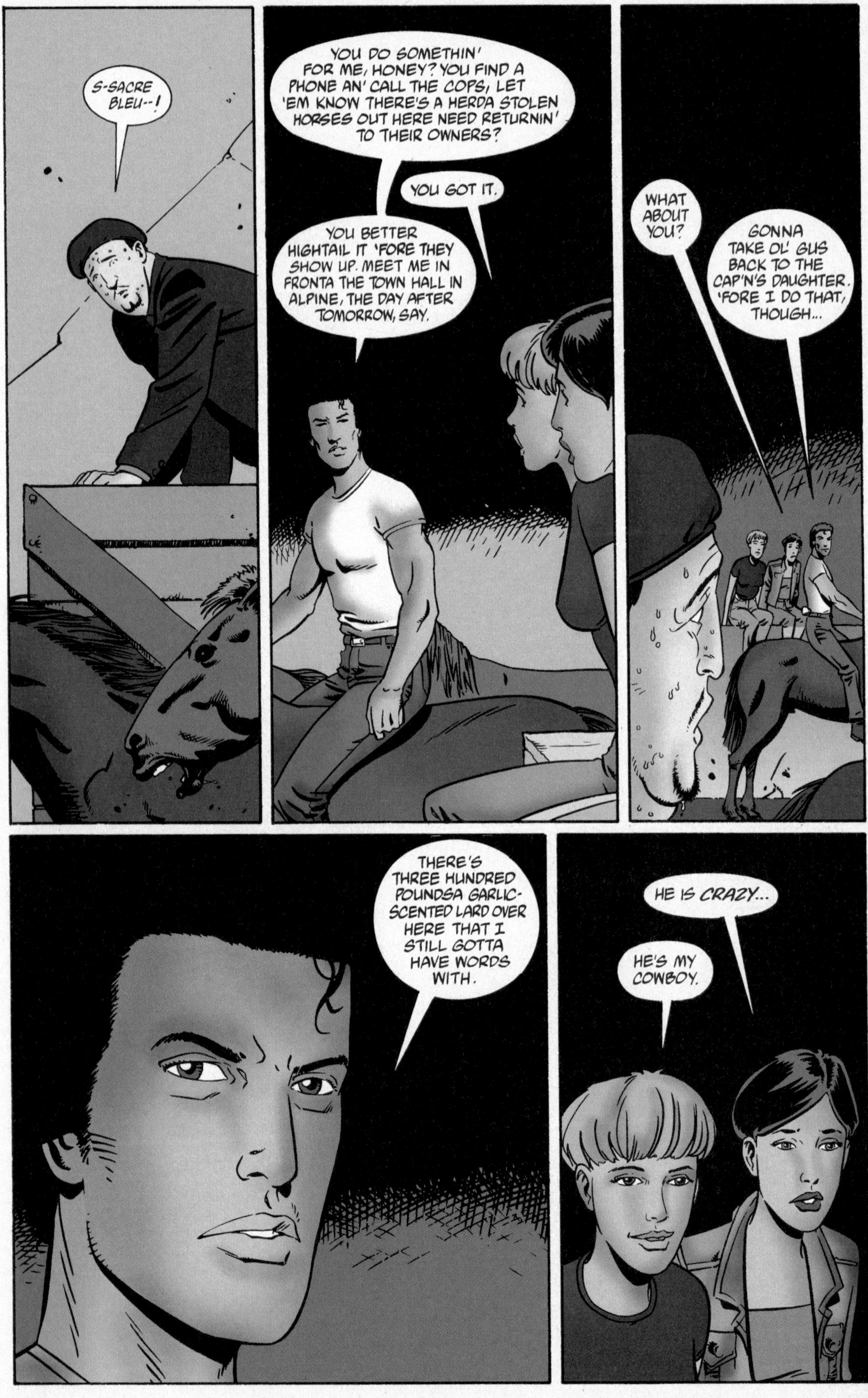
S-SACRE BLEU--!
YOU DO SOMETHIN' FOR ME, HONEY? YOU FIND A PHONE AN' CALL THE COPS, LET 'EM KNOW THERE'S A HERDA STOLEN HORSES OUT HERE NEED RETURNIN' TO THEIR OWNERS?
YOU GOT IT.
YOU BETTER HIGHTAIL IT 'FORE THEY SHOW UP. MEET ME IN FRONTA THE TOWN HALL IN ALPINE, THE DAY AFTER TOMORROW, SAY.
WHAT ABOUT YOU?
GONNA TAKE OL' GUS BACK TO THE CAP'N'S DAUGHTER. 'FORE I DO THAT, THOUGH...
THERE'S THREE HUNDRED POUNDSA GARLIC-SCENTED LARD OVER HERE THAT I STILL GOTTA HAVE WORDS WITH.
HE IS *CRAZY*...
HE'S MY COWBOY.

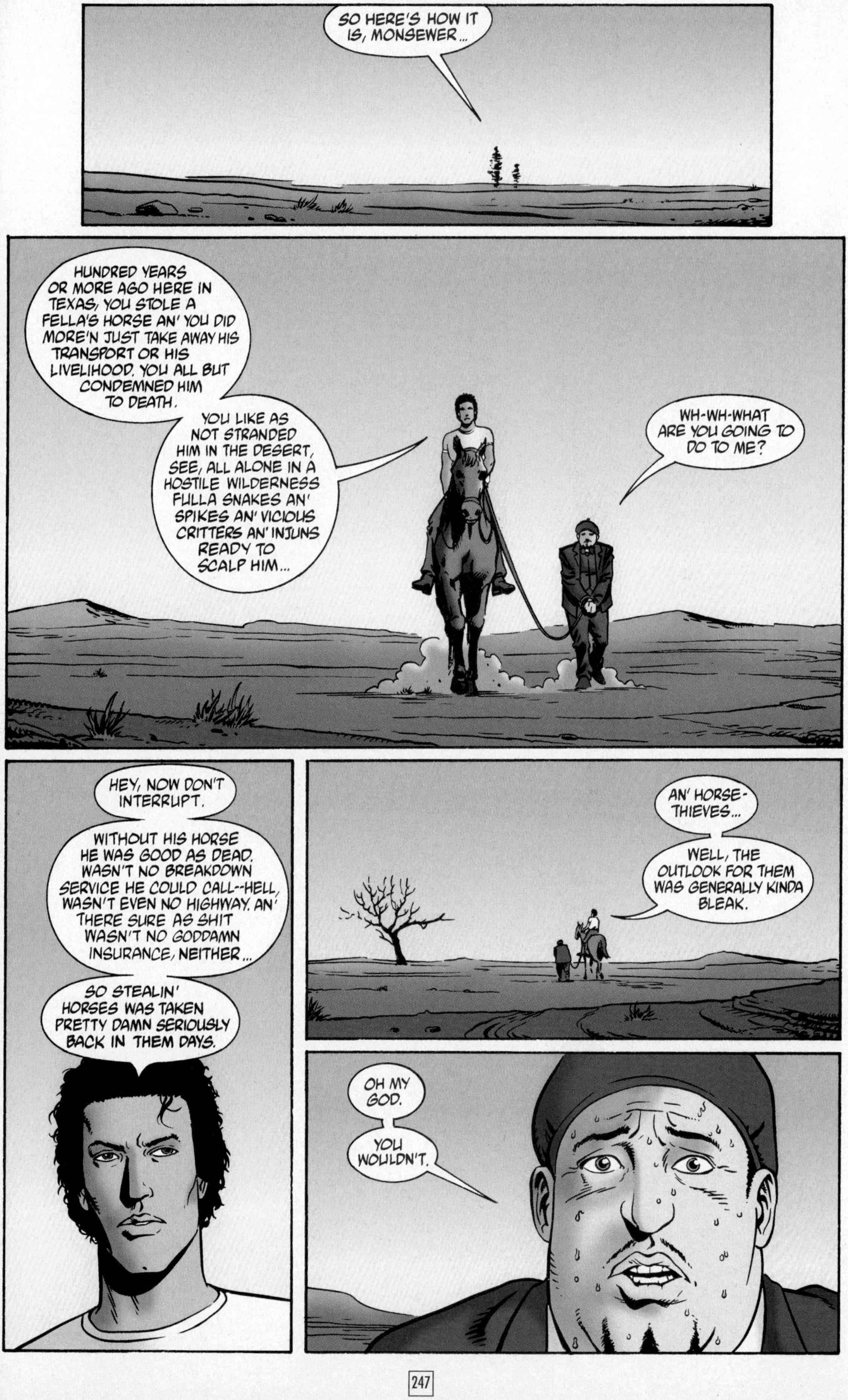
SO HERE'S HOW IT IS, MONSEWER...
HUNDRED YEARS OR MORE AGO HERE IN TEXAS, YOU STOLE A FELLA'S HORSE AN' YOU DID MORE'N JUST TAKE AWAY HIS TRANSPORT OR HIS LIVELIHOOD. YOU ALL BUT CONDEMNED HIM TO DEATH.
YOU LIKE AS NOT STRANDED HIM IN THE DESERT, SEE, ALL ALONE IN A HOSTILE WILDERNESS FULLA SNAKES AN' SPIKES AN' VICIOUS CRITTERS AN' INJUNS READY TO SCALP HIM...
WH-WH-WHAT ARE YOU GOING TO DO TO ME?
HEY, NOW DON'T INTERRUPT.
WITHOUT HIS HORSE HE WAS GOOD AS DEAD. WASN'T NO BREAKDOWN SERVICE HE COULD CALL--HELL, WASN'T EVEN NO HIGHWAY. AN' THERE SURE AS SHIT WASN'T NO GODDAMN INSURANCE, NEITHER...
SO STEALIN' HORSES WAS TAKEN PRETTY DAMN SERIOUSLY BACK IN THEM DAYS.
AN' HORSE-THIEVES...
WELL, THE OUTLOOK FOR THEM WAS GENERALLY KINDA BLEAK.
OH MY GOD.
YOU WOULDN'T.

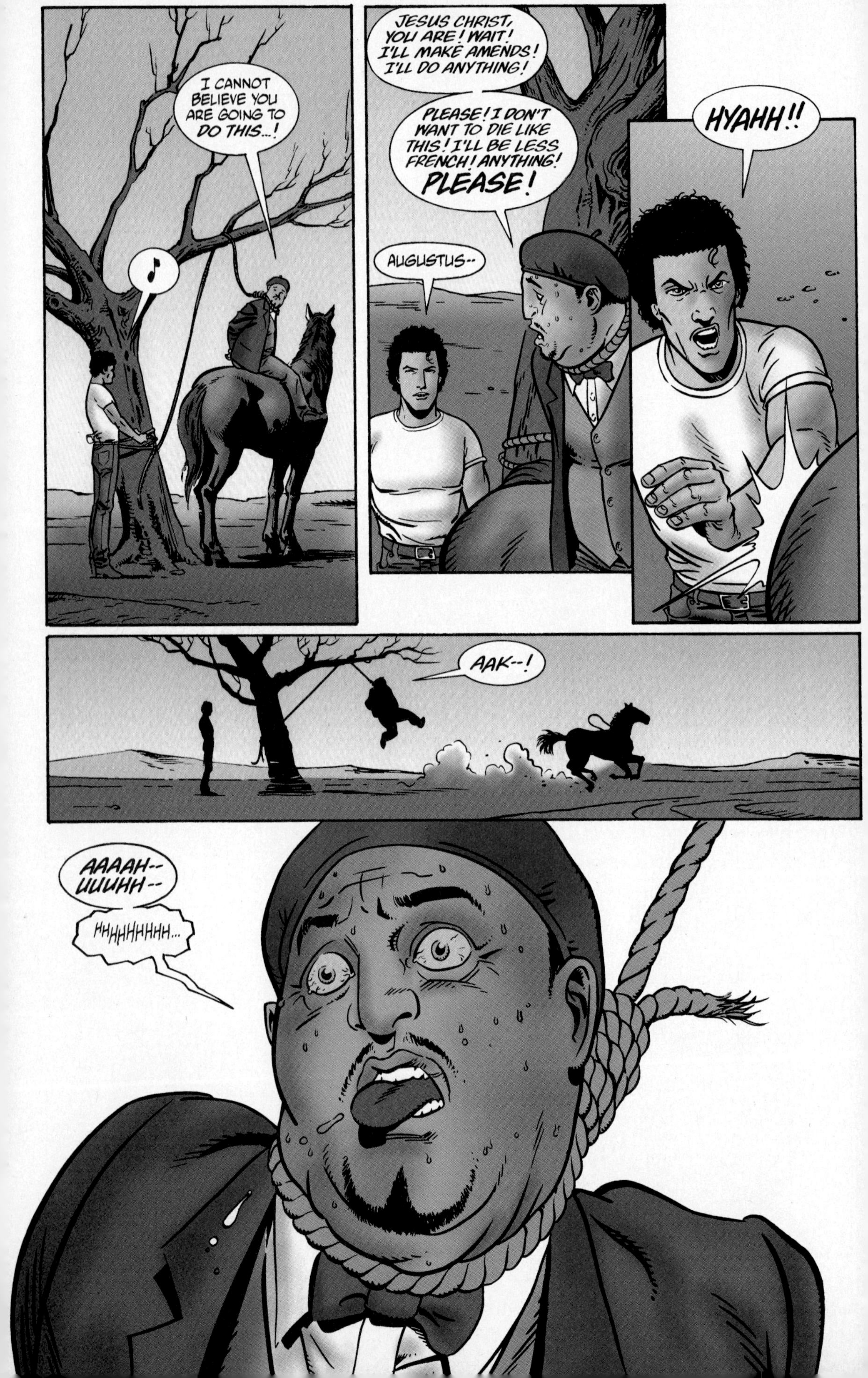
I CANNOT BELIEVE YOU ARE GOING TO DO THIS...!
♪
JESUS CHRIST, YOU ARE! WAIT! I'LL MAKE AMENDS! I'LL DO ANYTHING!
PLEASE! I DON'T WANT TO DIE LIKE THIS! I'LL BE LESS FRENCH! ANYTHING! PLEASE!
AUGUSTUS--
HYAHH!!
AAK--!
AAAAH-- UUUHH--
HHHHHHHHH...

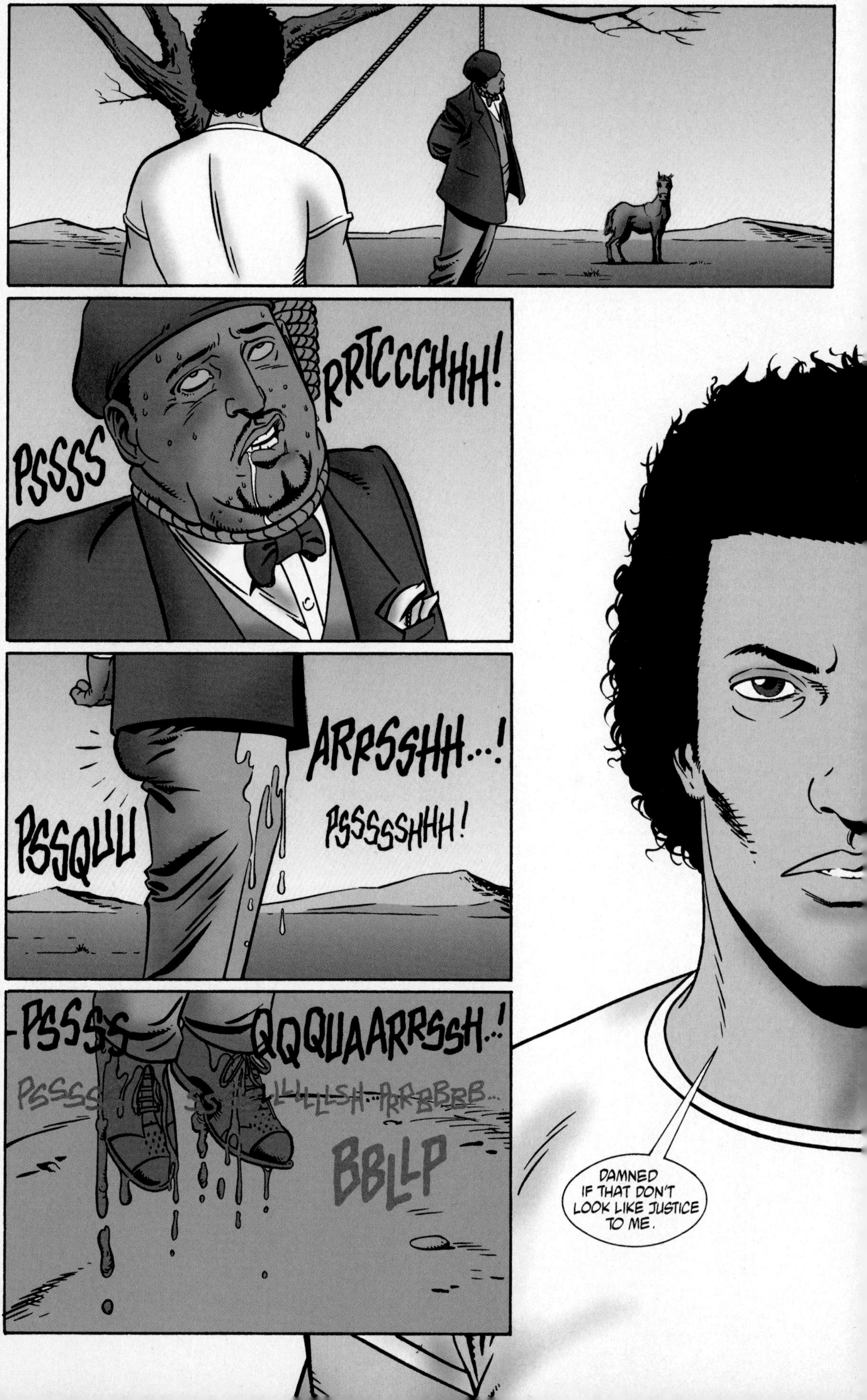
RRTCCCHHH!
PSSSS
ARRSSHH...!
PSSQUU
PSSSSSHHH!
PSSSS
QQQUAARRSSH..!
BBLLP
DAMNED IF THAT DON'T LOOK LIKE JUSTICE TO ME.

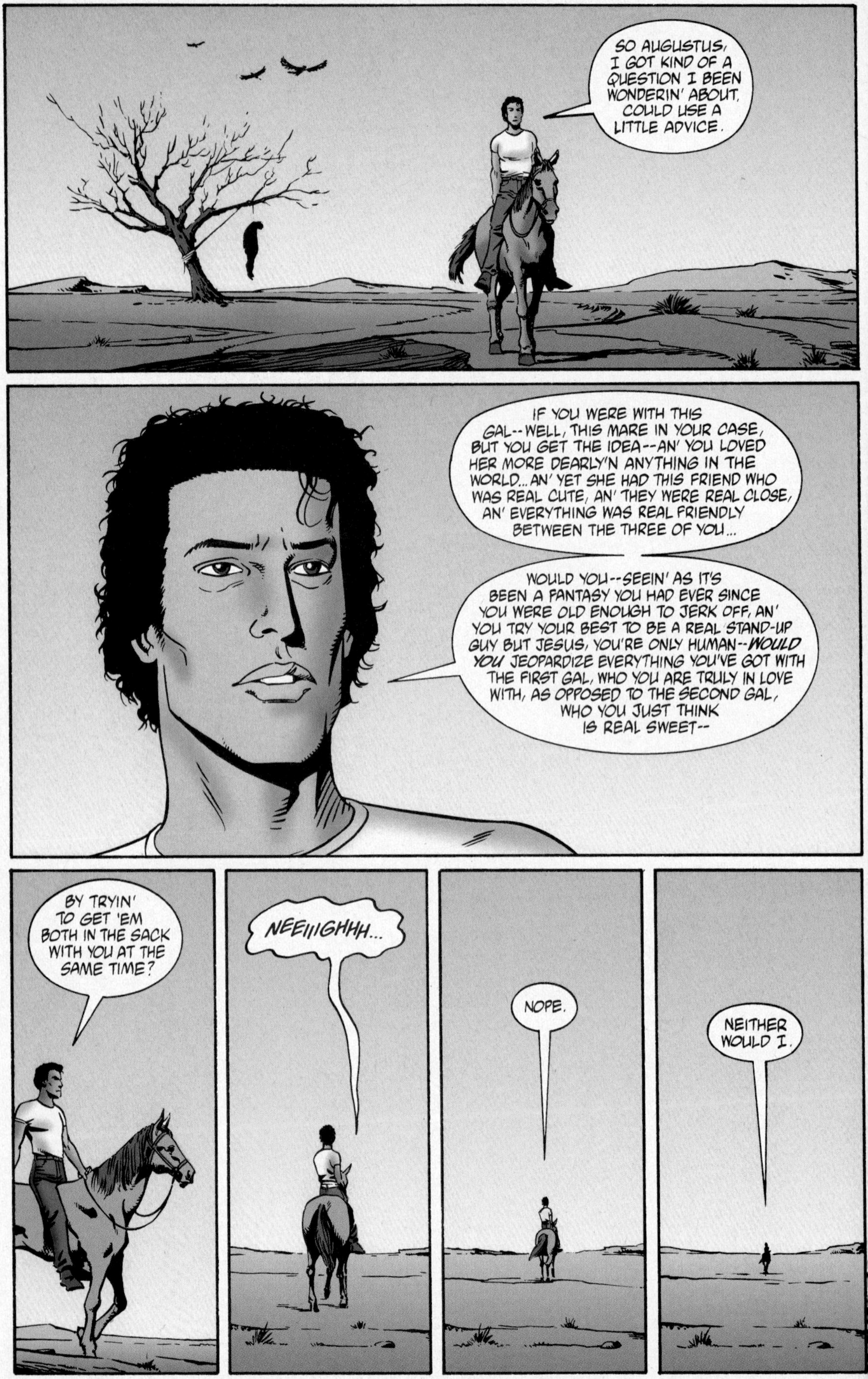
SO AUGUSTUS, I GOT KIND OF A QUESTION I BEEN WONDERIN' ABOUT, COULD USE A LITTLE ADVICE.
IF YOU WERE WITH THIS GAL--WELL, THIS MARE IN YOUR CASE, BUT YOU GET THE IDEA--AN' YOU LOVED HER MORE DEARLY'N ANYTHING IN THE WORLD... AN' YET SHE HAD THIS FRIEND WHO WAS REAL CUTE, AN' THEY WERE REAL CLOSE, AN' EVERYTHING WAS REAL FRIENDLY BETWEEN THE THREE OF YOU...
WOULD YOU--SEEIN' AS IT'S BEEN A FANTASY YOU HAD EVER SINCE YOU WERE OLD ENOUGH TO JERK OFF, AN' YOU TRY YOUR BEST TO BE A REAL STAND-UP GUY BUT JESUS, YOU'RE ONLY HUMAN--*WOULD YOU* JEOPARDIZE EVERYTHING YOU'VE GOT WITH THE FIRST GAL, WHO YOU ARE TRULY IN LOVE WITH, AS OPPOSED TO THE SECOND GAL, WHO YOU JUST THINK IS REAL SWEET--
BY TRYIN' TO GET 'EM BOTH IN THE SACK WITH YOU AT THE SAME TIME?
NEEIIIGHHH...
NOPE.
NEITHER WOULD I.

THE PREACHER LIBRARY

GARTH ENNIS/STEVE DILLON/GLENN FABRY/VARIOUS

A modern American epic of life, death, God, love, and redemption — filled with sex, booze, and blood.

ALL TITLES ARE SUGGESTED FOR MATURE READERS

VOLUME 1:
GONE TO TEXAS

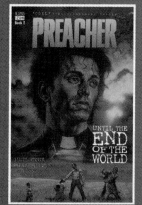

VOLUME 2:
UNTIL THE END OF THE WORLD

VOLUME 3:
PROUD AMERICANS

VOLUME 4:
ANCIENT HISTORY

VOLUME 5:
DIXIE FRIED

VOLUME 6:
WAR IN THE SUN

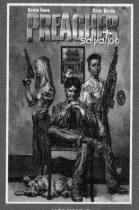

VOLUME 7:
SALVATION

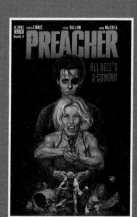

VOLUME 8:
ALL HELL'S A-COMING

VOLUME 9:
ALAMO

PREACHER: DEAD OR ALIVE
(THE COLLECTED COVERS)

Also from writer Garth Ennis:

THE HITMAN LIBRARY

GARTH ENNIS/JOHN MCCREA

With x-ray vision and a sniper's accuracy on the trigger, Gotham City's Tommy Monaghan is arguably the world's greatest hit man — and his power of telepathy ensures that he only kills the bad guys!

Garth Ennis & John McCrea
HITMAN

VOLUME 1:
HITMAN

Garth Ennis & John McCrea
HITMAN
10,000 BULLETS

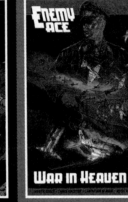

VOLUME 2:
TEN THOUSAND BULLETS

Garth Ennis & John McCrea
HITMAN
LOCAL HEROES

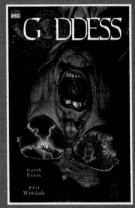

VOLUME 3:
LOCAL HEROES

GARTH ENNIS & JOHN McCREA
HITMAN
ACE OF KILLERS

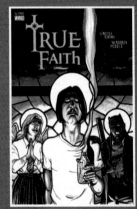

VOLUME 4:
ACE OF KILLERS

ENNIS, McCREA & LEACH
HITMAN
WHO DARES WINS

VOLUME 5:
WHO DARES WINS

TITLES BELOW ARE SUGGESTED FOR MATURE READERS

ENEMY ACE
WAR IN HEAVEN

ENEMY ACE: WAR IN HEAVEN
Garth Ennis/Chris Weston

VERTIGO
GODDESS
Garth Ennis
Phil Winslade

GODDESS
Garth Ennis/Phil Winslade

VERTIGO
GARTH ENNIS JOHN HIGGINS
PRIDE & JOY

PRIDE & JOY
Garth Ennis/John Higgins

VERTIGO
TRUE FAITH
GARTH ENNIS
WARREN PLEECE

TRUE FAITH
Garth Ennis/Warren Pleece

VERTIGO
UNKNOWN SOLDIER
BY GARTH ENNIS
& KILIAN PLUNKETT

UNKNOWN SOLDIER
Garth Ennis/Kilian Plunkett

THE HELLBLAZER LIBRARY

Where horror, dark magic, and bad luck meet, John Constantine is never far away.

ALL TITLES ARE SUGGESTED FOR MATURE READERS

**VOLUME 1:
ORIGINAL SINS**

JAMIE DELANO/VARIOUS

**VOLUME 2:
DANGEROUS HABITS**

GARTH ENNIS/VARIOUS

**VOLUME 3:
FEAR AND LOATHING**

GARTH ENNIS/STEVE DILLON

**VOLUME 4:
TAINTED LOVE**

GARTH ENNIS/STEVE DILLON

**VOLUME 5:
DAMNATION'S FLAME**

GARTH ENNIS/STEVE DILLON/

WILLIAM SIMPSON/PETER SNEJBJERG

**VOLUME 6:
RAKE AT THE GATES OF HELL**

GARTH ENNIS/STEVE DILLON

**VOLUME 7:
SON OF MAN**

GARTH ENNIS/JOHN HIGGINS

**VOLUME 8:
HAUNTED**

WARREN ELLIS/JOHN HIGGINS

**VOLUME 9:
HARD TIME**

BRIAN AZZARELLO/RICHARD CORBEN

**VOLUME 10:
GOOD INTENTIONS**

BRIAN AZZARELLO/MARCELO FRUSIN

**VOLUME 11:
FREEZES OVER**

BRIAN AZZARELLO/MARCELO FRUSIN/

GUY DAVIS/STEVE DILLON

OTHER GREAT COLLECTIONS FROM VERTIGO

ALL TITLES ARE SUGGESTED FOR MATURE READERS

100 BULLETS
Brian Azzarello/Eduardo Risso
With one special briefcase, Agent Graves gives you the chance to kill without retribution. But what's the real price for this chance — and who's setting it?
Volume 1: FIRST SHOT, LAST CALL
Volume 2: SPLIT SECOND CHANCE
Volume 3: HANG UP ON THE HANG LOW
Volume 4: A FOREGONE TOMORROW
Volume 5: THE COUNTERFIFTH DETECTIVE
Volume 6: SIX FEET UNDER THE GUN

ANIMAL MAN
Grant Morrison/Chas Truog/Doug Hazlewood/various
A minor super-hero's consciousness is raised higher and higher until he becomes aware of his own fictitious nature in this revolutionary and existential series.
Volume 1: ANIMAL MAN
Volume 2: ORIGIN OF THE SPECIES
Volume 3: DEUS EX MACHINA

THE BOOKS OF MAGIC
Neil Gaiman/various
A quartet of fallen mystics introduce the world of magic to young Tim Hunter, who is destined to become the world's most powerful magician.

THE BOOKS OF MAGIC
John Ney Rieber/Peter Gross/various
The continuing trials and adventures of Tim Hunter, whose magical talents bring extra trouble and confusion to his adolescence.
Volume 1: BINDINGS
Volume 2: SUMMONINGS
Volume 3: RECKONINGS
Volume 4: TRANSFORMATIONS
Volume 5: GIRL IN THE BOX
Volume 6: THE BURNING GIRL
Volume 7: DEATH AFTER DEATH

DEATH: THE HIGH COST OF LIVING
Neil Gaiman/Chris Bachalo/Mark Buckingham
One day every century, Death assumes mortal form to learn more about the lives she must take.

DEATH: THE TIME OF YOUR LIFE
Neil Gaiman/Chris Bachalo/Mark Buckingham/Mark Pennington
A young lesbian mother strikes a deal with Death for the life of her son in a story about fame, relationships, and rock and roll.

DEATH: AT DEATH'S DOOR
Jill Thompson
Part fanciful manga retelling of the acclaimed THE SANDMAN: SEASON OF MISTS, part original story of the party from Hell.

FABLES
Bill Willingham/Lan Medina/Mark Buckingham/Steve Leialoha
The immortal characters of popular fairy tales have been driven from their homelands, and now live hidden among us, trying to cope with life in 21st-century Manhattan.
Volume 1: LEGENDS IN EXILE
Volume 2: ANIMAL FARM

THE INVISIBLES
Grant Morrison/various
The saga of a terrifying conspiracy and the resistance movement combating it — a secret underground of ultra-cool guerrilla cells trained in ontological and physical anarchy.
Volume 1: SAY YOU WANT A REVOLUTION
Volume 2: APOCALIPSTICK
Volume 3: ENTROPY IN THE U.K.
Volume 4: BLOODY HELL IN AMERICA

Volume 5: COUNTING TO NONE
Volume 6: KISSING MR. QUIMPER
Volume 7: THE INVISIBLE KINGDOM

LUCIFER
Mike Carey/Peter Gross/Scott Hampton/Chris Weston/Dean Ormston/various
Walking out of Hell (and out of the pages of THE SANDMAN), an ambitious Lucifer Morningstar creates a new cosmos modelled after his own image.
Volume 1: DEVIL IN THE GATEWAY
Volume 2: CHILDREN AND MONSTERS
Volume 3: A DALLIANCE WITH THE DAMNED
Volume 4: THE DIVINE COMEDY
Volume 5: INFERNO

THE SANDMAN LIBRARY
Neil Gaiman/various
One of the most acclaimed and celebrated comics titles ever published — a rich blend of modern myth and dark fantasy in which contemporary fiction, historical drama, and legend are seamlessly interwoven.

Volume 1: PRELUDES & NOCTURNES
Volume 2: THE DOLL'S HOUSE
Volume 3: DREAM COUNTRY
Volume 4: SEASON OF MISTS
Volume 5: A GAME OF YOU
Volume 6: FABLES & REFLECTIONS
Volume 7: BRIEF LIVES
Volume 8: WORLDS' END
Volume 9: THE KINDLY ONES
Volume 10: THE WAKE
Volume 11: ENDLESS NIGHTS

SWAMP THING: DARK GENESIS
Len Wein/Berni Wrightson
A gothic nightmare is brought to life with this horrifying yet poignant story of a man transformed into a monster.

SWAMP THING
Alan Moore/Stephen Bissette/John Totleben/Rick Veitch/various
The writer and the series that revolutionized comics — a masterpiece of lyrical fantasy.
Volume 1: SAGA OF THE SWAMP THING
Volume 2: LOVE & DEATH
Volume 3: THE CURSE
Volume 4: A MURDER OF CROWS
Volume 5: EARTH TO EARTH
Volume 6: REUNION

TRANSMETROPOLITAN
Warren Ellis/Darick Robertson/various
An exuberant trip into a frenetic future, where outlaw journalist Spider Jerusalem battles hypocrisy, corruption, and sobriety.
Volume 1: BACK ON THE STREET
Volume 2: LUST FOR LIFE
Volume 3: YEAR OF THE BASTARD
Volume 4: THE NEW SCUM
Volume 5: LONELY CITY
Volume 6: GOUGE AWAY
Volume 7: SPIDER'S THRASH
Volume 8: DIRGE
Volume 9: THE CURE

Y: THE LAST MAN
Brian K. Vaughan/Pia Guerra/José Marzán, Jr.
An unexplained plague kills every male mammal on Earth — all except Yorick Brown and his pet monkey. Will he survive this new, emasculated world to discover what killed his fellow men?
Volume 1: UNMANNED
Volume 2: CYCLES
Volume 3: ONE SMALL STEP

BARNUM!
Howard Chaykin/David Tischman/Niko Henrichon

BIGG TIME
Ty Templeton

BLACK ORCHID
Neil Gaiman/Dave McKean

COWBOY WALLY
Kyle Baker

HEAVY LIQUID
Paul Pope

HUMAN TARGET
Peter Milligan/Edvin Biukovic

HUMAN TARGET: FINAL CUT
Peter Milligan/Javier Pulido

I DIE AT MIDNIGHT
Kyle Baker

IN THE SHADOW OF EDGAR ALLAN POE
Jonathon Scott Fuqua/Stephen John Phillips/Steven Parke

JONNY DOUBLE
Brian Azzarello/Eduardo Risso

KING DAVID
Kyle Baker

THE LITTLE ENDLESS STORYBOOK
Jill Thompson

THE LOSERS: ANTE UP
Andy Diggle/Jock

MR. PUNCH
Neil Gaiman/Dave McKean

THE MYSTERY PLAY
Grant Morrison/Jon J Muth

THE NAMES OF MAGIC
Dylan Horrocks/Richard Case

NEIL GAIMAN & CHARLES VESS' STARDUST
Neil Gaiman/Charles Vess

NEIL GAIMAN'S MIDNIGHT DAYS
Neil Gaiman/Matt Wagner/various

ORBITER
Warren Ellis/Colleen Doran

PROPOSITION PLAYER
Bill Willingham/Paul Guinan/Ron Randall

THE SANDMAN: THE DREAM HUNTERS
Neil Gaiman/Yoshitaka Amano

THE SANDMAN: DUST COVERS — THE COLLECTED SANDMAN COVERS 1989-1997
Dave McKean/Neil Gaiman

THE SANDMAN PRESENTS: THE FURIES
Mike Carey/John Bolton

THE SANDMAN PRESENTS: TALLER TALES
Bill Willingham/various

SCENE OF THE CRIME: A LITTLE PIECE OF GOODNIGHT
Ed Brubaker/Michael Lark/Sean Phillips

SHADE, THE CHANGING MAN: THE AMERICAN SCREAM
Peter Milligan/Chris Bachalo

SKREEMER
Peter Milligan/Brett Ewins/Steve Dillon

UNCLE SAM
Steve Darnall/Alex Ross

UNDERCOVER GENIE
Kyle Baker

V FOR VENDETTA
Alan Moore/David Lloyd

VEILS
Pat McGreal/Stephen John Phillips/José Villarrubia

WHY I HATE SATURN
Kyle Baker

THE WITCHING HOUR
Jeph Loeb/Chris Bachalo/Art Thibert

YOU ARE HERE
Kyle Baker

VISIT US AT WWW.VERTIGOCOMICS.COM FOR MORE INFORMATION ON THESE AND MANY OTHER TITLES FROM VERTIGO AND DC COMICS.

CALL 1-888-COMIC BOOK FOR THE COMICS SHOP NEAREST YOU, OR GO TO YOUR LOCAL BOOK STORE.